Encyclopedia of

Public Administration
and Public Policy

First Update Supplement

Encyclopedia of
Public Administration
and Public Policy

First Update Supplement

edited by

Jack Rabin

*The Pennsylvania State University—Harrisburg,
Middletown, Pennsylvania, U.S.A.*

Taylor & Francis
Taylor & Francis Group

Boca Raton   London   New York   Singapore

Published in 2005 by
Taylor & Francis Group
6000 Broken Sound Parkway NW, Suite 300
Boca Raton, FL 33487-2742

International Standard Book Number-10: 0-8493-3895-6 (Hardcover)
International Standard Book Number-13: 978-0-8493-3895-3 (Hardcover)

Library of Congress Cataloging-in-Publication Data

Catalog record is available from the Library of Congress

Taylor & Francis Group is the Academic Division of T&F Informa plc.

Visit the **Taylor & Francis** Web site at
http://www.taylorandfrancis.com

Göktug Morçöl
School of Public Affairs, Penn State Harrisburg, Middletown, Pennsylvania, U.S.A.

Bruce J. Perlman
School of Public Administration, University of New Mexico, Albuquerque, New Mexico, U.S.A.

Donijo Robbins
School of Public & Nonprofit Administration, Grand Valley State University, Grand Rapids, Michigan, U.S.A.

James Ruiz
School of Public Affairs, Penn State Harrisburg, Middletown, Pennsylvania, U.S.A.

Barbara Sims
School of Public Affairs, Penn State Harrisburg, Middletown, Pennsylvania, U.S.A.

Khi V. Thai
School of Public Administration, Florida Atlantic University, Fort Lauderdale, Florida, U.S.A.

Eran Vigoda-Gadot
School of Political Sciences, University of Haifa, Haifa, Israel

Jeffrey A. Weber
Penn State Harrisburg. Middletown, Pennsylvania; Senate of Pennsylvania, Harrisburg, Pennsylvania, U.S.A.

Robert K. Whelan
School of Urban and Public Affairs, University of New Orleans, New Orleans, Louisiana, U.S.A.

Chengfu Zhang
School of Public Administration, Renmin University, Beijing, China

Contributors

John Adler / *Arizona Department of Administration, Phoenix, Arizona, U.S.A.*

Michael Asner / *Michael Asner Consulting, Surrey, British Columbia, Canada*

Michael W. Austin / *University of Colorado at Boulder, Boulder, Colorado, U.S.A.*

David L. Baker / *Arizona State University, Tempe, Arizona, U.S.A.*

Daryl Balia / *Public Service Commission, Pretoria, South Africa*

Jane Beckett-Camarata / *Kent State University, Kent, Ohio, U.S.A.*

Lisa B. Bingham / *Indiana University, Bloomington, Indiana, U.S.A.*

Thomas A. Birkland / *University at Albany, State University of New York, Albany, New York, U.S.A.*

Deborah A. Botch / *New York State Unified Court System, Albany, New York, U.S.A.*

Ann O'M. Bowman / *University of South Carolina, Columbia, South Carolina, U.S.A.*

Brian Brewer / *City University of Hong Kong, Kowloon, Hong Kong*

Brendan F. Burke / *Bridgewater State College, Bridgewater, Massachusetts, U.S.A.*

Terry F. Buss / *National Academy of Public Administration, Washington, D.C., U.S.A.*

Ledivina V. Cariño / *University of the Philippines, Diliman, Quezon City, Philippines*

Jill Clark / *University of Texas at Arlington, Arlington, Texas, U.S.A.*

Richard K. Common / *The University of Hull, Hull, U.K.*

Krishna S. Dhir / *Berry College, Mount Berry, Georgia, U.S.A.*

Scott Fritzen / *National University of Singapore, Singapore*

Thomas Greitens / *Northern Illinois University, DeKalb, Illinois, U.S.A.*

M. Shamsul Haque / *National University of Singapore, Singapore*

Michael A. Harper / *University of Arkansas, Fayetteville, Arkansas, U.S.A.*

James R. Heichelbech / *University of Colorado at Denver, Denver, Colorado, U.S.A.*

Marc Holzer / *Rutgers, The State University of New Jersey, Newark, New Jersey, U.S.A.*

Yilin Hou / *The University of Georgia, Athens, Georgia, U.S.A.*

Helen Ingram / *University of California, Irvine, California, U.S.A.*

David Seth Jones / *National University of Singapore, Singapore*

Walter J. Jones / *Medical University of South Carolina, Charleston, South Carolina, U.S.A.*

Hwang-Sun Kang / *Seoul Development Institute, Seoul, Republic of Korea*

Bruce Kieler / *Wharton County Junior College, Wharton, Texas, U.S.A.*

Yvonne J. Kochanowski / *SteelEdge Business Consulting, Placerville, California, U.S.A.*

Steven G. Koven / *University of Louisville, Louisville, Kentucky, U.S.A.*

Dale Krane / *University of Nebraska at Omaha, Omaha, Nebraska, U.S.A.*

Wendell C. Lawther / *University of Central Florida, Orlando, Florida, U.S.A.*

Mordecai Lee / *University of Wisconsin-Milwaukee, Milwaukee, Wisconsin, U.S.A.*

Eric K. Leonard / *Shenandoah University, Winchester, Virginia, U.S.A.*

Jeroen Maesschalck / *Katholieke Universiteit Leuven, Leuven, Belgium*

Michelle Maiese / *University of Colorado at Boulder, Boulder, Colorado, U.S.A.*

Theo Edwin Maloy / *West Texas A&M University, Canyon, Texas, U.S.A.*

Gary S. Marshall / *University of Nebraska at Omaha, Omaha, Nebraska, U.S.A.*

Darin Matthews / *Multnomah County Schools, Portland, Oregon, U.S.A.*

Jack W. Meek / *University of La Verne, La Verne, California, U.S.A.*

Göktuğ L. Morçöl / *The Pennsylvania State University-Harrisburg, Middletown, Pennsylvania, U.S.A.*

Tina Nabatchi / *Indiana University, Bloomington, Indiana, U.S.A.*

Stuart S. Nagel / *University of Illinois, Urbana, Illinois, U.S.A.*

Brian Negin / *Israel Central Bureau of Statistics, Jerusalem, Israel*

Holona L. Ochs / *University of Kansas, Lawrence, Kansas, U.S.A.*

Jun Peng / *University of Arizona, Tucson, Arizona, U.S.A.*

Steven A. Peterson / *The Pennsylvania State University at Harrisburg, Middletown, Pennsylvania, U.S.A.*

Suzanne J. Piotrowski / *Rutgers, The State University of New Jersey, Newark, New Jersey, U.S.A.*

Jon S. T. Quah / *National University of Singapore, Singapore*

Rupert G. Rhodd / *Florida Atlantic University, Davie, Florida, U.S.A.*

Rainer Rohdewohld / *GTZ-SfDM, Jakarta, Indonesia*

John F. Sacco / *George Mason University, Fairfax, Virginia, U.S.A.*

Ishak Saporta / *Tel Aviv University, Tel Aviv, Israel*

Anne L. Schneider / *Arizona State University, Tempe, Arizona, U.S.A.*

Mary Schmeida / *Kent State University, Kent, Ohio, U.S.A.*

William D. Schreckhise / *University of Arkansas, Fayetteville, Arkansas, U.S.A.*

Alex Sekwat / *Tennessee State University, Nashville, Tennessee, U.S.A.*

M. Shamsul Haque / *National University of Singapore, Singapore*

Leiyu Shi / *Johns Hopkins University, Baltimore, Maryland, U.S.A.*

Noore Alam Siddiquee / *International Islamic University Malaysia, Kuala Lumpur, Malaysia*

Carlos Nunes Silva / *University of Lisbon, Lisbon, Portugal*

Linda L. Stanley / *Our Lady of the Lake University, San Antonio, Texas, U.S.A.*

Stuart C. Strother / *University of Louisville, Louisville, Kentucky, U.S.A.*

Mark Turner / *University of Canberra, Canberra, Australia*

Walter Vance / *General Accounting Office, Washington, D.C., U.S.A.*

Ryan J. Watson / *National Academy of Public Administration, Washington, D.C., U.S.A.*

Clay Wescott / *Asian Development Bank, Manila, Philippines*

Andrew B. Whitford / *University of Kansas, Lawrence, Kansas, U.S.A.*

Elisabeth Wright / *U.S. Naval Postgraduate School, Monterey, California, U.S.A.*

Habib Zafarullah / *University of New England, Armidale, New South Wales, Austalia*

Contents

Preface xi

Accounting and Reporting for Private Nonprofit Organizations—Balancing Economic Efficiency with Social Mission / *John F. Sacco and Walter Vance* 1

Acquiring Resources Through Price Negotiation: A Public Sector Approach / *Rupert G. Rhodd* 8

Administrative Law Judges and Agency Adjudication / *William D. Schreckhise* 12

Administrative Reform in Southeast Asia / *M. Shamsul Haque* 16

Alternative Dispute Resolution Processes / *Tina Nabatchi and Lisa B. Bingham* 21

Assessing the Validity of Constructive Change Proposals / *Elisabeth Wright* 26

Association of Southeast Asian Nations (ASEAN) / *Richard K. Common* 30

Budget Stabilization Fund / *Yilin Hou* 34

Bureaucrats and Politicians in Southeast Asia / *Scott Fritzen* 39

Cambodia / *Clay Wescott* 44

Capital Purchases / *Wendell C. Lawther and John Adler* 48

Community-Based Planning for HIV/AIDS / *Bruce Kieler and Ishak Saporta* 52

Cooperative Purchasing / *Alex Sekwat* 61

Court System Strategic Planning / *Deborah A. Botch* 63

Crisis Policy Making and Management in Southeast Asia / *Scott Fritzen* 69

Decentralization in Southeast Asia / *Ledivina V. Cariño* 74

Democracy and Public Policy / *Dale Krane and Gary S. Marshall* 78

Development Administration in Southeast Asia / *Mark Turner* 85

Environmental Policy / *Thomas Greitens* 90

Ethics and Administrative Reform / *Jeroen Maesschalck* 94

Ethics and Information and Communication Technology / *Brian Negin* 99

Financial Condition / *Jane Beckett-Camarata* 104

Foreign Policy Analysis / *Eric K. Leonard* 110

Freedom of Information Act—Federal / *Suzanne J. Piotrowski* 114

Government-Sponsored Enterprises (GSEs) / *Stuart C. Strother and Steven G. Koven* 118

Health Care, Assessment and Evaluation of / *Leiyu Shi* 123

Health Care Decision Analysis, Alternatives in / *Krishna S. Dhir* 129

Health Care Decision Making Behavior, Emerging Paradigms of / *Krishna S. Dhir* 133

Health Care Policy / *Walter J. Jones* 138

Humanitarian Intervention / *Michelle Maiese* 142

Impacts of Bureaucratic Reform on State Government Administration / *Brendan F. Burke* 148

Indonesia / *Rainer Rohdewohld* 153

Information Sources and State Policy Making / *Jill Clark* 157

Integrated Health Care Systems: New Trends, Emerging Models, and
  Future Shocks / *Yvonne J. Kochanowski* 162
John Rawls / *James R. Heichelbech* 166
Lao People's Democratic Republic (PDR) / *Clay Wescott* 170
Logistics and Transportation / *Linda L. Stanley and Darin Matthews* 174
Malaysia / *Noore Alam Siddiquee and Habib Zafarullah* 179
Milgram Experiments / *Holona L. Ochs and Andrew B. Whitford* 184
Models of the Policy Process / *Thomas A. Birkland* 188
National Security Policy / *Eric K. Leonard* 192
Ombuds and Ombuds Programs / *Tina Nabatchi and Lisa B. Bingham* 197
Pay-As-You-Go Financing / *David L. Baker* 200
Policy Design / *Anne L. Schneider and Helen Ingram* 204
Policy Implementation / *Ann O'M. Bowman* 209
Policy Networks / *Jack W. Meek* 213
Postpositivist Perspectives in Policy Analysis / *Göktuğ L. Morçöl* 217
Privatization / *Marc Holzer and Hwang-Sun Kang* 221
Public–Private Partnerships in Developing Countries / *Steven G. Koven and*
  Stuart C. Strother 224
Public–Private Partnerships for Economic Development / *Steven G. Koven and*
  Stuart C. Strother 229
Public Procurement Ethics / *David Seth Jones* 234
Public Reporting / *Mordecai Lee* 239
Reciprocal Relations Among Peace, Prosperity, and Democracy /
  Stuart S. Nagel 244
Restorative Justice / *Michelle Maiese* 248
Risk Management / *David L. Baker* 255
Singapore / *Jon S. T. Quah* 259
State Enterprise Zones / *Ryan J. Watson and Terry F. Buss* 264
State and Local Public Pension Fund Management / *Jun Peng* 271
Subnational Counter-Cyclical Fiscal Policy in the United States / *Yilin Hou* . . 276
Telehealth and State Government Policy / *Mary Schmeida* 281
Thailand / *Brian Brewer* 285
Transparency and Corruption in Southeast Asia / *Habib Zafarullah and*
  Noore Alam Siddiquee 290
Truth and Reconciliation Commission / *Daryl Balia* 295
Tuskegee Study / *Holona L. Ochs and Andrew B. Whitford* 298
Understanding the Basics of Refunding in the Municipal Bond Market /
  Jun Peng 302
United States Treasury Securities / *Theo Edwin Maloy* 306
Urban Planning and Ethics / *Carlos Nunes Silva* 311
Using Model Contracts to Reduce the Risks in Complex Information
  Technology Procurements / *Michael Asner* 317
Values and Policy Analysis / *Steven A. Peterson* 321
Whistle-Blowing: Corporate and Public Policy / *Michael W. Austin and*
  Michael A. Harper 323
Index 327

Preface

It is indeed an honor to write a Preface to the first Supplement to the *Encyclopedia of Public Administration and Public Policy.*

I make this statement for two reasons. First, I continue to be more than pleased with the quality and depth of each topical entry. I thank our Contributing Editors and Topical Entry Authors from around the world.

Second, I was told three years ago that the first Supplement probably would come out in 2007. Contributing Editor— and Topical Entry Author— productivity brought in the first Supplement two years earlier and, given that we have covered in the three printed volumes less than one-third of the topical entries which have been identified, I am sure that this productivity engine will continue to bear fruit.

As always, I want to thank W. Aaron Wachhaus, Jr., assistant to the Executive Editor, and Susan Lee for their contributions toward making this gigantic, international, cooperative endeavor work.

Jack Rabin
Executive Editor

Accounting and Reporting for Private Nonprofit Organizations—Balancing Economic Efficiency with Social Mission

John F. Sacco
George Mason University, Fairfax, Virginia, U.S.A.

Walter Vance
General Accounting Office, Washington, District of Columbia, U.S.A.

INTRODUCTION

This chapter discusses how the value of economic efficiency, which is typically associated with private business accounting and operations, is increasingly being used to measure private nonprofit accounting and operations financial performance. Since the mid-1990s, private nonprofit organizations under the Financial Standards Accounting Board (FASB) have begun to follow the full cost accrual and consolidation model that is associated with measuring economic efficiency. This change suggests that the public choice philosophy (business efficiency in government and nonprofits) has cast its shadow over the traditional progressive philosophy (social mission) that historically was the model of operations in private nonprofit organizations. Specifically, the use of full costing for every project, taking a hard look at projects that are not "breaking even," obtaining more outputs for less input, and putting extra emphasis on "earned income" in the form of donations are now all associated with the new nonprofit environment. Whether the pendulum will swing back to having social mission instead of economic efficiency being the primary criteria by which private nonprofits are judged is a critical question given the importance of the work that nonprofits undertake. With issues like environmental degradation, poverty, and international unrest in the forefront of the news, more pressure is placed on private nonprofit organizations to address these issues. How should the increasingly important private nonprofit sector account, measure, and report success?

DEFINITION

Private nonprofit organizations are not affiliated with a government, even though they may receive grants or aid from different levels of government. Much of their revenue comes from voluntary contributions or earnings for services provided—not taxes.

The range of functions provided by private nonprofit entities is wide. The traditional private nonprofit is a charity, such as Catholic Relief Services or the District of Columbia Capital Area Food Bank. They provide services to the needy. Trade associations are private nonprofit organizations but they serve their members as opposed to the public at large. The American Bankers Association is a trade organization. Like trade associations, business leagues such as local chambers of commerce are private nonprofit entities. Even political action groups that lobby for legislation can fall in the private nonprofit category. Private nonprofits are corporations and as such must obtain corporation status from a state government. To obtain tax-exempt status they must seek approval from the Internal Revenue Service (IRS). Many private nonprofits must report to the state in which they were incorporated and to the IRS. IRS form 990 is the usual way in which private nonprofits provide information to the IRS on a yearly basis.

THE ROAD TO FASB AND THE EMPHASIS ON COMPETITION

A private nonprofit does not have to follow FASB accounting standards. However, they cannot obtain a clean (unqualified) audit without fairly expressing their financial statements in accordance with generally accepted accounting principles (GAAP) as set by FASB. Even obtaining a bank loan may require financial reporting in accord with FASB standards. Although FASB is a private operation, it has permission form the Securities and Exchange Commission (SEC) to write accounting

---

The views expressed by the authors are theirs and do not reflect the views of their respective institutions.

Encyclopedia of Public Administration and Public Policy
DOI: 10.1081/E-EPAP 120025528

rules for business and provide nonprofit entities. When private nonprofit organizations use FASB accounting standards, they are subject to all FASB requirements. However, some FASB rules were written specifically for private nonprofit organizations. Four of the FASB standards that are specific to nonprofit entities will be discussed in detail.

The financial reporting model imposed by FASB is the accrual and consolidation model with some selective use of fair value accounting (discussed later). For the most part this accrual and consolidation model emphasizes economic efficiency. All costs, regardless of whether cash has changed hands must be matched against revenue to determine whether the cost (effort) generated adequate income to break even or show a surplus. The Statement of Activities for a private nonprofits (similar to the income statement of a business) differentiates among program expenses, administration (often called management and general), and fund-raising. If private nonprofit organizations are formed to serve a social mission in the community, then a high percentage of expenses going to fund-raising and administration might contradict the social mission orientation. With the Statement of Financial Position (the balance sheet in business), money restricted for certain purposes can be distinguished from money that is unrestricted. While all the money must benefit the social mission as defined by the charter, some monies may be restricted to address special aspects of the social mission.

Use of the Economic Efficiency Criteria and the Accrual and Consolidation Model

The inclusion of private nonprofit organizations into the FASB fold has a history behind it. FASB became concerned about the many sources of accounting rules for private nonprofit organizations. Specifically, FASB felt that users of financial reports were getting inconsistent information. In some cases, FASB and others felt the accounting and reporting rules for these private nonprofit organizations were too flexible and allowed the organizations to provide information that was not sufficiently candid.

Now that FASB is making the accounting and reporting standards for private nonprofit organizations, this means

private nonprofit organizations must recognize revenue when earned and account for all costs necessary to earn those revenues in that period. If a pledge is made late in the fiscal year with the cash anticipated during the next period, then it is revenue in the year when pledged, not when the cash is received. The work, the phone calls, the web site, and the direct mailing have been done to earn the contribution during the period when the pledge was made. Thus, the pledge is considered earned revenue. On the expense side, if employees have pension benefits or other accrued compensated absences (e.g., sick leave and vacation) the cost of those (usually some present value of the future payment) must be included during the period when they were promised even though the money will not be paid until a later date.

Consolidation is also part of the FASB approach. Separate funds to distinguish current donations from endowments are no longer used for external reporting. The total of all revenues (in consolidated format, not fund format) is reported. If the private nonprofit has a sizable endowment, that endowment is part of the consolidated assets and revenues. Thus, the private nonprofit may look very wealthy even in years when cash donations are low and the nonprofit is facing liquidity problems. In the past, those sizable endowments could be placed in a separate fund and not counted as part of the total wealth (now called net assets) of the nonprofit.

SFAS 116—ACCOUNTING FOR CONTRIBUTIONS RECEIVED AND CONTRIBUTIONS MADE

In examining Statement of Financial Accounting Standards (SFAS) 116, issued under due process by the Financial Accounting Standards Board, it is important to understand that the standard applies to private nonprofit organizations that receive contributions as well as organizations or individuals that make the contribution. If a company makes a contribution to a private nonprofit organizations, the timing of when (i.e., the basis) to incur the expense for the company and when to recognize the revenue for the nonprofit both come from SFAS 116.

Categories	Revenue?
Unconditional contributions	Recognized in period received at fair market value
Conditional promises	Recognized when conditions are substantially met because future uncertainty is attached to the conditions
Services	Only if a nonfinancial asset is created and special skills ordinarily contracted are used

Fig. 1 When to recognize revenue.

The main goal of SFAS 116 is to make sure that contributions are appropriately and consistently recorded, using the accrual logic for revenue recognition.

With respect to contributions, SFAS 116 has several broad categories that help determine when revenue should be recognized. Fig. 1 provides the categories.

Example of Revenue

Assume a private nonprofit organization has the following transactions and events.

What amount can be considered revenue and in which of these categories?

1. One party contributes a $1000 check with no conditions attached.
2. A company promises to contribute $10,000 contingent on the private nonprofit collecting $5000 specifically to match the promise made by the company.
3. Another individual pledges $2000 with the promise to make the donation in this current fiscal period.
4. An electrician donates his time to the organization by installing wiring. The electrician's time is valued at $500. If the electrician had not done this skilled work, the private nonprofit would have had to purchase the service.
5. One company, aware of the $5000 matching requirement of the other company, promises to give $1500 if the full $5000 matching requirement is reached.
6. A local government contracts with the private nonprofit organization. The organization receives $1200 for work to be performed in the next period.
7. An individual donates $1000 but restricts its use to a certain program.

Fig. 2 shows the results.

No conditions were applied to the $4000 revenue consisting of two $1000 cash contributions (Nos. 1 and 7) and one $2000 (No. 3) pledge contribution. The $11,500 of conditional promises (Nos. 2 and 5) would be placed in the notes to the financial statements if the conditions were not met this accounting and reporting period. For service

(No. 4) notice how the revenue ($500) from service is offset by an expense ($500). The money received (No. 6) from the local government contract is not revenue; rather, it is a liability because the nonprofit still owes the work to the local government. Having the cash is insufficient under the accrual logic to declare something a revenue. The revenue must be earned. In this case of the contract, the nonprofit must do the work later and thus has a liability or future sacrifice often called unearned revenue. In addition to liabilities, other distinctions are important in the revenue recognition logic.

Classifying Revenue into Net Assets—Permanently Restricted, Temporarily Restricted and Unrestricted

When revenue is earned by a nonprofit it needs to be placed in one of three categories as designated by the donor.

- Permanently restricted—Oftentimes, the corpus or original amount cannot be spent. It is permanently restricted. Only the interest or gains earned might be unrestricted and available for current expenses.
- Temporarily restricted—This can only be spent on a certain program, e.g., health program, or cannot be spent until a later period, e.g., 3 months from now. Other temporary restrictions are possible.
- Unrestricted—Can be spent in any legal manner related to the mission.

SFAS 117—FINANCIAL STATEMENTS OF NONPROFIT ORGANIZATIONS

The Three Required Financial Statements Under SFAS 117 are:

- Statement of financial position (balance sheet).
- Statement of activities (the term income is not used because nonprofit organizations carry out activities to benefit the community not earn a profit).

Categories	Revenue	Not revenue	Liability	Expense
Unconditional contributions	$4,000			
Conditional promises		$11,500		
Service as revenue	$500			$500
Work to be performed			$1,200	
Total	$4,500	$11,500		$500

Fig. 2 What are the amounts in the appropriate categories?

- Statements of cash flow (shows the sources of cash, cash payments, and increase or decrease in cash balance, or more technically, cash and cash equivalents).

Assume that the nonprofit has finished the fiscal year that went from 7/1/x0 to 6/30/x1.

Statement of Financial Position

In this first statement presented, the statement of financial position (or balance sheet) reflects the accounting equation (assets = liabilities + net assets) in that assets and liabilities are shown. Note that net assets are used in place of equity (the label to connote business ownership) and further that net assets are divided into permanently, temporary, and unrestricted categories. Net assets and the three categories are used to capture the not-for-profit nature and the types of restrictions that go with donations. Remember, also, the balance sheet is for a point in time and shows ability to pay short- and long-term obligations from the asset pool. It also shows the ability of the entity to take advantage of emerging opportunities by comparing things such as liquid assets with short-term obligations (Fig. 3).

The asset section does not have any nomenclature that is overly complex. It is arranged in terms of liquidity, from the most liquid, cash, to the least liquid, property, plant, and equipment, and long term investments. Contributions receivable parallel accounts receivable typical of private sector business operations. Liabilities are ordered from those that need to be paid the soonest to those that need to be paid later.

In the analysis of this balance sheet, total assets, $29,000, exceed liabilities, $13,000, by $16,000, suggesting a reasonably healthy financial status. For instance, the cash in unrestricted, $2000, is sufficient to cover the accounts payable (which total $500). A closer look reveals some possible problems. As is often the case with nonprofit entities, donor restrictions can limit flexibility. The entity has a note payable that might come due soon. The note payable is $5000, whereas the excess of unrestricted cash over accounts payable is only $1500.

	Private nonprofit organization name	
	Statement of financial position	
	6/30/x1	
Assets		
Cash – unrestricted	$2,000	
Cash – temporarily restricted	3,500	
Interest receivable	50	
Contributions receivable	1,450	
Property, plant, equipment (net of depreciation)	12,000	
Long-term investments	10,000	
Total	$29,000	
Liabilities and net assets		
Accounts payable	$500	
Notes payable	5,000	
Long-term debt	7,500	
Total	$13,000	
Net assets		
Unrestricted	$2,000	
Temporarily restricted	4,000	
Permanently restricted	10,000	
Total net assets	$16,000	
Total liabilities and net assets	$29,000	

Fig. 3　Statement of financial position (balance sheet).

Thus, the nonprofit may have to borrow. An examination of the net assets section shows the type and extent of restrictions. Of the total difference between liabilities and assets, $16,000, only $6000 is not permanently restricted. The rest, $10,000, is permanently restricted, which severely limits its ability to be used in the short term.

Statement of Activities

For the statement of activities, observe how the categories, unrestricted, temporarily restricted, and permanently restricted are included, just as they are in the balance sheet (Fig. 4). Notice too, the bottom line is not profit or loss but change in net assets. Unlike the statement of financial position, the statement of activities is for a period of time, not a point in time. In this case the statement answers the question, "What has been the financial success (revenues matched against expenses) for the period 7/1/x0 to 6/30/x1?"

Overall, as presented in the total column, net assets for the nonprofit have increased by $16,000 for the period. Total revenue was $91,000 and total expenses were $75,000. However, when the total column is dissected, only $6000 ($2000 from unrestricted and $4000 from temporarily restricted) of the change in net assets is not permanently restricted. Most of the change in net assets ($10,000) comes from the permanently restricted category. Overall, the organization brought in more money than it spent (on an accrual basis) but a significant amount of the financial success is permanently restricted.

Statement of Cash Flow

The statement of cash flow is designed to show where the cash came from and where it went. For instance, if a private nonprofit entity gets most of its cash from borrowing or grants, then future survival may be in question. Will the grants continue and will contributions be sufficient to repay amounts borrowed and any associated interest payments? Raising cash via heavy borrowing will show in the statement of cash flow and such information can be vital to outsider readers of the statements. The statement of cash flow also shows whether the amount of cash changed (grew, stayed the same, or dropped) during the period.

Revenue, gains, and other support	Unrestricted	Temporarily restricted	Permanently restricted	Total
Contributions	$75,000	5,000	10,000	$90,000
Income from investments	500			500
net unrealized and				
realized gains	500			500
Net assets released				
from restrictions				
satisfaction of program				
restrictions	1,000	-1,000		
Total	$77,000	4,000	10,000	$91,000
Expenses and losses				
Program A	35,000			
Program B	20,000			
Management and general	15,000			
Fund raising	5,000			
Total	$75,000			$75,000
Change in net assets	2,000	4,000	10,000	16,000
Beginning	0	0	0	0
End	$2,000	4,000	10,000	$16,000

Fig. 4 Private nonprofit organization name; statement of activities; for the period 7/1/x0 to 6/30/x1.

SFAS 124—ACCOUNTING FOR CERTAIN INVESTMENTS

Nonprofit entities often receive stocks and bonds as donations. SFAS 124 applies to equity securities (i.e., purchase or donation of stocks) with readily determinable market value and all investments in debt securities (e.g., purchase or donation of bonds). With SFAS 124 comes the interjection of "fair value" accounting and reporting (as opposed to historical cost accounting and reporting, which is used for most items such as property, plant, and equipment) and other rules related to investing in securities. On the surface, fair value accounting is not overly complex. Often called "mark to market," it means that even those increases or declines in the value of securities not sold (so called "paper changes") must be recognized at the end of the period. If the value goes up during the reporting period, that is an unrealized holding gain. It goes on the statement of activities as a part of revenue. If the value falls, even without a sale, that constitutes an unrealized holding loss. It too goes on the statement of activities as loss subtracted from revenues. Unrealized gains and losses would also affect the balance sheet value of the investment. Presumably, outside users of financial statements (e.g., donors) are better informed about the financial performance and quality of management with the application of fair value accounting for securities.

The simplicity of "fair value" reporting stops at the conceptual level and becomes much more complex in implementation. The use of fair value depends on an array of circumstances, including for stocks, the amount of a company that a private nonprofit owns. When a nonprofit holds a large stock endowment in one company, the accounting becomes complex. A private nonprofit may own 30% of a company from an endowment. If so, the accounting becomes even more complex and can likely move away from the fair value approach to an approach called the equity method where the nonprofit shows the earnings or losses of the company as part of their own revenue and value. For instance, if a nonprofit owns 30% of a company and the company loses $90,000 dollars, then the nonprofit shows a $30,000 loss.

SFAS 136—TRANSFER OF ASSETS TO A NONPROFIT

The complete title of this SFAS (136) indicates its focus. The full title is "Transfer of Assets to a Not-for-Profit Organization or Charitable Trust that Raises or Holds Contributions for Others." As might be expected from the title, this SFAS is designed to answer the question about how a nonprofit reports a contribution when the donor specifies another entity to ultimately or potentially receive the donation. SFAS 136 is of particular interest to federated fund-raising organizations. The United Way is an example of a nonprofit that will be affected by this standard. It often collects donations and contributions that will be transferred to another nonprofit organizations.

In the terminology of SFAS 136, the unit receiving the assets is the recipient while the unit that will or can ultimately get the assets is the beneficiary. The contributor is the donor. It is the donor's specifications that affect the answer to how the recipient and beneficiary account for the donation. As with other accounting rules, SFAS 136 can become more complicated as is the case when the recipient and beneficiary are economically interrelated (one is a subsidiary of the other). Then both can share a stake in the donation.

SOP 98-2—ACCOUNTING COSTS OF ACTIVITIES OF NOT-FOR-PROFIT ORGANIZATIONS AND STATE GOVERNMENT ENTITIES THAT INCLUDE FUND-RAISING

People who donate assets to nonprofit organizations as well as auditors who render opinions on nonprofit financial statements have been concerned that amounts spent on fund-raising can be underreported to make it look like the nonprofit is putting most of its expenses in mission-oriented programs. As a result, the American Institute of Certified Public Accountants wrote a statement of position (SOP) to clarify accounting and reporting for fund-raising, SOP 98-2.

Generically, the accounting term used to deal with this issue of allocating costs when more than one type of product is generated from the same process is "joint costs." In business, a typical example is allocating a portion of a cost on one cut of meat when there is only one expense for the entire carving process. In a nonprofit, an example is allocating the costs of postage, envelopes, labor, and machinery when educational or program information and fund-raising are included in the same mailing.

If an effort includes both fund-raising information and another activity such as the educational aspect of the social mission, allocation of joint cost to both program and fund-raising expenses can be used only if certain criteria are met. The activity must call on the audience to do something about the social mission. If the letter, for example, is directed toward environmental cleanup, then the letter must call for specific action such as attending a Saturday morning neighborhood cleanup. Simply saying that clean neighborhoods are important is insufficient for allowing the cost to be counted as program expenses as opposed to fund-raising expenses. If a specific, mission-oriented action is requested, an allocation between fund-raising and program expenses can be made.

Even the call for action may not be sufficient to allocate costs between fund-raising and program expenses. The audience selected should be people who believe in the mission. If the audience is selected because of past contributions, then all costs go to fund-raising. If the outside firm developing the campaign receives compensation on the basis of the assets donated, then all costs must be assigned as fund-raising costs.

CONCLUSION

Traditionally, private nonprofits were considered to be driven by a social mission. In the mid-1990s, the accounting rule-making body for publicly traded companies, FASB, became a part of the life of private nonprofits. As a result, private nonprofit organizations have a significant economic efficiency criterion to meet, and they did so, in part, by following the accrual and consolidation model (complemented by fair value) that FASB place on them. The new model demands more output for less input and

hard decisions about projects that fail to break even—not exactly a "kinder, gentler" type of accounting!

Private nonprofit entities are still adjusting to the dual forces of the competitive mentality of global markets and the world of social upheaval. In short, charity is in a new realm of competing in the market place for money and even for delivering services. Many for-profit agencies wish to sell the same services nonprofits provide. The demands on private nonprofit operations are considerable. They have their social mission to pursue, they must compete perhaps more so than in the past, and they are considered to be an important part of maintaining world social order.

FURTHER READING

Larkin, R.F.; DiTommaso, M. *Wiley Not-for-Profit GAAP 2003*; John Wiley & Sons Inc.: New York, 2002.

McLaughlin, T.A. *Streetsmart Financial Basics for Nonprofit Managers,* 2nd Ed.; John Wiley & Sons Inc.: New York, 2002.

McMillian, E.J. *Model Accounting and Financial Policies & Procedure Handbooks,* Revised Edition; American Society of Association Executives: Washington, DC, 1999.

Salomon, L.M. *America's Nonprofit Sector: A Primer,* 2nd Ed.; The Foundation Center: New York, 1999.

Acquiring Resources Through Price Negotiation: A Public Sector Approach

Rupert G. Rhodd
Florida Atlantic University, Davie, Florida, U.S.A.

INTRODUCTION

Commercial negotiation has been with us for a long time, some accounts going as far back as when ships first sailed to China to buy silk and spices. In the pre-Industrial Revolution era the small scale of manufacturing operations meant that the entrepreneurs had to be skilled in everything including the purchasing of raw materials. If entrepreneurs were able to determine the quality of the inputs and, at the same time negotiate a price to minimize the average cost of inputs, the greater the demand for their product and the higher the profit margin. With the coming of the Industrial Revolution and large scale production there was a role for purchasing agents. In this period negotiation focusing on quality, delivery, and service "as industrial sellers customarily set prices at or near cost plus 10%."[1] The focus of negotiation shifted in the 1930s when sales people were granted the authority to set price at any level. Today, negotiation focuses solely on securing the best possible price.

For any organization, achieving long- and short-term goals and objectives depends on a host of economic relationships including the demand and supply of resources, which determine the price of resources. With increasing population and demand for government services, and with budgetary constraints, negotiating the optimal price and quantity of resources that are required to deliver government services has become an important activity of government agencies. This is recognized by the increased role and prominence of procurement departments/personnel in government agencies. Through negotiation, the purpose of these departments/personnel is "to secure the best possible long or short-term agreement for the organization, consistent with the concept of lowest total cost."[1]

Negotiation, as an important component of the organization's strategy to acquire resources, can be considered a subtopic of game theory and can be analyzed using a similar approach as the broader topics of game theory. Alfred Chandler[2] defines strategy as the determination of basic long-term goals and objectives, and the adoption of courses of action to achieve these goals.[2] Strategy, which includes negotiation, is important to the organization's success, to the achieving of its long-term goals.

In a general way, a model of negotiation is an attempt to model in a specific way the interactions of competing utility or wealth maximizers, as it takes into account the strategies of competing players. Negotiation is therefore concerned with the analysis of strategic interaction in which the decision maker is assumed to interact with others in the environment, this causing the optimal decision to be affected by the action of others.[3] Although it uses the same players found in any market (buyers and sellers), it extends the analysis through which price is determined by including actual interaction such as asymmetric information and haggling over the price. As in any game of strategy, there may be *cooperation* in which the players use contracts and are able to plan long-term strategies. In other situations there could be *noncooperation* especially if enforcing the contract is difficult.

A model of negotiation could be included under the broader topic of "game theory" in which payoff functions and strategy sets are assigned to the participants, and the various outcomes are noted when particular strategies are chosen to maximize the payoff. "Game theory is concerned with the actions of individuals who are conscious that their actions affect each other."[4] Game theory is used mostly in situations where private decision makers are seeking to maximize wealth in the marketplace, not in situations where purchases are made by government agencies as they are not assumed to be "maximizers" of wealth or profit. However, because purchases by government agencies include contracts, are budget restricted, take place under various forms of competition, and oftentimes include some haggling, there is scope for analyzing government procurement through some form of game theoretic model using similar assumptions. The analysis presented below will not be a "pure form of game theory." It will seek to specify conditions under which government procurement takes place and theorize as to where the final price will settle; closer to the seller's offering or closer to the buyer's suggestion.

Encyclopedia of Public Administration and Public Policy
DOI: 10.1081/E-EPAP 120019560

VERTICAL INTEGRATION VS. OUTSOURCING

Vertical Integration

Public and private firms, seeking to acquire goods, generally do so through vertical integration or outsourcing. Whereas a vertical chain of production is the coming together of firms at various stages in the production of a good, outsourcing is that situation in which a firm gets an input to deliver a good or service, or the firm acquires the good or service to be delivered from an external source. With vertical integration, benefits such as 1) reduction in transaction and coordination costs, 2) continuity of supply, 3) the nonsharing of proprietary rights, and 4) greater control over the quality of inputs are often realized.

Organizing production through vertical integration means that firms are organized into a business unit. The implication from this is that measuring the performance of individual firms requires that a ''transfer price'' be established for goods and services exchanged. With a transfer price, total profits can be reallocated among firms in the business unit and this could impact the business unit's overall profit. Supplying goods through vertical integration may therefore not encourage least cost production by an individual firm because of subsidies by more profitable firms within the integrated business unit.

Transfer of goods between firms in a vertically integrated business unit can take place as follows. If there is a competitive external market for the good in question, the product can be transferred at the ''external market price.'' If there is no external market or if for some reason the market price does not truly measure the opportunity cost of producing the good, the ''marginal production cost'' could be used to determine the transfer price. With the marginal production cost being the cost to produce the last unit, this therefore represents the value of resources foregone to produce the last unit. Some firms in an integrated unit have also made use of ''full-cost transfer prices'' because it is felt that marginal cost of production focuses on variable cost and omits fixed cost.[a] This method is simple, is easily implemented, and is the most popular of the pricing mechanism used by firms in an integrated unit.[3]

Price negotiation can assist in the transfer of goods between firms in an integrated unit and also in the acquisition of goods through outsourcing. In an integrated unit, the price at which goods are transferred is aptly labeled the ''negotiated transfer price'' because it is de-termined by negotiation between the units. A negotiated price between firms in a business unit is expected to maximize the combined profits of the negotiating firms. The selling firm will not negotiate a price below its production cost, and the acquiring firm will not pay a price above that for which it can buy the product elsewhere. The reference to purchasing a good at a price not higher than that for which it can be purchased elsewhere indicates that the market does play an indirect role, and serves more as a reference point for the determination of a negotiated transfer price. Because it is possible for two firms in an integrated unit to negotiate a transfer price without at the same time agreeing on the quantity to be transferred at that price, there is no guarantee that the negotiated price will maximize the business unit's value. There is also the possibility of a long, drawn-out, and time-consuming process which when converted to a mon-etary value could increase the cost of acquiring goods and services.

Outsourcing

For the public sector in the United States, goods and services are acquired mostly through outsourcing, which is generally defined as obtaining goods and services from outside rather than providing them in-house. There are many possible reasons why the public sector may have decided to acquire goods and services through outsourcing. Among them are 1) heightened competition between supply firms and the relatively low cost of goods and services, 2) flexible production techniques and the willingness of producers to satisfy government needs, 3) the short tenure of government and the disruption that would be caused when the leadership/ruling party changes, and 4) improved communications and the relative ease with which goods and services can be obtained from outside agencies.

When firms seek to acquire goods and services through outsourcing, the cost of goods and services are determined by market conditions, or the price is determined through negotiation, especially where there are long-term contracts.[b] Buying goods in the competitive market could be advantageous as compared to a noncompetitive or negotiated situation because it could easily be argued that as competitive firms do not make surplus profit over the long-run period, the market-determined price tends to be lower than a negotiated price. However, even with the potential benefits from acquiring goods at market price, procurement officers in the public sector have used

---

[a]Whereas variable costs (e.g., direct labor costs and commissions to salespeople) increase with output, fixed costs (e.g., lease agreement and administrative expenses) remain constant when output increases.

[b]Long-term contracts could be in the form of long-term supply and distribution contracts, franchise contracts, leasing contracts, or strategic alliances.

negotiation with long-term contracts and a few vendors to acquire goods and services. There seems to be the feeling that through negotiation there is more control over price, quality, and delivery. Although this may be true for quality and delivery, the negotiated price is more dependent on the skillfulness of the parties "at the negotiating table" and conditions in the market.

GOVERNMENT PROCUREMENT AND MARKET CONDITIONS

Negotiation in general differs from a ball game or a war where only one side wins and the other side loses. In successful negotiations, both sides win something, giving rise to a "win–win" situation. When procurement officers or purchasing agents seek to acquire goods and services through negotiation, the objectives of negotiation are 1) to obtain the quality specified, 2) to obtain a fair and reasonable price, and 3) to get the vendor to perform the contract on time. Although all three objectives are important, budgetary restrictions on public sector agencies cause most attention to be paid to obtaining goods and services at a fair and reasonable price. Mention is often made of securing goods and services at the " right price," that which is fair to both buyer and seller.[5] And even with this definition, the "right price" is not static because firms are able (within limits) to adjust their asking and offering price, which could vary with market conditions.

In the United States we find the three forms of competition that are discussed in any elementary microeconomics textbook. At one extreme, there is the idealist form of perfect competition characterized by "atomistic" competition in which a large number of sellers trade a homogeneous good. This form of competition is also characterized by the availability of low cost of accurate information and the ability of firms to freely enter and leave the industry.

At the other extreme of the competitive spectrum is monopoly, where one firm controls the supply and hence the price of the product. Some reasons for the establishment of monopolies include the control of specific assets, production requiring large output and the realization of economies of scale, the availability of excess capacity and the ability to increase production at will, pre-commitment contracts, licenses and patents, and pioneering brand advantages.

Between the two extremes are conditions of imperfect competition where the number of sellers of a heterogeneous or homogenous good can be large or small. Under this market form, the supplier has some control over "brand" price. Studies have shown that in the United States, most goods are traded under conditions where

there is some freedom to adjust price, and this would imply conditions of imperfect competition.[c] We accept the conclusions of these studies as true, but we also believe that tightly budgeted expenditures and the encumbering of funds for future expenditure cause the government sector to secure goods under varying conditions of competition. To get the biggest "bang for the buck," government procurement is forced into markets where the price will be "right" or most beneficial to the agency.

Pricing of Goods

One of the tips given for conducting successful negotiation is "do your homework." For government agents, this includes knowledge of the product and market. Regarding the procurement of goods, one would be more inclined to believe that if quality and quantity are easily ascertained, pricing issues involving government procurement would be at a minimum. If this is so, the situation boils down to whether pricing should be based on full cost, marginal cost, or some method to benefit the government agency as well as the firm supplying the good.

In the most competitive market, substitute goods are differentiated by design, wrapping, or other such features. The market has a large number of sellers with the individual seller forced to sell at "near equal" prices. Furthermore, to remain in this market, suppliers must be very efficient. We could therefore infer from this that suppliers in this market will sell to government agencies at the lowest possible price, that the goods will be of the highest value, and that price is a true indicator of quality. Furthermore, if government procurement involves "large dollars" and contracts that can cover multiple years, firms selling to government agencies will endeavor to have a long relationship with the agencies by selling at a lower price. Based on the above, government procurement agents seem to have some amount of buying power.

Intense competition forces manufacturers to make their products intrinsically different. This gives room for different negotiated prices between suppliers and the government, and components such as service and delivery are included in the price. Also, as the number of producers/sellers in the market declines, suppliers will have more power over the price at which goods are purchased. It also follows that as the products become more differentiated, more effort will be required by government agencies to determine quality and similarity of prices. If procurement personnel is limited, government agencies could be forced to accept the seller's words, with the negotiated price more beneficial to the seller.

---

[c]See Ref. [5] p. 244, for a list of these studies.

If the government seeks to buy goods from traditional sellers, procurement agents could find themselves involved in a game. This is because traditional sellers see negotiation as a game in which they offer to sell their products at a very high price, expecting the buyer to counter at a very low price. Through haggling and counter-offers, the established price is set somewhere in between the seller's high price and the buyer's lower price. If the government procurement official is expecting this response, both buyer and seller will be using various means (tricks, creative lies, and artful badgering) to negotiate in their favor. This could compromise delivery, quality, and goodwill.

Pricing of Services

Research indicates that employee's compensation as a percentage of noncapital direct expenditure is between 30% and 40% at the state and local levels, and 15% and 20% at the federal level.[6] Economic theory proposes that labor should be paid according to its marginal revenue product, which is the marginal product of labor expressed in dollar value. This approach is only useful in the public sector where the output of labor is easily determined and where the government can determine the quality of the output. If quality and quantity are not easily determined, there is room for a negotiated wage rate. Many factors can determine the negotiated wages, these including union representation, skills of labor, demand by the public sector, and wage rate in other sectors of the economy.

There is also the additional issue of what price should the government pay labor when productivity of labor and wages in the other sectors of the economy increase faster than in the public sector. This issue is important because depending on the policy chosen, the supply of labor in the public sector could decline, efficiency could fall, and the average cost of services in the public sector could increase. Here again, negotiations are important. To reduce the above problems, the negotiated price of labor should be close to that which is offered in the more efficient private sector. Furthermore, because jobs in the public sector tend to be more secure and with the likelihood of more generous benefits, paying labor a rate close to that paid in the more efficient private sector could attract labor from the private sector and improve the efficiency of labor in the public sector.

Even with the analysis outlined above, we understand that each procurement project is unique and complex and thus defies the use of a general rule or policy. We also believe that for each purchasing organization, the regulations, and the rules are different. These complicate the procurement process. In the end, the procurement approach that is used and the manner in which it is implemented will determine the success or failure of government's projects. Because of the dynamic nature of today's market, it is imperative that government agencies continue their vigilance on procurement procedures.

CONCLUSION

With the increasing size of government spending, and with more pressure on the public sector to provide a wider range of goods and services, negotiating the "best" price for the highest quality of goods and services is of greatest importance. To facilitate this process government procurement officials must be well trained in negotiation, business decision-making, and economics and their departments must be adequately equipped with the latest technology to seek our suppliers. In the long run, a more informed procurement division will go a far way in maximizing society's benefits from public expenditure.

REFERENCES

1. Cavinato, J.; Kauffman, R. *The Purchasing Handbook: A Guide for the Purchasing and Supply Professional*; McGraw-Hill, 2000; 449, 500.
2. Chandler, A. *Strategy and Structure, Chapters in the History of the American Industrial Enterprises*; MIT Press: Cambridge, MA, 1962; 13.
3. Brickley, J.; Smith, C.; Zimmerman, J. *Managerial Economics and Organizational Architecture*; McGraw-Hill, 2001; 213, 448.
4. Rasmusen, E. *Games and Information*; Blackwell, 1990; 21.
5. Dobler, D.; Burt, D.; Lee, L., Jr. *Purchasing and Materials Management: Text and Cases,* 5th Ed.; McGraw-Hill, 1983; 242.
6. Hyman, D. *Public Finance*; Dryden, 1993.

Administrative Law Judges and Agency Adjudication

William D. Schreckhise
University of Arkansas, Fayetteville, Arkansas, U.S.A.

INTRODUCTION

Administrative law judges (ALJs) and agency adjudications are two things about which most people know very little, but both play an important role in the operations of government in the United States. Adjudications and agency hearings are an important component of regulatory enforcement, entitlement disbursement, and internal agency management. Administrative law judges preside over disputes between two or more parties, much like a judge presides over cases brought before a court. However, an administrative law judge is an employee of the *executive* branch of government and, often, one of the parties in the dispute is the agency for whom they are employed. Adjudications are the equivalent to cases and are the conflicts over which the administrative law judges preside. This entry will present the origins of administrative law judges and discuss the current role they play at the state and federal government adjudications.

ADMINISTRATIVE PROCEDURES LAWS AND ADMINISTRATIVE LAW JUDGES

Currently, 1286 ALJs serve in the federal government, holding positions in 26 different agencies (Table 1). They deal with such widely varying topics as disputes over continuing Social Security Disability Insurance benefits and the application of regulations of the U.S. Securities Exchange Commission.

The position of administrative law judge originated with the passage of the federal Hepburn Act (1906). In this act, Congress granted the Interstate Commerce Commission (ICC) the power to appoint "hearing examiners" to act on the commission's behalf in giving oaths, taking testimony, examining witnesses, and viewing evidence. The ICC's success with this new position prompted other agencies to follow suit. Between the years 1913 and 1940, Congress granted 18 other agencies the power to appoint their own hearing examiners. The federal Administrative Procedure Act (APA) of 1946 established the hearing officer as a clearly distinct judicial power in each agency. These positions were created to constitute an independent corps of judicial actors assigned powers to preside over agency hearings, but were to do it in a manner less formal

and more flexible than courtroom proceedings, and who could develop expertise in more technical areas of policy. These actors were to remain within each agency, yet through the APA, Congress erected institutional safeguards to ensure that ALJs would hear cases in an unbiased manner, ideally free from agency pressure to ensure due process for the parties involved.[1] State APAs created similar positions following a comparable logic of organization and institutional design. In 1972, the U.S. Civil Service Commission changed the title of "hearing examiner" to that of "administrative law judge" to reflect a recognition that, in many important areas of public life, ALJs would be hearing cases *independent* of agency pressure, i.e., carrying out the role of an impartial judge in the standard sense.

The Administrative Procedure Act granted federal ALJs a substantial degree of autonomy from their agencies. The APA gave to the Civil Service Commission (now the Office of Personnel Management) the power to determine the qualifications and compensation of individual ALJs. Under the APA, ALJs can be removed only for cause, and before one can be disciplined, demoted, suspended, or dismissed, they first must receive a hearing before the Merit Systems Protection Board. The Office of Personnel Management sets administrative law judges' qualifications, and the APA ties ALJ compensation to the Executive Schedule. The Civil Service Reform Act (1978) further protected ALJs by explicitly exempting them from annual performance appraisals by their agency, and today, ALJs are the only members of the federal Senior Executive Service who are exempt from them.[2] When these protections are considered along with the other protections afforded them under the APA, the federal administrative judiciary is clearly the single-most protected class of federal employees vis-à-vis employing agency influence.

However, ALJ independence is not absolute. In the eyes of the courts, federal ALJs are not "constitutionally protected" as are their regular courtroom colleagues. They are also subject to the agency in matters of interpreting the law and agency policy, and the courts have concluded that agencies can assign cases to specific ALJs as they see fit. All federal agencies using ALJs employ some type of review within the agency,[3] and the courts have ruled that in reviewing an ALJ decision under

Encyclopedia of Public Administration and Public Policy
DOI: 10.1081/E-EPAP 120024308

Table 1 Federal administrative law judges and their agencies

Agency	Number of ALJs
Commodity Futures Trading Commission	2
Department of Agriculture	2
Department of Education	1
Department of Energy	15
Department of Health and Human Services	9
Department of Homeland Security	7
Department of Housing and Urban Development	5
Department of Interior	11
Department of Justice	4
Department of Labor	47
Department of Transportation	2
Department of Treasury	2
Environmental Protection Agency	6
Federal Communications Commission	2
Federal Maritime Commission	3
Federal Mine Safety and Health Commission	9
Federal Trade Commission	2
International Trade Commission	4
Merit Systems Protection Board	5
National Labor Relations Board	54
National Transportation Safety Board	4
Occupational Health Safety Review Commission	11
Securities and Exchange Commission	5
Social Security Administration	1079
Total	1292

Source: Office of Personnel Management, FedScope, http://www.fedscope.opm.gov/employment.htm (accessed July 2003).

the APA, the agency maintains ''all the powers which it would have in making the institutional decision.''[4]

STATE ADMINISTRATIVE LAW JUDGES

On the heels of the passage of the federal APA, a working group of representatives from the American Bar Foundation and the National Conference of Commissioners on Uniform State Laws created a model state Administrative Procedure Act. The model act was fashioned after the federal APA and included provisions for the creation of state ALJs. The model APA has been adopted at least in part by all 50 states and by the government of the District of Columbia. Today, every state employs ALJs in a fashion similar to federal ALJs.[5]

State-level ALJs hear different types of cases from their federal counterparts. The bulk of federal ALJs hears

cases involving benefits for Social Security claims, with the remainder largely presiding over regulatory hearings (environmental, transportation, securities, mergers, labor, and tariffs). State ALJs hear cases involving workers compensation, alcohol sale permits, public health regulations, environmental protection, utilities regulations, and employment discrimination. Some states will even relegate to their ALJs the authority to preside over driver's license revocation proceedings.

The ways in which ALJs perform their duties vary somewhat from state to state. In some state jurisdictions, an ALJ is an employee of the agency for which he or she hears cases. In other states, ALJs are employed in a separate ''central panel'' agency. Central panel agencies were created at the state level to give state ALJs even greater decisional independence. The creation of central panels began after the Administrative Conference of the United States recommended the creation of such agencies for the federal government in the 1970s, and the idea was vigorously supported by state bar organizations.[6] By 2003, 26 states employed central panels systems, most of

Table 2 State central panel agencies

State	Agency
Alabama	Alabama Administrative Law Judge Central Panel
Arizona	Office of Administrative Hearings
California	Office of Administrative Hearings
Colorado	Division of Administrative Hearings
Florida	Division of Administrative Hearings
Georgia	Office of State Administrative Hearings
Iowa	Department of Inspections and Appeals
Louisiana	Division of Administrative Law
Maine	Division of Administrative Hearings
Maryland	Office of Administrative Hearings
Massachusetts	Division of Administrative Law Appeals
Michigan	Bureau of Hearings
Minnesota	Office of Administrative Hearings
Missouri	Missouri Administrative Hearing Commission
New Jersey	Office of Administrative Law
North Carolina	Office of Administrative Hearings
North Dakota	Office of Administrative Hearings
Oregon	Office of Administrative Hearings
South Carolina	Administrative Law Judge Division
South Dakota	Office of Hearing Examiners
Tennessee	Administrative Procedures Division
Texas	State Office of Administrative Hearings
Washington	Office of Administrative Hearings
Wisconsin	Division of Hearings and Appeals
Wyoming	Wyoming Office of Administrative Hearings

Source: National Association of Administrative Law Judges (2003).

them modeled after the California central panel system that was adopted originally in the 1940s[7] (Table 2). In states without central panels, it is often the practice for the ALJs to be watched over by a board or commission, whose members may be drawn from the interests in cases the ALJs are to hear, as some states require in statute representation on the boards of particular interests.[8]

It should be noted that some states recognize the difference between formal and informal adjudicative hearings. Generally speaking, state-level adjudications are even less formal than are federal adjudications, generally require less proof to prove a case, and are less likely to involve attorneys for private parties involved in the hearing.[8]

AGENCY ADJUDICATIONS

Administrative law judges are the most visible actor in state and federal agency adjudications because they hear the vast majority of them. However, they are not the only ones who can preside over adjudications. Namely, the agency commission, board, or agency head may also preside over them. There are no specific processes for how hearings are held. Although all federal agencies must adhere to portions of the APA, each agency is free to develop its own specific methods. In many respects, agency adjudications look like regular courtroom trials, but are less formal than a courtroom proceeding. Exactly how formal the proceedings are to be is up to each agency, and state-level adjudications tend to be even less formal than federal ones. At a minimum, administrative law judges (or whoever else is presiding over the adjudication) will manage the hearing (e.g., deciding who gives testimony and when), develop the record, maintain the integrity of the hearing, and render a decision based on the record generated in the hearing.

Who gets a hearing? The answer would seem to be a simple one, but it is not. Generally speaking, under the Fifth and Fourteenth Amendments to the U.S. Constitution, anyone in jeopardy of losing their life, liberty, or property at the hands of the government must be afforded due process. At the very least, this means they have to be given a hearing before an independent and unbiased decision maker. Because it is possible that an individual could lose his or her property at the hands of an agency (questions of life and liberty are handled exclusively by the courts), it seems anyone in this position should be given a hearing. However, the courts have been reluctant to require agencies to conduct adjudicatory hearings in *all* cases where a person stands to lose some type of property. When Congress has passed a law stating an agency must hold a hearing ''on the record'' for a particular type of case (such as in licensing radio stations), or when the

courts have inferred Congress intended to require the agency to hold such hearings (absent of any specific language on the matter), the adjudication provisions of the APA will apply. If there is no such statute, and the agency fails to grant the hearing, then it is up to the courts to decide whether a hearing is in fact required. However, scholars have been critical of the courts for failing to develop a coherent set of principles governing administrative due process and what constitutes a valid hearing.[9] Even if an individual can show a court they stand to lose property, the Supreme Court ruled in *Mathews v. Eldridge* (424 U.S. 319, 1976) that the agency can take into consideration the burden a hearing would impose on the agency when deciding to hold one, which means the court might not require the hearing even if a person's property is at stake. Furthermore, even if it is apparent that the individual has a right to a hearing, the Supreme Court has ruled that the hearing can be held *after* the property has been taken away by the agency.[10]

Generally speaking, adjudications can be grouped into one of four types, increasing in degrees of formality from alternative dispute resolution (ADR) hearings, paper hearings, oral hearings, to formal hearings.[11] In ADR proceedings, the parties in the case agree to reach a settlement through compromise and negotiation. So-called ''paper hearings'' are a bit more formal in the respect that the outcome is the product of the hearing officer (and not negotiation), but there is no actual hearing wherein oral testimony is presented. Instead, arguments are presented exclusively via written briefs. Even more formal are oral hearings where the parties present their arguments orally, but without discovery, prehearing conferences, or cross-examination during testimony, as in the case of formal hearings.

The federal APA does not provide a set of comprehensive procedures governing the holding of hearings. Generally, formal hearings will include opening statements, the presentation of the case by the proponent (usually the agency in regulatory hearings), the presentation of the case by the defendant, rebuttal (as allowed by the presiding officer), and closing arguments. Agencies vary by what can be admitted into evidence and are not bound by the Federal Rules of Civil Procedure's rules on allowable evidence, although each agency is required to generate their own rules. Agencies may base their decision on evidence that would not otherwise be admitted in a court case (such as hearsay), but the decision must also be based on enough evidence that would have been admitted or show why such evidence was not available.[12]

Depending on the type of hearing, the administrative law judge will issue an initial decision or recommended decision. Initial decisions are generally issued when the case deals with a well-established issue and, unless overturned by the agency, becomes the agency's decision.

If the case deals with a novel issue, the ALJ will issue a recommended decision that may require further action (such as additional proceedings) by the agency. The burden of proof is on the party bringing the case. Generally speaking, the standard of proof is "preponderance of evidence" if Congress has not set the standard already.[13] However, for immigration deportation cases, reviewing courts have required higher standards, such as the more stringent "clear and convincing evidence" standard.[14] Many agencies have internal appellate processes, having provisions that allow individuals to appeal the case to the agency board or an intermediate appellate body. Once all appellate remedies have been exhausted in federal adjudications, parties may appeal the case to a U.S. Court of Appeals, except cases from the Social Security Administration which are heard by U.S. District Courts.

CONCLUSION

Few of us who have not had contact with ALJs and agency adjudications know of their existence, but they warrant a degree of attention. Although the courts have recognized their constitutional legitimacy, their platypus-like characteristics of having both judicial and executive functions make them intrinsically interesting. The sheer volume of ALJ activity should garner our attention as well. In the case of the U.S. Social Security Administration alone, ALJs presided over 377,163 cases in fiscal year 1996; in contrast, in 1998, all 94 U.S. District Courts presided over only 280,293 civil cases.[15] Although the average dollar amounts at stake in District Court cases were probably greater, ALJs have been deemed an integral parting in the implementation of portions of the Social Security program, the largest of the federal domestic programs. They play important roles in state-level programs as well.

REFERENCES

1. Rich, M. Central panels of administrative law judges: An introduction. Judicature **1981**, *65* (5), 233–234.
2. Lubbers, J. The federal administrative judiciary: Establishing an appropriate system of performance evaluation for ALJs. Adm. Law J. Am. Univ. **1994**, *7* (3), 598–628.
3. 1992 A.C.U.S. 35.
4. See The Association of Administrative Law Judges, Inc. v. Heckler, 594 F. Supp. 1134 (D.D.C., 1984).
5. Schwartz, B. *Administrative Law,* 3rd Ed.; Little Brown: Boston, 1991.
6. Rosenblum, V. The central panel system: Enhancing administrative justice. Judicature **1981**, *65* (2), 235.
7. Rich, M.; Brucar, W. *The Central Panel System for Administrative Law Judges: A Survey of Seven States*; American Judicature Society: Chicago, 1983.
8. Bonfield, A. State law in the teaching of administrative law: A critical analysis of the status quo. Tex. Law Rev. **1982**, *61* (1), 95.
9. Carter, L.; Harrington, C. *Administrative Law and Politics: Cases and Comments,* 3rd Ed.; Longman: New York, 2000.
10. Cleveland Board of Education v. Loudermill, 470 U.S. 532 (1985).
11. Cooper, P. *Public Law and Public Administration*; F.E. Peacock: Itasca, IL, 2000.
12. Perales v. Richardson, 402 U.S. 389 (1971).
13. Steadman v. U.S., 450 U.S. 91 (1981).
14. Woodby v. INS, 385 U.S. 276 (1966).
15. Social Security Administration. *1998 SSI Annual Report*; U.S. Government Printing Office: Washington, DC, 1998.

Administrative Reform in Southeast Asia

M. Shamsul Haque
National University of Singapore, Singapore

INTRODUCTION

Since the end of colonial rule, administrative reform has been one of the most common domains of social change pursued by developing nations. In these countries, the process of administrative reform became quite intensive immediately after their decolonization to reduce their dependence on colonial administration, create more indigenous institutional structure, and expand the role of government in national economies.[1] Beyond this historical reason, there were inherent weaknesses in governing institutions—including bureaucratic inefficiency, administrative incapacity, social instability, market failure, and unemployment problem, which also required administrative reform. In more recent years, however, administrative reform in developing countries has been driven by the increasing local needs and demands as well as the contemporary global forces and pressures, in response to which the state has to restructure its administration and revive its managerial capacity in line with the similar reinvention in governance found in advanced capitalist nations.[2,3]

Administrative reform has traditionally been understood as a formal, planned, and deliberate change in various dimensions (e.g., structure, process, behavior, norms) of the administrative system to improve its efficiency, quality, coordination, motivation, responsiveness, accountability, and so on.[1,4] More recently, instead of administrative reform, many scholars and experts use the term "governance reform," which has much broader connotation, encompassing changes in the civil service, policy process, civil society, and state–market relations.[5] In terms of scope, administrative reform covers all major levels of government (federal, state, local) and public sectors (agriculture, industry, commerce, finance, transport, education, health).[3,6] Internally, it includes various structural, functional, procedural, normative, and attitudinal changes in the administrative system.

During the recent decades, there has emerged almost a paradigm shift, especially in terms of greater emphasis on the market-driven objective, role, structure, policy orientation, and norms of government administration. Compared to the earlier state-centered model, this newly emerging market-centered model of reform has become the major framework for undertaking administrative restructuring in most countries of the world. This current reform emphasizes the goal of efficiency and effectiveness, supportive or facilitating role, disaggregated and flexible managerial structure, result-based performance, promarket policies, customer orientation, and business sector norms.[7,8] Such an antibureaucratic mode of administrative reform largely represents the basic components of "reinventing government" prescribed by Osborne and Gaebler[9] as well as the principles of the so-called "new public management" presented by Hood,[10] and it differs substantively from the past reform initiatives undertaken by various governments in line with the traditional bureaucratic model.[9–11]

The above market-centered model of administrative reform, which emerged in advanced capitalist nations, was gradually adopted by developing countries often under the structural adjustment program prescribed or imposed by international aid agencies. In line with this global trend, in various degrees, Southeast Asian countries have embraced the major components of such reform agenda—including the downsizing of the public sector, deregulation of service delivery, divestment of state enterprises, liberalization of trade and investment, corporatization of public agencies, use of result-based budget and performance indicators, and so on—in the name of economic efficiency, competitiveness, service quality, value for money, and customer satisfaction.[12,13] There are some major causes and implications of this reform process in Southeast Asia.

FEATURES AND TRENDS OF REFORMS IN SOUTHEAST ASIA

Countries in Southeast Asia—including Brunei, Cambodia, Indonesia, Laos, Malaysia, Myanmar, Philippines, Singapore, Thailand, and Vietnam—vary significantly with regard to their territorial size, demographic pattern, ethnic and religious composition, colonial background, social structure, political system, and economic development.[14] In the past, this diversity created certain differences among these countries in terms of the nature and objectives of administrative reform. In recent years, however, most of these countries have adopted reforms in line with the globalized market-led model of public

Encyclopedia of Public Administration and Public Policy
DOI: 10.1081/E-EPAP-120024427

management mentioned above. This section discusses the major features and trends of current administrative reform, including the institutional, functional, structural, normative, and policy reforms in various Southeast Asian countries.

Institutional Reform

Most governments in Southeast Asia have undertaken major reform initiatives to restructure the public sector based on promarket assumptions. Examples of such initiatives include Public Service for the 21st Century (PS21) in Singapore, Panibagong Sigla 2000 (Renewed Vigor 2000) in the Philippines, Public Sector Management Reform in Thailand, Malaysia Incorporated in Malaysia, Resolution on Public Administration Reform in Vietnam, and National Development Program in Indonesia.[13,15] In addition, a new set of market-friendly state institutions has been introduced, such as the Public Sector Divestment Committee in Singapore, the Committee on Privatization and the Asset Privatization Trust in the Philippines, the Steering Committee on Reduction in the Size of the Public Service in Malaysia, and the Public and Private Sector Committee in Thailand.

A more critical institutional feature of administrative reform in the region, however, is the streamlining or downsizing of the public sector in line with the current global trend. For example, the Thai government adopted the downsizing strategies such as the recruitment freeze, early retirement scheme, abolition of postretirement vacancies, and replacement of underutilized employees.[15,16] The Philippine government also decided to downsize the number of public sector employees by 5–10% and Singapore government by 10%.[17,18] Similarly, the governments in Indonesia and Malaysia have decided to streamline state bureaucracy by cutting public expenditure and reducing the number of civil servants.[19,20] Even in communist Vietnam, the government has introduced unprecedented reform measures and reduced the number of ministries and agencies from 76 in 1986 to 48 in 2001 and the percentage of public sector employment from 10% in 1991 to 8.7% in 1994.[19,21]

Functional Reform

In Southeast Asian countries, the state bureaucracy played a crucial role in socioeconomic development, whereas the private sector took part in this development process under state regulation, control, and coordination. However, the recent administrative reform has moved away from such a dominant role of the monopolistic public sector and emphasized the role of market competition and private enterprise. This new mode of reform defines the function of public administration as that of a catalyst or facilitator

rather than main actor or leader—the purpose is to restructure the role or function of the administrative system in such a manner that it can enable (rather than control) the role played by the business sector.[22] In both Malaysia and Singapore, the role of the public sector has been redesigned to reduce its functional scope and to transform it into an enabling agent for the private sector, which now is supposed to play the leading role in economy and society.[11,20] Such a facilitating role of the public sector has also been prescribed in the Philippines, Thailand, and Vietnam in their recent initiatives of administrative reform.[23,24]

The functional dimension of the current administrative reform in the region has also greater emphasis on the satisfaction of public sector "customers," which represents a shift from the earlier focus on the *entitlement* of "citizens" to basic services provided by the state. Similar to the businesslike customer-oriented approach adopted recently in the public sector by most developed nations, the concern for customers or clients has gained increasing significance in public management in Singapore, Malaysia, Thailand, and the Philippines. Top public officials are now encouraged to develop customer-oriented outlook and customer-friendly attitude in these countries.[13]

Policy Reform

In most Southeast Asian countries, compared with their earlier state-centric public policies such as nationalization, regulation, and protectionism, the recent reform initiatives have moved toward more promarket policies such as privatization, deregulation, outsourcing, and liberalization. In the region, the privatization policy encompasses all major sectors, including telecommunications, electricity, airlines, railway, banking, finance, petroleum, transport, mining, construction, tourism, and so on. For instance, Malaysia introduced massive privatization under its Privatization Masterplan, Singapore adopted privatization policy planned by its Public Sector Divestment Committee, and the Philippines launched the privatization program through its Committee on Privatization. Similar privatization exercises were carried out in Thailand, Indonesia, Cambodia, and Vietnam.[19]

Southeast Asian countries have also pursued the deregulation and liberalization of trade, investment, and foreign ownership. For foreign investment, Indonesia has liberalized such sectors as electricity, railways, telecommunications, and airlines, which used to be under state control. Malaysia, Thailand, and the Philippines have withdrawn restrictions on foreign ownership and adopted incentives for foreign investors such as tax exemption, duty-free imports, and so on. The liberalization of trade and investment has also taken place in Cambodia, Laos, and Vietnam.[25] These recent changes certainly represent a significant policy reform in Southeast Asia.

Structural Reforms

Despite the diverse historical origins of the administrative systems in Southeast Asian countries, in general, they became increasingly based on the principles of a bureaucratic model that prescribes central control over financial, procedural, and personnel matters. However, in line with the abovementioned ''new public management'' model suggesting disaggregated and decentralized management practices, most countries in the region have moved toward reforming their administrative systems based on greater managerial and financial autonomy and flexibility. In Singapore, for instance, the government has restructured various agencies or departments into the so-called ''autonomous agencies'' assigned with considerable managerial autonomy in personnel and financial matters.[11]

In the case of Thailand, the government has also created various ''autonomous public organizations'' that have been provided with autonomy in their respective financial and personnel policies. In Malaysia, the traditional financial controls over government departments have been transformed into more decentralized financial management with greater autonomy in the budget matters. Similar trends of administrative reform in favor of operational autonomy in management can be found in Indonesia and the Philippines.[15]

Normative-Attitudinal Reform

In the past, in line with the bureaucratic model that emerged largely in Western liberal democracies, Southeast Asian countries adopted various reform measures to inculcate administrative norms and attitudes based on neutrality, equity, representation, and accountability, although such standards were not often observed in practice. However, under the recent reform in these countries, greater emphasis has been placed on values such as efficiency, economy, competition, value for money, service quality, and customer satisfaction. In Malaysia and the Philippines, there is greater concern for administrative efficiency, effectiveness, quality, partnership, and customer-orientedness.

Similarly, in recent development plans and programs, Indonesia and Thailand have emphasized these market-based normative and attitudinal standards. In the case of Singapore, the current reform initiatives for the public service, especially the PS21, also stress the realization of values such as competition, efficiency, quality, and customer orientation.[13] All these countries have also adopted various training programs to attitudinally reorient their public employees to make them more quality-conscious and customer-friendly.

CAUSES AND IMPLICATIONS OF REFORMS IN THE REGION

In general, the main factor or force behind the current market-driven reform in the public sector has often been attributed to the globalization of trade and investment, decline in state capacity, and erosion of state autonomy, which allegedly led to the crisis of the state and thus required substantive reforms in state policy and administration. According to Pereira,[3] this pressure of globalization on the state was reinforced by the international business interests and neoliberal policy elites demanding or advocating privatization, deregulation, liberalization, and other market-friendly institutional reforms. Because Southeast Asian countries were already integrated with the world capitalist system, they had to respond to the new globalized political economy and its forces by undertaking such reform initiatives often prescribed by international aid agencies.

For most developing countries, including those in Southeast Asia, the World Bank identified some major problems with the public sector, suggested reform measures such as downsizing, retrenchment, divestment, and so on, and extended loans mainly to those countries which could demonstrate commitment to these prescribed reforms.[5] To a certain extent, countries such as Thailand, Indonesia, the Philippines, and Vietnam introduced divestment, deregulation, and liberalization under the influence of the International Monetary Fund and the World Bank.[19] It is often the external debt and dependence of these countries that created an opportune context for these international financial institutions to exert such policy influence or pressure. However, it should be added that there are also internal factors—including domestic fiscal crisis, public sector inefficiency, and local business interests—which required such market-led reforms in these countries.

What are the implications of these contemporary administrative reforms? In terms of positive outcomes, the current promarket administrative reform represents a serious challenge to the traditional, centralized, monopolistic, and elitist state bureaucracy that existed in most Southeast Asian countries. This recent reform is likely to make the public sector more competitive, cost conscious, and performance-oriented and contribute to a greater degree of transparency, decentralization, service quality, and responsiveness to its clients or customers. However, there are critics who often point out various negative consequences of this contemporary reform. More specifically, for some scholars, the new model of administrative reform based on neoliberal assumptions and market-driven principles and policies has been largely imposed on developing nations, and it represents a form of ideological hegemony.[26]

It is stressed that under the current public sector reform, the privatization and restructuring may have diminished state sovereignty and increased foreign ownership in certain Southeast Asian countries (e.g., Thailand, Indonesia, Malaysia, and the Philippines) that suffer from heavy foreign debt and dependence and thus are vulnerable to external policy imposition.[27] Internally, on the other hand, policy reforms such as deregulation, divestment, welfare cut, and customer focus may not equally benefit all social sections or income groups—these reform measures are likely to benefit the business and political elites, overlook the concerns of ordinary citizens, and expand the gap between public officials and common citizens.[19,28]

In terms of the impacts of such market-led reform on the administrative system itself, the increasing similarities between public administration and business management may pose a challenge to the "public" nature of public service, perpetuate its identity crisis, and adversely affect the pride and morale of public employees.[13] In addition, under the current reform, the expansion of operational and financial autonomy of public managers and their growing interaction and partnership with business executives may generate new avenues for administrative corruption and thus compromise public service integrity. In other words, in the current context of managerial autonomy and partnership with the private sector, it may be necessary to introduce additional safeguards to prevent any kind of wrongdoing resulting from these recent changes.

CONCLUSION

It is evident from the above discussion that during the recent decades, Southeast Asian countries have introduced considerable administrative reforms based on market-based assumptions and principles, which include changes in the public administration system in terms of its institutional nature and scope, role and function, public orientation, structural pattern, and normative priority. Although there are some potential benefits from such administrative reforms, there are also some major adverse consequences. In this regard, there is a need to consider some major critical concerns by top policymakers in charge of initiating and implementing administrative reform in each of these countries.

First, in pursuing administrative reform, most developing countries, including those in Southeast Asia, have often followed models that emerged in advanced capitalist nations. In particular, the Weberian bureaucratic model

that evolved in Western nations was imitated by Southeast Asian countries in modernizing their administrative systems without much attention paid to their unique local contexts. On the other hand, the current process of administrative reform in the region has largely been based on the neomanagerial model ("new public management") that originated in countries such as America, Australia, Britain, Canada, New Zealand, and so on. This new model of reform, which is globally touted as "good governance" or "best practices" by international agencies, is also being reproduced in developing nations without much concern for the "peculiarities of public service problems and their settings" in these countries.[26] On this ground, countries in Southeast Asia should try to replace the imitative models of administrative reform borrowed from outside or imposed on them by external actors or agencies.

Second, to pursue a need-based, indigenous model of administrative reform, the policymakers in Southeast Asian countries should examine and seriously consider their respective contextual factors. It is stressed by some scholars that in general, administrative reform should not be based on the assumption of "ideological or cultural supremacy" of any particular society (especially the West); it should rather be determined by each nation's contextual factors such as political history, cultural tradition, nature of government, and constitutional features.[26,29] Each country in Southeast Asia has its own unique contextual factors—including the colonial legacy, state formation, political culture, social relations, cultural and religious beliefs, economic resources, and citizens' needs and expectations—which should be seriously taken into account in formulating administrative reform policies and their eventual consequences. As Heeks and Bhatnagar[30] mention, in general, "Public managers would do better to open their eyes and ears to their immediate surroundings rather than burying their noses in MBA textbooks in seeking guidance on reform."

Finally, it is essential to understand that administrative reform should be based on a comprehensive framework, which emphasizes reforms in other social domains (political, economic, and cultural) that affect and are affected by changes made in the administrative system. It is often emphasized that administrative reform can be successful only when it is complemented by corresponding reforms in other realms of society within which the administrative system exists and functions.[31] In Southeast Asian countries, most initiatives for administrative reform have been undertaken without much innovations made in politics, economy, society, and culture—this parochial or unbalanced nature of administrative reform represents a major obstacle to its successful realization or implementation. In this regard, the policymakers in each of these countries must reexamine the shortcomings of such a parochial approach to reform that focuses mainly on the administrative system and adopt a more comprehensive and multidimensional reform outlook that covers other relevant and important domains of society.

REFERENCES

1. Caiden, G.E. *Administrative Reform*; The Penguin Press: London, 1969.
2. Rosenbloom, D.H. Administrative Reformers in a Global World: Diagnosis, Prescription, and the Limits of Transferability. In *Rethinking Administrative Theory: The Challenge of the New Century*; Jun, J.S., Ed.; Greenwood: New York, 2001.
3. Pereira, L.C.B. *State Reform in the 1990s: Logic and Control Mechanisms*; Seminar on the Changing Role of the State (sponsored by The World Bank): Hong Kong, September 23, 1997.
4. World Bank. *The East Asian Miracle: Economic Growth and Public Policy*; The World Bank: Washington, DC, 1993.
5. Management Development and Governance Division (MDGD). *Civil Service Reform Paper*; MDGD, United Nations: New York, 2001; 30–36.
6. König, K. Administrative Sciences and Administrative Reforms. In *Strategies for Administrative Reform*; Caiden, G.E., Siedentopf, H., Eds.; Lexington Books: Lexington, MA, 1982.
7. Reyes, D.R. Public sector reengineering: Practice, problems and prospects. Philipp. J. Public Adm. **1998**, *42* (3–4).
8. Liou, K.T. Linking Administrative Reform to Economic Development: Issues and the National Experience. In *Administrative Reform and National Economic Development*; Liou, K.T., Ed.; Ashgate: Aldershot, 2000.
9. Osborne, D.; Gaebler, T. *Reinventing Government: How the Entrepreneurial Spirit is Transforming the Public Sector*; Plume Books: New York, 1993.
10. Hood, C. A public management for all seasons? Public Adm. **1991**, *69* (1), 3–19.
11. Haque, M.S. Structures of new public management in Malaysia and Singapore: Alternative views. J. Comp. Asian Dev. **2002**, *1* (1), 71–86.
12. World Bank. *World Bank Annual Report 1996*; The World Bank: Washington, D.C., 1996.
13. Haque, M.S. New directions in bureaucratic change in Southeast Asia: Selected experiences. J. Polit. Mil. Soc. **1998**, *26* (1), 96–114.
14. Aldaba, F.; Petilla, M.J. *Poverty Situation in Southeast Asia and NGO Responses*; Research Paper No. 1, March 2002, Catholic Institute for International Relations, South East Asia Research and Advocacy Unit, 2002.
15. Research Institute for Asia and the Pacific (RIAP). *Public Sector Challenges and Government Reforms in South East Asia: Report 2001*; RIAP, University of Sydney: Sydney, 2001.
16. Asian Development Bank. *Governance in Thailand: Challenges, Issues and Prospects*; Asian Development Bank: Manila, 1999.
17. Halligan, J.; Turner, M. *Profiles of Government Administration in Asia*; Australian Government Publishing Service: Canberra, 1995.
18. World Bank. *Philippines: The Challenge of Economic Recovery*; The World Bank: Washington, D.C., 1999.
19. Haque, M.S. Reinventing Governance in Southeast Asia: What Are Its Impacts on Economic Sovereignty and Self-reliance? The Second International Conference of Japan Economic Policy Association, Nagoya, Japan, November 29–30, 2003.
20. Kristiadi, J.B. *Administrative reform in Indonesia. The Conference on Public Sector Challenges and Government Reforms in South East Asia*; Research Institute for Asia and the Pacific, University of Sydney: Australia, March 12, 2001.
21. McCarty, A. Governance Institutions and Incentive Structures in Vietnam. In *The Conference on Public Sector Challenges and Government Reforms in South East Asia*; Research Institute for Asia and the Pacific, University of Sydney: Australia, March 12, 2001.
22. World Bank. *East Asia: Recovery and Beyond*; The World Bank: Washington, D.C., 2000.
23. United Nations. *Administrative Reforms: Country Profiles of Five Asian Countries*; United Nations Department of Economic and Social Affairs: New York, 1997.
24. Tiep, N.T. Government reform for socio-economic development in Vietnam. Asian Rev. Public Adm. **1998**, *10* (1–2), 172–185.
25. Montes, M.F. The Economic Miracle in a Haze. In *Growing Pains: ASEAN's Economic and Political Challenges*; Montes, M.F., Quigley, K.F.F., Weatherbee, D.E., Eds.; Asia Society: New York, 1997.
26. Blunt, P. Public Administrative Reform and Management Innovation for Developing Countries, Fourth Global Forum on Reinventing Government—Citizens, Businesses, and Governments: Partnerships for Development and Democracy, Marrakech, Morocco, December 11–13, 2002.
27. Higgot, R. The Asian economic crisis: A study in the politics of resentment. New Polit. Econ. **1998**, *3* (3), 333–356.
28. Cook, P.; Kirkpatrick, C. The Distributional Impact of Privatization in Developing Countries: Who Gets What, and Why. In *Privatization and Equity*; Ramanadham, V.V., Ed.; Routledge: London, 1995; 35–48.
29. Roness, P.G. Structural Features, Institutional Characteristics and Administrative Reforms: Theoretical Reasoning and Empirical Measures. In *The ECPR Workshop: Institutional Theory*; Issues of Measurement and Change: Edinburgh, UK, March 28–April 2, 2003.
30. Heeks, R.; Bhatnagar, S. Understanding Success and Failure in Information Age Reform. In *Reinventing Government in the Information Age*; Heeks, R., Ed.; Routledge: London, 1999; 71.
31. Haque, M.S. The contextless nature of public administration in third world countries. Int. Rev. Adm. Sci. **1996**, *62* (3), 315–329.

Alternative Dispute Resolution Processes

Tina Nabatchi
Lisa B. Bingham
Indiana University, Bloomington, Indiana, U.S.A.

INTRODUCTION

This chapter explores the basics of alternative dispute resolution (ADR). The chapter begins by defining ADR and examining its use in the public sector. It then discusses several processes within each of the three categories along the ADR continuum: unassisted negotiation, consensus-building, and quasi-adjudication.

WHAT IS ADR AND WHY IS IT USED IN THE PUBLIC SECTOR?

Alternative dispute resolution (ADR), also called appropriate dispute resolution, is an umbrella term for a wide variety of conflict management techniques and processes used in lieu of traditional judicial and administrative adjudication. In general, ADR processes are voluntary, and most use a third party neutral, such as a facilitator, mediator, or arbitrator. ADR processes are designed to resolve disputes in a faster, less expensive, and more amicable manner, and because the processes are less adversarial and formal than traditional litigation, ADR is often able to preserve, and sometimes strengthen, the relationships of the disputing parties. Today, ADR processes are used at all levels of government to resolve a wide variety of public sector disputes (see Table 1 for a list of government ADR web resources).

In the 1990s, several legislative acts incorporated ADR into all three branches of the federal government. The Civil Justice Reform Act of 1990 [28 U.S.C. §§ 471–482 (1994)] and the Alternative Dispute Resolution Act of 1998 [28 U.S.C. §§ 651–658 (Suppl. IV 1998)] brought ADR into the federal judicial branch. Legislative agencies were instructed to use ADR for employment disputes by the Congressional Accountability Act of 1995 [Public Law 104-1]. Executive branch agencies were encouraged to use ADR when Congress passed the Negotiated Rulemaking Act (NRA) of 1990 [5 U.S.C. §§ 561–570] and the Administrative Dispute Resolution Act (ADRA) of 1990 [Public Law 101-552 (codified in scattered sections of 5 U. S. C. and 9 U.S.C.)], as amendments to the federal Administrative Procedure Act (APA) [5 U.S.C. § 553]. The ADRA and the NRA were amended in 1996, making ADR and negotiated rulemaking permanent fixtures in federal agencies.[1,2]

State agencies derive their authority to use ADR from three sources. First, agencies may infer authority from the state Administrative Procedures Act (APA), which often provides for informal proceedings and the resolution of complaints by settlement.[3] Second, agencies may imply authority from a general enabling statute that gives them the power to enter into contracts.[3] Third, some state legislatures have passed statutes expressly authorizing state, and sometimes local, governments to use ADR and/or negotiated rulemaking.

Local governments and municipalities have also exercised their inherent police powers and budgetary and legislative authority to use ADR. Often, they collaborate with local community mediation programs, non-profit organizations with volunteers who are available to mediate typical neighborhood disputes.

Given the proliferation ADR legislation, such processes are now being used to address a wide variety of public sector disputes. ADR processes are used to resolve intra-agency disputes, interagency disputes among government agencies at the same or different levels, and disputes among agencies and private parties. In these contexts, ADR has been used in labor–management disputes, contracting and procurement disputes, regulatory and enforcement disputes, and for claims against the government. The following section of the chapter discusses the broad range of ADR processes that might be used in these different settings.

ADR PROCESSES

ADR processes can be arranged along a continuum ranging from informal, unassisted techniques to more formal adjudicatory arrangements. At one end of the continuum are certain approaches to negotiation; consensual ADR processes involving a third-party neutral fall in the middle of the continuum; and, at the other end of the continuum are quasi-adjudicatory processes involving a third-party neutral (see Table 2). Several ADR processes within each of these categories are discussed below.

Encyclopedia of Public Administration and Public Policy
DOI: 10.1081/E-EPAP 120024305

Table 1 ADR resources

For resources about ADR use in the federal government, see the Federal ADR Interagency Working Group web site at http://www.adr.gov
For resources about ADR use in state government, see the Policy Consensus Initiative (PCI) web site at http://www.policyconsensus.org
For resources about ADR use in local government, see the National Association for Community Mediation web site at http://www.nafcm.org
For a comprehensive gateway to ADR and conflict resolution resources, see the Conflict Resolution Information Source (CRInfo) web site at http://www.crinfo.org

Unassisted Negotiation

Although they do not require the use of a third-party neutral, certain approaches to negotiation, specifically principled or interest-based negotiation and partnering, fall on the ADR continuum.

Principled or interest-based negotiation

The terms principled negotiation and interest-based bargaining were developed to represent negotiation approaches that stand in contrast to traditional positional bargaining.[4] Positional bargaining, also called win–lose, competitive, or adversarial negotiation, is relatively confrontational; the disputing parties take sides (positions) and argue in such a manner as to prevail over the other. Conversely, principled or interest-based negotiation is relatively cooperative; the disputing parties seek a solution that is mutually beneficial. There are four steps in principled negotiation: 1) separate people from the problem; 2) focus on interests, not positions; 3) invent options for mutual gain; and 4) use objective criteria to assess possible solutions.[4] The goal of principled

negotiation is to find a solution that will meet the needs and interests of all parties in the dispute.

Partnering

Partnering is a relatively new ADR process developed by agencies for use in the area of procurement and government contracting. Partnering is intended to help avoid the occurrence of disputes by building strong, collaborative working relationships among the contracting parties before disputes arise. The goal is to establish channels of communication that are immediately used at the first sign of a dispute in order to catch and resolve potential problems before they become real disputes and to reduce the need for litigation in the future.[3]

Consensual Processes Involving a Third-Party Neutral

Consensus-building or consensus-based processes describe a number of collaborative decision-making techniques in which a third-party neutral assists diverse or competing interest groups in reaching an agreement about the issues in conflict.[5] These processes are typically used to foster dialogue, clarify areas of agreement, improve the information on which decisions are based, and resolve controversial issues in ways that all parties find acceptable. The most common consensus-based processes are conflict assessment or convening, facilitation, mediation, conciliation, negotiated rulemaking, and policy dialogues. In addition, there are processes intended to result in consensus that have adjudicatory elements, such as early neutral evaluation, minitrial, and summary jury trial. These processes supply the disputing parties with an expert opinion about the merits of their case and furnish more information about their best alternative to a negotiated agreement (BATNA). This, in turn, can provide the disputants with a loop-back to negotiation.

Table 2 The continuum of ADR process

Unassisted negotiation	Consensual process	Quasi-adjudicatory process
Principled or interest-based negotiation	Conflict assessment (convening)	Fact-finding
Partnering	Facilitation	Settlement judges
	Mediation	Private judges
	Conciliation	Arbitration
	Negotiated rulemaking	Med-arb
	Policy dialogues	
	Early neutral evaluation	
	Minitrial	
	Summary jury trial	

In all of the consensus building processes, the third party has no power to impose a settlement on the disputing parties, but rather simply aids the parties in reaching an agreement. The differences among these consensus-based processes stem from the third party's degree of activism in the dispute.

Conflict assessment (convening)

Conflict assessment, also known as convening, can be a valuable first step in many ADR processes. The assessment process begins with a discussion among potential stakeholders to evaluate the causes of the conflict and identify the entities and individuals who would be substantively affected by the outcome of the conflict. Next, the interests and needs of the stakeholders are assessed, a preliminary set of relevant issues is identified for discussion, and the feasibility of using various collaborative ADR processes to address the dispute is evaluated. In the final step, often called process design, the neutral recommends and assists in developing an appropriate ADR technique for addressing the dispute.

Facilitation

Facilitation is a collaborative process in which a neutral assists a group of stakeholders in constructively discussing the issues in controversy. The facilitator typically works with participants before and during discussions to assure that appropriate persons are at the table. The facilitator also helps the parties set and enforce the ground rules and agendas, assists the parties in effectively communicating, and helps keep them on track and working toward their goals. Facilitation is commonly used in negotiated rulemaking and to help resolve complex environmental or public disputes; however, the process may work in any number of situations where parties of diverse interests or experience are in discussion.

Mediation

Mediation, one of the oldest forms of conflict resolution and the most common ADR process used in the federal government, is a style of facilitated negotiation, where a skilled, impartial third party assists disputants in reaching a voluntary, mutually agreeable resolution to all or some of the disputed issues.[5] The mediator works with disputants to help them analyze the conflict, improve communication, identify interests, and explore possibilities for a mutually agreeable resolution. The mediator lacks power to impose any solution; instead he/she assists the disputants in designing their own solution. Typically, this involves supervising the bargaining, helping the

disputants find areas of common ground and understand their alternatives, offering possible solutions, and helping parties draft a final settlement agreement. Mediation usually occurs in the context of a specific dispute involving a limited number of parties; however, mediation procedures are also employed to develop broad policies or regulatory mandates and may involve dozens of participants who represent a variety of interests. Mediation is most often a voluntary process, but court orders or statutes mandate its use in some jurisdictions.

Conciliation

Conciliation involves efforts by a third party to improve the relationship between two or more disputants. Generally, the third party will work with the disputants to correct misunderstandings, reduce fear and distrust, and improve communication. The term conciliation was used in the early 20th century to refer to labor–management mediation, and was later used in Title VII of the Civil Rights Act of 1964 to refer to settlement efforts conducted by an investigator in the Equal Employment Opportunity Commission (EEOC) after reasonable cause to believe that discrimination under the Act has occurred.[3] Today, conciliation is often used to prepare disputants for a future ADR process, and can also be used as a synonym for mediation.

Negotiated rulemaking

Negotiated rulemaking, also known as regulatory negotiation or reg-neg, involves efforts by regulatory agencies to design regulations by negotiating with interested stakeholders.[6] In this multiparty process, a negotiating committee consisting of the rulemaking agency and interested stakeholders seeks to reach agreement on the substance of a proposed rule, policy, or standard. The purpose and intent of negotiated rulemaking is to avoid the litigation that may arise to challenge the new rule by generating agreement among the affected interests so that they abide by the decision and its implementation. Federal law requires a thorough conflict assessment before the use of reg-neg and the involvement and assistance of a skilled, neutral mediator or facilitator during the process.

Policy dialog

Policy dialogues are a relatively new form of ADR that are generally used to address complex environmental conflicts or public-policy disputes. In this process, representatives of groups with divergent views or interests are assembled to explore and discuss the issues in controversy. Unlike many other consensus-based ADR processes, policy dialogues usually do not seek to achieve a full, specific agreement. Rather, participants seek to assess the potential for developing a full consensus resolution at some later time or may put forward general, nonbinding recommendations or broad policy preferences for an agency (or other governmental entity) to consider in its subsequent decision making.

Early neutral evaluation

Early neutral evaluation (ENE) is a service often initially performed informally by mediators. In this process, a third-party neutral, usually someone with specifically relevant legal, substantive, or technical expertise, hears informal evidence and arguments from all the parties involved in the dispute and issues a nonbinding report advising parties about the strengths and weaknesses of their cases.[3] The report may also evaluate the likely reaction of a judge or jury if settlement is not reached, provide guidance about appropriate range of outcomes, and assist the parties with narrowing the areas of disagreement or identifying information that may enhance the chances of settlement.

Minitrials and summary jury trials

Minitrials and summary jury trials are commonly used to resolve litigation over complex environmental or public issues. In a minitrial, parties are generally represented by a counsel and an agent with the authority to agree to a settlement or decision, e.g., a CEO or agency official. Abbreviated versions of the evidence and arguments are presented, after which the decision-making representatives attempt to negotiate a settlement.[3] In a summary jury trial, the disputing parties impanel a jury and present short versions of the evidence and arguments. The jury deliberates and makes findings of fact and liability when appropriate, which are then released by the judge.[3] The parties are not bound by the jury's findings, but rather use the information to assist with settlement negotiations. Minitrials and summary jury trials are alike in that they both serve as a loop-back to future negotiations.

Quasi-Adjudicatory Process Involving a Third-Party Neutral

There are a broad range of ADR processes that resemble administrative agency adjudication. These processes can be nonbinding, with a decision that is advisory only and may serve as a loop-back to negotiation, or binding, with a decision that is final and enforceable by the courts. Some of the most common quasi-adjudicatory processes are fact-finding, settlement judges, private judges, arbitration, and med-arb.

Fact-finding

In this process, the neutral, called a fact finder, receives information and listens to arguments presented by the disputants. The fact finder, who may conduct additional research to investigate the issues in dispute, evaluates the evidence and submits a report that contains findings of fact and sometimes recommendations based on those findings.[3] Typically, this informal, nonbinding process is used in cases where the disputed facts involve highly technical scientific or engineering issues, thus requiring the fact finder to have subject-matter expertise.

Settlement judges

Settlement judges are used for litigation that has already reached administrative adjudication. In this process, a judge, who is different from the presiding judge in the case, acts as a mediator or neutral evaluator and meets both separately and jointly with the parties to find a mutually agreeable solution.[3] If the efforts of the settlement judge do not produce full agreement, the case returns to the presiding judge. A settlement judge often plays a more authoritative role than a private mediator, by sometimes providing parties with specific, nonbinding legal or substantive information and recommendations.

Private judges

Private judging is similar to both settlement judging and arbitration, and is used for cases that have already reached adjudication. In a private-judging process, sometimes called rent-a-judge, the disputing parties or the courts empower a private person, usually a retired judge or magistrate with special expertise, to hear and decide their case after private proceedings.[7] The private judge acts as an adjudicator and issues a binding decision based on both fact and law.

Arbitration

Arbitration is a quasi-adjudicatory process where the disputants present their case to an impartial third party, who then issues an opinion. Arbitration may be of rights or interests. Rights arbitration is retrospective; the issues involve an existing contract that one party claims the other has breached. Interest arbitration is prospective; the issues involve the determination of entitlements under some future contract. Arbitration has been used in both unionized and nonunionized labor settings, where it is referred to as rights arbitration, grievance arbitration, interest arbitration, employment arbitration, and final-offer or baseball arbitration.[8] The success of arbitration in labor relations has led to its use in commercial settings.

Commercial arbitration is used for disputes involving architectural, construction, consumer, and sales contracts, as well as for divorce, environmental, and other disputes.

In all forms arbitration, neither the decision-maker nor the parties are bound by the rules of evidence used in a court of law. However, the hearings themselves generally follow the steps of adjudication: the parties make opening statements; the party with the burden of proof presents its case, then the other party presents a rebuttal; witnesses may be cross-examined and the parties may make closing statements or present briefs arguing their cases.

Med-arb

Med-arb is a relatively new procedure in which a neutral first mediates the case, and if that fails, then goes on to arbitrate the dispute. Sometimes the same neutral mediates and arbitrates the case; at other times different neutrals act as the mediator and arbitrator. In this latter variation, the mediator and arbitrator may or may not be in contact, and the arbitrator may or may not consider the mediator's comments and recommendations.

CONCLUSION

The emergence and proliferation of ADR is one of the most significant movements in U.S. law in the latter half of the 20th century and has had profound effects on the way the government and public administrators handle conflicts. The institutionalization of ADR in administra-

tive agencies demonstrates both innovation and a concern toward amicable resolution of public disputes. The use of ADR in the public sector will continue to grow as governments recognize the potential of these processes to resolve disputes in a faster, less expensive, and more amicable manner, and as public managers develop expertise in using these processes in decision- and policy-making activities.

REFERENCES

1. Senger, J.M. *Federal Dispute Resolution: Using ADR with the United States Government*; Jossey-Bass: San Francisco, 2003.
2. Breger, M.J.; Lakfer, D.S.; Schatz, G.S. *Federal Administrative Dispute Resolution Deskbook*; American Bar Association: Washington, DC, 2001.
3. Bingham, L.B. Alternative Dispute Resolution in Public Administration. In *The Handbook of Public Law and Administration*; Cooper, P.J., Newland, C.A., Eds.; Jossey-Bass: San Francisco, 1997; 546–566.
4. Fisher, R.; Ury, W.; Patton, B. *Getting to Yes*; Penguin Books: New York, 1991.
5. Moore, C. *The Mediation Process*; Jossey-Bass: San Francisco, 1996.
6. Kerwin, C.M. Negotiated Rulemaking. In *The Handbook of Public Law and Administration*; Cooper, P.J., Newland, C.A., Eds.; Jossey-Bass: San Francisco, 1997; 225–236.
7. Ponte, L.; Cavenagh, T. *Alternative Dispute Resolution in Business*; West Educational Publishing: Cincinnati, 1999.
8. Elkouri, F.; Elkouri, E.A. *How Arbitration Works*; Bureau of National Affairs, Inc.: Washington, DC, 1985.

Assessing the Validity of Constructive Change Proposals

Elisabeth Wright
U.S. Naval Postgraduate School, Monterey, California, U.S.A.

INTRODUCTION

The theory of changes is unique to public contracting. While the parties to a commercial contract may negotiate the right to make subsequent changes to the contract in public sector contracting, the public entity generally retains the right, through the contractual language of a changes' clause, to make unilateral changes within some predetermined parameters. This right seeks to preserve the government's fiduciary duty in the expenditure of public funds.

However, changes outside of the contractual right to make changes can occur. Such changes are commonly known as constructive changes, i.e., the changes outside of the authority of a changes' clause. This article examines the nature of the constructive change and offers an approach for examining the validity of claims based on the constructive change argument.

THEORY OF CHANGES

Contracts between commercial and public entities generally contain a clause that permits the public party (i.e., the buyer) to the contract to make changes in specific areas related to or arising from the contract. Such a right protects the expenditure of public funds; that is, work or other contractual matters can be redirected or redefined to ensure that what is actually necessary is accomplished. The ultimate objective is simple and important: wise expenditure of tax dollars in pursuit of satisfying a government need.[1]

The changes' authority is specific and is limited to certain predefined actions that can be taken only by those who have actual delegated authority to make or direct changes. The authority and scope of changes is limited by design. Decentralized or informal authority to make changes to any contract would undoubtedly cause systemic havoc and chaos—from a contract performance perspective and from a financial management perspective.

Contract performance is framed by the boundaries of the written contract. The supplier is required to furnish the items required by the contract according to the terms and conditions of the written contract. Thus a fundamental requirement of changes is the ability to identify work performed, but not required by the contract. Changes that have been properly ordered according to the terms and conditions of the contract (i.e., a changes' clause) are considered to be formal changes and are recognized as within the changes' authority of the contract.[2] This clause gives the government the right to unilaterally change the contract after it has been awarded. The specific language of the changes' clause limits the extent and scope of changes. In consideration of this extraordinary right, the government agrees that it will compensate the supplier for the additional costs of the work as changed, will extend performance or delivery dates, if appropriate, or will compensate with money and time.

The contract requires the government to issue changes in a formal written manner. However, circumstances may arise in which the supplier is directed to perform outside of the formal written contract. For example, a government inspector may impose more stringent acceptance criteria on supplies tendered under the contract. In effect, the inspector will change the acceptance criteria of the written contract; this may cause the supplier to incur additional costs or to experience a schedule delay. When this manner of effecting a contract change occurs, the government can be liable for the costs the supplier incurs in complying with the change. In addition to a cost impact, a schedule impact can occur as the result of a contract change. Changes that take place outside of the explicit authority of the changes' clause are considered as "constructive changes." The supplier attempts a legitimate argument that a constructive change occurred and that compensation is appropriate. That compensation can be in the form of additional money, time, or both. Such compensation is referred to as equitable adjustment.

CONSTRUCTIVE CHANGE

The constructive change can be thought of as an "informal" change to the contract. A formal change is written direction from a government official with the specific authority to direct a change. The formal change is followed by the issuance of a "Change Order," generally in the form of a modification to the contract. The informal

Encyclopedia of Public Administration and Public Policy
DOI: 10.1081/E-EPAP 120019217

change lacks the formality of the written change; that is, it is a verbal or written act by a government employee that causes a change to the existing contract.

The constructive change can arise from any number of actions or inactions on the part of the government. If the government inspector failed to appear at the agreed upon time and date to accept the supplies, then a constructive change argument might be appropriate. Of course, it is necessary in any change situation that entitlement and quantum be proven. That is to say, mere failure to appear on time to accept supplies does not entitle the supplier to additional compensation. If the supplies were not ready for inspection and the inspector failed to appear, then a constructive change argument would not prevail.

Some examples of circumstances that have been held by boards and courts to constitute constructive changes are the following:

1. Impossibility of performance. Time, money, or impracticality makes it impossible to perform. Drawings or specifications tendered by the government that are impossible to meet would pass the test of practical impossibility. (Recognize that with unlimited time and money, many things are possible, but not practically possible.)
2. Defective specifications. Ambiguous or defective specifications that prevent the work from being accomplished. The supplier may have spent time and money after contract award attempting to comply with the specification as provided by the government.
3. Over-inspection and delays. Actions or inactions by government representatives that may place overly stringent inspection and testing requirements on the supplier after contract award. The supplier may have experienced delay and disruption when supplies rejected should have met the contractual inspection and testing requirements.
4. Additional tasking or direction. Actions that cause the supplier to perform work in excess of the level of work anticipated by the contract.
5. Failure to provide timely and/or suitable government-furnished equipment, property, or information. When the contract calls for items and/or information to be provided by the government, timely availability of those items may be critical to preserving contract price and schedule. Additionally, property or equipment provided as "suitable for its intended use" is warranted for its purpose. Unsuitable equipment that cannot be used by the supplier may constitute a constructive change.

There are many other circumstances that can occur during performance of the contract that provide grounds for claims of constructive change. Government contracting officers must ensure that all government personnel involved in postaward activities comply with stated terms and conditions and are fully aware of the scope of their authority and the potential consequences of their actions.

As a consequence of a constructive change, suppliers prepare and submit a proposal for compensation based on the changed work. The quality of the change proposal is of utmost importance because the government must evaluate the validity of the claim. The claim and its supporting documentation must undergo careful scrutiny and analysis. To that end, evaluators must look for specificity in all information provided. A claim that fails to support entitlement should be returned to the supplier. If entitlement is justified, then quantum may be subject to negotiation.

CONTENTS OF THE CONSTRUCTIVE CHANGE PROPOSAL

At a minimum, the supplier's change proposal should consist of the following elements:

1. Statement of the alleged change. This statement should clearly and precisely outline the basis of the claim and the equitable adjustment requested.
2. Statement of the relevant contract requirement. The contract requirements must be clearly established. The supplier's interpretation of the relevant contract requirement may be included. Attention must be paid to this interpretation because it may be unreasonable or inconsistent with the contract language. For example, the use of the word "shall" in the work statement connotes a requirement while "may" suggests a permissive state. Information given in this section of the claim is a critical component of the claim and forms the foundation for continued review and consideration. It defines what the supplier exactly perceived to be his responsibilities under the contract at the time it was signed.
3. Statement of the government action or inaction that caused the performance of work outside the boundaries of the contract. This statement provides detailed information regarding the government's action or inaction that caused the change. It must support the argument that a gap exists between the contract language and the government's action or inaction. In the absence of a well-written document pointing to government "interference," this statement becomes difficult to prove. For example, a letter rejecting all supplies tendered for failure to meet a tolerance of 1 in. compared to the contract requirement of a 1.5-in. tolerance makes entitlement easier to prove. Evaluators are reminded that government action needs only

contribute substantially toward the changed work for a supplier to successfully argue a constructive change.

4. Detailed discussion of the additional work performed. This portion of the claim must include a detailed discussion of the excess work performed. For example, specific information regarding increased scope of duties, increased performance levels, higher personnel standards, etc., must be provided. It is not sufficient for the supplier to make a broad-sweeping statement that "delay occurred as a result of government action." The link between cause and effect must be clearly established. For example, if an item required rework because of overly stringent testing requirements, then the claim should include amount of rework (hours, dates, etc.) and the detailed bill of material substantiating additional material costs.

5. Detailed cost proposal supporting the additional work performed. The claim must also include a detailed cost proposal showing the actual costs of the changed work. While some suppliers may attempt to use the total cost method approach toward justifying quantum, evaluators are cautioned that using such a method does not provide a causal link for purposes of additional costs incurred. To avoid such a circumstance, contracts should include a change order accounting clause that requires suppliers to have an accounting system in place that segregates costs of changed work. The cost proposal should contain the direct and indirect costs strictly associated with the constructive change. Sometimes, constructive change determinations are retroactive making the total cost approach the logical choice. However, total cost approach suggests that the difference between the contract price and the new cost of the work (plus profit) represents the total new value of the work. Oftentimes, this is not the case. Inefficiencies and other matters unrelated to the change may find a way into the cost proposal when the total cost approach is used. Detailed cost data should be included as a supplement to the claim and should include all pertinent cost back-up information. Detailed records, such as timesheets, supplier's invoices, and payroll records, should augment the cost proposal.

6. Compensation requested. The supplier should state the specific compensation requested, i.e., time, money, or both. Remember that the existence of a constructive change does not automatically confer rights of compensation. The supplier must demonstrate a direct link between the alleged cause of the change, the change, and the additional costs incurred.

In addition, the well-documented claim should include supporting information that augments or "backs up" the alleged claim. Information, such as records of conversations, technical write-ups, copies of relevant portions of the contract, data analysis, and basis of cost estimates, are useful in analysis of the claim. Photographs can also lend credibility to the claim. In reviewing the content of the request for equitable adjustment, the evaluator should be cognizant of information that is noticeably absent or of conflicting information either among the documents submitted or among documents not submitted. For example, the supplier's initial technical proposal may address some aspects of the work in a manner that challenges the constructive change argument.

Evaluators must also be alert to the submission of superfluous information that has no relevance to the constructive change itself. Well-organized, clear, and unambiguous information should provide support to the claim. If necessary, additional information should be requested.

IDENTIFICATION AND INVESTIGATION OF THE ALLEGED CHANGE

As part of the review process, the government must conduct an independent review and analysis. This will include a thorough review of all contractual records not only those contained in the official contract file but any that might exist in other government files. Interviews and meetings with government personnel involved or alleged to be involved provide a valuable opportunity to understand the facts and circumstances surrounding the alleged change.

A detailed technical review of the alleged change must be conducted if technical matters are relevant. Experts in the field are best suited to conduct a review and analysis of the supplier's technical arguments and presentation of the alleged facts. An independent comparison of the supplier's information and the government's information must be made to identify any areas that are not in agreement. Such a comparison may form the basis for the denial of the claim or for negotiation of the claim. The evaluation must focus on the extent to which a cost and/or schedule overrun resulted from the government's action or inaction.

The government team must establish the baseline contract requirements. Reviewing the contract and any extrinsic evidence, such as precontractual correspondence and records, may point to discussions or clarifications with the supplier. Additionally, the supplier's proposal can provide important information about the supplier's intent and understanding when entering into the contract. Review of the supplier's proposal is a critical part of the investigation that cannot be overlooked. In many contracts, the supplier's proposal is incorporated into the contract by reference. This most often occurs when the government elects to pay a premium for a better technical solution. In such cases, the supplier's proposal forms the baseline for technical expectations.

Recreating the history of what happened and who was involved is important. This can be a difficult task because of personnel change and records transfer. File documentation may not adequately represent the events surrounding the constructive change making the recollections of government personnel important. In such cases, oral findings must be documented and added to the government record.

This investigation is important for several reasons:

1. It enables the government to assess the validity of the claim.
2. It allows the government to isolate the extent to which the government may have caused the constructive change.
3. It enables the government to reconstruct the events for purposes of establishing a monetary and/or time value.
4. It prepares the government to support its position in the event of litigation.

RECOVERABLE COSTS

If entitlement has been determined, then every conceivable type of cost analysis should be performed. However, recognize that the extent of resources used during this effort should be commensurate with the value of the claim. Solid cost analysis will place the government in a solid position when negotiating the quantum aspect of the constructive change claim.

It is generally recognized that in a firm fixed-price bid, a supplier does not include contingency costs. A firm fixed-price contract type indicates a well-defined work statement for which no contingency costs are necessary. Additionally, firm fixed-priced contracts are often awarded to the low-priced bidder. That being the case, suppliers are not motivated to include ''unnecessary costs'' into their bid price. If it is possible to reconstruct the bid price using some fundamental assumptions, then analysis of various cost elements and cost-estimating

relationships may help develop a good negotiation position. Richard Newman's *Supplier Price Analysis* contains useful information that may assist evaluators in developing solid assumptions about a supplier. Typical examples of recoverable costs include increased labor costs caused by productive time problems, additional man hours, wage increases due to extended performance periods, overtime costs; increased material costs, increased overhead costs and repair and alteration costs. The causal relationship must be established prior to any establishment of reasonableness.

Suppliers are not expected to add costs for anticipated changes to their bid price. The costs caused by such changes, if they occur, are expected to be paid by supplemental agreement to the contract. Although a supplier may identify and quantify all costs incurred that are associated with the change and a reasonable profit, such costs may not be an accurate representation of due compensation. In fact, federal procurement regulations caution that costs incurred are not presumed to be reasonable. For example, inefficiency on the part of the supplier may have contributed to the additional costs. Constructive changes does not provide a supplier the opportunity to recover acquired losses that are not related to the change.

CONCLUSION

Constructive changes present unique challenges for government contract managers. Great care must be taken to avoid situations that can result in constructive changes. However, if such a claim is made, then a thorough identification and investigation of the circumstances and facts surrounding the allegation will ensure that the government's findings and conclusions result in a justifiable position that leaves the parties whole.

REFERENCES

1. Sherman, S.N. *Government Procurement Management*; Wordcrafters Publications: Germantown, MD, 1995.
2. Cibinic, J.; Nash, R. *Administration of Government Contracts*; The George Washington University: Washington, DC, 1996.

Association of Southeast Asian Nations (ASEAN)

Richard K. Common
The University of Hull, Hull, United Kingdom

INTRODUCTION

Despite the diversity across a myriad of policy areas, the nation states that comprise the membership of the Association of Southeast Asian Nations (ASEAN) have developed a mechanism for "cooperation" in matters pertaining to public administration and policy across its member states. ASEAN now provides a regional rival to the older and arguably more important organization for public administration affairs in Asia, the Eastern Regional Organization for Public Administration (EROPA). Although ASEAN was established in 1967, it was not until the second meeting of the ASEAN Standing Committee in 1980 that the ASEAN Conference on Reforms in the Civil Service (ACRCS) was established as an ASEAN activity. The ACRCS was renamed the ASEAN Conferences on Civil Service Matters (ACCSM) in 1987, with a stronger emphasis on collaboration between member countries. Clearly, much of the impetus surrounding these developments was based on a desire among member states to facilitate economic integration in addition to positioning the region as an attractive place for foreign direct investment underpinned by strong administrative and policy capacities. A fundamental founding principle of ASEAN is cooperation between member states, and the ACCSM is regarded as one of its key cooperation initiatives. This entry will aim to evaluate the extent of cooperation between administrative systems in the region and the nature of the reforms that are being promulgated by the ACCSM.

PUBLIC ADMINISTRATION IN ASEAN

It is beyond the remit of this entry to describe in any detail the direction and nature of administrative reforms in each member nation of ASEAN (see other entries in EPAP). However, it is useful at this stage to pick up some major themes and points of difference within these countries. There are roughly three groupings within ASEAN based on the extent of modernization within the various administrative systems where there is a strong correlation between political stability and economic development.

Brunei Darussalam, Malaysia, Singapore

In this group, there have been considerable attempts by stable political leaderships to orientate administrative systems close to Western models.[1] In particular, Malaysia and Singapore have come the closest to replicating the New Public Management observed in western nations, particularly Britain and New Zealand. However, even here it is difficult to generalize. For example, Malaysia's "Look East" policy explicitly emulated the example set by Japan and to a lesser extent, Korea, in terms of economic and human resources policy. Brunei's civil service has consistently looked to the United Kingdom for inspiration despite its unique monarchy.[2] Arguably, these three nations are also the most economically successful in ASEAN.

Indonesia, Philippines, Thailand

This grouping has experienced varying degrees of political turmoil when compared to the first grouping, in addition to a similar variance in economic development. Both Indonesia and Thailand suffered particularly damaging consequences as a result of the Asian economic crisis of the late 1990s, and had to seek International Monetary Fund (IMF) loans. For Thailand, in particular, the program of economic reform that constituted the IMF response in 1997 included civil service reform. Economic progress in the Philippines has also been exacerbated by political instability. However, attempts have been made to modernize administrative systems in all three countries, but here generalizations remain difficult. For instance, Thailand's system of government remains highly centralized when compared with that of Indonesia and the Philippines.

Cambodia, Laos, Myanmar, Vietnam

The third group of countries represent the most recent members of ASEAN, with Cambodia being the newest, joining ASEAN in 1999. However, with the exception of Cambodia, these countries are characterized by authoritarian rule and command economies, although Vietnam and Laos are engaged in cautious reform strategies. For

Encyclopedia of Public Administration and Public Policy
DOI: 10.1081/E-EPAP 120024428

the purposes of this entry, what is clear is that administrative modernization has not been high on the agenda of any of these countries until very recently.

KEY COMPONENTS OF ACCSM

Under the auspices of ASEAN, it is proposed here that ASEAN acts as a forum for learning in terms of policy and administrative development. Comparisons with the European Union (EU) are largely futile in this area as a key component of the ''ASEAN way'' is to rely ''on national institutions and actions, rather than creating a strong central bureaucracy.''[3] However, the 1992 declaration of an ASEAN free trade area (AFTA) and the Asian economic crisis created pressures for ''greater coordination and institutionalization.''[3] Thus the ACCSM is pivotal to understanding developments in public policy and administration within ASEAN.

The main forum for discussing developments in relation to public administration policy occurs within the ACCSM biannual conferences. At each conference, technical and country papers are presented. The rest of this section will briefly review developments from the 8th ACCSM in Manila mainly because it marked the beginning of ASEAN enlargement and it signaled the start of closer cooperation and institutionalization of public administration practice within ASEAN member states.

At the 8th ACCSM in Manila in 1995, an Action Plan was endorsed entitled ''Building Dynamic and Responsive 21st Century Civil Services'' outlining the following objectives:

- Human resources development.
- Recruitment and selection.
- Information exchange.
- Research and development.

These objectives were to be met by resource sharing and through the use of ICT.[4] For instance, in relation to human resources development, it was declared that member countries who have a ''special interest in a particular field of public administration'' set up ASEAN Resource Centers (ARCs) to disseminate information to other ASEAN members. The establishment of the Resource Centers has emerged as a key plank in the strategy of strengthening cooperation in public administration within ASEAN to allow the exchange of best practice within ASEAN member states.[5] The ASEAN Covenant, ''Toward Building Better Bureaucracies'' formalized the establishment of the ARCs ''to optimize the movement of goods and services across traditional boundaries.''[5] What is apparent is that the ARCs are concerned with the micromanagement aspects of public administration and policy only.

The 9th ACCSM was held in 1997 in Singapore, where it was proposed that each ACCSM was to be held on a biannual basis. Thus it was the 10th ACCSM, in 1999 in Thailand under the theme of ''Good Governance: A Challenge for Economic Revitalization and Democracy Development,'' that further consolidated the Covenant of the 8th ACCSM. In addition, it was the first ACCSM to be attended by all the current members of ASEAN. The conference also took place under the backdrop of the repercussions of the Asian financial crisis.

At the 11th ACCSM in Hanoi in 2001, the theme was ''ASEAN Civil Services for Dynamic and Sustainable Development,'' with the focus shifting to the post-1995 new member states. Both Cambodia and Laos proposed the establishment of ASEAN resource centers on Capacity Development of Civil Servants and Civil Service Performance Management, respectively. Only Myanmar has yet to submit a proposal.[a] In addition, the ACCSM prescribed a role for member states with more developed administrative systems to guide others in terms of human resource development.

The theme of the last and 12th ACCSM in 2003 in Brunei was ''E-Government: An Opportunity for National Development and Public Sector Modernization.'' This represents macro-level cooperation within ASEAN and builds upon the creation of an e-ASEAN task force to develop a regional ICT strategy, linked to wider ''E-Government'' initiatives.[7]

OBSTACLES TO COOPERATION

What is the likely outcome of closer cooperation between the ASEAN nations with regard to public administration? The sheer diversity of the nation states in question immediately militates against any generalizations. In terms of modernizing public administration and policy making within ASEAN, a strong ''colonial legacy'' could be a basis to predict whether a nation's reform program will replicate those being undertaken in the West. Turner and Hulme[8] identify the common features of the colonial legacy including a tendency toward centralization, ambiguity about the roles and relationships of public administrators and politicians, and a tradition of appointing ''generalist'' administrators to senior positions.

Although these features are readily identified in the majority of ASEAN countries, the colonial imprint is uneven across ASEAN. Britain colonized Brunei, Malaysia, Myanmar, and Singapore and likewise France in

---

[a]For details of ASEAN resource centers, go to Ref. [6].

Cambodia, Laos, and Vietnam. The Dutch administered Indonesia until 1949, while its neighbors, the Philippines, were under the control of the United States until 1946, and Spain before that, until 1898. Thailand is the only ASEAN country never to be under the administration of a foreign power. However, Thailand's hierarchical society and bureaucratic polity, although unexposed to modernization early in its development, is typical of most countries in ASEAN. In the Philippines, U.S. colonial administration was influential, which helped some aspects of modernization but "the American emphasis on political and civil, rather than bureaucratic, action did not result in a highly trained Filipino officialdom."[9] In Indonesia, the Dutch relied on local officials, which sided with the Dutch during the nationalist revolution, so they were politicized after independence.[9] Overall, the "indigenization" of systems of public administration that followed colonization has served to preserve bureaucratic systems, which in turn, has made them resistant to reform.[10]

Secondly, the elite domination of administration and politics in the ASEAN countries would suggest that ACCSM has important symbolic value. As Turner and Hulme[8] have argued, bureaucracies dominated by technocrats tend to welcome reforms that give "legitimacy or the appearance of substance to the regime and state." Moreover, political legitimacy in the ASEAN countries requires strong economic performance; thus the appearance of administrative modernization has a strong appeal.[10] For instance, the Philippines' policy making is "subject to the *particularistic* demands of a wealthy elite or oligarchy" supported by the bureaucratic management of the economy that compromises national economic development.[11] The same is true of Indonesia.

In Vietnam, the major turning point for administrative reform was the Eighth Plenum of the Central Committee in January 1995, which focused on the reform of state institutions, the reform of administrative procedures, and the creation of a corps of administrative officials. It is the latter that addressed the civil service in particular as it was reported that only a minority of civil servants "were fully qualified to do their jobs... The reform involved the design of a new system and code, a new salary structure, and a new recruitment process based on examination and the retraining of old cadres."[12] This development happened to coincide with accession to ASEAN the same year.

The newer group of ASEAN nations have had to quickly adjust to the Association's initiatives. Market reforms, implicit in the thrust of ASEAN initiatives, have also challenged the newer group in terms of bureaucratic management of the economy. Vietnam's historically bureaucratically managed economy has been "progressively dismantled."[13] For Laos, joining ASEAN was traumatic, as it "struggles to pay its ASEAN fees and

lacks enough English-speakers and skilled diplomats to make an impression at the 300 yearly meetings of the organization and its various committees."[14] In Myanmar, the problems are different and possibly more acute. Any colonial impact by Britain was negated by military rule, which "drove most of the trained civil officials from office" in 1962.[9] The subsequent excessive corruption was recently exacerbated by a freeze on civil servants' salaries.[15] Thus of all the ASEAN countries, it is probably Myanmar's administrative structure that is least developed. In a stark warning by Matthews,[16] "there is simply no infrastructure to sustain a modern nation." Finally, Cambodia has had to respond to economic initiatives within ASEAN, which have required new institutional arrangements. This has demanded modernization of the civil service system in addition to developing appropriate human resources, developing appropriate incentive structures, and rooting out corruption.[17] In addition, Cambodia faces similar problems to Laos when engaging with ASEAN. There is concern about a general lack of competence in English, the language of ASEAN, and the requirement to upgrade technical knowledge to be able to represent the interests of Cambodia within ASEAN.[18]

CONCLUSION

Although ASEAN has explicitly promoted cooperation among its members in terms of policy, the overall picture tends to be one of divergence rather than convergence. This is partly explained by the political context as for most of ASEAN rule by military or civil bureaucracy or both, rather than rule by party is the norm. Convergence between such contrasting economies and political elites through strategies such as the e-ASEAN ICT task force is unlikely.[7] However, the main objective of ASEAN, which is to enhance regional cooperation, as outlined in the Bangkok Declaration of 1967, looks more likely to be achieved through the ARCs and the dissemination of "best practice," rather than through any conscious attempt at the impossible task of converging administrative systems.

REFERENCES

1. Common, R.K. *Public Management and Policy Transfer in Southeast Asia*; Ashgate: Aldershot, 2001.
2. Halligan, J.; Turner, M. *Profiles of Government Administration in Asia*; Australian Government Publishing Service: Canberra, 1995.
3. Tay, S.; Estanislao, J. The Relevance of ASEAN: Crisis and Change. In *Reinventing ASEAN*; Tay, S., Estanislao, J.,

Soesastro, H., Eds.; Institute of Southeast Asian Studies: Singapore, 2001; 3–24.

4. Civil Service Commission, Republic of the Philippines. *ASEAN Conference on Civil Service Matters*; 1995. http://www.csc.gov.ph/asean1.html (accessed October 2003).

5. ACCSM. *The ASEAN Covenant: Towards Building Better Democracies*; National Institute of Public Administration: Kuala Lumpur, 1995. http://dls.intan.my/accsm/accsm.htm (accessed October 2003).

6. http://aseansec.org/12953.htm.

7. Wescott, C. E-government in the Asia-Pacific region. Asian J. Polit. Sci. **2001**, *9* (2), 1–24.

8. Turner, M.; Hulme, D. *Governance, Administration and Development*; Macmillan: Basingstoke, 1997.

9. Crouch, H.; Morley, J. The Dynamics of Political Change. In *Driven by Growth*, Revised Ed.; Morley, J., Ed.; Institute of Southeast Asian Studies: Singapore; M.E. Sharpe: New York, 1999; 313–354. (see previous data).

10. Common, R.K. *Public Management and Policy Transfer in Southeast Asia*; Ashgate: Aldershot, 2001.

11. Hutchison, J. Crisis and Change in the Philippines. In *The Political Economy of South-East Asia*, 2nd Ed.; Rodan, G., Hewison, K., Robison, R., Eds.; Oxford Univ. Press: Oxford, 2001; 42–70.

12. Vasavakul, T. Vietnam: Sectors, Classes, and the Transformation of a Leninist State. In *Driven By Growth*, Revised Ed.; Morley, J., Ed.; Institute of Southeast Asian Studies: Singapore, M.E. Sharpe: New York, 1999; 59–82.

13. Gates, C. The ASEAN Economic Model and Vietnam's Economic Transformation. In *ASEAN Enlargement: Impacts and Implications*; Than, M., Gates, C., Eds.; Institute of Southeast Asian Studies: Singapore, 2001; 322–361.

14. Mallet, V. *The Trouble with Tigers*; HarperCollins: London, 1999.

15. Steinberg, D. Burma/Myanmar: Under the Military. In *Driven By Growth*, Revised Ed.; Morley, J., Ed.; Institute of Southeast Asian Studies: Singapore; M.E. Sharpe: New York, 1999; 25–58.

16. Matthews, B. Burma/Myanmar. Round Table **January 1999**, (349), 77–97.

17. Kato, T. Cambodia's Accession to AFTA. In *ASEAN Enlargement: Impacts and Implications*; Than, M., Gates, C., Eds.; Institute of Southeast Asian Studies: Singapore, 2001; 164–199.

18. Zasloff, J. Emerging Stability in Cambodia. Asian Aff. Am Rev. **2002**, *28* (4), 187–201.

Budget Stabilization Fund

Yilin Hou
The University of Georgia, Athens, Georgia, U.S.A.

INTRODUCTION

The budget stabilization fund (BSF), popularly called the ''rainy-day fund'' (RDF), is a fiscal device used by subnational governments to store extra revenues during economic booms for use in economic downturns to supplement inadequate resources for meeting outlay demands. Since the early 1980s, this countercyclical device has attracted increasingly more academic attention.

ORIGIN

The concept and practice of countercyclical reserves date back to Biblical times: Joseph saved Egypt from a great famine by storing up food in years of harvest.[1] In the American government system, the BSF also enjoys a relatively long history, tracing back to the second half of the 19th century.[2] With ineffective controls and too frequent transfers, many cities then had difficulty keeping departmental spending within budgeted levels; so the cities created contingency funds for emergencies.[3] Early contingency funds were very small as a percentage of the budget or in absolute amounts[3] (for example, Boston reserved only a quarter to half a percent of appropriations for emergencies and Cincinnati reserved $50,000 for each half-year period). Rules regarding the use of the funds were developed involving consensus between the executive and legislative branches[3] (in Boston, the city auditor could transfer from this fund only when he was directed to do so by the mayor, with approval of the council's committee on finance. Council approval often had to be majority. In Cincinnati, mayoral direction had to be accompanied by consent of two-thirds of the council, while Minneapolis demanded supermajority approval—20 out of 26 council votes).

The earliest use of the name ''rainy-day fund'' was by New York City in the 1930s. The NYC rainy-day fund had inadequate restrictions on approval procedures and an insufficient mandate on replenishment; its balance was very ''modest'' by the early 1960s. ''When NYC borrowed for operating expenses, it also decided to make use of its rainy day fund''[4] (this is a comment by Mr. Ted Weiss who, in the early 1980s, was chairman of the House Subcommittee on Intergovernmental Relations and Human Resources. Mr. Weiss was on the New York City Council in the early 1960s). The fund soon went into disuse and was forgotten. The lesson is apparent: a BSF cannot exist long without restrictive approval procedures. A consensus mechanism between the executive and legislative branches is a necessary feature.

At the state level, New York was the first to adopt a formal BSF (1946)—the tax stabilization reserve fund—''as a safeguard against possible future declines in revenues.''[5] It should be noted that states give their BSFs different names. Ohio first used the name ''budget stabilization fund'' (1981); Michigan adopted a more descriptive name—''countercyclical budget and economic stabilization fund'' (1977).

EVOLUTION

From Contingency Funds to General Fund Balances

Early contingency funds were created out of operational necessity, but maintaining the funds, especially when the financial condition was strong, often encountered intense political pressure. Clow[2] mentioned that although they saw the strong management and operational rationale behind the fund, most finance officers involved in setting up the reserves were unwilling to stand the related outside pressures. They even preferred not to have a reserve fund.[2]

As a consequence, finance officials often resorted to ''unofficial'' ways to end up with general fund balances (GFB)—money that they could use for contingencies. One way was to intentionally underestimate revenue or overestimate expenditures. Another way was to designate GFB for some purpose they knew would not occur or on which the entire designated amount would not be spent. This represents a tacit transformation of a contingency fund into GFB through management gimmicks.[2] [Clow records that such dilemma had led to the purposeful complication of the contingency account by financial officers (e.g., treasurers), so that politicians could not easily make clear how much balances were available.

Encyclopedia of Public Administration and Public Policy
DOI: 10.1081/E-EPAP 120024101

Countercyclical Role of General Fund Balances

The development of GFB as a countercyclical fiscal tool is closely related to balanced budget requirements (BBR) in the states. The requirements, in one form or another, are all in stock instead of in flow by nature.[6–8] Thus instead of rigidly requiring each state to balance their budgets in each fiscal year (or each budget cycle for those biennial budget states), the BBRs allow states to balance over the years, creating the need and chance for the establishment of countercyclical reserves. A good illustration is that while most states require their governor to submit and sign and their legislature to pass a balanced budget, allowing deficit carryover into the next budget cycle is a common article in state BBRs. Gradually, states developed the practice of building up their GFB during boom years to help mitigate revenue shortages in downturns. Historical data confirm this proposition. From 1957 to 1984, over the cycles of six national recessions, GFB of the state and local sector in aggregation grew substantially during boom years (Table 1, Panel B) and the balances depleted very quickly in lean years (Table 1, Panel A). Professional organizations such as the National Association of State Budget Officers (NASBO) and Government Finance Officers Association (GFOA) have also advocated maintaining a certain amount of GFB as one of the ''best practices'' (for details, see Refs. [9,10]).

General Fund Balances to Budget Stabilization Fund

General fund balances, however, became easy targets of attack by voters in more recent times, as in the case of Proposition 13 in California. Taxpayers in many states through referendum voted into effect tax and expenditure limitations to restrain state and local governments from keeping large GFB. The vulnerability of GFB made officials increasingly aware of the advantages of a properly structured countercyclical fiscal tool as a more reliable and easier-to-operate vehicle that is protected by law from spending pressure.[4,11,12] This device is the budget stabilization fund.

DEFINING BUDGET STABILIZATION FUNDS

The fact that the BSF is a useful instrument to save assets during booms for use during recessions has been recognized by state as well as federal legislators,[4,13,14] professional organizations[10] rating agencies,[15] and scholars.[12] While there is a consensus regarding the utility of BSF, there does not seem to be consensus yet on what a BSF is or what key structural features a BSF must possess to qualify as a real BSF. GFOA and NASBO, for example, list different features as essential for a BSF. The lack of consensus has led to confusion and misuse of the concept, which in turn causes inaccuracy in data collection.

Synthesizing past literature and related legislative history and examining the finance laws of the states identify three overarching features of the BSF. First, a BSF must have an enabling legislation as its legal basis. Second, a BSF is a countercyclical reserve fund across fiscal years or budget cycles. Finally, a BSF must be a government-wide reserve for general purposes.

Enabling Legislation

Budget stabilization funds are established with enabling legislation which describes the details of a BSF, such as its purpose(s), funding source(s), allowable balance level, procedure for use approval, replenishment after use, and so on. This legislation is the legal basis of the fund. It is very significant in several fundamental ways. First, the legislation serves as a firewall between the fund and elected officials. Executive officials cannot easily use the money at their discretion because the procedure for use approval is fairly strict in most cases. Legislators cannot readily engage in pork barrel spending with this fund either because the money is available only for predetermined purposes.

Second, the legal language creating BSFs provides a defense for elected officials against popular pressure for tax returns/refunds or overspending during boom years, especially in the era of tax revolts and expenditure limitation movements. Third, the law makes it compulsory to save when the economy is strong and state revenue goes above the expenditure needs and to replenish the fund after use, so the state can stay better prepared for revenue shortfalls.

Finally, the existence of a legal basis for a BSF serves as a dividing line between a countercyclical fiscal reserve fund and GFB, which is maintained more out of practice than as a legal requirement in response to daily operational needs. The fact that a few states do have a legally required fiscal year-end balance of the general fund does not diminish this distinction: such required balances do not go across fiscal year/budget cycles. Findings from a previous study indicate that when downturns hit, general fund balances are always the first to be depleted, followed by budget stabilization funds and other useable funds.[12] When these resources are almost

Table 1   State-local fiscal behavior, 1957–1984—average quarterly growth rates of aggregate general fund balances

Panel A: Behavior during recessions

Contraction		Revenue growth (%)	Expenditure growth (%)	Surplus change (bil $)
Peak	Trough			
1957 III	1958 I	1.7	2.9	− 0.55
1960 I	1960 IV	1.9	2.1	− 0.1
1969 III	1970 IV	2.8	3.2	− 0.46
1973 IV	1975 I	2.6	3.3	− 1.32
1980 I	1980 II	0.5	1.9	− 4.7
1981 III	1982 IV	1.3	1.8	− 1.66

Panel B: Behavior during expansions

Expansion		Revenue growth (%)	Expenditure growth (%)	Surplus change (bil $)
Trough	Peak			
1958 I	1960 I	2.4	1.5	0.34
1960 IV	1969 III	2.5	2.4	0.08
1970 IV	1973 IV	2.9	2.5	0.8
1975 I	1980 I	2.5	2.1	6.15
1980 II	1981 III	1.8	1.3	3.06
1982 IV	1984 IV	2.1	1.8	4.95

Sources: 1957–1977 data, Advisory Commission on Intergovernmental Relations (ACIR), *State-Local Finances in Recession and Inflation, Report-70.* Washington, DC, 1979; 1978–1984 data, Ronald Fisher, "Statement before the Intergovernmental Relations and Human Resources Subcommittee of the Committee on Government Operations," in U.S. Congress, *Federal and State Roles in Economic Stabilization—hearings before a subcommittee of the Committee on Government Operations House of Representatives, Nov. and Dec. 1984.* U.S. Government Printing Office, 1985; 107.

gone, tax increases, expenditure cuts, and accounting gimmicks come into use.

Countercyclical Reserves Fund Across Fiscal Years/Budget Cycles

The BSF is designed as a countercyclical mechanism. As a reserve to be accumulated in boom years for use in lean years, it is necessarily a mechanism that operates across fiscal years (for those states that adopt biennial budgets, it operates across biennial budget cycles). The focal point of a BSF is to "balance," or smooth out the peaks and troughs of, revenues and expenditures through the business cycle, instead of merely the fiscal year or budget cycle.

This feature separates the BSF from working capital funds and legally required year-end general fund balances. A working capital fund serving cash flow purposes operates mainly within the fiscal year so that the government does not have to resort to the debt market for current spending before tax revenues stream in. In some cases, the working capital fund does go beyond the fiscal year, but even in those instances, its focus remains on filling in the revenue gap between two budget cycles.

In a few states (Colorado, Kansas, New Mexico, and Wisconsin), their finance laws require a balance (surplus) of the general fund at the end of fiscal years, ranging in size between 2% and 5% of the current year general fund revenue. Given the spending pressure from politicians and taxpayers, these required balances are not guaranteed to accumulate across fiscal years or budget cycles. As such, these required year-end balances cannot serve as a BSF.

Government-Wide Reserve for General Purposes

The U.S. General Accounting Office (GAO) classifies state reserves into three categories: 1) government-wide reserves for general purposes; 2) government-wide reserves for specific purposes; and 3) agency-specific reserves for specific purposes.[16] A BSF should be a government-wide reserve for general purposes. Any reserves for single or special purposes are not in this category. Reserve funds that are set up for use by only certain agencies in the government are not in this category either. Contingency funds as currently in use by many state governments are across-fiscal-year reserves, and they can be government-wide or agency-specific; but on the whole, these funds are reserves *for specific purposes*, e.g., natural disasters, litigation settlements, self-insurance, and so on. Therefore contingency funds are not the same as BSF.

Strict Definition of the Budget Stabilization Fund

Thus two distinct definitions of BSFs emerge, one relatively strict and the other loose. Adopting the strict or the loose definition of BSFs will end up with quite different data sets and thereby results of empirical analysis. The strict definition is clear and straightforward with regards to the accumulation of the fund (during good times) and purpose (to cope with revenue shortfall during recessions). It is:

> A budget stabilization fund is money set aside while good economic conditions prevail and then drawn down during poor economic times to lessen the extent to which state governments will have to reduce expenditures or raise taxes to cope with a recession.[4,9,12]

Table 2 Recessions and creation of BSF

Recession	State	Creation	Fund name	First balance
1945	New York	1946	Tax Stabilization Reserve Fund	1946
1957–1958	Florida	1959/65	Working Capital Fund/Budget Stabilization Fund	1965
1969–1970	Tennessee	1972	Reserve for Revenue Fluctuations	1972
1973–1975	California	1976	Special Fund for Economic Uncertainties	1977
	Georgia	1976	Revenue Shortfall Reserve	1976
	Delaware	1977	Budget Reserve Account	1979
	Michigan	1977	Countercyclical Budget and Economic Stabilization Fund	1978
	South Carolina	1978	General Reserve Fund	1978
	New Mexico	1978	General Fund Tax Stabilization Reserve	No balance
	Connecticut	1979	Budget Reserve Fund	1981
1980	Ohio	1981	Budget Stabilization Fund	1985
	Washington	1981	Emergency Reserve Fund	1989
1982	Indiana	1982	Countercyclical Revenue and Economic Stabilization Fund	1985
	Mississippi	1982	Working Cash-Stabilization Reserve Fund	1983
	Wyoming	1982	Budget Reserve Account	1983
	Kentucky	1983	Budget Reserve Trust Fund Account	1987
	Nebraska	1983	Cash Reserve Fund	1984
	Idaho	1984	Budget Stabilization Fund	1984
	Minnesota	1984/1996	Cash Flow Account/Budget Reserve Account	1984
	Maine	1985	Maine Rainy Day Fund	1985
	Maryland	1985	Revenue Stabilization Fund	1987
	Massachusetts	1985	Commonwealth Stabilization Fund	1987
	Oklahoma	1985	Constitutional Reserve Fund	1988
	Pennsylvania	1985	Tax Stabilization Reserve Fund	1986
	Rhode Island	1985	Budget Reserve and Cash Stabilization Account	1985
	Wisconsin	1985	Budget Stabilization Fund	No balance
	Utah	1986	Budget Reserve Account	1987
	New Hampshire	1987	Revenue Stabilization Reserve Account	1987
	North Dakota	1987	Budget Stabilization Fund	1990
	Vermont	1987	General Fund Budget Stabilization Reserve	1987
	Texas	1988	Economic Stabilization Fund	1990
	Alaska	1990	Constitutional Budget Reserve Fund	1992
	Louisiana	1990	Revenue Stabilization and Mineral Trust Fund	1999
	New Jersey	1990	Surplus Revenue Fund	1993
1990–1991	Arizona	1991	Budget Stabilization Fund	1994
	Nevada	1991	Fund to Stabilize Operation of State Government	1994
	North Carolina	1991	Savings Reserve Account	1991
	South Dakota	1991	Budget Reserve Fund	1992
	Iowa	1992	Economic Emergency Fund/Cash Reserve Fund	1993
	Missouri	1992	Budget Stabilization Fund	1992
	Virginia	1992	Revenue Stabilization Fund	1993
	West Virginia	1994	Revenue Shortfall Reserve Fund	1995

The loose definition purports that the fund is not only for temporary shortfalls, but also for any nonrecurring expenditures. The latter gives this definition a much broader scope. Consequently, the loose definition is broad enough to count a *contingency fund* as a BSF. The loose definition of the BSF runs:

> A budget stabilization fund is money set aside...against the chances of 'reducing service levels or raising taxes and fees because of temporary revenue shortfalls or unpredicted one-time expenditures.'[10]

ADOPTION OF BUDGET STABILIZATION FUND BY THE STATES

The creation of budget stabilization funds by the states has been slow. But recessions and tax revolts have highlighted the usefulness of BSF as an effective fiscal tool. Gold[6] noticed that the chronology of BSF adoption shows close correlation between establishment of BSF and recessions (Table 2).[17]

Every one of the earliest state adopters of the BSF—New York, Florida, Tennessee, and Michigan—came within 3 years of a previous recession. The recessions in the early 1980s made the correlation more apparent: fiscal stress that led to spending cutbacks and increased taxes as an effort to sustain funding for public services prompted 16 states (from 1981 to 1985) to establish their BSFs.[18] Once initiated, the adoption of BSFs spread broadly among the states. Then the 1990–1991 recession further increased the number of states with BSFs.

BUDGET STABILIZATION FUND DATA

Up to now, the *Fiscal Survey of the States* series compiled and published twice a year by the National Association of State Budget Officers (since 1977) is the only readily available source that provides BSF data of the states. Many empirical studies have based their analysis on this data source. A drawback with this series, however, is that the BSF figures provided by the states and reported in the series often do not match with those in the *Comprehensive Annual Financial Reports* (CAFR) of the states. The discrepancy may be a result of various reasons. However, because the CADRs are audited financial documents, they carry weight that should not be ignored. Therefore researchers and practitioners should exercise caution in their choice of data sources.

The usefulness of the budget stabilization fund as a subnational countercyclical fiscal device is now widely recognized—over 40 states have adopted the fund and researchers have begun to pay increasing attention to its study. However, comprehensive and conclusive examinations of this instrument are still lacking.

REFERENCES

1. The Old Testament, Genesis: 41.
2. Clow, F.R. *A Comparative Study of the Administration of City Finances in the United States, with Special Reference to the Budget*; MacMillan: New York, 1901. Sponsored by the American Economic Association.
3. Rubin, I. *Class, Tax & Power—Municipal Budgeting in the United States*; Chatham House Publishers, Inc.: Chatham, NJ, 1998; 35–36.
4. United States Congress. *Federal and State Roles in Economic Stabilization—Hearings Before a Subcommittee of the Committee on Government Operations House of Representatives, Nov. and Dec. 1984*; U.S. Government Printing Office: Washington, DC, 1985.
5. *Annual Report of the Comptroller, State of New York, for the Fiscal Year Ended March 31, 1946*; Comptroller's Office: Albany, NY, 1946; 5.
6. Gold, S.D. *State and Local Fiscal Relations in the Early 1980s*; The Urban Institute Press: Washington, DC, 1983.
7. National Association of State Budget Officers (NASBO). *State Balanced Budget Requirements: Provisions and Practice*; 1992. Washington, DC.
8. Briffault, R. *The Balanced Budget Debate: Balancing Acts—The Reality Behind State Balanced Budget Requirements*; The Twentieth Century Fund Press: New York, 1996.
9. National Association of State Budget Officers (NASBO); National Governors' Association (NGA); National Conference of State Legislators (NCSL). *The Fiscal Survey of the States*; February 1985; 6. Washington, DC.
10. Government Finance Officers Association (GFOA), Develop Policy on Stabilization Funds. In *Recommended Budget Practices*; 1999; 17.
11. *Michigan Legislation 1977*. Michigan Compiled Laws, Chapter 18: Dept. of Management and Budget, Sec. 351–359.
12. Sobel, R.S.; Holcombe, R.G. The impact of state rainy day funds in easing state fiscal crises during the 1990–1991 recession. Public Budg. Finance **1996**, *16* (3), 28–48.
13. State of Michigan Act 76 of 1977 (repealed).
14. State of Michigan Act 431 of 1984.
15. Larkin, R.P. Impact of Management Practices on Municipal Credit. In *Special Report in Public Finance*; FITCH IBCA, May 4, 2000.
16. United States General Accounting Office. *Budgeting For Emergencies—State Practices and Federal Implications*; Government Printing Office: Washington, DC, September 1999.
17. National Conference of State Legislatures. *Preparing for the Next Recession: Rainy Day Funds and Other Tools for the States*; Legislative Finance Paper No. 41, 1983.
18. Douglas, J.W.; Gaddie, R.K. State rainy day funds and fiscal crises: Rainy day funds and the 1990–1990 recession revisited. Public Budg. Finance **2002**, *22* (1), 19–30.

Bureaucrats and Politicians in Southeast Asia

Scott Fritzen
National University of Singapore, Singapore

INTRODUCTION

Ever shifting relationships between bureaucrats and politicians have played a direct or indirect role in several major debates in Southeast Asia since colonization. One theme concerns the *contradictions of the colonial inheritance,* with its ideology of a politics–administration separation coupled with extreme executive dominance in practice. A second theme involves the role of the bureaucracy in *promoting economic transformation* in several Southeast Asian states modeling themselves after the successful newly industrialized countries (NICs). Finally, more recent calls for good governance in the wake of the East Asian financial crisis coupled with democratization trends in the region have raised the salience of the concept of *democratic accountability* of both politicians and bureaucrats. This review examines each of these areas, concluding that the dynamics of the bureaucrat–politician relationship are likely to continue to be a central point of theoretical and practical contestation in the coming years.

THE COLONIAL LEGACY

A seminal concept dominating the "modern" democratic notion of the bureaucrat–politician relationship harkens back to Woodrow Wilson's politics–administration dichotomy: "The field of administration is a field of business. . .removed from the hurry and strife of politics" (1887, quoted in Ref. [1]). Both politics and administration, it was understood, were to be underpinned by accountability to the public and to the rule of law. This normative ideal, whatever the realities in the home country context, did not travel well to Europe's Southeast Asian colonies. There, the appointed (European) "man in the field" was the ultimate bureaucrat-cum-politician ruling with great discretion with no democratic accountability.[2] This was, in practice, usually consistent with indigenous patterns of rule in kingdoms of Siam and Burma or the sultanates of the Malay Peninsula.[3–5]

The task of crafting modern polities, whether as part of the decolonization agenda or revolutionary struggles, was one of developing and cementing elite consensus within functioning organizations capable of commanding a sufficient degree of legitimacy and of exercising state power. This task expressed itself in different forms, depending on the contingencies of the political process. Three models are evident.

The first pattern, found in Malaysia, Indonesia, the Philippines, and Burma, involved a semisponsored, more or less orderly handover of power from the colonial authorities to a local elite. Colonial authorities looked to the civil service as the logical—often the only—source of "acceptable" nationalist leadership. In some places, these authorities explicitly endeavored to leave behind more ethnically representative bureaucracies (reversing earlier policies that favored Indians and Chinese in Malaysia, for instance) and political movements.[6] When such promotion led, in practice, to uncomfortably close ties between aspiring politicians and bureaucrats (because of the shallow pool of politically acceptable talent that colonial administrators could tap), principle gave way to political expediency. These former colonies were left with weakly institutionalized political systems that had but a semblance of political–administrative separation—and none at all following the military coups that subsequently occurred in all of the above countries except Malaysia.

Thailand, which avoided colonization, must stand in its own category. Here, at least until recent years, a military–bureaucratic alliance dominated. The 1932 coup d'etat that overthrew the absolute monarchy was motivated as much by bureaucratic–clientelistic objectives as by calls for greater modernization or democracy per se.[4] The ensuing pattern of Thai institutional life as "a matter of competition between bureaucratic cliques for the benefits of government" (David Wilson, quoted in Ref. [4]) remained, in some ways, institutionally consistent for several decades.

The third pattern—most costly in terms of human suffering and developmental trajectories—involved prolonged violence and instability in Indochina. It began in the immediate postwar period with the North Vietnamese struggle to unify the country under communist rule and ended only in 1993 with UN-sponsored elections initiated a decade of political consolidation and a semblance of stability.[7] Prolonged strife, combined with attempts to implement radical socialist programs, left Vietnam, Laos, and Cambodia without a professional bureaucracy or even

Encyclopedia of Public Administration and Public Policy
DOI: 10.1081/E-EPAP-120024429

rhetorical norms limiting regime powers. The bureaucracy was subsumed under the overriding necessity of developing revolutionary administrations utilizing neo-Stalinist forms of political organization.

To summarize, the internal contradictions of colonialism, coupled with the political turbulence that followed decolonization and modernization period, left bureaucracies in all of these countries (save Thailand) decisively dominated by political masters. The systems that emerged, however, varied greatly in their developmental effectiveness, for reasons explored in the next section.

THE BUREAUCRACY IN NEWLY INDUSTRIALIZING CONTEXTS

Beginning with the Japanese transformation, several East Asian countries, together with one Southeast Asian— Singapore—were able to rapidly transform their economies, attaining within some 20 years levels of per capita income that placed them in the ranks of advanced, industrial countries. Several Southeast Asian countries, which collectively became known as the new "tigers"— Malaysia, Thailand, and Indonesia—appeared to model certain aspects of the NIC's developmental recipe and appeared to achieve considerable success in doing so.

How had the NICs achieved such a feat? This became the dominant question in practical and theoretical debates that continue to this day and in which the relationships between bureaucrats and politicians came to play a key role. Contrasting explanations were offered by those[8,9] who advocated that the state's role in economic decision making was decisive and others[10] claiming that state success in achieving macroeconomic stability and an external orientation was far more important than bureaucratic interventions. An influential explanation among the former group[11,12] held that the key to developmental effectiveness, both in the NIC case and potentially in other countries, was the "embedded autonomy" of the bureaucracy. Bureaucracies could, by this theory, successfully serve as "midwives" to economic development if they enjoyed four conditions. The first was a political leadership determined to pursue a transformational agenda with little fear of electoral backlash. The second was a meritocratic, technically competent bureaucracy (or an elite, "piloting" segment of it). The third and fourth requirements were special characteristics of this bureaucracy that would allow it to successfully intervene in the economy. The bureaucracy was to be both "embedded"—enjoying dense informational links to the companies and market sectors to be promoted—and "autonomous," i.e., not captured by any special interest

and therefore being capable of "disciplining" capital by, for instance, stopping subsidies where this was necessary.

To what extent did Southeast Asian countries put these purported conditions of success in place? Singapore, as one of the original NICs, was in many ways the archetypical example of the process. One must only make the proviso that the bureaucratic "autonomy" in question was not autonomy from the ruling People's Action Party itself. Rather, it reflected the overall autonomy of the regime, with its technically competent bureaucrats clearly in position as "implementers" of policies.[13,14]

Malaysia, Thailand, and Indonesia were all held up at one time or another as exemplary "new tigers" primarily because of their success in achieving, for extended periods, high rates of economic growth. Malaysia and Indonesia shared considerable regime stability (at times enforced by repression), a commitment of the leadership to economic modernization, and development outcomes that were broadly based, whether through programs of outright redistribution (as in the case of Malaysia's New Economic Policy) or successful strategy to boost agricultural productivity (as in Indonesia).

The bureaucracy in all of these cases was thought to be reasonably capable and "technocratic." Yet economic interventions were of a generally smaller scale than in the NICs themselves, and the "disciplining" of capital was heavily constrained by the need to promote the "illegitimate" (i.e., nontransformational) interests of the ruling clique itself, as expressed in soaring levels of corruption. Only in Malaysia did the high degree of unity of the Malay political–bureaucratic establishment consistently promote an agenda of redistribution from the Chinese economic elite to ethnic Malay majority. As shown in the next section, however, the developmental model employed by the "tigers" clearly involved less of a "steel-frame" bureaucracy than that implied by the embedded autonomy theory.

Vietnam has more recently emerged as arguably a vital member of the "tiger" community, with economic growth rates consistently among the highest in the world throughout the 1990s. Scholarly debates continue as to whether the far-reaching *doi moi* (renovation) reforms it introduced were driven by local bureaucratic responses to failed central planning or by a far-sighted central leadership.[15] Whatever the case, the rapid growth that ensued initially reflected gains brought on by the one-off removal of "artificial" constraints on growth imposed by poor institutions (such as collective agriculture) but was later sustained by a political–bureaucratic Communist Party elite calculus that rapid growth and modernization was the best chance the party had to maintain its legitimacy.[16] This strategy of economic reform with continued political authoritarianism has generated some tensions in Vietnam, as it has in countries such as Singapore and Malaysia, a trend reflecting of democratic pressures for reform.

PRESSURES FOR REFORM: THE GOVERNANCE AGENDA COMES OF AGE

The last 15 years or so have seen a shift in the parameters of the debate over the politician–bureaucrat relationship throughout Southeast Asia. Two overlapping categories of influence are particularly important in this context: democratization and the rise of the "good governance" agenda.

Calls for greater political accountability have been on the increase throughout the region. A "third wave of democratization"[17] saw civilian, multiparty rule return in Thailand (1992), Philippines (1986), Indonesia (1998), and Cambodia (1993). Public anger over the closed workings of the political–bureaucratic elites dominating the first three countries was a key factor in bringing down autocratic rulers. This increased mobilization and citizen consciousness has carried over into democratic politics in these countries; use of the bureaucracy for the enrichment of the political elite continued to feature prominently in calls for both political and bureaucratic reform in several contexts, for instance, the ouster of President Joseph Estrada during "People's Power II" (2002) and more positively, in the introduction of an ambitious new constitution in Thailand in 1997. Citizens throughout the region showed themselves eager and willing to envision democratization as a check on both unaccountable political and bureaucratic power.

In Singapore, Vietnam, Laos, and Brunei, governance remained both authoritarian and (for practical purposes, although via very different mechanisms) uncontested, whereas in Myanmar (Burma), a small group of generals continued to block any political normalization. Even here, the *ersatz* vocabulary of democratization—articulated in terms of improved governmental responsiveness to citizen feedback—was an increasingly prominent feature in officially sanctioned political discourse, although practical reform efforts betrayed the significant contradictions of their contexts. For instance, Singapore's establishment of district-based "Community Development Councils" in 1996 was touted as an attempt to promote greater citizen involvement in local decision making, despite the fact that council members were all appointed by the ruling party.[18] In Vietnam, much-hyped "grassroots democratization" reforms introduced in 1997, in practice, meant a clarification of standards (e.g., regarding local government budget transparency) that higher levels of the party-

state apparatus could use selectively to "discipline" lower levels.[16]

The "good governance" agenda that arose contemporaneously with the democratization movement above was given impetus primarily from donors, academic work highlighting the impact of governance qualities on development outcomes, and various think tanks and nongovernmental organizations. One variant of the agenda, driven by increasing financial integration of the region, was concerned corporate governance. Explanations for the Asian financial crisis beginning in 1997, which afflicted Indonesia, Thailand, and the Philippines more than other Southeast Asian countries, came to center on a pernicious set of incentives—of politicians to use capital markets for personal purposes; of banks to lend funds for unsound investments; and of bureaucratic regulators to overlook all of the above.[19] The financial crisis led to a fundamental reassessment of the supposed strengths of the region's political–bureaucratic systems. More specifically, the call was for greater transparency and disciplined oversight systems that reinforced the call for a clear separation of bureaucratic from political authority and for both to be underpinned by a reinforced rule of law.

Another "good governance" agenda lies in the promotion of decentralized decision making and management, whether in a democratic, fiscal, or administrative context. Here there was also much to discuss on the regional scene, with virtually all countries in the region engaged in some form of formal decentralization policy. For most countries, this went beyond rhetorical support for the concept as an ideological smokescreen. In Cambodia—arguably the least hospital environment for devolution in the region—authorities astounded observers with the speed with which it established democratically elected Commune Councils, even before presumably easier administrative reforms supporting such arrangements were in place. Through the rapid introduction of two decentralization laws (Nos. 22/1999 and 25/2000) in the immediate aftermath of Soeharto's resignation, Indonesia moved "from being one of the most centralized countries in the world to one of the most decentralized."[20] Thailand and the Philippines both continued to decentralize decision making to provinces and districts, the latter quite vigorously.[21]

There is, finally, a managerialist variant of the good governance agenda. The New Public Management (NPM) can be seen as an attempt to reengineer relationships between politicians, bureaucrats, and the public.[22] Key strategic elements in this broad family of reforms include: 1) delinking policy formulation (or "steering") from implementation functions to concretize the specific accountability borne by all actors; 2) introduction of competitive pressures to the bureaucracy using market mechanisms such as privatization where possible and systems of performance measurement where not; and 3) deregulation of internal operations to promote flexible, creative implementation.[23] Application of such ideas to developing country contexts, where the predictability and transparency of bureaucratic processes is limited, has been hotly contested.[24] But attempts to apply NPM principles to governance reforms are standard policy in the higher capacity countries covered here (Singapore and Malaysia), increasingly, if hesitantly, being applied in the newly democratic countries of Southeast Asia and are prominent in public administration reform strategy.

CONCLUSION

In the aftermath of colonialism, bureaucratic–politician relationships were, like government systems themselves, weakly institutionalized in Southeast Asia, regardless of whether they had inherited the ideological veneer of a politics–administration dichotomy. The ''tigers'' of Southeast Asia were able to grow quickly by drawing on a combination of transformational leadership, an external orientation, and core bureaucratic agencies of at least moderate capacity. The politician–bureaucrat relationship was driven in these cases by a substantial unity of elite interests (as in Malaysia) or domineering executives or parties (as in the Philippines, Indonesia, and Vietnam). Political systems were, in many cases, highly fragile and, in others (such as Myanmar), rigid but nontransformative; in all cases except Singapore and possibly Malaysia, however, bureaucratic capacities and incentives fell well beneath the threshold levels of ''embedded autonomy'' that theorists argued were necessary to sustain economic transformation over a period of not years but decades, as in the newly industrialized countries.

Democratization and good governance pressures, driven by the increased sophistication of societies and by global financial integration, have propelled the politics–administration link into the center of political discourse throughout the region. In a few countries (notably Myanmar, Laos, and Brunei), there is no discernable movement toward a more institutionalized, professional bureaucracy. Other authoritarian contexts (such as Singapore and Vietnam) are attempting to make their bureaucratic systems more responsive to their publics without threatening (indeed, while bolstering) the position of ruling elites. In more democratically competitive settings, a wider range of reforms—from formal regulation of civil servants via asset disclosure requirements to democratic decentralization to increase the direct accountability of service providers and local politicians to the public—is being introduced. Capacity to implement such ambitious reforms is, in all cases, limited. The outcomes of attempts to establish transparent relationships between politicians and bureaucrats, where these have never sat easily within the region's political economy, will be hotly contested in the years to come, both theoretically and on the ground.

REFERENCES

1. Starling, G. *Managing the Public Sector*, 6th Ed.; Harcourt College Publishers: Fort Worth, TX, 2002.
2. Tarling, N. The Establishment of Colonial Regimes. Chapter 1. In *The Cambridge History of Southeast Asia, Vol 2. Part 1. From c.1800 to the 1930s*; Tarling, N., Ed.; Cambridge University Press: Cambridge, 1992.
3. Crouch, H. *Government and Society in Malaysia*; Cornell University Press: Ithaca, NY, 1996.
4. Riggs, F. The Bureaucratic Polity as a Working System. In *The Political Economy of East Asia*; Ravenhill, J., Ed.; Edward Elgar: London, 1994.
5. Silverstein, J. The Evolution and Salience of Burma's National Political Culture. In *Burma: Prospects for a Democratic Future*; Rotberg, R.I., Ed.; Brookings Institution Press: Washington, DC, 1999.
6. Puthucheary, M. *The Politics of Administration: The Malaysian Experience*; Oxford University Press: Kuala Lumpur, 1978.
7. Roberts, D. From 'communism' to 'democracy' in Cambodia: A decade of transition and beyond. Communist Post-Communist Stud. **2003**, *36*, 245–258.
8. Wade, R. *Governing the Market: Economic Theory and the Role of Government in East Asian Industrialization*; Princeton University Press: Princeton, NJ, 1990.
9. Amsden, A. *Asia's Next Giant: South Korea and Late Industrialization*; Oxford University Press: New York, 1989.
10. World Bank. *The East Asian Miracle: Economic Growth and Public Policy*; Oxford University Press: New York, NY, 1993.
11. Evans, P. *Embedded Autonomy: States & Industrial Transformation*; Princeton University Press: Princeton, NJ, 1995.
12. Evans, P. Transferable lessons? Re-examining the institutional prerequisites of East Asian economic policies. J. Dev. Stud. **1998**, *34* (6), 66–86.
13. Leong, H.K. *The Politics of Policy-Making in Singapore*; Oxford University Press: Singapore, 2000.
14. Hamilton-Hart, N. The Singapore state revisited. Pac. Rev. **2000**, *13* (2), 195–216.
15. Fforde, A.; de Vylder, S. *From Plan to Market: The Economic Transition in Vietnam*; Westview Press: Boulder, CO, 1996.
16. Fritzen, S. Growth, poverty and the future of poverty reduction in Vietnam. J. Asian Econ. **2002**, *13* (5), 635–657.

17. Diamond, L. *Developing Democracy: Toward Consolidation*; Johns Hopkins University Press: Baltimore, 1999.

18. George, C. *Singapore: The Air-Conditioned Nation: Essays on the Politics of Comfort and Control 1990–2000*; Landmark Books: Singapore, 2000.

19. Dwivedi, O.P. Challenges of Culture and Governance in Asian Public Administration. Chapter 41. In *Handbook of Public Administration*; Peters, B.G., Pierre, J., Eds.; Sage: London, 2003.

20. Hoffman, B.; Kaiser, K. The Making of the Big Bang and Its Aftermath: A Political Economy Perspective, Conference Paper: ''Can Decentralization Help Rebuild Indonesia?'' Atlanta, Georgia, May 1–3, 2002; Georgia State University.

21. Brillantes, A.B., Jr. *Philippines: Sustaining the Gains of Decentralization*; Brillantes, A.B., Jr., Cuachon, N.G., Eds.; Asian Resource Center for Decentralization, 2002. Available at http://www.decentralization.ws/srcbook_main.asp [accessed December 29, 2003].

22. Peters, B.G.; Pierre, J. Civil Servants and Politicians: The Changing Balance. In *Politicians, Bureaucrats and Administrative Reform*; Peters, B.G., Pierre, J., Eds.; Routledge: London, 2001.

23. Osborne, D.; Plastrik, P. *Banishing Bureaucracy: The Five Strategies for Reinventing Government*; Addison Wesley: Reading, MA, 1996.

24. *The Internationalization of Public Management: Reinventing the Third World State*; McCourt, W., Minogue, M., Eds.; Edward Elgar: Cheltenham, UK, 2001.

Cambodia

Clay Wescott
Asian Development Bank, Manila, Philippines

INTRODUCTION

After over 40 years of frequent, and unusually drastic, changes in its political and economic regimes, Cambodia has made headway since 1991 in rebuilding its governance institutions. Considerable progress has been achieved in maintaining public order, increasing revenues, rationalizing public expenditure policy and management, introducing new audit mechanisms, launching democratically elected commune councils, and facilitating a vibrant civil society, private sector, and free media.

PUBLIC SECTOR

Since independence in 1953, Cambodia has experienced frequent, and unusually drastic, changes in its political and economic regimes.[1,2] Over the period, it has moved from constitutional monarchy, to republic, to extreme Maoist agrocommunism, to Communist party rule, and back to a constitutional monarchy with an elected legislature. The most unstable period was the period of Khmer Rouge rule from 1975 to 1979. During this period, the market economy and business activities were completely abolished, and there was no money or trade. No private ownership of any kind was allowed. Cambodia was cut off from the rest of the world except China, the regime's main supporter. The entire urban population was forcibly relocated to rural areas to perform agricultural work. Many educated civil servants, professionals, and military officers were executed or died from starvation or disease. People wearing glasses or able to speak a foreign language, both seen as symbols of higher education, were killed. Estimates indicate that more than 1 million people, or about 15% of the population, died of unnatural deaths.[3]

Since the 1991 Paris Peace Agreement, Cambodia has rebuilt its key governance institutions. National Assembly members were selected in an election supervised by the United Nations Transitional Authority in 1993. Cambodia's sixth constitution was adopted in 1993 and amended in March 1999 to establish the Senate as a political compromise between Cambodia's two main political parties. The National Assembly holds primary legislative power and has become more active since the formation of a new coalition government in late 1998. Although there was renewed political violence in 1997, the trend has been toward peaceful resolution of political disputes and increased democratic participation. The National Assembly has enacted several new laws critical for improving governance, such as the Financial Institutions Law and the Audit Law. In addition, television broadcasts of debates have increased the transparency of the legislative process. Meanwhile, the Senate is investigating complaints about illegal confiscation of land and has recommended amending the constitution to ensure that it has adequate time to review proposed laws.

The power to initiate legislation rests jointly with the Prime Minister and members of the National Assembly and Senate. Most draft legislation originates with the Royal Government of Cambodia (RGC), led by the Council of Ministers. The assembly has simply tended to review and enact bills drafted by the RGC, often without being given sufficient time and lacking the requisite expertise. In addition, there is no central repository for all regulations or subdecrees, and the legislature rarely receives copies of regulations or decisions by ministries related to laws enacted. Finding them consists of visiting each ministry to see what they have, making it difficult for citizens to know how to comply.

The imbalance between the legislature and executive is paralleled by an imbalance of financial and technical resources available, with far more donor resources going to the latter.

Executive power rests with the RGC, which directs the civil administration and armed forces. In 2003, Cambodia has 166,672 civil servants (including defense forces, but excluding police, whose numbers are unknown). In comparison to other low-income countries, the Cambodian civil service is about average in terms of cost (the wage bill as a percentage of GDP, current expenditures, and revenues) and size (civil servants as a percentage of population).[4]

Low salaries in the public sector are one of the most fundamental structural problems, with direct implications for the sector's accountability and transparency (or lack thereof). If this issue is not addressed, it is likely to remain as a major obstacle to other governance reforms.

The RGC approved a *Governance Action Plan* in 2001, and the Council for Administrative Reform had made good progress on completing the civil service census and on a Priority Mission Group scheme (identification of

Encyclopedia of Public Administration and Public Policy
DOI: 10.1081/E-EPAP 120024438

staff groups to receive enhanced salaries linked to performance benchmarks). Perhaps the area of reform that had the clearest government commitment and leadership is decentralization. Following the announcement of the intention to hold elections in the country's 1,621 rural communes and urban sangkats in February 2001, the Law on Commune Elections and the Law on Administration of Communes were promulgated, and the interministerial National Committee for Support to Communes/Sangkats and its subcommittees responsible for implementing the decentralization reforms were established. The commune and sangkat elections were held in February 2002, and elected councils are increasingly taking on local government functions guided by the RGC's Decentralization Roadmap.

In addition, downsizing the huge defense and security forces is an urgent issue that requires a new vision for the armed forces and police. However, their ideal size is difficult to assess without determining their new roles in postconflict Cambodia. Military and security agencies need to promote professionalism, train their staff to observe new codes of conduct, and develop relevant skills. A reassessment of the roles of the military and police is under way.

The Governance Action Plan also identifies issues concerning the management of natural resources (including land, forestry, and fisheries) as critical to ensuring social peace, environmental sustainability, poverty reduction, and economic development. There are three important areas: 1) the resolution of land issues (i.e., ownership, classification, registration, and tenure); 2) combating corruption and mismanagement of forests; and 3) ensuring long-term sustainability of fisheries. Communities need to be empowered to play appropriate roles in the management of natural resources and to help ensure accessibility by the poor.

The RGC has undertaken several key reforms of public finance and administration since 1993. For example, the 1993 Organic Budget Law (basic law that defines the overall legal framework), combined with prudent fiscal and monetary policy, has helped fight inflation and bring about macroeconomic stability. The 1997 Law on Taxation has improved the government's revenue-raising capacity.

In 2001, total public revenues were only 11.7% of gross domestic product (GDP), one of the lowest proportions among countries, although up from 8.3% in 1998. The introduction of a value added tax in 1999 contributed to the revenue increases, while simplifying the tax structure, widening coverage, and reducing cascading (taxation of something more than once). Improvements in tax administration have included better collaboration among government departments and strengthening tax auditing. Collection of tax arrears is expected to be stepped-up through several enforcement measures, including freezing bank accounts. However, further reforms in tax adminis-

tration need to be considered, such as setting up a semi-autonomous revenue authority and reducing the use of ad hoc tax and duty exemptions.

Over the period 1998–2001, the RGC has generally maintained fiscal discipline, and there has been a shift in expenditures away from the military and security toward social and economic development, with education spending doubled and health spending tripled; yet social spending is still too low to meet development goals. Furthermore, budget execution has suffered from delays and unpredictable release of funds because of cash constraints, thus undermining operational planning. The system is plagued by gate keeping, deficient accounting and reporting systems, and the use of cash rather than the banking system, leading to a weak control environment. The Ministry of Economy and Finance is currently undertaking several measures to improve budget execution and revenue-enhancing capacity, planning to raise total revenue to 14–15% of GDP by 2007.

The Governance Action Plan includes provisions to improve gender equity and to reduce systemic barriers to accessing services for women and girls. However, until an output-based, medium-term expenditure framework system has been implemented, it will be difficult to ensure that policies designed to increase gender equity are properly prioritized and funded.

Legislation establishing the National Audit Authority consistent with international standards was passed in March 2000. The authority is independent of the executive, reports to the National Assembly, enjoys financial and administrative autonomy, and is authorized to determine the scope and methods of audits. An auditor general and two deputy auditor generals are appointed for 5-year terms by royal decree at the recommendation of the government and approved by a two-third-majority vote of the National Assembly. The current auditor general is from the ruling party, and the deputies are from minority parties. Although these are promising developments, more training and additional equipment will be needed, along with considerable political will, for the authority to be fully effective.

The judiciary has four distinct components: the Constitutional Council, formed in 1998; the Supreme Council of Magistracy, established in 1994; the courts; and the prosecutors. The Constitutional Council safeguards the constitution and decides cases involving the election of National Assembly and Senate members. The Supreme Council is the prime guardian of the judiciary's independence and is the only body empowered to discipline and appoint judges and prosecutors. The Supreme Court and Appeals Court are located in Phnom Penh, and each province and municipality has lower courts. There is also a military court. As of 1999, Cambodia had 117 judges and 54 prosecutors.

An independent, capable, and uncorrupted judiciary is the foundation of the rule of law and underpins the development of a market economy. Unfortunately, Cambodia's judiciary does not yet meet acceptable standards in this regard. The decimation of the legal sector in the 1970s and the socialist legal principles and processes instituted in 1980s still have a strong influence on the legal system.

Only 33% of judges and prosecutors have any formal legal education and like other civil servants receive a salary that is less than a living wage. Budget allocations are inadequate to cover other basic costs. Thus the general perception that the court system is riddled with corruption is hardly surprising.

The procedures for forwarding draft laws to the Constitutional Council are applied inconsistently. Only organic laws are consistently sent to the council for review. Contrary to the constitution, other laws are sometimes forwarded directly to the king for promulgation without prior council review. Rules governing how judges, prosecutors, and the judiciary in general function leave many issues of jurisdiction among courts unsettled and provide no standard for resolving jurisdictional disputes, although a modern set of rules has been drafted and is under discussion.

In 2002, the government made commitments to the following: 1) a time-bound legal and judicial reform strategy would be completed; 2) the Supreme Council of Magistrates would be restructured; 3) a Law on the Statute of Magistrates would be submitted to the National Assembly; 4) reported cases of corruption would be immediately investigated and prosecuted appropriately within the existing legal framework; and 5) an anti-corruption law would be submitted to the National Assembly. In addition, Cambodia in 2003 became the 19th country to endorse the Anticorruption Action Plan for Asia-Pacific, designed in collaboration with the Asian Development Bank and the Organization for Economic Cooperation and Development. The goal of this initiative is to help countries work together to build effective anticorruption mechanisms.

CIVIL SOCIETY AND PRIVATE SECTOR

Since 1993, the government has vigorously promoted the transition to a market economy. Laws regulating the private sector include the 1994 Law on Investment, the 1995 Law on Organization and Functioning of a Council for Development in Cambodia and the Cambodia Investment Board, and the 1997 Law on Taxation. New institutions were created to enforce these laws. The economy has started to recover since the downturn of 1997–1998, with real growth rate of 6.3% in 2001 and 4.5% in 2002. While the RGC's efforts thus far deserve credit, challenges

remain in reducing transaction costs, both formal and informal. Weaknesses in land law and enforcement need to be addressed. Businesses need clear rules that guarantee their property rights, resolve commercial disputes, regulate anticompetitive conduct, and limit state interference. Promoting fair and consistent enforcement of laws is also important. Setting up monitoring systems to enforce newly enacted laws and to strengthen the enforcement capacities of relevant agencies may be useful.

Although nongovernmental organizations (NGOs) had an important role prior to 1991 in the absence of other donor agencies, their numbers and the value of their assistance have increased dramatically since then, with NGO disbursements equal to over 11% of external assistance during the period 1999–2001. The government's attitude toward international NGOs is liberal while somewhat more restrictive toward national ones.

Other civil society organizations have also emerged since 1991. Establishment of the Cambodian Bar Association in 1995 was a notable development. Among civil society organizations, the financial position of Cambodian NGOs is generally weak and highly dependent on foreign sources of funding. Some NGOs appear to be under the strong influence of political parties, while others reportedly abuse their NGO status. However, many are providing much needed development services.

The lack of a legal framework for NGOs may allow some NGOs to abuse their status or give government officials the discretion to issue arbitrary decisions on the status of NGOs. To address these concerns, a draft legal framework is being finalized for discussion.

In the 1980s, media organizations were used for political party propaganda, and no privately owned media existed. Currently, Cambodia has more than 200 newspapers and magazines, including several foreign language newspapers, and a number of television and radio stations. The constitution guarantees the freedom of expression, press, and publication. The Press Law creates a legal framework.

While the Press Law guarantees more freedom than equivalent laws in other countries in Southeast Asia, journalists worry that vague definitions of terms present a risk that they could be used as excuses to suppress the freedom of the press. The media needs mechanisms to curb irresponsible reporting, sometimes influenced by political parties.

CONCLUSION

Cambodia's experience in rebuilding its governance institutions since 1991 highlights that reform is a long-term process that requires setting achievable goals and providing consistent support. Considerable progress has been achieved in maintaining public order, increasing revenues, rationalizing public expenditure policy and management, introducing new audit mechanisms, launching democratically elected commune councils, and facilitating a vibrant civil society, private sector, and free media. While many challenges lie ahead, the commitment to the reform process demonstrated by the government and the achievements made to date are heartening.

REFERENCES

1. Summary of Cambodia Governance Assessment. In *Key Governance Issues in Cambodia, Lao PDR, Thailand and Viet Nam*; Wescott, C., Ed.; ADB: Manila, 2001; 5–19. http://www.adb.org/Documents/Books/Key_Governance_Issues/default.asp?p=govpub (accessed August, 2003).
2. ADB and Cambodia Development Resources Institute. *Cambodia: Enhancing Governance for Sustainable Development*; ADB: Manila, 2000. http://www.adb.org/Documents/Books/Cambodia_Enhancing_Governance/default.asp?p=govpub (accessed August 2003).
3. Chandler, D.P. *The Tragedy of Cambodian History*; Yale University Press: New Haven, CT, 1991.
4. World Bank; ADB; IMF. *Cambodia, Enhancing Service Delivery Through Improved Resource Allocation and Institutional Reform: Integrated Fiduciary Assessment and Public Expenditure Review. in press.*

Capital Purchases

Wendell C. Lawther
University of Central Florida, Orlando, Florida, U.S.A.

John Adler
Arizona Department of Administration, Phoenix, Arizona, U.S.A.

INTRODUCTION

Capital equipment is usually defined as any equipment with a useful life of at least three years.[1] In the public sector, it is usually funded by the capital budget. In many ways, capital purchases differ from purchase of services and other relationships defined by contracts between public sector agencies and private vendors.

These differences often produce controversial issues that the purchasing staff must face in buying this equipment, often coming into conflict with the agency that requests the equipment. First, there is conflict between those who wish equipment with the latest technological advances and those who argue in favor of the equipment with the lowest price. Although this equipment may be more expensive and the use of the new technology cannot be fully justified by the using agency, the attractiveness of owning the fastest personal computer in anticipation of future uses is very appealing.

Second, ignoring the issue of productivity may result in purchasing inappropriate equipment. Part of the analysis in deciding what equipment to purchase depends upon how the purchased equipment impacts productivity. To achieve this information, outputs of the equipment must be identified and analyzed. The number of copies per minute for a copy machine, as well as the number of copies made by a using agency should both be identified. In this manner, a unit cost—cost per unit of output for a given time period—is calculated. The purchase of more expensive equipment may not be justified if the unit cost is much higher than that of less expensive equipment. This may be the case if the number of outputs and the resulting productivity of using the equipment is low.

Third, life cycle costing (LCC) assesses the total cost of owning, operating, maintaining, and disposing of the equipment. As early in the acquisition process as possible, LCC should be performed. The lowest initial cost equipment model may not be the wisest purchase because repair and maintenance costs may be higher than a more expensive model.

The increased technological advances for equipment such as personal computers and customer service systems based on on-line access have significantly altered the capital purchasing process. As writing specifications for such equipment may be difficult, as in-house purchasing staff may not have sufficient knowledge to do so, obtaining the equipment relies more heavily on processes such as Invitation to Negotiate (ITN) in which the purchasing process is very different from the acceptance of the lowest cost item.

THE CAPITAL PURCHASING CYCLE

An overview of the procedures and methods used in purchasing capital equipment will help to illustrate the unique aspects of capital purchasing. Because the process repeats itself as old equipment is replaced, it is most accurately viewed as cyclical in nature.

Need Determination

Various factors contribute to determining the need for capital equipment. Changing service or workload may require additional equipment to maintain acceptable levels of productivity. Advances in technology may make the currently operating equipment obsolete because it cannot maintain new standards of responsiveness.

Also, accompanying a replacement policy and set of procedures are decision rules chosen by an agency that identifies the need for new equipment to be purchased (or leased). For example, when the cost of repair reaches 60% of the value of the equipment, the agency may determine that replacement is necessary. Police vehicles may be replaced after 80,000 miles of usage.

Planning and Budgeting

Depending on the requirements of the budgeting process of the government, capital equipment needs must be identified one or two years into the future. In many cases

Encyclopedia of Public Administration and Public Policy
DOI: 10.1081/E-EPAP 120019221

these needs must be prioritized, justification provided by the using agency, and funds identified to support the purchase. The impact of the capital purchase on the operating budget is usually part of the projections that need to be made.

Specification Development

A specification is a description of the physical and/or functional characteristics of the equipment to be purchased. It may include the requirements to be met by the equipment and the procedures used to assess whether these requirements have been met.[2] There are many aspects to developing specifications that provide challenges to the procurement official. First, the specifications should not be restrictive so that competition among potential suppliers is not dampened. Second, the use of brand names may be too restrictive and should be avoided unless it can be justified by the using agency. The purchasing official must guard against the possibility that the agency has been persuaded by sales personnel that their brand is superior.

The issue of standard specifications vs. customized specifications must be resolved in many instances before purchasing can proceed. The using agency may request more customized equipment, stating that "it's our money." Unless a specific need can be identified, it is the role of the purchasing official to explore with agency personnel using standardized specifications as much as possible. The more standardization that is possible, the more "off- the-shelf" software and hardware, for example, can be purchased, usually at a lower cost to the government.

In some CE areas, such as the purchase of information technology (IT) and related telecommunications products, the fast-changing technology may make it difficult to identify and write accurate descriptions of what hardware and software is needed to meet a customer service need. In the field of advanced traveler information systems, for example, governments have had to state the goals of the system they wish to acquire without detailed specifications identified. It is expected that with this ITN or similar purchasing process, that specifications will be identified as a result of a negotiation among purchasing and agency personnel and potential suppliers.

Sourcing

This part of the process involves identifying and maintaining a list of those vendors or suppliers that produce or can obtain the required equipment and would respond to an invitation to bid (ITB), request for quotation (RFQ), or request for proposal (RFP) provided by the government. To maintain competition, the list should be updated as much as possible by adding new vendors. Purchasing staff can obtain these from agency personnel who are more likely to be in contact with relevant vendors. Also, those suppliers who have failed to respond to an ITB or who have provided unsatisfactory performance should be removed from the list.[3]

In many cases bidders are required to pre-qualify. This process not only is more efficient for the purchasing department, as vendor qualifications do not have to be reviewed after every bid award. It also facilitates the bid review and award process by assuring that all vendors considered have the capability to provide the equipment as required.

Source Selection

The process of selecting which equipment to buy is different for capital equipment compared to purchasing services or other supplies. No matter what source selection process is chosen, there is likely to be more negotiation with capital purchases. Other items are consumed relatively quickly after purchase, while capital equipment may be with the agency for years. Even if standard specifications can be chosen for the equipment, and an ITB, RFQ, or RFQ is used, there may be the expectation by the supplier that a counteroffer from the government or agency will be forthcoming, and that negotiation will resolve differences.[1]

If the equipment is customized, or complex enough so that specifications cannot be written in great detail, or part of a larger system, e.g., information technology, a RFP or invitation to negotiate may be the source selection process chosen. These are multistep processes that may involve extensive negotiation with more than one vendor. Usually, there is a proposal review process that involves creating a bid rating scale, establishing a team of raters from purchasing, the using agency, and from other governments or agencies, and prioritizing the bids received.

At the highest degree of complexity, when the agency goal or problem is clear/well-defined but the equipment and the means to accomplish that goal are unclear, the agency may use the source selection process to assist it in choosing the means. The Commonwealth of Kentucky, for example, has established a pre-qualification process for obtaining agreements with information technology. As of fall 2000, 15 IT vendors were pre-qualified: 5 for "full-service" while the other 10 fill specific niches. Once private vendors are qualified, then any state agency sends a letter to all vendors outlining the problem that needs to be solved, and inviting vendor to propose solutions. If there is an interest, negotiations begin. The final result is a fixed price contract, with specific deliverables identified.

Contract Administration

This function ideally should be performed by a team of purchasing and agency personnel. The activities involved are similar to the administration of all contracts, including 1) monitoring the delivery of equipment to ensure that it is provided in a timely fashion according to the dates specified in the contract; 2) resolving problems/complaints if deadlines are not met and/or equipment does not meet specifications; 3) assessing the capability of the supplier to provide the equipment as required; and 4) assessing penalties or other sanctions including termination of the contract.

In the case of capital equipment, however, there must be a process testing the delivered equipment to ensure that it produces the required output. In addition, administering the warranty, including knowing when and under what conditions the warranty applies, is part of contract administration.

Maintenance and Service

The primary decision rules adopted by the agency pertain to the use of routine or preventative maintenance (PM). Without such maintenance, the equipment is repaired when it fails to operate. This is known as failure maintenance (FM).

The obvious benefit of PM is that frequent usage will extend the useful life of the equipment. The assumption here is that the more funds invested in PM, the lower the costs of FM. Failures will be less frequent, and resulting downtime less costly as well. Preventative maintenance costs include the cost of materials, the time/salary of those performing the repairs, the cost of spare parts that may be installed, and the downtime of the equipment while being maintained.

The issue of downtime becomes important in determining the usefulness of PM. In many cases, the cost of downtime is negligible. Alternative equipment may be available. If a personal computer needs PM for one day, email may be accessed via another computer. A laptop computer may substitute for the PC. If a vehicle is ''in the shop'' for PM, work can be rescheduled or another vehicle may be available. If downtime incurs realistic costs, however, and requires renting replacement equip-

ment, then these costs must be factored into the need for PM.

An opposing view is that PM is not needed. When the equipment fails, it should be repaired at that time. This approach can be adopted under certain conditions. If the assumption expressed above about PM is not accurate: increased PM does not lessen or has little impact on the cost of FM, then PM may be of little value. Preventative maintenance for a personal computer may have little bearing on whether a hard drive crashes.

A second condition is relevant to the value of the equipment when FM is likely to be necessary. If the value depreciates quickly, so that when the equipment breaks down the cost of repair is a high percentage of its value, then replacement instead of repair is a more feasible option.

Replacement Planning

As indicated above, many agencies have a replacement plan or policy in place that will start the purchasing cycle. Decision rules exist that are often implemented based on industry standards and/or past experience. These will trigger replacement of existing equipment. Agency or government committees may be established to monitor and oversee vehicle and equipment replacement.

Disposal

In many respects the capital purchasing cycle ends and begins again with the disposal of the equipment and the planning for its replacement. There are several disposal options available, including 1) trade-in for new equipment; 2) sell to a used-equipment buyer; 3) used for spare parts; and 4) pay to have the equipment removed.

The option chosen depends upon the availability of a market for the used equipment. In some cases, if upgrades have been added to the equipment over its useful life, it may be worth more when disposed than its initial cost.

CONCLUSION

With the need to purchase computer hardware and software, especially in the context of creating information technology systems, the importance of capital purchasing has risen dramatically. The stakes are higher, as the risk of failure increases with the complexity of the equipment purchased. Countless numbers of examples are similar to the following instance.

Florida state legislators plan to audit a child welfare computer system that is seven years behind schedule and more than $200 M over budget. The system, designed to replace paper files and several separate computer systems that track abused and neglected children in Florida, was first approved by the legislature in 1990. It was originally supposed to be completed in 1998 at a cost of $32 M. It is now scheduled to be completed in 2005 and cost nearly $232 M.[4]

The greater need for a partnership approach to capital purchases is evident from this example.[5] Public sector purchasing and agency personnel need to partner with private vendors so that the requisite knowledge needed to accomplish the goals is shared by all. Problems need to be identified early in the implementation process, and solutions sought with the input of all concerned to avoid waste, delays, and cost overruns.

REFERENCES

1. Newman, R.G.; Simkins, R.J. *Capital Equipment Buying Handbook*; American Management Association: New York, 1998.
2. The National Institute of Governmental Purchasing, Inc. *Dictionary of Purchasing Terms*; Herndon, VA, 1996.
3. Council of State Governments. *State and Local Governmental Purchasing*; Author: Lexington, KY, 1988.
4. Kestin, S. *"Legislators to Conduct Audit as Computer System Goes $200 Million Over Budget" South Florida Sun-Sentinel.Com News*; January 7, 2002. http://www.sun-sentinel.com/news/local/florida/sflcomputerjan07.story.
5. Lawther, W.C. *Contracting for the 21st Century: A Partnership Model*; The Pricewaterhouse Coopers Endowment Business for Government: Arlington, VA, 2002.

Community-Based Planning for HIV/AIDS

Bruce Kieler
Wharton County Junior College, Wharton, Texas, U.S.A.

Ishak Saporta
Tel Aviv University, Tel Aviv, Israel

INTRODUCTION

During the past decade, the devolution of responsibility for health care and social support services programs for persons infected and affected by human immunodeficiency virus (HIV)/acquired immune deficiency syndrome (AIDS), from the federal and state levels to the local level, was accompanied by an increasing utilization of community-based participatory planning entities. These entities became the primary means used for prioritizing services and allocating resources to meet the needs of persons living with AIDS, caused by the HIV, and for implementing HIV prevention programs throughout the United States. These participatory planning entities are also being used in other service areas including mental health, substance abuse counseling, housing, tobacco control, and disease prevention and education programs. They include such organizations as health services planning councils, health care consortia, disease prevention planning groups, tobacco control coalitions, and housing planning committees.

Despite their widespread usage, very little is known about community-based participatory planning entities, their formation, operations, development, and effectiveness over time. The study of community-based participatory planning entities can be based on a variety of theoretical perspectives including small group formation, authority in groups, procedural justice, group decision making, conflict resolution, organizational environment and form, institutionalization of new organizational forms, population ecology of organizations, organizational innovation and change, organizational alignment with the environment, management of strategic alliances, and coordination of services. The goals of this chapter are to examine several of the leading theoretical perspectives that are relevant to the study of the expanding organizational population of community-based participatory planning entities, and to suggest a methodology for conducting case studies of these entities.

BACKGROUND

This article is an update of Chapter 11, "Community-Based Planning," by Kieler.[1]

The rapidly changing health care industry in the United States suggests a dynamic and turbulent organizational environment. Into this complex and unpredictable environment, an unusual type of planning organization is being embedded, namely, the community-based participatory planning entity. This type of organization is variously called a community-based planning council, committee, consortium, coalition, or group. Establishment of these new organizations is mandated by both federal and state legislation. The premier examples of these new entities are the HIV health services planning councils mandated by Title I of the Ryan White Comprehensive AIDS Resources Emergency Act of 1990 (i.e., the CARE Act), under Public Law 101-381 as amended, and the HIV health care consortium mandated by Title II of the CARE Act. Another such planning entity is the HIV prevention community planning group (CPG) that is mandated by the Centers for Disease Control and Prevention.[2] The HIV prevention CPG has responsibility for addressing the needs for education about and prevention of HIV infection in almost all public health jurisdictions in the United States.

Community-based participatory planning entities have many of the characteristics that define a coalition.[3,4] Definitions of each of these entities, as well as enumeration of their respective roles, responsibilities, and mandates, are usually provided in the specific legislation or program announcements authorizing their use. Specific instructions to local governmental or health jurisdictions about establishing these entities are usually contained in the program guidance issued by the federal or state agency responsible for implementing the program. For example, Minkler[5] provided guidance in community organization and community building for health, whereas the Academy for Educational Development[6] and McKay[7] both provided extensive discussions of the HIV prevention community planning process.

Encyclopedia of Public Administration and Public Policy
DOI: 10.1081/E-EPAP 120014919

Several papers on Title I planning councils look at: 1) various issues and challenges that confront planning councils;[8,9] 2) the initial stages of development of a typical planning council;[10,11] 3) institutionalization and legitimation of a planning council process;[11] 4) decision making by a planning council;[11] and 5) organizational environment and organizational form of a planning council.[11,12] Other papers on the Title I process focus on the types and availability of HIV/AIDS services before and after the allocation of Title I funds,[13–16] as well as on the impacts of the various CARE Act titles.[17–23] Several major unpublished manuscripts focus on the implementation of the various CARE Act titles, including a report on challenges facing Title I and Title II planning entities that was submitted to the AIDS Action Foundation in 1993[24] and a report on the implementation of Title I in six major U.S. urban areas that was submitted to the Kaiser Family Foundation in 1994.[25]

Funding for the various CARE Act titles[26–28] and the effectiveness of services provided by these funds[29–31] are explored in a number of reports and position papers. The general conclusion is that the CARE Act has resulted in substantial additional services and increased access to services for persons living with HIV disease. The recurring challenges that the CARE Act community-based planning entities must face in their decision-making processes are noted both in news reports and published research. These would include reports on contractual disputes, program management, program effectiveness, and use (and misuse) of funds.[32–34]

In reporting on a multiyear observational study of the Oakland HIV health services planning council, Kieler et al.[8] noted that, at the time the CARE Act was enacted by the U.S. Congress, the use of community-based participatory planning entities was popular with HIV/AIDS advocates, HIV/AIDS service organizations, and federal officials alike. This model of health care and support services planning provided a way for community-based organizations and public sector agencies, as well as individuals infected and affected by HIV disease, to play key roles in these newly initiated and federally mandated planning councils. Additionally, this model appealed to local agencies because it offered local control over the allocation of funds to meet local needs for health care and support services. It appealed to federal officials because this model placed AIDS constituency groups in the position of having to work collaboratively at the local level to achieve expanded availability of services, rather than constantly appealing to Congress and the federal executive branch in an ad hoc fashion for more funds.

The experiences of a number of planning councils in different parts of the country, most notably the Oakland HIV health services planning council, suggest that this model of planning does work, but not in the collaborative,

rational fashion envisioned in Title I of the CARE Act. As Kieler et al.[8] reported, local control of the program in the Oakland area was accompanied by interorganizational conflict, accusations of personal and organizational misconduct, frequent challenges to the legitimacy of the process, and a general sense that local political factors played too great a role in priority setting, resource allocation decisions, and contracting for services. Not only in Oakland, but nationwide, local governmental entities and community-based groups have experienced challenges in grass roots decision making regarding implementation of Title I. In his study of planning council decision-making behavior, Slack[35] applied a political model (the zero-sum model) and a bureaucratic model (the Herbert thesis) to identify the factors triggering conflictual zero-sum behaviors.

However, the Kieler et al.[8] study found that, in spite of these difficulties, the Oakland planning council was able to distribute funds approximately on schedule to local service providers, and the availability of needed services was increased. The findings of the Oakland study suggest a number of ways that a planning council could be structured to increase its effectiveness while reducing interpersonal and interorganizational stress among service providers that the process induced in the past.

Additional work needs to be done to develop a theory-based literature that will document, explain, and analyze all aspects of the establishment, operation, development, and effectiveness of these newly mandated community-based participatory planning entities, and guide the establishment and development of future participatory planning entities. Such a literature might also serve as the basis for building organizational theory specific to participatory planning entities such as planning councils, consortia, CPGs, and coalitions.

AN INTEGRATED THEORETICAL MODEL

Federal and state programs mandating the use of community-based participatory planning entities in local health care and support services environments are only a part of the major changes that are resulting in the restructuring of health care and health-related services. Scott[36] observed that the medical care field is a multifaceted and dynamic scene that it is complex and rapidly changing, that health care organizations in the United States have undergone a revolution during the past half century, and that particularly dramatic changes have occurred during the past two decades. ''To throw some light on the current situation,'' Scott described the nature of the changes that have occurred in health care organizations, particularly those in the medical care delivery system. Scott was convinced that ''we will not make much headway in our understanding of complex societal systems until we begin to examine the ways in which institutional and technical environments, organizational fields, [organizational] populations, organizational sets, and individual organizations act and interact to constrain and change each other'' (p. 296).

In describing the nature of the changes that have occurred in health care organizations and the medical care delivery system, Scott formulates a general theoretical framework within which to view, interpret, and explain such changes. This framework may provide us with a basis for studying the formation, operations, and organizational development of numerous new organizations, including community-based participatory planning entities, that are emerging in the health care and support services environment.

Scott begins by noting that the various organization theories (e.g., population ecology, strategic management, resource dependency, transactions costs, and institutional theory), which are used by analysts to account for one or another feature of the changing health care scene, ''have only recently been developed (most appeared after 1975) and are typically treated by organizational analysts as offering contradictory or competing explanations'' (p. 272). Scott feels, however, that each of these perspectives is limited and provides only a partial account of the complex phenomena being observed. Although development of unified theory is beyond the scope of his paper, Scott does propose that ''the search for an improved, detailed understanding and for verifiable accounts will be advanced by the development of more integrative frameworks that seek to define where and when—to what types of phenomena and under what conditions—the various theory fragments apply'' (p. 272). Scott proposes that the ''effort to understand the medical care system should begin at the most comprehensive level—the institutional environment—and then proceed to examine more and more delimited systems and units'' (p. 273).

The key features of the organizational analysis model that Scott proposes include three levels, namely, the organizational environments level, the organizational fields/populations level, and the organizational sets/organizations level. For each level, Scott identifies the appropriate theoretical perspective to use in discussing activities at that level.

Scott then identifies the major trends in the development of the U.S. health care sector. These include such features as the increased scale of the medical care system, increased concentration of medical resources devoted to the delivery of health services, and increased specialization of both individual providers and medical care organizations. These trends also include greater diversification, such as in the range of services and types of clients served. Scott points out that other trends in the health care sector include increased linkages among provider organizations, increased governmental involvement in the health care system, increased privatization, increased managerial and reduced professional influence, and increased market orientation of the health care system.

Within this rapidly changing health care sector are embedded the newly established community-based participatory planning entities to which many must now turn for health care, support services, and prevention/education services.

ORGANIZATIONAL ENVIRONMENT AND FORM

Bidwell and Kasarda[37] noted that organizational form is not only composed of interpersonal relations of members of the organization, but also contains properties that pertain to the organization conceived of as a collectivity with a unitary character. Some of these properties can be regarded as aggregates of interpersonal relations, such as the division of labor and hierarchy. Others may not be so regarded, such as the size and composition of an organization's membership, its stock of technological and material resources, its own institutional characteristics (structure, bylaws, rules, policies, and processes), and the technological, physical, demographic, and institutional properties of its environment. The authors caution against using a behavioral approach to a theory of organizational form because of the likelihood that such an approach would yield a theory of ''unmanageable complexity and intellectual difficulty.'' Instead, they espouse a macrosocial approach that allows the treatment of aggregative properties of the organizational collectivity without appeal to the mediation of interpersonal ties or exchanges. They note that in ''taking this step, other properties of the collective unit (such as technology, rules, and laws) are introduced into the web of systemic relationships at the level of the collectivity'' (p. 25).

Bidwell and Kasarda next define organizational environment to include all external phenomena that affect or could affect an organization. They identify four aspects of the environment, namely, supplies of resources, actors who supply them or who in other ways may affect their supply, flows of resources to and among various populations of organizations within the environment, and relationships among the environmental actors that influence the flow and utilization of resources. The first two are compositional aspects of the environment and the third and fourth are relational aspects (p. 38).

Bidwell and Kasarda divide the organizational environment into an ''internal'' and an ''external'' environment. The internal environment is synonymous with the structure of the organization itself. They posit that organizational structure is the locus of opportunities for and constraints on the organization's further morphological evolution. The existence of the external environment, in its relational aspects (i.e., the surrounding social and normative order), is another principal source of these opportunities and constraints (p. 39).

In viewing community-based participatory planning entities, such as the CARE Act Title I planning councils and HIV prevention CPGs, as organizations, one finds that this particular population of organizations is continually expanding as additional metropolitan and rural areas turn to this type of organization to address local needs for health care, support services, and disease prevention/education. The specific organizational form that characterizes all community-based participatory planning entities is not a unique form. Although at first glance an argument might be made that these entities have the characteristics of "synthetic" organizations, as defined in Thompson,[38] their apparently increasing permanence and institutionalization in the local health care environment suggest something more. All such entities appear to have many of the characteristics of what is known in the organizational behavior literature as a "minimalist" organization.

The minimalist organizational form is identified by Halliday et al.[39,40] in a study of the vital events observed in the organizational population of state bar associations. Furthermore, Aldrich et al.[41] used a similar approach in their study of U.S. trade associations. Both of these studies focus on minimalist organizations in the private sector and use the population ecology of organizations perspective. (For comprehensive discussions of population ecology of organizations, see Hannan and Freeman,[42–44] Hannan and Carroll,[45] Singh,[46] and Tucker et al.[47])

The studies of minimalist organizations observe that such organizations are structurally flexible, frequently exist in relatively noncompetitive environments, and have long life spans. These organizations may not demonstrate the patterns of foundings and failures characteristic of most business organizations, and especially not the liability of newness. They are called "minimalist" because they require minimal resources for founding and sustenance.

The differences between minimalist and nonminimalist organizations can be stated in terms of four core dimensions. Halliday et al.[39] identified these dimensions as follows:

1) Initial Costs. Many organizations require extensive zcapital investments and labor commitments for birth, but minimalist organizations can be founded with very limited labor commitments and capital. In the case of Title I planning councils, the establishment of a council is mandated by federal law. To qualify for funding, an eligible metropolitan area (EMA) must use its own resources to form a council, the costs of which are not reimbursable. Following a metropolitan area's qualification for the program, application can be made for Title I formula and supplemental grant funding, and a small part of the total grant funds can be utilized for council support and development.

2) Maintenance Costs. Nonminimalist organizations require resource abundant environments for survival, but minimalist organizations can subsist in substantially poor resource environments. In the case of Title I planning councils, even when federal program funds are reduced or withheld, the work of the planning council continues.

3) Reserve Infrastructures. Most nonminimalist organizations have few shadow organizational structures or external resources to fall back on in times of hardship, but many minimalist organizations can supplement organizational resources with administrative and other infrastructures to be called on when necessary. In the case of Title I planning councils, numerous reserve infrastructures may exist, including assistance and staffing from the local public health jurisdiction, members who are only nominally or minimally reimbursed for their participation, agencies that maintain their employees on the payroll while they serve on the council, and various incidentals, such as travel time, out-of-pocket expenditures, and use of personal equipment and time for council business, all of which are usually not reimbursed by the Title I grant.

4) Adaptiveness. High sunk costs in capital and labor commitments impart structural inertia to many organizations, but low sunk costs enable minimalists to adapt readily to changes in their environments. Minimalists may also gain an advantage from normative flexibility: their conception of what the organization is about can more readily be altered. In other words, the minimalist organization can easily adapt or evolve to fit the particular environment in which it must function. In the case of Title I planning councils, there is an expectation that individual councils will develop in response to the constraints found in each of their local health care and services environments.

In addition to these four critical dimensions, Halliday et al.[39] identified a subclass of minimalist organizations that have a unique distribution of vital events because they evidence a high standing on two additional dimensions (p. 457). These dimensions include the following:

5) Niche Definition. Most organizations have overlapping or poorly defined niches that encourage

competition, but many minimalist organizations have well-defined niches and segmented competitive environments that require minimal defense. This dimension pertains, in some instances, to government-sponsored corporations. In the case of Title I planning councils, a specific niche has been defined by the CARE Act, namely, the planning, prioritizing, and allocation of resources to meet the needs of persons with HIV disease for health care and support services in a specific geographical area. Originally, HIV prevention and education were specifically excluded from the purview of Title I councils. In the case of the HIV prevention CPGs, the Centers for Disease Control and Prevention defined the niche to include HIV prevention planning in a specific geographical area, usually a health jurisdiction or a combination of jurisdictions.

6) Norms of Competition. Competition is tolerated in many organizational populations, but a number of minimalist organizations tend to discourage competition. In most cases of this type of minimalist organization, a specific niche has been preserved for a particular minimalist organization (i.e., the minimalist organization has a ''regional monopoly'' in a clearly delineated territory and no other similar organization is permitted to function within the confines of that specific niche).

In the case of Title I planning councils, the boundaries of each respective EMA define the area in which a particular planning council has the responsibility and authority to plan, prioritize, and allocate resources for health care and support services for persons with HIV disease. Except for the required periodic submissions of supplemental grant applications, through which the metropolitan areas participating in the Title I program receive additional grant funds based on the merits of their application, there is supposedly no competition among the organizational population of Title I planning councils or the EMAs in which they operate. The same is said for each regional HIV prevention CPG. There is no competition among CPGs for funding.

Kieler et al.[12] posited that the HIV health services planning council, as mandated by Title I of the CARE Act, have all four of the core dimensions manifested by minimalist organizations as well as the dimensions of the subclass of minimalist organizations enjoying a monopoly in a particular environmental niche. They conclude that the Title I planning councils represent a new organizational population of mandated minimalist organizations in the public sector. Use of the population ecology of organizations perspective in the study of these planning councils could contribute to a greater understanding of this particular organizational population

as well as other organizational populations of community-based participatory planning entities such as consortia, CPGs, and coalitions.

COORDINATION OF SERVICES

The responsibility for developing a regional comprehensive plan for the delivery of health care and support services for persons with HIV disease makes the HIV health services planning council mandated by Title I of the CARE Act a key element in the coordination of such services at the local level. Therefore it can be expected that the planning council could face many of the same problems and barriers that Aiken et al.[48] found to be impeding efforts in the planning and implementation of integrated and coordinated mental health service delivery systems. These barriers include fragmentation of services, inaccessibility of services, lack of accountability of service delivery agencies, discontinuities in services, dispersal of services, wastefulness of resources, ineffectiveness of services, short-term commitments, and multiple local governments. Barriers to coordination are linked to aspects of the service delivery system including organizational autonomy, professional ideologies, conflicts among various client interest groups, and conflicts over who is to control the resources (p. 4). Many of these same barriers to coordination and issues of ideology that Aiken et al. observed in the 1970s were also observed by Kieler et al.[8] during the Oakland planning council case study in 1992–1995, or 20 years after they were first identified in a similar study of mental health service delivery systems.

Aiken et al. noted that professional ideologies often prevent professionals in one field from wanting to cooperate with professionals in another field. They observe that competing client interest groups may work at crosspurposes, cancel out each other's efforts, and present a less than united front in the community. They also note that service organizations frequently put their own survival and prestige ahead of the needs of the clients. They point out various studies which show that acceptance of clients by service organizations depends on social, cultural, and historical factors, and not just on the needs of the clients; that agencies refer clients to places that profit the agency, rather than to places good for clients; and that agencies like to have the ''right'' clients rather than those with the most pressing problems.

Aiken et al. suggested that one way to conceive of a coordinated delivery system was to view it as a change process having several stages. These stages of development are identical to those noted by Hernandez and Kaluzny[49] and include awareness, initiation of effort, implementation, and routinization or institutionalization. In each stage, specific critical problems emerge:

1) Awareness Stage. The coordination effort usually has an initial period of increasing agitation by community groups and awareness by professional groups that treatment requires specialized services and new programs (p. 22).

2) Initiation of Effort Stage. Problems of gaining power, legitimacy, and funding usually occur in the initiation stage of the coordination effort (p. 22). Kieler[11] elucidated this stage of development in the Oakland planning council study.

3) Implementation Stage. The problems that arise during implementation usually stem from the choice of the organizational structure for the service delivery system, internal conflicts among key participants, and lack of effective control over other organizations (i.e., resistance to implementation by some of the participants). Another problem that might arise is the transformation of the goals of the change agent. As failures in achieving objectives occur, goals of the program may become displaced (i.e., the change agent might scale down its objectives and begin to concentrate on particular goals that reflect its inherent interests and values) (p. 23). Again, Kieler[11] found evidence of this stage in the Oakland planning council study.

4) Routinization Stage. The primary problem that might emerge lies with the resource controllers. Without their continued support, even the best of programs or service delivery systems would be jeopardized (p. 23). In the study of HIV planning councils, one recent example of this stands out, namely, the suspension of health care and support services for a person with HIV disease in Norfork, Virginia, because of a contract dispute between the resource controllers (i.e., the city manager of Norfork) and the service provider (i.e., Eastern Virginia Medical School Clinics).[32]

Not only could the Title I planning council process in a particular metropolitan area face the various problems associated with the first three stages noted by Aiken et al.,[48] it could also face the uncertainty of continued funding. Beginning in spring 1995, efforts were initiated in the U.S. Congress to secure reauthorization of the Ryan White CARE Act for an additional 5-year period. As of January 1996, the fate of the CARE Act had not yet been decided, nor had any funds been appropriated for the act's various titles for the fiscal year to begin in fall 1996. Nonreauthorization of the CARE Act would have resulted in major changes in the organizational environment of all Title I planning councils, and possibly in their demise as a regional planning and coordinating process for health care and support services for persons with HIV disease. However, Fortunately, final reauthorization was approved by Congress in March 1996. Since that time, Congress has periodically reauthorized the CARE Act.

IMPLICATIONS OF THE OAKLAND STUDY FOR PRACTITIONERS

Analysis of the data pertaining to the Oakland metropolitan area's HIV health services planning council includes a systematic examination, discussion, and critique of several key aspects of the Ryan White CARE Act, the organizational form of the planning council, and the organizational environment in which a planning council must function. It also includes a description of the organization of the Title I process in the Oakland EMA and a discussion on the major issues that the planning council successfully dealt with during the period 1992–1994. It applies a process model of organizational development and change to the planning council's efforts to reform its organizational structure, bylaws, processes, and procedures, and it examines the planning council's efforts to assure adherence to the planning council's own bylaws and Robert's Rules of Order, and to assure the compliance by all planning council members with the conflict-of-interest requirements.

The Oakland study also presents the implications for practitioners of the issues that arose to challenge the planning council during the period of observation. The primary issues and challenges that the Oakland HIV health services planning council faced are probably typical of all such community-based participatory planning entities. These include multiple complex interorganizational relationships, conflicts of interest, preexisting societal tensions, factionalism and competition for influence by the major social groups in the area, changing trends in the epidemic, consumers' conflicting demands for services, competition among service providers for funding, membership burnout, accountability, compliance with bylaws and rules of order, dealing with financially troubled service providers who were understandably reluctant to relinquish grant funding, and competition with other metropolitan areas for a fair share of the Title I funds. Kieler et al.[8,12] and Kieler[11] presented discussions on several of these major issues challenging community-based planning entities.

In mandating the establishment of the HIV health services planning council as the mechanism for assessing needs, setting priorities, and allocating Title I funds to health care and support service providers in an EMA, the CARE Act mandated the creation of a population of new minimalist organizations in the public sector. The CARE Act embedded this new organizational population in local HIV/AIDS-related health care and support services environments that are characterized by uncertainties and limitations of multiple complex interorganizational relationships, rivalries between services providers competing for limited funds, and conflicting demands of various populations that the planning council is mandated by Title I to serve. In other words, the CARE Act set the planning council into a multifaceted, diverse, and dynamic environment (i.e., a turbulent environment). Such an environment can have unpredictable impacts on the membership, functioning, credibility, and viability of the planning council process.

Any new organization, including community-based participatory planning entities, may face a liability of newness. A new planning entity could conceivably face an enormous burden in establishing its organizational legitimacy, in settling on an appropriate organizational structure to facilitate the accomplishment of its legislative mandates, and in adopting a standard operating procedure that would accommodate and satisfy its various stakeholders. The effort to achieve organizational legitimacy could consume an inordinate amount of time and effort during the first years of such an organization's existence.

The Oakland data suggest that a Title I planning council, even though it is a government-mandated organization, can have serious organizational legitimacy problems. These problems with legitimacy were reflected both in the various letters of complaint and in the opinions of providers and consumers about the planning council's prioritizations, allocations of funds, request-for-proposals process, appeals process, and contracting process. Additionally, the periodic efforts to change the planning council's organizational structure, prompted by internal opinion as well as by concerns expressed by federal program monitors, indicated a minimalist organization that was attempting to structure itself in response to environmental challenges to its legitimacy. The challenges to the legitimacy of the Oakland planning council stemmed primarily from the planning council's involvement in the direct allocation of Title I funds to local-level service providers, a role that more appropriately should have belonged to the grantee. However, removal of the planning council in the mid-1990s from involvement in provider-specific allocations served to increase the perceived legitimacy of the planning council process in the Oakland metropolitan area.

If the organizational ecology concept of failure to survive could be defined to include abrupt and significant changes (i.e., massive changes) in a planning council's membership, organizational structure, bylaws, policies, processes, and/or interorganizational relationships (i.e., its core features), then strong evidence of failure to survive by certain members of this new organizational population could be expected and probably be at a much higher rate than is found in the event histories of other populations of minimalist organizations. However, it should be noted that an initial high rate of "organizational death" typifies many organizational populations, but that this initial high rate declines over time as the population of organizations is legitimated and as the population's members successfully compete with each other for limited resources.

Because it is almost inconceivable that the chief elected official of an EMA and the various stakeholders in the Title I planning council process would condone a nonfunctional or dysfunctional planning council for very long, massive changes in a planning council's core features might suggest that the planning council is in the process of rapidly adapting itself—it is being adapted—to fit the specific social and organizational environment in which it must function. That is to say, the planning council is evolving to fit the local environment, and its evolutionary track is characterized by punctuated patterns of morphological change. In other words, it is experiencing periods in which changes are unusually significant when compared to its prior state.

However, given the event history of the Title I planning council in the Oakland metropolitan area through 1995, the case for evolution seems weak. The Oakland data from this period suggest an alternative hypothesis concerning massive changes in a particular planning council's core features, namely, that a replacement of an existing planning council by a successor planning council occurred. Furthermore, it appears that replacement of a planning council by a successor planning council is highly feasible, basically without cost, and might even serve to enhance the acceptability, credibility, and viability of the Title I process in an EMA. Swift replacement of an existing planning council, a dysfunctional planning council, or a collapsed planning council does not appear to jeopardize either the area's Title I status and eligibility, or its Title I-funded health and social services delivery system. However, the ramifications of the replacement procedure on perceptions of empowerment of the HIV/AIDS community are yet to be articulated.

CONCLUSION

An examination of the event histories of other Title I planning councils, or other similar community-based participatory planning entities, might provide additional evidence of the occurrence of replacement of an established planning entity by a successor planning entity. Quite possibly, it might be found that, in certain metropolitan areas and jurisdictions, there have been repeated replacements of the local participatory planning entity. Additionally, elaboration and analysis of the phenomenon of replacement of a planning council by a successor council may provide additional support for the hypothesis that environmental selection is occurring in this new population of public sector minimalist organizations.

ACKNOWLEDGMENTS

Preparation of this manuscript was begun during the Oakland HIV health services planning council study and was supported, in part, by a grant from the Henry J. Kaiser Family Foundation (Menlo Park, CA). Additional support came from the U.S. Public Health Service and the University of California's AIDS Research Program. Technical support was provided by the Institute of Industrial Relations at the University of California at Berkeley.

REFERENCES

1. Kieler, B.W.; Saporta, I.; El'Amin, Z. Community-Based Planning. In *Handbook of Health Administration and Policy,* 1st Ed.; Kilpatrick, A.O., Johnson, J.A., Eds.; Marcel Dekker, Inc.: New York, 1999; 195–206.
2. Centers for Disease Control and Prevention. *Supplemental Guidance on HIV Prevention Community Planning for Noncompeting Continuation of Cooperative Agreements for HIV Prevention Projects*; Centers for Disease Control and Prevention: Atlanta, GA, 1994.
3. Brown, C. *The Art of Coalition Building: A Guide for Community Leaders*; The American Jewish Committee: New York, 1984.
4. Feighery, E.; Rogers, T. *Building and Maintaining Effective Coalitions*; Stanford Health Promotion Resource Center: Palo Alto, CA, 1989.
5. *Community Organizing and Community Building for Health*; Minkler, M., Ed.; Rutgers University Press: New Brunswick, NJ, 1997.
6. Academy for Educational Development. *Handbook for HIV Prevention Community Planning*; Centers for Disease Control and Prevention: Atlanta, GA, 1994.
7. McKay, E.G. *Do's and Don'ts for an Inclusive HIV Prevention Community Planning Process: A Self-Help Guide*; National Council of La Raza/Center for Health Promotion: Washington, DC, 1994.
8. Kieler, B.W.; Rundall, T.G.; Saporta, I.; Sussman, P.C.; Keilch, R.; Warren, N.; Black, S.; Brinkley, B.; Barney, L. Challenges faced by the HIV health services planning council in Oakland, California, 1991–1994. Am. J. Prev. Med. **1996**, *12* (4), 26–32.
9. Bowen, G.S.; Marconi, K.; Kohn, S.; Bailey, D.M.; Goosby, E.P.; Shorter, S.; Niemcryk, S. First year of

AIDS services delivery under title I of the Ryan White CARE Act. Public Health Rep. **1992**, *107* (5), 491–499.
10. Kachur, S.P.; Sonnega, A.J.; Cintron, R.; Farup, C.; Silbersiepe, K.; Celentano, D.D.; Kwait, J. An analysis of the greater Baltimore HIV services planning council. AIDS Public Policy J. **1992**, *7* (4), 238–246.
11. Kieler, B.W. *The Oakland CARE Act Title I HIV/AIDS Planning Council: A Minimalist Organization Functioning in a Turbulent Environment*; University Microfilms, Inc.: Ann Arbor, MI, 1994.
12. Kieler, B.W.; Rundall, T.G.; Saporta, I. The Oakland HIV/AIDS planning council: Its organizational form and environment. Int. J. Public Adm. **1996**, *19* (7), 1203–1219.
13. Marconi, K.; Rundall, T.; Gentry, D.; Kwait, J.; Celentano, D.; Stolley, P. The organization and availability of HIV-related services in Baltimore, Maryland, and Oakland, California. AIDS Public Policy J. **1994**, *9* (4), 173–181.
14. Gentry, D.; Rundall, T.G. Staffing in AIDS service organizations: The volunteer contribution. J. Health Hum. Serv. Adm. **1995**, *18* (2), 190–204.
15. Rundall, T.G.; Kwait, J.; Marconi, K.; Bender-Kitz, S.; Celentano, D. Impact of the Ryan White CARE Act on the availability of HIV/AIDS services. Policy Stud. J. **1999**, *27* (4), 826–839.
16. Kwait, J.; Marconi, K.; Helitzer, D.; Rodieck, M.; Rundall, T.G.; Celentano, D. Ryan White CARE Act Title I funding priorities and unmet needs in Baltimore, Maryland. Policy Stud. J. **1999**, *27* (4), 855–871.
17. Fleishman, J.A.; Mor, V.; Piette, J.D.; Allen, S.M. Organizing AIDS service consortia: Lead agency identity and consortium cohesion. Soc. Sci. Rev. **1992**, *66* (4), 547–570.
18. Penner, S.J. *A Study of Coalitions Among Voluntary AIDS/HIV Service Organizations in California*; University Microfilms, Inc.: Ann Arbor, MI, 1992.
19. Penner, S.J. Problems with planning for the HIV epidemic. AIDS Public Policy J. **1992**, *7* (2), 120–127.
20. McKinney, M.M. Consortium approaches to the delivery of HIV services under the Ryan White CARE Act. AIDS Public Policy J. **1993**, *8* (3), 115–125.
21. McKinney, M.M.; Wieland, M.K.; Bowen, G.S.; Goosby, E.P.; Marconi, K.M. States' responses to title II of the Ryan White CARE Act. Public Health Rep. **1993**, *108* (1), 4–11.
22. Mor, V.; Fleishman, J.A.; Piette, J.D.; Allen, S.M. Developing AIDS community service consortia. Health Aff. **1993**, *12* (1), 186–199.
23. Mor, V.; Fleishman, J.A.; Allen, S.M.; Piette, J.D. Consortium Structure and Operation. In *Networking AIDS Services*; Mor, V., Fleishman, J.A., Allen, S.M., Piette, J.D., Eds.; Health Administration Press: Ann Arbor, MI, 1994; 55–74.
24. Doughty, R. *Lessons From the First Two Years: Issues Arising in the Implementation of Ryan White CARE Act Titles I and II*; AIDS Action Foundation: Washington, DC, 1993. (Unpublished report).
25. Ryan White Study Group; Rundall, T.G.; Principal Investigator. *Implementation of Title I of the Ryan White*

CARE Act of 1990: A Report to the Kaiser Family Foundation; The Kaiser Family Foundation: Menlo Park, CA, 1994. (Unpublished report).

26. HHS awards 1 billion in Ryan White grants. AIDS Policy Law **2003**, *18* (8), 1.

27. CAEAR Coalition. *Ryan White CARE Act Title I and Title III FY2003 Funding Needs*; Communities Advocating Emergency AIDS Relief Coalition: Washington, DC, (no date).

28. CAEAR Coalition. *Ryan White CARE Act Title I and Title III FY2004 Funding Needs*; Communities Advocating Emergency AIDS Relief Coalition: Washington, DC, (no date).

29. Oversight of spending for Ryan White CARE Act to receive review at HHS. AIDS Policy Law **2001**, *16* (14), 1–2.

30. McKinney, M.M.; Marconi, K.M. Delivering HIV services to vulnerable populations: A review of CARE Act-funded research. Public Health Rep. **2002**, *117* (2), 99–113.

31. Buchanan, R.J. Ryan White CARE Act and eligible metropolitan areas. Health Care Finance Rev. **2002**, *23* (4), 149–157.

32. Lesson From AIDS Flap: Don't Mess with Success. In *The Virginian-Pilot*; Pilot Media Companies: Norfolk, VA, July 9, 2003.

33. Los Angeles County Board of Supervisors Releases Results of Investigation into County AIDS Office. In *Kaiser Daily HIV/AIDS Report*; The Henry J. Kaiser Family Foundation: Menlo Park, CA, December 12, 2002.

34. New York Mayor Bloomberg's Decision to Transfer AIDS Groups to Health Department Sparks 'Bitter Power Struggle' Over AIDS Funds. In *Kaiser Daily HIV/AIDS Report*; The Henry J. Kaiser Family Foundation: Menlo Park, CA, April 29, 2003.

35. Slack, J. Zero-sum politics, the Herbert thesis, and the Ryan White CARE Act: Lessons learned from the local side of AIDS. J. Health Human Serv. Adm. **2001**, *24* (1), 80–102.

36. Scott, W.R. The organization of medical care services: Toward an integrated theoretical model. Med. Care Rev. **1993**, *50* (3), 271–303.

37. Bidwell, C.E.; Kasarda, J.D. *The Organization and Its Ecosystem: A Theory of Structuring in Organizations*; JAI Press, Inc.: Greenwich, CT, 1985.

38. Thompson, J.D. The Synthetic Organization. In *Organizations in Action: Social Science Bases of Administrative Theory*; Thompson, J.D., Ed.; McGraw-Hill Book Company: New York, 1967; 52–54.

39. Halliday, T.C.; Powell, M.J.; Granfors, M.W. Minimalist organizations: Vital events in state bar associations, 1870–1930. Am. Sociol. Rev. **1987**, *52* (4), 456–471.

40. Halliday, T.C.; Powell, M.J.; Granfors, M.W. After minimalism: Transformations of state bar associations from market dependence to state reliance, 1918 to 1950. Am. Sociol. Rev. **1993**, *58* (4), 515–535.

41. Aldrich, H.; Staber, U.; Zimmer, C.; Beggs, J.J. Minimalism and Organizational Mortality: Patterns of Disbanding Among U.S. Trade Associations, 1900–1983. In *Organizational Evolution: New Directions*; Singh, J.V., Ed.; Sage Publications, Inc.: Newbury Park, CA, 1990; 21–51.

42. Hannan, M.T.; Freeman, J. The population ecology of organizations. Am. J. Sociol. **1977**, *83*, 929–964.

43. Hannan, M.T.; Freeman, J. Structural inertia and organizational change. Am. Sociol. Rev. **1984**, *49* (2), 149–164.

44. Hannan, M.T.; Freeman, J. *Organizational Ecology*; Harvard University Press: Cambridge, MA, 1989.

45. Hannan, M.T.; Carroll, G.R. *Dynamics of Organizational Populations: Density, Legitimation, and Competition*; Oxford University Press: New York, 1992.

46. *Organizational Evolution: New Directions*; Singh, J.V., Ed.; Sage Publications, Inc.: Newbury Park, CA, 1990.

47. Tucker, D.J.; Singh, J.V.; Meinhard, A.G. Organizational form, population dynamics, and institutional change: The founding patterns of voluntary organizations. Acad. Manage. J. **1990**, *33* (1), 151–178.

48. Aiken, M.; Dewar, R.; DiTomaso, N.; Hage, J.; Zeitz, G. *Coordinating Human Services*; Jossey-Bass, Inc., Publishers: San Francisco, CA, 1975.

49. Hernandez, S.R.; Kaluzny, A.D. Organizational Innovation and Change. In *Health Care Management: Organization Design and Behavior*; Shortell, S.M., Kaluzny, A.D., Eds.; Delmar Publishers, Inc.: Albany, NY, 1994; 294–315.

Cooperative Purchasing

Alex Sekwat
Tennessee State University, Nashville, Tennessee, U.S.A.

INTRODUCTION

Cooperative purchasing refers to a variety of arrangements in which two or more entities buy goods and services under the same agreement or contract. The National Association of State Purchasing Officials (NASPO) (Ref. [1], p. 94) defines cooperative purchasing as ''buying through public solicitation of competitive bids or competitive proposal by two or more other public jurisdictions, authorities, or agencies.'' According to NASPO (Ref. [1], p. 94), cooperative purchasing ''may include the resale or exchange of goods and services without competitive bidding and the shared use of facilities, procurement information, and procurement personnel.'' Generally, cooperative purchasing arrangements require that participating entities sign a voluntary agreement or memorandum of understanding specifying, among other things, procedures for participation in contracts, warehousing, fee payments when applicable, contract dispute resolution, terms of agreement, and payment of invoices. Sponsorship of cooperative purchasing programs vary among states. However, all require participating jurisdictions to use best value in the procurement of goods and services.

OVERVIEW

There are many forms of cooperative purchasing agreements. The most common types include the join-bid contract, piggybacking, and joint administrative or consolidated purchasing. The join-bid method is popular among state and local government units. Under this technique, two or more jurisdictions take advantage of the benefits of centralized purchasing by reaching consensus on specifications, contract terms, and conditions for common products. The bidding requirements of the participating jurisdictions are pooled in a single invitation for bids to realize larger volume and better unit pricing. The piggybacking method requires a lead jurisdiction or large purchaser of product(s) to invite bids, enter into a contract, and arrange for other jurisdictions to purchase the same products under the same conditions.[2] Local jurisdictions often piggyback purchases on procurement done by state agencies especially of heavy equipment. The joint consolidated or administrative purchasing method is a formal contractual arrangement where several jurisdictions agree to set up an administrative agency responsible for partial or entire purchases for the participating entities. Under this method, each jurisdiction must give up its freedom to comply with terms of the formal contract. The lead agency is in charge of preparation of specifications, solicitation and evaluation of bids, monitoring participation, and administration of the contract. Participants share the administrative costs of the program. Joint purchasing is typically used by public agencies within a specific metropolitan area, agencies within a state, jurisdictions taking advantage of contract prices negotiated by a state, and educational institutions using contract prices negotiated by national educational associations.[3]

Other variants of cooperative procurement, especially among local jurisdictions, include the joint use of facilities and exchange of technical information and personnel.[2] Under the former method, two or more entities may agree to jointly use facilities such as a warehouse or a testing laboratory. Such an arrangement is intended to reduce procurement costs. In the event that jurisdictions are not in position to purchase cooperatively, ''they at least can help one another by sharing information, loaning their staff, or letting others use their facilities or product specifications'' (Ref. [2], p. 352).

Cooperative purchasing is used by private, public, and nonprofit sector entities. In the public sector, federal agencies, state agencies, and the approximately 87,000 local jurisdictions in the United States can engage in cooperative procurement. Nonprofit agencies, such as hospitals, colleges, universities, and religious organizations, are also major participants in cooperative purchasing. Although jurisdictions or organizations may have operational differences, they buy basically the same types of goods and services. The most jointly procured goods and services by state and local jurisdictions include vehicles, computer systems, software, office supplies, gasoline, automotive and heavy equipment parts, furniture and office equipment, asphalt, tires, pharmaceuticals, janitorial supplies, training services, travel services, and telephone services. In general, products or services, which are utilized by a large number of jurisdictions, are awarded by competitive bids.

HISTORICAL BACKGROUND

Cooperative purchasing is not new in the United States. The earliest known established practice in the public

DOI: 10.1081/E-EPAP 120019222

sector dates back to about 1930 in Alamosa, CO, when eight school districts formed a purchasing pool. Other early initiatives in cooperative purchasing included the formation of a joint procurement venture between the City of Cincinnati, OH, and the Hamilton County, OH, in 1931 and the purchase of fire hoses by the Michigan Municipal League for eight municipalities in 1938. The Cincinnati–Hamilton County plan was formed on a voluntary basis and managed by a coordinating committee of purchasing agents of Hamilton County composed of the purchasing agents of Hamilton County, the City of Cincinnati, the Cincinnati Board of Education, the Public Library of Cincinnati, and the University of Cincinnati.[4] By the late 1970s, intergovernmental cooperative purchasing reached its maturity. The publication in 1978 of the Model Procurement Code marked a milestone in the efforts of state and local governments to adopt laws and ordinances that encouraged and facilitated intergovernmental purchasing cooperation. Today, the practice is widespread among states, counties, cities, towns, villages, school districts, special school districts, colleges, universities, agencies, authorities, commissions, and other bodies with the power to award public contracts.

BENEFITS

Cooperative or pool purchasing has several benefits. First, by buying identical or similar goods and services in large volumes, participants save money and time. Volume purchasing provides participants with economies of large-scale purchasing by lowering unit costs of products. Pooling of purchasing functions further lowers administrative costs by substantially reducing duplication of efforts associated with competitive procurement. Second, cooperative purchasing programs save participants time to research specifications, to identify vendors, and to prepare, advertise, and administer a bid proposal or maintain a contract. Third, pool purchasing offers program subscribers standardized specifications, better quality control, and broader selection of goods and services. Finally, cooperative purchasing facilitates information sharing and expertise, especially among smaller jurisdictions that lack resources to hire full-time professional purchasing managers. Professional management of purchasing functions further benefits smaller jurisdictions in technical procurement functions such as preparation of specifications, training, economic analysis, development of buying strategies, testing and inspection of products, and disposition or exchange of surplus property.[1]

DRAWBACKS

Despite the benefits highlighted above, cooperative purchasing has some major drawbacks. First, certain legal and political obstacles impede the growth and development of cooperative purchasing programs. The major political obstacles include "preference of local vendors, the fear of loss of autonomy, the difficulty of settling on standardized items to all, and the feeling of the larger participants that their savings will be less than those of the smaller units."[3] Experience indicates that over time, political barriers are more difficult to overcome than legal barriers.[3] Second, sharing of administrative and technical overhead costs, especially under a join-bid arrangement, is problematic. Great effort is needed to assemble the participating jurisdictions, to draft and coordinate terms and specifications, to prepare bidders' lists and draft solicitations, and to tabulate and evaluate responses.[4] Last, if poorly designed, a cooperative purchasing program can increase the carrying costs for participating jurisdictions. Volume buying typically increases storage, insurance, coordination, and transportation costs. As noted by Reed and Swain,[5] "when items are purchased in large amounts, those items will need to be stored since products must be stored for an extended period of time. They must be stored so that they do not deteriorate, which may require special facilities. ... Clearly, considerable thought needs to be given to the costs of such enterprises."

CONCLUSION

Cooperative purchasing promotes sound administrative values, including economy and efficiency, by maximizing the time and resources of participating units. It is cost-effective and provides participants with the economies of large-scale purchasing. Thus it renders high value for taxpayers dollars. Well-rounded cooperative purchasing programs further foster intergovernmental cooperation and reduce duplication of work. However, as noted by NASPO (Ref. [1], p. 96), "successful programs need favorable laws, adequate implementing regulations, energetic leadership, and cooperation among the parties."

REFERENCES

1. National Association of State Purchasing Officials, NASPO. *State and Local Government Purchasing*; The Council of State Governments: Lexington, KY, 1988; 94, 96.
2. Gordon, S. Purchasing. In *Local Government Finance*; Petersen, J.E., Strachota, D.R., Eds.; Government Finance Officers Association: Chicago, IL, 1991; 339–353.
3. Zenz, G.J. *Purchasing and the Management of Materials*; John Wiley & Sons, Inc.: New York, 1994; 364, 365.
4. Page, H.R. *Public Purchasing and Materials Management*; Lexington Books: Lexington, MA, 1980.
5. Reed, J.B.; Swain, J.W. *Public Finance Administration*; Prentice Hall: Englewood Cliffs, NJ, 1990; 195.

Court System Strategic Planning

Deborah A. Botch

New York State Unified Court System, Albany, New York, U.S.A.

INTRODUCTION

The courts of the United States have experienced a quiet revolution over the past two decades. Once strictly neutral forums for case adjudication, courts have evolved into tribunals with a dual function. They remain the primary forum for resolving civil and criminal matters; but today courts also proactively seek ways to solve human and community problems. This fundamental change has brought with it new service demands and organizational challenges that have created a need for more systematic and integrative long-term planning. To confront this increasingly complex and dynamic environment, court systems have turned to long-established strategic planning tools and methods. This article explores concepts, models, and common practices adopted by federal, state, and local court systems in developing and implementing strategic plans.

PUBLIC SECTOR STRATEGIC PLANNING

By definition, strategic planning is a formalized and systematic process used by any organization, enterprise, or community to identify and achieve future goals through collective action. Long employed by large private sector corporations as a means of improving competitive advantage, strategic planning did not come into widespread public sector use until the 1990s.[1] Faced with ever-increasing social and technological challenges, coupled with vocal demands for improved performance and accountability, government and nonprofit organizations are now keeping pace with the private sector in instituting strategic planning processes as a matter of course. Today, strategic planning plays an important role in the management of many governments, government agencies, and nonprofit organizations.

The public sector has adopted strategic planning as part of its organizational management structure for a number of reasons. According to Mintzberg,[2] strategic planning processes serve multiple purposes. They are effective devices for self-assessment, improved communication, and consensus building. Bryson[1] points also to strategic planning's utilization of participative decision making, which is central to solving public problems in a

democracy, as a key reason why the approach has been widely adopted and persists.

Legislative mandate provides another impetus to public sector adoption of strategic planning. Some governments have enacted laws and regulations that call for the submission of regularly updated strategic plans to executive and legislative authorities. A case in point is the Government Performance and Review Act (1993) that directs federal agencies to develop and submit strategic plans to Congress and the Office of Management and Budget (OMB).[3] Strategic planning and routine submission of plans and performance reports to Congress and OMB are an ongoing part of the management processes of federal agencies.

The availability and proven track record of a number of strategic planning models have also contributed to the rapid expansion of public sector strategic planning. Bryson[1] has developed a widely recognized and frequently referenced model for public sector strategic planning in the United States. Bryson's[1] process consists of the following stages: initiate and agree on a strategic planning process; identify mandates; clarify mission and values; assess the organization's external and internal environments; identify strategic issues; formulate strategies to manage issues; review and adopt the strategic plan; establish a vision of success; develop an effective implementation process; and, reassess strategies and the strategic planning process.

COURT SYSTEM STRATEGIC PLANNING

Like its executive branch and local government counterparts, the judicial branch operates in an increasingly dynamic and uncertain environment. Increased case loads, public demands for greater accountability, and the introduction of grassroots problem-solving court programs are changing the environments in which courts operate. To respond to these changes, many courts have instituted strategic planning processes over the last decade and they continue to do so. The National Center for State Courts (NCSC) provides an extensive bibliography of court-related strategic planning materials as well as a comprehensive state-by-state reference list of court strategic plan documents. The NCSC also supplies access

Encyclopedia of Public Administration and Public Policy
DOI: 10.1081/E-EPAP 120011040

to many electronic documents and links to sites containing court strategic plans and process information at their web site, http://www.ncsconline.org/.[4]

Strategic Planning in Federal Courts

The federal judiciary has long operated under a formalized process of strategic long-term planning that reflects its unique Constitutional obligations. Administration of the federal courts, which includes long-range strategic planning among its various functions, is carried out under the policies and direction of the Judicial Conference of the United States. The Judicial Conference, made up of Senior Circuit and District Court Judges, directly oversees the Administrative Office of the Courts and authorizes and establishes standing and advisory committees that deal with specific areas of administration.[5] In 1990, the Judicial Conference began a (http://www.uscourts.gov/lrp/index) long-range planning process with its establishment of the Committee on Long-Range Planning. The Committee's work reflected a highly decentralized and consultative process consistent with the federal judiciary's organizational structure and legally defined operations.

In meeting its charge, the Committee reviewed key historical plans and reports and coordinated its work with other committees of the Judicial Conference. These committees collaboratively prepared a number of subject-specific long-term plans, which included input from individual judges, supporting documentation from several judiciary sponsored research projects, and extensive public review and comment. Four years later, in 1994, the final product was a comprehensive draft long-range strategic plan containing dozens of long-term goals and implementation strategies.

In December 1995, the Judicial Conference of the United States adopted a final version of the *Long-Range Plan for the Federal Courts*, which contained a Vision and Mission Statement and 93 goals and 76 implementation strategies. A complete copy of the *Long-Range Plan for the Federal Courts* is available at the federal courts web site, http://www.uscourt.us.gov/lrp.[6]

Strategic Planning in State and Local Court Systems

At the state and local level, while many different approaches have been applied to strategic planning development and implementation, most court systems have relied on only a few strategic planning methodologies and models to guide and coordinate the process. According to Martin and Wagenknecht-Ivey,[7] these methods and models address organizational improvement issues and reflect an external and community focus. They

invite broad-based public participation and include stakeholders from outside the court to assure sustained community involvement. According to Rottman et al.,[8] community collaboration in the court planning process inculcates greater understanding of the role of the courts and fosters public trust and confidence.

While the composition of planning committees varies, two distinct approaches are generally used in structuring court strategic planning committees. According to Martin and Wagenknecht-Ivey,[7] the first approach is broad-based, made up of judges, court personnel, local government officials, lawyers, citizens, and community groups. In the second approach, the committee is entirely composed of judges, court staff, and court system administrators.

In the following section, two models that illustrate the key attributes, processes, and methods common to court strategic planning will be discussed:

1. Court Community Planning Model (Judicial Council of California).
2. Nine-Step Court Strategic Planning Process (Center for Public Policy Studies).

COURT STRATEGIC PLANNING MODELS

State of California Court Community Planning Program

The State of California Court Community Planning Program is an excellent example of the application of the community-focused model of court planning. In keeping with the model, the California program has been designed to promote community outreach and development of court–community partnerships.[9]

The Judicial Council of California, the governance board for the State's judicial branch, is responsible for improving the administration of justice in California. The Council has adopted an official strategic planning process and management cycle that is integrated with other administrative processes, including annual judiciary budget preparation. In 1998, under the direction of the Judicial Council, the California courts launched its community-focused strategic planning process. The process fosters inclusion of community stakeholders as full partners in the planning process and relies on a five-stage community-outreach model developed in consultation with national experts.[10] Much of the planning in this model is delegated to courts at the county level and is accomplished by teams of county court judges, court staff, local government officials, bar representatives, and community groups.

Several features of the five-stage model are common to other public sector strategic planning models. For instance, there are similarities with strategic planning steps recommended in Bryson's[1] framework, such as clarifying vision and mission, scanning the environment to determine important issues and trends, and development of goals and measures of success. But what sets the California model apart is its emphasis on broad-based public participation and the "enablement" of public involvement.

To enable community participation, the California model recommends creation of planning teams that include broad-based representation both from within and outside the courts. In the enablement phase, training is provided to all planning team members in the basics of strategic planning and use of the five-stage model as a means of building planning capacity and group cooperation and cohesion.

The California Courts Community Planning Model has generated a variety of local ideas for improving court operations and making courts more responsive to the unique needs of the State's socially and economically divergent communities. This planning process has also spawned a variety of community justice partnerships. For example, court- and school-based education programs have been instituted in a number of small rural jurisdictions to enhance student understanding of the legal system. Elsewhere, a citizen advisory board has been established to build court and community trust and cooperation in the Los Angeles Superior Court.[8] The success of the collaborative model used in California can also be seen in the rapid response and participation in the planning effort. As of 2002, all 58 counties of the State had submitted court community strategic plans to the State's Judicial Council.[10]

Nine-Step Court Strategic Planning Process

By far, the most popular model used for court system strategic planning is that developed by John A. Martin and Brenda J. Wagenknecht-Ivey as consultants to the Center for Public Policy Studies (CPPS). According to Martin and Wagenknecht-Ivey, the *Nine-Step Court Strategic Planning Process* offers a standard systematic approach that can be readily adapted for use by any court system, court, or court subdivision. Although input from the wider community is a feature in the model, it is not a requirement. The nine-step model focuses on organizational change, learning, and improvement. As of the year 2000, more than 50 state and local courts and other justice agencies have reported adoption of this model for strategic planning (Fig. 1).[7]

According to Martin and Wagenknecht-Ivey,[7] because strategic planning requires significant resources and

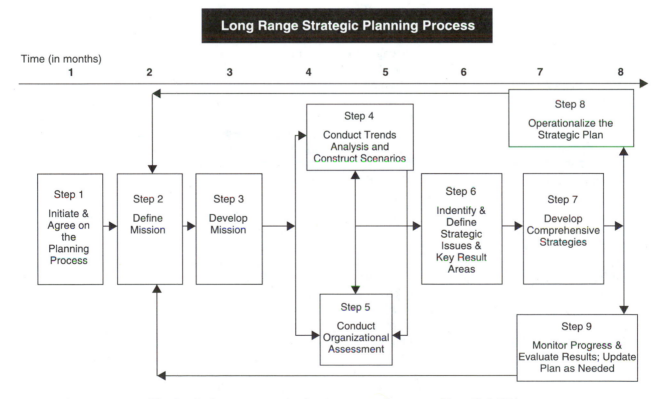

Fig. 1 A nine-step strategic planning process for courts. (From Ref. [7].)

time commitments, courts need to be sure that conditions are right for introducing strategic planning. The authors recommend that, prior to undertaking strategic planning, court leaders must be able to focus on long-term priorities, be ready to embrace organizational change, and be willing to involve a wide-range of participants in planning. Wagenknecht-Ivey has developed a tool to score and evaluate an organization's conditions of readiness.[7] If "readiness" criteria are met, court organizations are given the green light to move ahead with a strategic planning efforts.

Following the readiness assessment, the nine-step model begins with a commitment from court leaders and managers and an agreement from the planning group about the scope and purpose of the effort. Steps 2 and 3 focus on development of vision and mission statements. Step 4 consists of a trend analysis and scenario constructions. Scenario construction, according to the authors, can help planners picture how a variety of trends may impact on the courts and how courts can shape a positive future. They are creative tools that involve speculation and imagination, but are not predictions. Use of scenarios facilitate systematic future-oriented and "what if" thinking to help organizations better understand the potential forces impacting on desired future conditions.[11]

Step 5 in this model is an organizational assessment that, according to the authors, allows the court to see how its structures, policies, attitudes, and resources align with "expected" and "desired" future conditions. In step 6, strategic issues and key-result areas are identified. Strategic issues are the critical policies or challenges to the court organization that will impact on future effectiveness. Step 7 involves development of comprehensive strategies to respond to each strategic issue area. The authors consider this step to be the heart of the model and recommend that broad goals, objectives, and end targets be established.

Step 8 moves plan formulation into operational and action planning stages and involves project selection, setting time frames, and evaluating resource availability and impacts.[7] The model assumes that strategic planning will be an ongoing and continuous process. As a result, step 9 urges courts to set up methods for monitoring and evaluating results and developing plan updates.

Mentoring guidelines have been prepared as a practical tool to guide court strategic planners in using the nine-step model.[7] The guidelines provide a case study of the Florida judicial branch long-range strategic planning effort. This case study illustrates the application of the nine-step model in an actual court system environment and shows how the model facilitates a court strategic planning process. The value of the nine-step strategic planning approach is confirmed not only by the Florida courts example, but by the number of other strategic plans

it has helped foster. For example, see the plans of several statewide court systems—California, Michigan, and Wisconsin, and at the trial court level—Los Angeles County Superior Court, 36th District Court in Detroit, Michigan; and, Yakima County Superior Court in Washington State.

Other Tools That Aid Court Strategic Planning

Along with models that are used to guide, coordinate, and quicken the pace of strategic planning, several other practical tools are available to facilitate the strategic planning process in state and local court systems. One such tool is a set of performance standards that have been adopted and used by hundreds of trial and municipal courts across the country to improve the quality and accountability of court programs and services.[12] The Trial Court Performance Standards (TCPS),[13] developed by the Commission on Trial Court Performance Standards, provides 22 guiding principles covering five public interest areas:

1. Access to justice.
2. Expedition and timeliness.
3. Equality, fairness, and integrity.
4. Independence and accountability.
5. Public trust and confidence.

To support vision and mission statement, development state and local courts often rely on these national performance standards as a key resource.

A second tool available to state and local court systems is one that can help shorten the time frame and reduce the cost, complexity, and work required of strategic planning. This tool is referred to as the "environmental scan" and is a concept presented in detail in the *Environmental Scan for State Courts 2002*, developed by the National Center for State Courts and Futures.com.[14] As explained in the overview of the *Scan* report: "Environmental scanning attempts to identify events, trends, and developments or drivers, shaping the future...." Trends, for instance, can include those in social, scientific, technological, economic, political/governmental, and professional categories.[14] In its broadest sense, environmental scanning involves an effort to take a court beyond its current ways of doing things (or encouraging it to rethink its "paradigms"). The scan report can be used by a court or court system to support strategic planning either as the sole resource for identifying forces and changes in the external environment or in combination with locally prepared environmental trends information and analyses.

A third tool that can be used as a foundation for strategic planning is the information gathered in court "futures" reports. As indicated by the National Center for

State Courts web site, during the 1990s, 22 state court systems created futures commissions or committees. These study groups were generally initiated by visionary state judicial leaders whose objectives were to assess economic, social, cultural, technological, and political trends and to consider how court systems should adapt their structures, rules, workforce, operations, and intergovernmental and community relationships to effectively respond to expected changes.

The Ohio Courts Future Commission undertook one such ''futures'' study. Conducted by a variety of legal experts, community and business leaders, and citizens, the Ohio study provides a good example of the breadth of issues and long-range horizons generally reflected in court futures studies. The Commission's final report identified 10 key attributes of the Ohio courts that would be desirable by the year 2025, including, among other things, courts that are physically, economically, and functionally accessible to all citizens, a jury system that respects jurors and lets them take a more active role in court proceedings, selection of judges based on superior legal and personal qualifications (trained and continually reeducated on topics of relevance to the courts), and a workforce that is well trained and professional.[15]

Strategic Planning Issues and Future Directions

Even with its benefits, such as clearer mission and goals, coherent decision making, and improved performance, strategic planning may not be suitable for some court organizations or in all circumstances. Bryson[1] cites a number of difficulties and challenges that must be addressed to ensure success, including, foremost, the commitment of key leaders and stakeholders. Bryson further recommends that if implementation appears unlikely, strategic planning should not be considered. Martin and Wagenknecht-Ivey[7] also recommend that courts assess their readiness for change and the commitment of leaders and stakeholders before embarking on a strategic planning effort. Critics of strategic planning are also concerned with the costs and time-consuming aspects of the process. Hamel,[16] for example, argues that strategic planning is not only too costly but also does not provide for the fast-paced strategy development needed by today's organizations.

Henry Mintzberg,[2] in his classic work on the ''rise and fall of strategic planning,'' cites several other limitations of strategic planning including the conflict between the creativity necessary for innovation and the logical and systematic requirements of formal planning. For the public sector, he reiterates the challenge of ensuring that the desires of the people are adequately represented. Mintzberg[2] does not entirely dismiss the

process, but notes that while strategic planning may have benefits, at best, ''[it is] a process with particular benefit in particular contexts'' (p. 4). More recently, Raffoni[17] argues that strategic planning often founders at the execution stage because of a limited understanding by management of what it takes to successfully implement strategies. Raffoni also contends that few plans recognize the importance of translating broad-brush conceptual strategies into decisions about who will carry out the associated tasks and how much time and money will actually be expended.

In spite of these difficulties, the need for effective methods to deal with the dynamic forces of change remains a major challenge for court systems and other public sector institutions. Strategic planning and related techniques that facilitate communication, collaboration, goal setting, and accountability have helped many public sector organizations better prepare for the future. At the same time, there is recognition[18] that more robust, focused, coordinated, and democratic methods will be needed if strategic planning is to remain a viable and beneficial tool for the next generation of public leaders, managers, and citizens.

CONCLUSION

Strategic planning concepts, tools, and models have helped many court systems prepare for the future and transform themselves into more responsive public organizations. As the pace of change quickens and public expectations for effective performance increases, systematic planning processes will become even more critical in ensuring the effectiveness of courts and court/community cooperation at all governmental levels. Recognizing this, several state court systems have made strategic planning an integral and ongoing organizational management process. Also, the National Center for State Courts continues to expand its resources and services to help court systems build and sustain their strategic planning capacity. While public sector conditions have dramatically changed in recent years, those courts that have a history of long-range, systematic, and broad-based strategic planning are likely to be able to adapt to changing conditions and meet new demands for service and effectiveness now and in the future.

REFERENCES

1. Bryson, J.M. *Strategic Planning for Public and Nonprofit Organizations: A Guide to Strengthening and Sustaining Organizational Achievement*; Jossey-Bass Publishers: San Francisco, 1995.

2. Mintzberg, H. *The Rise and Fall of Strategic Planning*; The Free Press: New York, 1994.

3. GAO. *Executive Guide—Effectively Implementing the Government Performance and Results Act (GAO/GGD-96-118)*; U.S. General Accounting Office, 1996.

4. National Center for State Courts. **2003**, (http://www.ncsconline.org/ (accessed 3/20/03).

5. Judicial Conference of the United States. http://www.uscourts.gov/judconf (accessed March 5, 2003).

6. Long Range Plan of the Federal Courts. **1995**, (http://www.uscourts.gov/lrp (accessed March 5, 2003).

7. Martin, J.A.; Wagenknecht-Ivey, B.J. *Strategic Planning Mentoring Guidelines: Practical Tips for Court Leaders*; State Justice Institute: Alexandria, VA, 2000.

8. Rottman, D.; Efkeman, H.; Hansen, R.; Stump, S. *A Leadership Guide to Statewide Court and Community Collaboration*; 2002. http://www.ncsconline.org/WCDS/Pubs/ (accessed February 19, 2003).

9. Judicial Council of California. *Community Focused Court Planning Initiative: Fact Sheet*; January 2003. http://www.courtinfo.ca.gov/reference (accessed April 16, 2003).

10. California Courts. *Court Community Planning*; http://www.courtinfo.ca.gov/programs/planning (accessed March 6, 2003).

11. Martin, J.A.; Wagenknecht-Ivey, B.J. Courts 2010: Critical trends shaping the courts in the next decade. Court Manager **2000**, *15* (1), 6–15.

12. Keilitz, I. *Performance Based Strategic Planning (PSPB) in the Courts: A Planning Process Anchored in the Trial Court Performance Standards*; Sherwood Associates: Williamsburg, VA, 1997.

13. Bureau of Justice Assistance. *Trial Court Performance Standards and Measurement System*; National Center for State Courts: Williamsburg, VA. http://www.ncsconline.org/D-research/TCPS (accessed April 16, 2003).

14. *National Center for State Courts & Futurist.com 2002 Report on Trends in the State Courts*; National Center for State Courts: Williamsburg, VA. http://www.ncsconline.org/WCDSPubs/ (accessed March 21, 2003).

15. *A Changing Landscape: Ohio Court Futures Commission Report*; Ohio Courts Future Commission, May 2000.

16. Hamel, G. Strategy as revolution. Harvard Bus. Rev. **1996**, *74* (4), 69–82.

17. Raffoni, M. Three keys to effective execution. Harvard Manag. Update **2003**, *8* (2), 1–4.

18. Rubenstein, H. Strategic planning tools for futurists. Futures Res. Q. **Fall 2000**, *16* (3), 5–17.

Crisis Policy Making and Management in Southeast Asia

Scott Fritzen
National University of Singapore, Singapore

INTRODUCTION

Crises severely test the capacities of bureaucracies, politicians, and, at times, the overall resilience of political, economic, and social systems. Studying crisis management across country contexts enables the exploration of systemic capacities and policy-making patterns as these undergo (at times, extreme) stress. This review briefly introduces a framework for cross-country analysis and applies to Southeast Asia. It has four sections. First, it presents hypotheses for how different crisis types interact with country governance characteristics to influence decision making. Second, summary characteristics of crises influencing policy making and management are presented for a range of crises that have affected Southeast Asia in the past 10 years. Third, regional responses to the emergence and spread of the Severe Atypical Respiratory Syndrome (SARS) virus in 2003 are analyzed as one example of interconnections posited between governance characteristics and crisis management. The concluding section explores implications of the framework for those interested in improving the robustness of crisis management in the region.

CRISIS DECISION MAKING AND GOVERNANCE CHARACTERISTICS

Analytical frameworks for comparing crisis decision making across national boundaries are at an early stage of development, in contrast to the considerable literature that exists on individual types of crisis, such as terrorism or natural disasters (see the *Handbook of Crisis and Emergency Management*[1] for comprehensive coverage). Two types of generalizations are likely to be important for future work in this area.

The first stems from the pioneering work of Grindle and Thomas,[2] who analyzed ways in which problem characteristics and context help determine patterns of policy decision making. Distinguishing between ''crisis-driven'' and ''bureaucratic politics-as-usual'' reform contexts, they find that decision making in the latter case is likely to be addressed at senior levels of government and to be strongly influenced by the need to maintain regime stability. Together with Kingdon,[3] they also stress the importance of the leadership abilities of ''policy entrepreneurs,'' who are shown to make a profound difference on outcomes even in resource-poor environments.

Building on the Grindle and Thomas dichotomy, we can posit that ''not all crisis are created equal:'' Different types of crisis will ''trigger'' different decision-making modalities. Four characteristics seem particularly important:

1. Degree to which a problem threatens overall regime stability. Ability to threaten the tenure of senior leaders became in effect a defining characteristic of a crisis in Grindle and Thomas' framework, but it is clear that different types of crisis threaten *political* stability to very different degrees; it is also clear that the impact of the same type of problem on political stability will vary between regimes. The greater the degree to which regimes and incumbents are threatened by a crisis, the more decision making will tend to be dominated by the political calculus of senior officials.

2. Degree to which a problem is potentially amenable to a ''technical'' solution. The effectiveness of decision making in crises involving considerable technical complexity (such as environmental protection) will in large part be determined by the bureaucratic capacities that exist in a given system.

3. Degree of cross-national spillover involved. Interstate crises raise the complexity of problem solving by forcing decisions to be negotiated with multiple stakeholders, both within and outside of a polity. The greater the spillover effect, the more outcomes will be shaped by the effectiveness of regional forms of cooperation and by differentials in power between states.

4. The continuity of issue as crisis (whether short-acting or chronic). All crises, by definition, thrust themselves unpredictably onto the policy agenda. Some, however, are recurring in nature—sometimes over decades—such that precedents and ''organizational repertoires''[4]—patterned national and bureaucratic responses to a given problem—are triggered with each recurrence of the crisis. In unprecedented crisis

Encyclopedia of Public Administration and Public Policy
DOI: 10.1081/E-EPAP-120024572

contexts, the role of individual leaders in shaping responses may be highlighted to a greater extent than in the case of ''chronic'' crises.

A second broad generalization, to date insufficiently explored in the literature (but see Grindle[5]), is that state capacities matter in crisis management. A strategic approach to crisis policy making and management[6,7] focuses on three categories of capacities:

1. *Political and leadership capacities*, which, as the name implies, has two aspects depending on whether the capacities involved adhere primarily to an individual or to the system as a whole. A critical feature is the way political leaders (or, in rarer cases in Southeast Asia, policy entrepreneurs outside government) direct attention to a problem in a manner that shapes how the crisis is perceived.
2. *Bureaucratic and process capacity* involves the ability to manage a high-quality decision-making process during a crisis[8] and to execute decisions taken with predictability and control. This is a profoundly institutional capacity resting on many foundations: a well-functioning bureaucracy, clear information systems and resources (both manpower and fiscal) to tackle implementation challenges that arise.
3. *Social capacity* in times of crisis relates to the willingness of social or economic groupings to accept overall government coordination and/or to participate in the constructive response to the crisis.

Looking across these categories, one can make what might be called the ''weakest link'' hypothesis. Any given crisis may invoke multiple types of decision-making responses and rely for its resolution on multiple capacities. Yet some capacity constraints will be more binding for the ''successful'' management of crises than others. For politically sensitive crisis points, a governance system's political capacities will, in particular, be tested, and crises involving high technical complexity will depend heavily on a system's bureaucratic capacity. Crises with high spillover effects, in turn, will depend prominently on the strength of mechanisms for interstate cooperation—a capacity that in Southeast Asia has been growing steadily over the past two decades, but which is still stretched thin.

COMPARING CRISIS CHARACTERISTICS IN SOUTHEAST ASIA

Multiple kinds of crisis have affected Southeast Asian countries of the past 5 years or so, each with different characteristics based on the framework above (Table 1). These can be divided into three groupings that suggest different hypotheses for future research.

The first grouping includes chronic, largely political problems that are generally not amendable to any obvious ''technical'' solution, but are also unlikely to precipitate regime change on their own. Terrorism, internal violence, secession struggles, and human rights disputes all might fit into this category. In between inevitable crisis points, these problems have tended to simmer without resolution where they have affected low-capacity political systems (as in Indonesia or Cambodia). Their resolution will depend on the degree to which political and adaptive capacities develop in, as yet, weakly institutionalized democracies.

Table 1 Characteristics of crises buffeting Southeast Asia since 1997

	Technical solution	Spillover	Regime threat	Continuity
Health (SARS, bird flu)	High	High	Low	Low
Health (HIV–AIDS)	Moderate	Moderate–high	Low	High
Terrorism (e.g., response to Jemmah Islamiyah)	Low	High	Low	Moderate
Economic and financial crisis (1997–1999)	Moderate	Moderate	Moderate–high	Moderate
Regime challenge (e.g., ''People's Power II'' or the fall of Soeharto)	Low	Low	High	Low
Interstate dispute (e.g., Cambodia–Thailand ''Angkor Wat'' incident in January 2003)	Moderate	High	Low	Low
Internal civil violence (e.g., Maluku unrest)	Low	Moderate	Moderate	Moderate
Secessionist struggles (e.g., Aceh, Mindanao)	Low	Moderate	Moderate	High
Human rights problems in regional countries (e.g., ASEAN response to Myanmar's detention of Aung San Suu Kyi in May 2003)	Low	Moderate	Low	High
Environmental dispute (e.g., Indonesia–Singapore ''smog'' problem, 1997)	Moderate	High	Low	Moderate

A second category of problems includes technical problems with high "contagion," moderately capable of threatening regime tenure. Handling of epidemic outbreaks and regional economic crises, such as (notably) the East Asian financial crisis beginning in 1997, fall into this category. Outcomes in these cases depend, to a large extent, on problem continuity and the technical capacity and interest of the affected governments to address the problems. Addressing major problems of high contagion in this manner clearly goes beyond the capacity of less-developed Southeast Asian countries, which must therefore rely, to a large extent, on regional management mechanisms. As shown by the SARS example below, the degree to which bureaucratic capacity and interstate norms can simultaneously develop becomes critical to the eventual resolution of crises in this category.

The third category involves direct challenges to government tenure, extending in the extreme to challenges to the entire governance system (as in Indonesia during the fall of Soeharto). These are, of course, political crises points, the resolution of which depends on the balance of state capacity, legitimacy, and institutionalized conflict-management mechanisms built up over the history of the polity concerned.

RESPONDING TO A CRISIS OF UNKNOWN PROPORTIONS: THE CASE OF SARS IN 2003

Different responses in Southeast Asia to the outbreak of a new and deadly disease—Severe Atypical Respiratory Syndrome (SARS)—serve as an illustration of the interaction effects of crisis and governance characteristics. SARS originated in southern China in November 2002, reached Hong Kong in February 2003, and peaked in May 2003, by which time it had spread eventually to over 25 countries. It was to cause just fewer than 800 deaths before its chain of transmission was declared broken in all countries in July 2003. Of the 10 worst affected countries, seven were in Asia, foremost among them mainland China, which accounted for almost 90% of worldwide cases.[9] This health crisis gripped the public imagination in a manner much different from the far more devastating HIV virus, in part because it erupted in a short time, caused widespread uncertainty (including over transmission modalities and fatality rates) and massive economic costs to the countries worst affected. SARS posed a tremendous challenge above all to East and Southeast Asian countries and territories that bore the brunt of the disease—seven of the 10 worst affected countries were in Asia.[10]

The SARS epidemic had a high technical content; the policy response to SARS was predicated on getting better information on transmission routes and effective mecha-

nisms of control. It was moderately threatening in political terms, with fears concentrated on the potential economic costs as well as the social fallout from being seen to handle the virus incompetently. Of course, SARS had high international spillover (and therefore generated high amounts of pressure from the international community for affected countries to institute transparent control mechanisms). Despite sharing these crisis characteristics, the way the SARS virus was handled differed substantially in China, Vietnam, and Singapore in ways that shed light on the intersection of governance qualities and crisis-management modalities.

In Vietnam, early detection of the virus and a swift response led to eventual containment. The government's response drew praise from the World Health Organization (WHO):[11] "Vietnam demonstrated to the world how a developing country, hit by an especially severe outbreak, can triumph over a disease when reporting is prompt and open..." Partly, the response was one of luck, as a rapid initial effort to contain the spread was successful. As was shown eventually in neighboring China, this success was a function of effective dissemination of information through Vietnam's some 10,000 rural health centers, demonstrating that even in relatively poor countries, infrastructural and organizational capacities, once mobilized, may be impressive. The resolution of the SARS outbreak in Vietnam, and the slower but eventually effective response in China, was multifactorial, "involving improvements in management and triage in hospitals and communities of patients with suspected SARS and the dissemination of information to health care workers and the public."[12]

It is the initial Chinese response that calls for further analysis. Information regarding the true extent of the outbreak in China was suppressed for some weeks before the government launched a full-scale attack on the disease. The normally diplomatic (by necessity) WHO noted as much, saying, "SARS is now known to have begun in mid-November [2002] in Guangdong Province. Cases during the earliest phases of the SARS outbreak there were not openly reported, thus allowing a severe disease to become silently established in ways that made further international spread almost inevitable."[13] Harsher assessments were found in the international press, with *The Economist* magazine[14] likening the Chinese performance to that of the Soviet Union during the Chernobyl disaster. It was as the international spotlight fully glaring on the Chinese that the stakes, in terms not least of national image, became great enough for the central leadership to initiate its rapid and comprehensive course correction that finally led to an effective response.

Singapore generally drew high praise for its response to the outbreak. As an international trading and tourist hub, Singapore clearly stood to lose a great deal to the virus. The government's early response to it was to pull no stops; virtually all containment measures imaginable, including use of military forces to enforce quarantine requirements,[15] were taken with alacrity. The leadership was engaged in a high-profile manner in communicating information regarding the latest occurrences of the virus and its transmission mechanisms. A recent review of Singapore's experience, based on a survey of 1200 Singaporeans, found that respondents evaluated highly the authorities' management of the SARS crisis, with a special emphasis on their openness to communication. The authors also pointed to the importance of social capacity in responding to the virus, finding "a relatively high level of social discipline in the population."[16]

Singapore, Vietnam, and China are all authoritarian states generally capable of mobilizing society behind high-priority national decisions society unencumbered by legal niceties and challenges. However, in this type of crisis, technical capacities and leadership—the ability of the authorities to grasp the situation at the grassroots and their willingness to act in a transparent manner on this information—mattered more than the macrogovernance characteristics of the regimes. As a technologically savvy city–state, transaction costs to access information about what was "really" happening over the course of the disease were reasonably low in Singapore, whereas the complexity of governing the world's most populous nation, coupled with classic distortions in center-periphery communications in China, led to its central government initial incapacity to take action transparently to thwart this emerging crisis.

IMPLICATIONS

Regime characteristics and systemwide capacities clearly matter in determining crisis-management outcomes. Three types of capacities can be examined, in particular, country contexts—political, technical, and social. Overlapping their boundaries are two additional "meta-capacities:" for systemwide learning and adaptation and for effective international cooperation and lesson sharing. Mechanisms for responding collectively to problems of high technical complexity are still at an early stage of development in Southeast Asia, although—as demonstrated in part by the SARS example—they are improving.

The characteristics of crises themselves also matter, and this has implications for those seeking to shore up regional capacity to address crises in Southeast Asia. Technical capacities will be particularly important where the crisis context allows decision making to proceed in a relatively politically neutral fashion (unlike the early response to SARS in China). Reformers seeking better crisis management in such cases might hope to mobilize external parties affected by the issue—i.e., to raise the

"spillover" salience of an issue—in order to prompt better cooperation and national responsiveness.

Where political motives are paramount in responses to crisis, answers will be more complex. Systems of conflict resolution are needed at the regional level that are both technically and politically viable. The influence of NGOs and others in keeping unpopular issues on the policy agenda will be essential, as will ongoing attempts to open policy making to greater external scrutiny and input. Although state capacities to handle crises in Southeast Asia are highly uneven, robust institutions to manage political transitions and accumulated social pressures are in fairly short supply in most Southeast Asian countries.

REFERENCES

1. Farazmand, A. *Handbook of Crisis and Emergency Management*; Marcel Dekker, Inc.: New York, 2001.
2. Grindle, M.; Thomas, J. *Public Choices and Policy Change: The Political Economy of Reform in Developing Countries*; Johns Hopkins University Press: Baltimore, MD, 1991.
3. Kingdon, J. *Agendas, Alternatives, and Public Policies*; Harper Collins College Publishers: New York, 1995.
4. Allison, G.; Zelikow, P. *Essence of Decision: Explaining the Cuban Missile Crisis*, 2nd Ed.; Longman: New York, 1999.
5. Grindle, M. *Challenging the State: Crisis and Innovation in Latin America and Africa*; Cambridge University Press: New York, NY, 1996.
6. Nice, D.; Grosse, A. Crisis Policy Making: Some Implications for Program Management. Chapter 5. In *Handbook of Crisis and Emergency Management*; Farazmand, A., Ed.; Marcel Dekker, Inc.: New York, 2003.
7. Irving, K.J. Managing "Complex Emergencies": U.N. Administration and the Resolution of Civil Wars. Chapter 10. In *Handbook of Crisis and Emergency Management*; Farazmand, A., Ed.; Marcel Dekker, Inc.: New York, 2003.
8. Moore, M. *Creating Public Value: Strategic Management in Government*; Harvard University Press: Cambridge, MA, 1995.
9. Lam, W.K.; Zhong, N.S.; Tan, W.C. Overview on SARS in Asia and the World. Respirology **2003**, *8* (11).
10. World Health Organization. *Severe Acute Respiratory Syndrome (SARS): Status of the Outbreak and Lessons for the Immediate Future*; WHO: Geneva, 20 May, 2003.
11. *Severe Acute Respiratory Syndrome (SARS): Status of the Outbreak and Lessons for the Immediate Future*; WHO: Geneva, 20 May, 2003; 7.
12. Pang, X.H.; Zhu, Z.H.; Xu, F.J.; Guo, J.Y.; Gong, X.H.; Liu, D.L.; Liu, Z.J.; Chin, D.P.; Feikin, D.R. Evaluation of control measures implemented in the severe acute respiratory syndrome outbreak in Beijing, 2003. J. Am. Med. Assoc. **2003**, *290* (24), 1.
13. World Health Organization. *Severe Acute Respiratory Syndrome (SARS): Status of the Outbreak and Lessons*

for the Immediate Future; WHO: Geneva, 20 May, 2003; 8.

14. The Economist. In *"China's Chernobyl?"* *London*; 24 April, 2003. Available at http://www.taiwandc.org/economist-2003-01.htm [accessed January 10, 2004].

15. World Health Organization. *Severe Acute Respiratory Syndrome (SARS): Status of the Outbreak and Lessons*

for the Immediate Future; WHO: Geneva, 20 May, 2003; 5.

16. Quah, S.R.; Lee, H.-P. Crisis Prevention and Management During SARS Outbreak, Singapore. In *Emerging Infectious Diseases [serial online] [accessed December 20, 2003]*; Feb, 2004. Available from http://www.cdc.gov/ncidod/EID/vol10no2/03-0418.htm.

Decentralization in Southeast Asia

Ledivina V. Cariño
University of the Philippines, Diliman, Quezon City, Philippines

INTRODUCTION

Decentralization is an important political process that holds the promise of enhancing any society's enjoyment of democracy and development. This article focuses on how its two principal types, devolution and deconcentration, have been manifested in Southeast Asia. Specifically, it discusses how colonialism and the later struggle against home-grown authoritarian regimes have put a stamp on the efforts of the countries of the region to close the gap between the rulers and the ruled. The present trend is a movement from centralization to devolution, with even those states choosing deconcentration doing so within a larger governance framework of a limited state and popular participation. The article ends with warnings about possible pitfalls of decentralization and how these may be contained.

PRINCIPAL DECENTRALIZATION CONCEPTS: DEVOLUTION AND DECONCENTRATION

"Decentralization" refers to the transfer of powers, functions, and resources away from the central government. It is supposed to bring government closer to the people. How it does that depends on the type of decentralization chosen. Greater physical access to government offices and services can be accomplished through "deconcentration," which is the creation of a system of field units staffed by civil servants who draw their salaries from, and implement programs drawn up by, the central government. Deconcentration, also called "administrative decentralization," is more strictly defined as the transfer of functions and resources alone, because power remains at the center and the transfer is effected to agents of the central government that remain responsible to, and are controlled by, it. The expected main strengths of deconcentration are greater efficiency in service provision and the equal treatment of all localities within the national territory.

Government can also be brought closer to the people by granting them power to select their own officials, and, through them or directly, make the decisions for their own localities. This type of decentralization is called "devo-lution," where the central government transfers powers to elected local governments. Devolution, also called "political decentralization," is usually accompanied by local autonomy and is often regarded as the higher form of decentralization. In fact, "decentralization," unqualified, is usually used as a synonym of devolution.

Devolution shares with deconcentration the advantage of improved access and efficiency. However, the principal strengths of devolution lie in its accountability and responsiveness to the people. Although the center continues to see to it that all local governments maintain national standards and less developed ones are assisted in the performance of their functions, the accountability of local governments is primarily to its citizens. Because of this, it is expected to fashion programs more in tune with the particular demands of its local inhabitants, instead of being bound by the homogenizing ethic that deconcentration follows.

Deconcentration and devolution are two ends of a continuum rather than mutually exclusive categories. For instance, devolution in the Philippines is widely accepted as the most evolved in the region, with local governments elected for the last half-century and major functions transferred to these local units since 1991. However, education, the biggest sector (accounting for 18% of the state budget and a third of the civil service force), remains a deconcentrated function. Besides, the central government continues to perform some of the devolved functions instead of concentrating on national standard setting, monitoring, and incentives provision, its appropriate roles in a regime of devolution.

Also, federalism, being a union of autonomous subnational units called states, is usually associated with devolution. However, despite having the only federal structure in the region, Malaysia maintains a deconcentrated system of governance. Local chief executives of the states are either hereditary or appointed by the Malaysian king, the *Yang di Pertuan Agong*. In turn, the state governments appoint the heads of local bodies. Moreover, the federal government can make and has made binding decisions on matters in the State List, with nary a complaint from the local units. Besides, close to 85% of total government revenues accrues to the federal government, giving the states very little room to fund their own programs.[1]

Encyclopedia of Public Administration and Public Policy
DOI: 10.1081/E-EPAP 120024437

The wide variety of arrangements and processes that fall under the rubric of decentralization conveys a sense of the complexity of the concept. No nation has stuck to only one option, and the decentralization regime of each country is a product of its own history and culture; the pressures of its political, economic, and social forces; and even the demands of the global environment.

IMPACT OF COLONIALISM ON SOUTHEAST ASIAN DECENTRALIZATION

Western colonialism to a large extent drew the boundaries of the nations of Southeast Asia, and its legacy continues to be manifested in the decentralization status and struggles of these nations. What is now Malaysia consists of individual kingdoms until the 18th and 19th centuries. The British consolidated them as a federation under a British resident-general, with each territory ran by their respective sultans with a British adviser. Thus the federal structure of Malaysia has its roots in colonial times. Meanwhile, French Indo-China consisted of Cochin China, Tonkin, Annam, Laos, and Cambodia. Upon independence, Laos and Cambodia claimed the land of their precolonial kingdoms, while the first three territories formed the present Vietnam.

Perhaps the most problematic colonial bequests are the archipelagoes of Indonesia and the Philippines whose component islands were separate kingdoms until they were ruled as single colonies by the Netherlands and Spain, respectively. The idea of a single nation was born practically only in their respective struggles for independence.

The Netherlands imposed a federation of 15 republics on newly independent Indonesia in 1947. This was reversed with the creation of a unitary state in 1950. At present, most of the former Dutch East Indies have accepted the idea of national unity under one Indonesia, except for Aceh and Papua whose demand is for independence. Indonesia has responded with Law 18/2001 and Law 22/2001, granting them greater autonomy. East Timor, which was recently granted independence from Indonesia, used to be a Portuguese, and not a Dutch colony. For the rest of the country, resistance has been directed instead against the centralizing policies of Jakarta and the loss of regional identity and autonomy. Similarly, the Philippine territory is defined as it was when the United States (successor colonizers to Spain) left in 1946, but secessionist movements raged in areas not completely colonized by the West. The Philippine government countered with proposals to give autonomous status to Muslim Mindanao and the Cordilleras, upon approval by their inhabitants in a special plebiscite. The organic laws were accepted in parts of Mindanao but not in the Cordilleras; thus the former enjoys devolved powers while the latter remains simply an administrative region. In the case of both Indonesia and the Philippines, the autonomy afforded these territories is an exception to the general level of devolution provided to the rest of the local governments in these nations.

While there is no necessary historical sequence to decentralization, most countries experience it first as deconcentration. It has been said that in Thailand, anyone wishing to ignore the government simply disappears into the hinterlands.[2] However, a field unit makes that less possible. Thus deconcentration extends the reach of the State. Moreover, it also attempts to maintain equity and justice by treating all areas as homogeneous parts of the territory. Nevertheless, with no accountability to the people it serves while being so distant from the center to which it is supposed to be responsible, that unit may simply intone, as the Spanish colonial field officials used to say in the Philippines, ''obedezco pero no cumplo'' (''I obey but I do not comply'').[3] Thus rules and regulations that stream from the center may be followed to the letter, but the spirit of service and equity that animates them may be lost as they move down through several layers of the bureaucratic hierarchy.

GROWTH OF DEMOCRACY AND DEVOLUTION

The last decade of the 20th century has seen a clear trend in Southeast Asia toward devolution and a loosening of central control even in deconcentration. Devolution has commended itself as a result of the growth of democracy, or at least, the idea of democracy, in the region, and the rise of an awakened citizenry that demands a say in governance. These factors are associated with economic growth and an expanding middle class. They are complemented by the demonstration effect of experiences in neighboring countries, made visible and immediate by mass media, technological developments, intraregional information exchanges, and the support of international donor organizations for decentralization. The effects of these factors can be seen in the devolution experiences of the Philippines, Indonesia, Thailand, and Cambodia, all of whom emerged from authoritarian rule in the last 15 years of the last century.

The Philippines started the trend with the overthrow of Martial Law President Ferdinand E. Marcos in a peaceful 4-day ''People Power Revolution'' in 1986. In the redemocratization period that followed, it wrote into the Constitution of 1987 the principles of local autonomy and people's participation in governance. Although the Philippine decentralization movement has its roots in the 1960s with the election of councils at village level, the landmark devolution law was enacted only in 1991, with people power euphoria still in the air. The Local Government Code devolved major powers to local government units, and increased their revenues as well as their taxing powers. It also provided for citizen participation in local governance through the inclusion of people's representatives in five local special bodies.

Similarly, devolution in Indonesia is a component of *Reformasi*, the movement for reform that toppled the three-decade-long rule of President Suharto in 1996. Post-Suharto amendments to the constitution provide for wide-ranging autonomy to regional governments and democratically elected local legislatures at provincial, town, and city levels. Law 22/1999 and Law 25/1999 provide for devolution and its concomitant, fiscal decentralization, respectively. These laws are based on the principles of democracy, community participation, equity and justice, recognition of the potential and diversity within regions, and the need to strengthen local legislatures. Law 22 gives the provinces a dual status, as autonomous regions and as administrative arms of the center. Meanwhile, it gives full autonomy to districts and municipalities (rural and urban local governments, respectively), devolving powers to them except in security and defense, foreign policy, monetary and fiscal matters, and justice and religious affairs, similar to a federalistic allocation of powers.[4–7]

A peaceful revolution of the Thai middle class overthrew the military government in 1992, and gave rise to the new democratic Constitution of 1997. That constitution was both democratically written—because even ordinary citizens could submit their suggested drafts— and democratic in substance and spirit. It sought to enhance public participation in governance and to promote new channels for democracy, including a National Decentralization Committee that includes private citizens.[8] Nine articles on local self-rule and decentralization have served as the basis for a series of decentralization laws and policies passed since 1999. The most important of these is the National Decentralization Act, which specifies devolution in 4 years and change of the ratio of expenditure between central and local government from 91:9 in 1999 to 65:35 in 2006. Meanwhile, the Municipality Act of 2000 mandates that mayors of metropolitan municipalities and cities would be directly elected at the end of their current term.[9]

Cambodia, meanwhile, emerged from a bloody civil war that transformed it from a socialist state into a multiparty liberal democracy in 1993. Decentralization has been at the heart of its rehabilitation, being a feature of the *Seila* (Stone Foundation) Program and other reform initiatives of the Royal Government of Cambodia. A poverty-alleviation pilot program supported by the United Nations Development Program, Seila attacks poverty by strengthening local government structures from the commune level upward. The government has written Seila's decentralization mechanisms into the 2001 Law of Administration of Communes. In 2002, elected commune officials replaced state appointees and started to wield powers in order and security, health, economic and social development planning, cultural and environmental property, and general welfare.[10]

For the other countries, deconcentration remains the prevailing decentralization mode. However, recognizing the problems of central control that it represents, administrative decentralization is now embodied within a larger governance framework that involves providing field units more autonomy, the participation of the citizens, and fledgling efforts toward elected local units. The size of the city-state of Singapore gives it little option except deconcentration, but it is nevertheless moving away from classic central control to allowing more autonomy to be exercised by administrative units such as schools and health centers. This has happened even in Vietnam, a socialist State that recognizes the Communist Party as the force leading State and society and practices democratic centralism. The Government is the executive body of the National Assembly and the highest administrative body of the State. It directs the work of ministries at the central level as well as People's Committees (PCOMs), the executive bodies at the local levels. Although People's Councils are elected at provincial, district, and commune levels, they are supervised and guided by the Standing Committee of the National Assembly and the Government and are thus not autonomous local bodies. Nevertheless, as the program of *doi moi* (renovation) is moving the country from a centrally planned to a more market-oriented economy, Vietnam's Public Administration Reform (PAR) program embodies a complex decentralization agenda. Launched in 1995, PAR specifies the centralization of all regulation-making tasks and the decentralization of economic and social decision making. Thus the Grass-roots Democracy Decree (No. 29, passed in 1998) gave elected commune-level administrations the task of ensuring that the citizens exercise their rights, and that government be accountable to households for information about local activities and finances.

CONCLUSIONS: PROBLEMS AND CHALLENGES FOR DECENTRALIZATION

The popularity of decentralization in all the countries of the region does not imply that it is a panacea for all the ills of governance and development. There is a need for complementary policies and measures to be able to achieve poverty reduction, people's participation, and economic development.

Moreover, there are problems associated with decentralization itself. If power is transferred to officials who care more for their self-interest than the general welfare, decentralization can conceivably nurture fiefdoms of corruption and abuse. This suggests the need for decentralization to be accompanied by strong accountability mechanisms, such as local media and civil society, and impartial central oversight agencies. Many analysts also point to the issue of fiscal decentralization, which do not necessarily move concomitantly with power decentralization. Some countries decentralize power but keep the control of funds at the center, making the local units incapable of adequately serving their constituents. On the other hand, a generous center may keep local units dependent on its largesse and unable or unwilling to generate local revenues that could make them unpopular with the people. Other problems may arise because of the weakness of the new decentralized structures, the lack of competent officials and staff in many localities or their greed and power-hunger, and the absence of active citizens and institutions that can help both in capability building and in exacting accountability from the field units and local governments. Decentralization is a means of moving government closer to the people. Yet as has been seen, in many Southeast Asian countries, this is not a one-way street as the people have gotten new decentralization policies through their own demands and struggles. A similar militancy is necessary so that its gains are constantly monitored and defended and its ills minimized.

REFERENCES

1. Celestino, A.B. Malaysia: Does It Really Need Decentralization? In *Decentralization and Power Shift: An Imperative for Good Governance (A Sourcebook on Decentralization Experiences in Asia)*; Brillantes, A.B., Jr., Cuachon, N.G., Eds.; Asian Resource Center for Decentralization: Diliman, Quezon City, 2002; Vol. l, 137– 150.

2. Siffin, W.B. *The Thai Bureaucracy: Institutional Change and Development*; East-West Center Press: Honolulu, 1966.

3. Endriga, J.N. Historical notes on graft and corruption in the Philippines. Philipp. J. Public Adm. **July–October 1979**, *23* (3–4), 241–254.

4. Asanuma, S.; Brodjonegoro, B. *Indonesia's Decentralization Policy: Origins, Issues and Policy Directions*; 2003. http://www.gtzsfdm.or.id/documents/dec_ind/o_pa_doc/Shinji_Brodjonegoro_DecentralizationPolicy_Sept2003.pdf.

5. Esden, B. Indonesia: Rising Above Challenges. In *Decentralization and Power Shift: An Imperative for Good Governance (A Sourcebook on Decentralization Experiences in Asia)*; Brillantes, A.B., Jr., Cuachon, N.G., Eds.; Asian Resource Center for Decentralization: Diliman, Quezon City, 2002; Vol. 1, 115–126.

6. Mokhsen, N. *Decentralization in the Post New Order Era of Indonesia*; 2003. http://www.commonwealthseminar.org.nz/Papers2003/Nuraida%20Mohksen%20Indonesia%20-Decentralisation%20Case%20Study.pdf.

7. Rocamora, J. *Legal and Policy Frameworks for 'Participation' in Southeast Asia*; 2003. LogoLink Research. http://www.ids.ac.uk/logolink/resources/downloads/regionalreports/RegionalReportSoutheastAsia 20fmal.pdf.

8. Mutebi, A.M. *Thailand's Decentralization Experiment: Evolution, Dimensions, and Challenges*; 2003. http://www.fas.nus.edu.sg/ppp/wp/wp46.pdf.

9. Cuachon, N. Thailand: The Continuing Quest for Local Autonomy. In *Decentralization and Power Shift: An Imperative for Good Governance (A Sourcebook on Decentralization Experiences in Asia)*; Brillantes, A.B., Jr., Cuachon, N.G., Eds.; Asian Resource Center for Decentralization: Diliman, Quezon City, 2002; Vol. 1, 165–172.

10. Tumanut, M. Cambodia: Hitting the Road. In *Sourcebook on Decentralization in Asia*; 2002; 94–101. http://www.decentralization.ws/srcbook/cambodia.pdf.

FURTHER READING

International Development Research Center. *Some Socio-Economic Features Related to Decentralization*; 1997. http://www.idrc.ca/socdev/pub/vietnam/ch1.html.

Mok, K.-h.; Chan, D. *Decentralization and Marketization of Education in Singapore: A Case Study of School Excellence Model*; 2002. http://personal.cityu.edu.hk/~samiclee/middle_activities_501.html.

Quan, N.M. *Decentralization in Vietnam: Key Issues and Possible Solutions*; 2002. http://www.decentralization.ws.icd2.decent__vietnam.htm.

Rasyid, E.; Sugiyanto, C.; Ozeki, Y. *Local Government Capacity Constraints and Decentralization in Indonesia*; 2002. http://www.gtzsfdm.or.id/documents/dec_ind/o_pa_doc/LocGovtCapacity_Rasyid%20et.al.%20Sept2003.pdf.

Sutherland, H.; Raben, R.; Locher-Scholten, E. *Rethinking Regionalism: Changing Horizons in Indonesia 1950s–2000s*; 2000. http://www.knaw.nl/indonesia/transition/workshop/chapter3sutherlandrabenlocher-s.pdf.

Suwondo, K. *Decentralization in Indonesia*; 2002. http://www.infid.be/INFID%20Background%202002%20Decentralisation.pdf.

The Commune Council Support Project. *NGO Statement to the 2001 Consultative Group Meeting on Cambodia*; 2001. http://www.bigpond.com.kh/users/ngoforum/cg2001/commune_admin.htm.

Democracy and Public Policy

Dale Krane
Gary S. Marshall
University of Nebraska at Omaha, Omaha, Nebraska, U.S.A.

INTRODUCTION

Any discussion of the definition, the attributes, or the purposes of democracy invariably entails a consideration of public policy. The two terms, although distinct and different, are closely intertwined. Democracy is a form of government and, as such, refers to a system of authority and power. Discussions of democratic theory revolve around the organization and use of political power within a society—who should govern, how they should govern, and for what ends or purposes they should govern. By contrast, public policy refers to a purposive course of action established by public officials that is binding on the residents of a community or nation. Simply put, public policy is what governments choose to do or choose not to do.[1] Who exercises power or has authority to take actions binding on a community or a society will obviously affect what actions are selected or not selected. Likewise, the organization of authority will also shape its use as manifested in policy choice. Because of this link between form of government and performance of government, the theory of democracy, in Henry Mayo's[2] words, "... is one answer to the question of how the political policy decisions are made and should be made."

DEFINITIONS OF DEMOCRACY

Since its emergence in Greek political thought, the literal definition of democracy, "rule of the people," has remained more or less constant. But how this simple two-element formula of *demos* (people) and *kratos* (power) is interpreted and translated into actual practice has been a major industry in political theory circles from Socrates and Solon to Rousseau and Mills to the multitude of today's theorists. Books addressing questions such as "Who are the people?," Which people should exercise power?," and "How many people are required to make a decision binding on the community?" fill whole sections of libraries around the world. "Today the term *democracy* [italics in original]," Dahl observes,[3] "is like an ancient kitchen midden packed with assorted leftovers from twenty-five hundred years of nearly continuous usage." Yet, these definitional debates can be distilled down to the basic issue of identifying "... the best constitutional means of approaching the ideal, it already agreed that this ideal includes or involves a large participation of the common people in the forming of public policy"[2] (as quoted by Mayo from Robinson, Richard: *Definition.* Oxford 1949, 166).

Much of the theorizing about democracy falls into one of two perspectives. For much of its history, democracy was conceived as a form of government applicable only to communities of relatively modest populations such as the Greek city-states or the Italian and Swiss cities of the Renaissance period. Within small-scale societies, the people, usually defined as the (male) citizens, formed the government, typically an assembly of the whole, and decisions of the assembly were binding on citizens as well as all other residents of the community. This theoretical position is often labeled as *direct democracy* and "... is principally concerned with ensuring democratic rights for the *community* as a whole." [italics in original].[4]

Critical to direct democracy is the notion that citizens possess the capacity and the volition to govern themselves. Rule of the people requires "rule by the people," or self-government. Direct democracy rests on two core principles: 1) citizens are "sovereign"; that is, citizens make public policy and 2) each citizen is legally and politically equal to every other citizen. Also necessary to direct democracy are two important rules: 1) when unanimity does not exist among citizens, the preference of the largest number of citizens becomes public policy, and 2) freedom to express one's opinion about public policy is protected, and the majority may not "silence" the minority (though the minority must obey policy decisions until the decision is changed). Because policy decisions reflect the choice of the community, policy must be obeyed by all citizens, officials as well as nonofficials. Furthermore, the processes of deciding and then administering public policies are legitimate only if the established procedures have been followed. That is to say, political power is limited by a set of rules as to how it will be exercised. Instead of government by privilege or by force, government acts through popular consent.[5] Direct democracy, it should be noted, is not immune to the problems commonly associated with the exercise of power such as the difficulties of 1) arriving at a community-wide

Encyclopedia of Public Administration and Public Policy
DOI: 10.1081/E-EPAP 120011076

consensus, 2) controlling conflict among citizens with different preferences, and 3) ensuring compliance with the collective decision.

As modern nation-states developed between the 1600s and the 1800s, rapid population growth and urbanization posed a significant challenge to democratic theorists. The sense that direct, communal democracy in a large-scale city or country was untenable became increasingly widespread. If it was impossible for each person to participate in the deliberation and choice of public policy in a large city or country, then democracy had to be redefined. It was crucial to find ways for citizens to control the government as well as to be protected from actions by the government that would lessen or eliminate "popular sovereignty." Liberal ideas of representation were proposed as a solution, and rule by the people was redefined as the choice of one's rulers.

The ideas motivating the revolutionary break from the medieval order strongly influenced the second perspective to democracy. Instead of democracy embodied in a community-wide consensus, "general will," or "public interest," democracy became associated with the revolutionary ideal that each person, to quote Thomas Jefferson, has "certain unalienable Rights." If the people were to rule, then each person had to be guaranteed the exercise of certain rights such as belief, speech, assembly, and representation. Likewise, certain limits had to be established beyond which the community could not impose its will on the individual (NB: limits also had to be imposed on individual behavior). If every person was inherently equal, then a mechanism that allowed each person to express a preference for who would rule had to be developed. Furthermore, because most persons could not devote all of their energy and time to the occupation of ruler, then those few persons who would rule had to be held accountable to the ruled.

Elections became the set of procedures held to be most important to the operation and maintenance of a democracy. If the question is when do people exercise popular sovereignty, the answer, according to Sartori,[6] "is easy—during elections." Citizens would select rulers from candidates who sought votes by offering different visions of public policy, and the candidate that attracted the most support (votes) became the ruler, typically in the form of a representative to an assembly of elected officials who had the authority to make public policy.

Once elections became the mechanism through which the people ruled, then the procedural rules for the conduct of elections became a matter of high interest for citizens, candidates, and officials. Important procedural questions included the following: who may vote, who may be a candidate, how are votes counted, may candidates form groups of like-minded candidates (i.e., political parties),

how many representatives will serve in the legislative assembly, how will representatives be selected by voters (e.g., by geographic territory or by occupation), how long a term will each representative serve, and may a representative become a candidate in the next election? Because many different answers to these questions can be devised, different nations have developed different electoral procedures. Consequently, indirect or representative democracy is characterized by a variety of electoral procedures.

These two distinct perspectives on the definition of a democracy—communal vs. individual—bear directly on how one arrives at a policy decision as well as what constitutes legitimate public policy. Direct democracy holds that public policy emanates from decisions made by the whole community, or, to paraphrase Rousseau, sovereignty cannot be represented. Thus, only a collective body composed of all or as many members of the community as practical can truly determine the "... common identity, its life and its will."[7] The test of public policy in a direct democracy is whether it "embodies a moral imperative for people to promote common interests."[7] Indirect democracy, by contrast, holds that the realities of daily life make it impossible to involve all or most citizens in the continual process of policy making. Put another way, if every adult citizen devoted significant amounts of time to making public policy, there would be no one left to perform all the other tasks necessary to a functioning society. Therefore, some citizens must be selected to form a government and make public policy. Policy decisions are legitimate if they are made by the elected representatives of the people. The key to indirect democracy is the creation of one or more mechanisms by which the people exercise control over the representatives and the policy choices they make. Because each representative is presumed to express the views of the individuals who elected the representative, it is also presumed that a wide range of opinions will exist among the representatives. Consequently, policy will not reflect the "common will" or the "public interest"; instead, public policy will be, as Madison argued, the product of bargaining and negotiation among the individual representatives.

ATTRIBUTES OF DEMOCRACY

Democracy has always been a contested concept, not just in terms of what democracy means in the abstract, but also what constitutes an actual, functioning democracy. What are the identifiable attributes or features that make possible (or better, probable) "rule by the people?" On what bases or criteria can we decide that one nation (or community) is democratic, while another is not? Democracy as an ideal ultimately has to be translated and transformed into governing institutions that resolve societal problems and produce policy decisions that reflect the consent of the governed.

Citizen influence over policy makers and policy decisions occurs in both democratic and nondemocratic regimes. Benevolent dictators populate the pages of history, and even tyrants understand that it is often too costly to ignore popular opinion in every policy decision. If not popular influence, then what? The most typical single answer given by scholars is popular control of policy makers and policy decisions. But even this change of one word (control for influence) does not clearly distinguish democratic government from nondemocratic ones. Obviously then, multiple mechanisms are necessary to ensure "rule by the people," and so scholars of democracy have sought to construct lists of attributes by which they identify a government as democratic.

Although several scholars have offered particular lists, the most widely known and cited list of political institutions that characterize modern democratic government is the one proposed by Robert Dahl. Since his early masterpiece *A Preface To Democratic Theory* in 1956, Dahl has sought to identify the distinguishing marks of democratic government. His current version[8] includes 1) elected officials, 2) free, fair, and frequent elections, 3) freedom of expression, 4) access to alternative sources of information, 5) associational autonomy, and 6) inclusive citizenship.

Of the six that Dahl identifies, other scholars typically concur with his first four or five features of democratic government: elected representatives, noncoercive elections, basic political freedoms, associational autonomy, and access to independent information. In a very real sense, the marks of a modern democracy were first specified in the U.S. Constitution's initial 10 amendments, the "Bill of Rights."

It should be noticed that political equality is not specifically included in Dahl's list; rather, equality is implicit in the notion that (practically) all citizens have rights to vote, to run for public office, and to exercise a broad range of political freedoms. Also missing from Dahl's list is the requirement for majority rule. It is omitted because majority rule is simply one of several possible decision rules by which an assembly of citizens or representatives may arrive at a decision. Representative bodies in democratic nations function with different decision rules, including plurality, simple majority, and various forms of extraordinary majorities (more than 50%+1).

Dahl's list of fundamental requirements must be present in any political system that is to be considered

democratic, but they may be manifested in very different political institutions and policy processes. Comparative studies of democratic politics, to simplify a large body of research, recognize at least three distinct models of democratic political institutions, each of which exhibits a different style of policy making. Variations of each of the three models exist, but the basic institutional differences among the three models are critical to the particular styles of policy making and the way in which popular sovereignty is exercised.

Parliamentary institutions combined with a majoritarian political party system constitute the first model, sometimes referred to as the "Westminster" model, after the Palace of Westminster where the British Parliament meets. The key features (although not all) of Westminster majoritarian democracy are 1) fusion of executive and legislative power, 2) executive power concentrated in a ministerial cabinet, 3) asymmetric bicameralism, 4) exclusively representative government, 5) unitary, centralized government, and 6) two-party system. Majoritarian, parliamentary institutions provide for "rule by the people" through an emphasis on a responsible, strong political party model in that two parties contend for popular support by offering competing policy visions. The winning party gains essentially exclusive control over the instruments of government action and is expected to enact its policy platform. The leader of the majority party in the parliament is also the prime minister who selects the cabinet, thus there is unified control across legislative and executive institutions. Only a vote of no confidence or a loss at the next scheduled election can seriously undermine the party in power's control over public policy. The United Kingdom is the preeminent example of this model, and many of its former colonies exhibit this form of democratic government.[9]

Presidential government is a second model of indirect democratic government, and is characterized by a formal separation of powers between executive and legislative institutions. Instead of the fusion of legislative and executive powers that typify parliamentary government, the executive "head of state" in presidentialist governments is selected independently from the legislative branch and cannot be removed by the legislature, except for very serious reasons and through complex procedures. Presidents may propose new policy directions but cannot enact them into law because the legislature is independent of the executive. Instead, the president must build a coalition of legislators (of the president's party or other parties) that is willing to support the executive's policy preferences. Presidential systems may be unitary or federal, may have two or more political parties, and may have a bicameral legislature, especially if the country is large in territory.

Presidential governments provide for popular sovereignty through the following three key features: 1) the independent election of the executive from the legislative members of the government, thus reducing the concentration of power in the hands of one office or institution, 2) policy making requires bargaining within and between each legislative chamber as well as between the legislature and the executive, thus ensuring that a multiplicity of views are represented, and 3) because the executive is typically the only public official elected by the whole electorate, the president's policy positions are considered to be those of the electorate (or at least of those who voted for the incumbent).[10] The United States of America is the preeminent example of presidential government, and it can also be found in several Latin American nations.

A third model of representative democratic government combines the parliamentary form with the presidential to create what is labeled as a "dual power," or "semi-presidential" government. The key institutional features include the following: 1) an independently elected head of state [the president], 2) a legislatively selected head of government [the prime minister], 3) an executive cabinet presided over by the prime minister, and 4) a legislature elected independently from the head of state. These nations usually have unitary government, multiple political parties, and may have a unicameral or a bicameral legislature. The reputed benefits for popular sovereignty of a dual-power government are: 1) the stability associated with an independent president, 2) the flexibility of a parliamentary majority, and 3) the ability to avoid potential stalemates between the president and the legislature. France is the preeminent example of a "dual-power" democracy, and other examples can be found in Portugal, Finland, the Czech Republic, Poland, Estonia, Lithuania, and Slovenia.[10]

Each of these three models of democratic government vary by institutional features, style of leadership, nature of policy bargaining, and constitutional rules. The organization of these different types of democratic government affects differentially the ability of citizens to influence policy making. For example, in parliamentary governments, much of the bargaining and debate over policy choices occurs as part of the electoral competition, and once a party wins a parliamentary majority, it can enact its policy platform without any serious obstacles. By contrast, in presidential models, bargaining and debate over policy continue past the election of the president and the legislature, and as a consequence, it is often the case that each policy initiative requires an extensive effort to build a bipartisan majority to support the proposal. The point here is simply that the ideal of "rule by the people" must be transformed from ideas

to functioning institutions and rules by which governing institutions produce policy results that are acceptable and legitimate.

PURPOSES OF DEMOCRACY

Governments of whatever form exhibit some common purposes, among which are social order, dispute resolution, coordination of collective action, and protection from external attack. But many different forms of government have been established with the intent of achieving certain objectives. For example, a Communist government seeks to ensure a dictatorship of the proletariat and to alter the means of production to create a socialist utopia.[11] Fascism sought to develop and maintain "the glory of the State" so that all other activity in society was subordinate to the State.[11] But what objectives are to be achieved by establishing a democratic government? Although there is no agreement as to what purposes democracy is designed to attain, there are at least five distinct answers to the question, and each of these answers contains an expectation about the goals of public policy in a democracy.[2]

The first answer about the purposes of a democratic government is implicit in the core notion of rule of the people. To ensure popular sovereignty, democratic government is designed to constrain the emergence of an elite or a permanent ruling class and to encourage widespread civic participation. The rules of the democratic political game, as expressed in law, create opportunities and resources so that citizens may participate in policy decisions. To put this another way, democratic government is rule by a continually changing cast of amateurs. Furthermore, there are no preordained goals for public action; instead, public policy will be the product of the continually shifting diversity of interests within the community. "All policies will be compromises, and it is unlikely that we shall find any democracy committed to one all-consuming purpose."[2]

Second and probably the most widely accepted purpose of democracy is the protection of individual rights. Liberal democrats, in their revolutionary attacks on the absolutist State, defined freedom as independence from government control. Jefferson's (and Thomas Paine's) dictum that "the best government is the one that governs least" concisely captures this attitude, but it is important to understand that the context was one where the State controlled most spheres of human activity—commerce and trade, religion and culture, property and status. Locke, who was Jefferson's inspiration, argued that every power government exercised came at the expense of individual liberty and, therefore, the less public policy the better. Rousseau, on the other hand, argued that individual rights could be increased by government action, e.g., where public policy restricts the rights of employers in order to eliminate unacceptable practices such as gender and racial biases in hiring or child labor.[12] This debate over negative vs. positive conceptions of freedom does not detract from the basic point that an important purpose of democratic governments is to constrain government as well as individual action to ensure rule by free consent of the governed.

The struggles that produced modern democratic nations were motivated not only by efforts to freely exercise religion and to freely choose one's rulers, but also to protect one's property from confiscation by the State. Much of the justification for limited government rests on the protection of personal property rights, and, by extension, it is often held that an important objective of democratic government is the maintenance of a free or market economy. The fact that one can find market economies in nondemocratic nations undermines part of this idea that only under democracy can capitalism flourish. However, because all democracies support capitalist markets, there is obviously a connection between these two distinct societal institutions.[3,13,14] The link is through public policy, which creates and enforces the rules required to sustain these two institutions. Both democracy and capitalism depend on the freedom of individual choice. Just as democracy depends on a set of procedural rules that provide for competition among candidates, so also does a liberal market depend on rules that provide for competition among producers. Critical to the functioning of market economies is an extensive set of laws and regulations ensuring free choice for producers and consumers, employers and workers. The contemporary efforts to foster economic development in the nations of the former Soviet Union illustrate the necessity of an extensive body of public policy that establishes and maintains the institutions of a modern capitalist economy (e.g., property ownership, enforceable contracts).

A fourth purpose, it is argued, that democracy serves is the development of the individual. The pursuit of equality has been part of the pursuit of liberty because freedom for only some individuals leaves others unfree and unequal. The Christian ideal of the inherent equality and worth of all individuals predates the development of modern democracy, but this idea strongly shaped the earliest arguments for democracy.[5] Without equality for all persons, the notion of government by consent of the governed is hollow, and so the campaigns to end government by hereditary rulers promised equality as well as liberty. Equality first meant equal franchise—the right to vote—but usually only for males with certain attributes—education, property, and/or race. It is only within recent history that universal suffrage has become widely accepted.[15]

Closely associated with equal franchise is the importance of the vote as a means for citizens to communicate their policy preferences to candidates and elected officials. If a whole class of persons is denied the right to vote (e.g., women), then matters of concern to this class of persons is likely to be ignored by public officials. Similarly, if one's vote counts less than someone else's vote (the problem of malapportionment), then one's policy interests will be disadvantaged. Furthermore, if one is not provided with the means to participate in the electoral process (e.g., education, information, finances), then one's ability to participate is diminished. Over time many democratic governments have enacted policies to foster equal participation and one can see the results in the increased diversity of today's elected (and administrative) officials, compared to previous eras.

More recent views on equality have focused on equality of opportunity—the provision of sufficient resources to individuals to permit them to pursue and "fulfill' their dreams. "The notion of democracy has always contained the notion of equality. Not arithmetical equality of income or wealth, but equality of opportunity to realize one's human capacities."[16] Predemocratic societies where most persons were serfs or slaves used force or tradition to prevent individuals from realizing their potential. Democratic governments were the first to proclaim the establishment of justice and the promotion of the general welfare as their principal purposes. This has led over time to a policy cornucopia of goods and services that today is labeled as the modern welfare state. From education to employment, from health to social security, the bulk of public policy in a modern democratic state aims to ensure a minimal quality of life for all and to facilitate, in the words of modern psychology, each person's "self-actualization."[17]

Perhaps the most unique purpose allegedly served by democracy is that it makes possible a new type of human character. "Democracy, then, both presupposes and tends to promote a particular type of character or personality; or alternatively we may say—since character is a slippery concept—that the system relies on certain attitudes or dispositions or behavior patterns and these it tends to foster because they contribute to the working of the system."[2] This argument goes back at least as far the writings of J. S. Mills and de Tocqueville, and has been revisited by such writers as James Bryce and Harold Lasswell. But how is it that a form of government can shape character or personality? An important answer is found in the recent writings that advocate "participatory democracy" as a remedy to the ills of liberal representative democracy. Critics of representative democracy such as Benjamin Barber see the reliance on elections, interest groups, and political parties as producing a "thin democracy" in which "citizenship is only legal matter; people are bound together by self-interested contracts; and they are politically passive" (as quoted in Ref. [7]). Departure from "possessive individualist ways of thought and action" (Macpherson's phrase to describe consumerism and self-centeredness), Carole Pateman claims, "is facilitated by a change in people's values that results from political participation itself" (as quoted in Ref. [7]). Democratic citizens are, in a sense, forced to be free; that is, in order to solve problems in the community they must act together collectively—there is no ruler ordering them to act. In a society where all are free to hold and express different views, a democrat not only must tolerate these differences of opinion, but also must strive to find compromises to which a majority can consent. Such complex attitudes and behaviors, it is argued, depend on the development of a public-regarding spirit, and nothing does more to foster this new character than participation in public affairs; that is, action can alter attitudes.

That there are multiple purposes associated with the advocacy of democracy comes as no surprise. Democracy became the wave of the future in the 1600s because the purposes it alleged to serve "fit the minds of men," in Burke's phrase. Freedom and liberty, equality and individuality, were exciting ideas that pointed away from tradition and toward a new society. Democracy's purposes, open and indeterminate, do not constitute the stuff of a dogmatic ideology,[2] but instead offer a design within which individuals can shape public policy to fit the general interest of their community. Sen[15] tells us that "a country does not have to be deemed fit *for* democracy; rather it has to become fit *through* democracy" [italics in original]. Democracy, as rule of the people, allows the people to enact public policies designed to pursue purposes that are beneficial to the community. This is what makes democracy, according to Sen,[15] "a universally relevant system."

CONCLUSION

The establishment of a democratic form of government is a fundamental public policy decision and makes popular sovereignty the primary principle of the policy-making process. Democracy depends on a set of necessary attributes, but how these critical features are built into governing institutions may vary from place to place.

Parliaments and presidents are merely instruments through which popular sovereignty may be achieved; what is critical to democracy is a sufficient level of citizen participation so that the policies selected reflect the diverse preferences and values within a community or country. Abraham Lincoln proclaimed the core ideas of democracy in his famous aphorism, "government of the people, by the people, and for the people." The continuing challenge to theorists of democracy as well as to citizens and public officials is the adaptation of the institutional features of government to changing societal conditions without sacrificing the core ideas of popular sovereignty. Just as direct democracy was modified to accommodate population growth, so too must representative democracy be modified to ensure popular sovereignty in a world characterized by deep economic and social inequalities. Although universal suffrage is now widely accepted in most parts of the globe, public policy to provide a minimal quality of life to all citizens has not been attained. Long ago, Jefferson pointed out that certain public policies such as universal education were necessary to a functioning democratic government. The continued impoverishment of a majority of the world's population stands as a major obstacle to the spread of democracy. But the continued existence of nondemocratic forms of government in too many places also blocks action to reduce severe economic and social inequalities. Sen[15] explains the pragmatic connection between the democratic procedures of government and the substance of public policy:

> Political and civil rights give people the opportunity to draw attention forcefully to the general needs and to demand appropriate public action. The response of a government to the acute suffering of its people often depends on the pressure that is put on it. The exercise of political rights (such as voting, criticizing, protesting, and the like) can make a real difference to the political incentives that operate on a government.

Democracy offers citizens a set of instrumental procedures and rules that allow citizens to shape public policy so that "rule of, by, and for the people" is possible. Other forms of government are neither premised on this goal nor are designed to foster it.

REFERENCES

1. Dye, T. *Policy Analysis: What Governments Do, Why They Do it, and What Difference it Makes*; University of Alabama Press, 1976.

2. Mayo, H. *Introduction to Democratic Theory*; Oxford University Press, 1960; pp. 28, 31, 244–278.

3. Dahl, R. *Dilemmas of Pluralist Democracy*; Yale University Press, 1982; pp. 5, 108–115.

4. Grugel, J. *Democratization: A Critical Introduction*; Palgrave, 2002; 14.

5. Muller, H. *Freedom in the Ancient World*; Bantam Books, 1961; 176–179.

6. Sartori, G. *Democratic Theory. Based on the Author's Translation of Democrazia E Definizione*, 2nd Ed.; Praeger: New York, 1965; 73.

7. Cunningham, F. *Theories of Democracy: A Critical Introduction*; Routledge, 2002; pp. 124, 130.

8. Dahl, R. *A Preface to Democratic Theory*; Yale University Press, 1998.

9. Lijphart, A. *Democracies; Patterns of Majoritarian and Consensus Government in Twenty-One Countries*; Yale University Press, 1984; 1–20.

10. Keman, H.; Mallouk, M. Democratic Institutions, Governance and Political Performance. In *Comparative Democratic Politics: A Guide to Contemporary Theory and Research*; Keman, H., Ed.; Sage Publications, 2002; 257–285.

11. Morstein Marx, F. *Foreign Governments: The Dynamics of Politics Abroad*; Prentice-Hall, 1952; 417–418.

12. Muller, H. *Freedom in the Western World: From the Dark Ages to the Rise of Democracy*; Harper Colophon Books, 1963; p. 345.

13. Lindblom, C. *Politics and Markets: The World's Political Economic Systems*; Basic Books, 1977; 161–169.

14. Macpherson, C. *The Real World of Democracy: The Massey Lectures*; Oxford University Press, 1966; 4.

15. Sen, A. Democracy as a universal value. J. Democr. **July 1999**, *10* (3), 3–17.

16. Macpherson, C. *The Real World of Democracy: The Massey Lectures*; Oxford University Press, 1966; 47.

17. Bay, C. *The Structure of Freedom*; Stanford University Press, 1965.

Development Administration in Southeast Asia

Mark Turner
University of Canberra, Canberra, Australian Capital Territory, Australia

INTRODUCTION

Development administration was welcomed into newly independent countries of Southeast Asia after the Second World War as a vehicle for facilitating economic and social development. The rate and nature of its adoption varied between countries and have been mediated by factors such as resource endowment, development policies, political regimes, and history. Thus the contemporary profile of development administration in Southeast Asia varies significantly between countries in the region. The appreciation of the importance of development administration for improving human welfare and economic progress has never been stronger, with all the regions' countries currently engaged in a variety of reforms and innovations selected from a lengthening list of possible development administration initiatives.

FROM DEVELOPMENT ADMINISTRATION TO DEVELOPMENT MANAGEMENT

Development administration was a form of social engineering imported from the West in the 1950s and 1960s, which was built on a belief in the application of rational scientific principles and Keynesian welfare economics. Governments in the West and Southeast Asia perceived it as a managerial weapon in the war against communism, which would stem revolutionary appeal by delivering the benefits of modern capitalist development. Its success in this venture was circumscribed by the triumph of revolutionary forces in Vietnam, Laos, and Cambodia.

Development administration demonstrated faith in a "big government" and the leading role the state should play in development. It was also synonymous with public administration, although it was distinguished from practices in rich countries by "that inconvenient combination: extensive needs, low capacities, and severe obstacles."[1] A tool bag of development administration interventions was created and transferred to Southeast Asia via foreign aid programs. In the 1970s, questions over the efficacy of this approach resulted in "a period of self-criticism, reflection, and uncertainty."[2] Development administration had reached a "deadlock,"[3] or was seen to be in "crisis."[4]

A rethinking of development administration was urgently needed. This coincided with the rise of neoclassical economics in determining the development agenda. Big government was out, and private sector ownership and management techniques were in. Thus new public management (NPM) was soon being exported to the public sectors of developing countries in Southeast Asia, although its reception was less than welcoming in many instances. Participation also moved to the mainstream of thinking either by nongovernmental organizations (NGOs), or by a renewed interest in territorial decentralization. The agenda of development administration broadened considerably beyond its early public administration focus to embrace diverse activities from privatization to community participation.

Today, we can define development administration, or development management as it is often known, as:

- An academic subfield in the social sciences
- Built around a set of problems relating to the management of development, rather than being a distinct body of theory
- Heavily but not exclusively focused on public administration
- Embracing a wide range of approaches to managing development, including actions by nonstate actors
- Being concerned with power and politics as determinants of development policy making and its implementation
- Applying to almost 75% of the world's population, residing in countries displaying diverse characteristics.

CONTEMPORARY SOUTHEAST ASIA

Development administration operates in a variety of contexts in Southeast Asia (Table 1). At one extreme, there is Singapore with a GNI per capita above that of its former colonial ruler, the UK; whereas at the other extreme, there are impoverished nations such as Cambodia and Laos. Populations are as large as 212 million in Indonesia, but are as low as 350,000 in Brunei. There are countries that have functioning democracies, semidemocracies, and one-party or authoritarian states. Culture is variegated both between countries and even within them.

Encyclopedia of Public Administration and Public Policy
DOI: 10.1081/E-EPAP-120024430

Table 1 Selected environmental features of Southeast Asian countries

Country	Population of 2002 (millions)	GNI per capita PPP of 2002 (US$)	GDP growth rate per capita (%) of 1999–2002	Adult literacy (%) age 15 years and above of 2002	Life expectancy of 2002 (years)	Political regime of 2002	Leading religion of 2002
Brunei	0.35	19,210		91.6	76.6	Sultanate	Islam
Cambodia	12	1,590	3.7	69.4	54.0	Multiparty democracy	Buddhism
Indonesia	212	2,990	1.7	87.3	66.2	Multiparty democracy	Islam
Lao PDR	6	1,610	3.5	66.4	54.5	One-party state	Buddhism
Malaysia	24	8,280	2.2	88.4	72.8	Semidemocracy	Islam
Myanmar	49	1,027	9.9	85.3	57.2	Military authoritarian	Buddhism
Philippines	80	4,280	1.8	95.4	69.8	Multiparty democracy	Roman Catholic, Islam
Singapore	4	23,090	3.4	92.8	78.4	Semidemocracy	Various
Thailand	62	6,680	3.3	95.8	69.2	Multiparty democracy	Buddhism
Vietnam	81	2,240	4.4	92.9	69.7	One-party state	Buddhism

Source: Ref. [5].

Thailand is predominantly Buddhist, the Philippines is Roman Catholic, and Indonesia is Moslem. However, there are small but significant Islamic minorities in Thailand and the Philippines, whereas Indonesia has substantial Christian and Hindu minorities. What this means is that the environment for development administration in Southeast Asia differs between countries—often quite dramatically. Thus the practices and innovations that are employed under this broad umbrella are many and vary according to circumstances.

PUBLIC ADMINISTRATION AND ITS REFORM IN SOUTHEAST ASIA

In Southeast Asia, the concept of bureaucracy as set out in Weber's ideal type has retained a strong appeal among civil service elites, who have most often been able to direct the design and implementation of public administration reform. They are attracted to what the model appears to offer—efficient administration, reliance on formal rules, hierarchy, and upward accountability—rather than by dysfunctions that have frequently characterized public administration in the region. For example, the Philippine public administration has been criticized for being under the influence of ''partisan politics, geographical ties, the compadre system, familial obligation, and personal factors.''[6] In Indonesia, dysfunctional civil service practices have included the sale of positions, extortion of money for promotions, seeking bribes for favorable decisions, and marking up project costs to secure illegal payments. Among the problems in Thailand's public service have been ''patronage and corruption in appointments and promotions, lack of performance incentives, and overcentralization.''[7] In Vietnam, there has been concern with the failure to integrate public administration reform with political strategies, the poor quality of legal documents, the overlapping and unclear definition of organizational functions, and low skill levels and budgeting geared to the number of staff rather than functional priorities or results.[8]

The dysfunctions of public administration have not been ignored in Southeast Asia. There is a long history of reform, although there have been considerable contrasts between countries. For example, Singapore and Malaysia have almost 50 years of experience with successful incremental reforms, whereas in the Philippines, despite most presidents having a comprehensive public administration reform program, not one has ever been implemented.[9] The governments of Vietnam and Lao PDR have, until recently, been reticent to engage in substantial public administration reforms, perhaps fearing a diminution of political control.

However, today, all countries in Southeast Asia are engaged in public administration reform, often with great enthusiasm. The reasons for the growing importance of public administration are as follows:

- A perceived link between public administration and international competitiveness
- The potential contribution good public administration can make to sustainable human development
- Democratization requiring reconsideration of the relationship between state and society
- The promotion and support of good governance, including public administration reform, by multilateral and bilateral development agencies.

The dominant theme in public administration reform across Southeast Asia has been bureaucratic modernization. Although the preferred method of reform has been incremental adjustments, there is currently some interest in systemic reforms. For example, in Vietnam, a Public Administration Master Plan has been introduced for the period 2001–2010. It builds on prior incremental changes and includes the following:

1. Program to renovate the development, issuance, and quality improvement of legal normative documents
2. Program on roles, functions, and organizational structures of the agencies in the administrative system
3. Program on staff downsizing
4. Program on improving the quality of cadres and civil servants
5. Program on salary reform
6. Program on renovation of financial management mechanisms for administrative and public service delivery agencies
7. Program to modernize the administrative system.

These are not new ideas. The novel aspect is putting them together in an integrated program on a major scale, guided by a vision of what the government hopes to achieve. Thailand has also commenced an ambitious program of systemwide public administration reforms. The civil service has, in the past, been able to resist any radical reforms due to its powerful position in the Thai state. However, the gradual erosion of that power and the impact of the Asian financial crisis in 1997 provided the policy opportunity and impetus for the introduction of far-reaching changes to the public service. These include a move toward ''strategic performance-based budgeting''; the introduction of accrual accounting; a more efficient and transparent procurement process; improved procedures in revenue collection, especially through new information and communications technology; reorganization of the structures and functions of ministries; the introduction of results-based management; and the establishment of a Public Sector Development Commission (PSDC) to monitor public sector reform and advise the cabinet on policy.[10]

Although there has been considerable interest across Southeast Asia in public administration reforms in other countries, there has been only a limited adoption of NPM. If we view NPM as a menu of items, then we can classify the countries of Southeast Asia into three distinct groups according to the number of items selected for implementation.[11] Singapore and Malaysia are "enthusiastic diners" having introduced a wide range of NPM-style reforms. However, some initiatives are not new for these countries, whereas other items from the NPM menu have not been introduced. Borrowing reform initiatives and modifying them to suit local conditions have long histories in Malaysia and Singapore. The Philippines, Thailand, and Indonesia can be described as "cautious diners" because they are familiar with the menu but so far have experimented with a few reforms from the NPM menu. However, Thailand's new reform program may lift it into the "enthusiastic diners" category. Finally, there are those countries that are "unfamiliar with the menu," such as Lao PDR, Cambodia, and Vietnam. The governments appreciate the need for public sector reform and are, to some degree, engaged in it. However, they lack institutions and other environmental conditions necessary for NPM reforms.

There are several important variables that explain the differential adoption of NPM and the widespread persistence of bureaucratic modernization as the overriding reform theme across Southeast Asia. First, the most NPM-friendly countries are also the wealthiest, and, in the cases of Singapore and Malaysia, have many institutions derived from Britain—the heartland of NPM. In poor countries such as Lao PDR or Cambodia, NPM-style reforms may be unaffordable, impractical, and irrelevant. Second, state–society relations in Southeast Asia involve greater responsibility for national development being claimed by the state than in Organization for Economic Cooperation and Development (OECD) countries. Third, there are Southeast Asian values that may clash with NPM notions of public administration reform. These values could include group reference rather than individual reference; conflict avoidance; importance of "face"; respect for authority and seniority; paternalism; respect for academic credentials; undervaluation of the professional role of women; belief in cosmology and superstition; and the importance of family support.[12,13] Although these values may also be found in Western countries, their relative importance and particular combination in Southeast Asia produce different behavioral outcomes. Fourth, the political regimes of Southeast Asia show considerable diversity—ranging from authoritarianism in Burma,

through one-party regimes in Vietnam and Lao PDR, to semidemocracies in Malaysia and Singapore, to "elite democracy" in the Philippines. Some of these regimes are not receptive to particular NPM initiatives, especially those that could be seen to diminish regime power and legitimacy. Finally, some items on the NPM menu fit well with the longstanding Southeast Asian theme of bureaucratic modernization focusing on efficiency gains.

DECENTRALIZATION

One of the most significant trends in development administration in Southeast Asia has been decentralization. Power and authority have been taken from centralized bureaucracies and have devolved to elected local councils or deconcentrated offices of central agencies. The driving forces behind decentralization have been democratization and the belief that service delivery will be improved. The Philippines was the first country to decentralize through the Local Government Code of 1991. This legislation gave local government units responsibility for basic services in health, agriculture, public works, social welfare, and environment and natural resources. Funds to pay for these new functions were also given to the elected councils at provincial, city, municipal, and barangay (community) levels. Participation by NGOs and the private sector in local governance was also decreed in the Local Government Code of 1991. The general opinion is that the decentralization in the Philippines has been "fairly successful" in bringing devolved democratic governance to people across the Philippines.[14,15] Whether it has led to improved service delivery is more difficult to determine.

Indonesia was the next country to engage in decentralization. Under the authoritarian New Order regime of President Suharto, Indonesia had been a highly centralized state. Hasty legislation (Laws 22 and 25 of 1999) after Suharto's removal from office resulted in Southeast Asia's most radical decentralization program. The regional hierarchy was abolished, leading to a considerable reduction in the authority and importance of the province, and a great increase in the authority of the districts. A long list of functions was placed under the control of the autonomous districts. The list includes public works, health, education and culture, agriculture, communication, industry and trade, capital investment, environment, land, cooperatives, "manpower affairs," and the management of national resources. Locally elected assemblies have become very important as they now set regional policy and manage vastly increased resources. Implementation has been problematic. The schedule was too short; the legislation had some fundamental weaknesses and is to be revised; the regulatory program necessitated by Laws 22 and 25 has not been completed; there are regional inequities; accountability provisions are suspect; and "money politics" has arrived in the regions.[16]

Further experiments in decentralization have taken place in Thailand where the current government is enhancing the powers of the provincial governors—now referred to as chief executive officers (CEOs)—at the expense of central ministries, and is also trying to enhance the role of the grassroots Tambon Councils. In Cambodia, steps have been taken to both devolve and deconcentrate.[17] Devolution is to the elected Commune Councils while deconcentration is to the field offices of ministries such as health, education, and agriculture. Progress has been slow, with very limited resources and functions devolved to the Commune Councils, whereas deconcentration moves at a pace and in a manner determined by cautious central ministries.

CONCLUSION

All governments in Southeast Asia appreciate the importance of development administration for national development, and all are engaged in reform initiatives to improve the performance of their public service and local government institutions. The longstanding theme of bureaucratic modernization is still evident in public administration reforms to increase the efficiency of the government by initiatives such as reducing red tape, introducing ICT, and downsizing and strengthening budgetary procedures. This has been accompanied by decentralization experiments in the Philippines, Indonesia, Cambodia, and Thailand. The pace and content of reforms have varied between countries according to a range of environmental features. Interest in reform and continued activity in the field will undoubtedly persist as Southeast Asian countries seek to improve their international competitiveness, extend participation and democracy, and seek to improve the amount and quality of services delivered to their citizens.

REFERENCES

1. Schaffer, B.H. The Deadlock in Development Administration. In *Politics and Change in Developing Countries*; Leys, C., Ed.; Cambridge University Press: Cambridge, 1969; 177–211.
2. Turner, M.; Hulme, D. *Governance, Administration and Development: Making the State Work*; Macmillan: Basingstoke, 1997.
3. Hirschmann, D. Development administration? A further deadlock. Dev. Change **1981**, *12* (3), 459–479.
4. Dwivedi, O.P.; Nef, J. Crises and continuities in development theory and administration. Public Adm. Dev. **1982**, *2* (1), 59–77.
5. Statistics are from the websites of the World Bank (www.worldbank.org), United Nations Development Programme (www.undp.org) and Asian Development Bank (www.adb.org), accessed on March 10, 2004.
6. De Guzman, R.P.; Reforma, M.A. Administrative Reform in the Asian Pacific Region: Issues and Prospects. In *Administrative Reform Towards Promoting Productivity in Bureaucratic Performance*; De Guzman, R.P., Reforma, M.A., Eds.; EROPA: Manila, 1993; 2–14.
7. RIAP (Research Institute for Asia and the Pacific). *Building Institutional Capacity in Asia: Public Sector Challenges and Government Reforms in South East Asia*; RIAP, University of Sydney: Sydney, 2001.
8. GSC-PAR (Government Steering Committee for Public Administration Reform). *The Overall Report: Review of Public Administration Reform*; GSC-PAR: Hanoi, 2000.
9. Turner, M. Choosing items from the menu: New Public Management in Southeast Asia. Int. J. Public Adm. **2002**, *25* (12), 1493–1513.
10. World Bank. Thailand Country Development Partnership: Governance and Public Sector Reform, Monitoring Workshop, Bangkok, June 19, 2003; OCSC (Office of the Civil Service Commission). In *The Next Steps of Public Service Reform*; OCSC: Bangkok, 2000.
11. Choosing items from the menu: New public management in Southeast Asia. Int. J. Public Adm. **2002**, *25* (12), 1493–1513.
12. Mauzy, D.K. The human rights and 'Asian values' debate in Southeast Asia: Trying to clarify the key issues. Pac. Rev. **1997**, *10* (2), 210–236.
13. Mahbubani, K. *Can Asians Think?* Times Books International: Singapore, 1997.
14. Tapales, P.D. The Philippines. In *The Changing Nature of Local Government in Developing Countries*; McCarney, P.L., Ed.; Centre for Urban and Community Studies, University of Toronto: Toronto, 1996; 197–219.
15. Rood, S. *An Assessment of the State of Knowledge Concerning Decentralized Governance Under the 1991 Local Government Code. Paper Presented at the Third European Conference on Philippine Studies*; April 27–29, 1997.
16. Turner, M.; Podger, O. *Decentralisation in Indonesia: Redesigning the State*; Asia Pacific Press: Canberra.
17. Turner, M. Whatever happened to deconcentration? Recent initiatives in Cambodia. Public Adm. Dev. **2002**, *22* (3), 353–364.

Environmental Policy

Thomas Greitens
Northern Illinois University, DeKalb, Illinois, U.S.A.

INTRODUCTION

Federal environmental policies center around three pieces of legislation: the Clean Air Act, the Clean Water Act, and the National Environmental Policy Act (NEPA). These acts enhanced federal involvement in environmental policy and established a system of command and control regulation of industry. However, by the late 1980s this emphasis on command and control regulation diminished as policymakers started to emphasize concepts of decreased federal involvement that could help control environmental pollution. Among these concepts were notions of cooperative frameworks between industry and government as well as the concept of organizations implementing environmental management systems to improve economic efficiency through better environmental performance.

This decreased federal involvement in environmental policy is nothing new. In fact, initial federal statutes regarding clean air and water policies did not rely on direct federal involvement. Rather, these statutes typically allowed states to set environmental standards with no federal guidelines. Beginning in the 1960s and 1970s, this began to change as the public increasingly became aware of environmental problems and the federal government realized states implemented environmental standards inconsistently. By briefly analyzing the historical development of federal environmental policies, this changing pattern of federal involvement in environmental policy becomes clarified.

CLEAN AIR POLICY

Before 1955, air pollution statutes were mainly state or local affairs. This started to change with the 1955 Air Pollution Control Act. In this act, the federal government provided states with funds to conduct air pollution research and train personnel.[1] By 1963, this act was supplanted with the original Clean Air Act. The original Clean Air Act provided additional federal support for air pollution research, funded the development of state pollution control agencies, and allowed the federal government to assist states when issues of interstate air pollution occurred.[1] Although significant, these acts represented indirect federal involvement in air pollution policy.

Direct federal involvement began in 1967 with the passage of the Air Quality Act. This act required states to use federal research on air pollutants to develop air quality standards for areas with major air-pollution concerns.[1] Unfortunately, many states did not develop air quality standards by the time the act expired in 1970.[1] This set the stage for the 1970 amendments to the Clean Air Act; what many refer to when speaking of the Clean Air Act. Under these amendments, the federal government established national ambient air quality standards (NAAQS) for major air pollutants from stationary sources, states were given responsibility for implementing air pollution plans within federal guidelines, and both the federal and state governments enforced these plans on industrial polluters.[2] These NAAQS represented the maximum concentration of common air pollutants permitted and were divided into primary standards protecting human health and secondary standards protecting forests, agricultural products, and buildings.[3]

Further amendments to the Clean Air occurred in 1977 and 1990. Most significantly, the 1977 amendments formally added the prevention of increased air pollution in areas such as national parks or forests having minimal air pollution concentrations below NAAQS.[4] The 1990 amendments included provisions that established new emission standards for mobile sources of air pollution, phased out certain ozone depleting chemicals, and created a program of emissions trading for sulfur oxides.[2] Of particular interest, policymakers implemented the sulfur oxide trading program as a way to reduce command and control regulation of industry. Although the federal government was still actively involved in this program, it represented a move back to indirect federal involvement in clean air policy.

In 1955, federal clean air policy began as a program of grants to states for research and training. However, by 1970 federal clean air policy had evolved to a command and control system attempting to reduce certain types of air pollutants. This evolution of environmental policy occurred because of increasing public concern over environmental issues and an increasing awareness by the federal government that most states would not implement air pollution standards without compulsion

Encyclopedia of Public Administration and Public Policy
DOI: 10.1081/E-EPAP 120012941

from the federal government.[2] By 1990, political influences forced parts of this direct federal approach back to a more indirect approach, yet command and control regulations still constituted the majority of federal air pollution policy. A similar progression of federal involvement in environmental policies can also be observed in clean water policy.

CLEAN WATER POLICY

Federal involvement in controlling water pollution technically commenced with the Refuse Act of 1899. In an attempt to ensure navigable waterways, this act prohibited the discharge of waste such as sludge and sawdust into navigable waterways without a federal permit.[5] However, federal legislation emphasizing the improvement of water quality for purposes other than navigation began with the Water Pollution Control Act of 1948. In keeping with the prevailing view of the time, this act emphasized indirect federal involvement in controlling water pollution. Specifically, the act gave the federal government authority to conduct research on water pollution and to establish a loan program for municipalities wishing to construct municipal sewage treatment facilities.[5] This act was amended in 1956. The 1956 amendments created a federal grant program for municipalities constructing sewage treatment facilities and established the concept of holding conferences to determine who should clean up interstate water pollution.[5] However, because these statutes did not implement water quality or effluent standards and because the conference concept proved to be unworkable, these statutes were unsuccessful in controlling water pollution.

The Water Quality Act of 1965 had water quality standards. In this statute, states were required to develop water quality standards for interstate waters within state borders and determine the maximum discharge allowed into these interstate waterways.[3] However, as in controlling air pollution, states did not consistently implement or enforce these standards. Consequently, direct federal involvement in water pollution policy came in 1972 with the Federal Water Pollution Control Act. This act established federal standards for point source (i.e., industrial or commercial) discharges of conventional water pollutants based on available technology, gave the federal government initial responsibility for enforcing those standards on individual polluters within a certain time period (states could take over this enforcement duty at a later time), and expanded the federal grant program for municipalities constructing sewage treatment facilities.[6]

Further changes to clean water policy occurred in 1977 when Congress passed the Clean Water Act. This act delayed some of the deadlines included in the 1972 statute for establishing technology-based effluent standards for individual dischargers and added effluent limits on toxic pollutants.[7] Changes occurred again when Congress passed the Water Quality act in 1987. This act further postponed deadlines for establishing technology-based effluent standards, required states to implement plans for controlling non-point sources of water pollution such as runoff from agricultural land and urban areas, and reduced the amount of federal aid available to municipalities constructing sewage treatment facilities.[5]

Over time, federal involvement in water pollution increased because of state inconsistencies in controlling water pollution. However, by the late 1980s the prevailing political environment contributed to a decrease in federal involvement in clean water policy. This decreased federal involvement resulted in a reduced federal grant program for the construction of municipality sewage treatment facilities and the continued delay of establishing technology-based effluent standards for industry and businesses. During this time, policymakers started to advocate approaches to pollution control in which the organization voluntarily assessed environmental impacts. Ironically, policymakers first introduced the concept of organizations assessing environmental impact in the late 1960s with the NEPA.

THE NATIONAL ENVIRONMENTAL POLICY ACT

In contrast to the extended histories surrounding the Clean Air Act and the Clean Water Act, policymakers designed NEPA legislation within one year and passed it into law at the beginning of 1970. The most significant provisions of NEPA required federal agencies to assess the environmental impact of programs before implementation and submit environmental impact statements for programs impacting the environment.[8] An important provision of NEPA was increased citizen participation. Under the NEPA process, community groups could challenge the adequacy of an agency's initial environmental impact statement.[9] In response to these challenges, agencies often changed program designs or designed final environmental impact statements reflecting citizen concerns.

While focusing on federal agencies, NEPA introduced the concept of assessing environmental performance at the organizational level. This organizational idea of assessing environmental performance later became an emphasis of environmental management systems in the 1980s and 1990s. In environmental management systems, organizations voluntarily measure significant environmental impacts due to operations.[10] Consequently, organizations can use environmental management systems to ensure compliance with current federal regulations regarding pollutant discharges and also to focus on environmental issues not currently regulated such as the sustainability of natural resources.

Environmental management systems allow the organization to focus on improving environmental performance. Although the success of environmental management systems in decreasing environmental impacts has still not entirely been proven, the voluntary standard adopted by organizations using these systems represents a further reduction in federal involvement in environmental policy. As environmental policy progressed through the 1980s and 1990s this trend of reduced federal involvement became increasingly apparent in statutes dealing with clean air and clean water.

CONCLUSION

During the 1960s and 1970s, environmental policy at the federal level shifted from a system of indirect federal management regarding such issues as air and water pollution to a more direct system emphasizing command and control regulation. Generally, these command and control regulations focused on industrial causes to pollution and required the federal government to define pollution standards while state governments designed plans to achieve those standards. The passage of legislation such as the 1970 amendments to the original Clean Air Act and the 1972 Federal Water Pollution Control Act exemplified this command and control process. These acts, along with their numerous amendments through the years, resulted in a dramatic increase in air and water quality.[11]

While command and control regulations improved air and water quality, other environmental problems such as the depletion of natural resources and nonindustrial sources of pollution persisted. To address these types of problems falling outside of the command and control process, environmental policy in the 1980s and 1990s increasingly emphasized strategies of pollution prevention rather than pollution reduction.[12] Reflecting political concerns over the economic costs of direct federal involvement and a technical challenge of establishing national standards for less common pollutants, these pollution prevention strategies shifted federal environmental policy back to a more indirect involvement. Typically, this indirect strategy relied on

businesses and governmental agencies to engage in cooperative frameworks that often adopted voluntary standards of pollution prevention.[12] In addition, this strategy also emphasized the notion of businesses adopting environmental management systems, often independent of any governmental incentive, in order to increase efficiency by decreasing negative environmental impacts.[10]

These strategies of direct and indirect federal involvement currently comprise environmental policy. Command and control regulations implemented in the 1960s and 1970s operate with more voluntary standards emphasized in the 1980s and 1990s in an attempt to improve environmental quality. When operating together, both strategies may significantly improve many aspects of the environment. Nevertheless, the historical pattern of environmental policy development suggests that federal involvement in environmental policy will continue to vary to reflect new political trends and emerging technical challenges.

ACKNOWLEDGMENTS

I would like to thank Dr. Paul Culhane of Northern Illinois University and Dr. Patrick Stewart of Arkansas State University for providing thoughtful guidance on environmental policy.

REFERENCES

1. Portney, P. Air Pollution Policy. In *Public Policies for Environmental Protection,* 2nd Ed.; Portney, P., Stavins, R., Eds.; Resources for the Future: Washington, 2000; 77–123.
2. Rosenbaum, W. *Environmental Politics and Policy,* 5th Ed.; CQ Press: Washington, 2002.
3. Ringquist, E. *Environmental Protection at the State Level: Politics and Progress in Controlling Pollution*; M.E. Sharpe, Inc.: New York, 1993.
4. Smith, Z. *The Environmental Policy Paradox*; Prentice Hall: Englewood Cliffs, NJ, 1992.
5. Freeman, A. Water Pollution Policy. In *Public Policies for Environmental Protection,* 2nd Ed.; Portney, P., Stavins, R., Eds.; Resources for the Future: Washington, 2000; 169–213.
6. O'Leary, R.; Durant, R.; Fiorino, D.; Weiland, P. *Managing for the Environment: Understanding the Legal, Organizational, and Policy Challenges*; Jossey-Bass Publishers: San Francisco, 1999.
7. Portney, K. *Controversial Issues in Environmental Policy:*

Science vs. Economics vs. Politics; SAGE Publications, Inc.: Newbury Park, CA, 1992.

8. Kraft, M.; Vig, N. Environmental Policy from the 1970s to the Twenty-First Century. In *Environmental Policy: New Directions for the Twenty-First Century,* 5th Ed.; Vig, N., Kraft, M., Eds.; CQ Press: Washington, 2003; 1–33.

9. Rosenbaum, W. The Bureaucracy and Environmental Policy. In *Environmental Politics and Policy: Theories and Evidence,* 2nd Ed.; Lester, P., Ed.; Duke University Press: Durham, NC, 1995; 206–241.

10. Coglianese, C.; Nash, J. Environmental Management Systems and the New Policy Agenda. In *Regulating from the Inside: Can Environmental Management Systems Achieve Policy Goals?* Coglianese, C., Nash, J., Eds.; Resources for the Future: Washington, 2001; 1–26.

11. Ringquist, E. Evaluating Environmental Policy Outcomes. In *Environmental Politics and Policy: Theories and Evidence,* 2nd Ed.; Lester, P., Ed.; Duke University Press: Durham, NC, 1995; 303–327.

12. Press, D.; Mazmanian, D. Understanding the Transition to a Sustainable Economy. In *Environmental Policy: New Directions for the Twenty-First Century,* 5th Ed.; Vig, N., Kraft, M., Eds.; CQ Press: Washington, 2003; 275–298.

Ethics and Administrative Reform

Jeroen Maesschalck
Katholieke Universiteit Leuven, Leuven, Belgium

INTRODUCTION

Administrative or civil service reform has impacted the public sectors of many countries throughout the world since the 1980s. The reforms have included several strategies (maintain, modernize, marketize, minimize.[1]), but most prominent were the changes that Hood assembled under the conceptual umbrella "New Public Management" (NPM). This includes the introduction of performance management systems, more responsibility and accountability for public managers, more competition in the public sector, the introduction of quality management techniques, etc.[2,3]

The implementation of these reforms in governments throughout the world has sparked concern, both among academics and practitioners, about their impact upon the ethics of public servants. This article identifies four positions in this debate over the impact of the reforms on public servants' ethics and concludes with the observation that in spite of their seeming rivalry, the empirical claims underlying these positions are in fact complementary.

ETHICAL CONCERNS ABOUT ADMINISTRATIVE REFORM

The apprehension for the potentially negative impact of New Public Management (NPM) reforms on the ethics of public servants has been strengthened by highly publicized scandals in many Organization for Economic Cooperation and Development (OECD) countries. Many of these scandals are about individuals behaving unethically, and often also illegally, and causing their public sector organization financial and other difficulties. A case in point is Robert Citron in Orange County, CA.[4] Typically, these individuals were initially seen as exemplars or even heroes, who successfully managed to escape bureaucratic constraints in order to produce results and "get things done" until it was discovered that their escaping bureaucratic constraints also included manifest illegal behavior. It is argued that these excesses are caused by NPM reforms because the NPM-type rhetoric and reforms provided these individuals not only with the

opportunity to perform such behavior but also with the moral mindset to justify it.

NPM-type reforms are also alleged to lead to more collective or even systemic unethical behavior. A case in point are "creaming" strategies, a typical perverse effect of performance management systems. Suppose that the public servants who are in charge of vocational training of unemployed people would be assessed (and paid) on the basis of their "success rate," defined as the number of applicants who are able to obtain a job following the training. It is not unlikely that these public servants would only allow the most job-ready applicants into their training courses. This would leave a considerable category of unemployed people without training, which is unlikely to be an intended effect of this policy.[a] This is just one example of the ethically undesirable consequences that are alleged to be fostered by NPM reforms.

FOUR POINTS OF VIEW

The answer of public administration scholars to these scandals and to the more general concerns about the impact of administrative reforms on (un)ethical behavior of public servants is a discussion that can, in terms of Hood and Jackson, be conceived of as a "doctrinal debate."[5] Doctrines are "specific maxims about administrative whos, hows, and whats," they "denote specific ideas about what should be done in administration." Roughly summarized, four rival positions can be identified in this debate, each proposing their own administrative doctrines to foster ethical behavior in the public sector. The following paragraphs will summarize those positions. Although this overview will focus on the recent debate over the ethical impact of NPM reforms, it is in fact much broader because those against NPM reforms propose their own alternative, which is then in turn criticized by the other participants in the debate. Moreover,

---

[a]Although these creaming strategies are currently very relevant because of the popularity of performance management systems, they were already pointed out by Blau, P.M., 1955. *The dynamics of bureaucracy*. Chicago: University of Chicago Press.

Encyclopedia of Public Administration and Public Policy
DOI: 10.1081/E-EPAP-120024736

three of the four positions are rooted in a broader administrative philosophy, thus making this debate a contemporary version of older debates.[b]

New Public Management

The first position is anchored in the NPM administrative philosophy. NPM's heyday started with the seminal 1991 article of Christopher Hood[2] who conceived of NPM as a set of doctrinal ideas with a certain degree of coherence, (i.e., an administrative philosophy) that has come to be widely accepted. Hood[3] mentions six doctrines to define the NPM administrative philosophy.

1. "Unbundle" the public service into corporatized units organized by product.
2. More contract-based competitive provision, with internal markets and term contracts.
3. Stress on private sector styles of management practice.
4. Put more emphasis on visible "hands-on" top management
5. Make performance standards and measures explicit, formal, and measurable.
6. Greater emphasis on output controls.

One could add to this the doctrine: "Apply quality management and a customer service focus." This doctrine was not the initial focus of NPM reforms, but has become very important in a "second wave of reforms."[6]

The NPM proponents' consideration of the ethical consequences of administrative reform is rather modest. Sometimes, NPM proponents emphasize how competition mechanisms can reduce corruption, e.g., by lessening the opportunities of public servants to corruptly charge monopoly rents.[7] More often, however, they remain silent on the topic of ethics.[8] The assumption seems to be that ethical behavior will naturally follow from an implementation of NPM reforms. Ethical behavior is then mainly understood as behavior that strengthens "the three E's" (economy, efficiency, and effectiveness).

Traditional Public Administration

The second position is at the other side of the spectrum. It is rooted in "Traditional Public Administration" (TPA), also referred to as the "old public administration"[9] or the "orthodox model."[10] Of course, TPA contains many different ideas and it would be incorrect and simplistic to present them as one monolithic block of doctrines and justifications without any internal debates or changes. Nevertheless, there seems to be broad consensus over a limited number of core doctrines including the following:[c]

1. Public administration should be politically neutral.
2. The organizational structure should be a centralized bureaucracy.
3. Programs should be implemented through top–down control mechanisms, limiting discretion as much as possible.
4. Officials should be kept in a procedural straitjacket.

The administrative doctrine of TPA with regard to ethics management prescribes that the organizational processes be organized in such a way that "the individual ethical choice is limited to choosing to follow the rules (the ethical thing to do) or to violate them by commission or omission (unethical acts)."[11] In the debate over the ethical effects of NPM reforms, the proponents of TPA have "throw[n] up their hands in horror at recent trends, seeing them as marking the destruction of the public service ethos."[12] In the United Kingdom, Chapman and O'Toole[13–15] argue for a return to the traditional civil service ethos and to the traditional concept of "public duty." Writing from the U.S. context, Frederickson[16] also forcefully expresses his concerns about the ethical consequences of NPM innovations such as marketizing, privatizing, or contracting out, and he argues for a "re-regulation." One particularly prominent strand in the TPA tradition emphasizes the legal point of view and criticizes NPM "for its sometimes cavalier treatment of the rule of law, especially its free and easy slogans about eliminating red tape and letting managers manage."[17]

New Public Service

The third position is derived from what has recently been labeled the "New Public Service" (NPS).[9] Skidmore[18] describes a similar approach as the "classical" or "Aristotelian" mode of organizing (referring to its roots in MacIntyre's work), while others[d] have labeled it the "communitarian/citizen alternative." Denhardt and Denhardt present the NPS approach as a viable third alternative for the observed dichotomy between "the old

---

[b]An earlier version of this discussion of the four positions was published by Maesschalck, J, 2004. The impact of new public management reforms on public servants' ethics: Towards a theory. *Public Administration* 82(2):465–489.

[c]The first three doctrines are taken from Denhardt and Denhardt.[9] The fourth doctrine is taken from Ref. [2].

[d]For example, Fox, C.J., Miller, H.T., 1996. *Postmodern public administration. Towards discourse.* Thousand Oaks: Sage.

public administration'' and ''the New Public Management.'' Rather than traditional bureaucracies that are controlled from the top down and largely closed for citizens, Denhardt and Denhardt propose new mechanisms in which ''the primary role of the public servant is to help citizens articulate and meet their shared interests rather than to attempt to control or steer society.''[9] In order to achieve this overall aim, Denhardt and Denhardt propose seven doctrines that embody their administrative philosophy:

1. Serve, rather than steer.
2. The public interest is the aim, not the by-product.
3. Think strategically, act democratically.
4. Serve citizens, not customers.
5. Public servants should be attentive to the law, community values, political norms, professional standards, and citizen interests.
6. Value people, not just productivity.
7. Value citizenship and public service above entrepreneurship.

As for the recent debate over the impact of NPM reforms on ethics, those writing from an NPS point of view largely join the TPA advocates in their negative assessment of the ethical consequences of NPM reforms, but propose a different solution. Specifically, Denhardt and Denhardt argue that public sector organizations should be organized in such a way that public servants are not responsive to ''constituents and clients'' (TPA), nor to ''customers'' (NPM), but to ''citizens.'' Citizens are described as those people who ''demonstrate their concern for the larger community, their commitment to matters that go beyond short-term interests and their willingness to assume personal responsibility for what happens in their neighborhoods and the community.''[9] To make public servants capable of being responsive to these kinds of citizens, the doctrines described above should be the guide. Several other authors have criticized NPM from an NPS point of view. Although he also used TPA arguments to criticize NPM (see above), most of Frederickson's prescriptive claims (particularly in ''The Spirit of Public Administration'') rather correspond to the NPS administrative philosophy. One example of this is his plea for a ''combination of patriotism (the love of the regime values) with benevolence (the love of others).''[19] Gawthrop[20] fits the NPS philosophy even more neatly. He contrasts the ''democratic spirit'' with the NPM-type ''entrepreneurial spirit'' and argues that the former should prevail. He also strongly criticizes the TPA-type ''ethics of compliance'' he observed in the U.S. public administration the past five decades for leading to a soulless public administration, obsessed with procedural correctness. He argues that public servants should have a personal responsibility, with ''service as the center of value.''

Ethics Management

The fourth position in the debate does not clearly build on a single identifiable administrative philosophy such as the previous three. Its central argument is that public sector ethics management is an important and evolving subfield of public management, which deserves its own set of doctrines, hence the ''Ethics Management'' approach. Its core doctrine is that an ethics policy should be a combination of doctrines from the three aforementioned approaches, adapted to the specific circumstances of the organization. Admittedly, arguments for a combination of different approaches have been articulated before. Cooper,[21] for example, proposed such a combined approach in his seminal ''The Responsible Administrator.'' However, the success of the NPM discourse and the concomitant ethical concerns fostered a recent revival of this approach. The Public Management (PUMA) Department of the OECD[22,23] has been among its most prominent promoters, together with practice-oriented academics such as Gilman[24] or Uhr.[25] These and other recent proponents agree with the NPM advocates that NPM reforms can have many beneficial consequences, but are at the same time conscious of the undesirable effects (particularly unethical behavior). However, in contrast with TPA and NPS, their solution is not to do away with NPM innovations, but to complement them with a well-developed public sector ethics management that is adapted to the reforms. They see two possible approaches to such an ethics policy. The OECD, Gilman, and originally Paine[26] identify these as the ''compliance'' and the ''integrity'' approach, respectively. The distinction goes back to the famous Friedrich–Finer debate over the importance of internal and external controls on public servants, respectively.[e] The ''compliance'' approach to ethics management emphasizes the importance of external controls on the behavior of public servants (e.g., legislation, strict behavioral ethics codes, and extensive control mechanisms) and thus comes very close to the ethics management doctrines of TPA. However, the ''Ethics Management'' proponents observe that this compliance approach does not fit the NPM-style results-based managerial approach. It thus violates their basic doctrine of a management style adapted to the circumstances. Instead, NPM-type changes need to be complemented by an ''integrity'' approach to ethics management, which emphasizes internal control: control exercised by the public servant on herself/himself. This integrity approach is ''based on aspirations, relies on incentives,

---

[e]For a discussion, see Cooper, T.L, 1998. *The responsible administrator: An approach to ethics for the administrative role.* San Francisco: Jossey-Bass, pp. 131–163.

and encourages good behavior rather than policing and punishing errors and wrongdoing.''[23] Such an ethics management style is necessary because the increased discretion that goes with the reduction of hierarchy in NPM-type reforms needs to be paralleled by an ethics management style that supports the public servants in dealing with this discretion, rather than limiting their discretion by developing new rules and control systems.

CONCLUSION

This article presented four prominent positions[f] in the debate about the impact of administrative reform on the ethics of public servants. Although the positions in this doctrinal debate seem rival, all authors can easily point at empirical instances that support their claims. For example, while the NPM literature is ripe with success stories of NPM reforms and convincing examples of the undesirable effects of traditional bureaucracies, the TPA proponents can easily point at the scandals that followed NPM reforms and show how these would not have occurred in a more traditional bureaucracy. How should we deal with these diverse claims? If all participants in the debate can provide convincing examples of their position, who should we believe?

To answer this question, it might be useful to distinguish between the normative and the empirical claims made in this literature. The normative claims underlying the three first positions[g] are clearly rival. The proponents of these positions evidently disagree in their evaluation of both the desirability of particular types of ethical behavior and the seriousness of types of unethical behavior. In contrast with this rivalry among the normative claims, the empirical claims are rather complementary. While the proponents of a particular approach concentrate on its beneficial effects, the opponents point at its deficiencies. Although this might look rival, such claims can empirically be complementary: It is perfectly consistent to claim that a particular approach can be beneficial in particular circumstances, but engender undesirable effects in other circumstances. In fact, this is an important maxim in management: Each innovation, however well intended, carries with it the risk of particular excesses. Kathryn Denhardt[27] formulated this eloquently in the context of ethics management: ''Every organiza-

tional structure can promote an ethical stance yet at the same time contain the seeds of pathology.''

One prominent strategy to cope with this risk is to ensure that all main perspectives are taken into consideration and structurally anchored in the organization. The permanent tension between the approaches that follows from this then helps to avoid blind spots for the potential negative effects of one particular approach.[h] According to this strategy, the decision is not which of the three main administrative philosophies—New Public Management, Traditional Public Administration, and New Public Service—should be applied, but how all three of them should be combined. This is in fact what the Ethics Management approach, the fourth position in the debate, sets about to do. Proponents of this approach accept some NPM reforms, but also require that these are combined with two other approaches: a considerable degree of TPA (the ''compliance'' approach in the ethics management jargon) to delineate the discretion and ensure that the discretion is not abused and a considerable degree of NPS (the ''integrity'' approach) which stimulates public servants to use the remaining discretion to ''serve citizens, not customers.'' Such a complex balancing exercise will not guide us to clear-cut and neat solutions, but it does reduce the risk of administrative reforms leading to ethical disaster.

REFERENCES

1. Pollitt, C.; Bouckaert, G. *Public Management Reform. A Comparative Analysis*; Oxford University Press: Oxford, 2000.
2. Hood, C. A public management for all seasons? Public Adm. **1991**, *69* (1), 3–19.
3. Hood, C. *Explaining Economic Policy Reversals*; Open University Press: Buckingham, Philadelphia, 1994.
4. Cohen, S.; Eimicke, W. Is public entrepreneurship ethical? Public Integr. **1999**, *1* (1), 54–74.
5. Hood, C.; Jackson, M. *Administrative Argument*; Aldershot: Darthmouth, 1991.
6. Pollitt, C. *Managerialism and the Public Services*; Blackwell: Oxford, 1993.
7. Klitgaart, R. *Controlling Corruption*; University of California Press: Los Angeles, CA, 1988.
8. Menzel, D.C. The morally mute manager: Fact or fiction? Public Pers. Manage. **2000**, *28* (4), 515–527.
9. Denhardt, R.B.; Denhardt, J.V. The new public service: Serving rather than steering. Public Adm. Rev. **2000**, *60* (6), 549–559.

---

[f]It is obvious that these are four sets of doctrines and not four groups of authors. Although most authors clearly have one of the four positions as their favorite, several of them endorse doctrines from different philosophies. This goes for at least two of the most prominent authors that were discussed: Cooper and Frederickson.

[g]The Ethics Management position is an exception.

---

[h]For further development of this argument, see Maesschalck, J., forthcoming. Approaches to ethics management in the public sector: A proposed extension of the compliance–integrity continuum. *Public Integrity*.

10. Fox, C.J. The Use of Philosophy in Administrative Ethics. In *Handbook of Administrative Ethics*; Cooper, T.L., Ed.; Marcel Dekker: New York, 2001; 105–130.

11. Fox, C.J. The Use of Philosophy in Administrative Ethics. In *Handbook of Administrative Ethics*; Cooper, T.L., Ed.; Marcel Dekker: New York, 2001; 110.

12. Greenaway, J. Having the bun and the halfpenny: Can old public service ethics survive in the new Whitehall? Public Adm. **1995**, *73*, 357–374.

13. Chapman, R.A. Problems of ethics in public sector management. Public Money Manag. **1998**, *18* (1), 9–13.

14. Chapman, R.A. Change in the civil service. Public Adm. **1994**, *72*, 599–610.

15. Chapman, R.A.; O'Toole, B.J. The role of the civil service: A traditional view in a period of change. Public Policy Adm. **1995**, *10* (2), 3–20.

16. Frederickson, H.G. Public ethics and the new managerialism. Public Integr. **1999**, *1* (3), 265–278.

17. Rohr, J.A. *Civil Servants and their Constitutions*; University Press of Kansas: Kansas, 2002; xi. (For examples of this legal criticism on NPM, see, e.g., Cooper, P.J., 2000. *Public law and public administration. third edition*. Itasca, IL: F.E. Peacock.)

18. Skidmore, M.J. Ethics and Public Service. Ann. Am. Acad. Polit. Soc. Sci. **1995**, *537*, 25–36.

19. Frederickson, H.G. *The Spirit of Public Administration*; Jossey-Bass: San Fransisco, CA, 1997; 202.

20. Gawthrop, L.C. *Public Service and Democracy*; Chatham House: New York, 1998; 80.

21. Cooper, T.L. *The Responsible Administrator: An Approach to Ethics for the Administrative Role*, 1st Ed.; Kennikat: Port Washington, NY, 1982.

22. OECD. *Ethics in the Public Service. Current Issues and Practices*; OECD: Paris, 1996.

23. OECD. *Trust in Government. Ethics Measures in OECD Countries*; OECD: Paris, 2000; 25.

24. Gilman, S.C. Public sector ethics and government reinvention: Realigning systems to meet organizational change. Public Integr. **1999**, *1* (2), 175–192.

25. Uhr, J. Institutions of integrity. Balancing values and verification in democratic government. Public Integr. **1999**, *1* (1), 94–106.

26. Paine, L.S. Managing for organizational integrity. Harvard Bus. Rev. **1994**, (2).

27. Denhardt, K.G. Organizational Structure as a Context for Administrative Ethics. In *Handbook of Administrative Ethics*; Cooper, T.L., Ed.; Marcel Dekker: New York, 1994; 181.

Ethics and Information and Communication Technology

Brian Negin
Israel Central Bureau of Statistics, Jerusalem, Israel

INTRODUCTION

Information and communication technology, in particular the Internet, has benefited global society by enabling unfettered dissemination of, and access to, information on a scale previously unknown to mankind. At the same time, this technology has created challenges to the enforcement of existing regional norms, pitting the value of freedom of speech (and of information) against other equally important values, such as the protection of human dignity.

THE IMPORTANCE OF INFORMATION AND COMMUNICATION IN SOCIETY

Human life and society depend on the ability to communicate information. While this seemingly self-evident truth applies to human development over tens of thousands of years, the recognition of the importance of information to human society is only a relatively recent one, rooted in the Enlightenment. The Enlightenment signified a societal change of orientation from natural duties to natural rights.[1] One of the natural rights that has figured prominently in the development of Western society has been the *freedom of speech*, necessary for the actualization of democratic society. As recognized by the Supreme Court of the United States, *freedom of speech* includes the freedom to both access and disseminate information.[2] An alternative approach expressed in the draft *Declaration of Principles* of the World Summit on the Information Society views the freedom to access and disseminate information not as a corollary of the *freedom of speech*, but as an independent right.[3]

LIMITATIONS ON FREEDOM OF INFORMATION AND COMMUNICATION

Human society depends on the ability of human beings to communicate and also on the existence of norms that establish the borders of permitted behavior. Among these norms are those that define the permissible *content* of speech, as well as those that define permissible *access* to and *use* of that content. In a modern society, one may distinguish between such norms that are based solely on social or cultural pressures (*extralegal norms*) and those that are expressed in law (*legal norms*).

Extralegal normative control of behavior, including speech, generally occurs within social and professional networks that require *correct* behavior from their members or as a result of dedicated pressure groups promoting an agenda, such as those pressing for the removal of *controversial* reading material from school curriculums.[4] Legal control of the content of speech protects societal values considered at least equally important as the freedom of speech. Criminal laws, for example, prohibit sedition, incitement to violence, incitement to racism, and the dissemination of obscene material. Civil laws prohibit the dissemination of defamation, the invasion of privacy, the violation of trade secrets, and the infringement of copyright.

Thus we see that while *freedom of speech*, including freedom of access to, and the dissemination of, information, is a fundamental value of modern civilization, it is not an absolute and unlimited freedom. Restraints on freedom of speech usually reflect a fine balance among competing societal values as developed over time within evolving social and technological contexts.

THE PROMISE AND THE CHALLENGE OF THE INTERNET

The Internet has created an exceptional platform for the dissemination of, and the access to, information. As reflected in the World Summit on Information Technology, one of the primary global issues today is how to provide full and uncensored Internet access to the world's population, including those nations that either lack a sufficient technological infrastructure or that choose, for political reasons, to limit access. It is commonly believed that access to information over the Internet, including the ability to communicate through it, is an enabling factor in the positive development of all people around the world. However, this utopian spin on the Internet tends to overlook social, ethical, and legal problems that the new technology has created. As scholars have noted, new technology can bring good to society, but can also bear unexpected consequences.[5]

Encyclopedia of Public Administration and Public Policy
DOI: 10.1081/E-EPAP 120024738

One of the unexpected consequences of the Internet is that its technology has created challenges to the enforcement of accepted societal norms, legal and extralegal, that define the permissible content of speech and the permissible access to, and use of, information. The Internet also has created new difficulties regarding competing regional or national norms.

These challenges highlight the ongoing struggle of society to define and enforce normative values necessary for human survival. This struggle is apparent in Section 9 of the current draft Declaration of Principles of the World Summit on the Information Society, titled *Ethical Dimensions of the Information Society*. Article 52 in this Section states:[6]

> The Information Society should be subject to universally held cultural and ethical values such as truth, justice, solidarity, tolerance, human dignity, shared responsibility, transparency and accountability, and without prejudice to the moral, social and religious values of all societies. All actors in the Information Society should seek to promote the common good, protect privacy, and to prevent abusive uses of ICTs. The freedom of use of ICTs should not undermine the human dignity, human rights and fundamental freedoms of others, including personal privacy, matters of faith and other personal beliefs. These values are particularly relevant when commercial activities are conducted through networks.

Following are three topics that illustrate some of the ethical issues consequential to the development of information and communication technology and particularly the Internet. These are online defamation, protecting minors from sexually explicit content on the Internet, and online privacy and confidentiality.

ONLINE DEFAMATION

The prohibition against defamation is at least as old as the Bible. The prohibition in the Ninth Commandment, against bearing false witness, has been interpreted as also prohibiting gossip and slander.[7] In modern terms, the prohibition can be understood as protecting the value of human dignity, central to the modern worldview evolved in the Enlightenment. As a basic human value, its pedigree predates *freedom of speech*. At the same time, the content and enforcement of defamation law must be balanced against the value of freedom of speech.

A person can be held legally responsible for defaming another person. When defamatory speech is disseminated online, it must normally reside, if only temporarily, on the computer system of a service provider in order for it to be accessed. Barring the existence of specific legislation to the contrary, the common default legal position in most

Western countries would hold service providers liable for not removing such illegal content if duly requested to do so, analogous to the legal liability of distributors for the dissemination of third-party defamation in the physical world. This was the situation according to U.S. case law until 1995,[8] as well as the position expressly taken by Germany in its Act on the Utilization of Teleservices.[9]

However, in 1997, a U.S. Court of Appeals upheld a lower court decision immunizing service providers from all liability for *third-party* illegal content, including immunity from the equivalent of *distributor liability* in the physical world for not removing defamatory content when asked to do so.[10] The court was concerned that recognizing service provider distributor liability would chill free speech on the Internet by encouraging an onslaught of demands by purportedly injured parties for the removal of allegedly defamatory material from service providers' computer systems. Service providers would either comply, thus implicating themselves in prior restraint of free speech, or not comply and face enormous legal fees to defend themselves while passing on the additional costs to users in the way of higher fees.

The preponderance of U.S. case law, following the above precedent, today holds that an injured party to online defamation can only hold the creator of the defamatory content liable to pay compensation for damage.[11] The result is that the substantive law of defamation remains the same, while the ability to enforce it in the online environment has been reduced. This change reflects a weakening of the norm protecting human dignity while strengthening a competing societal norm, the freedom of speech. In this sense, the technology of the Internet has wrought a substantive change in the balance of societal values, at least in the United States, in the context of defamation law.

PROTECTING MINORS FROM SEXUALLY EXPLICIT CONTENT ON THE INTERNET

Freedom of speech includes the freedom to disseminate sexually explicit material, as long as it does not violate local community standards. However, even sexually explicit material that is legally available to adults might be harmful to vulnerable and innocent minors. The technology of the Internet has made access to sexually explicit content very easy, even for minors. In addition, a mistyped web address can inadvertently bring up a pornographic Web site, even to the most experienced adult. How can children be protected against the harmful effects of such material online?

While some argue that the best protection for minors against harmful content on the Internet is education and parental guidance,[12,13] the U.S. government has decided that this is a matter for legislative intervention. Two federal attempts at criminalizing the dissemination to minors, over the Internet, of constitutionally protected material that, for minors, would be considered *harmful*[14,15] have been judged to be unconstitutional because they were overbroad and limited adults' rights to otherwise legally protected speech.[16,17] A third legislative attempt to protect minors from such material, the Children's Internet Protection Act (CIPA),[18] has been upheld by the U.S. Supreme Court.[19]

Under CIPA, a public library may not receive federal assistance for the provision of Internet access, unless it installs software to block obscene or pornographic images and to prevent minors from accessing material deemed harmful to them. The legislation addresses, among other things, the problem that library patrons of all ages, including minors, regularly use public library Internet computers to access not only information, but also online pornography. In addition, library staff or patrons may at times be exposed to pornographic images left displayed on computer terminals or printed on library printers.

The Supreme Court held that public libraries, by necessity, must make value judgments about what material will be included in their collections. Public libraries may also make value judgments regarding the type of content they will make available to the public over their Internet computers. Just as most libraries exclude pornography from their print collection, they may exclude it from Internet access on library computers by using filtering applications—even if those applications are imperfect and might *overblock* access to legal and nonharmful information while *underblocking* access to some illegal or harmful sites. Therefore public library use of Internet filtering software does not violate adult patrons' First Amendment rights.

Notwithstanding the legality of the use of filtering software in public libraries, discussion continues as to the efficacy of the use of such software and the alternatives to it. In the settlement of a workplace harassment case brought by Minneapolis librarians regarding patron use of public library Internet computers to access pornography, it is reported that library officials will consider, in addition to filtering software, changes in the printing of Internet material, increased sanctions for those who violate library Internet policy, and consultation with staff about placement of terminals.[20,21]

The Children's Internet Protection Act also requires installation and use by schools of filtering or blocking software on Internet computers to be eligible to receive or retain universal service assistance. The Electronic Frontier Foundation, in its study on Internet blocking in public schools, criticizes the efficacy of the use of such software.[22] It concludes that because filtering or blocking software both *overblocks* permissible material and *underblocks* harmful material, it cannot sufficiently protect children while at the same time, it damages educational opportunities for students to access information.

PRIVACY AND CONFIDENTIALITY ON THE INTERNET

The technology of the Internet enables the collection of information about users of services such as the World Wide Web, even without the individual user being aware of such. This information might include data on the user himself (name, E-mail address, and perhaps more) and the web pages visited on any given site. Sometimes the information on the user is anonymous, in the sense that Internet technology enables, through the use of *cookies*, the tracking of a particular computer's navigation through a given Web site. The computer can be identified [by *cookie*[23] or Internet Protocol (IP) address], but unless personal information has been provided by the user of the computer, it is difficult to attribute web surfing habits to a particular, identified person.

However, the tracking of identified users on the Internet is becoming easier as more and more Web sites require *registration* to access the information on the site. The *New York Times* Web site is an example.[24] To receive free access to the online newspaper, one must first register and provide the following personal information: E-mail address, country, zip code, age, sex, household income, industry, job title, job function, and subscription status to the *New York Times*. The use of this information is in accordance with a privacy policy[25] that describes what personal information is collected, how usage is tracked on the site (*cookies* and IP address), and what use will be made of the information collected (statistical analysis and banner advertising, E-mail if you elect it as an option during registration, and sharing information with partners on an opt-in basis only). This example demonstrates the striking of a balance between commercial enterprise and the protection of privacy on a contractual basis. To receive a commercial commodity for free, a person gives up a bit of his or her own privacy under the terms of an agreement that delineates the permitted use of the information provided.

Noncontractual limitations on the use of personal information also exist, mandating maintaining the confidentiality of third-party private information stored on computer systems. For example, the U.S. government must abide by the Privacy Act of 1974 that prohibits use of personal information by the federal agencies for purposes other than those for which it was provided.[26] While U.S. legislation applies only to the federal government, the European Union Directive 95/46/EC on the protection of individuals with regard to the processing of personal data and on the free movement of such data applies to everyone.[27] It also requires that personal information be used only for the purpose for which it was provided. The directive has been implemented by the member states in their own internal legislation.[28]

Setting the boundaries of permitted use of private information in a digital environment requires taking steps to protect that information from unauthorized access or use. The person, business, organization, or government holding the information must establish administrative policies regarding the use of the information that conform with the privacy norms binding it. In addition, it must also take computer security measures to prevent unauthorized access to that information both from within and from without. Steps from within include limiting access to such information only to those who have been granted access privileges through user name, password, and access rights administration. The protection from outside access via public communication networks, including the Internet, will usually include, in addition to the above, firewalls and other software and hardware that can make unauthorized access by outsiders very difficult. These computer security measures are normally grounded in an organization's policy on computer security intended to set the guidelines not only for the protection against unauthorized access to sensitive information residing on the computer system, but also to protect the system itself against being compromised as a result of external attack, natural disasters, or simple equipment failure. For example, Appendix III of OMB Circular A-130 on the management of federal information resources requires that federal "[a]gencies shall implement and maintain a program to assure that adequate security is provided for all agency information collected, processed, transmitted, stored, or disseminated in general support systems and major applications.''[29,30]

CONCLUSION

The ease of use of the Internet as a means of accessing and disseminating information, its global reach, and the power of its technologies create challenges in enforcing established societal values or balancing among competing values. Freedom of speech enjoys a technological advantage in this environment, as does the ability to gather and process information about individuals. As a result, other values such as the protections against defamation, against harm to vulnerable minors, and against the invasion of privacy may suffer. Human society has always had to find the proper balance between these and other competing values, especially in the context of new information technologies.

This process is an ongoing one. Society continuously examines and reexamines its resolution of these conflicts even in the absence of new technologies, learning from experience as well as responding to external forces, such as the terror attacks of September 11. In this context, the conflicts discussed above in this entry continue to be scrutinized by the public, the courts, and the legislator and may remain unresolved for some time to come. At the same time, information and communication technologies shall continue to develop, providing new challenges to realizing their potential while maintaining the ethical balances necessary to promote the common good.

REFERENCES

1. Strauss, L. *Natural Right and History*; The University of Chicago Press: Chicago, 1953.
2. *United States et al. v. American Library Association, Inc. et al.* United States Supreme Court, 2003. http://supct.law. cornell.edu/supct/html/02-361.ZS.html (accessed September 2003).
3. *Draft Declaration of Principles*; Document WSIS/PC-3/2-E, The World Summit on the Information Society: Geneva, Switzerland, 2003. Section A. http://www.itu.int/dms_pub/itu-s/md/03/wsispc3/doc/S03-WSISPC3-DOC-0002!!PDF-E.pdf (accessed September 2003).
4. Ravitch, D. *The Language Police—How Pressure Groups Restrict What Students Learn*; Alfred A. Knopf: New York, 2003.
5. Dunlop, C.; Kling, R. Introduction—Social Controversies about Computerization. In *Computerization and Controversy: Value Conflicts and Choices*; Dunlop, C., Kling, R., Eds.; Academic Press: Boston, 1991; 1–29.
6. *Draft Declaration of Principles*; Document WSIS/PC-3/2-E, The World Summit on the Information Society: Geneva, Switzerland, 2003. Section 9. http://www.itu.int/dms_pub/itu-s/md/03/wsispc3/doc/S03-WSISPC3-DOC-0002!!PDF-E.pdf (accessed September 2003).
7. Scherman, N. *Stone Edition Chumash: The Torah, Haftaros and Five Megillos with a Commentary From Rabbinic Writings*; Artscroll Mesorah: Brooklyn, 1993; 412.
8. Negin, B. *Illegal Content on the Internet*; Israel Government Internet Committee: Jerusalem, Israel, 1998. http://www.itpolicy.gov.il/topics/docs/mso2F8.pdf (accessed September 2003).
9. *Act on the Utilization of Teleservices*. Germany. http://www.iid.de/iukdg/aktuelles/fassung_tdg_eng.pdf (accessed September 2003).
10. *Zeran v. America Online Inc.*, 129 F. 3d 327, United States Court of Appeals, 4th Circuit, 1997. http://laws.lp.findlaw.com/4th/971523p.html (accessed September 2003).
11. *Batzel v. Cremers*, United States Court of Appeals, 9th Circuit, 2003. http://caselaw.lp.findlaw.com/data2/circs/9th/0156380p.pdf (accessed September 2003).
12. Willard, N. *Choosing Not To Go Down the Not-So-Good Cyberstreets*. http://responsiblenetizen.org/pdf/nwnas.pdf (accessed September 2003).
13. *Welcome to ALA's Web Site on the Children's*

Internet Protection Act (CIPA); American Library Association. http://www.ala.org/Content/NavigationMenu/Our_Association/Offices/ALA_Washington/Issues2/Civil_Liberties,_Intellectual_Freedom,_Privacy/CIPA1/CIPA.htm (accessed September 2003).

14. *The Communications Decency Act (CDA)*. Section V of The Telecommunications Act, Pub. L. No. 104–104, 110 Stat. 56 (1996), codified at 47 U.S.C. §223(a) and §223(d).

15. *The Children's Online Protection Act (COPA)*. Pub. L. No. 105-277, 112 Stat. 2681 (1998), codified at 47 U.S.C. §231.

16. *Reno v. ACLU*, 521 U.S. 844, United States Supreme Court, 1997. http://supct.law.cornell.edu/supct/html/96-511.ZO.html (accessed September 2003).

17. *ACLU v. Ashcroft*, United States Court of Appeals for the 3rd Circuit, 2003. http://laws.findlaw.com/3rd/991324.html (accessed September 2003).

18. *Children's Internet Protection Act (CIPA)*. Pub. L. No. 106-554, 114 Stat. 2763A-335 http://www.ala.org/Content/NavigationMenu/Our_Association/Offices/ALA_Washington/Issues2/Civil_Liberties,_Intellectual_Freedom,_Privacy/CIPA1/cipatext.pdf (accessed September 2003).

19. *United States et al. v. American Library Association, Inc. et al.*, United States Supreme Court, 2003. http://supct.law.cornell.edu/supct/html/02-361.ZS.html (accessed September 2003).

20. *Librarians Settle Internet Porn Case*. Brainerddispatch.com, August 16, 2003. http://www.brainerddispatch.com/stories/081603/sne_0816030021.html (accessed September 2003).

21. Volokh, E. *Squeamish Librarians*; 2001. http://www1.law.ucla.edu/~volokh/harass/library.htm (accessed September 2003).

22. *Internet Blocking in Public Schools*; Electronic Frontier Foundation, 2003. http://www.eff.org/Censorship/Censorware/net_block_report (accessed September 2003).

23. Whalen, D. *The Unofficial Cookie FAQ*; Cookie Central, 2002. http://www.cookiecentral.com/faq/ (accessed September 2003).

24. New York Times On The Web. http://www.nytimes.com (accessed September 2003).

25. *Privacy Policy*. The New York Time on the Web, 2003. http://www.nytimes.com/ref/membercenter/help/privacy.html (accessed September 2003).

26. *The Privacy Act of 1974*. Codified at 5 USC §552a. http://www.usdoj.gov/04foia/privstat.htm (accessed September 2003).

27. *Directive 95/46/EC of the European Parliament and of the Council of 24 October 1995 on the Protection of Individuals with Regard to the Processing of Personal Data and on the Free Movement of such Data*; The European Commission. http://europa.eu.int/comm/internal_market/privacy/law_en.htm (accessed September 2003).

28. *Status of Implementation of Directive 95/46 on the Protection of Individuals with Regard to the Processing of Personal Data*; The European Commission. http://europa.eu.int/comm/internal_market/privacy/law/implementation_en.htm#ukingdom (accessed September 2003).

29. *Management of Federal Information Resources*. Circular No. A-130, Revised, (Transmittal Memorandum No. 4); Office of Management and Budget: Washington, DC. http://www.whitehouse.gov/omb/circulars/a130/a130trans4.html (accessed September 2003).

30. *Security of Federal Automated Information Resources*. Appendix III to OMB Circular No. A-130; Office of Management and Budget: Washington, DC. http://www.whitehouse.gov/omb/circulars/a130/a130appendix_iii.html (accessed September 2003).

Financial Condition

Jane Beckett-Camarata
Kent State University, Kent, Ohio, U.S.A.

INTRODUCTION

The regular reoccurrence of state and local governments' fiscal problems over the last 30 years has pointed to the need for an effective system to provide citizens, creditors, managers, legislative and oversight bodies, and others with early warning sings of pending fiscal stress. The widespread financial problems that occurred in the 1970s in cities throughout the United States resulted in changes in financial reporting nationwide. Pressure from the credit market and effective leadership of financial organizations have had major impacts, leading to improvements in financial reporting standards as well as compliance with those standards. Because of the implementation of those standards, potential fiscal problems are likely to be discovered sooner and prevented.

Thus, preventing financial problems requires early alert analysis to proactively identify trends and practices that may adversely impact financial condition. Assuring that government has the financial capacity to sustain desired public services is the primary reason for internal managers to monitor financial condition. Bond investors and creditors also have a similar interest in evaluating financial condition, particularly to assess a government's ability to make future interest and principal payments, even in the face of adverse economic trends or natural disasters. Knowledge that internal managers are employing a system to track financial trends provides investors and creditors with added confidence in the quality of the government's financial management. This is true particularly if such trend data are shared with credit analysts. Credit analysts also have more than a passing interest in the government's ability to provide services and pay down debt in the long run. Experience has shown that, in times of fiscal crisis, expenditures for critical services often take precedence over debt service payments.

Local governments produce many financial reports, both internal and external, every year. Financial data are presented in accordance with state and/or professional oversight bodies' requirements. Some states impose uniform financial accounting and reporting systems that all municipalities within the state must follow. Local governments may also be required to submit annual financial reports to a state oversight body. State legislatures are responsible for helping formulate sound fiscal poli-

cies for the government. However, oversight bodies are responsible for establishing and possibly monitoring fiscal policies of governmental units they are responsible for. Both legislative and oversight groups are responsible for monitoring executive compliance with relevant laws and regulations.

OVERVIEW

The Comprehensive Annual Financial Report (CAFR) includes useful information for financial condition analysis. The essential information is contained in the basic financial statements (BFS), including the notes that are part of them. The BFS are financial statements that must be included in a government annual report to comply with GAAP under the Governmental Accounting Standards Board (GASB) statement no. 34. The required statements are: a government-wide statement of net assets; a government-wide statement of activities; fund financial statements for governmental, proprietary, and fiduciary funds; and Notes to the Financial Statements. The notes are particularly important for determining the structure of the organization, accounting methods used, assumptions made, and other background information that gives the reader a perspective as the financial statements are reviewed. Careful review and analysis of management's discussion and analysis (MD&A) and other required supplemental information (RSI) are fundamental to the new process. Furthermore, financial condition analysis must also take into account additional factors such as debt per capita, tax rates, and citizen income and wealth. However, financial condition analysis can be very complex. Prior to GASB statement no. 34, ratio analysis was limited. However, with government-wide financial statements prepared on a full accrual basis, it will be somewhat easier to use ratios to analyze governments' financial condition. Government financial statements usually do not provide information for more than 1 year, probably because of the amount of information already being displayed on one page. MD&A provides 2 years' worth of data for some numbers. CAFRs frequently provide 2 years of statements. In performing a financial condition analysis, an understanding of financial trends

Encyclopedia of Public Administration and Public Policy
DOI: 10.1081/E-EPAP 120025947

is critical and, generally, 3 years' worth of data is considered adequate for ratio analysis.

What is the utility of the CAFR, given the complex analytical framework for analyzing financial condition? Many people who analyze public financial data find the introductory and statistical sections and the Notes to the Financial Statements to be more useful than the financial statements for assessing financial condition. This is because the introductory and statistical sections of the CAFR and Notes to the Financial Statements provide critical information on environmental and organizational factors and their relationship to financial factors. The BFS provide helpful information for calculating financial ratios essential to understanding the organization's financial position, which is an important component of financial condition.

WHAT IS FINANCIAL CONDITION?

Basically, financial condition is a local government's ability to finance its services on a continuing basis. It is the ability to: 1) maintain existing service levels; 2) endure local and regional economic disruptions; and 3) meet the demands of natural growth, decline, and change.[1] The International City/County Management Association (ICMA) defines financial condition as "a government's ability to generate enough cash over thirty to sixty days to pay its bills."[1] This definition of financial condition is called *cash solvency*. The Governmental Accounting Standards Board defines financial condition as: "The probability that a government will meet both its financial obligations to creditors, consumers, employees, taxpayers, suppliers, constituents, and others as they become due and its service obligations to constituents, both currently and in the future."[2] In both the ICMA and GASB definitions, financial condition is similar to the accounting term *solvency*. Whether a local government can maintain existing service levels or increasing service levels is related to the concept of *interperiod equity*. Interperiod equity is defined as: "whether current-year revenues are sufficient to pay for the services provided that year and whether future taxpayers will be required to assume burdens to pay for current services to future taxpayers may threaten the government's ability to sustain the current level of services or to expand services to meet future population growth."[3] Financial condition can also apply to a government's ability to provide services at the level and quality that are required for the health, safety, and welfare of the community and that its citizens desire. This is its *service-level solvency*. A government that does not have service-level solvency might, in all other respects, be in sound financial condition, but be unable to support police and fire services at an adequate level. If in such condition,

the local government tries to provide adequate services; it suffers cash, budgetary, or *long-term solvency* problems.

FACTORS AND INDICATORS USED IN ASSESSING FINANCIAL CONDITION

Financial condition analysis is the examination of the financial status of a government organization based on a financial statement analysis as well as an evaluation of many external factors that affect the financial condition of the government, such as the wealth of the citizenry, employment rate, and general economy. Financial condition analysis is a complex, multidimensional concept that requires the study of a multitude of factors. GASB identifies the major categories of these factors as: economy and demographics; revenue base; current and capital expenditures; debt, pensions, and other postemployment benefits; internal resources; management capabilities; infrastructure; and willingness to raise revenues and provide required public services.[2] Khan,[4] in his study of municipal bond ratings, listed several indicators used for assessing and making comparisons of financial condition. These include Per Capita Income, Percent Below the Poverty Line, Age of Housing, and Unemployment Rates. Economy and demography are two of the categories used by ratings agencies to assign bond ratings to municipalities. The ICMA uses indicators such as Vacancy Rates, Property Value, Population, Business Activity, Poverty, Households, Personal Income Per Capita, and Employment Base in its handbook for analyzing financial condition. It identifies these categories as "Community Needs and Resources Indicators." ICMA's financial trend monitoring system was developed for financial managers to use in tracking their governments' financial performance. The ICMA points out that these factors are important because they indicate the interrelationship between community demands for services and the ability of the government to provide them.

"Changes in community needs and resources are interrelated in a continuous cumulative cycle of cause and effect. For example, a decrease in population or jobs lowers the demand for housing and causes a corresponding decline in the market value of housing; this, in turn, reduces property tax revenues. The initial population decline also has a negative effect on retail sales and personal income, causing local government revenues to drop even further. But because of fixed costs in its expenditure structure that are impervious to declines in population or business activity, the government cannot always balance the revenue loss with a proportionate reduction in expenditures. The government may, in fact, be forced to raise taxes to make up for lost revenues: this puts a greater burden on the remaining population. As economic conditions decline and taxes rise, the community becomes a less attractive place to live and population may decline further. The cycle continues."[5]

WHAT IS THE DIFFERENCE BETWEEN FINANCIAL CONDITION ANALYSIS AND FINANCIAL POSITION ANALYSIS?

The primary difference between financial condition analysis and financial position analysis is that financial position "tends to be a shorter-run concept compared with financial condition."[2] According to GASB, "financial position for governmental funds focuses on assets and liabilities that require cash, or are normally converted to cash in the near future and can generally be determined from the financial statements alone."[2] Thus financial position is associated with the concept of liquidity.

Internal and external analysts can compare specific ratios to national and state medians published by Moody's Investors Service, Selected Indicators of Municipal Performance (Moody's annual), or comparative ratios published by Dr. Kenneth Brown for both cities and counties. Dr. Brown's Ten-Point Test[7] can be used to compare the financial position of cities or counties. The Ten-Point Test consists of a comparison of 10 key ratios for a city, county, or school district with similar entities across the nation. The *Test* measures the following elements of financial condition.

- Revenues—the ability of annual revenues to finance government services
- Expenditures—the manner in which revenues are utilized to provide government services
- Operating Position—the extent to which a positive balance between revenues and expenditures exists and the level of sufficiency of liquid assets and reserves
- Debt Structure—the levels of debt, both short term and long term, and the burden of annual principal and interest payments.

Of the 10 key ratios, three measure the adequacy of revenues, one measures expenditure allocation, three measure operating position liquidity, and three measure the debt structure of the entity.

DR. BROWN'S TEN-POINT TEST OF FINANCIAL CONDITION

1. Total Revenues/Population
2. Total General Fund Revenues from Own Sources/ Total General Fund Revenues
3. General Fund Sources from Other Funds/Total General Fund Sources
4. Operating Expenditures/Total Expenditures
5. Total Revenues/Total Expenditures
6. Unreserved General Fund Balance/Total General Fund Revenues
7. Total General Fund Cash and Investments/Total General Fund Liabilities
8. Total General Fund Liabilities/Total General Fund Revenues
9. Direct Long-Term Debt/Population
10. Debt Service/Total Revenues.

The analysis in Table 1 uses data from the four similar Ohio cities to compare financial position.

CITY OF CANTON, OH

The City of Canton is the county seat of Stark County in northeastern Ohio. It was incorporated as a village in 1828 and became a city in 1854. The 1998 U.S. Census Bureau estimate of population for the City of Canton was 79,259, a decline of 5.8% from the 1990 census figure of 84,161. Canton is a statutory city under the laws and regulations set forth in the Ohio Constitution. It operates under the mayor–council form of government. The main source of revenue for the operations of the city government is the collection of a 2% income tax. The city provides police protection, firefighting and prevention, street maintenance and repairs, building inspection, parks and recreation, water, and sewer and sanitation.

The results of the ratio analysis for Canton show relative strength in ratios 1, 5, and 10. Ratio 1, Total Revenue/Population, shows Canton to be in the upper quarter of cities. Higher per capita revenues indicate that the city has adequate annual resources to meet its obligations. Ratio 5, Total Revenues/Total Expenditures, is a measure of operating position and measures relative levels of operating surpluses or deficits. Canton's high score indicated that in FY 1998, it ran a relatively high operating surplus, which helps to build margins for the future. Building margins in good times helps soften the blow of bad times.[6] The third ratio, where Canton scored in the upper 25th percentile, was Debt Service/Total Revenues. A relatively low indicator of debt structure is important for a city's ability to meet its debt service obligations in a timely manner.

Although Canton did not score in the lower 25th percentile in any of the ratios, there are some areas of comparable weakness (25th–50th percentile score). Canton is somewhat reliant on intergovernmental revenue in its general fund (see ratio 2). This leaves the city more exposed to the whims of the Congress or the State legislature. Another area where the city may need more work is in ratio 4, Operating Expenditures/Total Expenditures. Its higher score indicates that the maintenance and building of infrastructure may not be getting adequate

Table 1 Comparison of financial condition

		Springfield	Canton	Loraine	Mansfield
Ratio 1	Numerator (US$)	70,628,228	37,502,751	39,124,038	47,261,029
	Denominator (US$)	79,259	68,857	49,802	65,568
	Ratio	891.107	544.647	785.592	720.794
	Score	2	(1)	2	1
Ratio 2	Numerator (US$)	40,781,273	18,758,142	5,269,803	24,045,204
	Denominator (US$)	49,138,452	23,228,448	10,152,822	28,572,261
	Ratio	0.830	0.808	0.519	0.842
	Score	0	0	(1)	0
Ratio 3	Numerator (US$)	0	0	10,866	0
	Denominator (US$)	49,138, 452	23,228,448	10,162,688	28,571,261
	Ratio	0.000	0.000	0.001	0.000
	Score	1	1	1	1
Ratio 4	Numerator (US$)	60,468,964	39,817,799	33,725,217	38,045,931
	Denominator (US$)	66,850,333	42,319,044	38,065,918	47,282,401
	Ratio	0.905	0.886	0.886	0.805
	Score	0	0	0	1
Ratio 5	Numerator (US$)	70,628,338	37,502,751	39,124,038	47,261,029
	Denominator (US$)	66,850,333	42,319,044	38,065,918	47,282,401
	Ratio	1.057	0.866	1.028	1.000
	Score	2	0	2	1
Ratio 6	Numerator (US$)	7,801,374	3,068,901	2,139,373	4,659,711
	Denominator (US$)	49,138,452	23,228,448	10,153,688	28,571,261
	Ratio	0.159	0.132	0.210	0.163
	Score	0	(1)	0	0
Ratio 7	Numerator (US$)	5,351,800	1,889,351	2,033,739	3,301,564
	Denominator (US$)	5,754,138	4,086,572	2,941,238	2,935,719
	Ratio	0.930	0.462	0.691	1.125
	Score	0	(1)	(1)	0
Ratio 8	Numerator (US$)	5,754,138	4,086,572	2,941,238	2,935,719
	Denominator (US$)	49,138,452	23,228,448	10,163,688	28,571,261
	Ratio	0.117	0.176	0.289	0.103
	Score	1	0	(1)	0
Ratio 9	Numerator (US$)	16,530,000	9,202,634	4,300,000	17,289,225
	Denominator (US$)	79,259	68,857	49,802	65,568
	Ratio	208.557	133.648	86.342	263.684
	Score	1	1	1	0
Ratio 10	Numerator (US$)	2,726,289	6,292,582	1,189,939	93,527,285
	Denominator (US$)	70,628,228	37,502,751	39,124,038	47,261,029
	Ratio	0.039	0.168	0.030	1.979
	Score	2	0	2	(1)
Total score		Canton	Loraine	Mansfield	Springfield
		9	(2)	5	3

attention. Canton also scored lower in unreserved fund balances and relative liquidity. Lower relative fund balances indicate that Canton might not be as well suited to meet a fiscal emergency as a similar city. Lower levels of cash and short-term investments could indicate an inability to meet short-term obligations.

Canton's overall score was nine. This puts Canton in the 75th percentile according to Dr. Brown's Test. The relative strength in the current position means that Canton, at least in the short run, should be able to meet its obligations in both providing services to its citizenry and meetings its financial commitments.

CITY OF LORAINE, OH

Loraine is the largest city in Loraine County, located in northeastern Ohio. It was incorporated in 1874, and is located about 30 miles west of Cleveland. The 1998 U.S. Census Bureau estimate of population for the City of Loraine was 68,857, a decline of 3.4% from the 1990 figure of 71,245. Lorain, too, operates as a statutory city under the laws and regulations set forth in the Ohio Constitution. Legislative authority is vested in a city council and the executive authority in the mayor (mayor–council government). As in Canton, the main source of revenue from the operations of the city government is the collection of income tax, which represented 63% of general fund revenues. Loraine provides police protection, firefighting and prevention, public health services, street maintenance and repairs, building inspection, parks and recreation, water, and sewer.

Ten-Point Test scores for Financial Position were very low (e.g., no score in the upper quarter in any ratio, two scores in the 50th–75th percentile, and four scores in the bottom quartile of the 10 ratios). Scores for the ratio of revenues to population indicate a deficiency in annual resources. The ratio of operating expenditures to total expenditures is too high, indicating substandard attention to infrastructure. The unreserved general fund balance is too low compared with total general fund revenues, and Loraine seems to have relatively low short-term liquidity as evidenced in its low ratio of cash and short-term investments to total general fund liabilities.

Overall, the City of Lorain scored a −2, putting it in just the 5th percentile. That means that 95% of cities scored higher. A long-term trend analysis would seem to be prudent to rule out whether there are some underlying long-term issues that need to be addressed.

CITY OF MANSFIELD, OH

Mansfield is the county seat and the largest city in Richland County, located approximately 65 miles northeast of the city of Columbus. Mansfield was incorporated in 1808 and operates with the mayor–council form of government. The 1998 U.S. Census Bureau population estimate was 49,802, a decline of 1.6% from the 1990 figure of 50,627. Like most cities in Ohio, Mansfield relies on municipal income tax as its main source of revenue (50.5%). Mansfield provides traditional municipal services (police, fire, recreation, streets, etc.) as well as operates an airport, a parking garage, and water and sewer utilities.

Mansfield had three areas of relative strength (75th percentile), and they were the same as Canton. The city's per capita revenue indicated adequate resources, its ratio of total revenues to total expenditures was strong, and its debt service levels were manageable. Mansfield did score in the lower quartile in three areas. The city seems too dependent on intergovernmental revenues in its general

fund, indicating some vulnerability to outside governmental entities. Its liquidity was relatively low, whereas the ratio of general fund liabilities to general fund revenues was too high, indicating that short-term obligations might not be easily serviced by the normal flow of annual revenues. Mansfield scored a five overall on Dr. Brown's Ten-Point Test, which puts the city firmly in the middle at the 50th percentile. That means half of the cities analyzed will score higher and half will score lower.

CITY OF SPRINGFIELD, OH

Springfield Ohio is the county seat and largest of Clark County, located in southwest Ohio. It is the only city in this analysis that is located in the southern part of the state. It was incorporated in 1850, although its roots date back to the 18th century. The city enacted a charter in 1913 that provides home-rule powers to the city under a city commission–manager form of government. The 1998 U.S. Census Bureau estimate of population for the City of Springfield was 65,568, a decline of 6.96% from the 1990 figure of 70,487. Municipal income taxes represent 71.5% of general fund revenues. The city provides traditional municipal services, as well as operates an airport, golf courses, and a sewer system.

Springfield did not score in the upper quartile in any ratio in Dr. Brown's Ten-Point Test. It did score in the 50th–75th percentile range in 4 of 10 ratios. Per capita revenues seem relatively healthy, whereas the general fund seems relatively independent from outside revenue sources. The city appears to be investing an adequate amount in infrastructure, and its current year operating position (total revenues/total expenditures) was also slightly above the median.

Springfield scored in the 25–50th percentile in 5 of 10 ratios. Fully 90% of its scores was within the 25th–75th percentile. Springfield scored in the lowest quartile in the 10th ratio, Debt Service to Total Revenues, indicating a weakness in its ability to meet debt service requirements. This performance was reflected in its final score, a three. The score puts Springfield in the 25th percentile, which means that 75% of the cities analyzed scored higher.

In summary, according to Dr. Brown's Ten-Point Test, the four Ohio cities rank as follows:

Rank	City	Score	Percentile
1	Canton	9	75th
2	Mansfield	5	50th
3	Springfield	3	25th
4	Loraine	(2)	5th

The data to calculate the 10 financial ratios are readily obtainable from most CAFRs. Except for population, which is usually disclosed in the statistical section, data for the first four ratios can be obtained from the Statement of Revenues, Expenditures, and Changes in Fund Balances—Governmental Funds and Balance Sheet–Government Funds. Data for the remaining ratios usually can be found in the Notes to the Financial Statements. In determining ratios 1–8, some analysts prefer to utilize general fund data only, whereas others use combined data for all governmental fund types. This decision will depend, in part, on how large the general fund is relative to all governmental fund types. In determining operating revenues, capital project fund revenues should be excluded because the capital project fund is not an operating fund.

In addition to analyzing ratios, the stability, flexibility, and diversity of revenue sources; budgetary control over revenues and expenditures; adequacy of insurance protection; level of overlapping debt; and growth of unfunded employee-related benefits should also be evaluated. Socioeconomic and demographic trends should be analyzed as well, including trends in employment, real estate values, retail sales, building permits, population, personal income, and welfare. This information is found in the CAFR and the U.S. Census.

CONCLUSION

Financial condition analysis relies heavily on analysis of BFS, including the notes that accompany them. The notes are especially useful for determining the structure of the entity, accounting methods used, assumptions made, and other background information that gives the reader a perspective as the financial statements are reviewed. In addition, financial condition analysis must take into consideration additional external factors such as debt per capita, tax rates, and citizen income and wealth. The use of ratios, such as Dr. Brown's Ten-Point Test or ICMA ratios, is also appropriate for financial condition analysis. Financial condition analysis is complex because the business of government is complex. For example, a local government's population might be growing but property values might be stagnant. There may be high property values but also high debt per capita. In any financial condition analysis, comparison with a relevant group should be made, and strengths and weaknesses should be considered as a whole in making a reasoned assessment about financial condition.

REFERENCES

1. Nollenberger, K. *Evaluating Financial Condition: A Handbook for Local Government (Revised)*; International City/County Management Association: Washington, DC, 2003; 1pp.
2. Berne, R. *The Relationships Between Financial Reporting and the Measurement of Financial Condition*; Governmental Accounting Standards Board: Norwalk, CT, 1992; vii, 16–17, 25.
3. Governmental Accounting Standards Board Concepts Statement No. 1. In *Objectives of Financial Reporting*; GASB: Norwalk, CT, 1987. Part 61.
4. Kahn, A. Classification models and municipal bond ratings. Public Budg. Financ. Manage. **1994**, *6* (2), 183.
5. Groves, S.M.; Valente, M.G. *Evaluating Financial Condition: A Handbook for Local Government*; International City/County Management Association: Washington, DC, 1994; 112 pp.
6. Pollock, R.; Suyderhoud, S.J. The role of rainy day funds in achieving fiscal stability. Natl. Tax J. **1986**, *39* (4), 197–485.
7. Brown, K. The 10-point test of financial condition: Toward an easy-to-use assessment tool for smaller cities. Gov. Finance Rev. **1993**, *9* (6), 21–26.

Foreign Policy Analysis

Eric K. Leonard
Shenandoah University, Winchester, Virginia, U.S.A.

INTRODUCTION

In the 1950s, the field of international politics (IP) split in two. The study of IP became a systemic view of foreign relations, whereas foreign policy analysis (FPA) began the process of "opening up the state" and examining its contents. These two divergent paths examined very different causal factors for global events. However, the overlap between these two fields was always undeniable. This article begins by examining the split between IP and FPA, with a focus on the difference between the traditional theoretical perspectives of these two fields of study. I then turn to the primary goal of this article, which is to show how we can bring these two fields back together. The method of unification is social constructivism and its emphasis on the co-constitutive relationship between agent and structure. If employed as a method of FPA, it may assist scholars in a more complete understanding of the decision-making process.

THE EMERGENCE OF FPA

Prior to the 1950s, IP, as a field of study, was more or less cohesive. Those who studied IP tended to blend the analysis of state relations with an assessment of foreign policy decision making. Although the early study of IP contained its fair share of disagreements (in particular, the realist–idealist debate of the 1930s and 1940s), the field remained unitary. Foreign policy analysis, although clearly a part of our world since at least the rise of the modern state system, did not emerge as an autonomous academic field of study until the early Cold War era. Foreign policy analysis evolved as a part of IP, finding its voice in the classical realist and idealist writings. However, the scientific or behavioralist revolution within the social sciences allowed the study of FPA to branch out on its own.[1]a

Foreign policy analysis "refers to a complex, multi-layered process, consisting of the objectives that govern-

ments pursue in their relations with other governments and their choice of means to attain these objectives."[2] Clearly, this form of analysis lies within the study of IP. However, during the 1950s, the IP scholars began to focus their attention on "actor-general" theories and turn away from any acceptance of "actor-specific" theories.[3] The best way to describe the actor-general type of analysis is that it is systemic in nature. This model describes the state as a rational unitary actor which acts in accordance with the national interest. If scholars of international relations are searching for a causal factor for world events, they need to look at systemic factors and not within the black box of the state. In effect, this form of analysis entails the study of like units acting within an anarchical system. What this perspective does not take into account, at least not to any large extent, is the inner workings of the state and its domestic relations.

Realism is the quintessential example of actor-general theory, as one can see by examining its core assumptions. First, realists view the state as the most important actor within the international system. No other actor rivals the importance of the nation-state. Second, they consider the state a unitary, monolithic actor. In other words, the state is considered a "black box" that acts, at least in the international arena, in a unified fashion. The turmoil of domestic politics is not a consideration for realist scholars because the primary causal factor for states' actions is external or systemic, not internal or domestic. Third, realists consider states rational actors. This "rational hypothesis" allows an IP scholar to view state motives as similar and unitary. This hypothesis also constructs a system of states that always act according to their national interest—which, for realists, is defined by security and relative power. Finally, the anarchical structure of the system is the underlying factor for all actions within the international system. Due to the fact that there is no overarching authority, states will act to maximize their relative power position within the system.[4,5]b

The systemic turn of IP study is what FPA scholars find so unpalatable. Foreign policy analysis scholars believe that if we are to understand the relationship among states,

---

a Provides and excellent description of this split along with a detailed discussion of the divergent models within IP and FPA.

b Morgenthau is the quintessential classical realist, while Waltz is the definitive text on neorealism and its structural emphasis.

Encyclopedia of Public Administration and Public Policy
DOI: 10.1081/E-EPAP-120024800

we must first and foremost open up the black box of the state. This entails moving from an actor-general model of understanding to an actor-specific model of understanding. Foreign policy analysis scholars began the process of unpacking the black box of the state in the 1950s.[6] This break from traditional understandings of foreign policy decision making—understandings that are predicated on viewing the state as a rational unitary actor—forever changes the field of FPA.

TRADITIONAL FOREIGN POLICY MODELS

When foreign policy scholars opened up the black box of the state, they discovered a plethora of factors that influence foreign policy decision making. Foreign policy analysis was no longer tied to the static thinking of structural models. Foreign policy analysis scholars could now engage the inner workings of the state and examine their impact on the decision-making process. Although numerous different perspectives emerged from this new form of analysis, this article will examine the three most influential models: bureaucratic politics model, small group context model, and individual decision-making model.[7]c

The statement, ''where you stand depends on where you sit,'' best describes the bureaucratic politics model. A bureaucratic politics assessment of foreign policy centers on the debate and negotiations that occur between competing bureaucratic agencies. Instead of focusing on the rational decision-making process of the state, bureaucratic politics analysts focus on the self-promotional style of competing organizations. Foreign policy, according to this model, is created from a negotiation process between competing organizations, which are each attempting to implement policies that benefit or highlight their organizational strengths. Thus rational unitary decision making is no longer sufficient for understanding the reality of intergovernmental competition.

This model gained credibility with the publication of Allison's seminal text, ''Essence of Decision: Explaining the Cuban Missile Crisis.'' In Allison's analysis of the crisis, three competing paradigms of decision making are compared. Allison concludes that the first model, the rational actor model, is insufficient due to the simplicity of its conclusions. Allison asserts that the decision-making process during the crisis was much more complex and involved a negotiation process among several competing governmental organizations. Therefore Allison tends to

favor the examination of intraorganizational debate and interorganizational debate (both of which engage an assessment of bureaucratic politics) as a means of FPA.

The small group context model focuses on the inner circle of foreign policy decision makers and the debate, or lack there of, that arises within the group. Within the realm of American foreign policy, the analysis would center on the presidential cabinet. Most small group context analysts agree that this form of decision making is not the best. According to this model, the sociological dynamics of such a group tends to homogenize the perspectives of its participants. The result, often times, is a lack of policy options due to the desire for personal acceptance and group cohesion.

The seminal text on small group context, or at least its negative consequences, is ''Victims of Group Think'' by Janis. Janis' sociological analysis of the dynamics of small group decision making asserted that group consensus was the prime motivator for many foreign policy decisions. This form of political decision making hinders the ability to ascertain good policy because of either the lack, or complete loss, of viable options. The small group becomes homogenized, thus prohibiting any of the positive components that may have resulted from a multiplicity of perspectives. In fact, there is a loss of multiple perspectives to the one dominant group consensus. Janis tested this hypothesis on several foreign policy case studies, including the Bay of Pigs incident, the Cuban Missile Crisis (which actually shows the positive attributes of small group decision making), the escalation of Vietnam, and others.

The individual decision-making model focuses on the primary authority figure within the nation-state—usually the President or Prime Minister. This psychological analysis of the leader depicts the decision-making process as one in which the ultimate ability to create foreign policy resides in one person. If, according to this model, FPA scholars are to understand the decision-making process, then they must examine the individual characteristics of the primary actors. This microlevel analysis would include an examination of personal characteristics (such as leadership style, conflict management, and personal perception/political history), along with the context within which the individual is making one's decision.

There is not one seminal text for this model of FPA. However, one of the more influential texts is George's, ''The 'Operational Code': A Neglected Approach to the Study of Political Leaders and Decision-Makers.'' This text describes the importance that a leader's core political beliefs have on the foreign policy process, thus placing emphasis of foreign policy decision making on the individual. George's assessment of the role of personal political beliefs, along with management styles within

---

cSee Ref. [3] for a comprehensive discussion of foreign policy models and their historical evolution.

the decision-making process, exemplifies this most microlevel of analysis—the individual. Ultimately, the message of individual-level FPA scholars is that decision making in the world of foreign policy can turn on the perceptions, personality type, or management style of the world's leaders.

What all of these FPA models have in common is a general acceptance that individual actors have the greatest influence on the foreign policy decision-making process. This conclusion completely counters the traditional understandings of FPA that emerged from the field of IP. These traditional understandings focused on the state as a rational unitary actor whose decision making is affected primarily by the systemic construct. But why does an analysis of foreign policy have to exist within this dichotomous relationship? Is the best understanding of foreign policy achieved by engaging in an either/or framework of analysis? Currently, many scholars feel that there is a way to incorporate both IP and FPA understandings of decision making into their analysis. The link between these two divergent understandings is social constructivism.[8]d

SOCIAL CONSTRUCTIVISM AND FPA

Social constructivism rests on the premise that the world around us is irrevocably social, and that an examination of global social relations will provide us with a more complete understanding of IP and, in the case of this article, the foreign policy decision-making process. According to this analytical perspective, the world exists in its current form because we—agents in the world— have made it that way. Such a perspective is very amenable to the FPA scholars and their models of decision making because the focus rests on the agents involved in the process. However, social constructivism does not view the decision-making process as a one-way street. Yes, agents do make the world, but conversely, social relations also make agents.

Thus social constructivists also acknowledge the causal factors of the traditional IP literature. This complex form of analysis provides us with a co-constitutive model of foreign policy, with both agents and structures making each other. In general, social constructivists do not privilege one perspective over another, but recognize the complexity of decision making in world politics, thus acknowledging the importance of both actor-general and actor-specific perspectives. It is the co-constitutive relationship of these two perspectives that social constructivists want to examine.[9,10]e

When thinking about foreign policy, the first attribute that social constructivists purport is that no concept, term, institution, or agent of foreign affairs is static. Because of the socially constructed nature of the world, the reproduction or reconstruction of everything is possible. This reconstruction simply depends on the interaction between the relevant agents and social arrangements, and, more importantly, the rules that guide those agents and social arrangements. Therefore we cannot think of the defining concepts of world politics/foreign policy as static institutions or discourses.

Second, social constructivists agree that foreign policy decision making does not come about through one causal factor, as traditional FPA or IP scholars would have us believe. Instead, decision making results from the interplay between actors (which include more than just states and individual leaders) and context. Social constructivists privilege neither factor. However, what social constructivists do privilege is the social relationship between the two (agent and structure), which causes a certain decision-making process to occur.

One problem that arises from this rich and complex understanding of foreign affairs is qualifying the relationship that exists between agent and structure. If social constructivists hope to study foreign policy from both agent-general and agent-specific perspectives, how do we link the two forms of understanding? The link occurs in the form of action and interaction. Social constructivists do not accept that agents/actors and or context/environment are simple and static. Both agents/actors and structure/context are malleable entities, and the change that may or may not occur in both of these entities comes about via action and interaction. This is, in fact, the making of our world, or, in the case of FPA scholars, the making of foreign policy. An example from the current global context may help to clarify this approach.

The current situation in Iraq—and, in particular, the Unites States' decision to invade—is a hot topic of conversation among FPA scholars. How does one understand the motives behind the U.S. invasion? Was this action generated primarily by the agents involved, or were these agents simply acting according to the current structure? A social constructivist would answer yes to both questions. How does one understand the decision to

---

dKubalkova's ''Foreign Policy in a Constructed World'' is one text that attempts to bring together these two divergent areas of policy study by engaging in constructivist ontology.

e''Constructivism: A User's Manual'' and ''Making and Remaking the World for IR 101: A Resource for Teaching Social Constructivism in Introductory Classes'' provide two excellent introductory sources to the study of world politics through a social constructivist perspective.

invade Iraq if you disregard either the actors involved or the structure? The fact that George W. Bush is President of the United States is crucial to understanding the decision to invade. His boisterous, do-it-alone (unilateralist) attitude is a primary causal factor in the decision-making process, as is the individuals that he has surrounded himself with. However, an analysis of the President's personal perceptions, management style, etc., along with an analysis of the aforementioned traits of the presidential cabinet, are not sufficient to understand the decision to invade. One major question looms: would the United States have invaded Iraq if 9/11 had never happened? I would argue no, thus showing the importance of context and its impact on the agents involved. 9/11 made the foreign policy decision to invade possible, but so did the election of George W. Bush. The crucial area to study for FPA scholars is not simply the context nor the individuals, but the interaction between these two. Social constructivism may be more complex then previous FPA approaches, but it is also more complete in its assessment of foreign policy.[11]f

CONCLUSION

So where is the field of FPA headed in the coming years?[12]g This article has attempted to show both the divergent positions within the study of FPA and a new form of analysis that might serve as a bridge within the field. With that said, the future of FPA may or may not find its theoretical basis in social constructivism. Constructivism may not solve the long-standing debate between traditional FPA and IP scholars, along with the subdebates contained within FPA. However, if FPA scholars are willing to engage in a social constructivist assessment of foreign affairs, they may find the bridge that brings these seemingly opposed fields of study back together. As this form of analysis grows in acceptance, I believe that its applicability to multiple fields of study will grow. Nevertheless, ontological shifts are slow, but constructivists can serve as a repairperson for the IR/FPA split, if the analysts allow it. The result would only bene-

fit the field and our understanding of foreign policy decision making.

REFERENCES

1. Holsti, O.R. Models of International Relations and Foreign Policy. In *Diplomatic History*; 1989, *13* (1), 15–43.
2. Kubalkova, V. Foreign Policy, International Politics, and Constructivism. In *Foreign Policy in a Constructed World*; Kubalkova, V., Ed.; M. E. Sharpe: Armonk, NY, 2001; 15–37.
3. Hudson, V.M. Foreign policy analysis yesterday, today, and tomorrow. Mershon Int. Stud. Rev. **1995**, *39* (1), 209–238.
4. Morgenthau, H. *Politics Among Nations*; Alfred Knopf: New York, NY, 1947.
5. Waltz, K.N. *Theory of International Politics*; Addison-Wesley: Reading, MA, 1979.
6. Snyder, R.C.; Bruck, H.W.; Sapin, B. *Decision Making as an Approach to the Study of International Politics. Reprinted in Foreign Policy Decision Making: An Approach to the Study of International Politics*; Free Press: New York, NY, 1962.
7. Hudson, V.M. *Foreign Policy Analysis*; Encyclopedia of Policy Studies, 1994; 281–304.
8. *Foreign Policy in a Constructed World*; Kubalkova, V., Ed.; M. E. Sharpe: Armonk, NY, 2001.
9. Onuf, N. Constructivism: A User's Manual. In *International Relations in a Constructed World*; Kubalkova, V., Onuf, N., Kowert, P., Eds.; M. E. Sharpe: Armonk, NY, 1998; 58–78.
10. Ba, A.; Hoffmann, M.J. Making and remaking the world for IR 101: A resource for teaching social constructivism in introductory classes. Int. Stud. Perspect. **2003**, *4*, 15–33.
11. Campbell, D. *Writing Security: United States Foreign Policy and the Politics of Identity*, revised edition. Minnesota University Press: Minneapolis, MN, 1998.
12. Karbo, J. Foreign policy analysis in the twenty-first century: Back to comparison, forward to identity and ideas. Int. Stud. Rev. **2003**, *5* (2), 156–163.

FURTHER READINGS

Allison, G.T. *Essence of Decision: Decision Making and the Cuban Missile Crisis*; Little, Brown, and Co.: Boston, MA, 1971.
George, A.L. The 'Operational Code': A neglected approach to the study of political leaders and decision-makers. Int. Stud. Q. **1969**, *13*, 190–222.
Janis, I. *Victims of Group Think*; Houghton Mifflin Company: Boston, MA, 1972.

f"Writing Security: United States Foreign Policy and the Politics of Identity" is an excellent example of constructivist work and its relation to foreign affairs.

g"Foreign Policy Analysis in the Twenty-First Century: Back to Comparison, Forward to Identity and Ideas" provides a good assessment of probable future forms of study.

Freedom of Information Act—Federal

Suzanne J. Piotrowski
*Rutgers, The State University of New Jersey,
Newark, New Jersey, U.S.A.*

INTRODUCTION

The Freedom of Information Act (FOIA) is the premier open government statute in the U.S. federal government. FOIA works to ensure a more transparent federal administration. The openness afforded by FOIA has become a central aspect of federal administration. After a long debate, FOIA was passed by Congress in 1966 and has been amended periodically. FOIA allows individuals or organizations to request documents from a federal agency. While not all documents are releasable, many are. Federal agencies may withhold documents that fall into nine broad exemption categories. Included within this entry is an overview of the theoretical underpinnings of the act, a legislative history of FOIA, and a short description of the major provisions of the act.

WHAT IS FOIA?

The Freedom of Information Act is one federal law that deals with open government. Other open government federal laws include the Privacy Act (1974), the Government in the Sunshine Act (1976), and the Federal Advisory Committee Act (1972). Implementation of FOIA is a major administrative function which cost over $270 million in fiscal year 2001. Open government laws are not unique to the federal government. All 50 states have laws governing the release of government documents. Freedom of information and the free exchange of information is a global concern. Over 50 countries ranging from Albania to Zimbabwe have laws facilitating access to government documents. Over half of these international freedom of information laws were passed within the last 10 years.[1]

Governmental transparency and democratic accountability are the underlying tenets behind FOIA. Governmental transparency refers to the ability to find out what is going on inside of government. Democratic accountability is holding elected and unelected government officials responsible for their actions. While the initial Freedom of Information Act was passed in 1966,[2] the debate surrounding transparency in govern-

ment long predates the act. James Madison wrote in a personal correspondence:

> "A popular Government, without popular information, or the means of acquiring it, is but a Prologue to a Farce or a Tragedy; or, perhaps, both. Knowledge will forever govern ignorance: And a people who mean to be their own Governors must arm themselves with the power which knowledge gives."[3]

Madison's sentiments were included in the *Senate Report*, which accompanied the initial FOIA.[4]

The idea of opening up the government and holding officials accountable is an essential aspect of democracy. Francis Rourke[5] made this point eloquently: "Nothing could be more axiomatic for a democracy than the principle of exposing the processes of government to relentless public criticism and scrutiny." Policies which work toward a more transparent government combat administrative and executive secrecy. As explained later in the section "How FOIA Works?" not all types of documents are releasable through FOIA requests; however, at its core, FOIA is a disclosure statute.

FOIA also has two other provisions. The first requires agencies to disclose information automatically by publishing it in the *Federal Register*. Information that must be disclosed includes descriptions of agency organizations, functions, and procedures; substantive agency rules; and statements of general agency policy. The second requirement is the reading room provision of FOIA. Final agency opinions and orders rendered in the adjudication of cases, specific policy statements, certain administrative staff manuals, and some records previously processed for disclosure must be made available in agency reading rooms. Some of these disclosed documents must also be posted in an agency's electronic reading room. Failure to disclose some types of information precludes agencies from enforcing or relying on them.

LEGISLATIVE HISTORY

Varying proposed pieces of freedom of information legislation were prepared and debated in Congress for

Encyclopedia of Public Administration and Public Policy
DOI: 10.1081/E-EPAP-120024306

over a decade before the final bill was passed. An early advocate of freedom of information laws, Senator Thomas C. Hennings, Jr. (D-Missouri), referring to a proposed freedom of information legislation, noted that: "The aim...of this bill...is to make it clear beyond any doubt that the basic purpose of this section is to insure the dissemination of the maximum amount of information reasonably possible."[6] FOIA, which amended the Administrative Procedure Act of 1946, was passed on July 4, 1966 and went into affect in 1967.

Since the initial law was passed, a series of amendments have modified the statute. Some changes strengthened the statute while others weakened the reach of the law with regard to access of government. The first series of major amendments came in 1974 in the wake of the presidential Watergate scandal. These amendments significantly strengthen the reach of FOIA disclosures. A little more than a decade later in 1986, another series of amendments were passed by Congress during the Reagan administration. These changes weakened access to government afforded through FOIA by expanding the exemption for law-enforcement documents.

The last major set of amendments came in 1996 and are referred to, collectively, as the Electronic Freedom of Information Act or E-FOIA. These amendments brought FOIA into the Internet age. Electronic documents are now accessible through FOIA requests, and agencies are obligated to proactively post their most frequently requested documents in their electronic reading rooms. In 2002, the Homeland Security Act was passed which also included an amendment to FOIA. Senator Patrick Leahy (D-Vermont) called this amendment the "most severe weakening of the Freedom of Information Act in its 36-year history."[7] The Homeland Security Act amendment exempts all information deemed related to homeland security which corporations voluntarily disclose to the Department of Homeland Security. This is a very broad exemption that ensures the department will keep the disclosed information secret and allows companies to be free of potential civil liability and antitrust lawsuits if the information indicates wrongdoing.

HOW DOES FOIA WORK?

Essentially, FOIA is a disclosure statute. All agency records are accessible to the public unless specifically exempt from disclosure. Documents, not information, are requested and released under FOIA. This is a meaningful distinction. One cannot request the federal government to make a report or compile and summarize information. Under FOIA, one can only request preexisting agency records. There is no clear definition of what is an agency record. Typically, documents must be in control of the

agency from which they are requested. After the 1996 E-FOIA amendment, electronic files may be requested and will be released in electronic form. Prior to the 1996 amendments, databases released to requesters would usually have been printed and sent in hard-copy form. Currently, requesters may receive data sets electronically in the electronic format of their choosing. Generally, e-mails are considered agency records although the line between agency and personal records is at times blurred. For a comprehensive discussion of relevant case law, see *Litigation Under the Federal Open Government Laws 2002: Covering the Freedom of Information Act, the Privacy Act, and the Government in the Sunshine Act, and the Federal Advisory Committee Act.*[8]

Virtually, anyone can make a FOIA request including U.S. citizens, foreign citizens, corporations, and governments. FOIA is a disclosure statute, meaning it opens up documents in the federal government for release. With that said, there are nine exemptions written into FOIA:

1. National security information.
2. Internal agency rules.
3. Information exempted by other statutes.
4. Business information.
5. Inter- and intra-agency memoranda.
6. Personal privacy.
7. Law-enforcement records.
8. Records of financial institutions.
9. Oil well data.

Most of these exemptions are discretionary; that is, if a document falls under one of the exemption categories, then the federal agency has the option whether to release the document or not. However, the first exemption is not discretionary. Documents that have been classified for national defense or foreign policy are not releasable. Documents that are properly classified are not appropriate for a discretionary disclosure. The second exemption refers to documents which relate to internal personnel rules and practices. Documents falling under exemption 2 may be discretionarily disclosed. The third exemption is one of the broadest. If documents are exempt from disclosure through another statute, then they are also exempt under FOIA and cannot be discretionarily disclosed. Examples of statutes that exempt the release of material include the Department of Homeland Security Act, the Immigration and Naturalization Act, the Federal Aviation Act of 1958, and the Ethics in Government Act.

Trade secrets and business information are exempt from release through FOIA by the fourth exemption and rarely are discretionarily disclosed. At times, corporations or businesses seek to prevent the release of information gathered by an agency to a third party. These challenges are referred to as "reverse" FOIA litigation. Documents

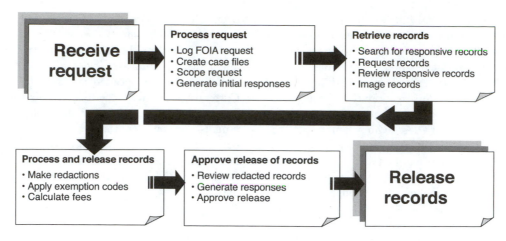

Fig. 1 Overview of generic FOIA process. (U.S. General Accounting Office (2002). *Information Management: Update on Implementation of the 1996 Electronic Freedom of Information Act Amendments* [GAO-02-493]. Washington, DC: U.S. General Accounting Office, p. 5.)

such as inter- or intra-agency memos regarding predecisional policy formation are covered under exemption 5. Documents falling under exemption 5 may be discretionarily disclosed. Individual's personnel or medical files are not releasable because of the privacy exemption, number six, and generally not deemed appropriate for discretionary disclosures. The law-enforcement provisions, which were strengthened by the 1986 amendment, are covered under exemption 7. Records dealing with financial institutions and oil wells are covered by exemptions 8 and 9, respectively. Documents falling under exemption 7, 8, or 9 may be discretionarily disclosed.

To make a FOIA request, one must send a written request to the individual agency you would like to release the documents. This can be carried out either by the mail or, increasingly, by fax or e-mail. It is essential that you write to the correct agency and you are as specific as possible about your request. There is a wealth of good references on how to write a FOIA request. The U.S. House of Representative Committee on Government Reforms publishes *A Citizen's Guide to Using the Freedom of Information Act and the Privacy Act of 1974 to Request Government Records*. This report is linked to the committee's homepage: http://www.house.gov/reform. A summary of the steps a FOIA office takes to fill a request are presented in Fig. 1.

However, not all requests are filled. If a request is denied, either in full or in part, the requester has the right to appeal. Frequently, appeals are settled informally by the agency and never make their way to court. Judicial remedy is the last recourse, however.

By law, agencies are required to make a determination on a FOIA request within 20 working days. Agencies are also required to make a determination on administrative appeals within 20 working days of receipt of the appeal.

Many agencies do not meet these requirements and some have construed the 20 days as the time frame within which the request needs to be acknowledged. This was not the intent of the law. Agencies frequently do not meet the statutorily prescribed timelines and subsequently have large backlogs of unfulfilled requests. Some agencies have requests that are years old. The 1996 E-FOIA amendments attempted to address this issue by setting up a multitrack processing system. Instead of a first-come first-serve basis, they now have a system where simple requests are filled within the order they are received and complex requests are put into a different queue.

Agencies can charge requesters for the direct costs associated with searching for documents, the direct costs associated with reviewing documents to determine which portions are releasable, and the duplication costs. Depending on the category of requester, all, some, or none of these fees may be charged. Review, search, and copy charges are set by the Office of Management and Budget. Certain categories of requesters can apply and receive fee waivers. Individuals or organizations that fall under the category of public interest groups, representatives of the news media, or educational or noncommercial scientific organizations may receive these waivers. Fee waivers are also granted to any requester who can show that the disclosure of the information is in the public interest and will likely contribute to public understanding of governmental operations and activities.

CONCLUSION

Implementation of the Freedom of Information Act is a complex process. Inherent in this process are multiple tensions. The first tension is between efficiency and transparency. FOIA is expensive and FOIA offices are periodically underfunded. FOIA functions are not associated with the missions of most federal agencies. When budgets are tight, it is essential to continue funding nonmission-based functions such as FOIA.[9] Budgetary constraints are a major impediment to FOIA implementation. Statutorily FOIA requests must be filled and lack of funding does not absolve this responsibility. Most agencies have significant backlogs of unfilled requests and requests may take years to be filled. Requesters have little recourse for delayed filling of requests other than litigation.

The tension between privacy and transparency is perennial. Privacy advocates consistently want to decrease the amount of information that can be released with regard to personal privacy, while other groups of people, such as journalists, may push for greater release of personal information. Other areas of tension include national security, homeland security, and business information. These tensions are inherent in any freedom of information law and are most likely never going to be resolved. The need to periodically strike new balances among FOIA's major concerns is not necessarily a problem. Competing interests will help shape the nature of future Freedom of Information Act amendments.

REFERENCES

1. Banisar, D. *The www.freedominfo.org Global Survey: Freedom of Information and Access to Government Record Laws Around the World*; The National Security Archive, The George Washington University: Washington, DC, September 28, 2003. http://www.freedominfo.org/survey/survey2003.pdf downloaded September 30, 2003.

2. Freedom of Information Act 1966 (as amended 1974, 1986, 1996).

3. Madison, J. Letter to William T. Barry, August 4, 1822. In *James Madison: Writings*; Literary Classics of the United States: New York, NY, 1999; 790.

4. *Freedom of Information Act and Amendment of 1974 Source Book: Legislative History, Texts, and Other Documents*; U.S. Government Printing Office: Washington, DC, 1975.

5. Rourke, F.E. Administrative secrecy: A congressional dilemma. Am. Polit. Sci. Rev. **1960**, *54* (3), 691.

6. Braverman, B.A.; Chetwynd, F.J. *Information Law: Freedom of Information, Privacy, Open Meetings, Other Access Law (Books 1 and 2)*; Practicing Law Institute: New York, 1985; 12.

7. *Homefront Confidential: How the War on Terrorism Affects Access to Information and the Public's Right to Know*, 4th Ed.; Dalgish, L.A., LaFleur, J., Leslie, G.P., Eds.; Reporters Committee for Freedom of the Press: Arlington, VA, September 2003; 67. March.

8. *Litigation Under the Federal Open Government Laws 2002: Covering the Freedom of Information Act, the Privacy Act, and the Government in the Sunshine Act, and the Federal Advisory Committee Act*; Hammitt, H.A., Sobel, D.L., Zaid, M.S., Eds.; Epic Publications: Washington, DC, 2002.

9. Piotrowski, S.J.; Rosenbloom, D.H. Nonmission-based values in results-oriented public management: The case of freedom of information. Public Admin. Rev. **2002**, *62*, 6. November/December.

Government-Sponsored Enterprises (GSEs)

Stuart C. Strother
Steven G. Koven
University of Louisville, Louisville, Kentucky, U.S.A.

INTRODUCTION

Government-sponsored enterprises (GSEs) are large financial institutions that function in secondary finance markets for the purpose of making credit more available to borrowers for home mortgages, agricultural loans, and student loans. Originally established by the federal government, most GSEs are now privately owned, although they still retain many characteristics of a public agency. Most GSEs are restricted by law to function only in the secondary market—they purchase or guarantee loans originated by primary lenders such as banks, thrifts, and mortgage banks. Because they have little direct interaction with the general public, GSEs function under the radar screen, but they are some of the world's largest financial institutions. Three of the major GSEs—the Federal National Mortgage Association (Fannie Mae), the Federal Home Loan Mortgage Corporation (Freddie Mac), and the Student Loan Marketing Association (Sallie Mae)—consistently appear in *Fortune*'s list of the 500 largest companies. In this entry, we describe the creation of the GSEs, explain how GSEs function, explore the public and private characteristics of GSEs, and note some current issues facing GSEs.

THE BEGINNING OF GSEs

The first GSEs, collectively called the Farm Credit System, were created by the federal government in 1916 to help stabilize financial fluctuations in the farm sector of the economy. The individual enterprises that comprise the Farm Credit System as well as other enterprises are shown in Table 1. The Farm Credit System was designed to "encourage the flow of credit for farm mortgage loans... make farm operating loans... and lend to agricultural producer cooperatives."[1] Farm Credit System institutions functioned as "cooperatives owned and controlled by the borrowers."[1] Wild fluctuations in agricultural operations were smoothed out primarily through the organizational structure of the Farm Credit System, rather than through outright government subsidies of farmers.

Housing-related GSEs have their origin in the federal government's post-Depression efforts to rebuild the na-tional economy. After the collapse of the national housing market, which was characterized by numerous mortgage defaults by borrowers, local bankers grew discouraged from investing in home loans. Government officials were convinced that access to affordable housing and higher levels of home ownership represented key components to a national economic recovery from the Great Depression. To spur such a recovery, the Federal Home Loan Bank System (FHLBS) was created in 1932. The objective of the FHLBS was to provide loans, called "advances," to financial institutions such as community banks. To secure advances, member banks put up collaterals such as traditional mortgages, agricultural loans, and small business loans. The FHLB system consists of 12 banks. The FHLBS is not publicly traded, but is owned by over 8000 member institutions that hold equity stakes. The increased availability of funds made possible by this arrangement allowed member banks to offer more home mortgages to their customers.

Another GSE, the "Fannie Mae," was created in 1938 as a latent component of President Franklin D. Roosevelt's New Deal.[2] The goal of Fannie Mae was to enable local banks to make more loans for purchases of private homes. If private banks would agree to make low interest home loans to individuals, Fannie Mae would purchase these mortgages with federal funds, thereby assuming all of the investment risks. Once private home loans were guaranteed by the federal government, local banks were able to extend credit to individuals without danger of loan default. This arrangement worked well and Fannie Mae's purchases of mortgages became known as the "secondary mortgage market." With the backing and strength of the federal government behind them, private banks again invested in home loans, resulting in higher rates of home ownership.

As part of President Lyndon B. Johnson's efforts to streamline the federal government during the Vietnam era, Fannie Mae was sold to shareholders and became a privately owned enterprise in 1968. Fannie Mae's mortgage-backed securities (MBS) operations were retained in the newly created federal agency, Government National Mortgage Association ("Ginnie Mae"). Ginnie Mae operates the federal government's MBS programs, which are described below. For three decades, Fannie Mae had

Encyclopedia of Public Administration and Public Policy
DOI: 10.1081/E-EPAP-120040370

Table 1 Comparison of major GSEs

Enterprise	Established	Ownership	Key function
Farm Credit System			
Federal Land Banks	1916	Privatized in 1968	Encourage credit for farm mortgages
Federal Intermediate Credit Banks	1923		Make farm operating loans
Banks for Cooperatives	1933		Make loans to cooperatives
Federal Home Loan Bank System	1932	Over 8000 member institutions have equity ownership since 1951	Provide advances (loans) to member institutions (banks, credit unions, and thrifts) so they will offer more home loans
Fannie Mae	1938	Publicly traded private company since 1968	Make home loans more available to individuals by purchasing mortgages from primary lenders in the "secondary market"
Ginnie Mae	1968	Federal agency within HUD	Operate the federal government's mortgage-based securities program
Freddie Mac	1970	Publicly traded private company since 1970	Same as Fannie Mae
Sallie Mae	1972	Publicly traded private company since 1972	Make student loans more available to individuals by purchasing student loans from primary lenders
Farmer Mac	1988	Publicly traded private company since 1988	Guarantees mortgage-backed securities to make agricultural loans more available

Source: Refs. [1] and [6].

operated as a monopoly in the secondary mortgage market, but in 1970, Congress created another GSE, the "Freddie Mac." Freddie Mac conducts the same financial functions as Fannie Mae, including buying loans from primary lenders, advancing funds to lenders, and issuing debt obligations (bonds).

In 1972, Congress created another GSE, the "Sallie Mae," to provide greater financial support for guaranteed student loans. At that time, student loans were perceived as "small, expensive to service, and generally unattractive" to private lenders such as commercial banks.[1] Like other GSEs, Sallie Mae's primary function was to provide a "secondary market," such that primary lenders would be encouraged to invest in student loans. Sallie Mae eventually expanded into home equity loans based on the idea that families sometimes take out home equity loans to pay for a child's college expenses.

The Federal Agricultural Mortgage Corporation (Farmer Mac) was established in 1988 to act as a guarantor for MBS issued by private lenders and the Farm Credit System. In general, GSEs have used their access to federal agency credit markets to create greater access to capital for borrowers, and have provided greater stability in housing, agricultural, and student loans. Table 1 provides basic information about the function, ownership, and establishment of major GSEs.

HOW GSEs FUNCTION

Government-sponsored enterprises have three major functions: lending money, raising money, and community investment. With the exception of the Farm Credit System that lends directly to borrowers, GSEs mainly lend money in secondary markets. Government-sponsored enterprises "loan" funds to primary lenders (i.e., banks, thrifts, and mortgage banks) by purchasing the home mortgages or student loans that were issued by the primary lenders. Government-sponsored enterprise also make collateral loans, called "advances," to primary lenders who can use "any acceptable market-worthy collateral" to secure the loan.[1] Figure 1 illustrates how GSEs interact with primary lenders and investors.

To make direct loans to individual borrowers, to purchase loans from primary lenders, or to offer collateralized loans, GSEs need capital. In the beginning, GSEs received federal government capital contributions, which were later repaid or forgiven once the enterprise was fully privatized.[1] Government-sponsored enterprises now raise funds by borrowing money through debt obligations (such as Series MM bonds), by directly selling MBS, or by guaranteeing the MBS issued by private lenders. Almost 400 private companies issue MBS, including mortgage companies (70%), commercial banks

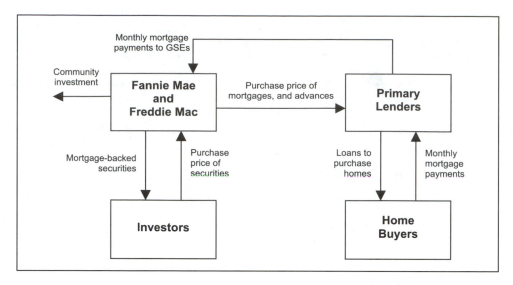

Fig. 1   Interactions between GSEs, primary lenders, and investors. (From Ref. [2].)

(14%), and savings and loan associations (10%).[3] After these companies have lent money to home buyers in the form of mortgages, a number of mortgages are pooled together and sold to investors in the form of MBS. Once the pooled mortgages are sold, the GSE guarantees payment to investors even if individual home buyers default on their mortgage payment obligations. The 30-year "Ginnie Mae" MBS is a favorite of investors. It can be purchased through any ordinary securities broker for US$25,000 and has historically yielded 4–6%. Because these are "pass-through" securities, shareholders are paid back their principal, with interest, each month over the life of the security.

In addition to improving communities through increased consumer access to homeownership, GSEs also have also contributed through community investment programs. Government-sponsored enterprises have contributed billions of dollars to the affordable housing program and the community investment program. These programs provide housing subsidies for low-income and moderate-income families, and provide funding for community and neighborhood economic development programs.

ARE GSEs PUBLIC OR PRIVATE?

At first glance, GSEs appear to be government agencies, but their core functions and operations have characteristics of both public agencies and private firms.

Notable public agency characteristics of GSEs relate to mission, limitations, leadership, regulation, taxes, access to capital, and quasi-monopoly status. When GSEs were

established, their stated mission was to serve a distinctly public purpose—to stimulate and stabilize the economy by providing a secure secondary market for loans. The congressional charters that established the GSEs also limited them to perform only certain functions. Fannie Mae and Freddie Mac, for example, are "limited to providing a secondary market for residential mortgages" of specified size.[1] Farmer Mac is limited by its charter to only provide specific types of agricultural lendings. Government-sponsored enterprise leadership also resembles public agencies in that the U.S. President appoints some members to each GSE's board of directors. Of Sallie Mae's board of directors, seven are elected by financial institutions, seven are elected by educational institutions, and seven are appointed by the U.S. President.[1] Government-sponsored enterprises also resemble purely public agencies in that they are not subject to certain regulations such as securities registrations; they are exempt from state and local taxes; and, most importantly, their securities receive preferential treatment due to the implied federal government guarantee. Another public characteristic of GSEs is that they operate as quasi-monopolies—a competitor cannot compete on a level playing field with the GSEs unless they first secured a similar charter from Congress, which is highly unlikely. These public characteristics represent a competitive advantage for the GSEs, making it difficult to assess whether they are efficient providers of financial services, or if they have displaced competitors who are wary of competing against a federally subsidized enterprise.

Notable private characteristics of GSEs relate to ownership and oversight. With the exception of Ginnie

Mae, the major GSEs are privately owned corporations. Like other privately owned enterprises, GSE management decisions seek to maximize shareholder wealth. Therefore the balance between the profit motive and social responsibility is a perpetual struggle for the GSEs. In the 1970s, the HUD Secretary tried to force Fannie Mae to invest more of its resources in subsidizing loans to low-income and inner-city areas. Fannie Mae's supporters claimed that the charter did not require such subsidies, essentially arguing they are not required to give away shareholder money. Government-sponsored enterprises raise money through bond issues like a federal agency, but their decisions to loan money largely mirror a private firm's decision-making process.

CURRENT ISSUES CONCERNING GSEs

Over the past two decades, GSEs have played an increasingly important role in the U.S. economy largely due to changes in consumer investment behavior. Throughout the 1980s and 1990s, consumers shifted their long-term savings from depository institutions (i.e., certificates of deposit at banks and credit unions) into equity investments (i.e., mutual funds and stocks). With their deposits declining, banks sought new sources of money and turned to GSEs, especially the FHLBS.[4] However, greater reliance on GSEs caused them to come under increased scrutiny and criticism. Government-sponsored enterprises have recently been chastised for wielding too much power, being too politically active, holding too much risk, and lending discriminatorily.[5]

Those who criticize the GSEs for having too much power claim that the government "subsidies" the GSEs enjoy amount to an unfair quasi-monopoly that prevents healthy competition in secondary loan markets.[5,6] Another criticism of the GSEs is that they are too politically active. They face only minimal oversight, which perhaps accommodated the June 2003 accounting misdeeds that resulted in the ouster of top executives at Freddie Mac.[7] Members of Congress have suggested that oversight of the GSEs should be consolidated in one place—the Treasury Department, where the GSEs' complex books are more likely to be understood.[8] The GSEs have responded to these suggestions by sending an army of high-powered lobbyists (mostly career politicians with little experience in mortgage finance) to Capital Hill to argue on their behalf.[9]

Another criticism of the GSEs is that they are holding too much risk. In February 2004, Federal Reserve Chairman Alan Greenspan called for actions to prevent the GSEs from further increasing their already US$3 trillion debt.[10] Much of this debt comes from the GSEs borrowing money from the U.S. Treasury to fund their purchases in the secondary mortgage market. A related complaint is that GSEs are retaining too much risk in their portfolios by holding on to mortgages rather than pooling them and reselling them.[5] In the event a GSE defaults on its own debt obligations, U.S. taxpayers are faced with a bailout much more painful than the savings and loan bailout of the 1980s.

A final criticism of the GSEs is that they have not eliminated discriminatory lending. An empirical study by Myers[11] concluded that "blacks and other minority group members are more likely than whites to be denied loans because their loans are less likely to be sold on the secondary market to Fannie Mae and Freddie Mac." Therefore the low-income home market is not as well served as it should be. It is likely that the profit motive of the GSEs directs investments away from housing loans for low-income home buyers and toward the more lucrative middle-income and upper-income housing loan markets.

CONCLUSION

Government-sponsored enterprises are large quasi-public financial institutions created by Congress to stabilize specific capital markets, especially the markets for mortgages, agricultural loans, and student loans. The GSEs fulfill this purpose by providing advances to financial institutions and by purchasing mortgages in the secondary market. Government-sponsored enterprises raise funds by issuing bonds and MBS, and by guaranteeing the MBS offered by private lenders. Government-sponsored enterprises have characteristics of both public agencies and private firms. They serve a public purpose, but operate based on private profitability. This hybrid organizational structure allows them to earn lucrative profits in capital markets while enjoying the stability and protection of the federal government's backing. Critics of the GSEs such as Stanton[1] argue that GSEs have served their public purpose and have concluded their life cycle. When Congress created the GSEs, no workable exit strategy was put in place, and, consequently, GSEs have grown to be powerful financial institutions that will probably continue to play an important role in U.S. capital markets.

REFERENCES

1. Stanton, T.H. *A State of Risk: Will Government-Sponsored Enterprises Be the Next Financial Crisis?*; Harper Collins: New York, 1991; pp. 19, 20, 23, 50, 59.

2. Koppel, J.G.S. Hybrid organizations and the alignment of interests: The case of Fannie Mae and Freddie Mac. Public Adm. Rev. **2001**, *61* (4), 468–482.

3. Ginnie, M. *Our History*; Retrieved on April 7, 2004 from http://www.ginniemae.gov/about/Our_History.asp? Section=About.

4. FHLB. *The FHLBank System: Partners in Community Credit*; 2001. Retrieved on February 4, 2004 from http://www.fhlbanks.com/Pages/template1.asp?P=131.

5. Donlan, T.G. Cut Fannie and Freddie down to size. Barron's **2004**, *84* (9), 35.

6. Stanton, T.H. *Government-Sponsored Enterprises: Mercantilist Companies in the Modern World*; AEI Press, 2002.

7. Barta, P.; McKinnon, J.D.; Zuckerman, G. House money— Behind Freddie Mac's troubles: A strategy to take on More risk; U.S.-chartered middleman of mortgages transformed into financial highflier. Wall Str. J. **September 22, 2003**, A1. (Eastern edition).

8. Cochran, J., III. A new watchdog for Freddie and Fannie? Regulation **Fall, 2003**, 6–7.

9. Murray, A. Fannie, Freddie use political prowess to parry regulators. Wall Str. J. **June 17, 2003**, A4. (Eastern edition).

10. Serwer, A. Greenspan sounds off: Is it politics or passion? Fortune **2004**, *149* (6), 69.

11. Myers, S.L. *The Effects of Government-Sponsored Enterprise (GSE) Secondary Market Decisions on Racial Disparities in Loan Rejection Rates*; U.S. Department of Housing and Urban Development: Washington, DC, 2000; 26.

Health Care, Assessment and Evaluation of

Leiyu Shi
Johns Hopkins University, Baltimore, Maryland, U.S.A.

INTRODUCTION

This article provides an overview of assessment and evaluation of health care. It describes the purposes, characteristics, and applications of health care evaluation. It delineates the process to conduct evaluation including determining the scope of evaluation, getting acquainted with the program to evaluate, finalizing the methodology for evaluation, collecting data, analyzing data, and reporting findings. The article will benefit those intent on conducting evaluation studies or critiquing evaluation work.

BACKGROUND

Assessment and evaluation of health care, or health care evaluation for short, is the systematic application of scientific research methods for assessing the conceptualization, design, implementation, impact, and/or generalizability of health services programs. It may be used for program monitoring and refinement, or for policy application and expansion.[1,2] The first purpose centers on the health service or program itself. It aims at finding out how a program actually operates, whether the program has fulfilled its objectives, and what improvements can be made toward program operations. In particular, evaluators are interested in addressing the following questions: How has the program been implemented compared to program plans? What are the characteristics and numbers of the beneficiaries? What are the strengths and weaknesses in its operations? To what extent has the program served its intended beneficiaries? What is the dropout rate? How cost-effective is the program? How cost-efficient is the program? What is the impact of the program? How can the program be improved for the future?

The second purpose goes beyond the program itself by analyzing the extent to which health policies achieve particular effects and assessing whether the program can be expanded or applied to a different setting. Evaluators are concerned about the following: How generalizable are the findings regarding the program? What is the potential of the program being applied to other settings? What are the conditions for such an application? What will be the costs and intended benefits?

The difference between these two purposes is that the first purpose is limited to improving effectiveness of a specific program within that setting. There is no attempt to generalize findings beyond the setting in which the program is operating. The second purpose serves to enlighten policy makers or funders by providing relevant information for decision making regarding program modification, refinement, expansion, or promulgation. Such evaluation can inform action, enhance decision making, apply knowledge to solve health problems, help set priorities, and guide the allocation of scarce resources.

Health care evaluation has a number of characteristics.[3] First, it is technical. Using established research methods, researchers design, implement, and assess a health-related project in a way that is reproducible by others. Rigorous application of scientific methods is necessary for the evaluation results to be valid and legitimate. Thus evaluators must be conversant with research methods commonly used for evaluation.

Second, health care evaluation is applied. In contrast to basic research, evaluation is undertaken to solve practical health problems and to have some real-world effect. It seeks to understand pressing organizational or societal problems and identify potential solutions. It studies the processes and outcomes of the attempted solutions. The researcher translates between the academic discipline and the world of action. The evaluator is often paid by the client who may be manager or administrator in a business, government, service, or private funding agency. The criteria for judging evaluation include its ability to provide useful knowledge, its utilization by decision makers, and its impact on health programs or conditions. Because the value of evaluation depends on its utilization by others, evaluators must be knowledgeable about the social dynamics of the setting in which they perform evaluation as well as the subject matter related to the evaluation.

Adapted from Shi, Leiyu, *Health Services Research Methods*. Albany, NY: Delmar Publishers, Inc., 1997, Chapter 9. Evaluation Research. pp. 182–214.

Third, evaluation should be objective. Program funders, administrators, and evaluators all have the duty of making the evaluation objective. On the part of program funders and administrators, the results of evaluation should not be tied to the current or future reward for the evaluator. If evaluators are personally or financially tied to the project they evaluate, they may be loath to report negative findings. Evaluations conducted under these circumstances may err in the direction of praise. On the part of evaluators, planning and conducting an evaluation often requires rapport, trust, and frequent interaction with program administrators. Evaluators should not let the process of gaining trust and rapport color their perspectives. Regardless of where or how they are employed, they need to find viable ways to maintain integrity, objectivity, and an appropriate sense of differentiation.

EXAMPLES OF HEALTH CARE EVALUATION

The field of health care evaluation is marked by diversity in disciplinary training, perspectives on appropriate method, and diversity in evaluation activities and arrangements. The major types include needs assessment, process evaluation, outcome evaluation, and policy analysis.[2-4]

Needs Assessment

The purpose of needs assessment is to identify weaknesses or deficiency areas (i.e., needs) in the current situation which can be remedied or to project future conditions to which the program will need to adjust. The decisions following a needs assessment usually involve allocation of resources and efforts to meet high identified needs.

Needs assessment has several applications. It can be used to identify goals, services, problems, or conditions which should be addressed in future program planning. Important questions to be addressed include: What are the goals of the organization or community? Is there agreement on the goals from all groups within the organization or community? To what extent are these goals being met? What are the areas in which the organization is most seriously failing to achieve goals? What do clients perceive they need? What problems are they experiencing? How effective is the organization in addressing problems perceived by clients? What are the new challenges affecting the organization or community? How can those challenges be met? What additional resources are necessary in meeting the challenges?

Needs assessment is also used to determine the need for additional health services or providers in a community. First, the need for the particular health service or provider in the relevant service area is examined. A trend study is usually necessary because the new service is likely to impact the service area population not immediately, but rather some time in the future. The second step is to look at the supply component in the given service area. Similarly, a trend analysis is necessary to project the future service level when the new competitor will be in the market. The third step is to assess if a gap exists between estimated requirements and estimated supplies. Finally, a determination is to be made regarding new entrance need based on the size of the gap and the impact the new service and provider will have on existing services and providers.

Process Evaluation

Process evaluation focuses on how a particular program operates. It is concerned with the activities, services, materials, staffing, and administrative arrangements of the program. Process evaluation is conducted not so much as to decide whether to continue or drop a program. Rather, it is conducted to monitor the implementation of the program, to find out how a requirement or procedure has been implemented by program administrators, where things are going as planned, where they may deviate from planned directions, and what factors are associated with such deviation. Monitoring also may include assessing whether program activities comply with legal and regulatory requirements—for example, whether affirmative action requirements have been met in the recruitment of staff and whether discrimination exists in the selection of clients. As a result of process evaluation, modifications may be made in the activities, services, staffing, organization, and other aspects of the program either to correct an unintended deviation from the plan or to address an unexpected problem encountered in the implementation stage.

There are many reasons for monitoring the process of implementing a program. First, program monitoring ascertains that program administrators conduct their day-to-day activities efficiently and, if not, identify ways to enhance efficiency. Second, program funders, sponsors, or stakeholders require evidence to indicate that the program is being implemented as planned and for the purpose that it was paid for. Third, process evaluation identifies unexpected problems that need to be corrected immediately rather than wait for the end of the normal duration of the program. Fourth, process evaluation is often a prelude to outcome evaluation. There is no point in assessing the impact or outcome of a program unless it has indeed taken place in the way intended. Finally, monitoring program costs and resource expenditures provide essential information for estimating whether the benefits of a program justify the costs.

Important questions to be addressed include: What are the critical activities, services, staffing, and administrative arrangements, etc. in the program? How are resources including staff, money, and time allocated? What is a typical schedule of activities and of services? How are program activities supposed to lead to attainment of program objectives? How many participants and staff are taking part in the program? How are the important components of the program operating? To what extent has the program been implemented as designed? To what extent has the program reached its target population? What are the resource expenditures for providing a service? Is the program implemented efficiently? How can the program be more efficiently carried out? What adjustments in program management and support are needed? Are there any problems encountered in program operation? If yes, what is the nature of the problems? How can they be solved?

Many of the data elements required for process evaluation can be incorporated in a Management Information System that routinely collects information on a client-by-client basis about sociodemographic data, services provided, staff providing the services, diagnosis or reasons for program participation, treatments and their costs, impressions of outcome, and other comments. The information is essential for program monitoring as well as assessment at a later stage.

Outcome Evaluation

Outcome evaluation is concerned with the accomplishments and the impact of the program, and the effectiveness of the program in attaining the intended results. The purpose is to collect and present information needed for summary assessment about the program and its value. Program effectiveness is tied to its intended goals which are usually stated in terms of participants' outcomes. Examples can be health status (e.g., recovered from an illness), behaviors (e.g., primary care visits), performance (e.g., stop smoking), cognitive (e.g., knowledge or skill gained), or affective (e.g., satisfaction level). While evaluators primarily emphasize explicit program goals, they also notice unanticipated or unstated outcomes, both positive and negative. Outcome evaluation examines the extent to which a program's goals are or are not being achieved. The results of outcome evaluation may assist the sponsors or decision makers in deciding whether to continue or discontinue a program, or whether (and how) to expand or reduce it.

To judge whether the program is successful or not, evaluators often compare program's accomplishments with some comparable standards, such as the results of the status quo or some competing alternative programs with the same goals. Even if a program is not totally successful, evaluators may conduct an impact assessment that gauges the extent to which the program causes change in the desired direction. Because of resource constraints, in most cases, knowledge of program accomplishments alone is insufficient; the results produced by a program must be judged against its costs. The program's effects and costs are contrasted with those produced by an alternative program with the same goals. Programs that are cost-effective are preferred to those that are either ineffective or effective but costly.

Important questions to be addressed include: What are the goals of the program? How are they measured or assessed? What programs are available as alternatives to this program? How are the program's essential components (e.g., activities, services, staffing, and administrative arrangements) tied to achieving program goals? Why should these components contribute to achieving goals? Does the program move toward goal achievement? How successful is the program in accomplishing its intended results? What conclusion can be made about the effects of the program or its various components? Has progress been made toward meeting the program goals? Which activities or services best accomplish each of the program goals? What gaps exist in meeting the program goals? What adjustments in the program might lead to better attainment of the goals? Is the program or some aspects of it better suited to certain types of participants or certain settings? How effective is this program in comparison with alternative programs? How costly is this program in comparison with alternative programs? Are there unanticipated outcomes associated with the program? If so, what are they? Should the program be discontinued, continued, expanded, or modified?

Policy Analysis

Policy analysis lays out goals, uses logical processes to evaluate identified alternatives, and explores the best way to reach those goals. It rarely aspires to the standards of traditional academic research which are supposed to be able to withstand the scrutiny of time, and the continuing probes of fellow investigators. An analysis that can be finished until after the decision must be made is not useful to the decision maker. The purpose of policy analysis is to inform the decision maker, providing the best analysis possible given the limitations on time, information, and resources. Analysis is presented not to overwhelm the decision maker with methodological details, rather in such a way that the essential points can be readily grasped. By relying on the analytic techniques developed in economics, mathematics, operations research, and systems analysis, policy analysis strives to improve our ability to predict the consequences of alternative policies, provide a framework of valuing those consequences, and make rational and better decisions.

The five-step framework[4] for policy analysis includes 1) establishing the context; 2) identifying the alternatives; 3) predicting the consequences; 4) valuing the outcomes; and 5) making a choice. Each of these steps contains important questions and issues to be addressed by the policy analysts. For example, to establish the context of analysis, policy researchers must find out the underlying problem that must be dealt with, and the goals to be pursued in confronting the problem.

To lay out the alternative courses of action, analysts need to be knowledgeable about the particular policy and program and know how to obtain further information for analysis. It is also an opportunity for creative thinking so that alternatives may be designed to take advantage of additional information as it becomes available and the decision process becomes flexible, enabling decision makers to change the course of action as they learn more about the real world.

In predicting the consequences or estimating the likelihood of the alternatives, researchers rely heavily on the analytic techniques of management sciences, in particular economics, and operational research (e.g., forecasting and simulation, benefit–cost analysis, discounting, decision analysis, linear programming, critical path method, Markov models).

To value the predicted outcomes, analysts try to choose objective (often quantitative) standards or criteria against which policy choices can be evaluated. Since some alternatives will be superior with respect to certain goals and inferior with respect to others, evaluators need to decide how different combinations of valued goals are to be compared with one another. When valuation problems do not lend themselves easily to quantification, analysts may have to address the issue descriptively.

In selecting the alternative, analysts draw all aspects of the analysis together to identify the preferred course of action. Sometimes, the analysis is straightforward and the alternative that is best may be selected. At other time, the analysis may be so complex that researchers have to rely on a computer to keep track of all the options and their possible outcomes. In most situations, the choice among competing policy alternatives is never easy, for the future is always uncertain and the inescapable tradeoffs painful.

PROCESS

There are many ways to conduct health care evaluation. The following is a description of a six-step process to conduct evaluation.

Determine the Scope of Evaluation

To determine the scope of evaluation, first, the evaluator reviews all pertinent information about the evaluation assignment. Then, some background investigation is conducted to find out more about the nature of the assignment. Finally, the evaluator negotiates and reaches agreements with the sponsor about their mutual expectations of the evaluation assignment.

Get Acquainted with the Program

Once the contract has been signed, the evaluator officially proceeds with the evaluation. The first task is to get fully acquainted with the program you are going to evaluate. Specifically, you should find out about the program's goals and objectives, its principal activities, organizational arrangements, staffing, roles, and responsibilities, relationships between program operations and outcomes, profiles of the clients and services provided, financial performance, and its primary problem(s). In addition, some contextual information about the organization that administers the program may be useful. Such information includes organization's mission, history, services or products, characteristics of staff and clients, etc.

Often, your collaborators or evaluation coordinators are the best source of information and can provide you with materials containing the abovementioned information. Or they may suggest places you can obtain the information. Some common sources that the above information may be obtained include the program proposal written for the funding agency, the request for proposals (RFP) written by the sponsor or funding agency to which this program's proposal was a response, brochures of the program, program curricular or other materials, program implementation directives and requirements, administrative manuals, annual reports, an organizational chart or description of the administrative, decision-making, clinical, and service roles played by various people in the program, patient or client records, daily schedules of services and activities, the program's budget and actual spending reports, memos, meeting minutes, newspaper articles, document describing the program's history or the social context which it has been designed to fit, legislation, administrative regulations, completed evaluation studies, and perspectives and descriptions from program managers, participants, sponsors, or users. If feasible, you may want to personally "scout" some or all of the program components and activities. At a minimum, you should conduct one site visit to obtain first-hand impressions of how programs actually operate.

The evaluator then directs attention to the goals, objectives, and outcomes of the program and their measurements. The goals and objectives specified for the program will be used as a benchmark. Program staff and planners will be consulted with to make sure these indeed are the goals and objectives of the program. They may be asked to write a clear rationale describing why the particular activities, processes, materials, and administrative arrangements in the program will lead to the goals and objectives specified for the program. Some adjustments may be necessary to add or delete some of the objectives. Reasons for the adjustments should be clearly documented. However, the program's major goals may not be changed. The evaluator may look for additional sources for program goals and objectives. For example, are there written federal, state or local guidelines about program processes and goals to which this program must conform? What are the needs of the community or constituency which the program is intended to meet? Utilizing the above information, the evaluator can recreate a detailed description of the program, including statements identifying program goals and objectives, and cross-classifying them with program elements or components, comparing how the program is supposed to operate with how it actually operates.

Information about the outcomes of the program may be obtained from the program's published documents, performance records, productivity indicators, patient or client data base, and cost data such as financial performance records, insurance claims records, workers' compensation claims records. Often it may be necessary to conduct additional studies to find out more about the program and its performance. For example, participant and/or staff survey or interview may be conducted to obtain additional or supporting data to back up depiction of program events, operations and outcomes. Past evaluations of this or similar program, if available, will provide insight into how measurements can be constructed. Books and articles in the evaluation literature that describe the effects of programs such as the one in question are also valuable. If feasible, you may want to personally observe or monitor the program outcomes.

Finalize the Methodology for Evaluation

Although you should have considered the evaluation plan at the start, now that you have become acquainted with the program, it is time to finalize the method(s) of evaluation. Specifically, you will decide the evaluation design, data instruments and measures, data collection methods, and data analysis techniques. You may consider involving the primary potential users in planning for the evaluation to facilitate their ownership of the study, and encourage trust and cooperation. As you plan for the evaluation activities, you should draw a detailed time

schedule indicating when each activity will be performed by whom using what types of resources, and the duration of these activities. The schedule will be used to monitor the progress of the tasks so that the evaluation can be completed in a timely fashion.

Collect Data

Once the evaluation methodology has been finalized, the evaluator then proceeds to perform the tasks as scheduled. Much of the initial research will involve implementing the planned methodology including design, sampling, data collection and processing. Usually, there will be different kinds of data and different ways of collecting them. Data may be collected cross-sectionally or longitudinally. They may be collected from program staff and/or participants themselves. Staff survey might indicate that services have been delivered. Participants' survey is valuable for a number of reasons. First, it provides evidence to corroborate the staff's response. If not, different perspectives can be obtained. Second, securing participant data enables providers and program planners to know what is important to clients, including their satisfaction with and understanding of the intervention. Finally, it is an important way to find out not only whether services were delivered, but what was actually delivered, how they are perceived, and whether they are utilized as intended. Collecting a variety of information enables you to gain a thorough look at the program, and obtain more indicators of program effects.

The evaluator should make sure that the instruments are administered, interviews and observations conducted and coded, secondary data gathered and processed, and the scheduled deadlines met. If necessary, the evaluator should see to it that proper training has been given to those responsible for data collection (sending out questionnaires and monitoring their return, or conducting telephone or face-to-face interviews, observations, field work, etc.).

Analyze Data

Data analyses are conducted according to the techniques specified in the methodology section. The major objective is to find out the net outcome of the program, i.e., whether or not a program produces desired levels of effects, reflected by the outcome measures, over and above what would have occurred either without the program or with an alternative program. Net outcome may be expressed as gross outcome subtracting effects from non-program-related, extraneous confounding factors and design effects. The net outcome may then be compared with that from other programs or some objective standards.

Report Findings

Evaluators have many ways to report the findings of their evaluation, including informal meetings with program and evaluation sponsors, memos, newsletters, formal presentations, formal written reports, and scholarly publications.[5] To program sponsors, a formal written report perhaps is the most important product of evaluation and is required from the evaluator. To enhance their utility, valuation results should be presented in a way that nonresearchers can easily understand. The evaluator may share any draft reports with the clients for review before turning in the final product.

CONCLUSION

In sum, assessment and evaluation of health care is the systematic application of scientific research methods for assessing the conceptualization, design, implementation, impact, and/or generalizability of health services programs. Health care evaluation is technical, applied, and should be objective. The process to conduct evaluation consists of determining the scope of evaluation, getting acquainted with the program to evaluate, finalizing the methodology for evaluation, collecting data, analyzing data, and reporting findings. Health care evaluation is likely in high demand given the increase in publicly funded health care programs and the need to establish their efficacy for continued funding.

REFERENCES

1. Stecher, B.M.; Davis, W.A. *How to Focus an Evaluation*; Sage Publications: Newbury Park, CA, 1987.
2. Herman, J.L.; Morris, L.L.; Fitz-Gibbon, C.T. *Evaluator's Handbook*; Sage Publications: Newbury Park, CA, 1987.
3. Patton, M.Q. *Qualitative Evaluation and Research Methods*; Sage Publications: Newbury Park, CA, 1990.
4. Stokey, E.; Zeckhauser, R. *A Primer for Policy Analysis*; W. W. Norton & Company Inc.: New York, NY, 1978.
5. Morris, L.L.; Fitz-Gibbon, C.T.; Freeman, M.E. *How to Communicate Evaluation Findings*; Sage Publications: Newbury Park, CA, 1987.
6. Rossi, P.H.; Freeman, H.E. *Evaluation: A Systematic Approach*; Sage Publications: Newbury Park, CA, 1993.

Health Care Decision Analysis, Alternatives in

Krishna S. Dhir
Berry College, Mount Berry, Georgia, U.S.A.

INTRODUCTION

Health care professionals routinely face complex decisions. There are a number of factors that contribute to increasing complexity in practically all aspects of health care professions. Research knowledge is growing rapidly. Technological sophistication is increasing. Health care organizations have become more complex. Laws are not simple. The challenge of decision making in the health care industry is becoming more and more daunting. Adding further complexity to health care decision-making process is the fact that physicians are no longer the sole arbitrators of patients health care provided to the patients. The process has become democratized, and even politicized, with the entry of other parties, such as health insurers, regulators, politicians, lawyers, ethicists, family members, and indeed, patients, in the decision-making arena. These parties are not necessarily adequately trained to tackle the problems that confront them. They may not understand the dynamics involved in regard to the various factors to be taken into account. Often the relationship between actions taken and desired outcomes is uncertain. All options available to the decision maker may be poorly specified or understood. Therefore, unassisted, decision makers may make poor decisions. In this article we review some of the theories and frameworks available for the analysis of decisions, which could assist the decision-making process. However, before we explore the alternatives available to decision makers, we further explore the nature of clinical decision making.

THE NATURE OF CLINICAL DECISION MAKING

Subjectivity plays an important role in practically every aspect of medical practice, including the tasks of diagnosing, assessing, and treating. Although clinical as well as laboratory techniques continue to become increasingly sophisticated and precise, the integration of the information obtained by health care professional remains a subjective process. Clinical judgment has its limitations. To make a decision based on judgment, the health care professional processes social information. This information is obtained from the environment and could come from a variety of sources. The decision maker must integrate this information. The cognitive image provides a representation of the environment based on the professional's past training and experiences, essentially predisposing the person to interpret, integrate, and respond to the information in predictable ways. This adds to the complexity of the interaction between the clinician and the patient. Each may bring very different sets of beliefs, values, experiences, and perspectives to the decision. Additionally, the information may be imperfect or incomplete. The outcome may be uncertain. The value placed by the patient on the outcome may not be clear. In light of all these considerations, clinical judgments are probabilistic. The process of clinical judgment is fundamentally a covert process. Individuals seldom describe their judgment process accurately. Ordinarily, the only means of explaining judgments are introspection and guessing at reasons. These explanations are generally incomplete and misleading. Subjective reporting is fallible. Judgments are thus inaccurately reported and are observed to be inconsistent. Identical circumstances do not always lead to identical judgments. Observations of inconsistencies may send an observer looking for hidden motives or incompetence on the part of the decision maker.[1] Robust evidence from randomized controlled clinical trials often does not support clinical decisions by health care professionals. Therefore, many clinical decisions have to be made on the basis of limited evidence, even when robust information is absent.[2,3] Additional considerations impact the decision-making process of health care professionals. The pressure on them to take account of both costs and effectiveness of alternative treatment strategies is mounting. Technological and pharmacological innovations have generated a range of treatment options where hitherto options were limited. For instance, kidney inefficiencies may be treated either by drugs, or dialysis, or through transplant. Hypertension may be treated with beta-blockers or diuretics. Patient may prefer increased quality of life to longevity, or vice versa.

Fortunately, a number of theories and frameworks are available that offer considerable promise to health care professionals. Approaches based on these frameworks deal with the difficulties described above by formalizing the manner in which the health care decision problems are structured, and making explicit the manner in which they

Encyclopedia of Public Administration and Public Policy
DOI: 10.1081/E-EPAP 120014357

are then analyzed. If the parameters of one's judgmental policy orientations could be identified, then we might model the process of that person's judgment and develop support systems to aid clinical judgment. This process may be explored by posing the following questions:

(a) What is being judged? This refers to the clinical or medical criteria being assessed.

(b) What factors influence the individual's judgments? Answers will identify variables that influence the professional's assessment of the criteria. These factors should have mutually exclusive characteristics or properties.

(c) What relative emphasis or weight does the individual put on each of these factors? This question refers to the relative weights assigned to the factors the professional takes into account in making the clinical assessment. One source of disagreement between health care decision makers arises from the fact that different weights are likely to be attached by different decision makers to the factors.

(d) How does the health care professional integrate the information regarding each factor to arrive at an overall judgment? Identification of the mathematical relationship, which describes the dependence of the overall judgment on the factors considered, is important. The relationship between each factor and the overall judgment may be linear or nonlinear, and the contribution of each factor to the overall judgment may be positive or negative. The nature of dependence of the overall judgment on each factor is referred to as that factor's function-form.

(e) How consistent is the health professional in making judgments? An individual may make different judgments about the same situation on different occasions. At least two characteristics of the judgment task are known to affect consistency: task complexity and task uncertainty. Studies show that consistency is lower when the judgment task is complex and when the task requires the use of nonlinear rather than linear function forms. Even when a decision maker intends to use a specific judgment rule as defined by a specific set of factors, relative weights and function forms, his or her judgments or assessments may deviate from those suggested by that rule. In the absence of explicit and immediate feedback on judgment, the decision maker may be unaware of the degree to which the actual judgment or assessment deviates from that intended.

Consistency is different from accuracy. A decision maker can be accurate but inconsistent, consistent but inaccurate, both consistent and accurate, or neither. Consistency has to do with the reliability of the decision maker in executing the intended judgmental policy as defined by a specific set of factors, relative weights and function forms. When deviation between the actual judgment and that intended is low, consistency is greater. On the other hand, accuracy has to do with the validity of the policy itself—whether the judgmental policy executed (the specific set of factors, relative weights and function forms) is indeed the one that was to be executed.

ALTERNATIVE APPROACHES

Among the various theories and frameworks for analysis of the decision-making process available to the health care professionals are the following: Decision Theory and Multiattribute Utility Theory,[4] Behavioral Decision Theory,[5] Analytic Hierarchy Process,[6] Prospect Theory,[7] Social Judgment Theory,[1,8,9] Information Integration Theory,[10] Attribution Theory,[11] Conflict Theory,[12,13] Constraint Theory,[14] Bazerman's bargaining and negotiation framework,[15] and Fuzzy Decision Theory.[16] While Decision Theory evaluates unidimensional utility functions over single attributes, Multiattribute Utility Theory seeks to maximize the overall utility derived from a set of criteria or attributes. They both are prescriptive in nature. Both these theories assume rational behavior. Decision making is reduced to knowing the various alternatives available to the health professional for choice, the probability of the respective alternatives occurring, and the worth or value of the outcomes of the respective alternatives to the decision maker. The decision is made by mathematically discounting the expected value to be realized from each alternative by the probability of realizing them. The probability may be objectively known through historical or empirical observations, or be subjectively estimated.[4] Behavioral Decision Theory is based on the subjective expected utility concept, and like Decision Theory and Multiattribute Utility Theory, attempts to prescribe rational decisions. It attempts to explain the less-than-optimal behavior of decision makers in psychological terms.[5] Analytic Hierarchy Process provides a unique mathematical approach for the analysis of multiattribute decision making that does not require the direct assessment of utilities or probabilities as demanded by decision theory and behavioral decision theory approaches. It describes a decision problem in terms of linked hierarchical layers of considerations. Paired comparisons among factors considered are made with respect to a consideration of the next highest level of hierarchy to yield a final set of ranking among the various options.[6] Prospect Theory, which is sometimes also referred to as the psychological decision theory, moves beyond description of decision-making process to explanation and prediction of decision behavior. It attempts to explain why decision makers deviate from rational prescriptions. It argues that decision makers psychologically transform probabilities of outcomes into decision weights or emphasis, and value of outcomes into psychological or perceived worth, before indicating their preference or making their choice. It seeks the cognitive sources of departure from the criteria of rationality and attempts to make decision makers aware of their own errors and biases.[7] Social Judgment Theory, which evolved from the work of Brunswik,[9] explores interpersonal conflict arising from different judgments and lends itself to applications in policy analysis. The "social" element in social judgment theory is derived from the interaction it affords among two or more parties through improved communication.[1,8] Information Integration Theory combines a psychological theory of measurement with a theory of information integration to produce a coherent expression of the subjective nature of human judgment. It seeks to discover the metric form of the cognitive algebra employed in cognitive activities, e.g., is the information integrated in one situation by one algebraic principle, and in another situation by another algebraic situation?[10] Attribution Theory draws from Gestalt psychology, and focuses on one's explanation of one's own behavior and the behavior of others. It views people as observing events in their environment and seeking causes of events by evaluating available information. It does not seek models of individual judgment or decision.[11] Conflict Theory relates to the group decision-making theory of groupthink. It provides a descriptive theoretical perspective on how people handle decisional conflicts where potential outcomes are of some consequence to the ones making the decision. It accounts for the effect of psychological stress on group decision-making behavior.[12,13] The more comprehensive Constraint Theory seeks to explain how cognitive (time, knowledge, ability, personality, attitudes, etc.), affiliative (need for recognition, acceptance, conformity, obedience, etc.) and egocentric (personal motives, prestige, stress, self-esteem, and other emotional needs, etc.) constraints influence the decision-making process, often resulting in suboptimal outcomes.[14] Bazerman's adaptation of Prospect Theory to bargaining and negotiation is also of interest, especially in view of increased democratization of the decision-making process in the health care industry. He extends the application of the Prospect Theory to situations where multiple parties jointly make decisions to resolve conflicting interests.[15] Fuzzy Decision Theory assumes that human judgment and decision making is based on a complex system whose elements were fuzzy, yielding imprecise, even vague, measures of information. It deals with possibility and believability (e.g., can the event happen) instead of probability (e.g., will the event happen).[16] Cooksey,[8] on pages 26–54, offers detailed

discussions of these theories, and also of some others not discussed here, in the context of their applicability to the analysis of judgment and decision.

CHOOSING A FRAMEWORK

Health care professionals encounter a variety of decision-making scenarios. When confronting problems that require coherence, they would likely prefer to project their clinical judgment competence in terms of logical, mathematical, or statistical rationality. In such cases, they are likely to benefit from analytical frameworks that are primarily mathematical or econometric in approach, such as those offered through Decision Theory, Multiattribute Utility Theory, and Analytic Hierarchy Process, with their emphasis on prescription of how rational decisions should be made; Behavioral Decision Theory and Prospect Theory, which explore *why* decision makers depart from rational prescriptions; and Bazerman's approach on bargaining and negotiation that is philosophically based on rational prescription. The objective in the health care profession, however, is not always to prescribe an approach to clinical health care professional. When confronting problems that demand clinical judgment, the health care professional may benefit more from an *explicit description* of his or her own judgment process rather than a *prescription* of what the judgment process ought to be. In such situations, frameworks offered through Social Judgment Theory, Information Integration Theory, Conflict Theory, and Constraint Theory may be of particular benefit. Social Judgment Theory is particularly useful where the objective is to obtain a model of individual judgment process, which may then be used to develop judgment and decision aids. Attribution Theory does not do this. Attribution Theory generally assumes that the person making the judgment does not influence the cognitive processes underlying causal judgments. The Information Integration Theory has generally stayed away from applications. The framework offered by the Social Judgment Theory is also easy to use. The methodology involved yields relatively straightforward and mathematically clean results that are easily understood by decision makers. Further, literature reports that the simple additive models of decision making based on regression analysis seem to be at least as accurate as the more complex models and are preferred by many users with respect to most criteria of desirability.[1]

CONCLUSION

In this article we explore the complex nature of clinical decision making. We identified the various factors that contribute to the complexity of the clinical decision-making process. Information is usually incomplete. Clinical decision-making process is becoming increasingly democratized. The various decision makers bring their own beliefs and values to the decision problem at hand and are predisposed to interpret, integrate, and respond to information in predictable ways. The judgment process itself is fallible and covert. Self-reporting of judgmental policies is inaccurate. However, it is possible to describe a decision maker's judgmental policies underlying the decision-making process in terms a set of parameters. These are identified.

Various theories and frameworks available to the health care decision maker to analyze the decision-making process are discussed. Some of these facilitate logical, mathematical, or economic rationality. These tend to be prescriptive, offering what rational decisions might be taken, or explaining why the decision taken may differ from rationality. Others facilitate a description of the decision-making process as it is, avoiding a prescription. Yet others facilitate analysis of the decision-making process when the information available is imprecise and vague, and the decision maker also brings to the decision-making process his or her own perceptions of possibilities or believability. Suggestions are offered as to how the health care professional might choose an approach to analyze the decision-making process from among the alternatives available.

REFERENCES

1. Dhir, K.S. Analysis of Clinical Judgment. In *Handbook of Health Administration and Policy*; Kilpatrick, A.O., Johnson, J.A., Jr., Eds.; Marcel Dekker: New York, 1999; 557–569.

2. Detsky, A.S.; Naglie, G.; Krahn, M.D.; Naimark, D.; Redelmeier, D.A. Primer on medical decision analysis: Part 1—getting started. Med. Decis. Mak. **1997**, *17*, 123–125.

3. Tavakoli, M.; Davies, H.T.O.; Thomson, R. Decision analysis in evidence-based decision making. J. Eval. Clin. Pract. **2000**, *6* (2), 111–120.

4. Keeney, R.L.; Raiffa, H. *Decision with Multiple Objectives: Preferences and Value Tradeoffs*; John Wiley and Sons: New York, NY, 1976.

5. *Utility Theories: Measurements and Applications*; Edwards, W., Ed.; Kluwer Academic Publishers: Boston, MA, 1992.

6. Saaty, T.L. *The Analytic Hierarchy Process: Planning, Priority Setting, and Resource Allocation*; RWS Publications: Pittsburgh, PA, 1990.

7. Kahneman, D.; Tversky, A. Prospect theory: An analysis of decision under risk. Econometrica **1979**, *47*, 263–291.

8. Cooksey, R.W. *Judgment Analysis: Theory, Methods, and Applications*; Academic Press: San Diego, CA, 1996.

9. Brunswik, E. *Perception and the Representative Design of Psychological Experiments*, 2nd Ed.; University of California Press: Berkeley, CA, 1956.

10. Anderson, N.H. *Methods of Information Integration Theory*; Academic Press: New York, 1982.

11. Kelley, H.H. The process of causal attribution. Am. Psychol. **1973**, *28*, 107–128.

12. Janis, I.L.; Mann, L. *Decision Making: A Psychological Analysis of Conflict, Choice, and Commitment*; The Free Press: New York, 1977.

13. Janis, I.L. *Groupthink*, 2nd Ed.; Houghton Mifflin: Boston, MA, 1982.

14. Janis, I.L. *Crucial Decisions: Leadership in Policymaking and Crisis Management*; The Free Press: New York, 1989.

15. Bazerman, M.H. *Judgment in Managerial Decision Making*, 3rd Ed.; John Wiley and Sons: New York, 1994.

16. *Fuzzy Sets and their Applications to Cognitive and Decision Processes*; Zadeh, L.A., Fu, K.-S., Tanaka, K., Shimura, M., Eds.; Academic Press: New York, 1975.

Health Care Decision Making Behavior, Emerging Paradigms of

Krishna S. Dhir
Berry College, Mount Berry, Georgia, U.S.A.

INTRODUCTION

In this article we examine some of the decision-making processes found in the health care industry. We review a set of paradigms to assist the understanding of emerging health care decision-making behaviors. The concept of paradigms should be differentiated from the concept of models. A model is an empirical, sometimes idealistic representation of a particular process in the real world. However, a paradigm embodies a distinctive and more or less coherent set of general ideas and principles, whether intellectual, ideological, ethical, or otherwise, which serve to make sense of and provide guidance for the understanding of the process.

Decision-making processes in the health care industry are becoming increasingly complex. In this day and age of exciting medical developments, it is easy to conjure up images of patients going to hospitals routinely for replacement of various parts of their anatomy, no matter how critical their function. However, new medical technologies are complicating clinical practice. The emergence of technologies that make heart, liver and other organ grafts, transplants and prosthetic replacements feasible demands reconsideration of definitions of life and death. Difficult decisions, many with consequences not well understood or not previously encountered, have to be made. As we come to grip with these, new paradigms are evolving to assist in the understanding of corresponding behaviors. Some of the emerging paradigms of health care decision-making behavior are discussed below. Specifically, we present a discussion of ethical, courageous, and virtuous decision-making behaviors.

ETHICAL DECISION-MAKING BEHAVIOR

An ethical dilemma is characterized by a requirement of 1) a choice to be made between equally desirable or equally unsatisfactory alternatives; 2) an assignment of different or competing priorities and responsibilities to alternatives; or 3) solving a problem that has no satisfactory solution.[1] The dilemma may emanate from the decision maker's system of values, principles, or sense of duty, and may be exacerbated by uncertainties of outcome or consequences resulting from the choice, assignment, or solution.

In the health care industry, the Hippocratic Oath is among the earliest representation of an ethical decision-making behavior paradigm. Nevertheless, some writers have observed that in America medical ethics may not be getting the attention it needs,[2] and several medical schools have abandoned the practice of new students taking the Hippocratic Oath. Others see reason for hope in the transition from the personal ethics of oaths to the communal professional ethics of codes, and applaud the "revolutionary" transition from personally interpreted "gentlemanly" ethics sworn to by individual practitioners to collaboratively interpreted professional ethics.[3] Through past few decades, the interest in the teaching of *ethical* decision-making behavior in the professions has been growing. Epstein has offered a sweeping review of the development of professional ethics and corporate social policy.[4]

Practically every aspect of medical practice involves ethical considerations. These include issues pertaining to balancing between morbidity and mortality, the development of treatment methods, cultural contexts, obtaining informed consent, and whistleblowing. Today, health care decision makers are forced to cope with unprecedented legal, socio-political, economic and other issues, such as having to decide who gets an expensive treatment and who does not; and whose treatment gets funded by the grants for experimental treatment and who must pay from his or her own resources. They must determine whether societal resources of sizeable amounts are better spent on development of a mechanical heart or on a prophylactic public health program.

New technologies take physicians, insurers, regulators, politicians, ethicists, family members, patients, and indeed the entire society, through uncharted territory. Not all consequences of new technologies are known. Bates highlights the ethical issues of consent to surgical treatment, linking the issue with law, conditions that render the consent invalid, and implications of poor handling of the consent process.[5] Weijer points to the need for placebo-controlled trials for novel surgical intervention.[6] However, what should serve as the placebo control remains controversial. Furthermore, while blinding is a desirable feature of a randomized controlled trial, it is not indispensable. Efforts to preserve blinding become unduly burdensome on patients, as in the case of trials comparing chemotherapy and radiation therapy for cancer treatment. Typically, placebo drug trials are viewed as a therapeutic intervention. In surgery trials, could sham surgery be viewed in the same way? This poses an interesting challenge for ethical analysis of risk.

Medical science is based on a strong scientific bias that demands clinical trials to mirror laboratory experiments in which variables are manipulated one at a time to facilitate attribution of effects to cause. In reality, clinical care and human response to disease are simply too complex. While the physicians' decisions are based on the state-of-the-art knowledge of medicine, it is also by necessity based on assumptions of the cause–effect relationships between biological factors, and between intervention and consequences. What further complicates matters is that physicians are no longer the sole arbitrators of health care provided to the patients. Other parties, such as health insurers, regulators, politicians, lawyers, ethicists, family members, and indeed patients, have a say in the matter. These parties have now entered the arena that was once the sole concern of physicians. Democratization of the decision-making process has added to the complexity of the emerging paradigms of ethical decision-making behavior in the health care industry. For instance, most adult Americans continue to favor the right to euthanasia and physician-assisted suicide, while lawyers, politicians, and ethicists continue to have difficulty in dealing with their implications. To deal with ethical issues emerging from innovation in medicine and surgery, health care decision makers are increasingly referring to what Agich calls the regulatory ethics paradigm.[7] The paradigm holds that deviations from standard care involves experimentation requiring the application of a set of procedures designed to assure the protection of the rights and welfare of the subjects of research. This paradigm regards innovative treatment as a departure from standard or accepted treatment, irrespective of whether the accepted treatment is effective or a burden. Innovative treatments are regarded as suspect and questionable until they are framed in a research protocol with prerequisite informed consent mechanisms. The paradigm requires that to be ethically defensible, 1) a research protocol must be prescribed to test the innovative treatment, based on scientific research methods; 2) formal mechanisms of informed consent must be implemented; and 3) professionally competent review board must review the prescribed protocol. Unfortunately, in practice "the complex processes characteristic of clinical innovation

are often not reducible to a scientific protocol...The demand that a clinical trial be undertaken in a field of medicine undergoing rapid and dynamic development can actually thwart innovation."[7] The recent revision of the *Declaration of Helsinki* recognizes that with informed consent of the patient, the physician should be free to apply unproven or new preventative, diagnostic or therapeutic strategies where proven methods are nonexistent or ineffective, if in the physician's judgment these strategies offer hope of saving life, alleviating suffering, or restoring health.[7]

COURAGEOUS DECISION-MAKING BEHAVIOR

Ethical decision-making behavior may or may not demand courage. Similarly, courageous decisions may have little to do with ethics. Generally, courageous behavior is "characterized by efforts to be productive, make contributions, and help others and results in a sense of personal integrity and thriving."[8] It is recognized as a complex phenomenon that is promoted and sustained by various interpersonal and intrapersonal factors. In the health care industry, courageous decision-making behavior has received little empirical scrutiny although anecdotal accounts of courageous behavior by patients exist.[9] Psychologists such as Deutsch and Kohut have reflected on its nature.[9,10] Deutsch pointed to the need for the use of actual social situations, especially ones of conflict and crisis, as a kind of laboratory for the study of social process.[11] He concluded that courage is manifested when the inner conviction (regarding the situation relevant to the courageous act) exceeds the perceived punishment potential; it is not manifested when the reverse holds true. He also differentiated between nonconformity, independence, and courage. Philosophers such as Rorty[12] and Walton,[13] and theologians such as Tillich,[10] too, have speculated about the nature of courage.[8] Unfortunately, little attention has been given to the role of courage in the behavior of health care professionals as they innovate, discover, and practice their professions. In recent decades, however, attempts have been made to understand courageous behavior among patients with long-term health concerns.

Finfgeld conducted a meta-interpretative study of courage among individuals with long-term illness based on two extant works in psychology, and four in nursing.[8] A meta-interpretative study is one in which findings from a number of qualitative works are synthesized to yield a deeper interpretation of the phenomenon of interest. The goal of such a study is to enrich the theoretical basis of a concept. This study offers a paradigm for courageous decision-making behavior in the health care industry. Finfgeld's meta-study included studies of courage in 1) a middle-aged woman with terminal cancer; 2) hospitalized adolescents with a variety of long-term health concerns; 3) sexual assault victims, individuals with severe physical disabilities, and people who had contracted human immunodeficiency virus or had acquired immunodeficiency syndrome; 4) chronically ill elderly; 5) young adults; and 6) middle-aged adults.[8]

Through the meta-study, Finfgeld found that the ability to be courageous develops over time and requires efforts to fully accept reality, solve problems based on this discernment of reality, and push beyond ongoing struggles.[8] Becoming courageous involves a lifelong learning process. The learning process begins in youth and continues through efforts of coping with persistent threats to well being. Being courageous is preceded by perceived threat such as uncertainty, loss, personal limitation, and powerlessness, helplessness, lack of control, pain, and embarrassment. The ability to be courageous is acquired through an ongoing bi-directional progressive–regressive process in which disappointments and frustrations can hinder or reverse the evolution of courageous behavior. Throughout its ongoing emergence and manifestation, courage lies on a continuum of behaviors, with noncourageous behavior at one end, courageous behavior at the other end, and different degrees of coping between the two ends. Courageous individuals take responsibility and are productive, and push themselves beyond coping.

The meta-study revealed that struggling to fully accept and comprehend a threatening situation is an essential component of being courageous. Comprehensive acceptance and understanding are enhanced by active acquisition of information, and helping others with similar problems. With full awareness, issues of well being, such as threats, struggles, and even death, are reframed and perceived to be manageable challenges. As a result of living their lives courageously, individuals experience an altered self-perception; enhanced sense of personal integrity, self satisfaction, and pride; and a sense that life has been lived well. Health care providers facilitate this process by demonstrating competence and communicating effectively. Outcomes of being courageous include personal integrity and thriving in the midst of normality. Thriving includes a feeling of power; vitality, zest; and joy and involvement in life.

Finfgeld's meta-study concluded that courage is not limitless, and the process of becoming and being courageous is dependent on intrapersonal and interpersonal factors.[8] Cuff suggests that courage is based on a motivating purpose or mission in life.[14] Finfgeld indicates that values promote and sustain courage by rendering powerful goals and expectations. Individuals strive to be fearless, avoid cowardice, help others, and live up

to personal expectations. Hope is another factor that helps to instill courage. Patients hope that their conditions will not deteriorate, if not improve. They also hope that if conditions do worsen, they would experience peaceful death. Individuals with ability to be courageous demonstrate a positive attitude, going beyond the norm to help others and contribute to the society. Behavior not demonstrated by them include persistent anger and pessimism, hopelessness, relinquishing of responsibility for self-care, risk avoidance, ignoring the welfare of others, and substance abuse.[8]

VIRTUOUS DECISION-MAKING BEHAVIOR

In the evolving literature on ethical decision making one can discern emergent interest in *virtuous* decision-making behavior.[15,16] Virtuous behavior is demonstrated by the courage to act toward protecting human welfare even with incomplete information about the potentially significant cost to the decision maker. Ethical behavior need not necessarily be virtuous or courageous. It may very well be motivated by self-interest. Unethical behavior can also demand courage. However, virtuous behavior is both ethical and courageous. Various models suggested for the study of ethics are predominantly rule-based or rule-directed. Students are presented with a narrative case and warned of the presence of an ethical dilemma. In practice, however, decision makers do not usually enjoy the benefit of being forewarned. They identify problems, formulate solutions, and implement plans, while performing under varying degrees of stress, engaging in parallel sets of concomitant activities, and interacting with a number of people over a range of decisions, all within a time constraint. Normative models of ethical decision making seek absolute truths about a decision. Positive models seek to explain actual decision-making behavior. Unfortunately, these models prove inadequate in their capacity to explain virtuous behavior.

The contemporary discussion on the ethics and moral obligation of decision making has been dominated by two major theories of principle: The deontological approach studies the decision-making behavior in terms of binding obligations, as in duty. The utilitarian approach studies decision-making behavior in terms of the importance of utility over beauty or other considerations. Unfortunately, these theories fall short of explaining behavior emanating from considerations of virtue. Other theories, such as Hobbes' nonutilitarian theory of egoism, too, are of little help in understanding virtuous decision making. However, Dhir has recently offered a new paradigm for the analysis of the virtuous decision making behavior.[15] According to him, the process of virtuous decision making is evident when an agent attempts to ameliorate a special class of ethical dilemma. The elements present in such decision-making process are as follows:

- Action is demanded of an agent.
- The situation is confronted unexpectedly, with little foreknowledge of the emergent situation.
- The situation is not of the agent's making.
- The situation consists of a conflict between alternative courses of action.
- At least one of the courses of action benefits the agent's self interests, satisfying the agent's individual obligations, often with relatively low associated costs or risks borne by the agent.
- Other courses of action are in interest of others, raising the issue of the individual's social responsibility, often with relatively high associated costs or risks borne by the agent primarily for the benefit of others.
- The timing may be awkward or inconvenient.
- The choice made may have significant consequences for the agent and for others.
- To be virtuous, the agent must first recognize the dilemma, that is, the agent must recognize that 1) there are conflicting obligations to be met; and 2) there is no solution that would satisfy all demands of the situation.
- Knowledge is a prerequisite for virtuous decision making. Through knowledge, the agent must seek to wisdom, or understanding, or deep insight.
- The individual must make an informed choice, with awareness of the consequences posed by the alternative actions available to the agent for all parties affected.

Consider the actions of whistleblower Jeffrey Wigand, who exposed corporate wrongdoing in spite of threats to his life and career. Dr. Wigand was Vice President of Research and Development at Brown & Williamson from 1989 to 1993. After 10 months with the company, he realized that he had a dilemma. His employers were denying that their tobacco-based products had harmful effects. He had an attractive income. He had a wife, and two daughters, of whom one required extensive medical coverage. So he looked the other way. He was not ready to face the consequences of taking an adversarial role against Brown & Williamson. Then, laboratory testing showed a controversial pipe tobacco additive, called Coumarin, to be a lung-specific carcinogen in mice and rats. In 1993, he took issue with the Brown & Williamson's continued use of Coumarin in pipe tobacco. They terminated him.

In 1994, the CEOs of seven major tobacco companies swore at congressional hearings on the effects of tobacco that nicotine was not addictive. Wigand had a confidentiality agreement with Brown & Williamson. He decided to expose the perjury. He broke the confidentiality agreement with his former employers and appeared on *60 Minutes* with Mike Wallace in 1996. He talked about the smoking issues. He also described how his family was being harassed with death threats. Initially, CBS shelved the interview, fearing a lawsuit from his former employer. Personal fallout from the stress included a divorce from his wife that same year and financial insecurity. The interview was subsequently aired. Brown & Williamson sued Wigand for breach of confidentiality. However, with the settlement between the tobacco industry and the states, this suit was dropped in 1997.

In relation to the paradigm presented here, Wigand recognized that he had a dilemma in terms of the conflicting demands of 1) his personal well being, security of his family, and continuity of his career; and 2) obligations to others, including 1) his confidentiality agreement with Brown & Williamson to protect their secrets, and 2) obligation to the society in terms of savings human lives and protecting human health. He had to make act, unexpectedly, within months of joining Brown & Williamson. The timing was awkward in that his daughter needed medical attention. Costs, both financial and otherwise, were high. Wigand made an informed choice after considerable contemplation.

CONCLUSION

In this article we have described a set of paradigms to aid the understanding of three different paradigms of decision-making behavior found in the health care industry. After differentiating between a paradigm and a model, we described paradigms of ethical, courageous, and virtuous decision-making behavior. Innovations and discoveries in health care have created ethical dilemmas never before encountered. The regulatory ethics paradigm, which has effectively guided ethical decision-making behavior of health care professionals, is now being questioned. New advances, as in the case of surgical techniques, show inadequacies of this paradigm. Greater degree of freedom for decision making by the physician is being demanded.

Courageous decision-making behavior of health care professionals has not been adequately studied. However, it has been found that becoming courageous is a lifelong process. Courageous behavior among patients with long-term health develops over time after full acceptance of reality by the patient. The patients are then able to manage their problems based on this discernment of reality, pushing themselves beyond coping to be productive and responsible.

Opportunities to manifest virtuous decision-making behavior arise when a decision maker must unexpectedly choose from alternative courses of action, of which 1) one benefits the decision maker's self-interest, satisfying his or her individual obligations with relatively low associated cost or risks borne by the decision maker; and 2) the other is in the interest of others, raising the issue of the decision maker's social responsibility, often with relatively high associated costs or risks borne by the decision maker. The decision maker must recognize the opportunity and then make an informed choice.

REFERENCES

1. Beauchamp, T.L.; Childress, J.F. *Principles of Biomedical Ethics,* 2nd Ed.; Oxford University Press: New York, 1983.
2. Smith, W.J. *The Culture of Death: The Assault on Medical Ethics in America*; Encounter Books: San Francisco, 2001.
3. Baker, R.B.; Caplan, A.L.; Emanuel, L.L.; Latham, S.R. *The American Medical Ethics Revolution: How the AMA's Code of Ethics Has Transformed Physicians' Relationships to Patients, Professionals, and Society*; Johns Hopkins University Press: Baltimore, MD, 2001.
4. Epstein, E.M. Business ethics and corporate social policy. Bus. Soc. **1998**, *37* (1), 7–40.
5. Bates, T. Ethics of consent to surgical treatment. Br. J. Surg. **2001**, *88* (10), 1283–1284.
6. Weijer, C. I need a placebo like I need a hole in the head. J. Law Med. Ethics **2002**, *30*, 69–72.
7. Agich, G.J. Ethics and innovation in medicine. J. Med. Ethics **2001**, *27* (5), 295–296.
8. Finfgeld, D.L. Courage as a process of pushing beyond the struggle. Qual. Health Res. **1999**, *9* (6), 803–815.
9. Rawnsley, M.M. Recurrence of cancer: A crisis of courage. Cancer Nurs. **1994**, *17*, 342–347.
10. Haitch, R. How Tillich and Kohut both find courage in faith. Pastor. Psychol. **1995**, *44* (2), 83–97.
11. Deutsch, M. Courage as a concept in social psychology. J. Soc. Psychol. **1961**, *55*, 49–58.
12. Rorty, A.O. The two faces of courage. Philosophy **1986**, *61*, 151–171.
13. Walton, D.N. *Courage: A Philosophical Investigation*; University of California Press: Berkeley, CA, 1986.
14. Cuff, W.T. The Experience of Courage and the Characteristics of Courageous People. Dissertation Abstracts International; University of Minnesota, 1993; Vol. 53, 5408B. Doctoral dissertation.
15. Dhir, K.S. A Paradigm for the Study of Virtuous Decision Making Behavior. In *Proceedings of the 2002 Western Decision Sciences Institute Conference*, Las Vegas, NV, April 2–5, 2002; Dhir, K.S., Ed.; Decision Sciences Institute, Georgia State University: Atlanta, GA, 2002; 94–99.
16. Pellegrino, E.D. Toward a virtue-based normative ethics for the health professions. Kentucky Inst. Ethics J. **1995**, *5*, 253–277.

Health Care Policy

Walter J. Jones
Medical University of South Carolina, Charleston, South Carolina, U.S.A.

INTRODUCTION

"Health policy" refers to the area of study that focuses on the outputs (products) and outcomes (final results) generated by a society that relate to the nature of the health services provided to the society's population. The term also refers to the processes by which societies create these outputs and outcomes. This entry examines and analyzes the various issues related to health policy making and policies.

THE NATURE OF HEALTH POLICIES AND POLICY MAKING

All societies produce health policies. During the twentieth century, as medical science developed, societies began to refine their health care systems through policies created by governmental and private bodies. In most of Europe, this process was soon dominated by national governments. By the end of the twentieth century, most economically advanced nations had enacted health policies that provided for universal health insurance coverage for all citizens. In contrast, the United States enacted policies that resulted in a very well-funded, but relatively unorganized, health care system, with health insurance provided not by citizenship, but by employment status and, more recently, by age category (Medicare) and "qualifying poor" status (Medicaid).[1]

THE HEALTH POLICY-MAKING PROCESS

Like other policy-making processes, health policy making is *cyclical*, not linear. It has no defined beginning or end. This also means that policy issues are never finally and completely resolved. Previous policy outputs and outcomes lead to further system inputs, which keep the process operating. In policy making, there are no final successes or failures.[2]

The health policy-making process comprises four phases.

1) Entry of Policy Inputs: In this phase, policy-making institutions and individuals are exposed to stimuli for action coming from individuals, groups, and institutions that comprise their relevant society. These inputs may include *demands* for policy making (or for opposition to proposed policy making), *supports* for previous policy making (including reelection to public office, or reappointment to an administrative or judicial position), *resources* for additional policy making (such as tax revenues), and *costs* incurred through previous policy making (such as budgetary debts, or the loss of political support as a result of previous policy decisions).

As a result of the relative impact of each input and their interactions, the *policy agenda* for the current cycle of policy making develops. The agenda includes the issues that policy makers will focus on in their current activities. Agenda setting is an important political skill for policy participants. It involves attracting public and policy maker attention through media publicity, published research, and other mechanisms. Some successful agenda settings are the result of such deliberative efforts (e.g., the efforts in the 1990s of groups such as ACT-UP to bring attention to the plight of people with HIV infection or AIDS). On the other hand, policy agendas are often set by the cumulative social results of previous policy making (for instance, the health care cost inflation in the United States mentioned below).[3]

2) Policy Formation: Once policy agendas are set, policy makers work through existing institutions to enact preferred policy responses. In democracies such as the United States and the UK, this usually involves the interaction of executive, legislative, judicial, regulatory, and private sector institutions.

Some democracies, such as the United States, have policy institutions that were designed to prevent hasty or dictatorial policy making. They feature the separation of policy-making powers between governmental branches, the further division of policy-making powers between the national and state governments, and the potential review of much executive and legislative policy making by the judicial branch.[4] Effective policy making in some areas (such as tobacco industry liability) ends up in the courts, with lawyers representing the various sides dueling over one or more lawsuits.

Because of divided power, U.S. health policy making is often characterized by *incrementalism*, with prevailing

Encyclopedia of Public Administration and Public Policy
DOI: 10.1081/E-EPAP 120011049

policy making consisting of only modest and gradual adjustments of current policies. Reforms of large, complex, and popular programs such as Medicare and Medicaid usually do not involve radical change. On the other hand, many other democracies, such as the UK, have more unitary systems of government. With the British Parliament in fact controlled by a government with a strong Prime Minister, and only modest judicial review, it is easier for British policy makers to enact new laws.[5] A countervailing advantage of the U.S. system may be flexibility and ease of experimentation. With some national programs such as Medicaid administered by the states with significant autonomy, it is possible for the United States to experiment with differing program coverages and methods of administration.

One other important feature of U.S. policy formation is the involvement of and, at times, control by private sector organizations. In the United States, slightly over half of health care spending comes from private sources, and most service deliveries are through private sector organizations. Consequently, private sector organizations have a significant amount of input into all health policy making. In some areas such as clinical certification and facilities accreditation, primarily private associations such the Joint Commission for Accreditation of Health Organizations (JCAHO) have de facto control over far-reaching public policy functions.

3) Policy Outputs: Policy formation by the various institutions described above leads to policy outputs. Some outputs are very tangible. *Laws* are passed; P.L. 89-97, the Social Security Amendments, established Medicare for U.S. senior citizens in 1965, whereas the Balanced Budget of 1997 substantially lowered Medicare hospital reimbursement to curb rapidly increasing Federal Government expenditures. Laws can also come in the form of *subsidies* to relevant individuals or institutions; in 1990, P.L. 101-381, the Ryan White Comprehensive AIDS Resources Emergency Act, provided AIDS treatment funding for states and metropolitan areas heavily affected by the HIV–AIDS epidemic. Laws result in money and/or legal authority being allocated to other government bodies (federal, state, or local), organized interest groups, families, and/or individuals.

In contrast, some policy outputs result from subsequent *regulatory decisions* rather than executive/legislative branch deliberations by elected policy makers. The Food and Drug Administration (FDA) effectively makes policy when it decides to withhold or withdraw medical products or devices from the market (as it did when it banned the use of the drug thalidomide in the 1960s). However, regulatory agencies derive their authority from executive and legislative branch mandates. At times, if their decisions create a sufficient public outcry, the other branches of government may act to rescind them. For example,

because of public opposition, Congress overrode the FDA ban on saccharine in the 1970s.[6]

In a similar fashion, policy making may flow directly from *judicial decisions*. A gridlock between the legislative and executive branches over tobacco policy was partially broken in the mid-1990s when public health lawyers and state attorney generals began to successfully sue tobacco companies in state courts over liability for Medicaid spending on tobacco-related illnesses. The hundreds of billions of dollars involved in the various suits prompted both sides to begin developing a nationwide settlement that would preempt further state legal action.

More nebulous, but very real, are variations in policy making that have been termed *symbolic politics* and *nondecision making*. Most policies have at least some symbolical intent, as the titles of some legislations suggest. For example, the 1996 law that ended the linkage between Medicaid and the primary public assistance program for families with children (Aid to Families with Dependent Children, or AFDC) was named the Personal Responsibility and Work Opportunity Act. This made the public point that there would be no more "free ride" for welfare recipients. The symbolical component of policies provides emotional satisfaction for political supporters of the policy makers and sends a more or less open warning to potential opponents.[7]

A nondecision is the output of a policy-making body when it defeats a proposed policy initiative through inaction, rather than any overt decision.[8] The most recent and important example of a nondecision was the 1994 defeat in Congress of President Clinton's proposed Health Security Act (HSA), which would have established a universal health insurance program for Americans. After President Clinton sent the bill to Congress, its opponents mounted an effective negative mass media campaign. Support for the bill dropped, and its opponents in Congress were able to prevent any vote on the legislation, either on the floor of Congress, or in any relevant committee. This nondecision preserved the decentralized status quo in U.S. health care organization and financing.

4) Outcomes: Health policies are intended to have some specific impacts, or to create a changed state of affairs, at some level of society. Examples of outcomes include situations in which enacted policies lead to defined groups of individuals receiving some enhanced access to health services, institutions receiving additional funding and/or legal authority, elected policy makers increasing their public popularity and ability to get campaign contributions, thus increasing their likelihood of reelection, and so forth. Most commonly, health policies aim to improve health care access, cost control, and/or quality.

However, policies often do not have their expected impact because their *implementation* varies in terms of

efficiency and effectiveness. Imperfections in implemen
tation will inevitably result in outcomes that are less
significant than expected. For example, one of the health
policy outputs of the 1997 Balanced Budget Act was
funding for the establishment of State Children's Health
Insurance Programs (SCHIPs). The intention was to
increase health insurance coverage for children. However,
current research shows that state implementation of these
programs has been quite uneven.[9]

Because health policy making usually involves considerable complexity and uncertainty, there is often a significant gap between intended and actual outcomes.[10]
Sometimes important policy outcomes are unintended and
unexpected. When enacted in 1965, the intended outcomes
of Medicare and Medicaid included increased access to
health services for senior citizens and some categories of
the poor. However, the increased health spending and
increased utilization were also primary factors in the U.S.
health care cost inflation that has persisted to this day.

U.S. HEALTH POLICY OUTPUTS
AND OUTCOMES: 1965–PRESENT

Since 1965, the United States has far outspent every other
nation in the world, both in the aggregate and per capita,
in health services. With the Federal Government taking
the lead, public policies that dramatically expand the
governmental role in organizing, financing, and delivering health services have been enacted.

The list of health policy outputs since 1965 is extensive. Programs such as Medicare and Medicaid have
significantly extended health insurance to defined population categories. The Federal Government has also spear-
headed a movement to improve health services through
more effective research into health outcomes, subsequently linked to clinical and organizational improvements. In 1989, the Agency for Healthcare Research and
Quality (AHRQ) was established. It works with academ-
ical and industry researchers to advance health outcomes
measurement, analysis, and applications.[11]

In reaction to the rapidly growing portion of the gross
domestic product devoted to health care, the Federal
Government has steadily put cost containment measures
into place, including a Prospective Payment System (PPS)
for hospital Medicare services in 1983 (P.L. 89-97) and a
Resource-Based Relative Value Scale (RBRVS) for physician Medicare reimbursement in 1989 (P.L. 101-239).
Most recently, the 1997 Balanced Budget Act reduced
Medicare and Medicaid provider reimbursements by an
estimated US $128 billion in 5 years (but recently, the
provisions of the Act have been significantly relaxed).

State governments have also been active health policy
makers.[12] Many states have experimented with new

delivery systems in their Medicaid programs, and the
general range and level of benefits have gone up steadily
in the last 20 years. Some states have instituted nearly
universal employer-based health insurance systems
(Hawaii), or have attempted to greatly expand health insurance coverage through state mechanisms (Tennessee).

With all of the above-mentioned public policy *outputs*,
how have health *outcomes* been affected? It appears that
public policies have, at best, a limited impact on population health. Some public health measures, such as
disease immunization and water purification, have dramatically affected life expectancy in the last century.
However, beyond that, it appears that most health outcomes are the product of overall environmental conditions
and individual lifestyle behaviors, not health policy measures.[13] Because of less effective prenatal care, along
with less healthy population lifestyles, Americans on
average have a shorter life expectancy than most citizens
of advanced Western European and Asian nations. To
improve these results, American policy makers must develop more effective methods of health education.

TWENTY-FIRST CENTURY HEALTH
CARE POLICY CHALLENGES

In addition to the ongoing task of cost containment balanced with reasonable access to the ever-expanding array
of medical technologies, the twenty-first century will see
the development of additional health policy challenges.

Health Disparities and the Market

As medical technologies develop, the gap between possible treatments and available resources to pay for these
treatments grows. All societies, including the United
States, will have to find some acceptable ways in which to
ration the most expensive medical technologies. How will
this be done? From a pure efficiency standpoint, the best
way to ration resources is through the use of market
mechanisms, such as price. The United States has already
gone farther than most countries in turning health care
over to markets as an economic commodity.

However, markets that are somewhat ''free'' imply
that those who cannot pay will go without. To what extent
are Americans willing to accept this? The United States
already has significant disparities in medical access. If the
United States wants to keep some semblance of rough
equality in the provision of essential health services, it
will have to increase its subsidies to the medically in-
digent to keep pace with the growing cost of care. If
Americans are unwilling to do this, the nation could wind
up with enormous and growing gaps in medical access

between social groups—gaps large enough to create future political unrest.

Genetic Technologies

With the ongoing mapping of DNA coming from the Human Genome Project, twenty-first-century health providers will increasingly have the ability to directly intervene in human genetic structures and functioning. This potentially means the ability to treat, or even prevent, the development of genetically based disorders, including cancer and cardiovascular diseases. Success here could materially increase average human life span, from the current 70–80 to 130 years or more.[14] This increase, if attained, would be a mixed blessing, bringing on funding challenges in geriatric health care that dwarf our current problems.

Growing abilities to manipulate human genetics would also give us the ability to eliminate almost *any* genetic feature, not simply those generally considered undesirable. Thus, there could be sharp policy debates over the social and ethical implications of using genetic medicine to select (or eliminate) actual or potential offspring by gender, physical appearance, or expected intelligence.

CONCLUSION

Based on the above suggestions as to twenty-first-century health policy challenges, one of the insights provided earlier should come to mind. Health policy making does not ''solve'' problems in a once-and-for-all fashion. Often, current problems that policy makers face result from prior policy initiatives that were and still are considered successes. It should not be hard to imagine future policy scholars drawing the same conclusion about such twenty-first-century advances as genetic medicine. The more things change, the more they remain the same.

REFERENCES

1. Anderson, O.W. *The Health Services Continuum in Democratic States*; Health Administration Press: Ann Arbor, MI, 1989.
2. Longest, B.B., Jr. *Health Policymaking in the United States*; Health Administration Press: Chicago, IL, 1998; Chap. 3.
3. Kingdon, J.W. *Agendas, Alternatives, and Public Policies*; HarperCollins College Publishers: New York, NY, 1995.
4. Ladd, E.C. *The American Polity*; W.W. Norton and Company: New York, NY, 1989; Chap. 5.
5. White, J. *Competing Solutions*; The Brookings Institution: Washington, DC, 1995; Chap. 10.
6. Foreman, C.H., Jr. *Plagues, Products and Politics*; The Brookings Institution: Washington, DC, 1994; Chap. 6.
7. Edelman, M. *The Symbolic Uses of Politics*; University of Illinois Press: Urbana, IL, 1974.
8. Crenson, M.A. *The Unpolitics of Air Pollution*; Johns Hopkins University Press: Baltimore, MD, 1974.
9. Bilheimer, L.T.; Colby, D.C. Expanding coverage: Reflections on recent efforts. Health Aff. **2001**, *20* (1), 83–95.
10. Thompson, F.J. The evolving challenge of health policy implementation. In *Health Politics and Policy,* 3rd Ed.; Litman, T.J., Robins, L.S., Eds.; Delmar Publishers: New York, 1997; 155–175.
11. Gaus, C.; Fraser, I. Shifting paradigms and the role of research. Health Aff. **1996**, *15* (2), 235–241.
12. Holahan, J.; Nichols, L. Health policy in the states: overview. In *Health Policy, Federalism and the American States*; Rich, R.F., White, W.D., Eds.; Urban Institute Press: Washington, DC, 1996; 39–70.
13. Feldstein, P.J. *Health Care Economics*; Delmar Publishers: New York, 1998; Chap. 2.
14. Schwartz, W.B. *Life Without Disease*; University of California Press: Berkeley, CA, 1998.

Humanitarian Intervention

Michelle Maiese
University of Colorado, Boulder, Colorado, U.S.A.

INTRODUCTION

Humanitarian intervention is the threat or use of military force primarily for the purpose of protecting the nationals of the target state from gross and systematic human rights violations. These violations result from either the conscious policies of a central regime or the general breakdown of that regime. The use of force may come in a variety of forms, including economic sanctions, arms embargoes, restrictions on income-generating activities, aviation bans, restrictions on diplomatic representation, and suspension of membership or expulsion from international or regional bodies. The discussion here focuses on the use of military force by one or more outside states to relieve grave human suffering.

OVERVIEW

Controversy surrounding humanitarian intervention arises from widely accepted constraints on the use of force among states. According to international norms discussed below and provided they do not threaten the legitimate claims of other states, sovereign states have a right to pursue their own destiny free from interference. They also have primary responsibility for the protection of their people's lives. Some believe that military intervention, even to protect human rights, denies the rightful autonomy of the state and constitutes an unacceptable assault on state sovereignty.

Others point out that passivity in the face of gross and systematic human rights violations is likewise unacceptable. They suggest that a government that engages in substantial violations of human rights forfeits both its domestic and its international legitimacy. If a state is unwilling to halt serious harm to its people, the principle of nonintervention yields to the international responsibility to protect.[1] To be legitimate under international law, military action to protect human rights should be authorized by the United Nations (UN) Security Council. Cases of ''unilateral'' intervention, undertaken by states without UN authority, are especially problematic.

There is a growing notion that the protection of human rights and dignity should be one of the fundamental objectives of modern international institutions. However,

because full-scale military operations may harm or kill many civilians, those who engage in intervention for human protection purposes should be careful to avoid doing more harm than good. The use of military force should produce substantial humanitarian benefits and be exercised according to principles of right intention, last resort, proportional means, and reasonable prospects.

POLICY OBJECTIVES

It seems clear that the issues faced in the 21st century differ from those the world faced in 1945 when the UN was founded. Cold War politics have imposed a brutal check on the political and economic development of many states. The amount of internal war and civil conflict has grown drastically over the last several decades and many countries have weak economic structures and government institutions.

Given the increase in intra-state conflict, the international community is faced with a dilemma: stand by while there is massacre, ethnic cleansing, and genocide; or take sides in civil conflicts, which may only further contribute to fragmentation of the state system.[1] Furthermore, humanitarian intervention entails military operations that may harm or kill many civilians. To destroy human life for the benign purpose of protecting human rights seems unacceptably paradoxical. Humanitarian intervention may also seem to go against many of our moral intuitions about the conduct of foreign policy. After all, states are typically concerned only with their own security and well-being; and international relations are commonly thought to be first and foremost relations among states and not individuals.

On the other hand, it seems clear that justice and rights protection no longer stop at the border of the nation-state.[2] When faced with gross human rights abuses, the international community should not accept that state sovereignty automatically trumps human rights claims. Instead, there is a need to balance the principle of state sovereignty against protection of human rights. Policy surrounding humanitarian intervention needs to meet at least four broad objectives:[1]

1. Establishing clearer rules, procedures, and criteria for determining whether, when, and how to intervene.

Encyclopedia of Public Administration and Public Policy
DOI: 10.1081/E-EPAP-120027809

2. Establishing the legitimacy of military intervention in those cases where all other approaches have failed.

3. Ensuring that military intervention is carried out for the purposes proposed, is effective, and is undertaken with proper concern for human costs and institutional damages that may result.

4. Helping to eliminate the causes of conflict while enhancing the prospects for a sustainable peace.

STATE SOVEREIGNTY AND HUMAN RIGHTS: A DILEMMA

The principles of sovereignty and nonintervention suggest that states can legitimately use armed force only in cases of self-defense. The international community, including the UN, is prohibited from intervening in matters that are considered wholly within the domestic jurisdiction of states. Article 2[2] of the UN Charter prohibits the use of force against a state's territorial integrity or political independence and suggests that states have exclusive jurisdiction within their own territory. If the duty not to intervene is violated, the victim state has the right to defend its territorial integrity and political independence. This effectively rules out interference, whether direct or indirect, with a state's political, economic, or cultural elements. It also seems to rule out a legal right to use force against another state even to promote human rights.

For many states, sovereignty is their only line of defense against major powers. The notion of sovereign equality guarantees that despite differences in economic, social, or political structure, less powerful states have the same legitimacy, rights, and duties as the developed Western states, as well as equal membership in the international community.[2] In general, sovereignty has meant immunity from external challenge and broad discretion with respect to methods of governance. Insofar as it serves as recognition of states' equal worth and dignity, their identity, and their right to self-determination, respect for sovereignty contributes to international stability.

Because the state is the ultimate repository of individual rights, a resolution should be sought within the state itself when states abuse human rights. If the people do not like what their government is doing, it is for them to rise up and reshape that government. When outside states impose their conception of rights on other countries, this may be viewed as a form of moral imperialism or intellectual arrogance. Moreover, even if human rights conditions are awful, an enduring remedy may require fundamental reordering of the whole society and its values; and an outside force is unlikely to be able to accomplish this. There is also a worry that widespread acceptance of humanitarian intervention will lead aggressive governments to use it as an excuse for their expansionist policies.[3]

However, others argue that humanitarian intervention does not represent cultural imperialism, but rather reflects the shared rights of humanity. Sovereignty has never meant the unquestionable right of government leaders and officials to do anything they please within their recognized space. Rather, a state's right of self-preservation is subordinate to individuals' rights of self-preservation.[4]

The fact that a state has been established according to traditional legal norms and has a fixed territory is not enough for legitimacy. Rather, the community grants limited powers to a central governmental authority to serve the interests of that community. Because states gain their legitimacy from the consent of persons, it is unclear that states that abuse human rights and obstruct social justice should be regarded as legitimate. In fact, governments that behave badly or misuse their authority undermine the one thing that justifies their political power and thereby become delinquent within the international community.[3] They should not be allowed to shield themselves behind international law and the principle of state sovereignty.

While Article 2[2] of the Charter establishes the norm of nonintervention, other provisions of the Charter list the protection and advancement of human rights as a primary purpose of the UN system. For example, Article 1[2] of the Charter commits the UN to promoting and encouraging respect for human rights and fundamental freedoms. The Universal Declaration of Human Rights (1948), the four Geneva Conventions, and the establishment of the International Criminal Court likewise set forth standards for state conduct. These agreements and mechanisms have changed expectations about what counts as acceptable state conduct and established a universal jurisdiction concerning matters of human rights. This emerging discourse implicitly recognizes a new kind of accountability and aims to protect oppressed minorities and excluded social groups against the domination of the powerful.[2]

Insofar as nations have agreed to promote universal respect for human rights and fundamental freedoms, these rights are a matter of international obligation and subject to the supervision of the international community. But does this warrant forceful intervention to secure that such obligations are met? Chapter VII of the Charter suggests that the UN Security Council may pursue economic, diplomatic, or military measures to maintain or restore international peace and security. Because widespread human rights violations create large numbers of refugees and often escalate domestic civil strife that can spill over into other countries, some maintain that such violations constitute a threat to international peace and security. As the international community becomes more and more connected, states that violate human rights come to pose a risk to people everywhere. According to this view, the UN has a right and a duty to respond to these situations. Passivity in the fact of gross and systematic human rights violations is unacceptable.

However, there is no express linkage in the Charter between the maintenance of peace and security and the protection of human rights. While the Charter does include many human rights provisions, it does not outline concrete powers and functions of the UN in promoting and protecting these rights. It seems that even if an intervention is for the purpose of protecting core human rights, it violates Article 2[2] by suppressing the political will of the target state. On the other hand, an expansive view of security sees it as extending beyond national or territorial security to include the security of individuals against threats to their life, safety, and well-being.[1] Over the last several decades, the UN Security Council has empowered itself to consider humanitarian emergencies a threat to international peace and security.

International human rights covenants and UN practice have begun to conceptualize sovereignty in terms of responsibility. In signing the Charter, a state takes on a dual responsibility: externally, to respect the sovereignty of other states; and internally, to respect the dignity and basic rights of people within the state. When states are unwilling or unable to do so, this responsibility should be borne by the broader international community. The responsibility to intervene stems from a general duty to assist victims of grave injustice and help them regain their autonomy and dignity.

CRITERIA FOR LEGITIMATE HUMANITARIAN INTERVENTION

Humanitarian intervention is a matter of delivering aid to ordinary people whose lives are at risk because their states are unwilling or unable to protect them. The international community has yet to develop consistent, credible, and enforceable standards to guide state and intergovernmental practice.

Growing practice among states and regional organizations, human rights provisions, and Security Council precedent suggest that the "responsibility to protect" is an emerging guiding principle for humanitarian intervention policy. The responsibility to protect implies an evaluation of the issues from the point of view of those needing support. It acknowledges that primary responsibility rests with the state concerned, but suggests that if the state is unwilling or unable to fulfill this responsibility, it becomes the responsibility of the international community to act in its place. This raises questions about legitimacy, authority, and operational effectiveness. The

use of military force for human protection purposes should be guided by the principles listed in Table 1.

Most turmoil within states does not require coercive intervention by external powers. The use of military force for human protection purposes should occur only in exceptional and extraordinary cases: situations of genocide, ethnic cleansing, forced expulsion or "disappearance," enslavement, and widespread and systematic acts of terror or rape. Situations of state collapse, mass starvation or civil war, or overwhelming natural or environmental catastrophes might also be included. Actions that fall short of outright killing, on the other hand, may not warrant military intervention. This includes cases of systematic racial discrimination or political repression.

In those cases where state action (or inaction) "shocks the conscience of mankind," military intervention should be guided by the principle of right intention. This means that the central purpose of the intervention should be the ending of gross human rights abuses and the restoration of peace. Because some level of self-interest may be required to justify expense of resources and troops, intervening states are likely to have mixed motives. In addition, there is often a gap between stated purposes and actual motivation. However, such cases should not be used as a rationale for abandoning the practice of humanitarian intervention altogether.[3]

There are various ways to ensure right intention. First, intervention should involve multilateral rather than unilateral state action. Second, those in need of help should welcome and support the intervention. Third, other countries in the region should support the actions taken.[1] These conditions reflect the general belief that interventions to safeguard commercial property or ideologically friendly regimes are impermissible.

Military intervention to protect human rights should be used only as a last resort, after all avenues for peaceful resolution of the crisis have been tried. Before sending troops into harm's way, endangering local civilians, and spending valuable resources, leaders have an obligation to attempt other peaceful alternatives. This includes negotiations, economic pressure, peacekeeping, pressure from regional organizations, international legal bodies, and other diplomatic efforts. In addition, all reasonable local remedies should be tried before calling on the international community for assistance. The people of the region should have a voice and accountability in negotiating solutions to humanitarian crises.[2]

In addition, the means used in humanitarian intervention should be proportional and limited to what is required to protect human rights. Foreign troops should not occupy the invaded territory longer than necessary, demand favors from a newly established government, or seek to dominate the targeted country. Intervention should preserve the territorial integrity of the target state

Table 1   Criteria for just humanitarian intervention

Just cause	Large-scale loss of life, with genocidal intent or not; or ethnic cleansing, whether carried out by forced expulsion, acts of terror, or rape. These atrocities may be actual or apprehended, and the product of either deliberate state action or inaction.	This excludes violations that fall short of outright killing: systematic discrimination, imprisonment, or political repression.
Right intention	Primary purpose must be to halt or avert human suffering. This is best assured by multilateral operations that are supported both by regional opinion and the victims.	This excludes the overthrow of regimes, the alteration of borders, or the advancement of ideologies or economic goals.
Last resort	Every nonmilitary option for the prevention or peaceful resolution of the crisis must be explored; and gross human rights violations must be imminent or actual.	This excludes use of military force before negotiations, economic pressure, and other diplomatic avenues have been tried; or there are reasonable grounds to suspect such efforts would not succeed.
Proportional means	The scale, duration, and intensity of the intervention should be the minimum required to protect human rights. The effect on the country's political system should be limited.	This excludes military operations that result in massive civilian deaths, lengthy military occupations, and the use of destructive modern weaponry.
Reasonable prospects	There must be a reasonable chance of success in halting human suffering; consequences of intervention should not be worse than the consequences of inaction.	This excludes cases where protection cannot be achieved, or where intervention is likely to escalate or trigger a larger conflict.
Right authority	The UN Security Council is the most appropriate body to authorize intervention. Its authorization should be sought prior to any military action being taken. If the Security Council fails to act, the matter of intervention may be considered by the General Assembly or regional organizations.	Unilateral action by states is prohibited by international law; however, emerging state practice suggests that states may take unauthorized action in certain cases of extreme necessity.

Source: From Ref. [1].

and interfere with the ruling structure only as necessary so as to promote an enduring peace. Whenever possible, military action should be directed not at the entire nation, but rather at those responsible for wrongdoing. Intervening states that contribute more to the deaths of innocents than the aid of the oppressed violate this principle of proportionality.

For states to engage in military action, there should be reasonable prospects of halting or averting human rights abuses. Intervening states need to calculate the damage that may be done to the target society and consider the possibility that the intervention will trigger a larger conflict. If humanitarian intervention leads to further escalation and war, it is likely to do more harm than good.

Note that humanitarian intervention differs from conventional warfare. Rather than seeking to defeat an enemy, it aims to protect and rescue populations. This calls for a new type of military operation, one that is preceded by preventive actions and followed by post-conflict rebuilding. The operational procedures used should promise quick aid to those under attack and reflect the principle of proportionality. Forces should uphold military law governing the use of force and refrain from using destructive modern weaponry. Because the use of military power may lead to further human rights abuses, quick success through surprise or the use of overwhelming force may not be feasible. There is need for ''incrementalism'' with respect to the intensity of operations and ''gradualism'' with respect to phases of the operation. The use of military force should be carefully tailored to the objective of protecting human rights. Finally, intervening military forces should collaborate with civilian authorities and humanitarian organizations to bring assistance to populations at risk. This is the best way to ensure an effective intervention.

THE IMPORTANCE OF UN AUTHORIZATION

Many believe that to be legal and permissible, military action against a sovereign state requires UN authorization. Under the UN Charter, the Security Council has primary responsibility for peace and security matters. Chapter VII of the Charter suggests that when the Security Council considers nonmilitary measures to be inadequate, it may take military action to maintain or restore international peace and security. The Security Council has expanded the traditional conception of what constitutes a "threat" to peace so that human rights violations are increasingly on the agenda.

Reliance on the Security Council for authorization establishes a legal framework by which humanitarian intervention can and should be conducted. Collective intervention endorsed by the UN is widely regarded as legitimate because it is duly authorized by a representative international body. The Security Council is the principal institution for mediating power relationships and consolidating the authority of the international community. Advantages of relying on the UN include its universal membership, political legitimacy, administrative impartiality, convening and mobilizing power, and expertise.

Many believe that the UN is ineffective and point to inherent limitations in its capacity to conduct interventions. First, some question the democratic legitimacy of the Security Council and suggest that it does not have broad enough representation. The founders of the UN were not interested in creating an ideal system of collective security in which all states would participate equally.[4] Instead, special responsibilities and privileges were given to the most powerful states. As a result, any of the Permanent Members can use their veto power to override the majority on matters of grave humanitarian concern. This sometimes leads to inertia on the part of the UN.

The UN does not have its own military force or the resources needed to carry out humanitarian intervention. Nor does it have facilities for the training of officers and troops in rules of engagement, command and control, or civic reconstruction. When the UN decides to deploy forces, they must be hastily recruited, and forces from different countries rarely have the opportunity to train with each other. It is likely that the UN will continue to authorize states to deploy forces under their own command in support of Security Council resolutions.[4]

One alternative to Security Council authorization is to seek support for military action from the General Assembly in an Emergency Special Session under the established "Uniting for Peace" procedures. While the General Assembly lacks the power to authorize military action, it could help to legitimize an intervention that has taken place and put pressure on the Security Council to rethink its position. A General Assembly resolution would engage the views of a wide range of states to determine whether intervention was warranted. However, a General Assembly recommendation for military action still requires approval from the Security Council to be fully legally legitimate.

THE QUESTION OF UNILATERAL INTERVENTION

In cases where the Security Council fails to act, states may be inclined to conduct an intervention on their own initiative. Unilateral intervention has both prospects and problems.

If unified Security Council action is not possible, human rights imperatives will be pitted against the Charter's rules governing the use of force. It seems we must choose between damage to the international order if the Security Council is bypassed or the slaughtering of human beings while the Security Council does nothing.[1] If the Security Council cannot uphold its responsibility to protect, unilateral action by states becomes more likely.

However, without the discipline and restrain of the UN, such interventions may not be conducted for the right reasons or in accordance with the proper precautionary principles. Some believe that discounting UN restrictions on the use of unilateral force guarantees the legitimization of barbarism in the name of human rights. There is a danger that the stronger powers will assert a new "duty" or "right" to assert "global leadership" on behalf of the world's vulnerable. Unauthorized humanitarian intervention poses a threat to the international constraints on the behavior of states and does serious damage to the UN's reputation and authority. Many believe that intervening states do not really intend to change international law, but rather to create new, exceptional rights for themselves. Providing an exception for a powerful state to violate the rules that continue to apply to all other actors severely undermines respect for international law governing the use of force.[5] The international legal system has a stake both in prohibiting unilateral intervention and preventing crimes against humanity.

Some point to the evolution of customary law and emerging state consensus as a legal justification for unauthorized humanitarian intervention in rare and exceptional cases.[6] Such instances of "extreme necessity" arise when there are extremely severe violations occurring, force is necessary to stop immediate harm to civilian populations, and humanitarian intervention is indeed the lesser wrong.[7] There should be widespread consensus that a situation of extreme necessity has in fact arisen, and states should proceed cautiously. Although the UN Security Council has not authorized action, the intervening states should maintain a close relationship with the council.

The intervention should be motivated primarily by humanitarian purposes, involve a coalition of states, and be welcomed by the population bearing the brunt of the atrocities. The consequences of the intervention should be more in keeping with the intent of the law than what would have ensued if no action had been taken.[7] This emerging consensus can help states to find a balance between what is lawful and what is right.

CONCLUSION

Military intervention for humanitarian purposes is controversial both when it happens and when it fails to happen. While there may be significant values of human dignity and justice advanced by intervention, there are also competing values favoring orderly and nonforcible resolution of such situations.[4] It seems clear that the tension between UN authority to address human rights issues and the demand that it not interfere in the internal affairs of states has been resolved to some extent by an expansive view of peace and security. This expansion raises questions for the future. Will this expansive view of ''threats to peace'' unleash a new era of just wars? Is the international community seeing a return to warfare ''for the right reasons'' that it may ultimately regret? Will the Security Council act merely as a tool of imperialism and colonialism, dominated by the most powerful nations?

Military intervention should always remain an option of last resort. However, when humanitarian intervention is required, it should reinforce the collective responsibility of the international community. National leaders should collaborate to mobilize both domestic and international support for intervention, and the UN should respond with timely authorization.

Finally, it is important to note that policymaking has focused almost exclusively on international reaction human rights violations. Little attention has been paid to the prevention of catastrophe or the need for peace building after abuse has occurred. To genuinely protect human rights, the international community should focus its attention both on conflict prevention and post-conflict rebuilding.[1]

REFERENCES

1. Evans, G.; Sahnoun, M. The Responsibility to Protect. In *Report of the International Commission on Intervention and State Sovereignty*; International Development Research Centre: Ontario, Canada, December 2001; pp. 5–6, 15, 36, 55, 69.

2. Chandler, D. *From Kosovo to Kabul: Human Rights and International Intervention*; Pluto Press: Sterling, VA, 2002; pp. 12, 120, 127, 179.

3. Garrett, S. *Doing Good and Doing Well: An Examination of Humanitarian Intervention*; Praeger Publishers: Westport, CT, 1999; pp. 26–28, 32, 118.

4. Murphy, S. *Humanitarian Intervention: The United Nations in an Evolving World Order*; University of Pennsylvania Press: Philadelphia, 1996; pp. 26, 28, 298, 305–308.

5. Byers, M.; Chesterman, S. Changing the Rules About the Rules? Unilateral Humanitarian Intervention and the Future of International Law. In *Humanitarian Intervention: Ethical, Legal, and Political Dilemmas*; Holzgrefe, J.L., O'Keohane, R., Eds.; Cambridge University Press: Cambridge, UK, 2003; 177–203.

6. Stromseth, J. Rethinking Humanitarian Intervention. In *Humanitarian Intervention: Ethical, Legal, and Political Dilemmas*; Holzgrefe, J.L., O'Keohane, R., Eds.; Cambridge University Press: Cambridge, UK, 2003; 232–272.

7. Franck, T. Interpretation and Change in the Law of Humanitarian Intervention. In *Humanitarian Intervention: Ethical, Legal, and Political Dilemmas*; Holzgrefe, J.L., O'Keohane, R., Eds.; Cambridge University Press: Cambridge, UK, 2003; 204–231.

Impacts of Bureaucratic Reform on State Government Administration

Brendan F. Burke
Bridgewater State College, Bridgewater, Massachusetts, U.S.A.

INTRODUCTION

State-level reform has taken several active paths during the past decade. This entry describes three distinct but potentially compatible directions for state reform—the enhancement of internal management subsystems, the movement toward a results orientation in agencies, and the expansion of customer and stakeholder accessibility to the functions of government via on-line technological advancements. For each reform line, this entry offers context and definition, specification of systems or process changes, and assessment of analytic endeavors to contrast state progress. State rankings on these reforms are compared, and a discussion of the measurement of potential outcomes of reform is initiated.

STATE LEVEL EFFORT AT ADMINISTRATIVE REFORM

Recent progress in state administration builds on a solid foundation of institutional advancement during the second half of the twentieth century. Since 1950, the states have acted to streamline organizations, update procedures, enhance the strength of institutions, and reduce the prevalence of independent authorities and commissions.[1] At the end of the century, the subnational level proved to be the most active in "reinvention"—the reorientation of policy and administrative systems toward concern for customer satisfaction and enhanced results.[2] The federal system facilitates a healthy competition across like units of government, wherein the 50 states view at least a comparable subset as competitors. The states strive not only to enhance conditions for their own citizens, but also to demonstrate their comparative advantage with regard to other states, or to leave their inferior status behind and climb up the ranks.

Table 1 displays a comparison in rankings for the most and least successful states on three different reform trends. Each trend, as well as a current measurement process and details of implementation, is discussed in turn. The table shows that certain states are successful under multiple definitions of reform, and that others rank poorly on multiple measures. However, certain states focus their reform efforts more narrowly, with leadership concentrating only on certain techniques (and for those at the lowest rankings, neglecting only certain narrower bands of reform option).

THE REFORM OF INTERNAL MANAGEMENT SUBSYSTEMS

Light[3] contends that reforms are like the tides—varying in force over time and potentially cyclical in nature. The historic focus of Light's "scientific management" tide is the enhanced efficiency of administrative systems as a precursor to the best direct service delivery processes. Early advocates, such as Luther Gulick, recognized the public administration specialist as the appropriate actor to ensure public management effectiveness and efficiency. In 1997, the Pew Charitable Foundation granted funds to Syracuse University's Maxwell School of Citizenship and Public Affairs to pursue the Government Performance Project (GPP), an effort to measure managerial performance at the federal, state, and local levels. The study results are displayed prominently on the project's web page[4] and through special issues of *Governing* magazine.

The management philosophy underlying the GPP is as follows: Government performance is a function of the cohesiveness and coherence of policy implementation efforts. But an important precursor of implementation is the strength of staff or administrative processes. Public management is seen as a kind of "black box" involved in the translation of government resources into varied direct results. Successful management includes an effective oversight of personnel, financial, planning, and information technology "subsystem" capabilities. In addition to these separate internal service functions, the integration of all four comes through the contemporary emphasis on "managing for results."[5] The unifying strand of the GPP model is a focus on enhancing the capacity of executive leadership and other top management to make well-informed choices and to disseminate them promptly throughout the organization.

The GPP assigned letter grades on an "A"–"F" scale for achievement on each of the five management subsystems, and a summary grade. The grades represent

Encyclopedia of Public Administration and Public Policy
DOI: 10.1081/E-EPAP 120025165

Table 1 Comparison of state rankings on alternative reform orientations

Rank	Internal management subsystems[1]	Results or "reinvention"[2]	Accessibility via e-government
1	**Michigan**	**Michigan**	Indiana
2	*Utah*	*Florida*	**Michigan**
3	*Washington*	Georgia	Texas
4	Delaware	Oklahoma	Tennessee
5	*Iowa*	*South Carolina*	*Washington*
6	Kentucky	*Ohio*	California
7	Maryland	Oregon	New York
8	Missouri	*Virginia*	Pennsylvania
9	Pennsylvania	*Iowa*	*Florida*
10	*South Carolina*	Utah	*Ohio*
11	*Virginia*	North Carolina	*North Carolina*
40	**Alaska**	**Alaska**	**Alaska**
41	*Arkansas*	*Mississippi*	*West Virginia*
42	*Connecticut*	**New Hampshire**	*Mississippi*
43	*Hawaii*	*Hawaii*	Vermont
44	*Nevada*	*Arkansas*	**Rhode Island**
45	**New Hampshire**	**Rhode Island**	*Oklahoma*
46	Oklahoma	New Jersey	Arizona
47	**Rhode Island**	Tennessee	New Mexico
48	*West Virginia*	*Nevada*	**New Hampshire**
49	*Wyoming*	*Connecticut*	Alabama
50	**Alabama**	**Alabama**	*Wyoming*

Source: Internal Management Subsystems: Government Performance Project, http://maxwell.syr.edu/gpp/ (accessed October 2003); Results or "Reinvention," Deil S. Wright, ASAP Data Files, Odum Institute for Research in the Social Sciences, University of North Carolina at Chapel Hill, Accessibility Via E-Government, http://www.insidepolitics.org/egovt01us.html (accessed November 2003).
Bold print indicates states in all top or bottom groupings for all three reform orientations; *italics* indicates states in two of three top or bottom groupings.
(1) Under Internal Management Subsystems, states ranked 1–3, 4–11, and 40–49 receive tie scores.
(2) The results or "reinvention" ranking does not include missing data from California, and thus ranks from 1 to 49.

an accretion of effort mostly during the 1980s and 1990s—not an evaluation for a given time unit. But because the state survey was reported in 1999 and 2001, there is some evidence of rising, steady, and falling performance at the turn of the century. The following are examples of "top-grade" activity within each of the categories:

1. Human resource management: Leading states consolidate job categories, where possible, in the civil service system; use prompt hiring and vacancy review processes; provide pay-for-performance systems; and practice long-term human resource planning. This can include an assessment of future human resource needs—both the potential types of jobs and responses to hard-to-serve markets within the state. Human resource management remains a relatively weak internal function overall for the states—only three received an "A" or "A–" grade in 2001 (South Carolina, Washington, and Wisconsin), and the average state grade was "B–."

2. Financial management: Successful states use broad budget authority so that appropriations can be flexibly matched with agency-spending needs; emphasize cost accounting and enterprise fund use; provide effective policies for investment and maintenance of fund balances; perform long-term revenue and expenditure forecasting; and stipulate performance-based contracting rules. Ten states received an "A" or "A–" grade in 2001, providing evidence that this is a relatively strong internal focus (average grade: B).

3. Information technology management: Powerful chief information officers are present to coordinate technology needs; to bridge statewide and agency plans; to optimize the use of the Internet for state web sites; and to ensure quick turnaround in technology replacement plans so that systems are current in a rapidly changing field. This is an improving subsystem, but still with some room for enhancement. The 1999 average grade was "C+" and the 2001 grade was "B–."

4. Capital management: The capital plan is not "one year of reality and four years of fantasy;"[6] the future needs are well prioritized and will be implemented to schedule; and the management of maintenance and operations funding is an adjunct to the construction of projects. The states were relatively successful at this management function in the initial GPP study, but there has been some decline since then. Nine states received "A" or A–" grades in 1999, but the number fell to five in 2001. The average grade remained a "B–" across the two studies.

5. Managing for results: The leading states pursue strategic planning between legislatures and agencies; effective performance measures are used in most agencies; performance is compared across agencies and across comparable states in benchmarking programs; and state auditors ensure the effectiveness and accuracy of performance information. Only five states received "A" or "A–" grades on this integrating reform in 2001, with an average grade of "C+."

THE RESULTS ORIENTATION

Although internal subsystems reform has brought greater efficiency and an enhancement of managerial capacity, it neglects an important determining point for the quality

Table 2 Progress on reinvention in the American states—agency implementation levels for specific reinvention features, 1998

Reinvention feature	Percent of agencies	
	Partially implemented	Fully implemented
1) Strategic planning to produce clear mission statements	37	50
2) Training programs to improve customer service	54	29
3) Quality improvement programs to empower employees	56	23
4) Benchmarks for measuring outcomes	49	24
5) Systems for measuring customer satisfaction	45	19
6) Decentralization of decision making	42	18
7) Reduction in hierarchical levels	23	21
8) Greater discretion in procurement	33	13
9) Simplification of human resource needs	27	7
10) Privatization of major programs	17	7
11) Greater discretion to carry over funds	14	8

Respondents are agency heads asked: ''From time to time, state agencies undertake to change the way they do things. Please indicate the extent to which your agency has implemented each of the following changes in the 1990s.'' Responses range from ''no changes considered'' to ''fully implemented'' ($n = 1075$).
Source: Deil S. Wright, ASAP Data Files, Odum Institute for Research in the Social Sciences, University of North Carolina at Chapel Hill.

of governmental effort—the transaction between the government and the service user or recipient. ''Street-level'' bureaucratic effort may benefit from better managerial guidance, information, and control of resources, but it serves also to benefit from enhanced flexibility in decision making and allocation of resources. In Light's vocabulary, this is the ''liberation management'' tide, but the most common moniker for this movement is ''reinventing government.'' The Winter Commission Report, *Hard Truths/Tough Choices*, and Vice President Gore's National Performance Review (NPR) documented the problems and the possibilities for reinvention at the subnational and national levels, respectively.[7,8] During the past decade, the most salient theme of reinvention has been the movement from government dialog away from processes, and toward service results.

The American State Administrators Project (ASAP) survey includes questions that track the prevalence of specific ''reinvention features'' underlying the results-oriented reform wave. Based at the University of North Carolina at Chapel Hill, with funding from the Earhart Foundation, the survey has been performed twice each decade since the 1960s, including inquiries about reinvention in 1994 and 1998. State agency heads respond to the mail survey, making ASAP a valid and expert-based source of knowledge about various trends across American state governments. For a full description of the ASAP survey and its methodology, see Ref. [9].

Eleven features of reinvention were included in the survey, with the request that the respondent indicate a degree of implementation from ''no consideration'' to ''full implementation'' of the different reinvention possibilities (Table 2). A primary difference between the ASAP and GPP studies involves the unit of analysis. The

GPP developed state grades on the internal management subsystems, whereas the ASAP results tracked agency activity and breadth of implementation across all states. Here, the findings describe the prevalence of the reform technique, without a detailed analysis of a state-specific nature. The state ranking in Table 1 was developed from the summation of results gained from the agency heads within each state, deleting California from the ranking because of a low response rate.

The ASAP inquiry gained information about the scope of reinvention across three of the same four categories as the NPR: reducing regulation by cutting red tape (reinvention features 8, 10, and 11); empowering employees (3, 6, and 7), and refocusing on the customer (1, 2, 4, and 5). The NPR focus on ''cutting back to basics'' is probably better served at the state level through the requirements for balanced budgets. Contracting out may be downplayed in this summary of reinvention techniques, but elsewhere in the ASAP survey, it is reported that 72% of state agencies contract out some services to private companies, nonprofit agencies, or other governmental units.

ACCESSIBILITY REFORMS VIA E-GOVERNMENT

A third reform trend has quickly gained stature in the twenty-first century. Light contends that the tides of reform can overlap one another, and this is certainly the case with state-level e-government initiatives embracing the Internet. (For an assessment of governmental techniques underlying E-government, see Ref. [10]. For a more

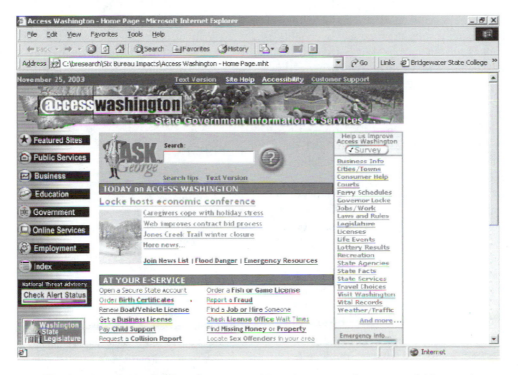

Fig. 1 The Washington State home page. (*View this art in color at www.dekker.com.*)

theory-based assessment, see Ref. [11].) States, through the use of the World Wide Web, have enhanced customer access to governmental services and have enhanced the citizens' ability to understand and affect governmental processes. As a reform tide, accessibility enhancement unites the results orientation with a portion of what Light calls the ''watchful eye.'' Earlier legislation under this tide included the Administrative Procedures Act of 1946 and various ''sunshine'' laws around processes such as public hearings. Citizen access, to be heard by a large number of governmental actors via e-mail and to read primary documents and databases, has been made much easier via the e-government focus. The Internet is rapidly becoming the facilitator of informed participation.

The accessibility reforms did not arise because of a specific problem; instead, some potential problems could now be treated because of new technology. The Washington State home page on the Internet (Fig. 1) immediately shows the enhanced value for the government's customers and interested citizens. Citizens have immediate and easy access to a number of services, including the renewal of vehicle licenses and payment of child support. The accesswashington site also shows how it may serve ''watchful eye'' interests, with information links to the state legislature and contract bid processes. Within the state legislature link, one can track legislative actions, their history, and their sponsors.

Darrell West, director of the Taubman Center for Public Policy at Brown University, studied a variety of characteristics of state effort underlying their Internet presence through surveys in 2000 and 2001. At that time, all states except Wyoming provided a variety of services on-line, including the filing of taxes, purchase of vehicle registration and hunting licenses, and the purchase of governmental documents. Forty-eight of 50 states enabled secure access for on-line transactions. All states had some web sites with disability access features, but in some cases, the percentage of accessible sites was low. Between the surveys in 2000 and 2001, West found that most states improved their Internet presence in these service areas and their on-line administration. West ranked the states on their implementation of these citizen services based on the following criteria: user accessibility, interactivity, and ease of use in both years; the 2001 rankings are reported in Table 1.[12]

MEASURING THE IMPACTS OF REFORM

Many of the intermediate impacts of bureaucratic reform have been specified to this point—public administration techniques bring about improvement and change to administrative systems. But what of the ultimate impacts of reform? More specifically, in what ways have state government reforms improved the status of the citizens? The transaction-enhancing nature of the results-oriented and accessibility-based reforms is too situational or contextual to aggregate into summary measures. One common goal of both the results-oriented and accessibility-oriented reforms is the enhancement of citizen trust in the government. There is situational evidence of the contrasting possibilities regarding this goal and the reform effort. Michigan and Florida are two states with high rankings on both their ''reinvention'' and e-government initiatives. In Florida, overall trust in the government has risen along with reform implementation; in Michigan, reform implementation does not correlate with higher trust in the government.

The impact of the internal management subsystem reforms is more readily analyzed because of their nature as an intervening variable on the path toward better governmental results. If the GPP grades can be considered a correlate of the ''scientific management'' movement, then they should illuminate efficiency gains within government processes. One way to test this is to link the GPP grades and a measure of financial strength—the state bond rating from Standard & Poor's (S&P). Bond ratings constitute a relatively stable factor that affects the cost of governmental debt issues. Small reductions in the interest rate for debt issuance, which correspond to the reduced investor risk of a highly rated governmental entity, can save that government many millions of dollars on a large bond issue. The GPP and S&P measures, when converted to rank order, have a relatively strong 0.50 correlation (0.01 statistical significance). The tie between GPP measures and bond ratings indicates an efficiency impact directly beneficial to citizens within the internal subsystem reforms.

CONCLUSION

During the 1990s and into the twenty-first century, the states have been active implementers of a variety of reform types, designed to enhance efficiency and responsiveness, and to reduce the psychic distance between government agents and varied stakeholders. The intermediate administrative impacts are clear with the types of improvement introduced by state leadership and bureaucracies. The ultimate or substantive impact is clear on internal subsystem reforms, but is harder to track on transaction-based reform tools and techniques. The

measurement of service outcomes is a growing advancing area. With effective measures for the results of the myriad of governmental activities, there may prove to be an acceptable method to aggregate these to a higher level, thus giving us a comparative basis across the waves of administrative reform.

REFERENCES

1. Bowman, A.O'M.; Kearney, R.C. *State and Local Government*, 5th Ed.; Houghton Mifflin Company: Boston, Massachusetts, 2002.
2. Osborne, D.; Gaebler, T. *Reinventing Government: How the Entrepreneurial Spirit is Transforming the Public Sector*; Addison-Wesley: Reading, Massachusetts, 1992.
3. Light, P.C. *The Tides of Reform: Making Government Work, 1945–1995*; Yale University Press: New Haven, Connecticut, 1997.
4. http://www.maxwell.syr.edu/gpp/ (accessed October 2003).
5. Ingraham, P.W.; Kneedler Donahue, A. Dissecting the Black Box Revisited: Characterizing Government Management and Capacity. In *Governance and Performance: New Perspectives*; Heinrich, C.J., Lynn, L.E., Jr., Eds.; Georgetown University Press: Washington, DC, 2000; 292–318.
6. Barrett, K.; Greene, R. Grading the States. Governing February **1999**, *12* (5), 50.
7. National Commission on the State and Local Public Service. *Hard Truths/Tough Choices: An Agenda for State and Local Reform*; Nelson, A., Ed.; Rockefeller Institute of Government: Albany, New York, 1993.
8. Gore, A. *Creating a Government that Works Better and Costs Less: The Report of the National Performance Review*; Penguin Books: New York, NY, 1993.
9. Brudney, J.L.; Wright, D.S. Revisiting administrative reform in the American States: The status of reinventing government during the 1990s. Public Admin. Rev. **2002**, *62* (3), 353–361.
10. Barrett, K.; Greene, R. *Powering Up: How Public Managers Can Take Control of Information Technology*; CQ Press: Washington, DC, 2001.
11. Fountain, J.E. *Building the Virtual State: Information Technology and Institutional Change*; Brookings Institution Press: Washington, DC, 2001.
12. http://www.insidepolitics.org/egovt01us.html (accessed November 2003).

Indonesia

Rainer Rohdewohld
GTZ-SfDM, Jakarta, Indonesia

INTRODUCTION

More than 5 years after the downfall of the "Orde Baru" regime of ex-President Suharto, Indonesia continues to face a multitude of challenges. The political transformation into a competitive multiparty system reduced the political influence of the armed forces and realigned power between the state institutions. The emergence of vocal, but yet disorganized and therefore often still ineffective, civil society organizations is supported by a free but not yet fully professional mass media. The public sector continues to be characterized by inefficiencies, corruption, and lack of regard for the needs of the society at large. Last but not least, consolidation of economic recovery to provide employment opportunities for the millions of school graduates entering the labor market every year faces an increasingly competitive Southeast Asian environment.

In this context, the Indonesian public administration system needs thorough and far-reaching structural and procedural reforms. It is under increasing pressure to improve performance and accountability. However, public sector reform (with the exception of privatizing selected state-owned enterprises) has largely been neglected in the reform agendas of both President A. Wahid (November 1999–July 2001) and Megawati Soekarnoputri (since 23 July 2001). Institutional or individual "champions of reform" are lacking.

BACKGROUND AND TRADITION

The present Indonesian system of public administration reflects a variety of influences: Dutch colonial rule, indigenous (especially Javanese) customs and values, and the legacy of the "New Order" period of President Suharto (1965–1998).[1] Centralization of power and the paternalistic attitude of the bureaucracy toward the public have been reinforced by the Suharto regime's instrumentalization of the public administration to stimulate and direct economic and social development after 1967. Accelerating economic growth, improving social welfare, and maintaining political stability were major achievements of the administration during that period,[2] during which the bureaucracy, together with the military, became the most powerful state institution. Despite frequent initiatives for economic deregulation since the early 1980 which increased the role of the private sector in economic and social development, and despite the widespread absorption of public sector reform concepts from abroad, the notion of "development administration" continues to find much sympathy with civil servants and political leaders.

THE CIVIL SERVICE

Indonesia has a civil service system based on life-long appointments of civil servants. There are four service ranks (*golongan*) according to educational background, which are divided into four to five grades, giving the civil service a total of 17 service levels. Civil service positions are either staff positions with no specific professional or managerial responsibilities, managerial positions (*jabatan struktural*), or professional/technical positions (*jabatan fungsional*). The latter have their own specific recruitment requirements and career paths, based on technical/professional skills and expertise. Managerial positions are divided into four levels (*eselon*), echelon I level being the highest.

The total size of the Indonesian civil service was around 3.9 million in 2002, thus being slightly below the regional average of 2.6% of the population.[3] In addition, there is a huge number of contractual staff (especially at the regional level) who do not have civil servant status. There are concerns about the sectoral and geographical distribution of staff[4] and about the quality of available skills and competencies: only around 25% of the civil servants have tertiary education, and nearly half (around 1.8 million) are classified as administrative-auxiliary staff (*tenaga administratif*).[5] A civil service survey in mid-2003 found more than 100,000 fictitious civil servants on the public sector payroll, indicating the weakness of existing internal management and control mechanisms (Table 1).

The Indonesian civil service has been observed to show the negative features associated with closed career systems: lack of managerial flexibility and accountability, limitation of the pool of leadership talent to insiders, dominance of seniority and patronage in promotion and

Table 1 Distribution of civil servants, 1989–2002

	1989	in %	1994	in %	1999	in %	2002	in %
Central Government	3.151.661	86.9	3.471.595	87.5	3.519.959	87.9	930.602	23.7
Regions	475.954	13.1	494.183	12.5	485.902	12.1	3.002.164	76.3
Total	3.627.615	100	3.965.778	100	4.005.861	100	3.932.766	100

Source: Ref. [9].

appointments, and lack of incentives to perform well.[3] Low pay has often been cited as a reason for low performance and for the widespread corruption in the administrative system; however, World Bank studies have concluded that wage bill increases will not by themselves achieve improved outcomes from the public sector,[6] and that low pay cannot be regarded as the main driving force for corrupt civil service behavior.[7]

In May 2002, the State Ministry for Administrative Reform presented an outline of reform initiatives, which included reviewing the role and functions of government agencies, regulating working mechanisms, increasing human resource capacities, improving performance appraisal systems, curbing corruption, and increasing the quality of public services.[8] Considering the disappointing track record in public sector reform and the lack of strategic direction from the political leadership, observers have little optimism about the chances of such a reform program succeeding.

Several government agencies compete in the management of the civil service system: formally, the State Ministry for Administrative Reform [*Kementerian Perdayagunaan Administrasi Negara*—(MenPAN)] is the lead agency for formulating and coordinating public administration policies, including civil service policies, policies regarding the procedures and mechanisms of delivering public services, and policies regarding the institutional setup of government agencies. The National Civil Service Agency [*Badan Kepegawaian Nasional* (BKN)] is in charge of personnel administration and sets national norms and standards for recruitment, promotion, and staff rotation. The National Institute for Public Administration [*Lembaga Administrasi Negara* (LAN)] determines national policies for civil service training, implements key training programs, and conducts research on public administration. The Ministry of Finance determines the budget ceilings for the government's personnel expenditures and for the formation of the individual central government agencies.

The revision of the civil service law in 1999 included the stipulation to establish an independent Civil Service Commission; however, this has not been implemented yet because of shifting policy priorities and internal resistance in the government's bureaucracy.

STRUCTURE OF THE CENTRAL GOVERNMENT ADMINISTRATIVE SYSTEM

The central government bureaucracy consists of several types of organizations: coordinating ministries (*Kementerian Koordinasi*) which oversee a range of government institutions, departments (*Departemen*) with policy making and implementing functions, state ministries (*Kementerian Negara*) which develop and coordinate government policies in specific areas such as research and technology, and nondepartmental (technical) agencies [*Lembaga Pemerintah Non-Departemen* (LPND)] which implement government policies in their respective fields of jurisdiction. Currently (October 2003), there are 3 coordinating ministries, 17 departments, 10 state ministries, and 25 technical agencies. The state and cabinet secretariat, which includes the secretariat of the vice president, is the administrative institution supporting the work of the president and the cabinet. The president is formally at the apex of the central government administration and determines the government's policies, while the ministers are regarded as "assistants" to the president.

The organizational structure of a department consists of the minister as the politically appointed head of the department. A secretariat general is in charge of policy coordination and of internal services (such as personnel management, finance, and public relations), while directorate generals are the main operational units. All are headed by an echelon I official. Most departments have their own training, as well as research and development units. Departments can have subordinated implementation units [*Unit Pelaksana Teknis* (UPT)] in charge of more technical or administrative matters. Before decentralization, departments used to have deconcentrated offices in the regions. This is now limited to those departments implementing exclusive central government functions.

While the total number of management positions in central government agencies has decreased by around 60% since 1999, the number of echelon I positions nearly doubled during the same period. Some departments have drastically reduced their personnel expenditures, and others report drastic increases.[9] Contrary to expectations, there has been no comprehensive reconfiguration of the central government administration as a result of the decentralization policy.

THE CHALLENGES OF DECENTRALIZATION

The decentralization policy included the administrative transfer of more than 2 million civil servants from central government agencies to the regions. Regions had no discretion to select or to reject staff in line with the regions' quantitative or qualitative needs. As a result, all regions are overstaffed, and many have created a vast landscape of local government agencies that does not reflect their actual needs. Nepotism and the need to buy in political support have contributed to this mushrooming of local government agencies. Recently, the central government issued a new and controversial regulation on the organizational setup of local governments (Government Regulation No. 8/2003) in an attempt to limit the overall size of the local government sector.[10]

The decentralization law grants the regions full authority to manage their regional civil service in accordance with national regulations, norms, and standards. The revised civil service law maintains key features of the Indonesian civil service as a unified system, in which entry requirements, preconditions for promotion, performance appraisal system, and all issues related to remuneration are determined by the national level and apply to all civil servants irrespective of whether they work at central or regional level. The continuing existence of a unified national civil service is regarded as a major factor in the context of maintaining national unity.

In general, the structure of administration at the local level consists of a regional secretariat [sekretariat daerah (Setda)], which coordinates the formulation of regional policies and provides administrative support to the head of region, of technical agencies (dinas) which implement services in the main sectors (such as infrastructure, health, and education), of other technical institutions (lembaga teknis daerah) including a regional development coordination agency [Badan Perencanaan Pembangunan Daerah (BAPPEDA)], and subordinated implementation units [unit pelaksana teknis daerah (UPTD)]. Local government agencies not only implement decentralized tasks (tugas desentralisasi), but can also be tasked to implement central government tasks in their respective geographical areas (tugas dekonsentrasi).

Part of the decentralization policy was a radical overhaul of the system of local government financing. The percentage of public funds managed by the regions nearly doubled, and in 2002, regions controlled public funds representing 5.6% of the GDP.[11] The new system of fiscal transfer consists of untied block grants [Dana Alokasi Umum (DAU)], regional shares on certain taxes and revenues from natural resources, and specified grants [Dana Alokasi Khusus (DAK)] in priority policy areas of the government. Regions continue to be financially dependent on central government transfer, with own-source revenue in most cases remaining below 10% of the total regional revenue.[12,13]

PUBLIC ADMINISTRATION REFORM

The lack of pace in reforming the public administration is deeply linked with the issue of public sector corruption. Indonesia has consistently been rated as one of the most corrupt countries in Asia and the world. Public sector corruption involves petty corruption where citizens have to pay a few thousand rupiah to obtain certificates and official documents, the taking of commissions and kickbacks by officials for the procurement of goods and services, the large-scale embezzlement of public funds by senior officials, and corruption within the civil service where appointments and promotions are being bought.[14] Any attempt to streamline the public administration and to introduce innovative concepts of public sector management is facing the major hurdle of how to eradicate corruption first. Some steps have been taken after 1998: in 1999, parliament passed the Clean Government Law No. 28/1999 which requires state and public officials to declare their assets before assuming their posts. They also have to agree to have their assets officially audited during and after their terms of office. Law No. 31/1999 on the Eradication of Criminal Acts of Corruption provides the legal basis for establishing charges and procedures for prosecution. Political support for a consistent enforcement of both laws has been lacking, and only recently has the required Anti-Corruption Commission been set up. Because corrupt behavior is so deeply embedded in public sector behavior, only a concerted effort with full political support can hope to achieve significant improvements.

There are some areas where reforms have been initiated to improve public sector performance and to make public administration more accountable. Efforts are being made to reform the public financial management system,[15] with the recently enacted Law on State Finance (Law No. 17/2003) being a key building block in this reform strategy.[16] Two other laws (on state treasury and on state audit) are currently being debated in the parliament. Efforts are being made to reform the public procurement system.[17] The emphasis of Law No. 17/ 2003 on performance budgeting is being complemented by a Ministerial Decree of the Ministry of Home Affairs (KepMendagri No. 29/2002) which requires all regions to use performance budgeting as of 2004. While these efforts have their own merits, they lack integration in a wider public sector reform strategy, which is certainly not on the present agenda of the political leadership.

CONCLUSION

In its 2002 Governance Assessment of Indonesia, the Asian Development Bank (ADB) came to the conclusion that "the national system of administration and the civil service system are not sufficiently conducive to good governance and improved performances. Both systems need fundamental reform taking internationally recognized good practices into account.''[14] Increasing the demand for accountability of public institutions and public officials is one option to press for public sector reform. It is no coincidence that if positive changes of the public administration occur, they occur at the local level,[18] where decentralization and democratization put increasing pressure on local governments to justify their performance toward their electorate. Improving public finance management by fully enforcing the new law on state finance and by concentrating public finance functions in the Ministry of Finance will also have a positive impact on public sector performance. Incremental reform efforts will be more effective if integrated in wider, medium-term reform strategy which receives the political report needed.

REFERENCES

1. Rohdewohld, R. *Public Administration in Indonesia*; Montech Pty Ltd.: Melbourne, 1995. (For the Graduate School of Government, Monash University).
2. Legowo, T. The Bureaucracy and Reform. In *Indonesia: The Challenge of Change*; Baker, R.W., Hadi Soesastro, M., Kristiadi, J., Ramage, D.E., Eds.; Institute of Southeast Asian Studies: Singapore, 1999; 81–98.
3. Research Institute for Asia and the Pacific, University of Sydney. *Public Sector Challenges and Government Reforms in South East Asia (Report of the Building Institutional Capacity in Asia Project Commissioned by the Ministry of Finance, Japan)*; University of Sydney: Sydney, 2001; 56–57.
4. MenPAN (Menteri Pendayagunaan Aparatur Negara). Sambutan, Delivered at the Workshop Pemantapan Kebijakan Rasionalisasi (Penataan) Pegawai Negeri Sipil, Jakarta, 2 July 2002; 2. (mimeo).
5. Hardijanto. Pokok-pokok Pikiran Tentang Rasionalisasi Pegawai Negeri Sipil, Paper Delivered at the Workshop Pemantapan Kebijakan Rasionalisasi (Penataan) Pegawai Negeri Sipil, Jakarta, 2 July 2002; 2–3. (mimeo).
6. World Bank. *Indonesia Civil Service Review, Summary Report*; 1999. Unpublished paper, Jakarta. (mimeo).
7. Filmer, D.; Lindauer, D.L. *Does Indonesia Have a "Low Pay" Civil Service?*; Policy Research Working Paper, Development Research Group, World Bank: Washington, D.C., 2001; Vol. 2621.
8. MenPAN (Menteri Pendayagunaan Aparatur Negara). Kebijakan Pendayagunaan Aparatur Negara, Disampaikan pada Sidang Kabinet Terbatas Tanggal Mei 23, 2002, Jakarta 2002; (mimeo).
9. Rohdewohld, R. Decentralisation and the Indonesian Bureaucracy: Major Changes, Minor Impact? In *Local Power and Politics in Indonesia. Decentralisation and Democratisation*; Aspinall, E., Fealy, G., Eds.; Institute of Southeast Asian Studies: Singapore, 2003; 259–274.
10. GTZ-Support for Decentralization Measures (SfDM). *Comments on Government Regulation No. 8/2003 Regarding the Organisational Structure of Regional Governments*; GTZ-SfDM Discussion Paper, 2003; Vol. 1/2003. GTZ-SfDM: Jakarta. Download from http://www.gtzsfdm.or.id/ documents/about/sfdm_pa_doc/DiscussionPaper_Perang-katDaerah_FinalFebr2003.pdf (October 2003).
11. Kadjatmiko. Perimbangan Keuangan Pusat dan Daerah dalam Kaitannya dengan Kebijakan Perhitungan Belanja Pegawai, Paper delivered at the Workshop Pemantapan Kebijakan Rasionalisasi (Penataan) Pegawai Negeri Sipil, Jakarta, 2 July, 2002. (mimeo).
12. Lewis, B. *Revenue-Sharing and Grant-Making in Indonesia. The First Two Years of Fiscal Decentralization*; 2002. Unpublished paper. (mimeo). Download from http://www. gtzsfdm.or.id/documents/dec_ind/o_pa_doc/BLewis_FiscalDecen2002.pdf (October 2003).
13. Fane, G. Change and continuity in Indonesia's new fiscal decentralisation arrangements. Bull. Indones. Econ. Stud. **2003**, *39* (1). 87, 159–176.
14. Asian Development Bank (ADB). *Country Governance Assessment Report—Republic of Indonesia (draft)*; Asian Development Bank: Jakarta, 2002. (mimeo).
15. Ministry of Finance (Republic of Indonesia). *The White Paper. Reform of the Public Financial Management System in Indonesia: Principles and Strategy*; Ministry of Finance: Jakarta, 2002. (Publication Series: 2002/KPMK/ VII/MK/003).
16. MacIntyre, A.; Resosudarmo, B.P. Survey of recent developments. Bull. Indones. Econ. Stud. **2003**, *39* (1), 133–156.
17. World Bank, Indonesia. *Country Procurement Assessment Report. Reforming the Public Procurement System*; World Bank Office Jakarta: Jakarta, 2001. (Report No. 21823-IND).
18. Kusumaatmadja, S. Indonesia's Current Crisis and the Impact on Civil Service Reform, Paper Presented at the Public Policy Challenges for Indonesia Symposium, Jakarta, 18 September, 2002. (mimeo).

Information Sources and State Policy Making

Jill Clark
University of Texas at Arlington, Arlington, Texas, U.S.A.

INTRODUCTION

In the last three decades, many American state legislatures have adopted reforms that expand institutional information sources (more professional staff and fewer committees) and encourage legislative independence from information provided by interest groups or the executive department. Studies suggest that individual legislators sometimes prefer information from constituents, other legislators, and legislative staffs. However, interest groups are also key information sources. Committees rely heavily on information from the executive department and interest groups, but information from legislative staffs is important as well.

Outside information (e.g., from other states or from national policy organizations) is transmitted through contacts made by the legislative and executive staffs and legislators, or through interstate interest group networks. This outside information may be most important for scientific issues, economic development policies, and, perhaps, for legislative leaders and minority representatives. Future research might focus on whether different information sources are more or less important at different stages of the policy-making process, for various policy areas or types, in different legislative contexts, or for particular legislators such as leaders.

LEGISLATIVE REFORMS: INFORMATION SOURCES

In the 1960s, "good government" reformers (e.g., The Citizens Conference on State Legislatures) advocated that American state legislatures enhance their policy-making capacity by developing institutional information sources: legislative research bureaus and larger and more professional committee staffs.[1] Reformers also favored the reduction of committees so that legislators could develop substantive policy expertise with a limited number of committee assignments.[2] Reformers argued that as a result of professional staffing and "expert" legislators, committees would become islands of policy information and recommend workable, efficient legislation. More

importantly, legislators would no longer need to rely so heavily on information from interest groups.

Reformers also encouraged the adoption of an executive budget for the governor, so that professional staff could provide information for policy making. However, some reform groups maintained that legislative reliance on information from the executive department would compromise the independence of the legislature. Thus, preserving the independence of the legislature became another rationale for developing professional information sources inside the legislature.[3]

STATE LEGISLATURES: THE RELATIVE IMPORTANCE OF INFORMATION SOURCES

Research on information sources in state legislatures initially focused on the adoption of institutional reforms (fewer committees and larger legislative staffs).[4] Researchers also surveyed legislators about the relative importance of information sources both for individual voting choices and for committee decision making. Constituents, the media, policy organizations, think tanks, and universities were included as possible information sources along with legislative and executive staffs, interest groups, and expert legislators.[5–7] One expectation was that constituent information would be the most important source because a legislator's primary concern was likely to be reelection or career advancement.[8] In other words, legislator motivations for information were assumed to be quite different from those of reformers. Another expectation was that certain characteristics of information would be salient to legislators. As a result, legislators would prefer information from legislative colleagues or staffs (insiders) because insider information was likely to be reliable, timely, and easily accessible.[9]

Overall, research findings suggested that there were multiple sources of information for legislative policy making, and that constituents and insiders were sometimes the most important information sources for individual members.[10,11] A recent survey of legislators in 12 states indicated that grass-roots organizations, legislative staffs,

Encyclopedia of Public Administration and Public Policy
DOI: 10.1081/E-EPAP 120024883

statewide lobby groups, and national ethnic organizations were the four most important information sources.[12] Furthermore, there were differences in information source preferences among legislators: Minority representatives used more sources of information than other legislators and were more likely to rely on information from conferences, the Internet, ethnic associations, and local branches of national organizations. Other legislators were likely to rely more heavily on information from the media and statewide lobby groups.

Legislative committees tended to rely most heavily on information from executive agencies and interest groups.[13] In other words, legislative staffs had not made committees independent of interest groups or executive agencies as primary information sources. However, policy information from legislative staffs was also important particularly on technical policy issues.[14] Specialist committee members made the most contacts with outside sources.[15,16] However, in general, policy organizations, the media, and universities did not rank highly as legislative information sources for committee decision making.

Most of the research on information sources has relied on surveys of legislators' reported preferences for information sources, and only a few studies analyzed the legislators' information use.[17] Furthermore, some findings are based on a single state, and most are based on a small group of states. As a result, study results are tentative, and it is difficult to generalize across states or over time. There has been some interest in determining whether states with professional staffs and fewer committees choose different policies from those with fewer institutional resources. In general, the conclusion is that they do not; instead, policy differences are tied to differences in state environments. The most affluent states are those most likely to adopt legislative reforms and to choose generous expenditures for programs such as education.[18] The same is true for policy innovation: Professional legislatures had little independent effect on whether states are leaders in adopting new policies.[19]

However, in 1971, The Citizens Conference on State Legislatures found that reformed legislative institutions were more efficient;[20] and the Advisory Commission on Intergovernmental Relations, in 1982, suggested that reformed state legislatures were more professional, open, responsive, and representative than unreformed legislatures.[21] However, some observers argued that legislative staffs had developed too much power for influencing elected officials. Later, legislative reforms came under scrutiny by citizens who believed that state legislatures have become remote, careerist, and elitist. These arguments have resonated in some states: Legislative term limits have been enacted in 21 states, and both annual legislative meetings and staff size are targets for change in several other states.

INFORMATION SOURCES: INTERSTATE POLICY DIFFUSION

Although information sources research underscored the importance of information sources within a state, cross-state diffusion research suggested that states quite frequently borrow policies from other states, especially neighbors. States often have similar policies, suggesting a flow of policy information among them and the use of that information in legislative policy making.[22,23] Moreover, the tendency of states to adopt similar policies has increased in recent decades,[24] perhaps in part because information technology facilitates both easier and timely access to information about other states' policies. Interstate tax base competition has stimulated similar business incentives policies,[25] tax types or rates,[26] state-run lotteries,[27] and educational reforms.[28] The notion of ''welfare magnets'' may encourage some states with the most generous welfare benefits to reduce those benefits in comparison with other states.[29]

One possibility for reconciling the findings of the information sources and policy diffusion literatures is a two-step communication process where staffs, expert legislators, or interest groups acquire information about other states' policies and then provide that information to legislators. Surveys of executive department staffs suggest that bureaucrats are actively involved in professional networks and are aware of policy developments in other states.[30–32] Specialist legislators typically report more contacts with information sources outside the state than other members. Certain individual characteristics such as ethnicity, educational level, or years of experience[33] may differentiate specialists from other members. Some interest groups rely on interstate advocacy coalitions to diffuse policy innovations to state legislatures.[34,35]

Although interstate staff and interest group networks have received some attention, there has been no research on the role of governors in acquiring information from outside the state.[36] The National Governor's Association is typically described as an organization that presents governors' views to the national government as a means of enhancing the reputation of governors with presidential aspirations. The assumption seems to be that governors rely primarily on political parties or executive department staffs to provide specific policy solutions. Legislators, like governors, have access to several national policy organizations (e.g., the National Conference of State

Legislators, the Council of State Governments, the National Legislative Exchange Council, and the State Government Affairs Council), and there is some evidence that legislators acquire information independently of staffs.

In fact, legislators now have more incentives for outside searches for policy information because legislators are more "careerist." Policy accomplishments or campaign issues can be part of a strategy to stay in office.[37] In other words, policy information from outsiders may have political uses for legislators: job security and/or career advancement. Moreover, pressures from constituents, citizen groups, the media, public opinion polls, and, in some cases, direct democracy[38] could also motivate legislators to initiate their own policy proposals. Independent policy information could make the legislature an initiator of policy, rather than a more passive institution that responds to proposals from either the executive department or from the citizens.

National policy organizations (such as the Council of State Governments) offer a number of advantages as information sources for legislators. Professional staffs prepare research, and organizational meetings offer legislators contacts with peers from other states. Information is available on political feasibility, and there is policy evaluation on programs that are in place in other states.[39] Internet communications make it possible to gain information quickly, and legislators can interact with peers. Thus, the same characteristics of information that appealed to legislators inside the institution are now available from national organizations: peer information and information that is reliable, timely, and easily accessible.

Policy solutions borrowed from national organizations can be adapted to the political context of a particular state or to a legislator's political agenda.[40] One possibility is that constituents or interest groups inside the state define problems, but solutions are borrowed from national policy organizations. Alternatively, policy information may be more relevant to the initial formulation of legislation and constituent or insider information, to agenda setting, or to the adoption of legislation. Policy information may also be useful in persuading other legislators or the public, or in justifying existing political beliefs.[41]

INFORMATION SOURCES: LEGISLATIVE LEADERS

Given their positions, legislative leaders may be most attuned to legislative independence, election agendas, and career advancement. As a result, leaders may engage in more outside information searches than members. Recent research from a national survey has focused on legislative

leaders' (speakers, senate presidents, and minority and majority leaders) contacts with information, and their use of information from national policy organizations.[42,43] Results suggested that leaders from "springboard legislatures" and/or from states without legislative term limits relied more on national organization information than leaders from dead-end or term-limited legislatures. Perhaps the most active leaders are motivated by the value of outside information in the context of legislatures that provide long-term career opportunities.

Additionally, both majority and minority leaders from states with one-party control of the legislative and executive institutions are more active in joining national organizations and in attending meetings than those from states with divided-party control. It could be that for these leaders, national organizations provide possible policy solutions independent of instate actors, and leaders can claim credit for policy accomplishments.

Compared with leaders in states with larger staffs, leaders in states with small legislative staffs reported that national organization information was more important. Leaders from small states were more active in joining professional associations and in attending meetings than those from large states, possibly because small states have fewer instate information sources. Perhaps these leaders seek more independence from the executive department, or they see political advantages associated with outside information.

CONCLUSION

Future research might investigate the information sources of policy makers other than legislators. There has been no attention to information sources for governors, and there has been little interest in executive department staffs. Future research on legislative policy making might focus more on identifying information sources utilized at different stages of the policy-making process (agenda setting, formulation, and adoption) and in further distinguishing the information sources of committees from those of individual legislators. Information uses should include not only policy making, but also political advantage (career advancement). Perhaps, ironically, the reformers' goal of legislative independence may be embraced by legislators who see career opportunities in acquiring policy information. Furthermore, interstate policy diffusion may be at least partially a product of politicians' political ambitions.

Additionally, different information sources may be more or less important for certain policy areas. For example, outside information may be more salient for policies that involve interstate competition for economic development, or for scientific or technical issues. Information use may also be influenced by differences in legislative context. Perhaps outside information is more important in legislatures with limited staff capabilities and/or in legislatures with the most career opportunities. Legislative leaders may be more attuned to the political advantages of outside information than to its members. Women and minority legislators may be more likely to seek information from national organizations that emphasize their concerns.

REFERENCES

1. Bowman, A.O.M.; Kearney, R.C. *The Resurgence of the States*; Prentice-Hall: Englewood Cliffs, NJ, 1986; 84–88.

2. Morehouse, S.M. *State Politics, Parties and Policy*; Holt, Rinehart, and Winston: New York, 1981; 287–290.

3. Bingham, R.D.; Hedge, D. *State and Local Government in a Changing Society*, 2nd Ed.; McGraw-Hill, Inc.: New York, 1991; 287–290.

4. Wissel, P.; O'Connor, R.; King, M. The hunting of the legislative snark: Information searches and reforms in U.S. legislatures. Legis. Stud. Q. **1976**, *1* (2), 251–267.

5. Sabatier, P.; Whiteman, D. Legislative decision making and substantive policy information: Models of information flow. Legis. Stud. Q. **1985**, *10* (3), 395–421.

6. Shaw, G.M. The role of public input in state welfare policymaking. Policy Stud. J. **2000**, *28* (4), 707–720.

7. Bradley, R.B. Motivations in information use. Legis. Stud. Q. **1980**, *5* (3), 393–406.

8. Webber, D.J. State legislators' use of policy information: The importance of legislative goals. State Local Gov. Rev. **1985**, *17* (2), 213–218.

9. Mooney, C.Z. Peddling information in the state legislature: Closeness counts. West. Polit. Q. **1991**, *44* (2), 433–444.

10. Mooney, C.Z. Information sources in state legislative decision making. Legis. Stud. Q. **1991**, *16* (3), 445–455.

11. Bradley, R.B. Motivations in information use. Legis. Stud. Q. **1980**, *10* (3), 393–406.

12. Jackson-Elmoore, C.; Knott, J.H.; Verkuilen, J.V. *An Overview of the State Legislators' Survey: Sources of Information and Term Limits Impacts*; W.K. Kellogg Foundation: Battle Creek, MI, 1998. http://www.wkkf.org/Programming/ResourceOverview (accessed September 2003).

13. Hamm, K.E. Patterns of influence among committees, agencies and interest groups. Legis. Stud. Q. **1983**, *8* (3), 379–426.

14. Guston, D.H.; Jones, M.; Branscomb, L.M. The demand for and the supply of technical information and analysis in state legislatures. Policy Stud. J. **1997**, *25* (3), 451–469.

15. Porter, H.O. Legislative experts and outsiders: The two-step flow of communication. J. Polit. **1974**, *36* (3), 703–730.

16. Sabatier, P.; Whiteman, D. Legislative decision making and substantive policy information: Models of information flow. Legis. Stud. Q. **1985**, *10* (3), 395–421.

17. Webber, D.J. State legislators' use of policy information: The importance of legislative goals. State Local Gov. Rev. **1985**, *17* (2), 213–218.

18. Dye, T.R.; McManus, S.A. *Politics in States and Communities*, 11th Ed.; Prentice Hall: Upper Saddle River, NJ, 2003; 200.

19. Nice, D.C. *Policy Innovation in State Government*; Iowa State University Press: Ames, IA, 1994.

20. The Citizens Conference on State Legislatures. *State Legislatures: An Evaluation of Their Effectiveness*; Praeger: New York, 1971.

21. Advisory Commission on Intergovernmental Relations. *State and Local Roles in the Federal System*; U.S. Government Printing Office: Washington, DC, 1982; 75–88.

22. Mooney, C.Z. Citizens, structures, and sister states: Influences on legislative professionalism. Legis. Stud. Q. **1995**, *20* (1), 47–67.

23. Walker, J.L. Diffusion of innovations among the American states. Am. Polit. Sci. Rev. **1969**, *63* (3), 880–899.

24. Savage, R.L. Diffusion research traditions and the spread of policy innovations in a federal system. Publius **1985**, *15* (4), 1–28.

25. Eisenger, P.K. *The Rise of the Entrepreneurial State: State and Local Development Policy in the United States*; University of Wisconsin Press: Madison, WI, 1988.

26. Berry, F.S.; Berry, W.D. Tax innovation in the states: Capitalizing on political opportunity. Am. J. Polit. Sci. **1992**, *36* (3), 715–742.

27. Barry, F.S.; Berry, W.D. State lottery adoptions as policy innovations: An event history analysis. Am. Polit. Sci. Rev. **1990**, *84* (2), 395–415.

28. Mintrom, M.; Vergari, S. Policy networks and innovation diffusion: The case of state education reform. J. Polit. **1998**, *60* (1), 126–148.

29. Peterson, P.; Rom, M.C. *Welfare Magnets: A New Case for a National Standard*; Brookings Institution: Washington, DC, 1990.

30. Chi, K.S.; Grady, D.O. Innovators in State Government: Their Organizational and Professional Environment. In *The Book of the States*; Council of State Governments: Lexington, KY, 1995; 382–404.

31. Freeman, P.K. Values and policy attitudes among state legislators and administrators. Public Adm. Q. **1984**, *7* (4), 483–497.

32. Gray, V. Innovation in the states: A diffusion study. Am. Polit. Sci. Rev. **1973**, *67* (4), 1174–1185.

33. Freeman, P.K. Interstate communication among state legislators. Publius **1985**, *15* (4), 99–112.

34. Glick, H.R.; Hays, S.P. Innovation and reinvention in state policymaking: Theory and the evolution of living will laws. J. Polit. **1991**, *53* (3), 835–850.

35. Mintrom, M. Policy entrepreneurs and the diffusion of innovation. Am. J. Polit. Sci. **1997**, *41* (3), 738–770.

36. Dresang, D.L.; Gosling, J.J. Governors. In *Politics and Policy in American States and Communities*; Allyn and Bacon: Boston, 1999; 216–218.

37. Loomis, B.A. *Time, Politics and Policies: A Legislative Year*; University Press of Kansas: Lawrence, KS, 1994.

38. Rosenthal, A. *The Decline of Representative Democracy: Process, Participation, and Power in State Legislatures*; CQ Press: Washington, DC, 1998.

39. Robertson, D.B. Political conflict and lesson-drawing. J. Public Policy **1991**, *11* (1), 55–78.

40. Hays, S.P. Patterns of reinvention: The nature of evolution during policy diffusion. Policy Stud. J. **1996**, *24* (4), 551–566.

41. Mooney, C.Z. Information sources in state legislative decision making. Legis. Stud. Q. **1991**, *16* (3), 445–455.

42. Clark, J.; Little, T.H. National organizations as sources of information for state legislative leaders. State Local Gov. Rev. **2002**, *34* (1), 38–44.

43. Clark, J.; Little, T.H. State legislative leaders' contacts with national legislative organizations: Differences in cosmopolitanism, resources, and political environments. Polit. Policy **2003**, *31* (2), 282–295.

Integrated Health Care Systems: New Trends, Emerging Models, and Future Shocks

Yvonne J. Kochanowski
SteelEdge Business Consulting, Placerville, California, U.S.A.

INTRODUCTION

Integrating the continuum of health care providers both vertically across different levels of care and horizontally within a level has been an ongoing trend during the last two decades. The degrees of success in these ventures, however, have varied greatly. Some emerging models are incorporating more than traditional health organizations and are embracing new methods of governance, structure, and financing to reinvent the integrated holistic health care system of the future. This e-paper provides an overview of these new trends, emerging models, and future shocks.

HISTORICAL AND THEORETICAL BACKGROUND

To understand why health care organizations are evolving into integrated systems, it is important to study the unique development of health care in the United States. The history of this development can be identified in three specific categories:

- Individualism and autonomy transitioning to formal medical study: When the country was being settled, experienced lay healers were called upon to use herbs and folk medicines to cure ills and ease pain. As towns developed, fledgling physicians would apprentice with a more experienced doctor and would then move into a solo practice. Knowledge was shared by way of professional journals. The advent of medical schools after the War of 1812, credentialing and standards of practice with a medical license in the mid-1800s, and consultations between physicians in the mid- to late 1800s contributed to the reorganization of medicine.
- Facilities transitioning from dying wards to places of healing: Early facilities could do little to heal those who were unfortunate enough to enter their doors. Until capital was invested by the wealthy or by the physicians, hospitals did not have the resources to perform healing. The move from social welfare to medical science began when the profession of nursing was formalized and when antiseptic surgery became available well after the Civil War. By 1900, hospitals had changed from voluntary structures to religious and ethnic-sponsored organizations and eventually evolved into a for-profit business run by physicians and corporations.
- Payors transitioning from social programs to risk insurance: Originally intended to guarantee wage replacement, to cover medical fees, and to pay the indirect costs of illness to society, insurance became a right to health benefits and shifted the focus to expanding the access to medical care in the early 1930s. By the 1950s, health insurance became a standard employment benefit, extended to the family as well as to the wage earner. Sophisticated systems of cost containment and utilization management provided the final shift in the past two decades.

According to Starr,[1] five trends shifted the individualized pieces of the health system toward the integrated structures existing today:

- Changes in type of ownership and control from nonprofit and government organizations to for-profit companies.
- Horizontal integration of similar providers into multi-institution systems.
- Diversification and corporate restructuring to corporations that strongly influence a geographic market.
- Vertical integration across the continuum of care at all levels of services.
- Industry concentration covering multiple regional and national geographies.

Four recent significant trends can be added to this list:

- Shifts from facility-based to outpatient, ambulatory, and home-care services, reducing the hospital power base.
- Changes in staffing patterns of care providers, reducing the impact of specialist physicians and increasing the emphasis on alternative staffing models.
- Increased pressures to reduce insurance premium costs, placing greater burdens on insurance companies

Encyclopedia of Public Administration and Public Policy
DOI: 10.1081/E-EPAP 120010757

to manage limited financial resources without being accused of withholding quality patient care.

- Recognition that social services play an integral part of a successful system, providing the infrastructure of supports that meets the functional needs of those receiving care.

It is within this new framework that the need for collaboration and alliances between physicians, providers, payors, and social services organizations to serve the individual has arisen. This framework requires integrating all levels of patient care and stakeholders interested in the efficiency and the effectiveness of American health care.

INTEGRATED SYSTEMS DEFINED

Integrated health care delivery models are patterned on horizontal and vertical combinations of different levels of the continuum of care, types of providers, categories of payors, and needs of patients. This organizational realignment is traditionally performed to dominate the market—provide services to a greater portion of the patient population in a given geographic area. Theoretically, this realignment reduces the costs of services, improves service delivery for patients, and increases satisfaction of the various clients of the system.

A fully integrated delivery system is most typically defined as a system that ties the financing for services to the provision of all services, with all the parties sharing risk. Care is provided at the most appropriate level of care—clinically and from a cost-effective perspective. Accountability for community health status—wellness as well as treatment of illness—is also a cornerstone. Conrad and Dowling[2] expanded this definition:

> A vertically integrated health care system is an arrangement whereby a health care organization (or closely related group of organizations) offers, either directly or through others, a broad range of patient care and support services operated in a functionally unified manner... Full functional integration requires both administrative and clinical integration.

While this definition identifies the clinical continuum and support services that are necessary to the design of an integrated system, little is mentioned about the cost-effective provision of care. In responding to economic realities, the financial component must be built into the integration paradigm.

Coddington et al.[3] define an integrated system as:

> ...a system that combines physicians, hospitals, and other medical services, along with a health plan (or the ability

of the system to enter into risk contracts), in order to provide the complete spectrum of medical care for its customers. In a fully integrated system, the three key elements—physicians, hospital(s), and health plan(s)— are kept in balance by common management and financial incentives so they can match medical resources with the needs of payers and patients.

The key characteristics of this definition include providers and payors, shared risk for the success of the venture, and cost effectiveness and information management systems which can maintain the efficacy of the system overall.

Shortell et al.[4] add the following key characteristics to the definition:

> We define an organized delivery system as a network of organizations that provides or arranges to provide a coordinated continuum of service to a defined population and is willing to be held clinically and fiscally accountable for the outcomes and the health status of the population served.

These researchers further point out that common ownership is not mandatory, and that a variety of strategic alliances and contractual arrangements is appropriate. Expanding the organization further, this structure takes the perspective from the individual to the organization and from the organization to the industry overall. What emerging trend and models can we expect based on this theoretical background?

EMERGING TRENDS AND MODELS

In a 1994 study, 71% of hospital and health network leaders said that their organizations are trending toward integrated delivery systems, with 81% saying that they would not exist as stand-alone institutions within 5 years.[5] Four indicators—strategic direction, economic processes, organizational culture, and unique clinical capabilities—are normally used to gauge an organization's readiness for integration. With this framework in mind, more recent trends have emerged in the integrated health care marketplace. A sample of three—legal structure issues, incentive alignment, and organizational evolution—is discussed here.

Legal Structure

With the formation of a new or reorganized legal relationship, single ownership gives way to shared ownership management contracts, external party contracts, affiliation agreements, informal or formal memorandums of understanding, and formal acquisitions and mergers. However, many individual providers, poised on the brink of integration with an established or fledgling system, face difficult issues in determining and then gaining approval for their legal structure. These approvals are not only internal to the organizations (governance, decision-making authority, responsibility for services) but also external (antitrust, market power, tax status).

According to Teevans,[6] "...Antitrust laws seek to protect health care consumers from persons or entities that seek to, among other things, increase prices of, lower the quality of, or limit access to health care services." In both urban and rural settings, health care organizations are coping with the realities of the external controls by demonstrating that the creation or expansion of an integrated network not only improves access, but also allows the organizations to continue to operate, thereby providing vital services to a community. For example, if individual physicians were each to recreate information systems, contract negotiations, and risk coverage, they would have little time left for patient care. Furthermore, many may be forced to leave a market simply based on the economics of investing in all of these support systems.

Incentives Alignment

Clinical, financial, and patient satisfaction incentives are most commonly used to measure the improvement in health status of the community. Clinical integration occurs through the development of critical paths, care tracks, and collaborative case management plans, resulting in an interactive patient care process. Financial incentive alignments come about through capitation, contracting, and more closely managed cost and reimbursement. Improved patient satisfaction typically results from better communications, data sharing, and consumer inclusion in decisions about their care and services.

It is difficult, however, to develop these alignments quickly. Some, such as the integrated care tracks across different levels of care, can take months of education and negotiation between providers who had previously worked independently. In the financial incentives arena, Linenkugel[7] asks, "How do providers keep going financially when the incentives are misaligned—when a lack of rewards for keeping people healthy is coupled with diminishing reimbursement from payers (government and commercial insurances) to care for persons who don't keep themselves out of health care trouble?" Finally, how can organizations consistently engage consumers in developing and implementing processes and systems that improve patient satisfaction?

Many organizations are addressing this through systems that:

- Include nonmedical determinants of health, considered within a framework of health behaviors, living and working conditions, personal resources of patients/consumers, and environmental factors.
- Place greater emphasis on population health status, with indicators such as mortality and morbidity, balanced scorecards of changes in population health status, and self-reports of patient changes.
- Examine health status throughout the life cycle, considering both ends of the spectrum and all points in between, from babies to the senior population.
- Assess the coordination at all levels, both between levels of care and within care levels.[8]

Organizational Evolution

While it is generally recognized that the theories behind the organization development, evolution, and utilization of system tools such as information systems have generally lagged in the health care practice field behind other industries, health systems have, in more recent years, begun to catch up. Barber et al.[9] have applied a standard organizational evolution model to the health care field with the following findings:

> The evolving IHS (integrated health system) will need to address the following infrastructure issues: a system-wide mission statement; a corporate culture that welcomes and integrates previously independent entities; an information system that will clinically and financially integrate the system; a clinical support system that emphasizes clinical efficiency and patient-focused care; and an actuarial approach to health care planning. The IHS's human resource challenges include recruiting and retaining administrators to initiate and manage complex arrangements among acute, subacute, long-term, and ambulatory care services; requiring governance to be proactive, structured, and focused on the resources and services of the entire system versus individual entities; and preparing physicians for the transition from independent fee-for-service ambulatory and hospital practices to integrated, clinically efficient managed care.

These researchers further state that external factors will influence and alter the life cycle of the organization. The keys are to continue to reexamine and reinvent the integrated system to better meet the needs of its community and to plan for contingencies that may arise from the external factors.

FUTURE EXPECTATIONS

How then can a forward-thinking health care organization continue to reinvent itself and remain a vibrant, contributing member of its community? According to some thinking, integrated health care systems are failing at an alarming rate, at a time when other industries that have long attempted integration (such as manufacturing, telecommunications, and services) are refocusing on core competencies.

According to Friedman and Goes,[10] the reasons for failure are both structural and functional:

Structural problems:

- Information system conflicts.
- Focus on hospital/physician/payer rather than on the patient.
- Unwillingness of network partners to surrender autonomy.
- Inefficient supply chain processes.
- Supremacy of financial performance measures.
- Difficulty in determining and measuring meaningful outcomes.

Functional and process problems:

- Misalignment of cultures and incentives.
- Problems associated with building trust between and among key stakeholders.
- Inadequate time and attention paid to managing employee responses to change.
- Problematic leadership.
- Uncertain vision of the desired outcome.
- Lack of overall organizational commitment and understanding.
- Poor or inadequate communication.

Focusing on community as well as organizational needs is critical to integration effectiveness. If the community needs a large network of primary care providers and the organization is attracting specialists, it will not be competitive. Similarly, reengineering the cost of health care delivery at the expense of community programs will disconnect the health care network from its greater purpose. Improved communications and requisite data collection will similarly meet community needs. As community report cards become more widely used, providing and maintaining measurable and superior health care quality which responds to community needs will become the true measure of integrated network strength.

REFERENCES

1. Starr, P. *The Social Transformation of American Medicine*; Basic Books, 1982; 429.
2. Conrad, D.A.; Dowling, W.L. Vertical integration in health services: Theory and managerial implications. Health Care Manage. Rev. **1990**, *15* (4), 9–22.
3. Coddington, D.C.; Moore, K.D.; Fischer, E.A. In pursuit of integration. Healthc. Forum J. **1994**, *37* (2), 53–59.
4. Shortell, S.M.; Gillies, R.R.; Anderson, D.A. The new world of managed care: Creating organized delivery systems. Health Aff. **1994**, *13* (5), 46–64.
5. Bartling, A.C. Integrated delivery systems: Fact or fiction. Healthc. Exec. **1995**, *10* (3), 6–11.
6. Teevans, J. Applying legal analysis to integrated rural networks. Calif. State Rural Health Assoc. E-Newsl. **Jan–Feb 2001**, 1–14.
7. Linenkugel, N. Integrated health networks are not created equal. Front. Health Serv. Manag. **2001**, *17* (4), 41–44.
8. Green, C.J.; Moehr, J.R. Performance evaluation frameworks for vertically integrated health care systems: Shifting paradigms in Canada. J. Am. Med. Inform. Assoc. **2000**, *7*, 315–319. Supplement.
9. Barber, J.B.; Koch, K.E.; Parente, D.; Mark, J.; Davis, K.M. Evolution of an integrated health system: A life cycle framework. J. Healthc. Manag. **1998**, *43* (4), 350–377.
10. Friedman, L.; Goes, J. Why integrated health networks have failed. Front. Health Serv. Manag. **2001**, *17* (4), 3–28.

John Rawls

James R. Heichelbech
University of Colorado at Denver, Denver, Colorado, U.S.A.

INTRODUCTION

John Rawls was the most significant political philosopher in the United States during the 20th century. His work revitalized discussions of social equity in public administration and provided a focal point for critical reflection about social institutions. Publishing in over a hundred articles and books between 1950 and 2002, Rawls presented most of his ideas in three books: *A Theory of Justice*,[1] *Political Liberalism*,[2] and *Justice as Fairness: A Restatement*.[3] The following includes a summary of the development of the theory of justice within these three books, a discussion of its significance for public administration and public policy, and a summary of criticisms.

A THEORY OF JUSTICE

A Theory of Justice is presented in three parts dealing with Theory, Institutions, and Ends. The first of these is undoubtedly the most important, as it presents the very idea of justice as fairness. Parts two and three concern the application of principles of justice and the relationship between these principles and *the good* (following the Kantian tradition of distinguishing the "right," which concerns minimally necessary moral requirements, and the "good," which concerns maximum positive happiness. Rawls explains the theory by clarifying the subject of justice, offering two principles of justice, and then presenting an argument for those principles from an *original position* behind a *veil of ignorance*.

The subject of justice, he says, concerns the basic structure of society—the way that social institutions distribute rights and duties resulting in division of advantages gained from social cooperation. The primary role of justice is to provide a standard for assessing the distributive aspects of the basic structure of society. Such principles are those that "free and rational persons concerned to further their own interests would accept in an initial position of equality as defining the fundamental terms of their association." Justice as fairness views principles of justice as the basis for determining which kinds of social cooperation and forms of government are acceptable.[1]

Rawls defines the basic structure of society as "the arrangement of major social institutions into one scheme of cooperation," where an institution is understood as "a public system of rules which defines offices and positions with their rights and duties, powers and immunities, and the like," and says that, ideally, "the rules should be set up so that men are led by their predominant interests to act in ways which further socially desirable ends." To that end, Rawls offers two principles: "Each person is to have an equal right to the most extensive basic liberty compatible with a similar liberty for others," and "Social and economic inequalities are to be arranged so that they are both 1) reasonably expected to be to everyone's advantage, and 2) attached to positions and offices open to all."[1]

An important feature of these principles concerns equality of opportunity. "The natural distribution," he says, "is neither just nor unjust; nor is it unjust that persons are born into society at some particular position. These are simply natural facts. What is just and unjust is the way that institutions deal with those facts." Accordingly, he suggests that a liberal interpretation of these two principles "mitigate the influence of social contingencies and natural fortune on distributive shares," by requiring, for example, that "free market arrangements ... be set within a framework of political legal institutions which regulate the overall trends of economic events, and preserves the social conditions necessary for fair equality of opportunity."[1]

The Original Position

The argument for these two principles uses the idea of the *original position*, a perspective from which we can devise a "fair procedure guaranteeing that any principle agreed to will be just." As a preliminary step, Rawls lays out the formal constraints of the concept of right: "Principles should be general...It must be possible to formulate them in such a way that they are not tied to particulars... Principles are to be universal in application...The parties assume that they are choosing principles for a public conception of justice ...[and] a conception of right must impose an ordering on conflicting claims."[1]

The appropriate position from which to arrive at principles within such constraints is that situated behind a

Encyclopedia of Public Administration and Public Policy
DOI: 10.1081/E-EPAP 120024735

veil of ignorance. Although persons in the original position are rational, which means that "in choosing between principles each tries as best he can to advance his interests," those behind the veil of ignorance do not know how their choice will affect their particular case and they are obliged to evaluate principles solely on the basis of general considerations. In other words, "while they know that they have some rational plan of life, they do not know the details of this plan, the particular ends and interests which is calculated to promote."[1]

This strategy for devising principles of justice reflects the deontological character of the theory. Rawls tells us that his aim is "to work out a theory of justice that represents an alternative to utilitarian thought generally," which he describes as the idea that "society is rightly ordered, and therefore just, when its major institutions are arranged so as to achieve the greatest net balance of satisfaction summed over all the individuals belonging to it." The primary difference between a theory of justice as fairness and utilitarianism, according to Rawls, is that "utilitarianism is a teleological theory whereas justice as fairness is not." It follows, then, that justice as fairness "is a deontological theory, one that either does not specify the good independently from the right, or does not interpret the right as maximizing the good." Priority of the *right* over the *good* is an important deontological feature of justice as fairness, for it restricts the basic structure of society in ways that a utilitarian account could not. Whereas any and every desire has some value from a utilitarian perspective, those in the original position agree "to conform their conceptions of their good to what the principles of justice require." In other words, principles of justice, as principles of right, allow us to distinguish satisfactions that have value from those that do not and thereby define a reasonable conception of one's good.[4]

Political Liberalism

Political Liberalism is also presented in three parts, Fundamental Ideas, Three Main Ideas, and Institutional Framework. And again, the first part is critical for understanding the development of Rawls's position. Here Rawls attempts to show how it is possible that "there may exist over time a stable and just society of free and equal citizens profoundly divided by reasonable though incompatible religious, philosophical, and moral doctrines," and how "deeply opposed though reasonable comprehensive doctrines may live together and all affirm the political conception of a constitutional regime." In other words, Rawls hopes to "work out a conception of political justice for a constitutional democratic regime that the plurality of reasonable doctrines ... might endorse."[2]

One of the primary tasks is to clarify justice as fairness as a *political* conception. Given the fact of reasonable

pluralism, that a "diversity of reasonable comprehensive religious, philosophical, and moral doctrines found in modern democratic societies...is a permanent feature of the public culture of democracy," justice as fairness is presented as "a conception of justice that may be shared by citizens as a basis of a reasoned, informed, and willing political agreement." Such a conception, he says, should remain "independent of the opposing and conflicting philosophical and religious doctrines that citizens affirm" so that we "gain the support of an overlapping consensus of reasonable religious, philosophical, and moral doctrines."[2]

Rawls explains that a political conception of justice has three characteristic features. First, it is a moral conception to the extent that it is worked out for political, social, and economic institutions. Second, it is a "freestanding view," which means that it is distinguishable from any comprehensive doctrine that it might be part of or derived from. Third, it is expressed in terms of ideas that are implicit in the public political culture of a democratic society.[2]

Although the remainder of *Political Liberalism* certainly provides important details, most of the discussion serves to clarify concerns related to this political conception of justice. However, it is worth noting the three main ideas of political liberalism described in the second part. The first is the idea of an "overlapping consensus," in which "the reasonable doctrines endorse the political conception, each from its own point of view." The second is the priority of the right, which means that a political conception of justice limits conceptions of the *good*. And the third is the idea of public reason. Rawls explains that public reason is public in three ways: as the reason of citizens, its subject is the good of the public and fundamental justice, and its content is public.[2]

Justice as Fairness: A Restatement

Here Rawls revises the two principles of justice. Second, he reorganizes the argument for those principles. Finally, he revises his understanding of justice as fairness, now understood "as a political conception of justice rather than as part of a comprehensive moral doctrine."[3]

While Rawls has quite a bit to say about his revised principles, there are no radical changes and the arguments for them are more of an adjustment than a departure from the original formulation. The revised principles are: "1) Each person has the indefeasible claim to a fully adequate scheme of equal liberties, which scheme is compatible with the same scheme of liberties for all. 2) Social and economic inequalities are to satisfy two conditions: first, they are to be attached to offices and positions open to all under conditions of fair equality of opportunity; and second, they are to be to the greatest benefit of the least-advantaged members of society (the difference principle)."[3]

On the other hand, while the explanation of justice as fairness as a political conception is similar to what Rawls presented in *Political Liberalism*, he provides additional clarification of the idea of free and equal persons within such a conception. "Justice as fairness," he says, "regards citizens engaged in social cooperation, and hence as fully capable of doing so, and this over a complete life." Accordingly, persons are assumed to have two moral powers, the capacity for a sense of justice and a capacity for a conception of the good. He describes a conception of the good as "an ordered family of final ends and aims which specifies a person's conception of what is of value in human life or, alternatively, of what is regarded as a fully worthwhile life." Such persons are equal in having these two moral powers and are free both because they "conceive of themselves and of one another as having the moral power to have a conception of the good," and because they "regard themselves as being entitled to make claims on their institutions so as to advance their conceptions of the good."[3]

RAWLS AND PUBLIC ADMINISTRATION

Rawls's work had and continues to have a profound impact on the normative dimensions of public administration and public policy. According to Terry Cooper, the publication of *A Theory of Justice* coincided with the development of administrative ethics as a field of study, especially significant with respect to social equity as an important part of the New Public Administration emerging in the late 1960s. In particular, he says, two essays contributed directly to administrative ethics as a field of study: "Social Equity and Organizational Man: Motivation and Organizational Democracy" by Michael Harmon and "Social Equity, Justice, and the Equitable Administrator" by David K. Hart.[4,5] Both focused on the Rawlsian conception of social equity as applicable to public administration, "thus providing evidence of the practical significance of administrative ethics and building confidence in the possibility of developing it as a field of study."[6]

In practical terms, two aspects of the Rawlsian perspective have been important within discussions of ethical public institutions. First, the requirement of impartiality, which is implicit within the very idea of neutral competence or merit system, gained theoretical grounding as an axiom of ethical decision making in the public sector. Second, the Rawlsian conception of political justice required attention to distributive inequities and helped articulate the basis for various policy

initiatives, such as affirmative action. In other words, Rawls provided a practically useful argument for demanding equity both in decision-making processes and in determining who should benefit from them.

CRITICISMS OF RAWLS

The primary sources of criticism have come from communitarian and feminist perspectives. Stephen Mulhall and Adam Swift present a concise summary of various communitarian criticisms of Rawls offered by such theorists as Charles Taylor, Michael Sandel, Michael Walzer, and Alasdair MacIntyre, who argue that the liberal emphasis on the individual implies a "neglect of the formative significance of their social context and the moral significance of relations between them."[7] Mulhall and Swift identify four types of criticisms along these lines. First, the Rawlsian conception of the person requires a radical detachment from one's nature and ends that is psychologically impossible and deprives one of resources needed to reason about social justice. Second, this asocial individualism neglects the extent to which the societies in which people live shape who they are and what values they have. Third, while Rawls requires the theory to be universally applied, it cannot take into account the different ways in which different cultures embody values and practices. Finally, while Rawls emphasizes the neutrality of the theory with respect to comprehensive doctrines, he "smuggles" in particular ideas of the good life for human beings.

Feminist criticisms of Rawls are of two sorts. One is a methodological concern about the legitimacy of the detached perspective of the original position. Another deals with concerns about the application of principles of justice to particular institutions, such as family.

Just as communitarian criticisms focus on the culturally nonneutral conception of rationality reflected in the original position, feminists point out that the original position reflects a gendered conception of rationality. For example, Carol Gilligan's account of differences in moral reasoning between boys and girls helped clarify the ways in which abstract, detached, and rule-oriented conceptions of moral reasoning can be considered gender-specific. "Listening to people talking about morality and about themselves," Gilligan "began to hear a distinction in these voices, two ways of speaking about moral problems, two modes of describing the relationship between other and self." She distinguishes these two voices in terms of a contrast between an ethic of *justice* and an ethic of *care*— "the logic underlying an ethic of care is a psychological logic of relationships, which contrasts with the formal logic of fairness that informs the justice approach." The ethic of care "evolves around a central insight, that self and other are interdependent'' and ''a consciousness of the dynamics of human relationships then becomes central to moral understanding.''[8]

These insights have been developed further in various ways. Martha Nussbaum provides a succinct overview of a rather diverse set of criticisms. For example, some argue that because ''rationality of the parties in the original position is described as self-interested prudential rationality,'' and ''the parties are characterized as mutually disinterested, unaware of strong ties to others,'' it discounts emotionally grounded approaches to moral reasoning and favors an egoistic conception of human beings. Those influenced by the work of Jurgen Habermas also question the ''monological'' nature of the original position in which ''the parties are imagined as basically all alike, and as reasoning on their own, rather than exchanging claims and counterclaims in a dialogue in which different perspectives can be presented and investigated.''[9]

In contrast to the methodological concern about how the principles of justice are chosen, feminists have also questioned the limited application of those principles of justice.

In *Justice, Gender, and the Family*, Susan Moller Okin suggests that Rawls's assumption that those in the original position are heads of families ''is far from being neutral or innocent,'' for it ''has the effect of banishing a large sphere of human life and a particularly large sphere of most women's lives from the scope of the theory.''[10] Although Rawls assumes that individuals have a sense of justice, he does not explain his assumption that family institutions are just. Still, Okin acknowledges that if we assume that those behind the veil of ignorance do no know their sex, there is implicit in Rawls's theory a potential critique of social institutions with respect to gender.[10]

CONCLUSION

Although Rawls has acknowledged that principles of justice have some application to social institutions, such as family, his responses to both communitarian and feminist criticisms tend to reemphasize the importance of a political conception of justice derived apart from more comprehensive conceptions. And it is worth noting that he consistently offers his account as merely part of a more complete story about social institutions. From the perspective of public administration and public policy, this resonates with the treatment of social equity as merely part of what we need to consider when we think about ethical public institutions. However, he argues that justice as fairness is implicit within a commitment to democratic institutions, and therefore the relative priority of social equity reflects the relative priority of democracy itself.

REFERENCES

1. Rawls, J. *A Theory of Justice*; The Belknap Press: Cambridge, MA, 1971; pp. 7–11, 30–31, 55–60, 73, 102, 130–136, 141–142.
2. Rawls, J. *Political Liberalism*; Columbia University Press: New York, 1993; pp. xviii–xx, 9–13, 36, 134, 174, 213.
3. Rawls, J. *Justice as Fairness: A Restatement*; The Belknap Press: Cambridge, MA, 2001; pp. xv–xvi, 18–34, 42–43.
4. Harmon, M. *Social Equity and Organizational Man: Motivation and Organizational Democracy*; Frederickson, H.G., Ed.; Public Administration Review Symposium on Social Equity and Public Administration, 1974; Vol. 34, 11–18.
5. Hart, D.K. *Social Equity, Justice, and the Equitable Administrator*; Frederickson, H.G., Ed.; Public Administration Review Symposium on Social Equity and Public Administration, 1974; Vol. 34, 3–11.
6. Cooper, T. The Emergence of Administrative Ethics as a Field of Study in the United States. In *Handbook of Administrative Ethics*, 2nd Ed.; Cooper, T., Ed.; Marcel Dekker: New York, 2001; 11–12.
7. Mulhall, S.; Swift, A. Rawls and Communitarianism. In *The Cambridge Companion to Rawls*; Freeman, S., Ed.; Cambridge University Press: Cambridge, UK, 2003; 460.
8. Gilligan, C. *In a Different Voice*; Harvard University Press: Cambridge, 1982; pp. 73–74, 149.
9. Nussbaum, M. Rawls and Feminism. In *The Cambridge Companion to Rawls*; Freeman, S., Ed.; Cambridge University Press: Cambridge, UK, 2003; 488–520.
10. Okin, S. *Justice, Gender and the Family*; HarperCollins: U.S., 1989; 95–105.

Lao People's Democratic Republic (PDR)

Clay Wescott
Asian Development Bank (ADB), Manila, Philippines

INTRODUCTION

The governance system in Lao People's Democratic Republic (PDR) has evolved from key historical events, in the context of a number of geographical factors such as being landlocked, mountainous, and thinly populated, with ethnically diverse people living in small, isolated villages. Although the poorest Association of Southeast Asian Nations (ASEAN) country, Lao PDR has seen modest improvements since the early 1990s due to market-oriented reforms and improved institutions.[1]

BACKGROUND

The fourteenth-century kingdom of Lan Xang broke up into three separate kingdoms in the late eighteenth century, and, some 100 years later, France took control and combined them under the rule of the royal house of Luang Prabang. With the exception of a brief period of Japanese control in World War II, French colonial rule continued until 1954. The Lao People's Party, later the Lao People's Revolutionary Party (LPRP), linked with the Pathet Lao resistance movement, established in 1955 under the leadership of Kaysone Phomvihan. In the 1960s, Laos, under the U.S.-supported government of Prince Souvanna Phouma, was subjected to heavy bombing as the United States sought to hinder the passage of North Vietnamese soldiers and supplies along the Ho Chi Minh Trail.

The Lao PDR was proclaimed in 1975. Prince Souphanouvong was named president, but the real power lay with Kaysone Phomvihan, secretary general of the LPRP. The new government faced severe challenges in the aftermath of 20 years of political struggle, civil war, and bombing; the emigration of skilled administrators and professionals; and a Thai economic blockade from 1975 to 1976. As many as 40,000 people were sent to reeducation camps, and anywhere from 30,000 to 160,000 were imprisoned for "political crimes." The former king, Savang Vatthana, had initially been assigned the position of supreme adviser to the president, but in 1977, Savang Vatthana was banished to a remote area of the country. Prince Souvanna Phouma was allowed to live quietly in Vientiane until his death in January 1984.

Attempts to collectivize agriculture encountered strong opposition, and production stagnated. The LPRP took the first steps toward market-oriented reforms in 1979 by easing restrictions on private trade and encouraging joint ventures between the state and the private sector. It reduced agricultural taxes and increased government procurement prices for most crops; however, it made no move to dismantle central planning.

More far-reaching reforms began in 1986 following the adoption of the New Economic Mechanism (NEM). The government abandoned the collectivization of agriculture, eased many restrictions on private sector activity, and gave state enterprises more decision-making power. By 1989, most political prisoners had been released and the camps had been closed. The number of state-owned enterprises (SOEs) was reduced from more than 800 in the early 1990s to about 90.

THE PUBLIC SECTOR

Although the 1991 constitution contains elements of an earlier revolutionary orthodoxy, it emphasizes that the economy is market-oriented, permits private property and all forms of economic ownership, and protects religious, gender, and ethnic rights. The constitution legally establishes executive, legislative, and judicial branches of government, whereas the leading role of the party is assured.

With about 65,000 members, the LPRP's highest authority is the Party Congress, a gathering of party cadres who meet to ratify decisions already taken by the party leadership. Next in the party hierarchy is the Central Committee—59 party elites who fill key political positions and lead the party between congresses, which are held every 5 years. The Central Committee is headed by the nine-member Politburo.

The LPRP has shown itself to be remarkably resilient. Transitions of power have tended to be smooth, the new generation of leaders has proven to be more open to reform, the Politburo has some ethnic diversity, and organized opposition is weak. Some improvements have been evident since the early 1990s in literacy, primary education for girls, and reduction of child mortality, malnutrition, and poverty.

Encyclopedia of Public Administration and Public Policy
DOI: 10.1081/E-EPAP-120024431

The central government consists of 16 ministries and equivalent organizations, down from 32 after the 1986 NEM reforms. The National Assembly elects the president for a 5-year term. The Council of Ministers is the highest executive body and includes the prime minister and three deputy prime ministers. There is also a vice president. None of the key political and government leaders is a woman; however, there are four women members of the 59-member Central Party Committee: three female vice ministers and one woman governor. When assessing Lao politics, it is important to distinguish between the formal political structure and the informal networks through which much of the decision making takes place. Nepotism and patronage are endemic within the party and the bureaucratic system. The lack of transparency makes it difficult for the majority of the population or outside observers to understand the political decision-making process.

Since a border conflict with Thailand in 1987, Lao PDR has been at peace with its neighbors. However, the Lao People's Army still maintains a regular armed force of 29,100 and a local militia of around 100,000. In addition, the military remains politically powerful: only two of the nine-member Politburo have no military background. Although the military is regarded as politically conservative, it has exploited the nexus between its powerful position and the opportunities provided by economic reform. At the heart of the military's commercial empire is the Import–Export Company, whose diverse activities include agriculture and forestry, construction, light industry, trade, and tourism. Yet for most soldiers, army life is austere. Pay is low, and uniforms and equipment are in short supply. Consequently, most young Laotian men serve only the minimum term after being drafted.

From 1975 until the early 1990s, Lao PDR relied heavily on Vietnamese and Soviet military aids. Once the internal security threat from resistance groups had been reduced and relations with the country's neighbors had improved by the early 1990s, the leadership was able to reduce the defense budget and, as of mid-1994, Lao PDR had the smallest defense budget in Southeast Asia.

Lao PDR is, at best, at the very beginning of democracy. The National Assembly is elected every 5 years. It currently has 109 members (25 of them women), and generally meets twice a year. There is ongoing work with donor support to promote debate, use secret ballots, televise sessions, and improve public consultation, legislative drafting, and floor deliberation processes. Between sessions, the Standing Committee of the National Assembly, consisting of the president, vice president, and an unspecified number of other members, prepares for future sessions and oversees activities of the administrative and judicial organizations.

Lao PDR is divided into 16 provinces, 112 districts, and more than 11,000 villages, yet there has been little real devolution of power. Most members of the government are members of the LPRP, and the party-controlled Lao Front for National Reconstruction must approve those who stand for election to the National Assembly. The present National Assembly includes only one non-party member.

Relations between Lao PDR and neighboring countries are cordial, in part the result of membership in regional groupings such as the Greater Mekong Subregion (GMS) and ASEAN. Despite its economic problems, Lao PDR has continued to take steps to meet tariff reduction targets to comply with ASEAN Free Trade Area commitments.

The civil service has about 90,000 employees (38% are women),[2] along with roughly the same number of other workers paid by the government but not part of the civil service, including the military. Although the official size and cost of government are less than for regional comparators, these figures may understate the actual size and cost due to weak information systems. Over four-fifths of civil servants work in provincial governments. Inflation has eroded the value of wages to the point that they are well below the minimum needed for food and basic necessities, despite a 20% wage increase in 2002.[3] Operating budgets are minimal. As a result, many civil servants lack the motivation to perform their jobs effectively. Low skill levels exacerbate this problem, along with recruitment and promotion based on factors other than merit, and frequent marginalization of talented staff through transfers and assignment to low-priority tasks. Job descriptions are only now being introduced and there is little clarification of roles and responsibilities. The civil service tradition is strongly top–down, and the staff are reluctant to make decisions or bring problems to their superiors' attention. Exchange of information is limited.

In 1991, the government established the National School of Administration and Management to train civil servants. It also created the Department of Public Administration and Civil Service in 1992, which is responsible for guidelines and policy issues. The Central Committee for Organization and Personnel appoints and manages staff at the director level and higher. Although there have been ongoing efforts supported by donors to address administrative weaknesses, progress remains slow.

Lao PDR is a member of the International Monetary Fund (IMF), which in 1998 laid down an international code for public financial management. The code covers four broad requirements: clarity of roles and responsibilities; public availability of information; open budget preparation, execution, and reporting; and independent assurances of integrity. The government has made some progress in moving toward these requirements.

The constitution requires the National Assembly to approve both the budget and the development plan, but contrary to the code, the National Assembly does not receive detailed information on the budget. There is also no indication that the National Assembly approves or reviews extrabudgetary spending, quasi-fiscal activities, or government equity holdings.

Lao PDR has made some progress toward complying with the code's requirement for public availability of information. Although increasingly detailed budget information has been released to the public since 1997, there are serious delays in publication, and no coverage of contingent liabilities, tax exemptions, and other required elements.

As concerns independent assurances of integrity, government accounts are incomplete, inconsistent, and difficult to comprehend, and there is no independent audit authority. The National Audit Office is under the Office of the Prime Minister; thus it is not in compliance with the minimum standard of independence.

On the revenue side, the government has introduced a number of fiscal reforms intended to reduce the budget deficit and inflation. A key aim has been to shift the revenue base away from a dependence on transfers from state enterprises toward income, property, excise, and trade taxes. As a result, revenue has gone up as a percentage of gross domestic product (GDP): from 10.6% in 1999 to 14.5% in 2002.[3,4]

The IMF's code also calls for the administrative application of tax laws to be subject to procedural safeguards. Various reforms have reportedly improved the filing rate from 30% to 80%, and have increased collections significantly. Customs procedures and clearance times have also improved, although customs revenues have not, probably because of low valuations of imported goods, smuggling, and tariff reductions required by ASEAN.

Weaknesses in public administration and financial management lead to problems in service delivery. For example, the country suffers from a shortage of schools and textbooks, poorly qualified teachers, and low enrollment and completion levels. Although educational expenditures have increased since the mid-1980s to 7.4% of the budget, with significant donor-funded investments, the amount would need to increase to around 15% to meet stated goals.[4]

Health standards are also lower than desired due, in part, to a weak public health system that is inaccessible to much of the population. Many poor people rely on private pharmacies that have sprung up in recent years for treatment, but their personnel are often inadequately trained. A positive sign is that government health expenditure increased from 2.5% in 1992 to 5.6% in 2001/2002, although this combines a sharp increase in the donor-funded capital budget with cutbacks in the recurrent budget. Overall, the budget remains heavily skewed toward capital rather than recurrent expenditure.

The government has initiated important reforms in the area of central–local government relationships. Fiscal and planning responsibilities were centralized in the 1990s, and then selectively transferred back to local authorities by decree in 2000, allegedly to speed up project implementation.[5]

Past and present decentralization efforts face challenges because of unclear legal and regulatory framework and enforcement, lack of capacity at the provincial level, weak central institutions, and poor communication and transport links. The lack of accountability of subnational authorities and an effective and transparent system of fiscal decentralization has reduced the transfer of tax revenues to the center. The economic gap between Vientiane and the rest of the country has widened since the reforms began, as most investments have gone to the capital and its environs.

Legal and judicial reforms began in 1989. A draft criminal code established procedures for criminal cases, set up a court system, and established a law school. The Supreme People's Court is now responsible for judicial appointments. Laws are published in the Official Gazette, but only for limited distribution each quarter.[2] The Ministry of Justice routinely publishes its decrees and those of other ministries it deems important. This leads to confusion in the application of unpublished decrees and arbitrary enforcement.

Access to justice is hindered by shortages of qualified judges and facilities, and administrative interference in judicial decisions. Outside of major urban centers, citizens rely on village-based conflict resolution committees to adjudicate disputes. Based on traditional systems, these parajudicial elected bodies relieve the underresourced civil courts of civil complaints.[2]

A key governance constraint is corruption at all levels. New opportunities for corruption opened up as economic reforms started to take hold in the 1980s. For example, giving provinces the right to trade directly with neighboring countries has opened the way for trade-related graft; the opening up to foreign investment has introduced opportunities to collect money to facilitate required authorizations. The enhanced political and economic roles given to the army have provided new opportunities for smuggling. Corruption also spread to personnel management, leading to the rapid promotion of those close to powerful leaders. Donor-funded procurements are commonly abused for personal gain. There are also reportedly 4–10% kickbacks paid for government contracts.[2]

The government has taken many actions to address the problem, adopting an Anti-Corruption Decree in 1999 and new directives at the Party Congress in 2002, placing new controls on illegal logging, publicly condemning lavish consumption, and strengthening the State Audit Authority, State Inspection Authority, and Inspection Department of the Ministry of Finance.

PRIVATE SECTOR, CIVIL SOCIETY, AND THE MEDIA

The private sector consists mainly of small family trading and food-related businesses, about 75% in rural areas. Although the government still views the emerging private sector—especially indigenous entrepreneurs—with suspicion, many initiatives are underway with donor support to improve the enabling and regulatory environment.

The National Chamber of Commerce and Industry represents 500 businesses, but still depends on party guidance. The party's mass organizations have extensive networks at the village level, and some accomplishments that point to, for example, the Lao Federation of Trade Unions have promoted the rights of textile workers and HIV/AIDS prevention as a right of all workers.

There are only a few indigenous organizations that might be viewed as the beginnings of an independent civil society. Nevertheless, there are increasing numbers of Laotian nongovernmental organizations (NGOs) working at the village level (e.g., Champa works on health issues and Padek Lao works on community-based agricultural issues). Foreign NGOs have developed further than indigenous ones because the government finds them easier to control.

Information and communication have been tightly controlled since French colonial times. During the years of revolutionary struggle, the LPRP relied heavily on radio broadcasts to a largely illiterate, mountain-dwelling audience. In recent years, the number of newspapers, televisions, and radio stations has increased. The government still controls all domestic radio, television, and newspaper outlets, and reacts harshly to expressions of political dissent. Despite government controls, the quality of reporting and scope of topics covered is increasing.[2]

Given the proximity of Thai radios and televisions, Thailand remains both an open window to a different economic system and provides an alternative perspective on the news. Satellite and cable broadcasting and the Internet are legal and progressively reducing government monopoly control of the media.

CONCLUSION

The resilient party and government apparatus that inherited the historical legacy and geographical constraints of Lao PDR has come a long way from its initial socialist orthodoxy to the nascent constitutionalism and market mechanisms of today. Yet Lao PDR is still a long way from operating as a modern constitutional state based on a clear separation of powers, and further reform will be required for Laos to meet its ambitious goals of poverty reduction, social development, and economic development.

REFERENCES

1. This is a personal view, and may not represent the views of the ADB. It summarizes and updates "Lao PDR." In *Key Governance Issues in Cambodia, Lao PDR, Thailand and Viet Nam*; Wescott, C., Ed.; ADB: Manila, 2001.
2. Lao, P.D.R. *Priority Areas for Governance Reform: Public Service Reform, People's Participation, Rule of Law and Sound Financial Management—Policy Paper*; Government of Lao P.D.R.: Vientiane, 2003; pp. 8, 39, 40, 47, 62–64.
3. ADB. *Lao PDR—Country Strategy and Program Update*; ADB: Manila, 2004; pp. 1, 2.
4. World Bank and ADB. *Lao PDR Public Expenditure Review Country Financial Accountability Assessment*; World Bank: Washington, 2002; Vol. 2, pp. 5, 15.
5. Chagnon. *Looking Back to See Forward*; Swedish International Development cooperation Agency: Vientiane, 2002; 22.

Logistics and Transportation

Linda L. Stanley
Our Lady of the Lake University, San Antonio, Texas, U.S.A.

Darin Matthews
Multnomah County Schools, Portland, Oregon, U.S.A.

INTRODUCTION

The management of transportation services is frequently an overlooked opportunity to contribute to the success of governmental operations that depend on purchasing's ability to evaluate transportation options and carriers, determine the means to reduce transportation and inventory carrying costs, expedite and trace shipments, and process claims. The selection of a transportation system is a specialized form of procurement in which services are purchased to provide a link among manufacturing sites, warehouses, distribution centers, and/or office sites. Components of the transportation service buy include 1) evaluating the prices of various transportation methods, 2) determining the effect of transportation service on operations, and 3) evaluating the effect of transit times, carrier dependability, and safe delivery on inventory levels.[1]

Traditionally, the procurement and management of transportation services were relegated to the supplier who provided a ''laid-down price''—the cost of transportation rolled into the price of purchased goods. This manner of operation was particularly popular prior through the late 1970s because rates were regulated by federal and state governments and were not negotiable. However, since deregulation, flexible pricing plans and more service options are available. Carriers are now logistics service companies and have integrated their expertise with that of their customers.[2] Thus savings opportunities are possible by paying closer attention to the costs of transportation, whether directly arranged by the procurement officer or managed by a supplier. Second, businesses and government agencies have begun to realize the value of evaluating the *total cost* of procuring goods, which may include transportation costs, carrying costs, disposal costs, etc.

This article is designed to provide governmental purchasers an introduction to transportation management, to offer strategies to effectively manage the procurement of these services, and to suggest some future trends. We will start with some definitions common to the transportation industry.

DEFINITIONS

Transportation is ''the physical movement of goods and people between points.''[3] Goods may include new materials brought into a production process or finished goods shipped to the customer. *Carriers* are those organizations that provide transportation services, and the primary *modes* include railroads, motor carriers, airlines, water carriers, and pipelines. Procurement officers may also hire *third parties*, or intermediaries, who serve to connect the various modes of transportation. Some examples include *transportation brokers*, *freight forwarders*, and *shippers associations*.

Transportation is part of both the inbound and outbound movement of goods. The inbound side is often referred to as *materials management*, which combines the activities of procurement, warehousing, transportation, inventory management, quality control, and scrap/disposal with the goal of improved customer service.[4,5] *Physical distribution* focuses on the outbound side, dealing with the flow of the finished goods to the final customer.[4] There may be several channel members in physical distribution of goods, including wholesalers and distributors.

Logistics management or *integrated logistics* management combines both inbound and outbound sides and can be defined as ''the art and science of obtaining and distributing materials and products.''[6] Factors that contributed to the move toward an integrated logistics function and beyond are provided in the next section.

EVOLUTION OF LOGISTICS

The term *logistics* was derived from military activities related to the deployment and the support of armed forces during the times of war.[7] In fact, logistics was referred to as early as 500 BC in Sun Tzu's *The Art of War*,[8] a book about logistical activities and their relationship to war tactics and strategies. During World War II, logistical activities contributed to victory for the United States and its allies. More recently, logistical activities were

Encyclopedia of Public Administration and Public Policy
DOI: 10.1081/E-EPAP 120019364

identified as a critical component of success for the United States during the Gulf War in 1990–1991. Involved was a massive movement of 122 million meals, 1.3 billion gal of fuel, and 31,800 t of mail.[9] Since the 1960s, logistics has come to the forefront of best business practices.

During the 1960s and 1970s, the impact of global competition on U.S. firms was significant. Companies were losing market share and revenues to firms from other countries, particularly Japan and Germany. Competitive pressures increased in the mid-1970s as trade barriers were reduced, forcing U.S. firms to improve the quality of their products and services, to focus on higher levels of customer service and satisfaction, and to reduce costs. The amount spent on logistics was identified as the final frontier for cost reduction and improved customer service.[10] Businesses turned their attention to the physical distribution of goods and materials for improved customer service and cost savings. They moved toward logistics management, the integration of transportation, distribution, warehousing, finished goods, inventory management, packaging, and materials handling. Deregulation of transportation played a large part as increased competition among carriers resulted in lower transportation rates and better management of inbound transportation.

Beginning in the late 1970s and continuing into the 1980s, the physical distribution management expanded to logistics management. This move led to purchasing's increased involvement in logistical decisions, including transportation management. Factors influencing this move included changes in the manufacturing environment and an increased emphasis on quality.[11] The environment had changed as manufacturers moved to outsourcing a greater percentage of the content of their products to outside suppliers. These suppliers were able to produce parts at a lower cost in part because of their nonunion environment. To replace the benefits of controlling all-part production, many firms moved to a just-in-time (JIT) manufacturing environment. In essence, JIT involved suppliers delivering parts to manufacturing sites just as needed for production and producing goods based on the actual customer need, rather than forecasts, resulting in lower inventory-carrying costs. However, it also meant relationships with both suppliers and transportation carriers needed to be stronger to assure the delivery within tight windows. In many instances, companies moved to single-sourcing arrangements. At the same time, the total quality management movement was in full force, enabling firms to compete with foreign goods producers. The selection of quality carriers was an important part of the equation because manufacturers had to be assured that the goods were moved safely and the customers were provided a proper level of service. Once the firms reduced the number of carriers in the pool, they focused on developing measures of performance and monitoring

carriers more closely. These measures included percentage of on-time shipments, percentage of damaged shipments, and percentage of complete orders shipped.

During the late 1980s and 1990s, the term *supply chain management* emerged and was defined as managing the total flow of goods and information from supplying agency to final "customer," realizing that each step in the flow of goods should add a value.[12] Potential savings within a supply chain were the driving factor behind this new trend. A supply chain has a series of "fixed points"—warehouses, distribution centers, offices, where goods are stored—linked together by transportation. This strategy includes developing partnerships between manufacturers, suppliers, and logistics-related members of the supply chain including transportation carriers. In particular, shippers spend more time qualifying their carriers. Carrier strategies that will lead to more successful relationships within the supply chain have been cited:[13]

1. Partnerships in which both shipper and carrier challenge each other to provide innovative solutions.
2. Working jointly with shippers to control transportation costs.
3. Providing services considered the highest priority by the shipper.
4. Committing to continuous improvement processes that are critical to positive change.
5. Implementing satellite communication systems.
6. Providing information systems, logistics consulting, and specialized services based on customer needs.

TRANSPORTATION STATISTICS

Logistics costs as a percent of gross domestic product (GDP) have continued to drop with the advent of deregulation. At a high of 17.9% in the early 1980s, costs have averaged approximately 10% since 1992 and were 10.1% in 2000.[14] In 2000, 5.9% of GDP was accounted for by freight transportation costs, the largest component of logistics costs, or $590 billion in 2000. The most recent figures available indicate that federal, state, and local governments spend approximately $129 billion annually on transportation.[15]

Table 1 breaks down where organizations spend their logistics dollars.

CARRIER SELECTION

Selecting a transportation carrier can be one of the most crucial decisions a government purchaser can make for their organization. Just as choosing the right supplier of goods can help ensure the operational success,

Table 1 Logistics cost breakdown, 2000

Logistics cost	Cost ($ billion)
Carrying Costs	
Interest	$95
Taxes, Insurance,	204
Obsolescence, Depreciation	
Warehousing	78
Subtotal	**$377**
Transportation Costs	
Motor Carriers	
Truck—Intercity	323
Truck—Local	158
Railroads	36
Water (International, Domestic)	26
Oil Pipelines	9
Air (International, Domestic)	27
Forwarders	6
Subtotal	**$585**
Shipper-related Costs	5
Logistics Administration	39
Subtotal	**$44**
Total Logistics Costs	**$1,006**

(From Ref. [14].)

determining how those same goods are transported to their final destination is vital.[16] While the initial choice made by an agency will be the type, or mode, of delivery, the choice of carriers will certainly be next.

When one contemplates how important quality deliveries are to an organization, they need only to look at the seven R's of customer satisfaction:[17]

1. The right product.
2. Delivered to the right place.
3. At the right time.
4. In the right condition and packaging.
5. In the right quantity.
6. At the right cost.
7. To the right customer.

The importance of quality, accuracy, and timeliness in the delivery of goods is apparent. Logically, this places major importance on which carrier the purchasing practitioner selects to make such deliveries. With the importance of the carrier selection determined, let us examine how these decisions are best approached.

One of the first considerations a buyer must make in carrier selection is whether or not these services will be purchased separately. The predominant method in the public sector is to shift the burden of carrier selection to the supplier.[1] By specifying Free on Board (FOB) Destination in the bidding documents, the public agencies have charged the selected vendor with handling all the aspects of delivery, with the agency taking ownership upon delivery.

However, there are many instances where an agency can contract directly for transportation services. Many organizations ship out goods and equipment from their own facilities and hire private carriers to transport them. For instance, a water treatment facility may need to ship specialized control equipment to a manufacturer for repair or upgrade. To ensure quality transportation services of such critical equipment, they would likely have a contract with a carrier already in place. Even for incoming freight, this approach can make a lot of sense. Rather than rely on a carrier someone else has selected, a public agency may want to hire a carrier to transport that replacement compressor from the supplier's dock. By doing so, buyers are essentially stating that they are better equipped to determine the carrier than their supplier.

If the government purchaser does elect to contract for transportation services, they will face many of the same issues encountered with other types of services. A determination of the best procurement method will need to be made. An invitation to bid may be employed or possibly a request for proposal (RFP). A bid process will be driven by the lowest cost, while the RFP process will take into account the other aspects the agency determines as valuable. These can include service quality, corporate experience, financial stability, customer satisfaction, and prior dealings among other factors. According to the research by McGinnis,[18] *service* is often more important than *cost* when selecting carriers.

As with other procurements, the opportunity for a contractor to have a large volume of guaranteed business by the agency will normally result in very favorable offers from the carrier community. Additionally, long-term agreements with multiyear options can provide an opportunity for a carrier to become a strategic partner of the public agency. Once a contract is executed and the business relationship is established, the agency has the ability to utilize the carrier whenever a transportation need arises. Similar arrangements can also be made with the third-party providers of transportation services. When an organization contracts with a freight forwarder or a broker, they can provide whatever type of transportation mode is needed, offering the buyer even more flexibility.

MODES OF TRANSPORTATION

There are five primary modes of transportation—motor carriage, rail, air, water, and pipeline. Each mode provides its own unique capabilities as well as disadvantages. The following paragraphs provide a short analysis of each mode.

The dominant mode of transportation is motor carriage, or trucking, where approximately $481 billion was spent in the United States in 2000 (Table 1), and they moved approximately one-half of all tonnage. The industry consists of a large number of small carriers, resulting in a high level of competition. The reasons for the heavy use of trucking include high availability, ability to provide service from and to almost any location, relatively fast transit times, and reliable service. Motor carriage has two roughly equal segments, for-hire and private carriage. Ninety-five percent of all for-hire carriage is moved by truckload, with the remaining 5% by less-than-truckload, or movements of less than 10,000 lb.[19] The average truckload delivery spans 350 mi, with a market dominance of up to 750 mi. Trucks move raw materials, component parts, and finished goods. Trucking companies are actually a good customer of the rail industry, loading their trailers onto rail flatcars.

There are a small number of relatively large railroads, called Class I carriers, in the United States. As seen in Table 1, the railroads account for about 6% of the revenues generated by all modes, although they move approximately 25% of all the freight tonnage.[20] Railroads carry primarily commodities including grain, metallic ores, crushed stone, and glass and clay products. Their advantage lies in moving goods long distances in large volumes with a low-cost structure. However, access is a significant disadvantage, resulting in the need for an additional mode of transportation such as trucks to complete deliveries. Another disadvantage is the long transit time as a result of consolidation and the transfer of boxcars at classification yards within the rail system. Shippers must also pay additional costs to maintain the safety of their goods. However, rail service is more reliable than other modes because it is mostly unaffected by poor weather conditions.

Water transportation also plays a significant role, accounting for $26 billion of total logistics dollars spent within the United States (Table 1). This mode is frequently used by the organizations located in strategic areas to move raw materials, heavy items, and low-value bulk materials. Road salt is one example of a common government commodity often transported by water. The oldest technology of transport, water transportation includes barges used on inland waterways as well as ocean-going ships. The cost of the pickup and the delivery of goods to the dockside need to be included in the total cost of shipping, as they are not included in the water freight rates. Water carriers normally base their charges on either weight or volume, depending on which one results in the highest revenue for the carrier.[1] The federal government has long been involved with improving the waterways within the United States. The Army Corps of Engineers is the agency that provides oversight and funding for river and harbor improvements. Projects such as enlarging the locks and deepening the channels are examples of such improvements.[3]

In 2000, a total of $27 billion was spent on international and domestic airfreight. This transportation mode includes all shipments made by air cargo carriers. The movement of goods through the air has certainly increased in recent years, but the relatively high cost has kept its use somewhat limited in the government. As a general rule of thumb, the freight rates for air cargo are approximately twice as high as motor freight. However, along with the higher costs do come certain advantages. Because the air travel is generally much smoother than the ground freight, it is very attractive for transporting delicate equipment.[1] Another advantage is the shorter delivery times involved with the air transport. A specialized repair part, for instance, can be shipped from New York to California in 1 day. Commercial companies that provide such service include the Federal Express and the United Parcel Service. When typical ground transportation would take several days, the decision to use airfreight is much more attractive. With such short lead times, organizations can normally reduce their inventories and carrying costs.

Referred to as the "hidden giant of American transportation," pipelines have been around since 1865 when Samuel Van Syckel constructed a 5-mi oil pipeline in Pennsylvania.[3] Besides its extensive use in the oil industry, pipelines are also used to transport other materials such as natural gas and coal slurry. The total transportation costs for oil pipelines alone was $9 billion during 2000. Within the United States, there are over 110 regulated oil pipelines. From 1906 to 1977, the oil pipeline industry was governed by the ICC. Since then, it has been regulated by the Federal Energy Regulatory Commission. The dependability of this transportation mode is extremely high, as far as obtaining the product to its destination when promised. Because pipelines are virtually unaffected by the weather, they really are unparalleled when it comes to dependability. One disadvantage to the pipeline transportation is the high costs associated with installing and maintaining the piping systems. The material, labor, and equipment costs can be extensive, including such things as speciality piping, journey level labor, pumps, and computerized flow controls. However, the pipelines continue to be a viable means of transportation in the United States, particularly in the oil industry.

CONCLUSION

Transportation has played an important role in the development of the United States and thus our economy.

City locations and their growth were often influenced by access to transportation. For example, Boston initially grew because of its origin as a port city; Chicago was a hub for the railroads; and Atlanta, initially a railroad stop, now has the world's largest airport.

Today, significant changes are occurring within the industry itself. A formerly heavily regulated industry now has the freedom to set prices, to determine where they want to operate and where they want to discontinue service, and to negotiate special services for customers. Cavinato[21] suggests watching for certain trends in the next 10 years, including:

1. Continuing turnover of truckload motor carriers.
2. More rail mergers with few capacity changes.
3. Consolidation of courier and express mail firms.
4. Airline volatility, including bankruptcies and mergers.
5. More extensive use of electronic information to provide inventory visibility and efficient billing and payment.
6. Industry consolidation that allows more one-stop shopping.

Wood and Johnson[3] also foresee an increase of environmental protection and safety laws. Additionally, recycling's impact on transportation will be significant because packaging choices will be based on reuse. Recycled materials and products mean additional hauls for transportation carriers. Finally, threats of terrorism will have a major impact on the international trade and the transportation carriers. The new challenge will be to reduce time and costs given increased security measures taken by the U.S. government. Given these trends, transportation and logistics will continue to be a dynamic and challenging part of the public procurement process.

REFERENCES

1. Corwin, S.H. *Intermediate Public Procurement*, 2nd Ed.; National Institute of Governmental Purchasing: Herndon, VA, 2000.
2. Stock, J.R. The maturing of transportation: An expanded role for freight carriers. J. Bus. Logist. **1988**, *9* (2), 15–31.
3. Wood, D.F.; Johnson, J.C. *Contemporary Transportation*; Prentice Hall: Upper Saddle River, NJ, 1996; p. 4.
4. Coyle, J.J.; Bardi, E.J.; Langley, C.J., Jr., *The Management of Business Logistics*, 6th Ed.; West Publishing Company: Minneapolis/St. Paul, MN, 1996.
5. Heizer, J.; Render, B. *Principles of Operations Management*; Prentice Hall: Upper Saddle River, NJ, 2001.
6. National Institute of Public Purchasing. *Dictionary of Purchasing Terms*; National Institute of Public Purchasing: Herndon, VA, 1996.
7. Gourdin, K.N. *Global Logistics Management: A Competitive Advantage for the New Millenium*; Blackwell Publishers: Oxford, U.K., 2000.
8. Tzu, S.; Gagliardi, G. *The Art of War: In Sun Tzu's Own Words*; Clearbridge Publishing: Seattle, WA, 1999.
9. Pagonis, W.G. *Moving Mountains: Lessons in Leadership and Logistics from the Gulf War*; Harvard Business School Publishing: Boston, MA, 1992.
10. Heskett, J.L. Logistics—Essential to strategy. Harvard Bus. Rev. **1977**, *55* (6), 84–95.
11. Gentry, J.J. *Purchasing's Involvement in Transportation Decision Making*; Center for Advanced Purchasing Studies: Tempe, AZ, 1991.
12. Ellram, L.M.; Cooper, M.C. Characteristics of supply chain management and the implications for purchasing and logistics strategy. Int. J. Logist. Manag. **1993**, *4* (2).
13. Wagner, W.B.; Frankel, R. Quality carriers: Critical link in supply chain relationship development. Int. J. Logist. Res. Appl. **2000**, *3* (3), 245–257.
14. Cooke, J.A. Steering through the storm. Logist. Manag. **July 2001**. Retrieved January 8, 2002, from http://www.manufacturing.net/lm/index.asp.
15. United States Department of Transportation, Bureau of Transportation Statistics. *Government Transportation Financial Statistics: Fiscal Years 1985–1995*; 2000. Retrieved January 8, 2002, from http://www.bts.gov/ntda.
16. Leenders, M.R.; Flynn, A.E. *Value-Driven Purchasing*; National Association of Purchasing Management and Irwin Professional Publishing: New York, NY, 1995.
17. Kuglin, F.A. *Customer Centered Supply Chain Management*; AMACOM, American Management Association: New York, NY, 1998.
18. McGinnis, M.A. The relative importance of cost and service in freight transportation choice: Before and after deregulation. Transp. J. **1990**, *30* (1), 12–19.
19. WEFA-DRIa. *Air Transportation Industry Yearbook 2001/2002*; WEFA-DRIa: New York, NY, 2001. Retrieved December 27, 2001, from Business Source Premier database.
20. WEFA-DRIb. *Railroad Transportation Industry Yearbook 2001–2002*; WEFA-DRIb: New York, NY, 2001. Retrieved December 27, 2001, from Business Source Premier database.
21. Cavinato, J.L. Buying transportation today. Purch. Today **2001**, *12*, 16–18.

Malaysia

Noore Alam Siddiquee
International Islamic University Malaysia, Kuala Lumpur, Malaysia

Habib Zafarullah
University of New England, Armidale, New South Wales, Australia

INTRODUCTION

With an area of nearly 330,000 km^2 and a population of 23 million, Malaysia is located at the heart of Southeast Asia. It is essentially a plural society where over 50% of the population are Malays and the rest are Chinese, Indians, and indigenous people. Politically, Malaysia is one of the most stable countries of the region. Yet despite the presence of multiparty democracy, Malaysia is often branded as a "semidemocracy"[1–3] and its political system as "hegemonic." A single party—the United Malays National Organization—has been dominating the political scene since independence in 1957. Economically, Malaysia has made impressive gains over the past decades; the economy is largely export-led, and it continues to enjoy high levels of growth notwithstanding the setbacks of the recent Asian financial crisis. With a human development index (HDI) ranking of 59 in 2002, Malaysia also fares well internationally in terms of other socioeconomic indicators. The economic success of the country is attributed, among other things, to political stability, dynamic and visionary leadership, and the efficiency of the administrative system in planning and managing programs of socioeconomic development.

THE GOVERNMENTAL SYSTEM

Malaysia is a constitutional monarchy within a federal and parliamentary structure. Of the 13 federating states, Selangor, Johor, Perak, Perlis, Pahang, Kedah, Terengganu, Kelantan, and Negri Sembilan are headed by hereditary *Sultans* who elect one of them as *Yang Di Pertuan Agung* (*Agung*), the supreme but nominal head of the federation for 5 years. The remaining states—Malacca, Penang, Sabah, and Sarawak—are headed by state governors appointed by the *Agung*. The Malaysian parliament consists of two chambers: a 219 member universally elected *Dewan Rakyat* (the lower house) with exclusive control over legislation and finance and a 69-member nominated *Dewan Negara* (upper house) performing the tasks of scrutiny and review.

The federal government, with overarching control over the entire country, is responsible for key public tasks such as finance, foreign affairs, defense, internal security, trade, commerce and industry, health, education, and social welfare, whereas the state governments have jurisdiction over local government, agriculture, land, mines, forestry, Islamic matters, and Malay customs. Although the federating states share certain functions[a] with the center, the balance of power is tilted heavily toward the federal government.

The Administrative Structure

The federal government is organized into ministries, departments, and statutory bodies. Currently, there are 25 ministries, 161 departments, and 75 statutory bodies through which the business of the federal government is transacted. Each ministry, headed by a minister, plays an important role in planning, coordinating, and implementing government policies and programs and has under its control a number of departments and statutory bodies which are primarily the implementing arms of the government. The secretary general, a career civil servant, as the administrative head of a ministry, assists and advises the minister and is responsible for the proper implementation of all policies and directives pertaining to the ministry. The departments are headed by directors-general and usually have their offices at the state and district levels.[4,5]

The prime minister and his cabinet, responsible to the *Dewan Rakyat*, exercise executive authority. At the apex, the prime minister's department serves as the nerve center of government administration and is vested with considerable powers to coordinate government policy-making and implementation. Its chief secretary, the highest-ranking civil servant and principal advisor to the prime minister, is responsible for smooth and efficient implementation of the decisions of the cabinet. The other

---

[a]Two eastern states of Sabah and Sarawak have been granted some additional powers relating to immigration and education.

Encyclopedia of Public Administration and Public Policy
DOI: 10.1081/E-EPAP-120024439

key central agencies include the Treasury within the Ministry of Finance, Public Service Department (PSD), Economic Planning Unit (EPU), Implementation and Coordination Unit, and Malaysian Administrative Modernization and Manpower Planning Unit, all under the prime minister's department.

At the state level, the governmental machinery replicates a similar fashion. The state executive council—the highest executive authority at this level—is headed by a *Menteri Besar* in states with hereditary *sultans* and a Chief Minister in other states. Although appointed by the federal government, he is required to contest and win in the state legislative assembly elections. The state secretariat is administered by the state secretary (the head of the civil service at the state level) who also acts as the chief advisor to the *Menteri Besar*/Chief Minister. Administratively, each state is divided into districts, *mukims* (subdistricts), and *kampungs* (villages). Although there are some additional levels in Sabah and Sarawak, districts play important roles throughout the country as most federal departments and agencies have their branches there, and almost all development projects planned at federal and state levels are implemented at this level.

The civil service in Malaysia has two broad divisions: the federal civil service and the state civil service. Although the federal civil service is organized into various cadres, the elite Malaysian Administrative and Diplomatic Service [*Perkhidmatan Tadbir dan Diplomatik* (PTD)] is the most important. Officers belonging to PTD enjoy more power and prestige, occupying as they do most top policymaking positions at both federal and state levels.[6] The civil service is also divided into three broad categories: top management group, professional and managerial group, and support staff. These groups are arranged vertically into 274 service schemes under 19 classifications based on similarities of roles and functions. Generally speaking, the service structure is rigid both vertically and horizontally[5] with little or no scope for interservice or group mobility. This, apart from huge differentials between/among various categories in terms of pay and perks, has caused considerable tension and resentment in the civil service. Although some states have their own civil services, almost all senior positions at the state level are filled by PTD personnel and other centrally appointed bureaucrats.

The PSD serves as the central personnel agency, with jurisdiction on personnel matters of federal, state, and local governments, but an independent Public Service Commission has responsibility over recruitment and selection in the civil services. There are another four specialized commissions for judicial and legal matters, railways, police, and education services. Civil servants in Malaysia are selected on the basis of merit and quota principles through a series of interviews, written examinations, and medical tests and placed on probation for 3 years before being confirmed and considered eligible for stipulated benefits and privileges.[5]

REFORM AND MODERNIZATION EFFORTS

Since the early 1980s, the administrative system, in general, and the civil service system, in particular, have undergone significant changes. A series of reforms aimed at enhancing efficiency and effectiveness have been introduced. These have modified the structure of the public service, rules, regulations and procedures, personnel management, planning, budgeting, and financial management systems. The worldwide recession of the 1980s and the growing budget deficits caused by falling exports and public revenues prompted the government to reduce its involvement in the economy and hence ''downsize'' the public sector. Following global trends in public management reforms, Malaysia has undertaken major programs of privatization and deregulation. Such drives along with subsequent institutional restructuring have led to considerable reductions in the size of the public bureaucracy; yet it remains relatively large vis-à-vis the population it serves.

Early initiatives such as the introduction of time clock systems, name tags for employees, codes of ethics, manuals on office procedures, and quality control signaled the government's commitment to bureaucratic efficiency and responsiveness and clean and trustworthy government. Other moves sought to enhance civil service capacity and its relationship with the private sector and creation of clearance centers for providing swift and hassle-free services to potential investors seeking business approvals. Public service networks provide a range of services besides acting as one-stop bill payment centers. The Client's Charter, introduced in 1993 along the lines of the Citizen's Charter in the United Kingdom, pursues enhanced bureaucratic accountability and improved service delivery systems. The charter is an assurance by agencies that their outputs and services will comply with stipulated quality standards that conform to customer expectations. More recently, internationally recognized total quality management, ISO 9000 series, and benchmarking have been adopted in the public sector, and a comprehensive award system for quality and excellence has been introduced. The multimedia super corridor was established to promote the application of information communication technology (ICT) in society and implement a variety of schemes such as e-government and e-services to enhance also the quality of public services.

Although there is a gap between promise and performance, generally, reforms are seen favorably; they have helped improve the delivery of public services, thereby contributing to customer satisfaction.[7]

PUBLIC ADMINISTRATION: TRENDS AND LIMITATIONS

The Malaysian administrative system has performed reasonably well compared with similar systems and traditions elsewhere in the region (except Singapore) and in other developing nations. Certain trends and limitations are perceptible, and these are explained below.

Centralization

Despite the arrangements for power sharing between the states and the center, the governmental system remains highly centralized. First, with exclusive control over all-important matters, the federal government plays a much bigger role than the state authorities. In the event of a conflict between the center and the states, federal laws have precedence. With its monopoly over resources and personnel, the central government exerts considerable influence on the states. Even with some autonomy in certain matters, the states rely on centrally deputed civil servants and federal grants and lack any degree of control on central agencies operating at the state or local level. Second, bureaucratic culture is characterized by a top-down approach to decision making, and there has been little or no attempt at delegating authority at lower levels. This has been reinforced by the concentration of power in central agencies. Prime minister's department symbolizes the concentration of extensive policy and managerial authority for planning and implementation of development activities at the state and local levels. The EPU serves as the center of national planning—conceiving and formulating major economic policies and strategies, including the 5-year plans. Even programs and projects initiated by individual agencies and departments need EPU approval and funding. Under such an arrangement, lower level agencies simply implement policies.

Dominant Executive

External control on administration has been weak in Malaysia mainly because of one-party hegemonic rule[3] and a series of constitutional amendments it has made over the years increasing the power of the executive in relation to the other branches of the government.[8] The dominance of the executive increased dramatically since the launch of the New Economic Policy (NEP) in the early 1970s. The NEP was a two-pronged scheme that sought to correct the problems of economic imbalance among major ethnic groups through redistribution of wealth and assets in favor of *bumiputeras*. Hence a large number of quasi-public enterprises were created under the scheme giving the public bureaucracy an important role in economic planning, public policy initiatives, and the management of large sectors of the economy. Consequently, Malaysia produced one of the largest public bureaucracies among countries of comparable size and level of economic development. Notwithstanding the drives for privatization and deregulation, the bureaucracy continues to play an active role in terms of setting developmental goals, stimulating economic growth through the promotion of private sector, and distribution of incomes and wealth among various ethnic groups. Given its pervasive role in the society, Malaysia is often described as an "administrative state"[9] where bureaucrats enjoy "positions and powers not to be found anywhere in the democratic world."[6]

Elitism and the Rule of Generalists

Public bureaucracy in Malaysia is characterized by elitism, a legacy of colonial administration. Members of the English-educated Malay aristocracy created by the British have continued to fill the highest positions in the bureaucracy since independence and enjoy extensive powers, privileges, and prestige.[6] They monopolize federal and state administrative structures. The elite PTD constituents occupy important decision-making positions in the field as well and are also privileged to provide leadership in the public service as the directors-general of various ministries and departments invariably come from its ranks. The continuation of the quota system guaranteeing 80% of positions to the *bumiputeras* endows native Malays the opportunity to dominate the ranks of the elite service. This Malay prominence in the PTD has created a feeling of disenchantment among members of other services, further heightening the longstanding tensions in the civil service.[5]

Politicization of Bureaucracy

An important feature of the public bureaucracy in contemporary Malaysia is the intimate relationship between politicians and bureaucrats. In theory, the Malaysian bureaucracy is governed by professional values and norms, and its members subscribe to the principle of "political neutrality;" in practice, the bureaucracy has never been separated from politics.[2,10] Although it is true that political leaders are generally capable of controlling the bureaucrats under their jurisdictions, senior bureaucrats share the same social and economic back-ground with political leaders and play an important role in the policy process. Consequently, civil servants not only see themselves as the ''paternal ruling group,'' but also often get enmeshed in party politics which, in reality, makes the Malaysian civil service a ''political bureaucra-cy.''[11,12] Although Malaysian public servants no longer stand for party positions, the law that prohibits them from being involved in party politics is not uniformly enforced. In recent times, the government has been prompt at taking disciplinary action against those public servants who have apparently supported the opposition, but has been wit-tingly indifferent to those who actively back the ruling coalition. Such a policy has encouraged many civil ser-vants, especially those who wish to build career in poli-tics, to become passive members of the ruling party/coalition and support its policies and programs. Whereas bureaucrats, in general, are expected to be sympathetic to government policies and programs, those who work in the state-controlled electronic media or the Ministry of Rural Development and the National Civics Bureau have little choice but to virtually act as the agents of the ruling coalition.[10]

Lack of Local Democracy and People's Participation

Local government in Malaysia is yet to emerge as a vibrant democratic institution. Presently, local agencies, established and regulated by state governments, are no more than subordinate offices of the state government. They suffer from limited capacity and resources and depend on federal and state grants to close their fiscal deficits. Furthermore, with local government elections remaining suspended since 1969, popular influence on local government and pressures for responsiveness is rather limited. In spite of administrative modernization, no significant drive has been mounted either to democratize governance at the grassroots or to rejuvenate local government bodies. Repeated overtures of the political opposition and civil society to reinstate a representative local government system have remained unheeded.

Likewise, public participation in governance has been lacking. Whereas impressive gains in eradicating poverty and promoting rapid socioeconomic development have been made, there has been no corresponding progress in creating opportunities for public participation. Reforms have fallen short of widening the presence of politically organized groups and civil society organizations in the policy process. As a result, the policy process continues to be insulated from political pressures and influences from outside the public sector. Instead, the use of restrictive laws to curtail political participation and the absence of transparency and scrutiny of governmental affairs by a

free media have not only undermined Malaysia's demo-cratic image,[1] but also thwarted the capacity of her citizenry to effectively influence public affairs. Without such capacities, the public at large remains simply passive recipients of government-directed services and facilities.

Corruption

The accountability system, despite changes brought about in various aspects of public management, has remained rather weak and inadequate.[13] The incidence of bureau-cratic malfeasance and corruption thus remains high. Corruption is believed to be rampant particularly at lower levels in the police service, road-transport department, immigration office, customs and excise office, and local government.[14] Contracts are often awarded on the basis of political and kinship ties and kickbacks, and underhand financial dealings are common business approvals. The Malaysian experience with privatization shows the scale and magnitude of such corruption and patronage distri-bution.[15] The anticorruption drives mounted by the government and the institutional mechanisms available to tackle the problem are yet to make any breakthrough in containing bureaucratic turpitude, and so Malaysia's position in the Transparency International's global corruption perception index has remained static over the past few years.

CONCLUSION

Public administration and the policy process in Malaysia operate within a federated pluralist political system with a dominant party playing the key role in all stages of the policy cycle. The prime minister and his cabinet deter-mine policy agenda, make the major decisions to frame and adopt policies, negotiate legislation in parliament, and oversee their implementation and evaluate their impact. An elite band of bureaucrats, selected by a merit-based recruitment system possessing considerable power and prestige and strategically placed in key central agencies, provides support to the political executive in managing governance at the center. The state and local bureaucra-cies are also active in implementing development pro-grams in their own jurisdictions.

A politically committed political leadership has suc-ceeded in introducing innovations, akin to the advanced industrialized countries, in public management practices. New institutions and structures have been created, and existing ones have been rejuvenated to inject efficiency in the delivery of public services. A range of reforms centered on economic rationalism as well as citizens' needs has enhanced the effectiveness of the administrative system. Deregulation and privatization have reconstructed the public sector for sound operation, and the application of ICT has simplified and improved communication both within government and between it and the private sector and citizens. Yet despite many positive features of these reforms, the administrative environment in Malaysia remains captive in enduring centralization, bureaucratic elitism, ineffective local governance, subdued public participation, bureaucratic corruption, and ineffective public accountability. These will need to be recalibrated, even if to a certain degree, to give the Malaysian administrative system a character correlating to the maxims of democratic governance.

REFERENCES

1. Case, W. Semi-democracy in Malaysia—Withstanding pressures for regime change. Pac. Aff. **1993**, *66* (2), 183–205.
2. Crouch, H. *Government and Society in Malaysia*; Cornell University: Ithaca, 1996.
3. Hilley, J. *Malaysia: Mahathirism, Hegemony and the New Opposition*; Zed Books: London, 2001.
4. Shafruddin, B.H. *The Federal Factor in the Government and Politics of Peninsular Malaysia*; Oxford University Press: Singapore, 1987.
5. Ahmad, A.S.; Mansor, N.; Ahmad, A.K. *The Malaysian Bureaucracy: Four Decades of Development*; Pearson: Kuala Lumpur, 2003.
6. Puthucheary, M. The Administrative Elite. In *Government and Politics of Malaysia*; Ahmad, Z.H., Ed.; Oxford University Press: Singapore, 1987; 94–110.
7. Siddiquee, N.A. Administrative reform in Malaysia: Recent trends and developments. Asian J. Polit. Sci. **2002**, *10* (2), 105–130.
8. Hai, L.H. Public Administration—The Effects of Executive Dominance. In *Democracy in Malaysia: Discourses and Practices*; Wah, F.L.K., Teik, K.B., Eds.; Curzon: London, 2002; 165–197.
9. Ahmad, Z.H. Introduction: History, Structure and Process in Malaysian Government and Politics. In *Politics of Malaysia*; Ahmad, Z.H., Ed.; Oxford University Press: Singapore, 1987; 1–10.
10. Funston, J. Malaysia: Developmental State Challenged. In *Government and Politics in Southeast Asia*; Funston, J., Ed.; Institute of Southeast Asian Studies: Singapore, 2001; 160–202.
11. Scott, J.C. *Political Ideology in Malaysia*; Yale University Press: New Haven, CT, 1968.
12. Common, R. Malaysia: A Case of Business as Usual. In *Governance and Public Sector Reform in Asia*; Cheung, A.B.L., Scott, I., Eds.; Routledge Curzon: London, 2003; 163–185.
13. See Chee, S. Public Accountability in Malaysia: Form and Substance. In *Public Administration in the 1990s: Challenges and Opportunities*; Pradhan, G.B.N., Reforma, M.A., Eds.; EROPA: Manila, 1991; 105–125.
14. *New Straits Times*; New Straits Times Press (M) Bhd., Kuala Lumpur, 15 April, 2002.
15. See Gomez, E.; Jomo, S.K. *Malaysia's Political Economy: Politics, Patronage and Profits*; Cambridge University Press: Cambridge, 1997.

Milgram Experiments

Holona L. Ochs
Andrew B. Whitford
University of Kansas, Lawrence, Kansas, U.S.A.

INTRODUCTION

Stanley Milgram's classic experiments, conducted between 1960 and 1963, sought to demonstrate the power of social influence by examining how subjects related to authority. The initial studies were later followed by several variants intended to test the factors mediating the conformity identified in those first experiments. The results of this research agenda are quite robust, having been replicated in numerous cultural contexts and appear to hold up well over time. In short, subjects of many social groups, and even some of arbitrary definition (i.e., men and women, and even Americans, Germans, Europeans, and Latinos), exhibit high levels of obedience to authority, and the overall levels of conformity remain relatively stable over time. Milgram shows that authoritarianism and conformity are not confined to particular social groups or "types" of people or even to types of situations. In fact, six out of every ten people will kill you if told to do so by someone in authority under a variety of circumstances.[1]

Moreover, Milgram's experiments are important because they have strong implications for ethical behavior on the part of experimenters who study authority relations in controlled settings. Many recent innovations in the protection of human subjects in experimental and other research settings are broadly due to the innovations introduced—and the resulting findings—by Milgram. For example, the American Psychological Association's *Ethical Principles in the Conduct of Research with Human Participants* (1982) make direct reference to these experiments and their findings on social authority in controlled settings. Most importantly, Milgram's experiments have great importance for the study of public policy generally, and public administration specifically. The current use of human subjects committees is particularly relevant, as well as the more pressing matters of social regulation and control in hierarchical settings.

HISTORICAL CONTEXT OF THE MILGRAM EXPERIMENTS

In the early 1960s a considerable amount of research was being conducted attempting to explain the atrocities of World War II. Generally, researchers sought an explanation for the human cruelty exhibited during this period, and there was a tremendous desire to attribute the violence to a readily identifiable characteristic that would allow people to identify that thing that must be something fundamentally different about someone who would participate in such depravity—or at least that the degeneracy of the circumstances produced such behavior in some individuals. Of course, efforts to assign responsibility for the atrocities exacted by the Nazi regime had resulted in many participants being charged during the Nuremberg Trials. The primary defense for the accused was that they were merely following orders. The vast majority of the research examined the authoritarian traits of the German people,[2–5] that is—with the exception of Milgram's studies.

The central importance of Milgram's studies[1,6–8] is that they attempted to pit moral values against the demands of authority in an experimental test of human behavior under social pressures to conform.[1] Milgram placed his experiments in the discursive field that linked his research with momentous examples of human barbarism, such as the treatment of the Jews by the Nazis in Germany and the My Lai massacre in Vietnam. He reasoned that most people would exact harsh consequences on others under certain conditions, particularly when given orders by someone in authority. Most importantly, he shows that people have an incredible tendency to conform and that in fact, most people would participate in violence under similar circumstances.

The Milgram experiments profoundly influenced the discourse on human nature, group behavior, ethics, public policy, and public administration. Specifically, the

Encyclopedia of Public Administration and Public Policy
DOI: 10.1081/E-EPAP 120024806

findings challenge some widely held beliefs about the capacity for human cruelty. The dispositional view that there must be something in the German character that makes them particularly cruel did not hold up when tested. Instead, the Milgram experiments undermine notions that human behavior is genetically determined or culturally determined. The results illustrate that human behavior is constrained by individual values to the degree that social influence and the situational characteristics are imposed.

METHODOLOGY

The initial experiment conducted by Milgram on obedience to authority began in a lecture theater where a group made up of psychiatrists, university students, and middle-class adults of various occupations and ages gathered for a lecture on obedience to authority.[8] Here we describe the situation Milgram asked his audience to imagine at the end of the lecture:[9]

> In response to a newspaper add offering $4.50 for one hour's work, you participate in a Yale University psychology experiment investigating memory and learning. You are introduced to a stern looking experimenter in a white coat and a mild-mannered individual introduced as your co-participant. The experimenter explains that the study examines the role of punishment in learning, and one of you will be the teacher and one will be the learner in this experiment. You are randomly assigned to the role of the teacher, and the three of you then proceed to an adjacent room, where the other participant, the "learner," is strapped into a chair. The experimenter explains that this is to prevent excessive movement during the experiment, but it is also obvious to you that the learner is unable to remove himself from the chair if he so chose. Then, conductive gel is applied to an electrode is subsequently attached to the learners arm, and the experimenter explains that this is to prevent burning and blisters. Both you and the learner are shown the electric shock generator that will deliver electric shocks that will serve as punishment for incorrect responses. The generator has 30 switches labeled with a voltage ranging from 15 to 450 volts. Each switch also has a rating, ranging from "slight shock" to "danger: severe shock," and the final two switches are labeled "XXX." The other participant assigned to the learner role asks if "the shocks will hurt" to which the experimenter replies, "although the shocks will be painful, they cause no permanent tissue damage."

> Your role is to teach the learner a simple association task, but you also are told by the experimenter that you are required to punish the learner for incorrect responses. You

are told that for every incorrect response you must increase the voltage by one more switch (15 volts). You are given a 15-volt shock to check that the generator is functioning adequately and to demonstrate the tingling sensation of 15 volts. The learner makes frequent errors during the experiment, each resulting in a higher voltage shock than the previous one. At 75 volts, 90 volts, and 105 volts, you hear the learner "grunt" through the wall. At 120 volts, the learner says the shocks are getting painful. At 150 volts, he screams, "get me out of here! I refuse to go on!" His protests continue as the voltage increases.

> At any point that you question whether you should continue, the experimenter tells you to keep going, saying, "you can't stop now," "he is getting paid to do this experiment" or "the experiment depends on your continuing compliance." He may even say "you have no choice." At 300 volts, the learner pounds on the wall and demands to be let out. After 330 volts, there is no longer any response from the learner, at which point the experimenter tells you that the learner's failure to respond should be interpreted as an incorrect response and to continue increasing the shock level. The experiment concludes when the highest shock level is reached or the learning task is completed.

Following the lecture in which the audience was asked to image the scenario described, each member of the audience was asked to anonymously record how he or she would have responded under the circumstances described. Members of the audience reported that they would have disobeyed the experimenter early in the experiment because they "didn't want to hurt anyone," and no one in the audience reported that he or she would continue beyond 300 V, the level indicating "danger: severe shock."[9]

What we now know is that when Milgram conducted the experiment described to the audience in the preliminary study, the "learner" was actually a confederate.[8] He found that more than 60% of the participants inflicted the maximum level of electric shock, and none of the participants disobeyed before 300 V.[1] Despite the prediction by the psychiatrists in the preliminary study that only "pathological sadists" would administer electric shocks to 450 V, the experiment revealed that ordinary people will inflict pain on another person under the right set of circumstances, particularly when told to do so by a legitimate authority.[8] The study also exemplifies the tendency to overemphasize dispositional factors and underestimate situational factors when making attributions about actions, referred to as a *fundamental attribution error*.[10] For example, people tend to assume that if someone has not done much today, it is because he is lazy; rather than assuming that he is tired or lacks the right resources.

Milgram conducted several variants of the experiment to test the factors that might mediate conformity, including surveillance by the experimenter and proximity of the learner to the teacher. Several characteristics of the study participants, experimenter characteristics, attributes of the confederate learner, and features of the experimental setting were manipulated in subsequent studies. In one variation, the learner asks for the shock, and not a single participant exceeds the constraints of the test manager.[1] It is evident that the presence and the demands of legitimate authority define the boundaries of behavior for the participants to a considerable extent.

It should be noted that a number of complaints about the Milgram experiments—beyond ethical considerations—are possible and have been voiced. For example, a central component in all of the Milgram experiments is the incremental shock procedure. By using a graduated series of shocks it may be possible that subjects faced an innocuous beginning that elicited compliance before any of the frightening implications of the procedure were clear to the subject. That means that subjects were not presented with any sort of "qualitative breakpoint" at which they might shift from obedience to disobedience. This procedure is held by some as a fundamental component that should have been varied within the experimental context.[11] Additionally, the studies took place during the epoch of behavioralism in the field of psychology. Consequently, the criticisms of a strictly behavioral approach are applicable to evaluating the Milgram experiments. In particular, Milgram's focus on the appearance of authority and the ambiguity of notions of authority and obedience make drawing conclusions about human nature a substantial leap.[12] However, subjects protections put in place because of the original protocol now make it difficult to replicate or extend it in any way that would meaningfully test these complaints.

IMPLICATIONS FOR PUBLIC POLICY AND PUBLIC ADMINISTRATION

Efficient and legitimate institutions can be used for constructive or destructive purposes.[13]

During Adolf Eichmann's testimony at the Nuremberg Trials, he claimed that he had nothing personal against the Jews or anyone else and stated that he found the concentration camps repugnant, but at the same time he described the meticulous organization of the deportation and extermination of several hundred thousand people.[2] He contended that he had an obligation to perform the administrative duties as assigned by the Third Reich because had he refused to be obedient and responsive to the political authorities, then every soldier from any army would have the right to disobey any order considered

personally objectionable. In fact, the Holocaust would not have been possible without the obedience and conformity of the public service, implementing the policies of the Nazi regime efficiently through routine practices.[13] In essence, latent tendencies toward dehumanization exist in the routinization of any process.[13]

However, some degree of conformity is necessary for the adequate functioning of any society. It is difficult to conceive of how decisions could be made and enforced—and actions implemented—without the recognition of some sort of authority. There is a reciprocal nature to the use and acknowledgment of authority. Public trust is essential to acquiring the compliance necessary to accomplishing civic purposes, and public servants are obligated to champion the public interest with empathy, respect, and consideration for future generations to obtain that trust.[14]

Additionally, hierarchy is an implicit component of any social regulatory regime because people vary in their readiness to obey and to extend trust. Useful hierarchical relationships require competence of the authority system.[1] For example, spectators in a concert hall do not respond to the instructions of the conductor. Authority is considered legitimate only by those who are incorporated into a system supporting that authority's legitimacy. This point is crucial when it comes to understanding policy and administration because those who are not integrated into the system have no investment in maintaining it. In fact, the alienation of people from society's institutions, processes, benefits, etc., undermines the legitimacy of the system, threatening the security and stability of the entire social group.

Conformity can also serve society in important ways.[1,15] For example, hierarchically organized groups are tremendously advantageous in addressing dangers or threats to security. Second, organizations provide stability and serve to facilitate cooperation among group members. Third, contesting hierarchical organization can lead to greater levels of violence. However, resolving the questions that arise when individual values and the demands of authority conflict remains among the central philosophical problems. Determining the nature of man and the role of values in society is integral to developing adequate policies.

Studies of public policy and public administration can draw several insights from the Milgram experiments. For example, Milgram outlines several preconditions for obedience.[1] Some basic attributes—such as the authority structure of parental authority within the family structure—directly conditions conformity. The larger institutional framework within which we all operate also solicits obedience. Even while institutional settings teach us that one's opinion is possible and important, for smooth functioning obedience is necessary. Rewards and sanctions of various types in a range of settings are structured to elicit conformity. This is essential to easing relations and facilitating transactions between individuals and groups.

In addition, an assortment of policy changes can be attributed to the Milgram experiments. The study itself raised numerous ethical considerations. First, participants volunteered for a learning experiment, a choice that is itself not a test of obedience. Although deception was essential to testing the obedience to authority, participants were not afforded critical information that may have affected their decision to participate, and they were deceived as to the nature of the experiment (i.e., the shocks were not real, and the learner was a confederate). Second, participants were filmed without their consent, with important implications for current practices about subjects' consent. Third, the strength of the social pressure made it very unlikely that participants could actually discontinue their participation if they so chose. Fourth, many of the participants exhibited severe and persistent psychological reactions to participating in the experiment. It is important to point out that the experiment itself exemplifies the principles under investigation. A study inquiring on the cruelty of humanity was continued through numerous trials despite the knowledge that there are detrimental effects on participants.

Eventually, the experiments were discontinued, and standards were developed for research that involved human subjects. The resulting policy requires research proposals to be reviewed by a *human subjects committee*. Only research meeting the standards for the treatment of human subjects is approved by the committee and capable of being carried out. The authority of human subjects committees and the standards of research practice hold considerable legitimate authority, and there are very high degrees of conformity to those standards in the United States. The federal policy for the protection of human subjects is implemented by the Department of Health and Human Services and is integrated into the procedural process of every public and private organization conducting research involving human subjects in the United States. Further, information about the federal human subjects research guidelines can be found at the United States Office for Human Research Protections (http://ohrp.osophs.dhhs.gov/index.htm).

CONCLUSION

Because the results of Milgram's research agenda are quite robust, having been replicated in numerous cultural contexts and over time (see Ref. [16]), we now have a fundamentally different understanding about how authoritarianism and conformity are not confined to particular social groups or ''types'' of people or even to types of situations. We have also discussed the strong implications for ethical behavior on the part of experimenters who

study authority relations in controlled settings, and recent innovations in the protection of human subjects in experimental and other research settings are broadly due to the innovations introduced—and the resulting findings—by Milgram. Readers seeking more information about the Milgram experiments should consult the works cited here, and general studies such as Ref. [17] but a most instructive introduction is located at the Milgram Reenactment (http://www.milgramreenactment.org/pages/index.xml), an online resource about the experiments and their lasting contribution to our understanding of authority, in all its forms.

REFERENCES

1. Milgram, S. Liberating effects of group pressure. J. Pers. Soc. Psychol. **1965a**, *1*, 127–134.
2. Adorno, T.W. *The Authoritarian Personality*; Harper: New York, 1950.
3. *Studies in the Scope and Method of 'The Authoritarian Personality'*; Christie, R., Jahoda, M., Eds.; Free Press: Glencoe, IL, 1954.
4. Scharrner, B. *Father Land; A Study of Authoritarianism in the German Family*; Columbia University Press: New York, 1948.
5. Shaver, J.P.; Hofmann, H.P.; Richards, H.E. The authoritarianism of American and German teacher education students. J. Soc. Psychol. **1971**, *84* (2), 303–304.
6. Milgram, S. Behavioral study of obedience. J. Abnorm. Soc. Psychol. **1963**, *67*, 371–378.
7. Milgram, S. Some conditions of obedience and disobedience to authority. Human Relat. **1965b**, *18*, 57–75.
8. Milgram, S. *Obedience to Authority: An Experimental View*; Harper-Collins: New York, 1974.
9. Adapted and Abridged from the Stanley Milgram Papers. Manuscripts and Archives, Yale University Library.
10. Kelley, H.H. Attribution in social psychology. Neb. Symp. Motiv. **1967**, *15*, 192–238.
11. Gilbert, S.J. Another look at the Milgram obedience studies: The role of the gradated series of shocks. Personal. Soc. Psychol. Bull. **1981**, *7* (4), 690–695.
12. Helm, C.; Morelli, M. Stanley Milgram and the obedience experiment: Authority, legitimacy, and human action. Polit. Theory **1979**, *7* (3), 321–345.
13. Adams, G.B.; Balfour, D.L. *Unmasking Administrative Evil*; Sage Publications: London, 1998; p. xxix.
14. Lewis, C.W. *The Ethics Challenge in Public Service: A Problem-Solving Guide*; Jossey-Bass: San Francisco, 1991.
15. Zimbardo, P.G.; Lieppe, M.R. *The Psychology Of Attitude Change And Social Influence*; Temple University Press: Philadelphia, 1991.
16. Smith, P.B.; Bond, M.H. *Social Psychology Across Cultures: Analysis and Perspectives*; Allyn and Bacon: Boston, MA, 1994.
17. Miller, A.G. *The Obedience Experiments: A Case Study of Controversy in Social Science*; Praeger: New York, 1986.

Models of the Policy Process

Thomas A. Birkland
University at Albany, State University of New York, Albany, New York, U.S.A.

INTRODUCTION

The simplest definition of the term "public policy" is "the things government chooses to do or not do." This very simple definition certainly raises more questions than it answers. How is public policy made? Who participates, inside and outside of government, to decide whether government should or should not act? Current models of the policy process seek to address these questions.

Since policy studies began as a distinct endeavor in the 1960s, two major categories of policy studies have emerged. First, the policy science and policy analysis tradition retains considerable influence and value in the study and practice of policy making.[1,2] This research tradition is rooted in the analytic tradition that prizes doing "the greatest good for the greatest number" of people in a society. Policy analysis often considers whether a particular policy proposal will yield net societal benefits (although the definition of what constitutes a "societal benefit" is open to interpretation). A major critique of this tradition is that it focuses too much on the economic aspects of policies without admitting the complexity of politics in policy making.[3] Policy process theories seek to understand how various elements of the sociopolitical environment interact with the structure and institutions of government to yield a set of policies. These theories are much more focused on the *politics* of policy, i.e., on the "who gets what, when and how" dimensions of politics famously outlined by Lasswell.[4]

EARLY THEORIES OF THE POLICY PROCESS

In 1965, Easton[5] conceived of politics and policy making as a *system* that contains inputs, outputs, and feedback. In Easton's systems model, policies are the product of inputs, such as public demands. The system takes in these inputs, which are influenced by features of the policy environment, and then produces, as outputs, policies. Policies are laws, rules, and other authoritative statements of what government does or has chosen not to do. Thus systems models view policy as the product of many influences inside and outside of government (Fig. 1).

Systems models help isolate the key elements of policy making, but have traditionally left the workings of the system—the "black box"—underspecified. The challenge for social scientists has come in opening up this box to understand how groups, political parties, the public, and elected and appointed government officials work to promote or oppose public policies.

Similar to the input–output model is the classic "how a bill becomes a law" model. This model is an idealized process model of how the process works in Congress. It fails to extend on the basic constitutional and institutional rules to explain how or why particular ideas are translated into laws while others are rejected. It is therefore not a useful model for understanding the policy process overall.

The Stages Model of Policy Making

The "stages" or "textbook" model of the policy process was, for many years, the preeminent model. In the stages model, policy making proceeds in stages, from *issue emergence and* agenda setting to *implementation* and then to *evaluation* and *feedback* (Fig. 2), and shares many features of the systems model.

A main critique of this model is that it is advanced as a one-way model, in which the stages happen in order.[6,7] In reality, policies are sometimes made without going through each step: some policies are quietly advanced without raising high on the agenda, and, in many cases, policies are not evaluated. In addition, the boundaries between stages of the policy process have never been particularly clear, when the stages are sometimes overlapping or intertwined, such as when implementation of a new policy causes problems to rise on the agenda to a level not seen during the agenda-setting phase. Still, the stages model has long helped social scientists to organize research around each stage of the process,[8] such as agenda setting[9–12] and implementation.[13–15]

MODERN THEORIES OF THE POLICY PROCESS

As scholars realized that policy making is more complex than the stages model suggests, researchers have developed increasingly sophisticated models of policy making. These theories include Kingdon's[16] "streams"

Encyclopedia of Public Administration and Public Policy
DOI: 10.1081/E-EPAP 120023078

The policy making environment

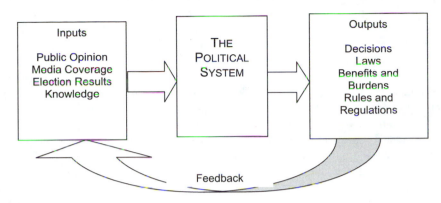

Fig. 1 A simplified input–output model of the political and policy system.

metaphor of public policy, Sabatier's Advocacy Coalition Framework,[17] and Baumgartner and Jones's[18] "punctuated equilibrium" model of agenda and policy processes.

Kingdon's Streams Metaphor

Kingdon built his idea of the "streams metaphor" by building on Cohen et al.'s[19] description of decision making in complex organizations. Kingdon argues that policy issues gain agenda status and alternative solutions are selected when elements of three "streams" come together. Each of these three streams contains various individuals, groups, agencies, and institutions that are involved in the policy-making process. One stream encompasses the state of politics and public opinion (the *political stream*). A second stream contains the potential solutions to a problem (the *policy stream*). The third, the *problem stream*, encompasses the attributes of a problem and whether it is getting better or worse, whether it has suddenly sprung into public and elite (i.e., the key participants') consciousness through a focusing event, and whether it is solvable with the alternatives available in the policy stream.

Within any particular problem area, these streams run parallel and somewhat independently of each other in a policy area or domain until something happens to cause one or more of the streams to meet in a "window of opportunity" for policy change. That trigger can be a change in our understanding of the problem, a change in the political stream that is favorable to policy change, a change in our understanding of the solvability of the problem given current solutions, or a focusing event that draws attention to a problem and helps open a window of opportunity. But the opening of the window does not guarantee that policy change will occur.

Kingdon provides a rich and multilayered description of policy making, from the early acceptance of new ideas about public problems to the active considerations of solutions as new public policy. However, one shortcoming of this model is that it does not describe the policy process beyond the opening of the window of opportunity.

The Advocacy Coalition Framework

Sabatier's Advocacy Coalition Framework (ACF) explicitly addresses two important features of the policy process: the role of groups and the importance of knowledge

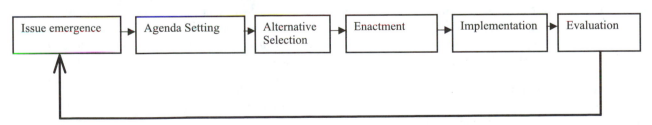

Fig. 2 The stages or textbook model of the policy process.

and learning in policy making. The pluralist tradition in political science argues that policy is made in a process of group competition. Sabatier understands, however, that dozens of groups working independently are unlikely to have as much power as they would have if they came together in larger groupings called *advocacy coalitions*.

In the ACF, two to four advocacy coalitions typically form in a particular policy domain when groups coalesce around a shared set of values and beliefs. These coalitions engage in policy debate and compete and compromise with other coalitions. Some actors, called "policy brokers," mediate competition between coalitions because the brokers are seeking particular policy outcomes or because they have an interest in promoting political harmony. Compromise is more likely when policies arise that do not threaten the advocacy coalitions' core beliefs and values. Policy change is much less likely if polarization of advocacy coalitions is so great that there is no room for compromise in groups' belief systems.

In the ACF, policy making is influenced both by "relatively stable" system parameters and by "dynamic (system) events," with the interaction between the two promoting or inhibiting policy making. The stable parameters include the basic attributes of the problem area, the basic distribution of natural resources in the society, the fundamental cultural values and social structure, and the basic legal structure, which, in the United States, is the constitutional framework and judicial norms.

The dynamic features of the system include changes in socioeconomic conditions and technology, changes in systemic governing coalitions (partisan balance in the legislative or the executive branch, for example), and policy decisions and impacts from other subsystems. Change in the governing coalition corresponds to one example of change in the political stream in Kingdon's model, while changes in socioeconomic and technological conditions influence the problem and policy streams. The activities of other subsystems can influence the policy, politics, and problem streams as their activities spill over into other policy domains. Like the streams metaphor, Sabatier's ACF encompasses a variety of individual and institutional actors, and it views policy making as a process over years or decades. The ACF also considers the mechanisms for policy change (not simply the possibility for change, as in the streams metaphor) and more consciously encompasses the influence of implementation and feedback on the system.

Punctuated Equilibrium

Baumgartner and Jones borrow the concept of "punctuated equilibrium" from evolutionary biology to describe the policy process. They argue that the balance of political power between groups of interests remains relatively stable over long periods of time, punctuated by relatively sudden shifts in public understandings of problems and in the balance of power of the groups seeking to fight entrenched interests.

Key to their theory of equilibrium is the idea of the *policy monopoly*, which corresponds with the idea of policy subsystems. A policy monopoly is a fairly concentrated, closed system of the most important actors in policy making. Such a monopoly has an interest in keeping policy making closed because it benefits the interests of those in the monopoly and keeps policy making under some measure of control. Under the older "iron triangle" conception of groups in the policy process, this system will remain quite closed and quite stable for a long time. But Baumgartner and Jones argue that there are instances where the "equilibrium" maintained by policy monopolies will break down, greater and more critical attention to issues will follow, and rapid policy change will be the more immediate result. The policy monopolies themselves can break down or at least become more open-issue networks.

How do policy monopolies and their dominant construction of problems break down? First, greater media attention to an issue can begin to break open policy monopolies. Media attention to issues can grow when a small, but compelling or influential, group of people calls for change, to which other members of the policy community do not effectively respond. Baumgartner and Jones use the breakdown of the nuclear power monopoly to illustrate the effect of greater attention on a problem: in a mere 12 years, this domain was completely reshaped by the greater attention paid to the safety and constant problems that accompanied nuclear power.

This example illustrates how Baumgartner and Jones found that increased attention to a problem usually means greater *negative* attention to it. In this way, the "policy image" of various issues and policies can change. In the nuclear power case, the increased scrutiny of the industry began to break down the image of nuclear power as "the peaceful atom" creating power "too cheap to meter" to an image of danger and expense. This negative image was further re-enforced by the accident at the Three Mile Island nuclear plant in Pennsylvania in 1979.

Policy monopolies also break down as groups that seek access *to* and change *in* the policy-making process go "venue shopping" to find the best venue in which to press their claims. The media are one venue, and groups can seek to gain access to the courts or other units of government to gain access to policy debate. The reform of the congressional committee system and, most importantly, the increasing autonomy of subcommittees starting in the early 1970s have led to a greater number of venues in Congress for groups to find a sympathetic ear to influence policy making.

An important aspect of this way of thinking about policy is the long periods of stability followed by rapid change, and followed again by long periods of stability. In this way, Baumgartner and Jones argue that policy change is not merely incremental and not always a state of constant flux: rather, policy remains stable, followed by a period of rapid change, then stability again, in sort of an S-shaped curve.

CONCLUSION

No one model of the policy process has yet been developed that can fully explain all the nuances and intricacies of the policy process. In addition, it is likely that the very complexity of politics and society will make a universal theory of the policy process impossible to achieve. But work continues on validating and improving on the models described in this article, with the goal of developing improved models to help us understand why public policy is or is not made.

REFERENCES

1. Weimer, D.; Vining, A. *Policy Analysis: Concepts and Practice*; Prentice Hall: Upper Saddle River, NJ, 1999.
2. Stokey, E.; Zeckhauser, R. *A Primer for Policy Analysis*; W. W. Norton: New York, 1978.
3. Stone, D. *Policy Paradox: The Art of Political Decision-making*; W. W. Norton & Co.: New York, 1997.
4. Lasswell, H.D. *Politics: Who Gets What, When, How*; Meridian Books: New York, 1958.
5. Easton, D. *A Systems Analysis of Political Life*; John Wiley and Sons: New York, 1965.
6. Nakamura, R.T. The textbook policy process and implementation research. Policy Stud. J. **1987**, *7* (1), 142–154.
7. Sabatier, P.A. Toward better theories of the policy process. PS: Polit. Sci. Politics **1991**, *24* (2), 144–156.
8. deLeon, P. The Stages Approach to the Policy Process: What Has It done? Where Is It Going? In *Theories of the Policy Process*; Sabatier, P.A., Ed.; Westview: Boulder, CO, 1999; 19–32.
9. Cobb, R.W.; Elder, C.D. *Participation in American Politics: The Dynamics of Agenda-Building*; Johns Hopkins University Press: Baltimore, 1983.
10. Cobb, R.W.; Ross, M.H. *Cultural Strategies of Agenda Denial: Avoidance, Attack, and Redefinition*; University Press of Kansas: Lawrence, 1997.
11. Hilgartner, J.; Bosk, C. The rise and fall of social problems: A public arenas model. Am. J. Sociol. **1988**, *94* (1), 53–78.
12. Schattschneider, E.E. *The Semisovereign People*; The Dryden Press: Hinsdale, IL, 1975.
13. Nakamura, R.T.; Smallwood, F. *The Politics of Policy Implementation*; St. Martin's Press: New York, 1980.
14. Pressman, J.; Wildavsky, A. *Implementation*; University of California Press: Berkeley, 1973.
15. Van Horn, C. *Policy Implementation in the Federal System: National Goals and Local Implementors*; Lexington Books: Lexington, MA, 1979.
16. Kingdon, J.W. *Agendas, Alternatives and Public Policies*, 2nd Ed.; Harper Collins: New York, 1995.
17. Sabatier, P.A.; Jenkins-Smith, H. The Advocacy Coalition Framework: An Assessment. In *Theories of the Policy Process*; Sabatier, P.A., Ed.; Westview: Boulder, CO, 1999; 117–166.
18. Baumgartner, F.R.; Jones, B.D. *Agendas and Instability in American Politics*; University of Chicago Press: Chicago, 1993.
19. Cohen, M.D.; March J.G.; Olsen, J.P. A garbage can model of organizational choice. Adm. Sci. Q. **1972**, *17*, 1–25.

National Security Policy

Eric K. Leonard
Shenandoah University, Winchester, Virginia, U.S.A.

INTRODUCTION

The events of September 11, 2001 dramatically altered the landscape of American national security. However, in many ways, this traumatic event may have clarified a flailing policy agenda, while reinvigorating the unilateralist position that is such a prevalent part of traditional U.S. national security policy. This article will examine the transformation of national security policy from the post–Cold War to the post–9/11 era. The primary method for examining this change will be the presidential doctrines/strategies that guided American national security policy during this period of history.[a] This article will conclude by analyzing the parallels between the early Cold War doctrines and the current National Security Strategy of the Bush administration. Although it appears that both exhibit similar understandings of how to engage the world, one primary difference exists—the employment of preemptive strikes.

POLICY OPTIONS

Within the realm of U.S. national security doctrine, the policy options available to U.S. decision makers tend to fall into two categories: isolationist and internationalist.[b] The isolationist option is probably the oldest form of national security policy dating back to George Washington's Farewell Address. In this address, Washington urged American policy makers to "steer clear of permanent alliances with any portion of the foreign world" because of the fact that "Europe has a set of primary interests which to us have none or very remote relations." The only rationale for extending foreign relations is "commercial interests." As for "political connections," Washington warned future policy makers against such ties. In short, the isolationist policy option advises that American decision makers avoid entangling relations with foreign nation-states. By heeding such prudent advice, Washington believed that the result would be a greater sense of national security.

Internationalists propose a more engaged form of national security policy. This policy option gained popularity as the international arena evolved from a disaggregated set of political entities to a more interdependent, globalized world. Internationalism promotes a national security policy agenda in which the United States actively pursues its national interest via involvement, not isolation. However, when discussing this policy option, one must also understand that several methods exist for achieving its goals. The two most prominent methods are unilateralism and multilateralism.

Unilateralism proposes that the United States promote its national security by pursuing its *own* agenda on its *own* terms. Any concern for allies and their interests, legal principles, and/or morality are all subservient to American national interest as defined by American policy makers. Thus a unilateralist policy agenda understands the need to engage the world, but always according to American interests and needs. There is no room for pandering to other global entities—whether they are nation-states or international organizations. Cooperation only occurs when those with whom the United States is cooperating accept the U.S. conditions for engagement. In short, a unilateralist perspective states that national security is best protected by a policy that engages the world according to U.S. national interest with no regard for compromise.

Multilateralists discuss engaging the world through more cooperative means, with cooperation meaning compromise between competing national interests. Advocates of this position recommend establishment of and adherence to international law, cooperative arrangements, and the defining of interests via a cosmopolitan perspective as opposed to an autonomous understanding of national interest. The resulting policy agenda would entail high levels of cooperation among nation-states and international organizations as a method for solving global problems, including issues of national security. Thus this perspective advocates the use of the UN as a forum for national security decision-making processes, along with a belief that international legal institutions are a quintessential tool for pursuing one's security interests. Consequently, multilateralists believe that cooperative/collective means are the best method for protecting American national security.

---

[a]Ref. [1] is an excellent source of analysis concerning these doctrines.
[b]Ref. [2] provides a detailed examination of these terms.

Encyclopedia of Public Administration and Public Policy
DOI: 10.1081/E-EPAP 120011074

HISTORICAL OVERVIEW

Historically, U.S. national security policy has dabbled in all three of these policy options. Most scholars consider the pre–World War II era a time of isolationism, with moments of unilateralism (such as the Spanish–American War).[c] However, with the outbreak of World War II, and, more importantly, the attack on Pearl Harbor, U.S. policy makers realized that an isolationist policy was simply not an option anymore. The world had become too interrelated for a rising hegemon to wall off its borders and exist in peace. Thus the United States began the modern period of internationalism.

In general, the Cold War appeared to be a time of unilateralism, with U.S. doctrine dominating any "cooperative" arrangements that may have existed. In other words, cooperative institutions did exist, but they existed on U.S. terms and were controlled by U.S. policy. American policy makers pursued their definition of national interest as they saw fit, with little regard for competing interests. But the Cold War period was more or less conducive to this type of environment. This was a time of ideological war in which the national security interests of two superpowers, the United States and the Soviet Union, dominated the global arena. Thus this power struggle not only defined American national security policy during the Cold War, but also the national security policies of the majority of the global community.

With the end of the Cold War, the United States enters a period of confusion concerning its national security policy. The Evil Empire is gone, the world appears safe from the scourge of global communism, and the liberal democracy stands alone as the victor. In such an environment, how does the global hegemon define and pursue its national security interests?

CLINTON'S POST–COLD WAR POLICY

With the onset of the post–Cold War era, President William Jefferson Clinton found himself searching for a national security directive. With the collapse of the Soviet Union, the United States lost its main adversary and the primary threat to its national security. As a result, the Clinton administration needed to redefine national security interests in an era devoid of liberal–communist ideological conflict. In September of 1993, President Clinton's first national security adviser, Anthony Lake, established an outline for a new national security agenda.[3] According to Lake, the new security strategy must entail an active engagement in the world "in order to increase our prosperity, update our security arrangements and promote democracy abroad." This engagement would entail an attempt to: 1) strengthen the world's market democracies; 2) foster and consolidate new democracies and market economies where possible; 3) counter aggression and support the liberalization of states hostile to democracy; and 4) help democracy and market economies take root in regions of greatest humanitarian concern. According to Lake, the justification for such a policy was that, "our own security is shaped by the character of foreign regimes." Thus it is imperative that the United States actively pursue a policy of engagement and enlargement.

This policy of enlargement had an air of multilateralism, or as UN Ambassador Madeline Albright characterized it, "assertive multilateralism."[4] According to the Clinton administration, American security was predicated on the proliferation of market democracy. If this ideological perspective took hold in all regions of the world, America's national security interests would be protected.[5] However, this meant that the United States must actively pursue a policy of enlargement through the means of engagement. Isolationism was simply not an option in an era of globalization.[6] The pursuit of national security now encompassed a broader definition of security than during the Cold War era, thus providing the Clinton administration with justification for a more active foreign policy agenda.

Somalia was the first and last real test for assertive multilateralism. Despite success in quelling the famine in Somalia, the catastrophic events of October 3, 1993 altered the direction of national security policy again. On that day, Somali rebels killed 18 American soldiers and then dragged their bodies through the streets of Mogadishu. As a result of the botched American mission and a public outcry against the American presence in Somalia, President Clinton began to rethink the notion of an expansive national security agenda. The result was Presidential Decision Directive 25 (PDD-25). This document, while still maintaining an internationalist foundation, initiated a period of more controlled multilateralism bordering on unilateralism.

PDD-25 limited the engagement policy to certain situations. According to this document, American intervention will only occur if the following conditions are present: 1) there must be an identifiable U.S. interest at stake in the operation; 2) the mission must be clearly defined in size, scope, and duration; 3) there must be sufficient resources, along with the political will to complete the mission; 4) there must be a tangible exit

---

[c]This statement on American isolationism is a generalization. True American internationalism did not take hold until the WWII era; however, moments of internationalism certainly permeated U.S. policy prior to the WWII period. One example of this internationalism is the Spanish–American War.

strategy in place; 5) must decrease the cost of U.S. involvement in multilateral peace operations.

The first attempt at a national security policy predicated on multilateralism appeared to have fallen by the wayside. Although President Clinton maintained the rhetoric of a multilateralist, the practice was much more unilateral.[d] Some prime examples of this unilateral pursuit of security are the following: the failure to engage in a multilateral military operation in Rwanda; the lack of support for the formation of a permanent International Criminal Court; the failure to pay UN arrears; the slow reaction to the decade-long crisis in the former Yugoslavia, among others. All of these situations are prime examples of the Clinton administration acting in a manner that benefits U.S. interests, but with little or no regard for the interests of others in the global community. Any intervention was to take place on U.S. terms with no room for debate or compromise. Consequently, one can classify the Clinton administration as striving for a multilateral security agenda, but ultimately falling into a more unilateralist one.[e]

GEORGE W. BUSH AND SEPTEMBER 11TH

George W. Bush's initial stance on national security bordered on isolationism, not internationalism.[f] At the outset of his term, Bush appeared to heed the advice of George Washington by publicly admonishing almost every multilateral arrangement that was under negotiation. Bush rejected the Kyoto Protocol, the land mines convention, and the small arms treaty; President Bush also unsigned the Rome Statute for the International Criminal Court and withdrew from the Anti-Ballistic Missile Treaty. The only form of multilateral arrangement that President Bush supported was economic/capitalist ones. If an international cooperative arrangement did not favor U.S economic interests, then his administration felt it prudent to turn inward. However, the events of September 11, 2001 changed everything concerning U.S. national security policy.[g]

---

[d]The National Security Strategy of Engagement and Enlargement [Ref. 7] document is one example of the constant struggle to find a middle ground between multilateral and unilateral methods.

[e]The Clinton administration did engage in some multilateral endeavors (such as leading the NATO airstrikes during the Kosovo crisis); however, if one is going to generalize about the administration's overall record on national security, unilateralism appears to be the primary method for achieving their defined goals.

[f]See Refs. [8,9] for an understanding of Bush's initial national security agenda.

[g]Refs. [10] and [11] provide excellent analyses of the post–9/11 policy options.

With the tragic events of 9/11, the Bush administration realized the need to engage the world in a more fundamental manner. The attack on the United States demonstrated that national security in the 21st century is not realized by isolating one's self. In fact, isolationism is not an option because of the globalization process. President Bush had to become an internationalist, but what means would he choose to pursue this policy of engagement?

In September 2002, President Bush published The National Security Strategy of the United States of America. In this document, President Bush outlines not only the means to national security, but also the enemy the United States is engaging and the values the United States must uphold. The explicit rhetoric of this document smacks of a multilateralist tone. For example, in the introductory section, the Bush doctrine states:

> we [the United States] do not use our strength to press for unilateral advantage. We seek instead to create a balance of power that favors human freedom.

Again, in the opening section, the doctrine states:

> We are also guided by the conviction that no nation can build a safer, better world alone. Alliances and multilateral institutions can multiply the strength of freedom-loving nations. The United States is committed to lasting institutions like the United Nations, the World Trade Organization, the Organization of American States, and NATO as well as other long-standing alliances.

However, the multilateral rhetoric is not about a cosmopolitan agenda of cooperation and compromise. Instead, the multilateral rhetoric extends only to situations in which the United States is in full control of the mission/ organization. Thus the United States is committed to institutions such as the United Nations (as stated in the doctrine), but this is because of the fact that the United States has veto power over the UN's actions. This is the form of multilateralism the Bush administration favors— multilateral arrangements that not only favor U.S. interests, but also are controlled by U.S. power. The post–9/11 situation in Iraq is a prime example of U.S. unilateralism in action.[12] The initial engagement of Iraq came in the form of multilateral efforts. The United States allowed the UN to play a role in the situation by collectively agreeing that the formation of a weapons inspection team was beneficial to the situation. However, when this team failed to find any weapons of mass destruction, the United States decided to intervene according to its own agenda.

At this point, the Bush administration disengaged the Iraq debate from the UN, in particular, the UN Security Council, because of the contentious nature of the topic.

The United States knew that France, Russia, and, possibly, China would veto any resolution authorizing a military intervention. Consequently, the United States chose to pursue its national security policy in a unilateral fashion, with the international community of states either standing by our side or getting out of the way. Some nation-states chose to stand by the United States and support our action (the coalition of the willing), but this ad hoc alliance of states was inconsequential to the action the United States was going to take. Bush had decided to invade, and no foreign power was going to alter this agenda. In the words of secretary of defense Donald Rumsfeld, ''The mission must determine the coalition; the coalition must not determine the mission.''

In the post–9/11 era, the United States begins a path toward unabashed unilateralism. In many ways, the events of September 11th have assisted U.S. policy makers in defining national security. During the Clinton years, the administration was left searching for a purpose for its national security agenda. There was no evil empire or ideological enemy. Instead, Clinton asserted that the promotion of free market liberal democracy would solidify American national security. However, in the post–9/11 era, a new focus/enemy exists—terrorism.

PREEMPTION AS A POLICY OPTION

As with the Soviet Union and its communist ideology in the immediate post–WWII era, U.S. national security policy now has a purpose—to combat terrorism. In the words of President Bush:

> Defending our Nation against its enemies is the first and fundamental commitment of the Federal Government. Today, that task has changed dramatically. Enemies in the past needed great armies and great industrial capabilities to endanger America. Now, shadowy networks of individuals can bring great chaos and suffering to our shores for less that it costs to purchase a single tank. Terrorists are organized to penetrate open societies and to turn the power of modern technology against us.[h]

The question that now looms is how to combat the enemy. During the Cold War years, the primary method for protecting American security interests was deterrence. In the post–9/11 period, the Bush administration has begun the use of preemptive strikes.[i] According to the Bush administration, because the enemy no longer fits the

traditional nation-state model, the old rules of engagement no longer apply. Deterrence was a plausible option when engaging other sovereign states that exerted a relative balance of power with the United States. However, the United States, or any other nation-state, does not have the ability to deter the current enemy (nonstate terrorist organizations). Consequently, the use of force in a preemptive and preventive manner is necessary. Engaging in a policy of deterrence would simply result in future terrorist attacks like September 11th. The only way to prevent such tragedies is to strike first—as in Iraq.

The use of preemptive force is a new form of national security policy. Never before has the United States publicly called for the employment of a first-strike policy. But according to the Bush administration, the current era of ''shadowy networks of individuals,'' whose use of weapons of mass destruction could perpetrate another September 11th or worse, necessitates the use of preemption. The Bush administration has altered the course of U.S. national security policy, but according to this administration, that is because the enemy has changed. A new enemy necessitates the initiation of new methods. The result is that preemption appears to be the future of national security policy.

CONCLUSION

The post-Cold War era is clearly a dynamic era full of rapid change. The national security policies of the two presidential administrations bear this fact out. With the onset of the post–Cold War era, President Clinton found himself having to redefine American national security. The ideological conflict between the Soviets and the Americans had disappeared and left U.S. policy makers with no clear security agenda. Clinton first initiated a multilateral policy agenda, but the conflict in Somalia quickly altered the method for obtaining and the definition of national security. The Clinton administration found it necessary to abandon much of the multilateral practices they had wanted to initiate for a more unilateral policy. However, even with this change toward unilateralism, the definition of what constitutes a national security threat was still unclear.

The events of September 11th provided President Bush with a specific enemy to center his national security policy around. Terrorism became the new threat to the American people, and in the vein of the Truman Doctrine and NSC-68, the Bush doctrine established a roadmap for how to protect the American people and eradicate the threat. The major difference between the post–WWII policies and the post–9/11 policies is notion of preemption. No longer does the United States wait to be attacked. President Bush, by

---

[h]Ref. [13] introductory section.
[i]Ref. [14] contains an expansive discussion of the Bush doctrine's policy agenda and the premise of preemptive action.

his actions in Iraq, has made it clear that when his administration perceives a viable threat to national security is in existence, the U.S. military will act. This sets the United States down an unprecedented course in security policy, one whose future, and the future of American national security, remains shrouded in doubt.

REFERENCES

1. Oliver, J.K. *The Foreign Policy Architecture of the Clinton and Bush Administration*. (*in press*).

2. Patrick, S. Multilateralism and Its Discontents: The Causes and Consequences of US Ambivalence. In *Multilateralism and US Foreign Policy: Ambivalent Engagement*; Patrick, S., Forman, S., Eds.; Lynne Rienner Publishers: Boulder, CO, 2002; 1–46.

3. Lake, A. *From Containment to Enlargement*; Speech given at the School of Advanced International Studies, Johns Hopkins University, September 21, 1993.

4. Albright, M. ''Myths of Peace-keeping.'' Statement before the Subcommittee on International Security, International Organizations, and Human Rights of the House Committee on Foreign Affairs: Washington, D.C. Dispatch **1993**, *4*, 464–467.

5. Brinkley, D. Democratic enlargement: The Clinton doctrine. Foreign Policy *Spring* **1997**, 106.

6. Berger, S.R. A foreign policy for the global age. Foreign Aff. **2000**, *79* (6), 22–39.

7. Clinton, W.J. *A National Security Strategy of Engagement and Enlargement*; White House: Washington, D.C., 1996.

8. Hirsh, M. Bush and the world. Foreign Aff. **2002**, *81* (5), 18–43.

9. Rice, C. Promoting the national interest. Foreign Aff. **2000**, *79* (1), 45–62.

10. Smith, S. The end of the unipolar moment? September 11 and the future of world order. Int. Relat. **2002**, *16* (2), 171–183.

11. Haass, R. *Defining US Foreign Policy in a Post-Post-Cold War World*; Department of State: Washington, D.C., 2002. http://www.state.gov/s/p/rem/9632.htm.

12. Nye, J.S., Jr. U.S. power and strategy after Iraq. Foreign Aff. **2003**, *82* (4), 60–73.

13. Bush, G.W. *The National Security Strategy of the United States of America*; White House: Washington, D.C., 2002.

14. Ikenberry, J. America's imperial ambition. Foreign Aff. **2002**, *81* (5), 44–60.

Ombuds and Ombuds Programs

Tina Nabatchi
Lisa B. Bingham
Indiana University, Bloomington, Indiana, U.S.A.

INTRODUCTION

This chapter discusses the role of an ombuds, a person within an organization who assists employees, stakeholders, or customers in resolving disputes by offering a wide variety of alternative dispute resolution (ADR) processes (for more information on ADR processes, refer to Nabatchi and Bingham in this volume; for more information on ADR in the public sector, refer to Nesbit and Bingham in this volume).

OMBUDS

Contemporary conflict resolution theory and practice suggest that organizations should design and build integrated conflict management systems, as opposed to a singular dispute resolution program, to better manage organizational conflict.[1] In turn, many scholars and practitioners have asserted that an ombuds office is both a desirable and cost-effective element in an efficient dispute resolution system.[2,3]

In Scandinavian countries, where the concept originated, an ombudsman, or an ombuds, is a public official appointed to hear citizen complaints and to conduct independent fact-finding investigations to correct abuses of public administration. The original word, *ombudsman*, is not gender-specific in Scandinavia; however, to avoid gender connotations, authors and scholars in the United States variously refer to an ombudsman as ombuds, ombudsperson, ombuds practitioner, etc. In the United States, the concept and function of an ombuds have developed differently, and have grown in both significance and prominence as they have blossomed in a number of public and private settings.

In the United States, an ombuds operates like a third-party neutral inside an organization by assisting employees, stakeholders, and/or customers of the organization in resolving workplace disputes through confidential, informal means. An ombuds has a diverse set of responsibilities and must serve many functions, such as supplying information and other resources, channeling communications, handling complaints, and resolving disputes.[4,5] For these many functions, the ombuds also plays a wide variety of roles, such as counselor, consultant, informal go-between, facilitator, formal mediator, and/or informal fact finder.[6] Moreover, the ombuds uses various conflict resolution skills, such as listening, conflict coaching, facilitation, mediation, and shuttle diplomacy,[6] but also has the ability to help individuals gain access to other informal or formal dispute resolution processes within the organization, such as traditional grievance procedures and equal employment opportunity (EEO) processes (for more information on grievance procedures, refer to Nabatchi and Bingham in this volume).

The ombuds serves an integrated function for the organization, and has the flexibility and capacity to handle numerous and varied disputes. In addition to providing assistance to people with complaints, concerns, and conflicts, the ombuds often also acts as an upward feedback mechanism, problem prevention device, and change agent in the organization.[6] In this respect, the ombuds serves as a troubleshooter for the organization. An ombuds generally works closely with all personnel in an organization, from top-level management to front-line staff; therefore, an ombuds is often able to identify processes and practices that create employee (and other) conflicts, or that otherwise have negative effects on the organization. In this respect, the ombuds serves as a bellwether of organizational problems that could develop into lawsuits and as an early warning signal for new and emerging problems. Moreover, the ombuds may notice a pattern of problems, which suggests the need for policy or procedural change within the organization. The ombuds will try to eliminate these sources of organizational conflict through problem solving or brainstorming meetings, retreats, trainings, and other conflict management sessions. These features of an ombuds not only result in a more integrative and systemic approach to managing conflict in an organization, but also allow the ombuds to serve both a corrective and preventative role as a resolver of conflicts.

The effectiveness of an ombuds office depends on its ability to demonstrate confidentiality and neutrality—key principles in the ombuds profession. In terms of confidentiality, ombuds generally do not keep case records, and the majority of their work is unknown to anyone except those who use their services.[7] However, in the federal sector, there are certain exceptions to confidentiality

Encyclopedia of Public Administration and Public Policy
DOI: 10.1081/E-EPAP-120037349

for ombuds; in some circumstances, federal employees must report information when it relates to a felony, waste, fraud, abuse, corruption, or crimes by government officers or employees.[8] These reporting requirements interact with federal statutes providing for confidentiality in dispute resolution.[8] Similarly, state and local governments vary in the degree of confidentiality they afford dispute resolution processes involving administrative agencies.

In terms of neutrality, the ombuds must: 1) resist taking sides during a conflict; 2) possess no stake in the outcome of a dispute; and 3) demonstrate fairness, objectivity, and evenhandedness in relationships.[4] To promote these qualities, the ombuds is outside of the organizational chain of command or reporting structure, and although all ombuds are made available and paid for by the host institution, not all ombuds are on the host organization's payroll. Some may work through a contract with another organization to provide an additional layer of neutrality.

OMBUDS PROGRAMS

Ombuds programs have been developed in both the public and private sectors. One reason for the growth of ombuds programs in the United States is that they are able to personalize the dispute resolution processes of large organizations such as corporations, municipalities, and government agencies. Thus, they provide people with individualized and flexible attention such that they are able to overcome the difficulties associated with the formalism and bureaucracy of large organizations. Today, ombuds programs are found in large corporations such as Haliburton (formerly Brown and Root), educational institutions such as the Massachusetts Institute of Technology (MIT), and government agencies such as the National Institutes of Health (NIH) and the Internal Revenue Service (IRS).

Ombuds programs can focus on different organizational constituencies. Traditionally, they provide services to those both within and outside the organization, including members of the public. In the federal government, most ombuds offices focus on organizational issues within the agency.[8] In some cases, Congress established ombuds offices through legislation (e.g., Federal Deposit Insurance Corporation, Office of the Comptroller of the Currency, Small Business Administration, and State Department).[8] In other cases, the agencies themselves created the office and staffed it with career employees insulated from politics (e.g., Customs Service, Federal Bureau of Investigation, Food and Drug Administration, and Department of Justice).[8]

Research on federal workplace ombuds offices suggests that they can be effective when the EEO office has too many non-EEO complaints, or the employee assistance program (EAP) is receiving workplace complaints outside of its mandate. In addition, ombuds programs can be effective when personnel-related offices are not working together, employee morale is low, and employee–management communication is poor. Finally, such programs can be effective when there are poor labor–management relations and when there are frequent employee claims of retaliation.[9]

BENEFITS AND RISKS OF OMBUDS PROGRAMS

Ombuds programs appeal to organizations for many reasons. First, many dispute resolution programs are accessible to a limited set of employees (e.g., those covered under collective bargaining agreements). In contrast, ombuds programs are accessible to everyone in the organization. Likewise, many dispute resolution programs are rigidly designed to handle specific types of disputes (e.g., those involving workplace contract or policy issues); however, ombuds programs are flexible enough to address typical workplace disputes related to contracts, policy, or law, but can also reach beyond these conflicts to handle individual and group disputes involving interpersonal issues, environmental problems, or racial and ethnic tensions. In short, ombuds programs are more inclusive of organizational personnel, can address a broader range of issues, and have greater ability to resolve conflict constructively and provide stability to the organization than single-process dispute resolution programs.

Second, most dispute resolution programs are reactive in that they only address conflicts that have been made "public." In other words, the programs respond only to disputes that have been formally expressed. Conversely, ombuds programs are both reactive and preventative: they can address formally expressed disputes, but can also address disputes where one party is unwilling or unable to publicly confront the other party.

Third, traditional dispute resolution programs focus on the symptoms rather than the source of problems. They engage in problem solving between the disputing parties, but not problem solving for larger organizational issues. Ombuds programs help identify and address the root causes of problems through systemic change. In theory, this allows an organization to decrease the highly visible costs of conflict and to increase organizational morale, productivity, and communication.

Finally, and perhaps most importantly, ombuds programs assist employees in finding fair solutions to problems, and may facilitate problem solving at lower levels than would be necessary through traditional dispute resolution processes. This not only saves valuable resources for the organization, but also promotes a sense of justice, fairness, and participation among organizational constituents. Research shows that higher perceptions of justice in an organization lead to higher employee productivity and morale. Moreover, evidence suggests that people who learn how to effectively resolve disputes are more likely to resolve future disputes independently and more likely to teach these methods to other colleagues.[10]

Despite the numerous potential benefits of ombuds programs, there are also some risks, especially if the ombudsperson violates guarantees of neutrality and confidentiality. One potential risk is that employers may distort the ombuds title in unilaterally adopted nonunion arbitration programs. For example, one employer had its ombuds represent employees as their advocate in arbitration and select the arbitrator on behalf of both parties. After repeated selection of the same arbitrator who always ruled for management, it was clear that this particular ombuds was not neutral. Similar structures, where the ombuds departs from a neutral role, give the appearance of a conflict of interest. This reduces stakeholder trust in the ombuds office, which is a critical element for program success.[11]

CONCLUSION

The use of ombudspersons continues to grow in a variety of settings, including educational institutions, hospitals, nursing homes, corporations, and government. Ombudspersons now have a professional association and a code of ethics.[12] (For additional information and resources about ombuds and ombuds programs, refer to The Ombudsman Association (TOA) at www.ombuds-toa.org). As the benefits of ombuds programs are increasingly measured and understood, and as conflict management theory and practice increasingly move toward dispute system design efforts and integrated conflict management systems, the prominence of such programs is also likely to increase.

REFERENCES

1. Lipsky, D.B.; Seeber, R.L.; Fincher, R.D. *Emerging Systems for Managing Workplace Conflict: Lessons from American Corporations for Managers and Dispute Resolution Professionals*; Jossey-Bass: San Francisco, 2003.
2. Rowe, M.P.; Perneski, T. Cost-Effectiveness of Ombudsman Offices. In *Corporate Ombudsman Newsletter*; May, 1990.
3. Slaikeu, K.A.; Hasson, R.H. *Controlling the Costs of Conflict: How to Design a System for Your Organization*; Jossey-Bass: San Francisco, 1998.
4. Gadlin, H.; Pino, E.W. Neutrality: A guide for the organizational ombudsperson. Negot. J. **1997**, *13*, 17–37.
5. Robbins, L.P.; Deane, W. The corporate ombuds: A new approach to conflict management. Negot. J. **1986**, *2*, 195–205.
6. Rowe, M.P. The ombudsman's role in a dispute resolution system. Negot. J. **1991**, *7*, 353–362.
7. Isenhart, M.W.; Spangle, M.L. Ombudsperson. In *Collaborative Approaches to Resolving Conflict*; Sage Publications, Inc.: Thousand Oaks, 2000; 169–175.
8. Senger, J.M. *Federal Dispute Resolution: Using ADR with the United States Government*; Jossey-Bass: San Francisco, 2003.
9. Meltzer, D.L. The federal workplace ombuds. Ohio State J. Dispute Resolut. **1998**, *13*, 549–609.
10. Rowe, M.P. Helping people help themselves: An ADR option for interpersonal conflict. Negot. J. **1990**, *6*, 239–248.
11. Bingham, L.B. Emerging due process concerns in employment arbitration: A look at actual cases. Labor Law J. **1996**, *47*, 108–126.
12. The Ombudsman Association. *Code of Ethics*; 1997. (available at www.naples.cc.sunysb.edu/Pres/ombuds.nsf/pages/ethics.

Pay-As-You-Go Financing

David L. Baker
Arizona State University, Tempe, Arizona, U.S.A.

INTRODUCTION

Some governmental budgets aggregate appropriations into one unified, or consolidated, budget (e.g., the federal government). Other governmental budgets are divided into 1) an operating budget and 2) a capital outlay budget. Within the operating vs. capital outlay distinction, an operating budget represents a financial plan that proposes expenditures based on estimated revenues to finance them for a fixed period (usually a defined fiscal year). An operating budget addresses everyday activities of an entity. A capital outlay budget represents a plan for investing in capital assets (also referred to as fixed assets) that are nonrecurring and endure beyond the operating budget cycle. Examples of capital assets with a long-term character include land, buildings, infrastructure, equipment, and furniture.

Pay-as-you-go financing (PAYGO) refers to public financing strategies that pay for spending increases or revenue reductions from current resources and without increasing a deficit or debt financing.[1–3] PAYGO financing serves as a means to achieve budgetary balance and to control deficits for consolidated and operating budgets. For capital budgets, it functions in contrast to PAYGO financing whereby capital outlays are paid for as they are used through debt service payments. PAYGO financing offers versatile features for consolidated, operating, and capital budgeting that require consideration within a public agency's overall budgetary and financial context.[4,5]

The following review of PAYGO financing unfolds through several sections. First, PAYGO financing for consolidated and operating budgets is discussed. Second, the review examines the role of PAYGO financing for capital outlay budgeting in comparison with debt financing. This analysis includes capital outlay examples and an example of transitioning PAYGO financing from capital to operational costs. Third, potential PAYGO financing sources are discussed. Fourth, and finally, the review closes with a summary regarding the usefulness of PAYGO financing.

PAY-AS-YOU-GO FINANCING FOR CONSOLIDATED AND OPERATING BUDGETS

Governmental entities operating under a consolidated budget employ PAYGO financing for budgetary balance and deficit control.[3] Federal budgeting serves as an example of this. The 1990 Federal Budget Enforcement Act (BEA) and subsequent amendments to the act establish PAYGO rules for spending and revenue legislation. Generally, congressional action is prohibited from adding to the budget deficit. Spending increases must be offset with other spending reductions or revenue increases. Conversely, revenue reductions must be offset by revenue increases or spending decreases. If full offsets are not made, funds are sequestered from certain expenditure areas.[6]

"PAYGO is a multiyear control enforced one year at a time."[6] Congressional budgetary actions are examined annually under the BEA on an aggregate basis, not by individual legislative bills. Federal PAYGO financing does not control spending influenced by population growth and inflation under existing law. Provisions are designed to limit growth in budgets and deficits by linking new spending to other expense reductions or revenue increases. PAYGO financing provisions shift the consequences for budgetary decisions to the stage in the process when spending increases or revenue reductions are first proposed.[7]

PAYGO financing also refers to the operating budget strategy of assuring that public agencies deal with financial liabilities as they occur. For example, PAYGO financing is at work when pension programs routinely fund the actuarially determined contribution to cover the pension liability accrued for each payroll. This avoids accumulating an unfunded pension liability. PAYGO financing mitigates the temptation to perceive resources as available for new initiatives by allocating funds to meet known obligations as incurred. Additionally, the political desirability of proposed spending confronts the task of selling other program cuts or tax increases to

Encyclopedia of Public Administration and Public Policy
DOI: 10.1081/E-EPAP 120025966

offset the new costs.[8] PAYGO financing acts as a cost-control measure.

PAY-AS-YOU-GO FINANCING FOR CAPITAL OUTLAY BUDGETS

Public agencies often rationalize PAYGO financing by the purpose of the appropriation. Deciding who will pay for a capital asset tends to be influenced by both the political and economic environments.[9] Financing methods also introduce conflict over opportunity costs because the amount spent on a capital outlay becomes unavailable for another use.[1] On the one hand, debt-financing advocates encourage capital assets to be purchased over time (usually the expected use cycle of an asset) by those who benefit from them. This promotes intergenerational equity in a community rather than permitting free riders to receive future capital asset benefits with no financial contribution. This also recognizes that capital assets may be needed today to support tomorrow's growth while such growth generates the revenue stream to retire the debt. On the other hand, PAYGO financing makes sense when short-term and long-term cost savings are desirable because of future fiscal uncertainty or the public agency already services substantial annual debt. Additionally, this strategy may be prudent where no significant concern exists about some citizens benefiting later while avoiding early cost participation.

PAYGO financing is the least expensive way of funding public agency capital outlays. Several relative, but material, agency cost components associated with debt financing are avoided through this financing method. The cost components identified in Table 1 are avoided in PAYGO financing. Costs identified do not include the varied, yet substantial, public agency staff and policy-maker costs associated with borrowing. These include the cost of the time involved in initiating capital asset financing, deal structuring, compiling supporting docu-mentation, managing the project, tracking funds, and filing required financial statements throughout the life of the financing.

In addition to cost avoidances associated with debt financing, other reasons explain why public agencies turn to PAYGO financing. First, PAYGO financing enables public agencies to manage their debt profile. A public agency's debt profile affects credit ratings.[1] A higher credit rating translates into lower interest costs on future financings, while a lower credit rating means higher interest costs.[10] Second, a PAYGO approach generates a certain amount of support. Because current residents often choose a specific capital outlay, there are sentiments that "the cost should not be imposed on future residents who have no say in the matter."[11] Third, PAYGO financing encourages government to live within its means. Fourth, PAYGO financing constrains the growth of interest costs as a portion of an agency's annual budget. Fifth, and finally, the fiscal capacity of a public agency may be sufficient to fund a needed capital asset from current revenue without burdening future fiscal years.

COMPARISON WITH DEBT FINANCING

Advantages of PAYGO financing for capital outlays require evaluation against the advantages of pay-as-you-use (debt) financing. Common policy and financial considerations with debt financing include the following:

- Does a public agency have the fiscal capacity to provide the necessary resources for essential capital assets from current revenues?
- Are there timing elements that must be factored into the decision calculus of PAYGO financing vs. debt financing (e.g., state- or federal-mandated requirements, pending litigation, or an advantageous, time-limited opportunity)?
- Can debt repayment schedules accommodate the community's ability to pay with synchronized payments aligned with the enjoyment of the benefits?[11]
- Can a public agency capitalize on low interest rates to stretch precious funds further?
- Does prudent debt financing maximize a public agency's options to invest current proceeds, to address other pressing priorities, and/or to meet unanticipated needs?
- Does borrowing avoid significant year-to-year funding variations that otherwise would be difficult for a jurisdiction to handle?
- Does excessive commitment to PAYGO financing prevent a public agency from capital outlays essential to the community?[4]

Table 1 Cost avoidance in pay-as-you-go financing for capital outlays

Debt interest on funds borrowed
Bond counsel
Disclosure counsel
Financial advisor
Trustee/pay agent
Official statement printing and distribution
Rating agency
Underwriter discount or premium included in the securities
 purchase
Insurance premiums
Credit enhancements

- Does debt financing allow the cost per capita for a capital asset acquisition to decrease over time, assuming population growth? Is this a desirable feature from the community's standpoint?

Public finance literature dealing with capital outlays occasionally refers to PAYGO financing as though it is an inviolate, overarching policy of particular public agencies.[12] A public agency either follows a PAYGO financing policy or it does not follow such a policy in this frame of reference. This portrayal diverges from the more common practice of public agencies employing a mix of financial strategies to meet capital outlay needs. Each capital outlay calls for individual assessment of financial and policy issues germane to that particular capital outlay.

PAY-AS-YOU-GO FINANCING CAPITAL OUTLAY EXAMPLES

Three PAYGO financing examples illustrate the utility of this mainstream public financing strategy. Each involves a public agency investigating PAYGO financing plans for the acquisition and development of a community park. An estimated $3.0 million is needed for the project.

Variation Examples

1. The public agency may appropriate $3.0 million, the total cost of acquisition and development, in one fiscal year offsetting the cost with increased revenues.
2. The public agency may appropriate $3.0 million over multiple years, assuming constant costs, in equal increments or nonequal increments that match available resources by fiscal year. Planned PAYGO financing appropriations may be advanced, suspended, or adjusted in future years based on available resources. Year-to-year funding may be assembled and preserved for a specific capital outlay purpose using an approved reserve (i.e., Good City community park reserve). Accounting treatments may vary by jurisdiction.
3. The public agency may budget and expend $3.0 million for community park acquisition and development on a PAYGO financing basis in definable phases that coincide with each fiscal year's funding availability. For example, the first year estimated land acquisition price of $700,000 and design development cost of $200,000 might be budgeted and expended. In the second year, park development and landscaping, estimated at $1.2 million, may be funded. The third year might include an estimated $900,000 for parking, picnic grounds, and specialty areas (i.e., tot lots,

volleyball courts, and nature center). At the federal level, this is referred to as "budgeting for stand-alone stages of larger projects."[13]

Pay-as-you-go financing may be used in conjunction with other funding. Typical examples include 1) PAYGO financing for some portion of a capital outlay while the remainder is debt-financed, 2) debt-financing a facility while cash-funding the furnishings that have a shorter useful life than the facility financed, and 3) PAYGO financing to match a grant or some other funding source dedicated to the capital outlay.

TRANSITIONING FROM CAPITAL TO OPERATIONAL COSTS

A more elaborate example demonstrates how PAYGO financing can be transitioned from a capital outlay to operating costs associated with a critically needed facility. In this instance, the capital outlay involves a $6.0 million expansion to an existing county jail. Upon occupancy, the jail expansion affects the operating budget in a dramatic manner.[14] Once operational, the project calls for approximately $2.0 million in new, annual operating costs for staffing, food, utilities, clothing, and supplies. Furthermore, operational costs will escalate at an estimated rate of 12–15% annually.

Several steps are taken to finance this facility and its operational cost. First, the public agency decides to use PAYGO financing because 1) it experiences a significant, ongoing increase in property tax revenue caused by development related to population growth and 2) this financing strategy minimizes the agency's debt profile because the jurisdiction anticipates a hospital expansion project requiring $50–75 million in debt financing within several years. Second, a $2.0 million surge in revenues is appropriated in two places for the first year of the project: 1) a reserve designated for jail expansion construction and 2) an initial construction project allocation to cover environmental work, architect and engineering fees, and project management. Third, in project year two, the continuing dedicated revenue stream of $2.0 million is split between building the reserve ($1.8 million) and ongoing preconstruction costs ($0.2 million). Fourth, in project year three, a third $2.0 million increment is budgeted along with the previously accumulated reserve to fully fund the construction. Fifth, once construction is completed, the annual $2.0 million dedicated revenue stream is applied to cover the ongoing operational cost of the jail expansion.

In the meantime, over the 4-year time span, the incremental growth on the base revenue stream of $2.0 million aids in addressing the annual operating cost

Table 2 Transitioning pay-as-you-go capital outlay funding to operational costs

	Project years			
	1	2	3	4
Revenue (in millions)	$2.0	$2.0	$2.0	$2.0
Appropriation (in millions)				
Capital outlay	0.6[a]	0.2[a]	5.2[b]	0
Reserve	1.4	3.2[c]	0	0
Operating costs	0	0	0	2.0[d]

[a]Preconstruction capital outlay costs (i.e., environmental work, architect and engineering fees, and project management costs).
[b]Comprised of $3.2 million accumulated reserve from year two plus $2.0 million revenue increment.
[c]Comprised of $1.4 million reserve from year one, plus $1.8 million revenue increment after covering ongoing preconstruction capital outlay costs.
[d]Anticipated annual operational cost.

increase of 12–15%. This overall strategy allows a smooth transition from capital outlay to funding the ongoing operational costs as part of the total budget. Graphically, this PAYGO financing is summarized in Table 2 with appropriation elements.

POTENTIAL PAY-AS-YOU-GO FINANCING SOURCES

Consolidated and operating budgets most frequently obtain PAYGO financing from three sources. First, revenue increases, both nonrecurring and recurring, may provide funds for PAYGO financing. Second, spending decreases, both nonrecurring and recurring, fortuitous or forced, can fuel a PAYGO strategy. Third, governmental entities may take action to rebudget funds from a lesser priority to a higher priority.[15]

For capital budgets, PAYGO funds most frequently come from nonrecurring and recurring revenue streams. However, there are other sources from which to derive such funds. Common sources after revenues include 1) use of unanticipated fund balance, 2) nonrecurring and recurring savings, 3) grants, 4) cancellation and rebudgeting of a designated reserve, and 5) rebudgeting from a lower priority to a higher priority appropriation.

CONCLUSION

PAYGO financing is an important tool in the public agency toolbox. It offers budget balancing and deficit control features for consolidated and operating budgets. PAYGO financing serves as a cost-effective, sensible

alternative to debt financing. Use of this financing method for a particular policy objective requires analysis in the overall financial context of a given public agency. PAYGO financing demonstrates versatility and can be integrated with other strategies. Finally, PAYGO financing may be utilized flexibly with a range of budgetary sources.

REFERENCES

1. Bland, R.L.; Clarke, W. Budgeting for Capital Improvements. In *Handbook of Government Budgeting*; Meyers, R.T., Ed.; Jossey-Bass Publishers: San Francisco, 1999; 653–677.
2. Mikesell, J.L. *Fiscal Administration: Analysis and Applications for the Public Sector*, 6th Ed.; Wadsworth Publishers: Belmont, CA, 2003.
3. Voorhees, W.R. Budgeting and Deficit Controls. In *Encyclopedia of Public Administration and Public Policy*; Rabin, J., Ed.; Marcel Dekker, Inc.: New York, 2003; 98–102.
4. Forrester, J. Municipal capital budgeting: An examination. Public budgeting and finance. Summer **1993**, *13* (2), 85–101.
5. Steiss, A.W. *Financial Management in Public Organizations*; Brook/Cole Publishing Company: Pacific Grove, CA, 1989.
6. Schick, A. *The Federal Budget: Politics, Policy, Process*; The Brookings Institution: Washington, D.C., 1995; 100.
7. Thurber, J.A.; Durst, S.L. Delay, Deadlock, and Deficits: Evaluating Proposals for Congressional Budget Reform. In *Federal Budget and Financial Management Reform*; Lynch, T.D., Ed.; Quorum Books: New York, 1991; 53–88.
8. White, B. Examining Budgets for Chief Executives. In *Handbook of Government Budgeting*; Meyers, R.T., Ed.; Jossey-Bass Publishers: San Francisco, 1999; 462–484.
9. Temel, J.W. *Fundamentals of Municipal Bonds*, 5th Ed.; John Wiley & Sons: New York, 2001.
10. Miller, G.J. Capital Asset Financing. In *Public Budgeting and Finance*, 4th Ed.; Golembiewski, R.T., Rabin, J., Eds.; Marcel Dekker, Inc.: New York, 1997; 633–651.
11. Horler, V.L. *Guidelines to Public Debt Financing in California*; Rev. Ed. Packard Press: San Francisco, 1987; 12.
12. Moody's Municipal Department. *Moody's on Municipals: An Introduction to Issuing Debt*; Moody's Investor Services, Inc.: New York, 1987.
13. Posner, P.L.; Lewis, T.V.; Laufe, H. Budgeting for federal capital. Public Budg. Finance **1998**, *18* (3), 11–23.
14. Bland, R.L.; Nunn, S. The impact of capital spending on municipal operating budgets. Public Budg. Finance **1992**, *12* (2), 32–47.
15. Forrester, J.P.; Mullins, D.R. Rebudgeting: The serial nature of municipal budgetary processes. Public Adm. Rev. **1992**, *52* (5), 467–473.

Policy Design

Anne L. Schneider
Arizona State University, Tempe, Arizona, U.S.A.

Helen Ingram
University of California, Irvine, California, U.S.A.

INTRODUCTION

Policy design refers to the content and substance of public policy—the tools, instruments, and other features or "architecture" of policy. Just as a city has a design, so also do public policies—whether constitutions, statutes, governmental pronouncements, agency guidelines, or practices of implementers. Moreover, just as a city's design can be characterized along many different dimensions, so too the description and analysis of policy design must encompass multiple dimensions.

Governments at all levels have many choices of tools or instruments with which they carry out their responsibilities. These responsibilities all fall within the broad framework of what we call public policy: allocating goods or distributing costs, regulating, extracting resources, persuading, controlling, listening to, and leading the population. The choices governments make in the details of policy designs, however, have long-term effects on politics, democracy, justice, and citizenship.

APPROACHES TO THE ANALYSIS OF POLICY DESIGN

The study of policy design traces to the very beginnings of the study of public policy and administration in the sense that the content and substance of public policy has always been central to these fields of study. The complexity of policy content, however, resulted in the early attempts to study policy design focusing mainly on case studies, without a common framework of description or analysis. More recent work attempts to identify systematic ways of describing policy designs that will enable researchers to compare designs across different policy arenas, and to compare the same kinds of policies across different countries or time periods.

The importance of policy instruments was highlighted by Dahl and Lindblom as early as 1953 when they noted that "this process [the invention and innovation in social techniques] is perhaps the great political revolution of our time."[1] They attributed the capacity of government to avoid having to make stark dichotomous choices between socialism on the one hand and capitalism on the other to the proliferation of techniques that blurred the lines between these seemingly absolute dichotomies.

Most of the initial efforts attempted to describe policy content in broad strokes. Dahl and Lindblom[1] posited five dimensions they believed could capture differences in designs: private to public; compulsory to informative; direct to indirect; compulsory to voluntary membership; and prescriptive to autonomous within the hierarchy. Ripley's work[2] cast the history of the United States in terms of three broad types of policy designs: subsidies (such as the Louisiana Purchase and the homestead act); regulation (of railroads, business, labor); and the most recent, manipulation, which included efforts to reduce the gulf between the indulged and the deprived. Bardach[3] suggested four types: prescription, enabling, incentives, and deterrence.

Lowi[4] is widely acknowledged as being the first scholar to propose a way of characterizing policy content that sparked theoretical and empirical development. His work emphasized that the study of policy design should not focus exclusively on why different kinds of designs emerge, but in fact, should recognize that policy content is an important cause of politics itself. The possibilities offered by policy, Lowi contends, create the arena in which politics is played out, with different types of policy-producing variations of pluralist or elitist politics.

Lowi's typology features two dimensions: the extent of coercion (i.e., whether benefits or burdens are being distributed); and whether the policy is directed at specific groups or whether it consists of rules that affect the more general environment. This fourfold typology produces four types of policies: distributive, regulatory, redistributive, and constituent. His theory suggested that distributive policy, which is the classic pork barrel in that benefits are being distributed to specific groups, will produce a form of particularistic politics with agencies or bureaus, the members of congressional committees and narrow clientele groups benefitting through log-rolling and bargaining. Regulatory policy, which imposes costs that impact many groups, will produce classic pluralist

Encyclopedia of Public Administration and Public Policy
DOI: 10.1081/E-EPAP 120016559

competition with various interest groups vying to gain regulations that benefit them or inflict costs on their competitors. The politics that results is often partisan, with contests between different coalitions of interest groups played out in congressional floor debates that are highly contentious. Redistributive policy, he believed, would create a form of elitist politics in which the President and close advisors, often including leaders in either business, labor, or other broad sectors of society, would formulate a policy and build support for it. This support often was built on the basis of appeals to class or economic divisions. The policies that were formulated would simply be ratified in the congress.

James Q. Wilson[5] also developed a typology for policy that offers an explanation of how policy content produces different patterns of politics. The two dimensions in his typology are whether benefits or costs are being distributed and whether the recipients are concentrated or dispersed. Majoritarian politics, he says, will ensue when benefits and costs are both widely distributed over a large number of people. The rationale here is that all will have about the same incentive to pay attention to politics. Interest group politics will emerge when benefits are concentrated on only a few, and costs are distributed among only a few (such as regulations that favor workers at the expense of business or vice versa). His reasoning is that the motivation of both sides will be about the same and both will mobilize to protect their interests. Clientist politics is when elected leaders distribute favors to small and concentrated groups (who then are highly motivated to protect such favors), whereas costs (through taxes) are broadly dispersed leading to no particular motivation to pay attention. Welfare policy is the main example of this type, and Wilson argues that government will always expand its clientist policies because they offer such high payoffs for elected leaders. Entrepreneurial politics occur when small portions of the population pay the costs to benefit large numbers of people. Taxation policies, for example, that impose especially heavy burdens on the rich and distribute the funds widely such as to education or social security, are examples. Wilson argues that government also will expand its entrepreneurial politics far more than is warranted because so many are motivated to continue gaining benefits at the expense of so few.

There are some difficulties with both of these typologies. Lowi's framework has sparked considerable research, but empirical studies are difficult because almost all policies contain elements of more than one of the types. There are almost no pure types. Wilson's framework has this same problem, but in addition, has over time been shown simply to be wrong in many respects. Welfare policy, which he believed would continually expand, has

not expanded but retracted. Federal policy has reduced (not increased) the taxation rate paid by the richest segments of society.

While Lowi and Wilson were interested in the broad relationship of policy content to types of politics, other researchers focused on fleshing out notions of policy elements and tools of government. In 1985, Stephen Linder and Guy Peters characterized policy design analysis as middle-level theory that was a mix of three dimensions: a theory of causality, evaluation, and instruments.[6] David Boborow and John Dryzek[7] concentrate on the process through which designs are constituted and legitimated. Their aim is to foster a broad dialogue among different design perspectives on issues such as instrumental and communicative reason so that the design process is open and democratic. Another group of researchers addresses in great detail the advantages and disadvantages of the adoption of certain specific policy instruments or tools. A volume edited by Lester Salmon[8] addresses a variety of policy tools including grants, tax expenditures, loan guarantees, contracting, public information, and other instruments. The concern of many authors in the tools field is that widespread policy designs embodying contemporary notions of decentralization and devolution may have unexpected and perhaps negative effects.

The understanding of policy design and development of theories of design have been advanced recently by scholars who factor into the analysis the power and social constructions of policy participants, particularly target populations. The basic argument is that variation in designs can be at least partly explained by differences in the power and social construction of target populations and other interested parties in the policy space.

TARGET POPULATIONS, SOCIAL CONSTRUCTIONS, AND THE ELEMENTS OF DESIGN

The symbolic aspects of public policy have long been recognized in the study of politics, but their incorporation into studies of public policy generally and policy design specifically has been more recent. Building on the work of Murray Edelman,[9] several policy scholars have emphasized the central role played by policy images, the way issues are framed, and the social construction of target populations, events, or the "items" of public policy.[10–18] What these approaches have in common is the incorporation of meaning, interpretation, symbolism, and social constructions into the description of policy design and into theories of both the causes and consequences of variation in policy design.

Schneider and Ingram[15,16] posited that policy designs—including constitutions, statutes, agency guidelines, and everyday practices of implementers—almost always contain a set of common elements including:

- Goals or problems to be solved.
- Target populations (those impacted directly or indirectly by the policy).
- Allocations of benefits or burdens (both material and symbolic).
- Tools (the devices used to insure the behavior needed by the policy).
- Rules (who is to do what, when, with what resources, to whom, with what constraints).
- Implementation structures (agencies, contractors, street-level case workers).
- Rationales (the logic, causal arguments, rhetorical devices, data).
- Underlying assumptions (implicit or explicit, agreed upon or contested).

Each of these has multiple dimension. For example, tools can be conceptualized in terms of their underlying behavioral assumptions producing several "types" of tools: positive incentives, negative incentives, force, information, capacity building, authority (pronouncements without penalties); persuasion; and learning.

Building from a framework of design elements, Schneider and Ingram developed a two-dimensional typology of target populations consisting of the political power resources of target groups and other interested parties (ranging from high to low) and the social constructions of target populations and other interested parties (ranging from positive to negative) (Fig. 1). The policy space created by examining political power and social constructions produces four "types" of target populations (although these are best thought of as a continuous rather than categorical characterization). *Advantaged* populations are those that have considerable political power resources and are positively constructed, usually as "deserving," or "good." Examples include business, the middle class, family farmers, and senior citizens. *Contenders* have political power resources to use but are negatively constructed, often as "greedy" or "undeserving" in some way. Examples of these groups include gun owners, the rich, and CEOs of large corporations. *Deviants* is the label given to those who have no legitimate forms of political power and are negatively constructed as dangerous and violent. Examples include criminals, terrorists, flag burners, and gangs. (Terrorists, of course, have the power to generate fear and take the lives of civilians; but by definition, the power of terrorists is not

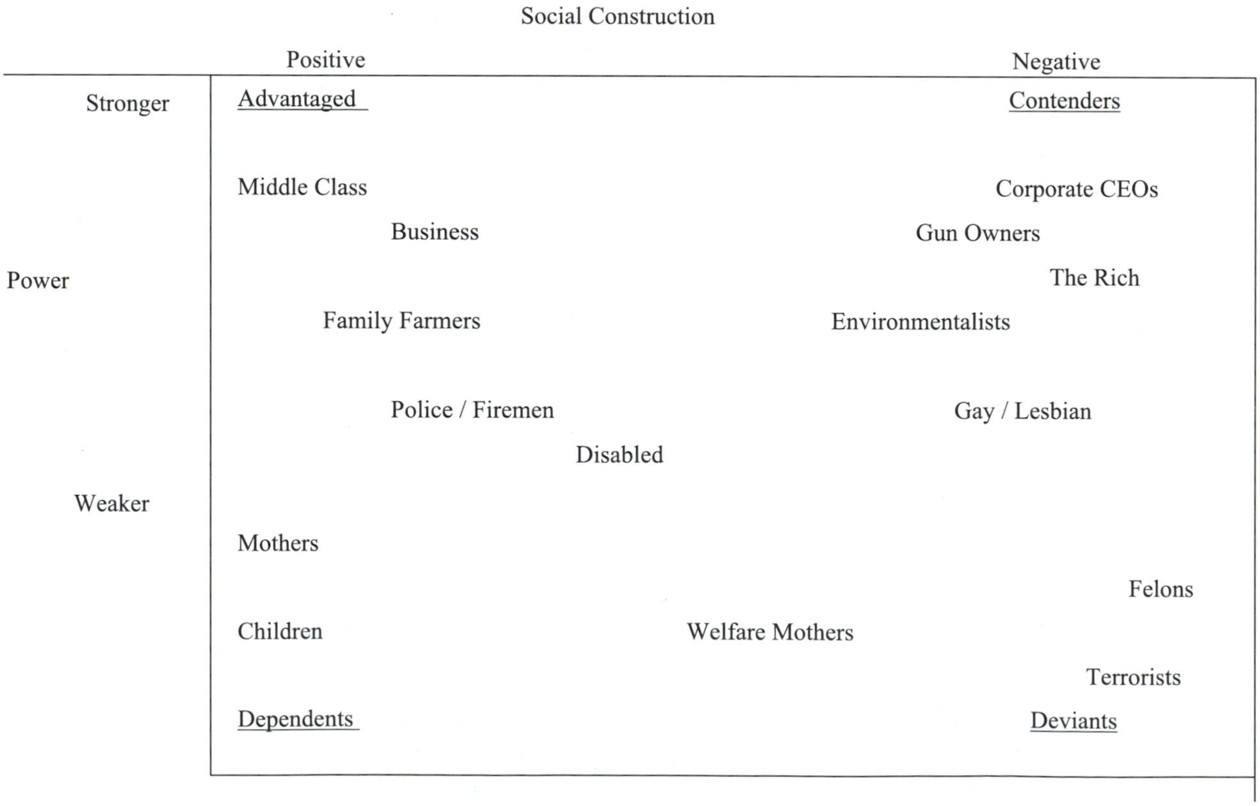

Fig. 1 Power and social constructions of target populations.

legitimate political power in the usual sense of that term.) *Dependents* are persons or groups with little or no political power but who have generally positive constructions, such as "good, deserving, people," although "helplessness" is also a common characterization of these groups who include children, mothers, the poor, homeless, and so on.

The theory of target populations and policy design that we propose is that each of these segments of the policy space will often be characterized by common types of design elements. Under conditions of pluralist or hyperpluralist political institutions, much can be learned about the characteristics of rationales, implementation structures, rules, tools, goals, and allocation patterns if one focuses on which type of target population the policy (or segments of it) is directed toward. For example, benefits are more likely to be oversubscribed to advantaged populations and undersubscribed to deviants, whereas punishments or costly regulations are more likely to be undersubscribed to advantaged and oversubscribed to deviants. The tools for delivering benefits to the advantaged typically will focus on capacity building (such as subsidies, entitlements, free information, and outreach programs), whereas the tools for delivering burdensome regulations to this same group are more likely to focus on self-regulation, learning, positive inducements, standards and charges, and only rarely, sanctions. Sanctions or regulations are likely to be imposed only when needed to protect one group of advantaged from another group of equally advantaged people. Tools for delivering benefits to dependents are expected to be income-tested subsidies in which the clients must establish their own eligibility, whereas tools for delivering benefits to advantaged groups are expected to be broad-based and not require means testing (social security, e.g., or farm subsidies). Rationales are expected to differ. When benefits are delivered to advantaged groups, rationales usually will be justified on the grounds of important national interests or an efficient means to the goal, whereas benefits to dependents are more likely to be justified on justice grounds such as equal opportunity, need, or fairness. Benefits to deviants generally do not occur unless required by courts on the grounds of fundamental rights or human decency.

This aspect of the theory has produced a significant amount of empirical research that generally supports the contention that social constructions of target populations are centrally implicated in the types of designs that emerge (or whether policy will be adopted). Donovan,[19–21] e.g., characterized target populations of persons with HIV/AIDS in terms of how they contracted the infection and found that allocations for HIV/AIDs research disproportionately allocated funds to those contracting the disease who were "advantaged" (medical workers, health professionals, people who got it through transfusions) compared to those who were not so "innocent" (i.e., drug users, homosexuals). Analysis of the generosity of government subsidies varies quite directly with the social construction and power of the target populations when one compares corporate welfare, e.g., with aid to those who are poor.

Other studies have shown that the manipulation of the social construction of target populations is a central aspect of discursive strategies used in legislative policy making. Jensen[22] shows how some types of veterans but not others came to be eligible for veterans pensions. Sidney[23] examines the ways in which a Black middle class was separated from "urban rioters" in debates about eliminating discriminatory practices in housing so that benefits could be provided to the former and denied to the latter. Studies of immigration policy document that underlying racist motivations have produced negative constructions as "undeserving" for many minority groups leading to highly restrictive immigration policy.[24,25] In a similar way, federal drug policy provides a much heavier penalty for crack cocaine than for powder cocaine, arguably because the former is used mainly by inner-city Black males and the latter by White middle-class professionals or athletes. The elimination of welfare as an entitlement owes much to the ability of moral entrepreneurs who have depicted welfare recipients as "welfare queens" or as unmarried, immoral teenagers who have children so that they can collect a welfare check.

Following the ideas contained in the Lowi and Wilson theories, we also have proposed that policy designs produce politics. Social constructions become embedded in public policy, producing messages to target populations that are interpreted and internalized with significant implications for political participation, attitudes toward the state, and citizenship. Mettler[26] documents that the GI bill was a crucial factor in the political participation of veterans. Soss's[27,28] empirical research on welfare compares the impacts of two very different policy designs: social security disability policy and Aid to Families with Dependent Children. His analysis presents strong evidence that differences in these designs have produced critical differences in trust of the state, efficacy, inclination to vote one's interest in elections, and overall participation patterns.

Theories of policy change also have begun to incorporate the importance of image, symbolism, and social constructions of policy participants in understanding whether policy change will occur and whether it will be incremental or sudden. Baumgartner and Jones,[13] e.g., in their analysis of punctuated equilibrium theories take into account the policy images and the social constructions of target populations.

CONCLUSION

The central contention of scholars who focus on policy design is that the content and substance of public policy is as important to study as the processes that produce policy. Furthermore, the policy design scholars emphasize that process cannot be well understood without a careful analysis of the product that has been produced. The power, social construction, and ideas that drive policy designs become embedded in the design elements. The goals, problem definitions, rules, tools, rationales, and implementation structures all reflect the dynamics of the policy production process. Policy designs also have significant impacts on target populations, others interested in the policy arena, and the general public. Differences in policy designs have been linked to important differences in attitudes about the state, conceptions of citizenship, and levels of political participation. The study of policy design offers rich potential for understanding how American democracy works, who benefits, and who suffers.

REFERENCES

1. Dahl, R.A.; Lindblom, C.E. *Politics, Economics, and Welfare*; Harper and Brothers: New York, 1953; 8.
2. Ripley, R.B. *Policy Analysis in Political Science*; Nelson Hall: Chicago, 1985.
3. Bardach, E. *The Implementation Game*; The MIT Press: Cambridge, MA, 1979.
4. Lowi, T. Four systems of policy, politics, and choice. Public Adm. Rev. **1972**, *11*, 298–310.
5. Wilson, J.Q. *American Government: Institutions and Policies*; D.C. Heath: Lexington, MA, 1979.
6. Linder, S.; Peters, G. From social theory to policy design. J. Public Policy **1985**, *4* (3), 237–259.
7. Boborow, D.; Dryzek, J. *Policy Analysis by Design*; University of Pittsburgh Press: Pittsburgh, 1987.
8. Salamon, L. *The Tools of Government: A Guide to the New Governance*; Oxford University Press: Oxford, 2002.
9. Edelman, M.J. *The Symbolic Uses of Politics*; University of Illinois Press: Urbana, 1964.
10. Stone, D. *Policy Paradox: The Art of Political Decision Making*; W.W. Norton: New York, 1997.
11. Kingdon, J. *Agendas, Alternatives, and Public Policies*; Little, Brown: Boston, 1984.
12. Baumgartner, F.R.; Jones, B.D. *Agendas and Instability in American Politics*; University of Chicago Press: Chicago, IL, 1993.
13. Schram, S. Putting a Black Face on Welfare: The Good and the Bad. In *Deserving and Entitled. Social Constructions and Public Policy*; Schneider, A.L., Ingram, H., Eds.; State University of New York Press: Albany, 2003.
14. *Deserving and Entitled. Social Constructions and Public Policy*; Schneider, A.L., Ingram, H., Eds.; State University of New York Press: Albany, 2003: and the introductory chapter, Public Policy and the Social Construction of Deservedness.
15. Schneider, A.L.; Ingram, H. *Policy Design for Democracy*; University Press of Kansas, 1997.
16. Schneider, A.L.; Ingram, H. The social construction of target populations. Am. Polit. Sci. Rev. **1993**, *87/2*, 334–347.
17. Ingram, H.; Schneider, A.L. Improving implementation by framing smarter statutes. J. Public Policy **1990**, *10* (1), 67–88.
18. Ingram, H.; Schneider, A.L. Target populations and policy design. Adm. Soc. **1991**, *23* (3), 333–356, 15.
19. Ingram, H.; Smith, S.R. *Public Policy for Democracy*; Brookings Institution Press: Washington, DC, 1993.
20. Ingram, H.; Schneider, A.L. Constructing Citizenship: The Subtle Messages of Policy Design. In *Public Policy for Democracy (Red)*; Ingram, H.M., Smith, S.R., Eds.; Brookings: Washington, DC, 1993.
21. Donovan, M.C. *Taking Aim: Target Populations and the Wars on AIDS and Drugs*; Georgetown University Press: Washington, DC, 2001.
22. Jensen, L.S. *Patriots, Settlers, and the Origins of American Social Policy*; Cambridge University Press: Cambridge, England, 2003.
23. Sidney, M.S. Contested Images of Race and Place: The Politics of Housing Discrimination. Schneider, A.L., Ingram, H., Eds.; 2003.
24. DiAlto, S. From ''problem minority to model minority: The changing social construction of Japanese Americans. Schneider, A.L., Ingram, H., Eds.; 2003.
25. Newton, L. It is Not a Question of Being Anti-immigration: Categories of Deservedness in Immigration Policy Making. Schneider, A.L., Ingram, H., Eds.; 2003.
26. Mettler, S. Bringing the state back in to civic engagement: policy feedback effects of the G. I. Bill for World War II veterans. Am. Polit. Sci. Rev. **2002**, *96* (2), 351–366.
27. Soss, J. Making Clients and Citizens: Welfare Policy as a Source of Status, Belief, and Action. Schneider, A.L., Ingram, H., Eds.; 2003.
28. Soss, J. *Unwanted Claims: Politics, Participation and the U.S. Welfare System*; University of Michigan Press: Ann Arbor, 2002.

Policy Implementation

Ann O'M. Bowman
University of South Carolina, Columbia, South Carolina, U.S.A.

INTRODUCTION

Implementation occurs in the middle of the policy process. It results from the stages that precede it, policy formulation and adoption, and it affects the subsequent stages: evaluation and redesign. The verb *to implement* means in its most basic sense, to carry out, to fulfill, or to accomplish. When applied to public policy, implementation is the process of putting into effect or carrying out an authoritative decision of government. This decision is most often enacted by a legislative body (e.g., the Congress, a state legislature, a city council), but it also can be a directive of the executive branch (e.g., a President's Executive Order, an agency's regulation) or a ruling by the judiciary. Implementation puts the objectives of policy adopters into action in an effort to accomplish desired results.

Implementation makes a policy happen, it gives a policy life. Policy formulation and adoption are necessary precursors, but implementation adds sufficiency. That may seem easy enough but several decades of research on policy implementation have demonstrated the complexity of putting policies into action. Few policies are self-implementing, most require concerted, coordinated action by actors other than those who adopted the policy. Implementation may stall, it may be diverted or subverted by implementors with conflicting interests, it may attenuate due to insufficient resources, it may encounter any number of pitfalls. A flawed implementation process makes the accomplishment of policy objectives all the more difficult. Since the early 1970s, researchers have sought answers to a fundamental question: What makes implementation successful?

DISCUSSION

"Policy implementation is what develops between the establishment of an apparent intention on the part of government to do something, or to stop doing something, and the ultimate impact in the world of action."[1] In the simplest cases, implementation is handled by a single agency at the governmental level where the policy was adopted. When implementation is multiagency, and when it is intergovernmental, the potential for slippage increases. Because the U.S. federal system is decentralized in design and, by the late 20th century, devolutionary in preference, most significant domestic policies are intergovernmental. Take, for example, environmental protection policies. Federal legislation such as the Clean Water Act requires the U.S. Environmental Protection Agency (EPA) to take certain actions but the bulk of the Act's implementation is the responsibility of state agencies. The Clean Water Act may have been enacted by the U.S. Congress and it may instruct the EPA to promulgate requisite rules, but it is Alabama's Department of Environmental Management and Vermont's Agency of Natural Resources, working with regional EPA offices, which are implementing the law. As it is in so many policy areas, implementation is increasingly a multiagency and multilevel process.

First-Generation Studies

Intergovernmental policy implementation is a complex process, a fact that emerged from a study of the "new towns in-town" program of the Johnson administration.[2] This was confirmed in 1973 with the publication of Jeffrey Pressman and Aaron Wildavsky's book, *Implementation.*[3] The subtitle said it all: *How Great Expectations in Washington Are Dashed in Oakland; Or, Why It's Amazing that Federal Programs Work at All.* Why did a well-intentioned, innovative employment policy enacted by Congress encounter so many obstacles during its implementation in the city of Oakland, California? The program provided funds for public works projects and business loans that would in turn produce jobs for unemployed minorities in Oakland. The level of enthusiasm for the program was high, agreement on the policy goals was substantial. But the program did not deliver on its promise. After three years, more than $1 million in business loans were made, but few jobs were created and major public works projects had not commenced. The Oakland EDA case reinforced the new towns finding: intergovernmental implementation is not easy. In Oakland, it was the "technical details," but most especially, the complexity of joint action required in the implementation process, that doomed the program. At more than 30

Encyclopedia of Public Administration and Public Policy
DOI: 10.1081/E-EPAP 120011068

decision points, multiple participants with diverse, often conflictual, perspectives collided.

Research in the Pressman and Wildavsky mold analyzed how a single authoritative decision was carried out—or, as more frequently, not carried out. One valuable result of these case studies was the recognition of the complex nature of implementation. But, although these accounts provided contextually rich, detailed information about a specific program, it was difficult to generalize from them. Implementation succeeded (or was delayed, or was subverted) for a host of seemingly idiosyncratic reasons.

Second-Generation Research

Even as these so-called "first-generation" studies continued, another type of implementation research was underway. This work sought to develop analytical frameworks that identified factors important to implementation. In other words, this "second-generation" research focused on the determinants of implementation success, defined primarily as the achievement of policy objectives. Conceptual models of the implementation process were developed and tested in several different substantive areas. Two approaches predominated: top-down and bottom-up.

Top-down approach

Top-down models of implementation focus on the authoritative decision (e.g., the new statute) and the formal actors (decision makers) in an almost hierarchical fashion. The questions flowing from this model include: What did the law specify? What decisions were made? Did compliance (with the directives of the statute) occur? Were policy goals met?

Top-down researchers found that successful implementation was more likely if the following conditions existed:

1. Clear and consistent policy objectives embodied in the statute (or other legal directive).
2. A sound theory underpinning the statute, one that specifies the factors affecting policy objectives and gives implementors sufficient authority.
3. The placement of the implementation function in a sympathetic agency with adequate structure, supportive decision rules, sufficient funding, and adequate access to supporters.
4. Implementors with substantial managerial and political skill, and commitment to statutory goals.
5. Active support from organized constituency groups and key elected officials throughout the imple-

mentation process, with the courts being neutral or supportive.
6. An absence of conflicting public policies and socioeconomic conditions that would weaken causal theory or political support.[4]

Other things being equal, a policy that possesses these conditions is more likely to experience successful implementation than a policy lacking in them. Although seldom are all six conditions met, even in suboptimal situations, several steps can be taken to enhance the likelihood of successful implementation. There is no "routine" or "natural" path to implementation, four implementation scenarios are plausible.[4] With the effective implementation scenario, as the label implies, implementation is smooth and swift. This is likely to occur in programs that seek only moderate changes in the status quo. In the gradual erosion scenario, implementation begins in a promising manner but slows precipitously as forces opposing the policy gain strength. The presence of numerous veto points wears down supporters and emboldens opponents. The link between the authorizing statute and the implementation process attenuates. The cumulative implementation scenario posits steady, slow progress toward implementation. Adjustments are made throughout the implementation process such that compliance from target groups is secured. In the rejuvenation scenario, initial start-up slows but then later resumes. Implementation is saved from the gradual erosion fate by changes in the statute (e.g., legislative clarification), in contextual factors (e.g., economic growth), and in agency characteristics (e.g., new leadership) that promote renewal of the implementation effort.

Bottom-up approach

Bottom-up approaches see implementation through a different set of theoretical and analytical lenses. Starting from the opposite end, bottom-up models focus on the existence of a public problem and the actors connected to it. To understand implementation, bottom-uppers look to the target population and the implementing environment.[5] Street-level bureaucrats are queried as to their goals for the program or service and relevant strategies, activities, and contacts. This information provides the basis for the next step: constructing a broader network that is multilocal and multilevel. In effect, implementation is mapped from the bottom-up. Rather than unfolding from the top, implementation builds from the bottom or "microlevel." To achieve successful implementation, local actors adapt policies and programs to fit local conditions. This helps explain how the same policy can produce very different implementation results from one setting to another. Implementation is determined by the bargaining (explicit or implicit) in the policy subsystem: members of an implementing organization and their clients. Alliances are formed, coalitions are created, and the implementation process is managed. When a new policy or program fits the local context, implementation proceeds. When it does not, implementors seek to delay it or to otherwise thwart the objectives of enactors.

Assessing the two approaches

Top-down approaches are criticized for overemphasizing the role of central decision makers while bottom-up models are said to overstate the amount of autonomy that local level implementers possess.[6] Regardless, second-generation research yielded several important findings about the implementation process. Chief among them was the recognition that implementation varies over time, across policies, and from one setting to another. Furthermore, it matters at what point in history implementation takes place and over what period of time.

Third-Generation Research

Third-generation research synthesizes the best features of both top-down and bottom-up approaches, in an effort to determine which variables, and in what setting, affect implementation. For example, policymakers are encouraged to engage in both "forward mapping" and "backward mapping."[7] In forward mapping, policy objectives, implementation guidelines, and evaluative criteria are stated clearly and explicitly. But backward mapping shifts the focus to the local level and to target groups. The question becomes: "What has to happen at the local level for this policy to be successful?" Once answered, the follow-up question is: "What has to happen at the next level for this policy to be successful?" This procedure is repeated all the way back to the point of enactment. By engaging in this hybrid top-down/bottom-up exercise, policymakers have a clearer understanding of the implementation process and therefore will select a better set of policy instruments. The result, the logic goes, is a policy that achieves its objectives.

Another way to conceive of implementation is as a multilevel subsystem full of messages, messengers, channels, and targets.[8] Implementation is a dynamic process as messages are designed, sent, received, interpreted, and responded to. The content and form of the policy messages, and the standing of federal-level communicators among the implementers, act to induce or constrain implementation. At the subnational level, inducements and constraints are generated by organized interests, elected and appointed government officials, and the focal state agency. These implementation-related interactions occur in a state setting that is structured by economic capacity, political conditions, and a set of situational variables such as the salience of the problem to a state, the amount of media attention given the problem, and a state's organizational capacity.

States decide how they will implement a federal directive. Four patterns or styles are possible. The first implementation style, compliance, reflects a state context in which the new federal policy (and /or program) fits, i.e., the goals of the policy are in sync with state goals, the funding is sufficient, and implementors have the required skills. Moreover, it may demonstrate the value of incentives built into the policy that encourage rapid, unmodified implementation. In the second implementation style, strategic delay, a state delays implementation in an effort to make the new policy conform to the state context. This assumes that the new policy contains ample flexibility and discretion for these adjustments to be made. The state's delay is strategic, thus it anticipates several rounds of negotiation and bargaining between federal-level actors and the state-level implementors. The third and fourth styles of implementation reflect a new policy at odds with a state context. In these instances, a state may simply drag its feet (the "delay" style) awaiting a judicial ruling, a change in the law, or a greater incentive to comply. Contrarily, a "defiance" state may opt to chart its own path, ignoring the dictates of the new policy. State policymakers may consider defiance preferable to the federal policy, but it may lead to the withdrawal of federal funding or the intrusion of federal enforcement officials.

Just as implementation is about communication, it is also about cooperation. However, implementation is often a matter of achieving cooperation among actors who are not necessarily inclined to cooperate.[9] These "reluctant partners" who may hold different values and may have conflicting interests have to be induced to cooperate. But, unlike the traditional top-down argument, it is not the national-level actors who hold all the cards. Instead, authority is diffuse and subnational actors possess resources that they can marshal strategically. Implementation regimes form to guide the interactions of the various participants as they jockey for position. These regimes are composed of rules, norms, and procedures that shape the way participants interact.

Another influence on implementation is the working relationship that evolves between federal and state personnel.[10] Two key dimensions of the working relationship are trust and involvement. In instances where trust and involvement are high, personnel at different governmental levels work together and achieve synergies, thereby facilitating implementation. Where one or both of the characteristics are low, the working relationships are suboptimal. To move these working relationships into the facilitating variety, implementors are encouraged to increase personal contact, use multiple communication channels, share information, promote interagency learning, and provide timely communication and feedback. To increase trust among the actors, open dialog is encouraged while back-door and end-run communication tactics are discouraged, ends rather than means are to be kept in sight, meaningful input by all participants is welcomed, and a re-centering of the relationship on shared visions, whether policy goals, problem dimensions, or available solutions, is to be sought.

The growing use of networks to deliver programs and services underscores the lessons of the third generation. Implementation is often indirect with programs managed through complex networks of nongovernmental providers such as nonprofit organizations.[1] Backward and forward mapping, effective communication, cooperative efforts, and increased trust and involvement are essential if implementation is to be successful.

CONCLUSION

The first generation of research on policy implementation produced fairly discouraging conclusions. Seldom, it appeared, were new governmental policies implemented as expected. Second-generation research sought to improve the situation by identifying solutions. However, the work was limited by an either/or definition of the problem: either top-down or bottom-up. This meant that the recommendations themselves were limited. The more recent third-generation research synthesizes the top-down and bottom-up approaches to produce more plausible explanations for why some policies are implemented successfully and others are not. It is not simply a matter of crafting a perfect piece of legislation for adoption. Nor is it enough to create a workable organizational structure or to rally a cadre of supporters to the cause. Instead, successful implementation involves converting the poten-

tial energy of diverse participants into concerted, positive action. Policymakers are instructed to engage in forward and backward mapping. Implementation managers are encouraged to improve communication and foster cooperation, and to increase the levels of trust and involvement among implementers. On balance, as the use of networks grows, perhaps the most likely implementation pattern is one of strategic delay.

REFERENCES

1. O'Toole, L.J., Jr. Research on policy implementation: Assessment and prospects. J. Public Adm. Res. Theory **2000**, *10* (2), 263–288.
2. Derthick, M. *New Towns In-Town*; Urban Institute: Washington, DC, 1972.
3. Pressman, J.L.; Wildavsky, A.B. *Implementation*; University of California Press: Berkeley, CA, 1973.
4. Mazmanian, D.A.; Sabatier, P.A. *Implementation and Public Policy*; Scott, Foresman: Glenview, IL, 1983; pp. 41, 42, 278–282.
5. Hjern, B. Implementation research—the link gone missing. J. Public Policy **1982**, *2* (3), 301–308.
6. Matland, R.E. Synthesizing the implementation literature: The ambiguity–conflict model of policy implementation. J. Public Adm. Res. Theory **1995**, *5* (2), 145–174.
7. Elmore, R.F. Forward and Backward Mapping: Reversible Logic in the Analysis of Public Policy. In *Policy Implementation in Federal and Unitary Systems*; Hanf, K., Toonen, T., Eds.; Martinus Nijhoff: Dordrecht, 1985; 33–70.
8. Goggin, M.L.; Bowman, A.O'M.; Lester, J.P.; O'Toole, L.J., Jr. *Implementation Theory and Practice*; Scott, Foresman/Little, Brown: Glenview, IL, 1990.
9. Stoker, R.P. *Reluctant Partners: Implementing Federal Policy*; University of Pittsburgh Press: Pittsburgh, PA, 1991.
10. Scheberle, D. *Federalism and Environmental Policy: Trust and the Politics of Implementation*; Georgetown University Press: Washington, DC, 1997.

Policy Networks

Jack W. Meek
University of La Verne, La Verne, California, U.S.A.

INTRODUCTION

Policy networks describe formal and informal social relationships among interested parties that form agreements to achieve individual and common goals in public arenas. Policy networks are viewed differently by political scientists interested in policy formation, by public administration scholars interested in policy implementation, and by sociologists interested in influence relationships among network partners. The influences of policy networks, and their great variety, provide evidence of social interaction that influence social behavior and influence public value. Some view these forms of associations as working alongside or even replacing formal government service and forming what has come to be described as governance. From another perspective, some forms of policy networks can be considered ''dark'' and there is a necessity to understand how these operate in addition to those policy networks that show promise.

POLICY FORMATION

Policy choices are expressions of social value traditionally thought to be developed by legislators who are representing the citizenry. In traditional theory, these choices are thought to be implemented by neutral public servants working in government bureaucracies. Political scientists have long observed that policy choices and governmental bureaucratic implementation are influenced by policy networks that are formed around the relationships and by participants closely involved in the policy choice. Those who decide (legislature), those who implement (bureaucracy), and those most affected (individuals, neighborhoods, industry or service) by policy form partnerships of interest that influence both the content and implementation of policy. These partnerships, referred to variously as subgovernments,[1] as iron triangles or as cozy triangles are characterized by the cultivation of continuing relationships that engage in mutual exchanges that favor the needs of clientele groups agencies and representatives. Hugh Heclo[2] broadened the frame of reference of these narrowly defined triangles to include a web of policy participants, with a variety of interests, that is character-

ized as an ''issue network.'' Self-interest and exchange held issue networks together, but this form of policy influence was considered broader than the subgovernment form of relationship.

One meaning of policy networks is that policy formation is subverted or at least influenced by the central participants of the issue and that citizenry are kept far from playing any form of influential role in the process. Indeed, of concern about policy networks are the mutual benefits generated from political-administrative connections. No longer is there a neutral bureaucracy implementing public policy; it is now understood that bureaucrats are policy advocates. Networks replaced neutrality with self-serving outcomes of elected officials, selected clientele, and bureaucracy. On the other hand, policy networks can also be viewed as functional necessities of the modern nation-state where relationships of the most central players usefully orchestrate public will in competition with other interests in the state.

POLICY ADMINISTRATION

Public administration scholars have observed that public programs are increasingly produced and managed through various collectives.[3] As networks, these collectivities include both governmental and nongovernmental partners. For Laurence O'Toole, these ''networks are structures of interdependence involving multiple organizations or parts thereof, where one unit is not merely the formal subordinate of the other in some larger hierarchical arrangement.''[4] These networks are policy networks that are characterized by a ''relatively stable relations between (different) governmental and (semi-) private organizations in which processes of policy making take place.''[5] Thus policy networks warrant much attention, not only from the policy or political demand or ''input'' side, but also from the policy ''output'' or implementation side. And there are different positions on how to view policy network outputs and their impact on public governance.

One position, as evidenced in the work of Hugh Miller, is that an emergent characteristic of policy network (implementation) is administrative discretion that approaches

Encyclopedia of Public Administration and Public Policy
DOI: 10.1081/E-EPAP 120024801

''political activism'' or even political professionalism by civil servants.[6] Such an outcome challenges the assumptions made by ''progressive'' public administration built around the principles of hierarchical control, scientific management, and neutral competence. The charge is that mutually supportive relationships spillover into the output/implementation side of policy where public administrators, motivated by a sense of agency expansion and self-promotion, become political administrators. The key issue is that administrators are hidden from direct public accountability and manipulate service design and delivery based upon a variety of reasons. It may very well be that administrators have captured and manipulated service implementation, which could serve many interests.

Another position among public administration theorists is to view the formation of networks as valuable tools in the implementation of public policy where administrative leaders face resource scarce environments.[7] The size and nature of policy implementation networks range widely from linkages between two or more organizations to a formal coalition of organizations formally designed to carry out a broad mission. Networks, viewed through this frame of reference, are forms of collaborations designed to effectively carry out policy directives. The privatization movement effectively constructs a web of networks managed by government engagement that oversees policy administration.

NETWORK MANAGEMENT

The unique feature of policy networks is that they can be considered a third form of social relationships, the other two relationships are categorized as hierarchy and market.[8] Whereas hierarchy and markets are usefully examined through the lens of superior–subordinate and rational self-interest, respectively, networks are much more elusive to understand. Network behavior is best matched with work on indeterminate behavior: participants come and go at will, there is no determinate pattern of leadership, power or hierarchy or leadership. Networks emerge and dissipate.

For public administration, accountability becomes a deep concern in policy administration networks. One study on the local management of economic development found that networks of multiple actors do represent an important form of governance. However, the management of networks adds to the tasks of public management and implies that both the capacity and policy making realm of cities becomes more decentralized and complicated.[9] Indeed, if governance means a pronounced reliance on exchange and a de-emphasis of the role and strength of government, then serious challenges to equity and accountability may undermine the ability and legitimacy

of government to govern. In addition, the concern for policy networks is how roles are conceived as well as their concomitant expectations of rights, responsibilities, obligations, and duties that guide behavior.[10]

The absence of hierarchy, the accountability vacuum, and the lack of role identity within networks have pushed public administration scholars to seek useful frames of reference that would guide public managers in determining what constitutes management cornerstones of policy networks. Robert Agranoff and Michael McGuire begin with examining the skills of the administrator and differentiating those required in traditional hierarchical public administration management (POSCORB) and those required of network management.[11] The class of behaviors they found relevant in networks includes the following: activation, framing, mobilizing, and synthesizing. Activation refers to the identification and development of stakeholders that might be part of the network. Framing is the ability to establish rules of operation for the network. Mobilizing is the ability to coordinate and accomplish the goals and objectives of the network. Synthesizing refers to providing an environment when conditions are created to enhance network productivity. The combined effect of these skills is nearly ''seamless in their applicability'' and may result in outcomes that emerge and evolve rather than those that are targeted and achieved. Current research in management behaviors in networks is focusing on propositions based on a strategic-contingency logic, that program performance will vary based upon the problem context of the network.[12,13] Drawing upon the examination of 12 network processes, Robert Agranoff has established 10 basic lessons in the management of networks (sharing burdens, sharing expertise, being creative, orchestrating agendas are examples), most of which reveal the fundamental need to be flexible within the fluid nature of network functioning.[14] These may have been valuable skills in hierarchies, but it is in networks that these skills are preeminent.

NETWORK PERFORMANCE

How well do these networks perform? Because policy networks involve many participants with multiple agendas, evaluating network performance becomes problematic, but necessary. One study[15] examined publicly funded health, human service, and public welfare organizations from three levels (community, network, and organizational/participant) each of which has unique effectiveness criteria that often may be in conflict. The authors argue that while ''service-delivery networks must be built and maintained at the organizational and network levels, overall network effectiveness will ultimately be judged by community-level stakeholders.''

To be successful, policy administration in networks calls upon different skills than those linked to successful administration in hierarchies. The very management of networks suggests the need for very different orientations and strategies of management.[5] Reliance on collaboration from participants with different interests and who are accountable to different "publics" offers constraints in determining and achieving common goals. Based on a "theory of network management," Meier and O'Toole found that managers who incorporated a networking management style (those who have greater interaction with environmental actors who are not direct line subordinates or superiors) had a significant impact on program performance and were able to influence program results.[16] While this is perhaps a limited measure of managerial networking, it is a beginning in the establishment of what is effective in managing policy network.

GOVERNANCE

With the growth and evolving complexity of urban areas, policy networks have appeared and approach policy problems and solutions side by side with governmental bureaucracies. These networks are forms of governance. These networks are seen to be more responsive to the citizenry, in terms of participation and accountability, than the traditional governmental structures although these networks often include governmental structures. In fact, there is evidence that networks are forms of governance that have very enlightening features.[17] Such features are more responsive to social problems that go beyond institutional boundaries set up by specific geographic jurisdictions that are represented by elected officials from that region. Administrative conjunction, the horizontal association of various networked public actors and the resultant administrative behavior of the network,[18] best describes the administrative city-state in urban arenas today. Region-like collaboratives, such as councils of governments, regional transportation, and air quality boards, represent emergent forms of governance that engage in a web of system interaction that, as a whole, act as an urban regime of linked participants of mutual and competing interests. Indeed, R.A. Rhodes may be quite accurate when he states that these networks are "inter-organizational linkages (that) are the defining characteristic of service delivery."[19] How these networks are held accountable, and to whom, are powerful questions within this emerging dynamic of networked public administration. O'Toole reviews the role of bureaucracy and the emergence of networks in relation to the central democratic political norms of responsibility, responsiveness, and enhancement of political deliberation, civility, and trust. He finds that networked public administration

possesses many challenges, yet the lessons of such a status provide "both complications and opportunities to facilitate parts of the democratic ideal."[20] According to Erik-Hans Klijn and Joop F.M. Koppenjan, a central role should be played by government in the management of policy networks. It is their argument, that the government's special resources and unique position can be used to represent the common interests of the public. This vital position means that government needs to play significant roles as network managers that arrange and facilitate interactive processes within communities.[21] The authors defend this network approach to governance based upon the various theoretical foundations of the network approach and the emerging ability of that approach to explain program success and failure based on network determinants, including power, network management, and network structure. It would seem that much of the judgment about the impact of networks, as to how they influence the implementation of public policy, will rest on the nature of each network and how each network is managed.

CONCLUSION

Because policy networks are viewed differently by various authors and disciplines, it will be difficult in the near term to develop a coherent theory of networks. However, the work of Laurence O'Toole provides valuable parameters from which we can begin to address the development of network theory.[4] O'Toole recommends that we explore the causal, conceptual, and descriptive dimensions of networks in order to improve our understanding of their role in public administration in a democratic society. LaPorte[22] also offers three approaches to examining and understanding networks: 1) from within the network (the net rider) or those organizational units that traditionally function within the network system; 2) from above (the net thrower) or those who have a view of the entire network, such as a policy maker; and 3) from the side (the net puller) or entities that view a network not as an integral network participant but one that has cross-cutting interests or influence, such as a professional association or those interested in some form of reform. Each of these perspectives allows for different insights, different research traditions, and addresses different interests of the same network phenomenon. There have also been several advances toward a typology of networks framed mostly from the context of a local government perspective.[7,9,15] Still others have felt that network theory for public administration and public policy is not likely to be advance on its own without considering networks as expressions of collective action.[23] Thus we have several valuable options from which to view policy networks. And, while most of the research on policy networks is focused on how networks and collaboration are quite positive, it is useful to note that networks can also have a dark side.[24] Here the work of Jorg Raab and H. Brinton Milward is instructive: there are ''dark networks'' such as drug cartels, terrorist networks, arms smuggling that require response. Surprisingly or not, these dark networks share the same characteristics as ''positive'' or legal networks. The exception is that these networks rely on secrecy and the use of physical force. The key contribution of this finding is that network analysis is useful not only in examining positive networks, but ''dark'' networks as well. As we examine further the wonderful dimensions of policy networks as forms of governance, we can expect many different research strategies to inform us about how these entities are formed, how they behave, and what impact they will have on our lives.

REFERENCES

1. Cater, D. *Power in Washington*; Random House: New York, 1965.
2. Heclo, H. Issue Networks and the Executive Establishment. In *The New American Political System*; King, A., Ed.; American Enterprise Institute for Public Policy Research: Washington, DC, 1978; 87–124.
3. Ketttl, D.F. *Sharing Power: Public Governance and Private Markets*; Brookings Institution: Washington, DC, 1993.
4. O'Toole, L. Treating networks seriously: Practical and research-based agendas in public administration. Public Adm. Rev. **1997**, *57*, 45–52.
5. Kickert, W.J.M., Klijm, E.H., Koppenjan, J.F.M., Eds.; *Managing Complex Networks: Strategies for the Public Sector*. Sage Publications: London, 1997; xvii.
6. Miller, H.T. Post-progressive public administration: Lessons from policy networks. Public Adm. Rev. **1994**, *54*, 4.
7. Mandell, M.P., Ed. *The Impact of Collaborative Efforts: Changing the Face of Public Policy Through Networks and Networks Structures*. Policy Studies Review: University of Tennessee Energy, Environment & Resources Center, 1999; Vol. 16, 1 p.
8. Powell, W.W. Neither market nor hierarchy: Network forms of organization. Res. Org. Behav. **1990**, *12*, 295–336.
9. Agranoff, R. Multinetwork management: Collaboration and the hollow state in local economic policy. J. Public Adm. Res. Theory **1998**, *8*, 1.
10. Knoke, D. *Political Networks: The Structural Perspective*; Cambridge University Press: New York, 1990.
11. Agranoff, R.; McGuire, M. After the Network is Formed: Process, Power and Performance. In *Getting Results Through Collaboration: Networks and Network Structures for Public Policy and Management*; Mandell, M.P., Ed.; Quorum Books: Westport, CT, 2001; 11–29.
12. McGuire, M. Managing networks: Propositions on what managers do and why they do it. Public Adm. Rev. **2002**, *62* (3), 599–609.
13. Mandell, M.P. Network Management: Strategic Behavior in the Public Sector. In *Strategies for Managing Intergovernmental Policies and Networks*; Gage, R.W., Mandell, M.P., Eds.; Praeger: New York, 1990; 29–53.
14. Agranoff, R. *Leveraging Networks: A Guide for Public Managers Working Across Organizations*; IBM Endowment for The Business of Government: Arlington, VA, March 2003.
15. Provan, K.G.; Briton, M.H. Do networks really work? A framework for evaluating public-sector organizational networks. Public Adm. Rev. **2001**, *61*, 4.
16. Meier, K.J.; O'Toole, L.J., Jr. Public management and educational performance: The impact of managerial networking. Public Adm. Rev. **2003**, *63* (6), 689–699.
17. Meek, J.W.; Schildt, K.; Witt, M. The Future of Local Government Administration. In *Local Government Administration in a Metropolitan Context*; Frederickson, H.G., Ed.; International City/County Management Association: Washington D.C., 2002; 145–154.
18. Peters, G.B. Governance without government? Rethinking public administration. J. Public Adm. Res. Theory **1998**, *8*, 223–243.
19. Rhodes, R.A. Foreword. In *Managing Complex Networks: Strategies for the Public Sector*; Kickert, W.J.M., Klijn, E.-H., Koopenjan, J.F.M., Eds.; Sage: Thousand Oaks, 1997; xii.
20. O'Toole, L. Implications for democracy in a networked bureaucratic world. J. Public Adm. Res. Theory **1997**, *7*, 443–459.
21. Klijn, E.-H.; Koopenjan, J.F.M. Public management and policy networks. Public Manage. **2000**, *2* (2), 135–158.
22. LaPorte, T.R. Shifting vantage and conceptual puzzles in understanding public organization networks. J. Public Adm. Res. Theory **1996**, *6*, 49–74.
23. Carlsson, L. Policy networks as collective action. Policy Stud. J. **2000**, *28* (3), 502–520.
24. Raab, J.H.; Brinton, M. Dark networks as problems. J. Public Adm. Res. Theory **2003**, *13* (4), 413–440.

Postpositivist Perspectives in Policy Analysis

Göktuğ Morçöl
The Pennsylvania State University—Harrisburg, Middletown, Pennsylvania, U.S.A.

INTRODUCTION

Postpositivism is a group of philosophical perspectives that are critical of positivist assumptions and methods. In philosophy and social theory, they emerged in the early- to mid-20th century and, in the policy analysis literature, in the 1980s.

Both positivism and postpositivism are vaguely defined terms. *Positivism* is sometimes used interchangeably with *empiricism*, *behaviorism*, and *naturalism*. Two philosophical movements called themselves positivist: the 19th century French sociologist August Comte coined the term and the Vienna Circle of philosophers of the early 20th century (Rudolp Carnap, Otto Neurath, Moritz Schlick, and others) adopted the name *logical positivist* (or *logical empiricist*). Some critical theorists of the Frankfurt School define positivism more broadly and label Karl Popper and the later writings of Karl Marx positivist.

The philosophical predecessors of postpositivism are the hermeneutic theories of the 19th and 20th centuries. The critiques of positivism by Karl Popper, the critical theorists of the Frankfurt School, and Thomas Kuhn established postpositivism as a philosophical perspective. Postpositivist philosophical arguments are reflected in the policy analysis and evaluation literature in five theory streams: the contextuality and presupposition theories, problem structuring and issue framing theories, the methodological critique, critical hermeneutics, and participatory policy analysis theories.[1]

Weimer[2] and others question the relevancy of postpositivist arguments to policy analysis, because, they think, most of policy-analytic theory and practice is not even positivistic. On the other hand, postpositivists such as Fischer[3] argue that the failures of the positivist policy analytic theory and practice in the 1960s and 1970s led to the surge of the postpositivist critique in the 1980s and that positivism survived despite the critique because it still is professionally, organizationally, and politically expedient. Morçöl[4] found in a survey that positivistic assumptions are prevalent at varying degrees among policy professionals.

ASSUMPTIONS OF POSITIVISM

Although the exact roots and scope of positivism are debatable, a set of assumptions can be identified as its core: a realist and deterministic ontology, an objectivist epistemology, and the belief in a fact-value distinction. Positivists use reductionist and analytical methods and believe in the primacy and superiority of quantitative methods.

Realism is the belief that the world exists independently of and prior to the knowledge of a knowing subject. The logical positivist of the early 20th century as well as August Comte and Karl Marx were realists. Positivist policy analysts assume that policy problems exist independently and can be identified and solved objectively.

Positivists also believe that this independent reality is composed of discrete and precisely identifiable objects whose relations and motions are determined. The notion that the universe is deterministic has a long history; the most recent version, one that undergirds the modern science, was articulated by Francis Bacon, René Descartes, and, most importantly, Isaac Newton in the 17th century. In the Newtonian deterministic universe, the relations between past and future events are fixed. Therefore if a complete knowledge of the past is obtainable, then future events can be predicted precisely. The deterministic worldview is reflected in policy research in the use of the experimental method, which attempts to establish causalities between variables; the forecasting methods that use information about the past to predict future; and the theory and methods of long-term planning.

The notion that the objective knowledge of an independent reality can be acquired is a core positivist assumption. The validity of the acquired knowledge can be verified by checking it empirically against the reality itself. What follows is that factual knowledge—knowledge that has referents in reality and is verifiable—can, and should, be separated from values—inner, subjective preferences of individuals. Positivist policy analysis attempts to keep the respective realms of politics and analysis apart, on the basis of the belief that while values belong to politics, facts should be the domain of analysis.

Encyclopedia of Public Administration and Public Policy
DOI: 10.1081/E-EPAP 120011080

APPLICATIONS OF POSITIVISM IN POLICY ANALYSIS

The reductionist/analytical methodology of positivism builds on the Newtonian scientific notion that objects are discrete and precisely identifiable and their characteristics (weight, length, etc.) can be counted, measured, and compared with one another. It is also assumed that a quantitative form of knowledge is inherently and under all circumstances more scientific and objective than a qualitative form of knowledge. Such assumptions are reflected in the notion that quantitative pieces of information are "hard facts," while qualitative ones are "soft," and in the extensive use of statistics in policy research and policymaking.

The assumption underlying cost–benefit analysis is that costs and benefits of a program or project can be identified objectively and measured. The experimental method is considered the most scientific, primarily in psychology and policy and program evaluation, because it is assumed that experiments can isolate variables and establish deterministic relations (causalities) among them definitively.

POSTPOSITIVIST CRITIQUE IN PHILOSOPHY

The philosophical roots of postpositivism can be traced to hermeneutics. In the most general sense of the term, hermeneutics is the study of meanings in symbolic interactions (speech, written text, rituals, cultural artifacts, etc.). Hermeneutic philosophers follow Wilhelm Dilthey's (1833–1911) distinction between the natural and social sciences: while the natural sciences aim to develop causal explanations of "outer" events, the social sciences are concerned about an "inner" understanding of meaningful human actions; therefore they should use different methods of inquiry.

Hermeneutic philosophers see social phenomena as texts to be interpreted. There are differences among hermeneutic philosophers as to whether there is a "true meaning" of a text, but the position of the German philosopher Hans-Georg Gadamer (1900–2002) is the most typical one. According to Gadamer, the meaning of a text is determined by an interaction between the intentions of the author and the interpretations of the reader, both of which are embedded in their respective particular historical contexts. It is not possible for a reader to know the entire historical context of the authorial intentions and hence the "true meaning" of his/her actions.

The Frankfurt School of critical theorists—Max Horkheimer (1895–1973), Theodor Adorno (1903–1969), Jürgen Habermas (1929–), and others—synthesized hermeneutics with Hegelian philosophy and Marxism. Habermas affirms the hermeneutic distinction between the natural and social sciences and argues that if we attempt to use the methods of the natural sciences in the social sciences, we turn the latter into "social technologies." This instrumentalist use of knowledge in the social sciences cannot be objective; in fact, it is used to perpetuate the social structures of domination. Habermas sees the task of the critical theory as to contribute to an emancipatory knowledge of society.[5]

In his critique of logical positivism, Karl Popper (1902–1994) aimed to show that scientific knowledge could not be positively verified and offered a *falsificationist* alternative: if a hypothesis has not been falsified, it can be accepted only as a tentative truth. Because Popper shared some of the core convictions of logical positivists (e.g., that science offers the most reliable form of knowledge because it is open to empirical testing), the critical theorists Adorno and Habermas characterized his work as an "internal critique" of positivism.[5] However, his demonstration of its weaknesses opened the door to a deeper critique of positivism.

Thomas Kuhn (1922–1996) offered a sweeping critique of the positivist understanding of science in his book *The Structure of Scientific Revolutions* (1962). He argued that scientists work in *paradigms*, belief systems that are "incommensurable." Paradigms are shaped in social and historical contexts. They determine which methods to be used and how the "facts" are "discovered." Therefore the positivist principle of fact-value dichotomy and hence its objectivist epistemology are not sustainable.

POSTPOSITIVISM IN POLICY ANALYSIS

Fischer[3] points out that the social crises and the failures of governmental policies in the United States in the 1960s and 1970s forced a rethinking of the assumptions and methods of the social sciences; those social scientists who were concerned about the role the social sciences played in the ideological manipulation of the poor and disadvantaged groups in the society began to formulate alternatives to positivist, instrumentalist, technocratic, and undemocratic forms of policy analysis. In the following decades, five theory streams emerged that are critical of positivism in general or some aspects of it: contextuality and presupposition theories, problem structuring and issue framing theories, the methodological critique, critical hermeneutics, and participatory policy analysis theories.

The *contextuality and presupposition theorists*, such as M.E. Hawkesworth, make the case that the theory and practice of policy analysis are predominantly positivistic.[6] They also argue that policy-analytic knowledge is presupposed—mediated by analysts' preconceived notions and values—and formed in historical, cultural, and political contexts. With such assertions, this group of theorists provided the general justification for a postpositivist critique of the mainstream policy analysis.

The *problem structuring and issue framing theories* also recognize the contextuality of policy-analytic knowledge and focus particularly on the significance of the way policy problems are structured. William Dunn points out that policy problems are typically ill-structured because they are socially constructed, dynamic, and interdependent.[7] He argues for a conscious, systematic, and continual structuring and restructuring of problems throughout the policy analytic process. Schön and Rein[8] point out that participants in policy processes construct problems through their mental frames in which facts, values, theories, and interests are intertwined. Schön and Rein call for a *frame-critical policy analysis*, in which the role of the analyst would be to understand frame conflicts and help participants reframe to reach policy resolutions.

In their joint and individual works, the late Donald Campbell (1917–1996) and Thomas Cook articulated a *methodological critique* of positivist methods. Campbell argued that positivists failed to recognize the equivocal and ambiguous nature of experimental research and the historical indexicality of the variables used. Cook and Campbell[9] offered quasi-experiments as an alternative to remedy the shortcomings of the experimental method. Cook[10] recognized the inability of positivistic methods to generate objective and precise knowledge by arguing for a *critical multiplist* methodology that would be anchored in realist ontology, but it would also use multiple methods, multivariate causal models, and multiple theoretical frameworks.

Hajer[11] and Fischer[3,12] represent the *critical hermeneutic* perspective in postpositivism. In his discourse analyses, Hajer shows that knowledge and power are articulated through discourse and human actors engage in struggles for discursive hegemony in policy processes. The influence of Habermas' critical theory can be seen most clearly in Fischer's works. He is critical of the instrumentalist and technocratic uses of the policy-analytic knowledge by analysts and policymakers because such uses support undemocratic practices. He proposes a participatory policymaking process, with the involvement of multiplicity of actors and interests. He emphasizes that the policy-analytic knowledge should also be transformational and emancipatory.

Participatory policy analysis has other proponents as well, although they do not necessarily come from a critical hermeneutic perspective. Kelly and Maynard-Moody,[13] for example, suggest that policy stakeholders should be involved in framing research questions and selecting the methods of inquiry. The task of an analyst should be to facilitate rational deliberations, help policymakers and citizens understand the limitations of their perspectives,

and synthesize multiple perspectives. Since the early 1990s, there is a growing literature on the use of participatory methods in the policy process—stakeholder analysis, Q-methodology, citizen panels, Internet-facilitated dialogue and analysis, and the like—in the leading journals of the field, such as *Policy Studies Journal*, *Policy Studies Review*, and the *Journal of Policy Analysis and Management*.

CONCLUSION

Postpositivists are not unified in their critique of or alternatives to positivism, but, in general, they emphasize the historical, social, and political contextuality of the policy-analytic knowledge, argue and demonstrate that facts and values are intertwined in the policy process, call for an understanding of the discursive nature of policy-making, expose the power relations in the policy process, and call for a more democratic and participatory policy process in which analysts would play a facilitative role.

There is another theory stream that shares some of the assumptions and aspirations of postpositivism: postmodernism/poststructuralism. *Postmodernist/poststructuralist* theories also have their roots in hermeneutics. Because of this commonality in philosophical roots and the vagueness in the uses of the terms postpositivism and postmodernism/poststructuralism, it is not easy to draw clear demarcations between the two. Fischer offers a distinction: while postpositivists see a chance of establishing a common basis for a valid discourse, truthfulness of interpretations, among different perspectives, postmodernists do not.[3]

Postmodernists/poststructuralists deny any "epistemological privilege" to any interpretation over another. In the works of Ferdinand De Saussure and Jacques Derrida, language is defined as a closed, self-referential system. As such, language does not have any reference to an "external reality"; therefore there is no basis for establishing truthfulness in knowledge. Poststructuralists use the method of deconstruction to demystify texts by revealing the arbitrary hierarchies and power bases in the seemingly rational and scientific discourses. They aim to delegitimize the socially constructed bases of authority and level the playing field for alternative, underprivileged discourses.

Schram's[14,15] works are examples of the postmodernist/poststructuralist approach in policy studies. He aims to expose the power relations embedded in the public policy process. Schram denies any "epistemological privilege" to social scientists and policy analysts in the analytical process and argues that the policy analysis practice should be abandoned and policy analysts and academics should join the political struggle for social change.

Postpositivism and postmodernism/poststructuralism are open-ended projects. What direction each will take and whether they will merge into a larger stream remain to be seen.

REFERENCES

1. Morçöl, G. *A New Mind for Policy Analysis: Toward a Post-Newtonian and Postpositivist Epistemology and Methodology*; Praeger: Westport, CT, 2002.
2. Weimer, D.L. Comment: Q-method and the isms. J. Policy Anal. Manag. **1999**, *18* (3), 426–429.
3. Fischer, F. *Evaluating Public Policy*; Nelson-Hall Publishers: Chicago, 1995.
4. Morçöl, G. Positivist beliefs among policy professionals: An empirical investigation. Policy Sci. **2001**, *34* (3–4), 381–401.
5. Giddens, A. *Politics, Sociology and Social Theory*; Stanford University Press: Stanford, CA, 1995.
6. Hawkesworth, M.E. *Theoretical Issues in Policy Analysis*; State University of New York Press: Albany, NY, 1988.
7. Dunn, W.N. *Public Policy Analysis: An Introduction,* 2nd Ed.; Prentice Hall: Englewood Cliffs, NJ, 1994.
8. Schön, D.A.; Rein, M. *Frame Reflection*; Basic Books: New York, 1994.
9. Cook, T.D.; Campbell, D.T. *Quasi-Experimentation: Design & Analysis Issues for Field Settings*; Houghton Mifflin: Boston, 1979.
10. Cook, T.D. Postpositivist Critical Multiplism. In *Social Science and Social Policy*; Shotland, R.L., Mark, M.M., Eds.; Sage: Beverly Hills, CA, 1985.
11. Hajer, M.A. *The Politics of Environmental Discourse: Ecological Modernization and the Policy Process*; Oxford University Press: Oxford, UK, 1995.
12. Fischer, F. *Technocracy and the Politics of Expertise*; Sage: Newbury Park, CA, 1990.
13. Kelly, M.; Maynard-Moody, S. Policy analysis in the postpositivist era: Engaging stakeholders in evaluating the economic development districts program. Public Adm. Rev. **1993**, *53*, 135–142.
14. Schram, S.F. Postmodern policy analysis: Discourse and identity in welfare policy. Policy Sci. **1993**, *26*, 249–270.
15. Schram, S.F. Against policy analysis: Critical reason and poststructural resistance [Book review essay]. Policy Sci. **1995**, *28*, 375–384.

Privatization

Marc Holzer
Rutgers, The State University of New Jersey, Newark, New Jersey, U.S.A.

Hwang-Sun Kang
Seoul Development Institute, Seoul, Republic of Korea

INTRODUCTION

The privatization movement in the public sector was accelerated by the New Conservatism under the Reagan and Thatcher administrations. Basically, new conservatists value economic and political liberalism that have emphasized free competition of market system. Under liberalism, small government and small tax are preferred. According to them, welfare state imposes so much tax and regulation on free-market mechanism as to distort the free flow of capital. Thus welfare state (big government) cannot but be faced with economic stagflation under which economic depression and inflation simultaneously occur. In addition to this basic belief of liberalism, new conservativists do not neglect the weak points of market mechanism. Thus they emphasize not only free-market system but also the inevitability of government intervention. In this context, new conservativists argue for ''small but strong'' government rather than simply ''minimal government.''

The privatization movement began from this reflection on the problem of welfare state. The rationale for privatization is government failure that public choice has criticized. According to public choice theorists, decision making in government is not made based on the principle of rationality; rather, most decisions are made by political bargain. In the political bargain process, many interest groups, politicians, and business groups are involved. And public policies produced by the process are implemented by big government. Public choice theorists consider government bureaucrats as self-interest seekers just like other business groups. As business groups pursue profit-maximization, government bureaucrats, according to public choice theorists, do ''budget maximization.''[1,2] As a result, interest groups, politicians, business groups, and government bureaucrats establish a ''budget-spending coalition.''[3] Public services provided by the budget-spending coalition cannot but be inefficient.

DEFINITION OF PRIVATIZATION

Strictly speaking, privatization means that government sells its property rights to state-owned institutions to the private sector. For example, currently government-owned companies are being sold to private companies. Thus many services that were once provided by government are now being provided by private companies. Even international companies can buy other countries' public companies.

In a broad sense, transition of government function can be included in privatization. For instance, government can make a contract with private companies in order to enable the companies to provide public services in lieu of government.

FORMS OF PRIVATIZATION

There are several forms of privatization. Here, four representative forms of privatization are discussed based on the Savas' classification: contracting out, voucher, franchising, and sale.[4]

Contracting Out

Government can delegate authority of a public service to a company via a competitive bid during a limited period. Through contracting out, government can provide better services with less cost because of competitive bids between private companies. Some state governments are using contracting-out strategy in order to stimulate public employees. Public employees can see that their jobs may be privatized unless performances of their organizations are satisfactory. When a government contracts out a service with a company, it should pay much attention to whether the company can sustain good quality of service after the service is contracted out. And government should check whether the company persistently holds to its responsibility to the citizens. Most of all, government should provide fair conditions for many private companies that are participating in a competitive bid.

Possible services that can be contracted out include public car maintenance, public hospital services, garbage collection, security services, and management of public facilities such as library, cafeteria, and other professional facilities. According to Savas' report, the average American city contracts out 23% of its 64 common municipal

Encyclopedia of Public Administration and Public Policy
DOI: 10.1081/E-EPAP 120010912

services to the private sector. The average American state contracts out 14% of its activities.[4]

Voucher

There are many limitations to a government's ability to take care of a citizen's specific demand. For instance, recipients of welfare services need very specific and various cares. By giving a voucher, government allows citizens who need a specific service to choose the service that meets their needs.

In this system, government should pay much attention to whether private companies can fairly compete with each other in the voucher market. Possible services for the voucher method include food, housing, education, health care, transportation, and other social services.

Franchising

Through franchising, government can award a company specific authority to provide a service for a limited period. A company, for example, can build a public parking lot and manage it in a public land. And the company should pay government a fee. Usually, building infrastructures is a great burden to governments. Through franchising, government can take advantage of private capital and provide better service for citizens with no great financial pressure.

Sale

Government can sell a public facility to a company. Of late, some governments have sold public-owned companies to private companies. In the globalization age, some international companies can purchase other countries' public companies.

In addition to those four methods, there are other methods of privatizations. Table 1 shows various methods of privatization based on Savas' study.[4]

EFFECTS OF PRIVATIZATION

In general, there are two advantages in the privatization of public services. First, privatization contributes to enhancing efficiency of government management. By transferring a portion of government function that the private sector can undertake, government is able to reduce its total size. By making government small, the private sector can play a bigger role in the total national economy. Thus privatization is known to relieve financial deficit in government. In fact, the privatization movement in America is closely related to the financial crisis of the public sector in the 1970s.

Second, privatization can give multiple choices to citizens choosing public services. Government loses its monopolistic authority in providing public services and has to compete with the private sector.

WEAKNESS OF PRIVATIZATION

The ideology of privatization is efficiency of government management. It is true that privatization has contributed to increasing the total efficiency (economic efficiency) of government management. However, it should be noted that privatization should be implemented under fair competition between private companies. In the same context, a certain class of people should not be excluded from the benefits of privatization. This is the issue of social equity.

Although the privatization of government function is widely preferred, it does not necessarily mean that

Table 1 Institutional arrangements for providing public services

Service arrangement	Arranger	Producer	Who pays?
Government service	Government	Government	Government
Government vending	Consumer	Government	Consumer
Intergovernmental agreements	Government[1,2]	Government[3]	Government[1,2]
Contracts	Government	Private sector	Government
Franchises (exclusive)	Government	Private sector	Consumer
Franchise (multiple)	Government and consumer	Private sector	Government and consumer
Grants	Government and consumer	Private sector	Government and consumer
Vouchers	Consumer	Private sector	Government and consumer
Free market	Consumer	Private sector	Consumer
Voluntary service	Voluntary association	Voluntary association	N.A.
Voluntary service with contract	Voluntary association	Private sector	Voluntary association
Self-service	Consumer	Consumer	N.A.

Source: From Ref. [4].

minimal state is the best form of modern government. In other words, privatization is not equated with "small government." Even in privatization periods, citizens still want government to do more work for them. Thus just as big government brings some problems, a big private sector will also bring some more problems. Stable development of modern societies would be possible in the status of equilibrium between the private and the public sectors.[5,6]

CRITERIA OF PRIVATIZATION

Before a public service is privatized, there are several points to be considered.

First, what is the original goal of the service that is going to be privatized? All public services have their targeted goals and recipients. If the services were provided by the private sector, would those original goals be maintained?

Second, should government really be responsible for the service? As it is well discussed by many scholars, the issue of responsibility is a very important point to be considered prior to privatization of public services.

Third, is the privatization policy of a country compatible with the societal needs and national goals of the country? It should be noted that privatization movement followed reconsideration of a welfare state in America and Britain. In other words, those developed countries already have a well-established welfare system. On the contrary, citizens in other developing and underdeveloped countries still need more extensive public services from government.

CONCLUSION

The core of privatization strategy is to imbue the public sector with competition and innovation mind. Transfer of property rights and government function from the pubic sector to the private sector has been a prevalent effort to institutionalize competition and innovation mind in the public sector.

Fundamentally, management strategy of public organizations should not be the same as that of private organizations because those two organizations have different organizational goals: profit maximization and pursuit of public interest. Considering the weaknesses of privatization, it would be more desirable to find more strategies to sustain competition and innovation mind along with the privatization forms mentioned above.

REFERENCES

1. Niskanen, W. *Bureaucracy and Representative Government*; Adline Publishing Company: Illinois, 1971.
2. Downs, A. *An Economics Theory of Democracy*; Harper & Row: New York, 1971.
3. Zahariadis, N. *Markets, States, and Public Policy; Privatization in Britain and France*; University of Michigan Press: Michigan, 1997.
4. Savas, E. *Privatization and Public–Private Partnership*; Chatham House Publishers: New York, 2000.
5. Mintzberg, H. Managing government management. Harvard Bus. Rev. **1996**, *74* (3), 75–83.
6. Nye, J. *Why People Don't Trust Government*; Harvard University Press: Massachusetts, 1998.

Public–Private Partnerships in Developing Countries

Steven G. Koven
Stuart C. Strother
University of Louisville, Louisville, Kentucky, U.S.A.

INTRODUCTION

In recent years, developing countries have been embracing innovative methods of service delivery including privatization, quasi-private arrangements, and public–private partnerships. Over time, officials in these nations have come to realize that government initiatives alone cannot properly address the enormous economic and social challenges that they confront. The needs of developing countries are truly vast and are beginning to be addressed through various combinations of partnerships between philanthropic organizations, nongovernment organizations, corporations, community-based organizations, and government entities.

Partnerships exist in developing countries for an array of activities including health care, transportation, energy policy, technology development, protecting the environment, making agriculture more productive, generating revenue from tourism, and many more activities. These partnerships offer the promise of generating profits for private companies, increasing government revenue, and improving the lives of people who often do not have access to safe water, electricity, or all-season roads.

Leaders in developing countries have come to recognize that government alone has failed to meet developmental goals. In turn, these leaders have begun to look at innovative partnership types in an effort to improve the living conditions of their constituents. This encyclopedia entry will describe why delivery systems such as privatization have grown in popularity, the decline of statist thinking, constraints on effective public–private partnering, and examples of successful partnerships.

WHY PRIVATIZE?

The movement away from monopolistic, government provision of goods and services has steadily advanced since the latter half of the 20th century. Numerous economic and social reasons have been presented to explain events such as the collapse of Soviet as well as Eastern European communism after 1989, the rise of leaders such as Margaret Thatcher in Britain and Ronald Reagan in the United States, and the renewed acceptance of neoclassical economics in developing countries.

Savas[1] identified five factors that have propelled the rise of privatization throughout the world. These factors include the impact of 1) pragmatic forces, 2) economic forces, 3) ideological forces, 4) commercial forces, and 5) populist forces. According to Savas, pragmatic forces promote privatization because there exists a need to continuously provide services to constituents in environments of rising costs and resistance to higher taxes. It is believed that privatization can assuage these pressures by enhancing productivity, reducing waste, and promoting efficiency. Productivity may be enhanced in a variety of manners. In instances where government-owned enterprises are dominant, they can be forced to compete with private companies. Competition between public and private entities can transpire for government contracts or for satisfying consumer desires. Economic forces that promote privatization relate to a growing affluence in some parts of the world and affluence's corollary of less dependence on government. For example, if more people own their own automobiles, there will be less reliance on public transportation.

Ideologically, some political theorists see an expanding government sector as a threat to freedom and liberty. This threat to individuals has been well documented historically. Nations such as Germany (during the Nazi regime of Adolf Hitler) and Russia (after the 1917 Bolshevik revolution) witnessed the growth of massive state entities that exercised almost total control over the lives of individuals. It is therefore not surprising that individuals living in pluralistic societies are wary about ceding power to impersonal government institutions. People in developing countries have often found themselves in situations where their individual rights were subsumed to a collective ideal that was defined by the state. Seizure of private property often preceded tight, central control over the economy, an economic paradigm that recently has been discredited.

Countries with large nationalized interests may also be pressured by business leaders to provide more business opportunities to private citizens (commercial forces). Savas[2] noted that much of the work performed by government consists of routine commercial activities such

Encyclopedia of Public Administration and Public Policy
DOI: 10.1081/E-EPAP-120039554

as maintenance of buildings, grounds, vehicles, and ships, data processing, collecting trash, and repairing streets. Business groups advocate the privatization of more of these activities to taxpaying, private companies. They claim that these services can be provided more efficiently and effectively if competition was permitted in contracting for services. Another segment of the private sector identifies business opportunities in financing, building, or operating large government projects, such as roads, bridges, airports, and waste-to-energy plants. In countries where nationalized industries exist, commercial pressure comes from business leaders who believe that the nationalized industries are mismanaged, slothful, and overtly underutilize existing assets. In such cases, denationalization (a particular form of privatization) is advocated. Denationalization presents the potential for innovation, whereas continued stagnation seems likely if nationalized industries remain protected from market forces. A lack of competition and protection of nationalized industries is viewed as counterproductive to innovation. State-owned enterprises or nationalized industries include a variety of enterprises such as manufacturing, mining, oil production, and transportation.

Finally, populist forces are believed to promote privatization based on widespread popular antipathy to the ideal of "big government." According to this viewpoint, government systems have become too institutionalized, too bureaucratized, too professionalized, and too protective of their own interest. Populist forces (common views of average citizens) advocate greater choice in public services, less reliance on cumbersome bureaucracies, and greater use of neighborhood, civic, church, and voluntary associations. Populist sentiment is believed to exist among citizens who are fearful of both big government and big business. These individuals find allies among advocates of family values and communitarians.

Other reasons to privatize are cited in the literature. Brinkerhoff[3] contends that enhancing efficiency and effectiveness represents just one of a number of reasons to privatize. In addition to improving efficiency/effectiveness, public–private partnerships can also provide more integrated solutions to problems, improve outcomes for stakeholders, and promote a broader conception of the public good. More integrated solutions and improved outcomes are likely to arise when diverse actors cooperate with each other, with diverse actors free to present their own perspective. Expertise and relationships are also enhanced with greater cooperation. For example, multinational corporations and national government agencies often partner with local health agencies to learn more about decentralized/local health-care needs. In partnerships, local agencies often gain access to more capital, which, in turn, is used to address their problems. Creativity may emerge as diverse actors come together to address specific issues.

Partnerships can also create a broader understanding of the public good. Through such an understanding, sustainable benefits can be created. Social capital can be created in public partnerships, and this capital can be applied to other issues. For example, the U.S. Agency for International Development found that social capital could be developed and could facilitate continued relationships between donor and recipient organizations. This would foster support for long-term cooperation on issues of common concern.

DECLINE OF STATIST THINKING

It is no coincidence that the ascendancy of privatization thinking has coincided with a decline in "statist" ideology.[4] Critics of countries characterized by "extreme statist experiments" (such as Cuba, Ethiopia, Mozambique, Vietnam, Laos, Cambodia, Burma, North Korea, and China) cite numerous reasons for the collapse of centrally planned societies. First, the assumption of self-centered behavior (looking out to maximize one's well being) is now recognized as applicable to both the public and private spheres. In statist societies, self-interest manifests itself in widespread corruption. Government officials use the pursuit of the common good and their ability to interpret the common good as a means to satisfy materialistic/individualistic desires. In the extreme, the selfless pursuit of common goals becomes a facade that masks individual self-interest. In contrast to classical economic thought, individual self-interest does not produce market competition/efficiency but allows public officials to extract personal rewards on the basis of their privileged government positions. Second, it is believed that "statism" fails to deal with the issue of incentives. Market incentives that imposed discipline on private sector managers and encouraged efficient production were simply not provided by the state. Third, building large-scale production units in urban areas of planned economies was detrimental to rural dwellers. Developing such units harmed those in rural areas and enriched only a small minority. Fourth, central planning neglected the question of quality. For example, Soviet oil fields were notorious for the amount of oil lost or wasted in production because Soviet managers were concerned with increasing output and not with making extraction less costly. Typically, managers in the Soviet Union were reluctant to develop new products for fear that production would temporarily lag. The private sector consumer-based market is more effective in promoting quality because profits are linked to a company's ability to attract customers. These customers are attracted on the basis of improved quality or reduced cost.[5]

Inefficient state-run farms were commonly associated with statist countries. Analysts claim that state entities consumed resources that would have better uses in other areas. For example, research has found that in developing countries where labor is abundant, small household farms are more cost-effective than large mechanized farms.[6] In some nations such as Cuba, the cost of agricultural workers was found to be greater than the value of the sugar they produced. Empirical data indicate that the consequences of collectivization were not positive. In many developing nations, real per capita incomes were lower at the end of the 20th century than they were when the nations achieved independence from their colonial rulers.[7]

Caustic criticism of the performance of statist regimes began to appear in the academic literature around the mid-1960s. By 1970, the Organization for Economic Cooperation and Development (OECD) published a study critical of state-centered import substitution industrialization (ISI) strategies that were prevalent in developing nations such as Argentina, Brazil, Mexico, India, Pakistan, the Philippines, and Taiwan. Soon after, the World Bank, in conjunction with the Inter-American Development Bank, published a study supporting the OECD's findings.

In 1983, the U.S. National Bureau of Economic Research (NBER) issued a report advocating export-oriented industrialization in contrast to import substitution characteristic of ISI-based regimes. According to the NBER, import substitution regimes were clearly less successful than regimes that focused on export-oriented industrialization. After adopting a market-based export model, some nations (particularly the Four Little Tigers or Dragons of East Asia: Hong Kong, Taiwan, Singapore, and South Korea) became models of efficiency, innovation, and prosperity. In per capita terms, these nations were the world's fastest growing in the latter decades of the 20th century.[7] Few now dispute the NBER study's assertion that nations adopting export-based policies have performed better than nations adopting import substitution. The NBER study was so widely accepted that some began to call it the core of the neoclassical critique of statism.[8]

As neoclassical economics regained acceptance, developing nations sought to forge partnerships with private sector companies in the developed world. In direct contrast to the prescriptions advanced in the ISI model (such as limiting imports of finished goods from developed countries and trade between poor countries), the neoclassical paradigm advocated trading between rich and poor nations.[8] This model was embraced by economists who proclaimed that there was no need to articulate an economics for development because the market offered the best mechanism for poor countries to develop. Leaders of developing countries, however, still confronted numerous impediments to economic advancement.

CONSTRAINTS TO PARTNERING IN DEVELOPING COUNTRIES

An array of factors clearly influences the feasibility of creating partnerships in developing countries. Two factors that impinge on the ability to create partnerships relate to governance and institutional capacity.[9] Governance in the form of laws, decrees, policies, actions, and regulations can encourage or discourage potential arrangements between public and private sector actors. Laws or decrees that inhibit profit-making, prohibit currency transfers, or limit market-based actions are likely to produce hostile environments for public–private partnerships. Governance factors considered hostile to partnerships include an absence of the rule of law principle, widespread corruption, and minimal access to policymakers. Legal impediments include overly burdensome administrative and financial requirements on potential partners. In the extreme, existing laws may outlaw the possibility of specific types of partnerships. Access to government decision makers and inefficient bureaucracies may be a source of concern. Finally, low levels of institutional capacity (witnessed in low levels of legitimacy and inexperience of major actors) can inhibit partnership creation.

Political risk also discourages investment. Five components of political risk have been identified in the literature. These risks include the danger of 1) violence or war, 2) currency restrictions, 3) contract interference, 4) expropriation, and 5) unfair regulatory environments.[10] Violence from civil war, insurrection, and coups clearly has a deleterious impact on partnership investments. Violence often coincides with property destruction, theft, arson, and an inability to attract dependable workers. Developing countries such as Sri Lanka, Pakistan, India, Algeria, Liberia, Rwanda, and others have been plagued by large-scale violence.

Government policies restricting the ability of foreign investors to convert local currency into their home currency also constrain partnership development. Flows of funds from host states can be entirely blocked by local/host country restrictions. Such restrictive policies will severely reduce the likelihood of foreign investment. Investors find no compelling reason to risk their capital unless they can convert future profits to the currency of their home country. In some instances, foreign-exchange brokers are licensed by the host government to handle foreign exchange.

Major international events may lead to repudiation of contracts between parties. For example, the U.S.-imposed embargo against Iraq caused the cancellation of some contracts between the previous government of Iraq and some European companies. Fears of expropriation (the government confiscation of property) represent another risk. Notable examples of expropriation of assets include the takeover of foreign property by the Castro regime following the Cuban revolution, the nationalization of foreign copper companies by the Chilean government, and the seizing of French assets by Tunisia following their independence in 1954. Finally, unfair regulatory treatment may inhibit investment. Unfair treatment includes government policies such as discriminatory tax treatment (taxes favoring the host's domestic firms), limits on access to materials needed for production, and limitations of access to local distribution systems. Private sector investors have an interest in clarifying these issues prior to making monetary commitments to enterprises in foreign nations. Whereas numerous constraints exist, there have been notable examples of successful public–private partnerships in developing nations.

EXAMPLES OF PUBLIC–PRIVATE PARTNERSHIPS IN DEVELOPING COUNTRIES

Innovative public–private partnerships have been created in both Africa and Asia. For example, in Africa, there is evidence that government officials have leveraged their niche as a center for tourism, particularly in regard to their notoriety in "big game" hunting.[11] In various African public–private ventures, contractual arrangements are formed between a community or local institution and a private investor. These parties work together in establishing and/or operating tourism or hunting enterprises. Both the community/local institution and the private investor have rights and responsibilities under the contractual agreement. Two common forms of partnership include 1) establishment of tourism lodges and 2) leasing of hunting quotas. In the case of tourism lodges, communities either have an equity stake or receive payments from lodge operators. In the case of the sale of hunting quotas, bids are taken, and the income from the sales is either distributed to residents in the area where the hunting takes place or is used for community projects.

Both lodge construction and quota agreements have grown in popularity as rights over wildlife have devolved from the central government to the local community level. Numerous cash-starved communities in Africa view tourism as an opportunity for local economic development. Private investors have identified African tourism for its profit potential. This confluence of interests led to the creation of joint ventures between public sector officials and private investors. Specific examples of tourism joint ventures include the sale of hunting quotas in Zimbabwe, the lease of large blocks of land around game reserve in Botswana, and the tripartite agreements in South Africa between public sector conservation departments, private

investors, and tribal authorities. The sale of rights to engage in trophy hunting (especially for the big five of lions, leopards, elephants, rhinos, and buffaloes) is viewed as a potential source of revenue. Attention to sustainability and mutuality of interest is thought to be essential to the development of successful joint ventures. Written agreements and contract are important in developing the shared vision.

Another case of public–private partnership is the development of a partnership between government officials and private sector shippers to upgrade efficiency in the South Korean port city of Pusan.[12] In the early 1990s, this was identified as a high priority of the South Korean government. The need for improved efficiency was evident to South Korean officials who were influenced by the fact that ports in general handled approximately 99.7% of Korea's trade, and the Pusan port handled about 90% of port trade. In 1998, the Pusan port was ranked as the fifth largest container port in the world.

South Korean officials focused on improving the flow of information, reducing the burden of government regulation, and shortening delays in unloading cargo. Prior to the 1990s, an estimated 50–150 documents were needed for delivering and unloading cargo. As a result of this and other factors, Pusan suffered from a perception of poor service. To improve the performance of the Pusan port, government officials concluded that better information was needed in regard to equipment availability (especially cranes and tractors for unloading), cargo losses/damages, and the availability of cargo pickup times. Each of these factors was dependent on accurate and timely flows of vital information.

To address the problem of poor service, the Korean government acquired state-of-the-art computer hardware and software between 1989 and 1990. This equipment was used in the creation of a new electronic information system termed electronic development interchange (EDI). Training of port workers for the system was instituted, and studies of the new system were conducted. In 1996, the new system was fully implemented by administrative fiat. Use of the new electronic system became mandatory among all private sector port users. Once it became clear that the Korean government had mandated participation, the private sector cooperated in the establishment of a public–private entity, the Korea Logistics Network Corporation (KL-Net). This company attracted investment from companies such as Hyundai Merchant Marine, Global Corporation, and others. By virtue of their investment, the private corporations became fully involved in KL-Net operations.

In this case, the government sector was a major initiator of the public–private partnership. The public sector invested in the creation of an EDI system, they used the coercive power of the state to guarantee use, and they received private sector contributions to run the system. From the perspective of improving port performance, the partnership is viewed as a great success and a model for others in developing countries.[12]

CONCLUSION

The repudiation of the centrally controlled economic system suggests that public–private partnerships will play an enhanced role in the economies of developing nations. These partnerships can be created as a consequence of state intervention (such as the case with the Pusan port) or more localized decision making such as the case of tourism in Africa. Whereas centralized economies such as those found in the former Soviet Union and Eastern Europe have been renounced, it is also doubtful that the 19th century style capitalism can be reintroduced. Given these parameters, it is likely that public and private sector officials will seek out cooperative arrangements as the mutuality of benefits becomes evident.

REFERENCES

1. Savas, E.S. *Privatization and Public–Private Partnerships*; Seven Bridges Press, LLC: New York, 2000; 5–14.
2. Savas, E.S. *Privatization and Public–Private Partnerships*; Seven Bridges Press, LLC: New York, 2000; 12–13.
3. Brinkerhoff, J.M. *Partnership for International Development: Rhetoric or Results?*; Lynne Rienner: Boulder, CO, 2002; 6.
4. Rapley, J. *Understanding Development: Theory and Practice in the Third World*; Lynne Rienner: Boulder, CO, 2002.
5. Rapley, J. *Understanding Development: Theory and Practice in the Third World*; Lynne Rienner: Boulder, CO, 2002; 42.
6. Young, C. *Ideology and Development in Africa*; Yale University Press: New Haven, 1982; 155.
7. Rapley, J. *Understanding Development: Theory and Practice in the Third World*; Lynne Rienner: Boulder, CO, 2002; 46.
8. Rapley, J. *Understanding Development: Theory and Practice in the Third World*; Lynne Rienner: Boulder, CO, 2002; 58.
9. Brinkerhoff, J.M. *Partnership for International Development: Rhetoric or Results?*; Lynne Rienner: Boulder, CO, 2002; 26.
10. Baker, J.C. *Foreign Direct Investment in Less Developed Countries: The Role of ICSID and MIGA*; Quorum Books: Westport, CT, 1999; 13–14.
11. Ashley, C.; Jones, B. Joint ventures between communities and tourism investors: Experience from southern Africa. Int. J. Tour. Res. **2001**, *3*, 407–423.
12. Bagchi, P.I.; Paik, S.K. The role of public–private-partnership in port information systems development. Int. J. Public Sect. Manag. **2001**, *14* (6/7), 482–500.

Public–Private Partnerships for Economic Development

Steven G. Koven
Stuart C. Strother
University of Louisville, Louisville, Kentucky, U.S.A.

INTRODUCTION

A public–private partnership is a formal complementary relationship between public and private entities to achieve a common objective. The formal partnership arrangement delineates each partner's roles and responsibilities, states the level of investment and risk of each partner, and describes how financial and nonfinancial benefits will be distributed between the partners. Although partnerships represent government "power sharing," they also entail "risk shifting" from government to the private sector. The basic purpose of partnering is "to take advantage of the potential for all parties to gain greater benefit than they could on their own." When public–private partnerships are created, the overall objective of the partnership is usually to increase jobs, to enhance the numbers of employers in a region, or to revitalize the physical assets of an urban area. This encyclopedia entry delineates various public strategies to achieve growth, privatization models, and future directions of public–private partnerships.

PUBLIC–PRIVATE STRATEGIES TO ACHIEVE GROWTH

State and local public actors enter into partnerships with private organizations to accomplish the objective of economic growth.[1] Some of the most common objectives of an economic development public–private partnership are to improve the general image of an area and to improve an area's business climate.[2]

Some public–private partnerships are specifically designed to market their area to outside firms. Surveys indicate that about 40% of U.S. cities engage in marketing their cities, and about 21% of cities partner with private economic development foundations. Private foundations typically engage in activities such as developing promotional materials, establishing Web sites, advertising in the media, hosting special events, and sponsoring trade missions abroad.[3]

Various strategies are utilized to improve the business climate of an area. In general, these strategies can be placed into categories of: 1) providing direct financial incentives; 2) improving the tax environment; and 3) providing nonfinancial incentives.[4] Each of these strategies involves some type of partnership and agreement between governmental entities and representatives of the private sector. These strategies are reviewed below.

Financial Incentives

Common financial incentives provided by government entities to the private sector include grants and loans. Grants have been a part of American history since its founding. Land grants to railroads and homesteading helped open up the nation's west. The Morrill Act of 1862 subsidized schools that offered instruction in agricultural and mechanical arts. Contemporary examples of federal grant programs include funding for urban renewal, small businesses, community development, and urban development. A federal government agency involved in providing grants to private entities is the Economic Development Administration (EDA). Initially, EDA programs were targeted to depressed rural communities. After the mid-1970s, programs were increasingly directed to urban areas. Public works grants, business loans, technical assistance grants, and grants to assist communities affected by economic dislocations are programs administered by EDA. Communities adept at marketing their needs were more likely than others to gain access to these federal programs.

Public entities provide loans for the private sector. The federal EDA provides loans under a Business Development Loan program. States provide loans to enterprises that promise to enhance economic development. These loans are often targeted for specific purposes. For example, the state of New Jersey targeted loans to firms that promise to locate in low-income/high-unemployment areas. Pennsylvania targeted a proportion of its loans to firms that deal with advanced technology. Alaska and Hawaii offer loans to owners of fishing vessels who are unable to secure conventional financing. Ohio gave priority for loans to businesses already operating in the state.

Public loan programs carry the risk of default and financial loss to taxpayers. This risk is assumed by the public sector in efforts to spur economic growth. Usually,

Encyclopedia of Public Administration and Public Policy
DOI: 10.1081/E-EPAP-120025971

state or local departments of economic development or industrial development authorities make direct loans. Revolving loan funds recycle payments of outstanding loans to other businesses. In theory, once a revolving loan fund is established, it exists in perpetuity and is self-financing as long as default rates as well as administrative costs are relatively low. Loans are often made by community development loan funds at below-market interest rates to help entrepreneurs start new businesses.

Tax Environment

Tax incentives are often offered to businesses in hopes of attracting major employers or retaining existing firms. Typical incentives offered to businesses include tax abatements, tax exemptions, tax credits, and tax increment financing.

Tax abatements are legal agreements between a government entity and a property owner to forgo taxing some share of assessed real estate value for a given period of time. It is expected that when the abatement period expires, rates will be reapplied, tax revenues will increase, and tax base will be strengthened. Tax abatements are the most popular type of tax incentive. They are often used to encourage economic development in depressed or blighted areas. Tax exemptions refer to reductions in the base upon which taxes are calculated. Businesses may be granted exemptions on corporate income taxes, commodities such as fuel, inventories, land, capital improvements, and equipment. Tax credits directly reduce tax obligations. They are more desirable than tax abatements and tax exemptions because they produce a dollar for dollar reduction in the amount of taxes one pays. Tax credits are often granted for activities (such as investment in new plant and equipment) that will produce long-term benefits for the jurisdiction.

Tax increment financing allows jurisdictions to borrow funds and earmarks increased tax revenues (attributable to improvements made with the borrowed funds) to repay debt. When bonds are fully paid, a tax increment finance district can be dissolved, and the full share of the tax increase is assigned to a jurisdiction's general revenue fund. Proponents of tax increment financing cite the facts that it does not incur out-of-pocket expenses, it does not obligate jurisdictions to raise taxes, and it does not place added obligations on property owners who reside outside the tax increment district. Critics of tax increment financing claim that it bypasses voter approval, it increases the need for essential services that must be paid by citizens living outside the increment district, it is more expensive than general obligation debt, and it subsidizes development that would have been undertaken in the absence of government assistance.

Nonfinancial Incentives

Site development, enterprise zones, and human resource development represent nonfinancial public activities that assist in attracting private development. These activities are not cost-free and are justified in the name of economic development.

State and local governments acquire and improve sites for industrial and commercial use. The object of site development is to attract private firms by offering land at a reduced cost. Capital improvements are often made to land in terms of water and sewer lines, landscaping, lighting, gutters, and curbs. The land is then sold to developers below cost. Jurisdictions provide catalogs of available industrial sites or build infrastructure to suit the needs of the private firm.

Jurisdictions often engage in land banking or the practice of acquiring and improving contiguous parcels of land suitable for development. To construct a land bank, public officials search for underused, underdeveloped, and/or misused properties. Officials catalog properties by size and location, keeping the information up to date for quick reference. Land banking usually requires a substantial amount of funds for purchases. Potential sources of funds include surtaxes on local real estate and the sale of bonds.

Enterprise zones provide tax incentives and regulatory relief to businesses that are willing to locate in a designated zone. Proponents of enterprise zones maintain that lowering taxes and red tape will induce companies to make investments in areas that typically are neglected. Such investments, in theory, can provide employment in declining neighborhoods. Critics of enterprise zones claim that they do not create new jobs but only shuffle jobs from one location to another. Furthermore, enterprise zones tend to benefit large, capital-intensive corporations with high tax liabilities. The public sector loses the tax revenue that would be generated from those large corporations when enterprise zones are created.

Many companies will not invest in areas where the workforce is viewed as inadequate. Inadequacies can be traced to insufficient numbers of the types of workers demanded by the enterprise. To alleviate workforce concerns, jurisdictions often provide customized training. This training is typically provided at the employer's work site or a local community college. Many state and local governments tailor training to the specific needs of the individual firm. In a specific example of an innovative public–private partnership, the commonwealth of Kentucky, colleges in the Louisville area, and the large package-handling firm United Parcel Service joined together in a collaborative arrangement that helped to expand the pool of nightshift part-time package-handling employees.[5] This partnership assured the retention of the largest employer in the commonwealth of Kentucky, increased tuition revenue for the participating colleges, and expanded access to education.

General economic development strategies that are discussed above have produced numerous success stories. These success stories generally occur when public leaders alter investment decisions of the private sector through the provision of inducements. An alternative perspective on public–private partnerships is viewed from the lens of service delivery. Government services can be delivered through a myriad of arrangements ranging from mostly public delivery to mostly private. Efforts on the part of public sector leaders to shift the delivery of services to private sector providers represent a major development in American governance. Some of the models that represent shifts from public to private provision of goods and services are described below.

PUBLIC–PRIVATE PARTNERSHIP MODELS FOR SERVICE DELIVERY

The level of collaboration between public and private actors in a partnership varies from case to case. Many public services have traditionally been provided directly by the government with no collaboration with the private sector. Intergovernmental agreements (such as a county and city sharing jail facilities, road maintenance responsibilities, or an airport) represent an example of collaboration between multiple public organizations. But the public sector is increasingly looking to the private sector for partners who can produce public services. Savas[6] lists 10 service delivery arrangements and ranks them by their degree of privatization or their degree of reliance on market forces. According to Savas,[6] free market, voluntary service, and self-service arrangements are the ultimate in privatization because they contain the least government involvement. Four other types of service delivery arrangements utilize private-sector production. Ranked in decreasing degrees of privatization, these arrangements include franchises, vouchers, grants, and contracts. Service delivery arrangements that utilize a government producer include government vending, intergovernmental agreements, and government service. Government service is considered to have the lowest level of privatization.

The *free market* provides most ordinary goods and services. Consumers select a producer, which is a private firm and pays the private firm. Government is not involved in the transaction in any significant way. *Voluntary service* is provided through organizations that provide services that ordinarily might be supplied by the public sector. Examples of such services include recreational programs run by sports enthusiasts, protective patrols run by neighborhood associations, and fire protection provided by volunteer fire departments. *Self-service* is the most basic of all delivery systems. It refers to people providing their own services such as installing burglar alarms in their homes to prevent crime.

Franchises are awarded by governments to private firms who agree to provide a unique public service such as airport operation, utilities, and toll roads. Government gives the firm permission to operate in a specific geographic area, and citizens pay the firm directly for services. *Vouchers* are subsidies given directly to consumers to purchase goods such as food (food stamps) or education (school vouchers). Unlike grants where the government decides which producers get the resources, consumers decide where to spend their vouchers. Job-training vouchers and the G. I. Bill are voucher programs designed to increase human capital and are therefore relevant from an economic development perspective. *Grants* are resources given by government to private firms who can then provide more affordable good or service to citizens. Grants are often subsidies, in the form of money, tax exemptions, tax abatements, or low-cost loans. For economic development, many state and local governments give away land at no cost to new firms. *Contracting* involves government payment to a private entity to provide a specific service. Virtually all governments procure some goods or services by contracting with private firms. Services related to economic development that are often provided by contractors include economic development attraction activity, road and building construction, convention center management, industrial development, and urban planning.

Government vending involves the purchase of goods or services from a governmental agency. An example of government vending is the sale of rights for water, mineral, timber, and grazing on livestock on government-owned land. *Intergovernmental agreements* involve one government hiring another to supply a service. For example, a state may contract with a city or county to provide social services, or a small community may purchase library services from a specialized government unit that was organized to sell services to other governments in the region. *Government service* denotes the delivery of a service by a government unit using its own employees. An example of government services is sanitation service provided by a municipal sanitation department or education provided by the local public school system.[6]

Infrastructure can also be supplied and delivered through various public–private partnerships. Some partnerships that utilize private sector arrangements to supply infrastructure include lease-build-operate, build-transfer-operate, build-own-operate transfer, and build-own-operate.[6]

Under *lease-build-operate* partnerships, a private firm is given a long-term lease to develop (with its own funds) and operate a facility. The firm pays a rental fee and reaps a reasonable return on its investment over the term of the lease. The facility remains publicly owned. Under the *build-transfer-operate* partnership, a private firm builds a facility and transfers ownership to a government agency. The government agency then leases the facility back to the private firm. The private firm operates the facility and has the opportunity to recover its investment. The firm earns a reasonable return from user charges and commercial activities.

In the *build-operate-transfer* arrangement, a private developer is awarded a franchise to finance, build, own, and operate a facility and to collect user fees for a specific period of time. At the end of the time period, ownership is transferred to the public sector. In contrast to a sale, government retains control over the project. Under the *build-own-operate* partnership, the private developer finances, builds, owns, and operates a facility in perpetuity under a franchise agreement. Long-term property rights provide a significant financial incentive for capital investment. Examples of build-own-operate transfer arrangements include the construction of a bridge in Shanghai, China, the construction of the "chunnel" under the English Channel, the development of private toll roads in California, and the creation of power plant facilities in Indonesia.[6,7] The build-own-operate arrangement resembles outright privatization.[8]

TRENDS AND DIRECTIONS OF PUBLIC–PRIVATE PARTNERSHIPS

The use of public–private partnerships is believed to be on the rise at the start of the 21st century because of partnership's ability to leverage private capital.[8] Public sector leaders primarily enter into public–private partnerships because "they are seeking additional capital for economic expansion."[9] In many instances, partnerships facilitate the construction of worthy goods, allow private sector contractor to make a profit, and permit eventual public sector ownership of facilities without government expenditure.

Another factor contributing to the popularity of public–private partnerships appears to be the decentralization of decision making from the national to local governments. Local governments often lack the fiscal resources necessary for public projects. Therefore creative entrepreneurial approaches, such as partnering with the private sector, are useful to provide needed public goods and services. Partnerships between public and private sector officials offer the promise of increasing efficiencies in the delivery of public services as well as increasing the

leveraging of private sector funds. These private sector funds are utilized for public projects.

A third reason for the rise in partnerships between government and industry relates to structural changes in the economy. In the new marketplace, firms increasingly compete across national boundaries, and public officials have a vested interest in maintaining international competitive advantages. In the United States, with its so-called "New Economy," economic growth relates to technological advances and corporate strategy.[10] In efforts to maintain and expand comparative advantages, technology partnerships between public and private actors have evolved.[11]

A leading example of a high-profile public–private partnership is SEMATECH, a partnership formed in 1987 between U.S. computer-chip makers and the U.S. federal government. Under this partnership, the federal government provided funding for a collaborative effort to increase the computer-chip market share of American companies. At the time of the creation of the SEMATECH, companies based in the United States lagged behind Japanese-based companies in the sale of semiconductors.[10] After almost a decade, the United States became the world leader in the semiconductor market, and the federal government withdrew public funding for SEMATECH.

A number of factors coalesce to expand the trend toward public–private partnerships. Decentralization of political power, an entrepreneurial public sector management style, fiscal stress, and the need for infrastructure all contribute toward this trend. The use of partnerships is viewed as especially critical in regard to infrastructure creation.[12]

CONCLUSION

Savas noted that privatization of government functions is in the ascendancy, and that a majority of Americans no longer believe that an expanding state is the answer. He stated that "throughout the world we are experiencing a reorientation of government away from a top-down approach, an abandonment of the reigning assumption that a powerful, active, and interventionist government, manned by a caring intellectual elite and driven by good intentions, is the basis for good society."[6] Public–private partnerships are likely to further evolve as acceptance of privatization as a basic strategy for societal governance grows in acceptance.

Some authors, however, caution against the blind acceptance of increased privatization. Rosenau[13] noted that private and public partnerships may suffer because of conflicting interests. Conflict is attributed to the fact that the private sector is oriented toward profit, risk, competition, and corporate goals, whereas the public sector is oriented toward legislation, public opinion, democratic decision making, minimizing risk, and realizing social goals. Because of this inherent conflict, policymakers must guard against providing services to vulnerable populations (the children, the elderly, the disabled, and the cognitively impaired) in such a manner as to maximize profit at the expense of quality, access, or equity. In addition, public–private partnerships should avoid cronyism or improper awarding of contracts to private firms who enrich themselves with public resources.[14] Public–private initiatives that erode participation, equity, access, and democracy concerns must be minimized. In general, however, public–private partnerships have proven to be an effective tool for economic development projects, and it is expected that they will continue to be utilized in the future.

REFERENCES

1. Linder, S.H. Coming to terms with the public–private partnership: A grammar of multiple meanings. Am. Behav. Sci. **1999**, *43* (1), 35–51.
2. Mullin, S.P. *Public–Private Partnerships and State and Local Economic Development: Leveraging Private Investment*; Economic Development Administration: Washington, DC, 2002.
3. *Economic Development 1999 [Data file]*; International City/County Management Association: Washington, DC, 2003.
4. Koven, S.; Lyon, T. *Economic Development: Strategies for State and Local Practice*; International City/County Management Association: Washington, DC, 2003; 27–53.
5. Koven, S.; Strother, S. Saving jobs in Louisville, Kentucky. Econ. Dev. J. **2002**, *1* (1), 19–22.
6. Savas, E. *Privatization and Public–Private Partnerships*; Seven Bridges Press, LLC: New York, 2000; pp. 67–86, 104, 243–247, 327.
7. Wu, A.; Wu, R. A Trip to the Construction Site of Dreams. In *Zhejiang Online*; 2003. Retrieved September 20, 2003, from http://www.zjol.com.cn/gb/node2/node138665/node139012/node149968/node162419/node162422/userobject15ai1729735.html.
8. Williams, T.P. *Moving to Public–Private Partnerships: Learning from Experience Around the World*; IBM Endowment for the Business of Government: Arlington, VA, 2003.
9. *Public–Private Partnerships for Local Economic Development*; Walzer, N., Jacobs, B.D., Eds.; Praeger: Westport, CT, 1998; 16.
10. Carayannis, E.G.; Alexander, J. Revisiting SEMATECH: Profiling public- and private-sector cooperation. Eng. Manag. J. **2000**, *12* (4), 33–43.
11. Stiglitz, J.E.; Wallsten, S.J. Public–private technology partnerships: Promises and pitfalls. Am. Behav. Sci. **1999**, *43* (1), 52–73.
12. Klitgaard, R.; Treverton, G.F. *Assessing Partnerships: New Forms of Collaboration*; IBM Endowment for the Business of Government: Arlington, VA, 2003.
13. Rosenau, P.V. The Strengths and Weaknesses of Public–Private Policy Partnerships. In *Public–Private Policy Partnerships*; Rosenau, P.V., Ed.; The MIT Press: Cambridge, MA, 2000; 217–241.
14. Rosenau, P.V. Introduction: The strengths and weaknesses of public–private policy partnerships. Am. Behav. Sci. **1999**, *43* (1), 10–35.

Public Procurement Ethics

David Seth Jones
National University of Singapore, Singapore

INTRODUCTION

One of the hallmarks of good governance in the modern state is adherence to strict ethical standards by government departments and agencies in procuring goods and services for public programs (these organizations are commonly referred to as government procurement entities or GPEs). Such standards are necessary for several reasons. The procurement of goods and services by public authorities often comprises a significant percentage of both the operating and capital budgets of a government and involves spending a substantial part of the revenue provided by the taxpayer. In addition, how public procurement is undertaken has a crucial impact upon the efficiency and effectiveness of public services and may also affect growth and employment within the wider domestic economy. For ethical principles to be upheld, there should exist a clear framework of rules and procedures based upon them, governing the various stages of the procurement process: devising specifications, advertising the intended procurement, evaluation of tender and quotation submissions, recommendation of a submission, final selection, drafting the contract, and postcontract adjustment.[1] Where they exist, such rules and procedures are usually enshrined in legislation and/or stipulated in administrative directives, often contained in public service operational manuals, with which procurement officers and other public officials as well as suppliers must comply.[2,3] Explained below are the key principles upon which such a framework of procurement should be based.

FAIRNESS

Principles of Fairness

An important part of the ethical responsibility of government and GPEs when purchasing goods and services is to follow fair practices. Fairness can be construed in various senses: rewarding desert, providing for need, avoiding harm to others, and honoring a promise. In the first sense, it entails providing rewards according to merit, achievement, or endeavor. In the second sense, it involves responding to the needs arising from circumstances or inborn disadvantages, regardless of merit, achievement, or endeavor.[4,5] These two interpretations of fairness have given rise to two different approaches to public procurement. The third interpretation of fairness prohibits actions which harm the legitimate interests of others, while the fourth sense of fairness, based on the duty to keep a promise, requires that the terms of a contract, freely entered into, be honored by the parties concerned.[6]

Desert Principle: Equal Access

Fairness related to desert requires that all potential suppliers be given equal access to the public procurement market through open competition, and that contracts be awarded to those who offer the lowest price or best meet the stipulated specifications.[2,7] To ensure equal access and a level-playing field, governments and GPEs must disseminate information about an intended procurement as widely as possible through the relevant advertising channels: the government gazette, the local and overseas newspapers, the trade journals, and, increasingly, the internet.[8,9] Equal access also necessitates, for the benefit of overseas companies and businesses, that a reasonable time be allowed for both the receipt of tender and quotation forms and other detailed documentation and also the submission of tender and quotation proposals. Once tenders and quotations have been submitted, the GPE is obliged to objectively evaluate the merits of each in terms of price and specification fulfillment to determine which proposal is the most advantageous.[7–9]

After the contract has been awarded, fairness based on desert prescribes that unsuccessful tenderers be informed of the reasons why they have failed. This would be helpful in enabling them to submit better proposals for future tenders and quotations. In addition, in the interest of fairness, any unsuccessful tenderer who has grounds to believe that his/her submission was not evaluated on the basis of merit or that procurement officers did not follow official procurement procedures should be given the right of appeal to a procurement adjudication body.[3,8]

Furthermore, postcontract adjustment should be carefully limited.[3] For contracts that extend over a lengthy period, some adjustments may be necessary as a result of

Encyclopedia of Public Administration and Public Policy
DOI: 10.1081/E-EPAP 120019220

changing rates of inflation, currency fluctuations (for overseas suppliers), newly improved product designs, and changing needs of the GPE itself. The contract alterations may be negotiated with the contracted supplier and should only be allowed under conditions stipulated in the contract or with the agreement of both parties. However, where the postcontract adjustments are either unrelated to the above and/or are substantial, then it is only fair to other potential suppliers that a new tender or quotation be called for.[3]

Open competition based on equal access has been enshrined as a central principle in the WTO's Government Procurement Agreement (GPA), which was drafted in 1994. More than 30 countries are now signatories to the agreement. The key objective is to liberalize the public procurement market in as many countries as possible and so enable foreign suppliers or foreign-linked suppliers to compete for government contracts on equal terms with local suppliers. Governments which acceded to the GPA cannot, under its provisions, discriminate against foreign suppliers, even those that do not include any domestic content in the their goods and services, nor can they discriminate against local suppliers with foreign affiliation or ownership and/or trading in goods and services originating in another country.[8] Goods and services of a security or strategic interest may be exempted (e.g., construction of a military building). In this respect, the GPA has followed the system of competitive procurement adopted in the European Union based on EU Directives following the creation of the European Single Market in 1987.[7,10,11]

Need Principle: Unequal Access

Alternatively, public procurement practices may be considered as fair if suppliers are chosen on the basis of their needs (or the needs of the population or section of the population to which they belong). Such suppliers are then given preferential treatment with contracts drafted which take into account those needs. Included in this category may be local suppliers within the country, small-scale suppliers, and those drawn from disadvantaged minority communities, most of whom could not compete effectively for government procurement contracts if equal access through open competition was permitted.[7,12] Affirmative access, it is argued, is necessary to enable such businesses to survive and expand and to generate income for owners and employees alike. For suppliers from a minority community, affirmative access may be important in raising living standards and creating business opportunities as part of a wider policy to improve its circumstances. To facilitate affirmative access, selective tendering may be adopted which restricts tender submis-

sions to suppliers that fall within the categories stated above. To the same end, open tendering may still be adopted, but with special consideration given to submissions from the favored categories during the evaluation stage.[2,12] Such special consideration may entail allowing a preferential percentage margin on the prices offered by the suppliers concerned.

Avoidance of Harm Principle

Fairness also imposes a responsibility upon GPEs and suppliers to ensure that goods and services are produced or supplied by means that do not lead to harmful consequences for others (negative externalities), especially in terms of health and safety. Examples of such externalities are the production of goods in which little care is taken to protect the safety of employees or which results in environmental waste or pollution. It is then justified for GPEs to restrict access to the public procurement market for businesses engaged in such practices. For this reason, certain governments, as a matter of principle, discriminate against businesses with poor industrial safety records or which despoil the environment or do not supply environmentally friendly products.[13,14]

Principle of Contractual Obligation

It is only fair, in accordance with the moral duty to keep a promise, that once a GPE and a supplier have signed a procurement contract, both then honor its terms. During the period of the contract, the GPE might want to alter the terms of the procurement, as a result of its changing needs, as mentioned above. This might be allowed under certain conditions and within certain limits, which should be stipulated in the contract. However, fairness dictates that, having entered the contract, the GPE should secure the agreement of the supplier to an alteration of the terms beyond what is allowable and should not terminate the contract if this is not forthcoming. Likewise, the supplier is duty-bound to honor his/her obligations under the terms of the contract, and any adjustment it wishes to make must have the consent of the GPE.[9] The key obligations for suppliers that relate to honoring a contract include not committing a novation of contract, refraining from unauthorized subcontracting, meeting the specifications in the type and quality of goods and services supplied, adhering to the price agreed, and abiding by the stipulated time frame for delivery.[9,15] Where the supplier is in serious default of the above, the GPE has the right to impose penalties, e.g., fines, termination of contract, and debarment from future contracts.

VALUE-FOR-MONEY

As major spenders of tax revenue, GPEs are under an obligation to provide value-for-money for the public as both taxpayers and recipients of public services. This reflects the "social contract" at the heart of a democratic state, by which voters/taxpayers are entitled to receive from an elected government efficient and effective public services in return for the income and wealth they have foregone through taxation.[7,16]

Value-for-money is achieved through the procurement of goods and services for a public program, appropriate to its specific requirements, which are of a sufficiently high standard and purchased at a reasonably low price. If such criteria are not adhered to, the taxpayers's money will be wastefully spent and public managers will be denied the means of providing a high standard of public services. Ensuring that a procurement meets the requirements of a public program may necessitate decentralizing the task of procurement to the implementing department or agency. However, where materials are commonly used in a standard form by all departments and agencies, then value-for-money can best be guaranteed by bulk purchasing by a centralized body.[1]

To ensure value-for-money, certain procedures must be established and observed. These include justifying the need for the procurement and devising procurement specifications in light of program requirements. In addition, tender proposals should be thoroughly vetted to determine which is the most advantageous, and contracts should be properly and precisely drafted. It is also important that procurement decisions are taken by committees and bodies that include not only procurement officers, but also technical specialists with the expertise to understand technical specifications and the end users who can determine if the products and services to be procured are appropriate to their programs.[7]

In most cases, value-for-money is most likely to be achieved through open competitive tendering. However, sometimes, even selective tendering and limited sourcing can result in equally positive outcomes. This depends upon negotiation and hard bargaining by procurement officers on matters of price, design, scope, and quality of the product or service to be purchased.[7] In such cases, procurement officers will be aided by having access to full information of the prospective supplier's cost breakdown, expected profit margin, and supply capacity.[17–19] Limited sourcing may involve the use of just one supplier for repeat procurements of the same goods or services. This is justified if the supplier is reliable and, on the basis of a guarantee of repeat orders, is prepared to offer discounts and improved products and services, resulting in better value-for-money.[11,19]

PROBITY

A further ethical obligation of governments and GPEs is to maintain strict standards of probity and avoid corruption and dishonesty in the procurement of goods and services. All too often, public procurement is undermined by corrupt practices in which political leaders, senior administrators, procurement officers, and other officials take advantage of the opportunities provided to make illicit personal gains or secure benefits for their family and friends. All the main forms of corruption can occur. One is misappropriation in which suppliers are overinvoiced and provide more goods than needed or specified, with the surplus then falling into the hands of public officials and used for their benefit or sold for personal gain. Another prevalent form of corruption is bribery. Money and favors (kickbacks) are offered to, or demanded by, officials in return for the award of a contract.[2,9,15] Equally common is nepotism and cronyism by which preferential treatment is accorded to businesses linked to the families and friends of government officials who influence or decide the choice of tenderer.[20] For their part, suppliers may act unethically not only by offering bribes, but also by committing fraud, such as by deliberately disclosing false information about their past financial record, resources and capital value, and their capacity to deliver the goods and services in question.[9]

To ensure high standards of probity, measures may be enforced to both prevent and deter corruption and dishonesty. Preventive measures may include a requirement that officers who are involved in any significant stage in the procurement process declare any possible conflict of interest. This especially applies to a personal or family connection with a business (or any affiliated business) submitting a quotation or tender, through ownership, partnership, shareholding, and loans.[9,20] As further measures to prevent corruption, the different functions and stages of the procurement process should involve separate officers (including separate officers for making procurement policy and undertaking procurement operations), and if manpower availability permits, they should be rotated on a regular basis.[2] In addition, more than one officer should be involved in the key stages of the procurement process.

Preventive measures should be reinforced by deterrence measures to punish those discovered to be engaged in corruption and dishonesty. Penalties would include stiff fines; in more serious cases, prison terms; in addition, for suppliers, debarment from future contracts; and for procurement officers, demotion or dismissal from post. In some countries such as Hong Kong and Singapore, legislation has been enacted under which an anticorruption agency has been created with wide-ranging powers to pursue inquiries and unearth any evidence of corrupt practices, with courts given powers to pass stiff sentences in such cases.[21] In many countries, the government audit agency is given the investigative powers and the responsibility to identify corruption in the procurement process.

TRANSPARENCY

Maintaining fairness, value-for-money, and probity in part depends upon making the public procurement process as transparent as possible. This requires the disclosure of all relevant information at critical points in the process.[3] At the outset, information relating to an intended procurement, including tender or quotation specifications, should be made available to all prospective suppliers, as mentioned above. The various tender or quotation proposals submitted should then be publicized, followed by the disclosure of the name of the successful bidder, together with the content of the contract and the cost of the purchase.[3] Transparency also requires that reasons be given to the unsuccessful tenderers why they had not been selected, as stated above. In addition, to ensure proper accountability in the procurement process, government auditors, internal regulatory authorities, and relevant watchdog committees within the legislature should be given details of how a procurement was undertaken, together with all the necessary documentation, if so requested. Where necessary, senior administrators and procurement officers of a GPE should be subject to cross-examination by relevant committees of the legislature.

Transparency underpins the three other ethical principles in public procurement in two senses. First, it is an essential condition in enabling open competition for tenders to prevail which is both the basis of fairness related to desert and arguably a guarantee of value-for-money. Second, it subjects GPEs to greater scrutiny and accountability in respect to various aspects of fairness, value-for-money, and probity. Any deviation from such standards can be readily identified and exposed, allowing action to be taken to rectify the shortcoming.

CONCLUSION

The above principles governing procurement in many respects supplement each other. For example, measures that promote fairness based on open competition necessitate transparency, arguably ensure increased value-for-money, and even safeguard standards of probity. Value-

for-money is more likely to be achieved with greater transparency that allows procurements to be open to scrutiny leading to greater political and public accountability. Value-for-money can be further enhanced if procurement practices are governed by probity, in view of the fact that corruption can lead to a lower standard of procurement and greater waste and inefficiency.

However, in one respect, one of the principles of procurement may be at variance with the others. While much may be said in favor of fairness based on the need to allow unequal access to the public procurement market, this may lessen the possibility of achieving value-for-money because the suppliers chosen for a contract through special preference may not offer the most advantageous terms. Equally, it may be at variance with fairness based on open competition and merit because suppliers offering better terms and more capable of meeting the specification requirements may be rejected. This requires the government or GPE to determine where the balance of ethical responsibility lies between need and value-for-money. If consideration of need-based fairness in the procurement process does not result in the acquisition of substandard goods and services at an excessive price to the tax payer, then preferential access may be allowable. However, if such access does indeed lead to procurements that fall well short of giving value-for-money, so impairing public programs and excessively draining tax revenue, then the alternative of selecting the best suppliers through open competition within a level-playing field may be the better option.

REFERENCES

1. Coe, C.K. *Public Financial Management*; Prentice Hall: Englewood Cliffs, NJ, 1989.
2. Coe, C.K. Government Purchasing: The State of the Practice. In *Handbook of Comparative Public Budgeting and Financial Management*; Lynch, T., Martin, L., Eds.; Marcel Dekker: New York, 1993; 207–224.
3. Sherman, S. *Government Procurement Management*; Wordcrafters Publications: Germanstown, MD, 1999.
4. Benn, S.; Peters, R. *Social Principles of the Democratic State*; George Allen & Unwin: London, 1961.
5. Barry, B. *Political Argument*; Routledge & Kegan Paul: London, 1965.
6. Thiroux, J. *Ethics: Theory and Practice,* 7th Ed.; Prentice Hall: Upper Saddle River, NJ, 2001.
7. Erridge, A. Competitive Tendering and Partnership in the Public Sector. In *Working in Partnership*; Burnes, B., Dale, B., Eds.; Gower: Aldershot, UK, 1998; 21–38.
8. WTO. *Plurilateral Agreement on Government Procurement*; Author: Geneva, 1997.

9. Farrington, B.; Waters, D. *Managing Purchasing: Organizing, Planning and Control*; Chapman & Hall: London, 1994.

10. Arrowsmith, S.; Linarelli, J.; Wallace, D. *Regulating Public Procurement*; Kluwer Law International: The Hague, 2000.

11. McDonald, F.; Winkelmann, T. Public Procurement Rules in the European Union and the Prospects for Efficient Supply: The Cases of UK and Germany. In *Innovations in Procurement Management*; Cox, A., Ed.; Earlsgate Press: Boston, UK, 1996; 283–304.

12. Leenders, M.R.; Fearon, H.E. *Purchasing and Materials Management,* 11th Ed.; Irwin: Homewood, IL, 1996.

13. Russel, T. Introduction. In *Greener Purchasing: Opportunities and Innovations*; Russel, T., Ed.; Greenleaf Publishing: Sheffield, UK, 1998; 9–21.

14. Pento, T. Implementation of Public Green Procurement Programmes. In *Greener Purchasing: Opportunities and Innovations*; Russel, T., Ed.; Greenleaf Publishing: Sheffield, UK, 1998; 22–30.

15. Finkler, S. *Financial Management for Public, Health, and Not-for-Profit Organizations*; Prentice Hall: Upper Saddle River, NJ, 2001.

16. Central Unit on Procurement. *Supplement to CUP Newsletter*; HMSO: London, 1989.

17. Fishner, S. *A Report on Government Procurement Practices*; Camelot Publishers: Merrifield, VA, 1989.

18. Baily, P. Procurement Policy. In *Handbook of Management,* 3rd Ed.; Lock, D., Ed.; Gower: Brookfield, VT, 1992; 339–406.

19. Deverill, N. Change and Innovation in Government Procurement. In *Innovations in Procurement Management*; Cox, A., Ed.; Earlsgate Press: Boston, 1996; 239–271.

20. Zenz, G. *Purchasing and the Management of Materials,* 7th Ed.; John Wiley: New York, 1994.

21. Quah, J. Controlling corruption in city states: A comparative study of Hong Kong and Singapore. Crime, Law Soc. Chang. **1995**, *22*, 391–414.

Public Reporting

Mordecai Lee
University of Wisconsin-Milwaukee, Milwaukee, Wisconsin, U.S.A.

INTRODUCTION

Public reporting refers to the actions of a government agency to account to the citizenry for its activities in the recent past, including its record of performance and its stewardship of public funds. The term refers both to the normative obligation of public entities in a democracy to perform such activities and to the internal management activities necessary to accomplish this external communications goal.

Public reporting was developed by public administration theorists in the first half of the 20th century in an effort to harmonize the emergence of the administrative state with democracy. Inasmuch as permanent and professionalized bureaucracies were not subject to elections, there was a need to define the role of public administration in democracy. By assigning to senior civil servants the duty to report directly to the citizenry on agency activities, theorists sought to make government departments accountable to the public-at-large, not just to elected officials. Public reporting would contribute to an informed citizenry, the ultimate source of power and decision making in democracy.

ORIGINS

With the emergence of the administrative state in advanced western societies in the late 19th and early 20th centuries, a natural concern arose regarding the need to harmonize democracy with the inherently undemocratic nature of bureaucracy. Political, legal, and constitutional responses were the understandable initial solutions. Administrative agencies would be formally accountable to the elected and appointed oversight institutions of democracy, such as through budget and policy controls possessed by the chief elected executive officer, oversight activities by legislative bodies, and the jurisdiction of the courts to rule on agency policies and procedures. These elected and appointed constitutional branches of government would be able to assure that democracy would reach into bureaucracy through external controls and interventions. Yet these approaches all assumed that bureaucracies were only *indirectly* accountable to the citizenry—the source of democratic sovereignty and power.

However, another line of thinking suggested that bureaucracies also needed to be *directly* accountable to the voters. It was not enough, this theorizing went, to be accountable to the citizenry through other democratic institutions. Instead, agencies should also be directly responsible to the electorate. Thus was born public reporting.

As it gradually developed in the 1920s and 1930s in the United States, public reporting referred to the duty of the public administrator to report regularly to the public-at-large on the activities of the agency. Inasmuch as an informed public was the sine qua non of democracy,[1] then government agencies should be one of the sources of information for the citizenry about the operations of the public sector. For public opinion to be the central engine of decision making in a democracy, the voters needed to have basic information upon which to construct their opinions. In the administrative state, information should come not only from traditional sources, such as newspapers, civic groups, and elected officials, but also from the newest component of the public sector, government departments. That meant government managers had the obligation of preparing and releasing reports on a regular schedule, helping to assure that the public would become familiar with agency activities.[2–4]

Public reporting first emerged as part of the efforts by reformers to ''clean up'' American city governments in the early 20th century. A knowledgeable citizenry would become a bulwark against patronage, waste, and corruption in city halls. One of the first references to public reporting was in 1912, when Bruère[5] argued that the concept of ''efficient citizenship'' required regular reporting by city government to the public. In the 1930s, the International City Management Association sponsored contests to promote improved public reporting[6] and through the 1950s continued actively encouraging municipalities to conduct robust reporting programs.[7]

The public reporting imperative of the government manager is one of the activities that operationalizes the difference between business and public administration. Given the public-sector environment it operates in, government management is qualitatively a different activity from business administration. The duty of public reporting is one of the components of public administration that reflects this inherent intersectorial difference.[8]

DEFINITION

Public reporting is only one element of the array of interactions that government agencies have with the public-at-large. In that respect, it needs to be delineated in a way that clearly separates it from other related, but distinctly different, activities.

In the context of an agency's external communication programs, public reporting is an activity that is not related to the efficient implementation of the agency's core mission. Many public relations programs are aimed at furthering the raison d'être of an agency, such as informing the public of new programs and services, using publicity as a substitute for regulation and encouraging the public to serve as the "eyes and ears" of the agency.[9] In that respect, public reporting is a communication activity that does not "do" anything in context of the pragmatic get-the-job-done pressures of daily management and communications. Rather, reporting simply provides information for information sake.

Similarly, public reporting focuses on efforts to contribute to an informed public. In that sense, reporting contributes to the functioning of democracy. However, public reporting focuses only on the transmission of information from the administrative agency to the public and not on the subsequent developments that it triggers. Thus public reporting is different from citizen participation in agency decision making or agency "listening" to customers and clients in an effort to improve the quality of consumer interactions.

Given that the modern definition of communication is a two-way flow of information, then public reporting focuses solely on the first half and front end of the entire communications loop and only on communication intended to inform for democratic purposes. Therefore public reporting is defined as:

> the management activity intended to convey systematically and regularly information about government operations, in order to promote an informed citizenry in a democracy and accountability to public opinion. It consists of direct and indirect reporting of the government's record of accomplishments and stewardship of the taxpayers' money. Public reporting is presented in many different communication formats, but always uses vocabulary that is understandable and meaningful to lay citizens.[10]

Public reporting occurs when an agency conveys information about its performance to the citizenry rather than to political and elected oversight institutions. Certainly, public opinion gains information about the operations of the government from elected officials, whether those from the executive or the legislative branches. However, the central concept of reporting focuses on government agencies communicating with the public *besides* the formal, legal, and constitutional channels they are subject to.

Generally, a bureaucracy can report to the public in two ways: directly and indirectly. Indirect reporting refers to communication efforts *through* the intermediary institution of the news media. Direct reporting focuses on nonmediated communications from the agency to the public-at-large for the purpose of conveying summary and performance information.

INDIRECT REPORTING

One way for an agency to inform the public is by facilitating media coverage of its operations. As an instrument of democracy, the news media can provide the public with ongoing information about the activities and performance of the government. Given this constitutional role of the press in contributing to an informed citizenry, agencies have a counterpart obligation to assist the press in its efforts to report about agency operations. This perspective is the underlying rationale for public-sector agencies to maintain media liaison offices, staffed with specialists trained in dealing with reporters.

Some news coverage of an agency is headline-driven. In those situations, the agency is passively reacting to inquiries from the press. This form of interaction rarely leads to providing the public with a more systematic and comprehensive understanding of agency performance. Instead, it provides highly selective—and often negative—snapshots driven by the media's need for controversy. Therefore a better opportunity for indirect reporting occurs when an agency is able to initiate and generate coverage. Events such as observing a milestone in a program's operations, the ribbon cutting at a new site, and the kickoff of a new service all provide an opportunity to report indirectly to the public about the general and overall activities of an agency. While, by necessity, an incomplete snapshot of the entire agency's operations, this category of news coverage is nonetheless a channel for reporting to the citizenry on the more routine and daily aspects of government, in contradistinction to news coverage that is crisis- and controversy-driven.

One of the advantages of indirect reporting is that it is free. The agency incurs no additional cost when the media reports to the public about it. Yet while agencies should make efforts to "tell their story" to the citizenry via the news media, indirect reporting—by itself—is rarely adequate to accomplish the broad democratic goals intended for public reporting.

DIRECT REPORTING

The more prominent and effective approach to public reporting is through direct contact with the citizenry. In the predigital era when public reporting first began, direct reporting often focused on printed materials. Items such as annual and quarterly reports were viewed as one of the basic ways that agencies could inform the public about their accomplishments. Two key elements have been identified as necessary for effective printed reports: contents and distribution.

First, printed reports should be prepared with the audience of the lay public in mind. Reports need to be in plain English and must focus on the key items that represent the agency's accomplishments. Long and detailed descriptions, use of technical jargon, and impenetrable statistical presentations are examples of what a good report should not contain. Besides use of plain language, effective public reports extensively rely on graphics, photos, and other visual techniques to make the documents user-friendly. Similarly, linking agency information to comparisons that are understandable to average citizens ("for the cost of an average breakfast, our agency delivers to each of our clients...") is another way to contribute to an effective public report. This focus on content and presentation also helps highlight the difference between public reporting and financial reporting. Annual reports prepared by accountants and auditors to satisfy various legal and constitutional requirements rarely qualify as public reporting. The density of numerical information in financial reports generally precludes creating a product that is meaningful to a lay reader.

Second, effective reporting also requires significant efforts to disseminate reports as broadly as possible. Some agencies indeed prepare annual reports, but their dissemination efforts are half-hearted and incomplete. Certainly, copies should be sent to elected officials, key civic leaders, the media, public libraries, and major civic groups. However, the concept of public reporting calls for efforts to put the report directly in the hands of the citizenry. In the middle of the 20th century, municipalities experimented with a wide variety of dissemination channels. Some examples included inserting the annual report in the annual property tax bill or in quarterly bills from municipal utilities, inserting the report in the daily newspaper, having sanitation workers distribute the reports while on their rounds and recruiting boy and girl scout troops to adopt, as their civic project, the distribution of the report door-to-door.

However, annual reports and other regularly issued publications (such as quarterly ones) are not the only way that government agencies can engage in direct public reporting. Referring again to examples from the mid-20th century, other efforts included open houses, speakers bureaus, billboards, signs on subways and buses, annual exhibits keyed to the budget adoption process, movie shorts, public service advertising, regular radio programs, and film versions of annual reports. Like other marketing and advertising efforts, multiple products and channels need to be utilized to maximize the potential of reaching as much of the citizenry as possible.

ROOSEVELT'S OFFICE OF GOVERNMENT REPORTS

In the federal government, the high water mark of traditional public reporting was the Office of Government Reports (OGR), which President Roosevelt established in 1939. In the Executive Order creating it, one of its central missions was to "distribute information concerning the purposes and activities of executive departments and agencies."[11] Roosevelt viewed OGR as the executive branch's agency that would report to the public on the activities of the federal government. In a national radio address, Roosevelt explained that once informed factually of the record of the Administration, public opinion could then express its will to Congress regarding the continuation or cessation of those federal programs.[11] As a reflection of the importance he assigned to OGR, Roosevelt made it one of the five original agencies comprising the Executive Office of the President (EOP), which he also established in 1939. However, OGR was a very controversial agency, especially with the conservative coalition in Congress. Overcoming strong resistance on Capitol Hill to the concept of such a federal reporting agency, in 1941, Roosevelt succeeded in shepherding through Congress a law authorizing permanent appropriations for OGR.[12] However, continued opposition to OGR by legislators forced Roosevelt in 1942 to merge it for the duration of World War II into the temporary Office of War Information (OWI). When President Truman tried to reestablish OGR after the war, as Roosevelt had intended, the Republican 80th Congress refused to appropriate any additional funding for it. OGR went out of existence in 1948.[12]

The political blowout relating to OGR presented a high-profile case of how easily public reporting can become politically controversial. Whether an accurate assessment or not, the lesson learned was that for public reporting to occur, it needed to be blander and less engaging. In fact, for the second half of the 20th century, public reporting gradually ossified into boring annual reports at most levels of government. Those half-hearted reports were given limited circulation and triggered even less interest.

21st CENTURY TRANSFORMATION: E-REPORTING

While the rationale for public reporting retained its validity in the post-OGR era of the second half of the 20th century, as a concrete activity, it gradually faded from prominence in both public administration theory and practice. However, the emergence of the communications age and the digital era has provided an opportunity to revive and reestablish the value of public reporting in the 21st century. New communications technologies now permit government agencies to communicate quickly, efficiently, and inexpensively directly to the citizenry. Annual and special reports posted on agency websites and distributed by e-mail provide an opportunity to perform public reporting in ways that could not have been envisioned a century earlier.

Similarly, the increased attention in public administration to performance measurement has provided a new format by which agencies can report on their operations to the public-at-large. While performance measurement was originally developed largely for management control purposes—whether for the senior management of the agency or for oversight by the executive and by the legislative branch—it has much potential and value to the lay citizenry as well.

Therefore the combination of digital technology with the focus on performance measurement has provided an opportunity to reformulate and reinvigorate the original conception of public reporting. Now called e-reporting, it consists of:

> the administrative activity that uses electronic government technology for digital delivery of public reports that are largely based on performance information. E-reporting is a tool of e-democracy that conveys systematically and regularly information about government operations that is valuable to the public-at-large, in order to promote an informed citizenry in a democracy and accountability to public opinion. E-reports are planned to be citizen-friendly, by being understandable and meaningful to the lay public.[10]

CONCLUSION

Public reporting has been making a comeback in public administration. Herzlinger[13] has suggested that one of the ways to restore public trust in government is through improved reporting. That would include an increase in the amount of important information disclosed to the citizenry as well as better and broader dissemination of such regular reports. The Organisation for Economic Cooperation and Development (OECD), an association of the most developed western countries, issued two reports in 2001 calling for improved public reporting and providing guidelines for such efforts.[14,15]

Whether widely or well practiced, public reporting is a permanent and inherent element of public administration in a democracy. Civil servants are expected to engage in systematic efforts to report to the citizenry on their agencies' activities, performance, and stewardship of taxpayer funds. The profession of public management entails more than effectively running an agency. It also involves contributing to the working of democracy. Public reporting is the vehicle for such efforts. For more information, see Refs. [16–20].

REFERENCES

1. Brown, R.D. *The Strength of a People: The Idea of an Informed Citizenry in America, 1650–1870*; University of North Carolina Press: Chapel Hill, NC, 1996.
2. Beyle, H.C. *Governmental Reporting in Chicago*; University of Chicago Press: Chicago, 1928.
3. National Committee on Municipal Reporting. *Public Reporting, With Special Reference to Annual, Departmental, and Current Reports of Municipalities*; Municipal Administration Service: New York, 1931.
4. Ridley, C.E.; Simon, H.A. *Specifications for the Annual Municipal Report*; International City Managers' Association: Chicago, 1948.
5. Bruère, H. Efficiency in city government. Ann. Am. Acad. Polit. Soc. Sci. **1912**, *41*, 3–22.
6. Simon, H.A. Inter-City Contests. In *Municipal Year Book, 1937*; Ridley, C.E., Nolting, O.F., Eds.; International City Managers' Association: Chicago, 1937; 137–144.
7. Snyder, R.W. Municipal Reporting in 1953. In *Municipal Year Book, 1954*; Ridley, C.E., Nolting, O.F., Eds.; International City Managers' Association: Chicago, 1954; 269–276.
8. Lee, M. Intersectoral differences in public affairs: the duty of public reporting in public administration. J. Public Aff. **2002**, *2* (2), 33–43.
9. Lee, M. Public information in government organizations: A review and curriculum outline of external relations in public administration. Public Admin. Manage. **2000**, *5* (4),

183–214. http://www.pamij.com/00_5_4.html (accessed February 2004).

10. Lee, M. *E-Reporting: Strengthening Democratic Accountability*; IBM Center for the Business of Government: Washington, DC, 2004, pp. 5, 9, also available online: http://www.businessofgovernment.org/pdfs/Lee_Report.pdf (accessed February 2004). Reprinted as Chapter 4 in *Managing for Results 2005*; Kamensky, J.M., Morales, A., Eds.; Rowman & Littlefield: Lanham, MD, 2004; 141–195.

11. Roosevelt, F.D. *The Public Papers and Addresses of Franklin D. Roosevelt*; Macmillan: New York, 1941; Vol. 1939, pp. 305–310, 494.

12. Lee, M. *The First Presidential Communications Agency: FDR's Office of Government Reports*; State University of New York Press: Albany, NY, 2005.

13. Herzlinger, R.E. Can public trust in nonprofits and government be restored? Harvard Bus. Rev. **1996**, *74* (2), 97–107.

14. Caddy, J.; Vergez, C. *Citizens as Partners: Information, Consultation and Public Participation in Policy-Making*; Organisation for Economic Co-operation and Development: Paris, France, 2001.

15. Gramberger, M.R. *Citizens as Partners: OECD Handbook on Information, Consultation and Public Participation in Policy-Making*; Organisation for Economic Co-operation and Development: Paris, France, 2001.

16. Campbell, O.W. San Diego's 1951 annual report. Public Admin. Rev. **1953**, *13* (1), 30–32.

17. Graves, W.B. Public reporting in the American states. Public Opin. Q. **1938**, *2* (2), 211–228.

18. Lee, M. Is there anything new under the sun? Herbert Simon's contributions in the 1930s to performance measurement and public reporting of performance results. Public Voices **2003**, *6* (2–3), 73–82.

19. Scott, J.D. Local Government Publications. In *Effective Communication: A Local Government Guide*; Wheeler, K.M., Ed.; International City Management Association: Washington, DC, 1994; 190–216.

20. Wall, N.L. *Municipal Reporting to the Public*; International City Managers' Association: Chicago, 1963.

Reciprocal Relations Among Peace, Prosperity, and Democracy

Stuart S. Nagel (Deceased)
University of Illinois, Urbana, Illinois, U.S.A.

INTRODUCTION

The leading controversial policy issues in developing nations like those of South Asia tend to be economic, political, and military in nature. The economic issues relate to making domestic economies more prosperous and facilitating investments, exports, and imports. The political issues relate to promoting democratic institutions, human rights, and self-determination. The military issues relate to advocating nonproliferation of arms and reduction in regional conflicts.[1]

The purpose of this article is to discuss some aspects of U.S. foreign policy as applied to these policy problems of developing regions and nations.[2] The context is in terms of win–win thinking where all nations involved are better off as a result of the interaction.[3] The context is also in terms of three tables, which give useful visual aids to clarify the mutually beneficial interaction.

TEN CAUSAL RELATIONS

The first six causal relations in Table 1 can be interpreted as follows:

1. Reduction in military conflicts is conducive to prosperity and investment.
2. Prosperity is conducive to reduction in military conflicts, especially prosperity based on buying and selling across countries that might otherwise be in conflict.
3. Prosperity is conducive to democratic institutions, human rights, and tolerance of minority ethnic groups.
4. Democracy, human rights, and ethnic peace are conducive to prosperity.
5. Democratic political institutions are conducive to a reduction in military conflicts.
6. Reduction in military conflicts is conducive to democratic political institutions.

The last four causal relations can be interpreted as follows:

7. U.S. policy is concerned with encouraging prosperity, investment, exporting, and importing because doing so is mutually beneficial.
8. U.S. policy is concerned with reducing military conflicts partly because of the favorable effect on prosperity and the economic issues.
9. U.S. policy is concerned with promoting a democratic political environment partly because of the favorable effect on prosperity and the economic issues.
10. U.S. domestic economic policy emphasizes U.S. prosperity and gross national product (GNP) growth, which partly explains why U.S. international policy emphasizes mutually beneficial trade and investment opportunities.

Miscellaneous points include:

1. In the context of South Asia, Pakistan is especially concerned with military security, India is especially concerned with political issues, and Sri Lanka is especially concerned with international economics, but all three countries are concerned with all three sets of issues.
2. The concept of mutual benefit is promoted through regional organizations, such as the South Asia Association for Regional Cooperation, as well as through interregional interaction between South Asia and the United States.
3. Social issues such as poverty and ethnic groups are also important, although they are considered under economic and political issues, respectively. Technology issues are also quite important, but they are discussed in the context of military, economic, and political issues.
4. There are positive relations among all five variables shown in Table 1. Those relations are positive in the sense of upward causation and being desirable relations, especially regarding the promotion of peace, prosperity, and democracy.

Encyclopedia of Public Administration and Public Policy
DOI: 10.1081/E-EPAP 120011054

Table 1   Win–win U.S. foreign policy

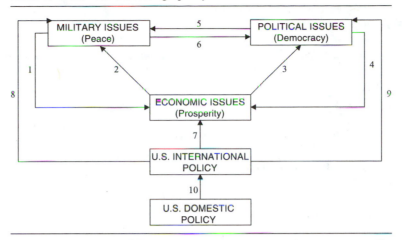

NOTE: All relations are positive. Thus there is no need for a plus sign on each arrow. For example, Relation 2 says prosperity causes peace because in time of depression, political leaders sometimes look for external enemies to distract people from being unemployed.

HISTORICAL DEVELOPMENT

The past was characterized by colonialism and the Cold War. The present is being characterized by investment, importing, and exporting of funds and foods. The future may be characterized by transfer of technologies and skills from the United States, which results in mutually beneficial investment—returns, buying, and selling. Those basic ideas are summarized in Table 2.

The arrows from the *past* indicate:

(1 and 2)   Colonialism-involved low wages going to the developing nations, and valuable resources going to the United States or other industrialized nations.

Table 2   U.S. foreign policy for 200 years

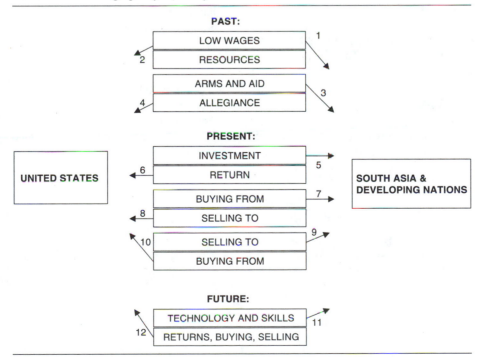

NOTE: Unlike Table 1, the arrows here are not causal arrows. The arrows on the left side show what the U.S. has generally received form its relations with developing nations in the past, present, and future. The arrows on the right side show what developing nations have received from the U.S.

(3 and 4)   The Cold War–involved arms and aid going to developing nations, and allegiance going to the United States or the Soviet Union.

The arrows from the *present* indicate:

(5 and 6)   Capital investment going to the developing nations with a reasonable return going back to the United States.

(7 and 8)   Cash or credits going to developing nations in return for their products.

(9 and 10)   Products going to developing nations in return for their cash or credits.

The arrows from the *future* indicate:

(11 and 12)   Technologies and skill go to developing nations, thereby improving their ability to be good places for investment, buying, and selling.

In the past, there was often an imbalance, with disproportionate benefits to the industrial nations and disproportionate detriments to the developing nations. In the present, there is generally mutual benefits from investments, exporting, and importing. In the future, the transfer of technologies and skills may enable all participating countries to exceed their best initial expectations simultaneously.[4]

ILLUSTRATIVE EXAMPLES

Tables 3–5 show how win–win analysis might be applied to three key issues in South Asia. The issues relate to trade vs. aid, secession, and nuclear arms.

Trade Vs. Aid (Prosperity)

The United States currently tends to favor trade over aid because trade is more mutually beneficial than aid, which

Table 3   Trade vs. aid in South Asia

	Goals	
Alternatives	Pro-United States (C)	Pro-South Asia (L)
C Mainly trade	+	−
L Self-determination	−	+
N	0	0
1) Some trade		
2) Some aid		
SOS or win–win	++	++
1) Skills transfer		
2) Technology transfer		

Table 4   Secession in South Asia (Kashmir)

	Goals	
Alternatives	Pro-United States (C)	Pro-South Asia (L)
C Self-determination	+	−
L	−	+
1) Retain rebellious provinces (pro-India)		
2) Release rebellious provinces (pro-Pakistan)		
N Partition	0	0
SOS or win–win	++	++
Autonomy like a U.S. state		

tends to mainly benefit the recipient nation unless there is a Cold War return.

Developing nations tend to favor aid with no strings attached, at least in the past, because they are fearful that[1] buying from the United States will disrupt local industries, and that[2] they have little to sell to the United States.

Skills and technology transfer greatly benefit the United States by virtue of improving places for 1) U.S. investment; 2) the buying of American products; and 3) the selling to the U.S. of products needed by the American people. Skills and technology transfer benefit developing nations by enabling them to upgrade their international competitiveness even more than offering them either trade or aid.

Seceding (Democracy)

The United States tends to favor self-determination out of a regard for democratic decision making, emphasizing the majority will within the rebellious provinces.

Table 5   Nuclear arms in South Asia

	Goals	
Alternatives	Pro-United States (C)	Pro-South Asia (L)
C No nuclear arms	+	−
L Retain the capability that exists	−	+
N	0	0
1) Reduce		
2) Inspect		
SOS or win–win	++	++
Peaceful conversion		

Developing nations tend to favor retaining their own rebellious provinces, emphasizing the majority will within the larger political entity.

Autonomy, like that of a U.S. state, refers to states having their own constitutions and governors that cannot be removed by Washington. States in India do not have their own constitutions and their governors can be removed by New Delhi.

Nuclear Arms (Peace)

The United States tends to favor the removal of nuclear arms from South Asia for fear that their presence may lead to nuclear warfare, which might involve the United States directly or indirectly by way of international disruption.

Countries that have nuclear capability like India and Pakistan are reluctant to weaken their deterrent power against each other.

Peaceful conversion in this context means providing India and Pakistan with the skills and technologies for converting their nuclear capability into peaceful and safe nuclear energy along with American investment funding.

REFERENCES

1. Stuart, N., et al. Co-effect diagrams and win–win analysis. Policy Eval. **2000**, *6*, 9–12.
2. Stuart, N., et al. Win–win domestic peace, prosperity, and democracy. Peace Prosper. Democr. **2001**, *1*, 35–42.
3. Francis, A. Prosperity: The Political Economy of Foreign Assistance. In *Multi-National Policy Toward Prosperity*; Stuart, N., Ed.; Kluwer, 2001.
4. Stuart, N. Win–win technology policy. Dev. Policy Stud. **1999**, *5*, 28–37.

Restorative Justice

Michelle Maiese
University of Colorado at Boulder, Boulder, Colorado, U.S.A.

INTRODUCTION

The dominant understanding of crime and justice in the United States is shaped by a retributive framework. This framework focuses on the establishment of guilt and understands crime as a matter of lawbreaking and an offense against the state. When a law is broken, this creates a debt that must be repaid to society. Offenders must receive their "just desserts" and endure their punishment. The United States has established elaborate legal mechanisms to administer "just" doses of pain to those who have willfully broken the law.

Restorative justice, on the other hand, understands crime as an offense against real people and relationships rather than the state. Making things right requires healing victims' wounds, restoring offenders to law-abiding lives, and repairing the harm done to interpersonal relationship and the community. Moreover, restorative justice recognizes that victims, offenders, family members, and affected communities are all key stakeholders in the restorative process and should play an active role in deciding how to repair the damage caused by the offense. Restorative justice thus represents a progressive way of thinking about crime and justice. The alternatives to punishment that it suggests can help to empower and heal victims, offenders, and communities.

NEEDS OF VICTIMS, OFFENDERS, AND COMMUNITIES

The safety, support, and healing of crime victims are the starting points for any restorative justice process. A primary objective is to attend to victims' needs: material, financial, emotional, and social.[1] Victims need to receive compensation for any property they have lost and any physical injuries they have suffered. Other central victims' needs include security, dignity, social support, and the sense that justice has been done.[2] They must have the opportunity to tell their story and express their feelings about what has happened. They also need to feel vindicated and to know that others recognize what happened to them was wrong.

Restitution often plays a central role not only in restoring material losses, but also in acknowledging wrongdoing. Restitution agreements symbolize the fact that offenders accept responsibility for the harm they have caused and wish to make amends. However, rather than focusing on punishing or defeating the wrongdoer, restitution aims to elevate the victim.[3] Restorative justice therefore advocates restitution to the victim by the offender rather than retribution by the state against the offender. Instead of causing further harm, it tries to restore relationships and stop the cycle of violence.[4]

Restorative justice also requires that victims be empowered. Because our current system defines the state as victim, this typically means that actual victims "are mere footnotes to the criminal justice process" and do not play an active role in their own cases.[3] Restorative justice, on the other hand, acknowledges that because part of the harm victims have suffered is loss of power, one dimension of justice is ensuring that this power is returned to them. Victims must have access to information about who the offender is, why they were targeted as victims, and what is being done about the crime. They must also have the opportunity to engage in dialogue with offenders. Victims should play an active role in directing the exchange that takes place and defining the responsibilities and obligations of offenders.

Offenders are likewise encouraged to participate in this exchange, to understand the harm they have caused to victims, and to take active responsibility for it. Both the rehabilitation of offenders and their reintegration into the community are vital aspects of restorative justice. Restorative processes encourage offenders to understand and acknowledge the harm they have caused and assume responsibility for making things right. This means making an effort to make amends for their violations by committing to certain obligations: reparations, restitution, or community work. In addition, offenders should share in the responsibility for deciding what needs to be done to repair the harm they have caused. This may increase their sense of accountability.

While fulfilling these obligations may be experienced as painful, the goal is not revenge, but rather the restoration of healthy relationships between victims, offenders, and communities. Moreover, if offenders can play an active role in the justice process and take responsibility for what they have done, this can contribute to their rehabilitation. Removing offenders from the

Encyclopedia of Public Administration and Public Policy
DOI: 10.1081/E-EPAP 120027808

Table 1 Comparison of retributive and restorative justice models

Retributive justice	Restorative justice
Crime is a matter of lawbreaking and an offense against the state.	Crime is an offense against individuals, relationships, and communities.
Those who commit crimes freely and willfully break the law.	Those who commit crimes act within a specific context. In many cases offenders themselves have suffered harm.
The process focuses on the establishment of guilt and is oriented toward the past.	The process focuses on offenders taking responsibility and is oriented toward the future.
To make things right, offenders must receive their "just desserts" and undergo pain.	To make things right, the harm caused to individuals and communities must be repaired.
Responding to crime centers on punishment.	Responding to crime centers on healing.
Victims' needs are peripheral.	Victims' needs are central.
Legal personnel process cases. Victims and offenders do not play an active role in the justice process.	Victims and offenders play an active role in determining outcomes.

Source: From Ref. [3].

community, or imposing any other severe restrictions, should be viewed as a last resort. The best way to prevent reoffending is reintegration.

Restorative justice is a forward-looking, preventive response that strives to understand crime in its social context. Although offenders are responsible for the harm they have caused, their behavior arises out of a social, economic, and psychological context. Moreover, crime often grows out of harm that the offender himself/herself has suffered. Restorative justice challenges us to examine the root causes of violence and the social conditions that give rise to crime.[4] It suggests that communities must take some responsibility for remedying those conditions that contribute to crime and work to promote healing. This means transforming relationships and communities so that crime does not recur.

Restorative justice processes thus aim to strengthen the community and promote changes that will prevent similar harms from happening in the future. Many believe that the implementation of restorative justice processes can improve the quality, effectiveness, and efficiency of justice as a whole.[3] A growing number of state and county justice systems in the United States have begun to incorporate "restorative" policies and programs (Table 1).

RESTORATIVE JUSTICE INITIATIVES

Restorative justice initiatives provide opportunities for dialogue and problem solving to interested crime victims and offenders so that they can more fully understand the events that have taken place. In short, the initiatives aim to put power and responsibility in the hands of those directly involved in the crime.

Such programs take on various forms. Victim–offender mediation is perhaps the most common and involves face-to-face dialogues between victims and offenders. Group conferencing is an extension of victim–offender mediation and involves more participants, including family members of the victim or offender, community contacts, teachers, neighbors, or counselors. In addition, community victim-support organizations work to provide victims with material, psychological, and social support to aid in the healing process. Other organizations assist in reintegration for offenders and provide literacy education, employment services, counseling, and housing accommodation.

Research has shown that these restorative justice programs provide higher levels of victim and offender satisfaction than do traditional criminal justice programs.[5] They are significantly more likely to result in victims' perceptions that their cases were handled fairly and help to humanize the criminal justice experience.[2] Below are more detailed descriptions of four restorative practices commonly used in North America and Europe: victim–offender mediation, group conferencing, community boards, and circle sentencing. These processess are nonadversarial, less formal than current criminal justice proceedings, and typically involve community members in planning and implementation.[6] The continued development of such initiatives indicates that the range of services available for crime victims is expanding (Table 2).

Victim–Offender Mediation

Victim–offender mediation (VOM) provides interested victims the opportunity to meet with their offenders in the presence of trained volunteers who act as mediators. A

Table 2 Comparison of four restorative justice processes

	Victim–offender mediation	Family group conferencing	Community reparative boards	Circle sentencing
Key participants	Mediator, victim, and offender.	Victim, offender, their close family members and friends, police, and social service persons.	Reparative coordinator, community board participants, and offender.	Victim, offender, support persons, and relevant community members.
Prior to meetings	Mediators have face-to-face meetings with victims and offenders to explain the process.	Coordinators contact the offender, the offender's family, and the victim (either by phone or in person).	There is no preparation for individual hearings. Board members receive general preservice training.	Community justice committees work extensively with offenders and victims to prepare them for the process.
Role of facilitator	Mediator manages dialogue and keeps conversation flowing. Victim and offender do most of the talking.	The coordinator calls on each participant to describe the impact the crime has had on his or her life and ensures that all participants have a chance to speak.	Board chairperson dictates the course the meeting takes and calls on participants to speak.	"Keeper" simply initiates the conversation. Dialogue proceeds by passing the talking piece.
Decision of outcome	The victim plays a central role in shaping the restitution agreement. Both victim and offender must consent.	All participants, including offender, work together to determine how the offender can best repair the harm caused. Participants typically sign an agreement.	Board members develop a list of proposed sanctions. The offender agrees to fulfill obligations within a certain time frame.	Participants gather in a sentencing circle to develop a sentencing plan and identify the obligations the offender must fulfill.

Source: From Ref. [6].

central goal of VOM is to actively involve both victims and offenders in addressing the emotional and material harm that has been done. Through a face-to-face meeting, victims and offenders can develop a better understanding of what has happened and work to develop mutually acceptable restitution plans.

This dialogue-driven form of ''mediation'' differs from traditional mediation insofar as the parties involved are not disputants and do not discuss the subject of guilt. Because the process is not focused on settlement, victims are not expected to compromise with respect to having their needs met and losses restored. Rather than passively taking their punishment, offenders take an active role in figuring out how to restore losses. Together, victim and offender determine the best way to repair the harms suffered.

Victim–offender mediation stresses the importance of extensive preparation for both victim and offender prior to the session. Before a dialogue takes place, the mediator meets with both offenders and victims to inform them about the process and invite them to participate. Preliminary meetings give the mediator a chance to establish credibility and rapport with the victim, provide information about the mediation program, describe the mediation process and its goals, and explain the possible benefits and risks of participation. Should the victim make an informed decision to participate, mediators also help to brainstorm about how losses and needs might be addressed. A dialogue with the offender should not be scheduled until the victim is ready and has realistic expectations about the process.[7]

Meetings should occur in a structured setting in a location that victims consider safe. The dialogue itself should be structured so as to neutralize differences in status and power and ensure that both parties' complete stories are heard. Parties are typically seated across from each other at a table, allowing them to have direct eye contact during the session. Support persons often accompany victims to the session to increase their sense of security and comfort. The mediator encourages participants to express their feelings and tries to facilitate an open dialogue in which victims and offenders do most of the talking. Although mediators must be careful not to intervene too frequently, they must also be prepared to step in immediately if a victim feels unsafe.[7]

In addition to the option to terminate the meeting at any time, victims have many choices throughout VOM. They decide when and where to meet, who should attend, and what restitution plan best meets their needs. In addition to reimbursement of monetary expenses, the victim may request that the offender do community service, perform a personal service, write a letter of apology, participate in treatment or rehabilitation programs, or complete some creative assignment. While the final restitution plan must

be negotiated with the offender, the process puts much decision-making power in the hands of the victim.

While VOM sessions typically result in signed restitution agreements, the dialogue itself is the most important part. Victims have an opportunity to express their feelings, speak about the impact that the crime has had upon their lives, and receive answers to important questions about what occurred. The opportunity to come face-to-face with their offender increases the likelihood that victims will receive an apology and gain emotional closure.[2] Offenders, on the other hand, come to understand the real human impact of their behavior and develop empathy for victims, which can help to prevent future criminal behavior. Thus mediated dialogue can satisfy the needs of the parties and aid in the healing process without resulting in a written restitution agreement.

At one time, people questioned whether victims would really want to meet with their offenders face-to-face. However, studies show that the majority of victims who are given the opportunity to engage their offenders in dialogue choose to participate.[7] Victims who meet with their offenders are also significantly less fearful of being revictimized and report that the opportunity to be actively involved in the justice process results in a heightened sense of emotional closure.[2] Research also indicates that offenders who meet with victims are more likely to fulfill their restitution obligations and less likely to commit future crimes.[6]

As a result, the American Bar Association has endorsed the use of VOM and dialogue in courts throughout the United States. In 2001, there were approximately 320 victim–offender mediation programs in the United States and more than 700 in Europe.[6] Many of the programs work only with juvenile offenders and handle mostly cases involving property offenses and minor assaults. However, advocates have begun to challenge the assumption that VOM is not suitable for violent or sexual crimes. Its use in these more serious cases is becoming more widespread.

Family Group Conferencing

Family group conferencing (FGC) involves all the people most affected by the crime: victim, offender, and the family and friends of both. The practice originated in New Zealand and emphasizes the role of family and community in addressing wrongdoing, reintegrating offenders, and holding them accountable. The process encourages the offender's support system to take collective responsibility for making amends and shaping the offender's future behavior. In addition to family members, conferences typically involve teachers, peers, and community resource people. Because conferencing involves more community members than VOM, some believe that it can contribute more to the empowerment and healing of the community as a whole.[5]

Prior to the conference, the facilitator contacts both victim and offender to explain the process and invite them to a conference. This in-person meeting provides an opportunity for coordinators to build trust, provide information, and prepare parties for the conference should they choose to participate. If victims and offenders are not prepared, they may not feel safe nor be able to participate freely in a genuine dialogue.

Once both parties have agreed to participate, they identify key members of their support systems to accompany them. With the help of the trained facilitator, the parties discuss how they have been harmed by the offense and how this might be addressed. After the offender has described why the crime occurred, each participant speaks about the impact the offense has had on his or her life. The offender is thereby faced with the real human impact of his/her behavior on the victim, those close to the victim, and his/her own family and friends. After this discussion, the victim helps to decide the obligations that the offender must carry out. All participants play a role in determining how the offender might fulfill these obligations and repair the harm he/she has caused. The session typically ends with participants signing a restitution agreement.

Family group conferencing is now being used in many states in the United States, including Minnesota, Montana, Pennsylvania, and Vermont.[6] It is used primarily with juvenile offenders and in cases of theft, arson, minor assaults, and vandalism. Police people, probation officers, or school officials often act as facilitators. The process is most often used as a diversion from the court process and can often provide a much quicker and more satisfying resolution than traditional criminal justice practices.

Community Reparative Boards

Community reparative boards are primarily used with adult offenders convicted of nonviolent and minor offenses. A small group of citizens who have received intensive training meet face-to-face with offenders (and sometimes victims) to discuss what has happened. During meetings, board members constructively discuss the nature of the offense with the offender and point out its negative consequences. A chairperson guides members through their questioning of the offender and their discussions with the other participants. The board members then propose and discuss a list of proposed sanctions. The offender agrees to take specific action within a given time period to repair the harm he or she has caused. A reparative coordinator, usually a State corrections em-

ployee, is responsible for monitoring the offender's compliance. This process enables offenders to take personal responsibility for what has happened and actually give something back to the community. It also reduces costly reliance on formal justice system processes. However, some criticize reparative boards for their minimal involvement of victims.[6]

Circle Sentencing

The practice of circle sentencing grew out of traditional sanctioning practices of aboriginal peoples in Canada and Native Americans in the United States. The first modern program was implemented in Canada and its use spread to the United States in 1996, when a pilot project was initiated in Minnesota.[6] It is a holistic integrative strategy that aims both to address the delinquent behavior of offenders as well as to consider the needs of victims and communities. Crime victims, offenders, family, friends, interested community residents, and justice and social service personnel all gather together to develop a better understanding of the event. The process tends to enhance respect and understanding among all involved and often produces innovative solutions.

Circle sentencing demands extensive presession preparation. To be admitted to a circle, offenders must petition the community justice committee, visit a respected community member for a conference, and begin work on a reparative plan. This plan typically involves some restitution to the victim and community service. The presession procedures act as a screening mechanism to ensure that offenders take the process seriously.

Circle sentencing typically involves a multistep process. First, there are separate healing circles for the victim and the offender. Next, there is a sentencing circle to develop a sentencing plan. After that, there are follow-up circles to monitor the progress the offender has made. Participants are expected to take responsibility for monitoring the offender's compliance with the sentence. Throughout the process, community support groups work to fulfill the needs of victim, offender, and community. A central function of these support groups is to protect victims, provide them a sense of security, and hear their stories.

A trained community member called a "keeper" initiates the dialogue and ensures the process is followed. Participants sit in a circle and pass around a "talking piece." When it is their turn to talk, they explain their feelings about the crime and express support for the victim and offender. Central goals of the process include promoting healing of all affected parties, empowering victims and community members by giving them a voice in the process, and providing an opportunity for the offender to make amends.[6] Circles also help to build a sense of community and address the underlying causes of criminal behavior.

CONCERNS ABOUT IMPLEMENTATION

Restorative justice is not yet a complete model. It is not entirely clear how it can address certain difficult issues, such as disputes over culpability, consequences of failure to reach an agreement, equity and proportionality in outcomes, or failure of the offender to comply with outcomes reached.[2] Also, it seems the notion of restorative justice has been developed largely within a white, male, North American perspective and has yet to be tested in diverse cultures and traditions.[3] Finally, it is unclear how restorative justice meshes with larger questions of social, economic, and political justice.

To prove successful, restorative processes must be highly sensitive to victims' needs. Programs that are overly offender-focused may treat victims simply as tools for rehabilitating offenders. In addition, restorative processes can perpetuate power imbalances already existing between victim and offender. Especially in cases where victim and offender have a prior relationship, power and coercion may operate in these informal structures to revictimize the victim. Facilitators must be careful not to exhibit bias toward the offender and to take the harms that victims have experienced sufficiently seriously. They must also be prepared to intervene should the victim feel threatened or uncomfortable. Processes that fail to adequately address victims' needs may have damaging effects.

Perhaps the most common argument against restorative justice practices is that the process and outcomes vary across programs, so that comparable crimes are not ''punished'' equally. Instead, restorative justice approaches yield individualized responses to crimes. This lack of uniformity contradicts some of our basic ideas about fairness. However, some suggest that issues of ''fairness'' could be mitigated if restorative justice initiatives were implemented system-wide. Furthermore, it seems that any worries that restorative processes might lead to random, inequitable, and overly severe sanctions are misguided.[8] In fact, the emphasis of restorative justice on healing and constructive goals suggests that such initiatives would actually have the opposite effect.

There is some debate about whether restorative justice should remain an unofficial alternative to the criminal justice system or whether such practices should be implemented system-wide. Some maintain that restorative justice is not likely to have lasting, significant effects if it continues to operate primarily at the grassroots level.

However, others suggest that even if restorative justice principles cannot transform the justice system, they may improve current criminal justice policies. Still others worry that government agencies will bureaucratize such initiatives and strip them of creativity. Spontaneity and grassroots ties are often what make these initiatives so successful.

Some advocate a double system of punishment, in which offenders are first processed through the traditional system and then move on to informal restorative justice programs to agree to a reparative contract. However, this may mean that they end up being subject to more sanctions. In addition, few resources will be saved if restorative initiatives are only a supplement to traditional punishment or are used only for minor crimes. It seems that for restorative justice initiatives to have a forceful impact, they must be implemented system-wide.[8]

Without official encouragement and support, restorative justice programs are likely to be concentrated in neighborhoods with relatively minor crime problems and to be used only with fairly minor offenses. However, the empirical data suggest that programs increasingly handle cases involving adult offenders, more serious crime, and disadvantaged urban communities.[8] Many believe that these experiments in applying restorative processes should continue. This will help to determine whether restorative justice is applicable in cases involving spouse and child abuse, rape, and murder, and what sorts of safeguards are needed. Testing of new programs will require creativity, risk-taking, and hard work.

CONCLUSION

To be sure, a restorative justice approach is not a realistic response in all situations. In cases where offenders are dangerous, it may be necessary to incarcerate and forego restorative tactics. There are also cases in which victims may experience meeting their offenders as threatening. In cases of emotional vulnerability, for example when victim and offender are well known to each other, a court process with its formality and impersonal procedures may be preferable.

However, the restorative justice paradigm shows promise of offering crime victims more justice than they currently receive in the dominant criminal justice paradigm. Such initiatives provide ''alternatives to punishment which offer possibilities for accountability, repair, and empowerment.''[3] While traditional justice practices tend to ignore victims' needs and treat crime as an offense against the state, restorative justice recognizes that crime involves real-life individuals. Rather than simply inflicting more harm via punishment, it seeks to heal individuals and repair communities.

REFERENCES

1. Marshall, T.F. *Restorative Justice: An Overview*; http://www.homeoffice.gov.uk/rds/pdfs/occ-resjus.pdf (accessed December, 2003).
2. Strang, H. *Repair or Revenge: Victims and Restorative Justice*; Clarendon Press: Oxford, 2002; pp. 48, 54.
3. Zehr, H. *Changing Lenses: A New Focus For Crime and Justice*; Herald Press: Scottsdale, PA, 1990; pp. 82, 221, 223.
4. Hutchison, P.; Wray, H. *What is Restorative Justice?*; http://gbgm-umc.org/nwo/99ja/what.html (accessed December, 2003).
5. Umbreit, M. *Family Group Conferencing: Implications for Crime Victims*; Center for Restorative Justice and Peacemaking United States Department of Justice: Washington, DC, 2000; pp. 1–10.
6. Bazemore, G.; Umbreit, M. *A Comparison of Four Restorative Justice Conferencing Models*; Juvenile Justice Bulletin United States Department of Justice: Washington, DC, 2001; pp. 1–19.
7. Umbreit, M.; Greenwood, J. *Guidelines for Victim-Sensitive Victim–Offender Mediation: Restorative Justice Through Dialogue*; Center for Restorative Justice and Peacemaking United States Department of Justice: Washington, DC, 2000; pp. 1–63.
8. Kurki, L. *Incorporating Restorative and Community Justice Into American Sentencing and Corrections*; Sentencing and Corrections 3 United States Department of Justice: Washington, DC, 1999; pp. 1–11.

Risk Management

David L. Baker
Arizona State University, Tempe, Arizona, U.S.A.

INTRODUCTION

Public agencies operate in a risky environment. Risk relates to the chance of injury, damage, or loss.[1] It represents a set of circumstances in which multiple outcomes are possible and the probability of each possible outcome can be estimated.[2] Losses affect the human, financial, physical, and natural resources under the care of a public agency.[3] Risk management seeks to conserve and to protect public resources from accidental loss. It proactively mitigates governmental risk through awareness, avoidance, assessment, containment, funding, and management oversight.

The following review discusses risks and defines exposures, perils, and hazards. It explicates six primary risk management concepts (risk awareness, exposure avoidance, risk assessment, risk containment, risk funding, and risk management). After highlighting macrotreatment and microtreatment strategies, common elements of governmental risk containment programs are described and the manners in which they minimize loss are examined. The review outlines the major tasks of risk management administration and introduces the notion of pervasive risk management. Following an appraisal of the organizational benefits arising from risk management, the review concludes with an overall summary of the topic.

RISKS, EXPOSURES, PERILS, AND HAZARDS

Two primary types of risk may be distinguished: speculative risk and pure risk. Speculative risk refers to situations where both loss and gain may occur. Pure risk involves unexpected loss without the opportunity of some gain. Public agency risk management deals with pure risk.

An understanding of exposures, perils, and hazards provides a common framework for analyzing pure risks.[1] Exposures have to do with risk circumstances that can result in a loss. It refers to vulnerabilities resulting from a public agency's existence and its operation. There is no exposure if there is no likelihood of loss. Perils are defined as the actual causes of loss.[4] For example, perils consist of death, injury, natural catastrophes, litigation, and illegal activity. Hazards boost the probability and/or severity of loss. Actions or conditions create hazards. For example, faulty brakes on school buses are a hazard that increases the likelihood of the peril of injury, property damage, and litigation.

Risk management seeks to reduce or eliminate losses by reducing hazards. Consequently, it is useful to evaluate hazards by segregating them into three categories: physical, moral, and morale (or behavioral) hazards.[1,4] Physical hazards are defined as conditions that increase the probability of loss. For instance, the absence of secure exterior doors on a public building constitutes a physical hazard. Moral hazards consist of dishonest behavior by individuals, either observed or unobserved, that affects the likelihood or magnitude of a loss[5] (e.g., a public employee stealing gasoline from a public agency for the employee's personal vehicle). Morale hazard comes from personal carelessness. An employee recklessly driving an agency's vehicle denotes an example of morale hazard. Within this framework of understanding, the review now turns to explaining the core concepts of risk management.

RISK MANAGEMENT CONCEPTS

Six risk management concepts capture the underpinnings of a comprehensive risk management program for governmental entities. First, "risk awareness" concerns identification of public agency resources that could be affected in unintended, adverse ways and to the detriment of the public interest. Resources face natural events (e.g., monsoons, volcanoes, and earthquakes) and human actions (e.g., terrorism, fires, and lawsuits) with serious consequences for governmental entities. Many exposures present indirect impacts involving expenses to meet essential operations and service responsibilities.[3] Wide-ranging exposure calls for persistent vigilance to discover and to address public agency risks.

Second, "exposure avoidance" means to avoid or to eliminate a given exposure.[6] The goal is to remove the likelihood of loss totally. A completely avoided exposure requires no further resource investment for risk containment or risk funding. Consequently, public agencies often attempt exposure avoidance when they first discover vulnerabilities.

Encyclopedia of Public Administration and Public Policy
DOI: 10.1081/E-EPAP 120010746

Third, after establishing risk awareness and attempting exposure avoidance, "risk assessment" encompasses the gray area between certainty (knowing exactly what will occur) and uncertainty (not knowing what will occur). It confronts Simon's[7] "bounded rationality" inasmuch as estimates are made about possible occurrences based on imperfect information.[8] Risk assessment entails measurement of risk by analyzing past loss frequency and severity probabilities. However, it is forward looking.[9] Exposures that present the greatest potential impact on an agency command the highest attention. Past loss history primes analysis as a public agency evaluates the extent of possible future losses and the relative likelihood of those losses.

Fourth, "risk containment" follows assessment. It refers to strategies designed to minimize risks and losses. This typically involves policy development and personnel training in many areas including security, safety, environmental protection, and emergency planning.[3] Risk containment activities require a well-coordinated effort through a designated risk manager. The risk manager functions under a defined system of accountability involving all levels of management, supervision, and front-line employees. Risk management administration is discussed more fully later.

Fifth, some risk losses may be inevitable despite a public agency's best efforts. As a result, part of a comprehensive risk management program involves "risk funding." The imperative to preserve a functioning public agency in the face of a significant risk obligates a governmental entity to maintain adequate funds and funding approaches to cover incurred losses. This calls for a mix of tactics designed to shield public assets at the least cost. The "least cost spectrum" ranges from 1) some risk retention by way of self-insurance, 2) risk sharing through some form of multiagency pooling arrangements, 3) the means to borrow from a financial institution, and 4) risk transfer with the purchase of insurance products.[3] Insurance solutions frequently provide a variety of intermixed methodologies to contain costs. For example, a public agency may be self-insured for the first $250,000 per incident, have a pooling arrangement for losses involving over $250,000 but less than $1.0 million, and purchase insurance to cover losses that exceed $1.0 million per incident.

Sixth, "risk management" combines governmental risk awareness, exposure avoidance, risk assessment, risk containment, and risk funding through a compelling, coordinated, and communicated effort to protect public assets. This usually involves various levels of policy development, training, staffing, organizing, and ongoing evaluation with periodic public reports to the community served. Conscientious risk management fosters the notion

of "pervasive risk management." This review introduces and explores that subject later.

RISK TREATMENT STRATEGIES

Risk treatment strategies commence with management fundamentals at the macrolevel. After analysis of an agency's strengths, weaknesses, threats, and opportunities, management initiates a risk management vision. This usually includes a statement of exactly what the agency seeks to accomplish, identification of resource allocations to support the desired accomplishments, measurable outcomes, and timelines for monitoring activities. Periodic performance review should include a regime of internal and external critique.

Moving to the microlevel, risk treatment strategies generally include many implementing measures that flow from macrolevel activities. For example, successful public agency risk treatment strategies require 1) briefing elected officials and public policy approvals, 2) communicating, coordinating, and educating the organization, 3) discussing and involving staff throughout the organization to identify and assess risk areas, 4) carefully constructing risk management policies, 5) implementing procedures and providing constructive assistance to organizational units in policy applications,[3] 6) monitoring and evaluating reports to review compliance, tackle problems, measure trends, and exploit emerging opportunities, and 7) periodic external critique through timely audits and review of data from comparable jurisdictions known for outstanding practices and performance.

RISK CONTAINMENT PROGRAM ELEMENTS

Risk containment is a central focus of risk management. It meets the objective of minimizing risks and losses through initiating activities that positively alter the probability that a loss incident occurs. When an incident does happen, the goal is to reduce the severity of the loss and provide a means for recovery. These activities, or program elements, are designed and modified based on specific risk exposure and assessment analysis. Common elements of governmental risk containment programs include the following.

- Security: Protecting people, possessions/property, information,[3] and the means to use information (information and communication technology) from illegal or unauthorized internal and external threats.
- Personal safety: Meeting all employee and citizen health and safety regulations,[3] taking preventative

measures, maintaining records of concerns and incidents, and training individuals as needed.

- Equipment safety: Developing and enforcing use standards on all equipment to assure safe operations. This may include checking weapons on law enforcement personnel, needle-stick and lifting protocols in public hospitals, and specialized forklift training in governmental warehouses.
- Emergency preparedness: Developing contingency plans to address natural and environmental disasters as well as human-induced actions. Such preparedness aims to safeguard human, private, and governmental loss.

Beyond these risk containment program elements, there are several techniques designed to minimize loss.[1] First, loss prevention hunts for ways to avoid harm before something occurs. For example, security guards may serve as a deterrent to theft. Second, loss reduction strives to cut the consequence of a loss. For instance, fire detection alarms and extinguishers may lessen a loss once a fire starts. Third, segregation relates to tactics taken to trim down potential harm. This is illustrated in the practice of insisting that several elected officials attending a conference use more than one aircraft for transportation. Fourth, and finally, duplication or redundancy protects an agency by assuring the availability of a replacement asset in critical situations should the primary asset be lost or malfunction. A case in point would be the provision for a backup generator to maintain computer services to law enforcement and fire suppression personnel during an electrical power shortage.

RISK MANAGEMENT ADMINISTRATION

Risk management programs require continuous direction and careful attention.[3] The staffing component dedicated to the effort varies depending on organizational size, complexity, and available resources. Effective programs administratively focus on the following activities.[1]

- Developing the overall mission and adaptive strategies, including periodic elected official briefings, generation of written policies, and constant performance monitoring and improvement.
- Defining responsibilities and organizing resources for risk awareness, exposure avoidance, risk assessment, risk containment, risk funding, and risk management.
- Communicating throughout the organization and to the public about the overall agency's challenges, objectives, and progress.

The job of risk manager requires a multistep process. The designated individual works as staff to the chief administrative officer in developing an organizational vision, mission, and objectives for the risk management effort. A comprehensive program is developed and implemented to contain and to manage exposures. Internal self-audit as well as external evaluation hone practices and refine strategies while identifying areas for continuous improvement and modification.

PERVASIVE RISK MANAGEMENT

Risk management requires deliberate attention throughout governmental activities. This does not mean that risk adversity should stifle governance and delivery of services with creativity crushing inertia. It does suggest that risk management needs to be addressed as part of everyday governmental activities. The notion of "pervasive risk management" calls for integrating macrorisk and microrisk management thinking into the daily activities of government. It brings systems thinking to bear on risk management holistically. Proactive problem solving emanates from examining the context of the system where the concerns arise.[10] Conserving and protecting public agency resources should not be an afterthought.

Public agencies need to push risk containment program elements back into program planning and strategic thinking at the earliest point possible to achieve risk management at the lowest cost. The pervasive risk management notion requires that the classical functions of planning, organizing, staffing, directing, coordinating, reporting, and budgeting[11] consider all these activities with sensitivity to risk management.

RISK MANAGEMENT BENEFITS

Several public agency benefits arise from risk management activities.[1,9,12] The more compelling involve 1) control of insurance costs, 2) enhanced communication, coordination, and record-keeping, 3) active case, or claims, management, 4) finely tuned risk sensitivity and training to curb injuries and claim expenses, 5) more sharply focused insurance decisions, 6) heighten security for citizens, employees, and public agency assets, 7) minimal operational disruptions, 8) immediate resources to address some losses and funding strategies to address larger losses, and 9) more proactive administrative leadership and an enhanced organizational culture to support it. Individually and collectively, these benefits boost the effectiveness of a public agency while conserving and protecting public resources.

CONCLUSION

All public agencies function with some level of risk.[13] Risk management seeks to conserve and to protect public resources from loss. It does this through a vigilant campaign of awareness, exposure avoidance, assessment, containment, funding, and overall management. There are macrorisk and microrisk treatment strategies, and public agencies are well served through implementing effective security, personal safety, equipment safety, and emergency preparedness programs. Risk management administration critically focuses on risk management leadership, responsibilities, resources, and communications. Execution of a comprehensive effort involves the notion of pervasive risk management where systems' thinking about risk management permeates the organization. The many benefits of a sound risk management program boost the effectiveness of a public agency while guarding public resources.

REFERENCES

1. Hampton, J.J. *Essentials of Risk Management and Insurance*; American Management Association: New York, 1993.
2. Parkin, M. *Microeconomics,* 5th Ed.; Addison-Wesley: Reading, MA, 2000.
3. Phelus, D.G. Risk Management: A Developed Discipline. In *Risk Management Today: A How-to Guide for Local Government*; Wasserman, N., Phelus, D.G., Eds.; International City Management Association: Washington, DC, 1985; 7–21.
4. American Institute of Certified Public Accountants. *Guide to Risk Management and Insurance*; American Institute of Certified Public Accountants, Inc.: New York, 1992.
5. Pindyck, R.S.; Rubinfeld, D.L. *Microeconomics,* 5th Ed.; Prentice-Hall: Upper Saddle River, NJ, 2000.
6. *Essentials of Risk Control, Volume I*; Head, G.L., Ed.; Insurance Institute of America: Malvern, PA, 1986.
7. Simon, H. *Administrative Behavior: A Study of Decision-Making Processes in Administrative Organizations,* 4th Ed.; The Free Press: New York, 1997.
8. White, M.J.; Clayton, R.; Myrtle, R.; Siegel, G.; Rose, A. *Managing Public Systems: Analytic Techniques for Public Administration*; University Press of America, Inc.: Lanham, MD, 1985.
9. *The Professional's Handbook of Financial Risk Management*; Borodovsky, L., Lore, M., Eds.; Butterworth-Heineman: London, 2000.
10. White, D. Application of systems thinking to risk management. Manage. Decis. **1995**, *33* (10), 35–45.
11. Gulick, L. Notes on the Theory of Organization. In *Classics of Public Administration,* 4th Ed.; Sharfritz, J.M., Hyde, A.C., Eds.; Harcourt Brace College Publishers: Fort Worth, TX, 1997; 81–89.
12. Wasserman, N.; Phelus, D.G. Case Studies in Risk Management. In *Risk Management Today: A How-to Guide for Local Government*; Wasserman, N., Phelus, D.G., Eds.; International City Management Association: Washington, DC, 1985; 159–168.
13. Borgsdorf, D.; Pliszka, D. Manage your risk or risk your management. Public Manage. **1999**, *81* (11), 6–10.

Singapore

Jon S. T. Quah
National University of Singapore, Singapore

INTRODUCTION

Singapore attained self-government in June 1959, when the People's Action Party (PAP) government assumed office after winning the May 1959 general election and after nearly 140 years of British colonial rule. The PAP government has governed Singapore for 45 years as it was reelected for the 10th time in the November 2001 general election. This article contends that the nature of public administration in Singapore is shaped by its British colonial heritage, its policy context, and the policies introduced by the PAP government.

PUBLIC ADMINISTRATION UNDER THE BRITISH (1819–1959)

In 1947, the Trusted Commission, which was appointed to review the salaries and conditions of service of public services in the Malayan Union and Singapore, recommended that a Public Service Commission (PSC) be formed as the adapted version of the Civil Service Commission in Britain; and that the Singapore Civil Service (SCS), following the example of the British Civil Service, be reorganized and divided into four divisions according to the duties and salaries of its members.

There are four major features of public administration in Singapore during the colonial period. First, the SCS did not play an important role in national development during the colonial period as it was preoccupied with enforcing colonial rule in Singapore and with economic exploitation of natural resources from the region for the benefit of the home government in Britain. In other words, the SCS focused on performing the traditional "housekeeping" functions of maintaining law and order, building public works, and collecting taxes.

Second, the SCS neglected administrative reform as it was responsible for introducing only two reforms: the fourfold division of the SCS in 1947, and the creation of the PSC in 1951. As the PSC was formed to keep politics out of the SCS by rejecting the spoils system and to speed up the localization of civil servants, its establishment led to the introduction of meritocracy in the SCS.

Third, the SCS was afflicted by the problem of corruption during the colonial period. Corruption was made illegal in 1871, when the Penal Code of the Straits Settlements was enacted. However, the first anticorruption law was only passed 66 years later in December 1937, when the Prevention of Corruption Ordinance came into force.

Fourth, the civil servants during the British colonial period were criticized for having "a colonial mentality and were insensitive to the needs of the population." The PAP leaders had serious misgivings about the SCS as its localization had not contributed to a national bureaucracy. Accordingly, the PAP leaders were compelled to introduce comprehensive reforms to transform the SCS after they assumed office in June 1959.

THE POLICY CONTEXT

A brief description of the policy context in Singapore is necessary as it is an important factor influencing the nature of public administration and the performance of the SCS. More specifically, Singapore's smallness, multiracial population, and level of economic development, and the PAP government's predominance will be discussed.

In terms of size, Singapore is a city-state with a total land area of 682.7 km^2, or the same size as Lake Biwa in Japan. Although Singapore's smallness has enhanced policy implementation as the SCS does not encounter the logistical and communications problems found in larger countries, its small size also constitutes a constraint as there is no large rural hinterland for the cultivation of crops or the mining of minerals. Indeed, as Singapore has no natural resources, it has to rely instead on its strategic location, deep harbor, and people.

In June 2002, Singapore had a population of 4,163,700 (including foreigners who have resided for at least a year) and a population density of 6075 persons/km^2. The resident population of 3,378,300 persons is heterogeneous in three aspects. First, it is multiracial as the Chinese constitute 76.5%, Malays make up 13.8%, Indians constitute 8.1%, and other races make up 1.6%. Second, although the resident population speaks many languages

Encyclopedia of Public Administration and Public Policy
DOI: 10.1081/E-EPAP-120024433

and dialects, there are four official languages: English (the language of administration), Mandarin, Malay, and Tamil. Finally, in terms of religion, 54% of Singaporeans are Buddhists and Taoists, 15% are Muslims, 13% are Christians, 4% are Hindus, and 14% have no religion.[1]

The resident population's diversity in race, language, and religion imposes two obligations on those governing the city-state. The first obligation is the necessity for any incumbent government to formulate and implement policies that contribute to nation building and racial harmony. Second, the political leaders must minimize discrimination of any kind by ensuring that all public and private organizations are fair and impartial in the treatment of members of the public, regardless of their race, language, or religion. The rights of the minorities and religious groups are also protected by the Presidential Council for Minority Rights and the Presidential Council for Religious Harmony, respectively.

In 1960, Singapore was a poor country with a per capita gross domestic product (GDP) of $443, a high unemployment rate, a serious housing shortage, and rampant corruption. However, the PAP government's success in promoting economic development, solving the housing problem, and curbing corruption has resulted in: a per capita GDP of $20,850 in 2001;[2] 85% of the population living in public housing today; and Singapore being the least corrupt Asian country and the fifth least corrupt country among the 133 countries included in *Transparency International*'s 2003 Corruption Perceptions Index.

The PAP government's predominance in Singapore can be attributed to four factors. First, during 1965–1970, it succeeded in garnering the support of the people to deal with the challenges of the withdrawal of the British military forces and the building of Singapore's own armed forces with the introduction of compulsory military service in 1967. Second, the PAP government acquired legitimacy among the population because of its effective response to communist and communal threats. Third, the PAP government's predominance in Singapore politics can be explained in terms of its ability to deliver goods and services to the population during its 45 years in power. Finally, there is no creditable alternative to the PAP government as the opposition political parties are weak organizationally, poorly funded, and unable to recruit professionals as members.

PUBLIC ADMINISTRATION UNDER THE PAP GOVERNMENT (1959–2004)

Public administration in Singapore during the 45 years of the PAP government's rule is characterized by these six features: meritocracy, minimization of corruption, comprehensive administrative reforms, competitive salaries for political leaders and senior civil servants, effective policy implementation, and policy diffusion.

Meritocracy

The PAP government retained the meritocratic system introduced by the British colonial government in 1951 with the creation of the PSC. However, Prime Minister Lee Kuan Yew expressed his disdain for the former British reliance on seniority and favored instead an emphasis on efficiency as the basis for promotion. Consequently, competent civil servants were promoted to more responsible positions regardless of their seniority. This focus on efficiency rather than seniority is responsible for the relative youthfulness of many of the permanent secretaries today. Lee's emphasis on meritocracy and the need to attract the ''best and the brightest'' to join the SCS can be attributed to his experience as the legal adviser to several trade unions in Singapore in the 1950s before his entry into politics. He won all his legal cases against the British colonial government as its lawyers were incompetent and poorly paid.

Accordingly, Lee reinforced the PSC's role in maintaining meritocracy by controlling the quality of personnel entering the SCS. The ''best and the brightest'' Singaporeans are recruited by the PSC for the SCS by awarding scholarships to the best students of every cohort to obtain university education in Singapore or abroad. In his 1996 study of the Economic Development Board (EDB), entitled *Strategic Pragmatism*, Schein[3] astutely observed that ''having 'the best and brightest' in government is probably one of Singapore's major strengths in that they are potentially the most able to invent what the country needs to survive and grow and to overcome the kinds of biases and blind spots.''

Minimization of Corruption

As corruption was a serious problem during the British colonial period, especially after the Japanese Occupation (1942–1945), the newly elected PAP government initiated its anticorruption strategy in 1960 with the enactment of the Prevention of Corruption Act (POCA), which increased the penalty for corruption and empowered the Director of the Corrupt Practices Investigation Bureau (CPIB) and the officers to investigate persons accused of corrupt offences. In 1989, the POCA was amended to enhance the penalty for corruption from 3 to 5 years imprisonment, and the fine was increased 10-fold from S$10,000 ($6000) to S$100,000 ($60,000).

The PAP government succeeded in minimizing corruption because it did not rely on the British colonial method of using the Anticorruption Branch (ACB) in the Singapore Police Force (SPF) to combat corruption. The ACB was ineffective in curbing corruption as it was inadequately staffed and funded, and had difficulty in dealing with police corruption. The theft of S$400,000 worth of opium by some detectives in the SPF in October 1951 forced the British colonial government to transfer the task of corruption control from the SPF to the CPIB in October 1952. However, the CPIB was ineffective during the next 8 years as its powers, personnel, and funds were limited.[4]

The PAP leaders, especially Lee Kuan Yew, were committed to eliminating corruption in Singapore as they relied on the CPIB to impartially implement the POCA against corrupt persons in both the public and private sectors. Moreover, the POCA is constantly reviewed and amendments are introduced whenever necessary to remove any loopholes. In other words, the key to Singapore's success in combating corruption is the impartial implementation of the POCA by the CPIB and the public's perception that corruption in Singapore is no longer a "low-risk, high-reward" activity but a "high-risk, low-reward" activity.[4]

Comprehensive Administrative Reforms

In contrast to the British colonial government, which neglected administrative reform, the PAP leaders initiated comprehensive administrative reforms after assuming power in June 1959 because of the favorable timing, their commitment, and the lower degree of risk in introducing reforms when compared with the maintenance of the status quo.

The timing was favorable for the PAP government to introduce major reforms as its assumption of power marked the end of nearly 140 years of British colonial rule. The PAP leaders emphasized both institutional and attitudinal reforms as they reorganized the SCS, established statutory boards, and changed the "colonial mentality" of the civil servants and their insensitivity to the population's needs. They were also committed to reform as manifested in their critical speeches in the Legislative Assembly on different aspects of the administration of the colony. The most important reason for the introduction of comprehensive administrative reforms was the PAP leaders' perception that the risk involved in not implementing the reforms was greater than the risk accompanying the implementation of the reforms.

The comprehensive reform of the public bureaucracy in 1959 involved these aspects: the formation of the Ministry of Culture and the Ministry of National Development; the creation of such statutory boards as the Housing and Development Board (HDB) and the EDB; the reduction of salaries of senior civil servants by discontinuing their variable allowances; and the establishment of the Political Study Center to change the "colonial mentality" of the civil servants. In short, the PAP government initiated a comprehensive reform of the public bureaucracy in 1959 because it needed the support of the civil servants to implement its programs.

During its 45 years in power, the PAP government introduced these administrative reforms: the 1959 reforms; the POCA in 1960; the 1978 and 1989 budgetary reforms; the establishment of the Public Service Division as the second central personnel agency in 1983; the formation of the Education Service Commission and Police and Civil Defense Services Commissions in 1990; the establishment of the Service Improvement Unit in April 1991; the creation of a system of 31 personnel boards in 1995; the revision of salaries from 1972 to 1993; the benchmarking of the salaries of political leaders and senior civil servants to several private sector professions in October 1994; and the launching of Public Service for the 21st Century (PS21) in May 1995.

Competitive Salaries

As Singapore's economy grew in the 1970s, the higher salaries paid by the private sector led to a brain drain from the SCS, and civil service pay was increased to curb the loss of talent. In 1972, the National Wages Council recommended the payment of an additional month's salary to minimize the gap between salaries in the public and private sectors in Singapore. The salaries of the political leaders and civil servants were periodically revised in 1973, 1979, 1982, 1989, and 1993 to reduce the salary gap in the public and private sectors.[5]

On October 21, 1994, a white paper on *Competitive Salaries for Competent and Honest Government* was presented to the Parliament to justify the pegging of the salaries of ministers and senior civil servants to the average salaries of the top four earners in six private sector professions. The white paper recommended the introduction of formal salary benchmarks for ministers and senior bureaucrats, additional grades for political appointments, and annual salary reviews for the SCS.

The adoption of the long-term formula proposed in the white paper has two advantages: it removed the need to justify "from scratch" every revision of the salaries of ministers and senior civil servants; and it ensured the building of an efficient SCS and a competent and honest political leadership, which are responsible for Singapore's prosperity and success. In short, the white paper institutionalized the PAP government's practice of "matching public pay to the private sector, dollar for dollar" as it enabled the government to revise automatically public sector salaries in response to increases or decreases in private sector salaries.[6]

Thus, by periodically revising civil service salaries to keep pace with rising wages in the private sector from 1972 to 1993, and by benchmarking these salaries with some private sector professions from October 1994 onward, the PAP government has enabled the SCS to retain its talented personnel and also to maintain its quality service.

Effective Policy Implementation

The SCS and statutory boards in Singapore are effective in policy implementation because, once a policy is formulated, the government ensures its successful implementation by providing the required manpower, legislation, financial resources, and equipment to the implementing agencies. Apart from political will, the emphasis on meritocracy and competitive salaries ensures that the public bureaucracy is staffed with qualified and competent personnel. The CPIB's success in minimizing corruption has removed a serious obstacle to policy implementation as scarce resources are not wasted on bribes and delays are avoided. Finally, the small size of Singapore is conducive to effective policy implementation as the public bureaucracy does not face the same logistical and communications problems encountered in larger countries. A good example is the HDB's effective implementation of the public housing program, which resulted in increase of the proportion of Singaporeans living in public housing from 9% in 1960 to 85% today.

Policy Diffusion

Finally, the PAP government has relied on policy diffusion, or the borrowing of policy ideas and solutions from other countries and adapting these ideas and solutions to suit the context of Singapore. As it is unnecessary and expensive to "reinvent the wheel," the PAP leaders and senior civil servants consider what has been done elsewhere to identify appropriate solutions for resolving policy problems in Singapore. Those solutions selected will usually be adapted and modified to suit the local context. Schein[3] has attributed the EDB's commitment to learning and innovation "to Lee Kuan Yew's and

Dr. Goh's willingness to learn from other countries and from various non-Singaporean advisers, and is most clearly demonstrated in the continuous changing and refining of social policy."

Soon after the attainment of its independence in August 1965, Singapore looked at Israel and Switzerland as role models to provide inspiration for devising relevant public policies for defense and other areas. Later, West Germany was added to the list for technical education, followed by The Netherlands (Schiphol Airport was the model for Changi International Airport) and Japan (for quality control circles and crime prevention). The critical lesson in these learning experiences is the adoption by Singapore of ideas that have worked elsewhere (with suitable modification to consider the local context, if necessary), as well as the rejection of failures in other countries.[7]

In sum, policy diffusion in Singapore remains an asset if there is intelligent sifting of relevant policy ideas and solutions tested in other countries by the policy makers, who must avoid blind acceptance or wholesale transplantation of foreign innovations without modification to suit the local environment.[8]

CONCLUSION

Public administration in Singapore is the product of its British colonial heritage, the constraints imposed by its policy context, and the various policies introduced by the PAP government during its 45 years in power. Indeed, the PAP government's success in transforming Singapore from a Third World state to a First World nation can be attributed mainly to its ability to attract the "best and the brightest" Singaporeans into the SCS. The high quality of Singapore's civil servants is manifested in the country's top ranking on the competence of public officials among 59 countries in the *Global Competitiveness Reports* of 1999 and 2000, and among 75 countries in the *Global Competitiveness Report 2001–2002*.[9–11] In sum, Singapore's lack of natural resources has been overcome by the quality of its political leaders and civil servants, who are responsible for its rapid transformation and progress during the past 45 years.

REFERENCES

1. *Singapore 2003*; Foo, S.L., Ed.; Ministry of Information, Communications and the Arts: Singapore, 2003.
2. The Economist. *Pocket World in Figures 2004 Edition*; Profile Books: London, 2003.
3. Schein, E.H. *Strategic Pragmatism: the Culture of the*

Economic Development Board; MIT Press: Cambridge, 1996; pp. 197, 221–222.

4. Quah, J.S.T. Singapore's Anti-Corruption Strategy: Is This Form of Governance Transferable to Other Asian Countries? In *Corruption and Governance in Asia*; Kidd, J.B., Richter, F.-J., Eds.; Palgrave Macmillan: Basingstoke, 2003; 180–197. Chap. 10.

5. Quah, J.S.T. Paying for the 'Best and Brightest': Rewards for High Public Office in Singapore. In *Reward for High Public Office: Asian and Pacific Rim States*; Hood, C., Peters, B.G., Lee, G.O.M., Eds.; Routledge: London, 2003; 145–162. Chap. 9.

6. Republic of Singapore. *Competitive Salaries for Competent and Honest Government: Benchmarks for Ministers and Senior Public Officers*; (White Paper presented to the Parliament on October 21, 1994, Command 13 of 1994).

7. Quah, J.S.T. Public Administration in Singapore: Managing Success in a Multi-Racial City-State. In *Public Administration in the NICs: Challenges and Accomplishments*; Huque, A.S., Lam, J.T.M., Lee, J.C.Y., Eds.; Macmillan Press: Basingstoke, 1996; 59–89. Chap. 3.

8. Quah, J.S.T. Singapore's Model of Development: Is It Transferable? In *Behind East Asian Growth: The Political and Social Foundations of Prosperity*; Rowen, H.S., Ed.; Routledge: London, 1998; 105–125. Chap. 5.

9. *The Global Competitiveness Report 1999*; Oxford University Press: New York, 1999.

10. *The Global Competitiveness Report 2000*; Oxford University Press: New York, 2000.

11. *The Global Competitiveness Report 2001–2002*; Oxford University Press: New York, 2002.

State Enterprise Zones

Ryan J. Watson
Terry F. Buss
National Academy of Public Administration, Washington, District of Columbia, U.S.A.

INTRODUCTION

President Reagan first introduced Enterprise Zones in the United States in his Urban Jobs and Enterprise Zone Act of 1980. Congressional interest, debate, and legislation concerning EZs continued over the years, but no federal EZ program ever materialized.[1] But, state officials loved the idea of building political capital by providing unbudgeted financial assistance to underdeveloped communities. By 1995, 2,840 zones had been established in 34 states: "no two states' enterprise zone programs are alike...unlike many other common state incentive programs that have been patterned after prominent federal income tax programs."[2] Tax incentives provided the most attractive incentives in recruiting businesses (see Table 1).

HOW DO STATES JUSTIFY TAX INCENTIVES?

EZ tax incentives have many advocates.[3] Public officials fear that their state or community will lose business to areas with more favorable business environments. Decision-makers want to rescue failing firms and shield businesses from competition.[4–6] Drawing in businesses from other areas or facilitating the start up of new firms can boost the economic well-being of a community.[6–9] Unsure about the intentions of private businesses, states offer tax incentives to hedge their bets.[5,6] Since most states and communities already offer tax incentives, policymakers simply follow the herd and offer similar incentives.[10]

Localities frequently perceive incentives as free money. The federal government underwrites some tax incentives and state taxpayers pay for state tax incentive costs, so localities receive free money.[11] Pervasive government intervention in markets means that tax incentives can go unnoticed,[12] especially since EZ incentives are generally not part of the state budget process. Tax incentives are viewed as a net benefit since the initial loss of tax revenue is eventually recaptured directly or indirectly-through taxes and growth. Market failures in state economies can be corrected by judiciously using

incentives.[13,14] But in reality, politicians mostly use EZ programs to appease constituencies or advocates for distressed places.

WHAT IS THE STATUS OF EZ PROGRAM EVALUATION?

States rarely perform evaluations to determine the effectiveness of EZ programs or to answer economic development questions.[15–17] A National Association of State Development Agencies survey of states concluded that states had not conducted rigorous cost-benefit evaluations of the incentives they offered. Likewise, the Council of State Governments' annual incentive survey found that only a few states used a formal cost-benefit model to gauge the impacts of tax and financial incentives.[18] The National Conference of State Legislators concluded: "Few states know the exact amount they spend on economic development initiatives."[19] A survey conducted by Lohman, et al.[2] found that while zone administrators believed that EZ incentives increased jobs and investment in zones, few states could offer adequate statistics to measure the effectiveness of these programs. The disregard for cost-benefit analyses is a significant factor in making EZ programs ineffective.

In his literature review, James[20] concluded that there has been no thoroughly acceptable evaluation of the impacts and cost-effectiveness of an EZ program (see also Ref. [21].) Nonetheless, existing studies offer important insights.

ARE EZ TAX INCENTIVES GOOD ECONOMICS?

EZs are largely unassailable in a political sense-Republicans favor them because they promote economic development using market-based incentives rather than entitlement programs, and Democrats support EZs since they represent a major source of social welfare funding for disadvantaged communities. EZ tax incentives are also good politics because policymakers can redirect resources to stimulate economic growth and development in the

Encyclopedia of Public Administration and Public Policy
DOI: 10.1081/E-EPAP 120026198

Table 1   Examples of state EZ incentives

- State income tax deductions, credits, or exemptions
- Local income tax reductions, credits, or exemptions
- Infrastructure improvement
- Property tax breaks
- Unemployment tax credits
- Sales tax refunds, credits, or exemptions
- Regulatory relief
- Job training assistance and subsidies
- Deduction for net interest income coming from loans to qualified zone firms
- Credit for wages paid to "disadvantaged individuals"
- Low interest loans
- Day care tax credits
- Business development assistance
- Contributions to enterprise zone associations
- Permission to carry forward 100 percent net operating loss for many years
- Reimbursement of insurance costs
- Expensing all or a portion of qualified property

Sources: Refs. [2,23,24].

poorest regions of their states, which theoretically increases long-term state tax revenues.

All political factions use tax codes to benefit certain projects or sectors. Businesses are strong advocates of EZ tax incentives, and the taxpayers who bear the financial burden of these incentives are largely unaware of their existence. EZ failure can be blamed on business cycles, market forces, dysfunctional business behavior, or in extreme cases on poor people in distressed places (e.g., high crime). When the economy is booming, policymakers can easily claim political dividends by saying that EZs contributed to the positive economic climate. These claims may be untrue, untested, or exaggerated, but citizens have no reliable way of evaluating these statements.

Setting aside politics, it is worth considering whether EZs are good economics. Economists offer various criteria that can justify public investment in EZs. In practice, the criteria outlined in the tax literature appear to be frequently ignored. Courant[22] suggests that if zone policies address market failures such as the inefficient utilization of resources or overly localized economies, zone incentives can increase economic efficiency. If investment is relocated from local labor markets with low unemployment to ones with higher unemployment, incentives may generate efficiency gains as underutilized resources are mobilized. Efficiency gains may also result if reductions in unemployment produce positive externalities such as reductions in welfare dependence or crime. Bartik[14] argues that net capital investment may be somewhat irrelevant, because redistribution, even within a state, may

be an end in itself. Investment, through tax incentives, may allow individuals to build job skills and experience that enhance their long run employability.

There is a large body of research that says EZs are not effective economics. Peters and Fisher[23] examined 75 EZs in 13 states by using a "hypothetical firm" computer simulation. They applied tax incentives to financial statements that they generated for hypothetical firms. Peters and Fisher came to largely negative conclusions about how well EZs work, as well as finding that the goals and policies of EZ programs are often confusing. Knowing that housing value growth rates are a quantifiable measure of EZ programs' effectiveness, Engberg and Greenbaum[24] conclude that EZs do not usually increase the growth rate in property values. In fact, zones that had high vacancy rates before being designated an EZ actually experienced a decline in the property value growth rate. Netzer[25] concludes that economic development tax incentives including those in EZs are, for the most part, neither good nor bad from the standpoint of economic efficiency. With imperfections in economies due to government interference at all levels (see also Ref. [12]), offering incentives does not parallel the efficiency operations of private competitive markets.

Research generally fails to measure how much market failures justify tax incentives. Skeptics believe that most tax incentives are poor economics.[26] Advocates believe that tax incentives work or do little harm, and that diverting economic development funding to assess them is a waste of money.[12] The majority of the research supports the skeptical view.

DO EZs STIMULATE GROWTH?

Some studies attribute economic growth to EZs, but more studies convincingly find negative or inconclusive results (e.g., Ref. [1]). Numerous studies of the same zones come to opposite conclusions, while some researchers reverse their positive conclusions in follow-up studies. Many correlations between taxes and economic growth are methodological artifacts (see Refs. [26].)

Multi-State Studies

Several researchers have undertaken multi-state EZ studies, the most extensive and rigorous among them are Peters and Fisher[27] and Greenbaum and Engberg.[28] Peters and Fisher studied manufacturing employment in 75 zones found in 13 states, comparing zone incentives and non-zone incentives to businesses. They found that during the 1990s, non-zone incentives grew in importance relative to EZ incentives, effectively lessening the potential impacts of zones. They concluded "EZ incentives tend to favor capital-intensive over labor-intensive industries; usually cause losses to public coffers and have very little impact on new investment; and do little to improve the job prospects of residents in the zones."

Greenbaum and Engberg[28] studied zones in California, Florida, New Jersey, New York, Pennsylvania and Virginia. Results showed that "the zone incentives do not significantly improve housing market, income, or employment outcomes either in the zones themselves or in adjacent neighborhoods."[28] They hypothesize that the lack of impact may be attributable to 1) zone programs crowding out other beneficial policies, 2) zone incentives may subsidize businesses that lack long-term viability, or 3) zone designation may carry a stigma.

Indiana Zones

Papke[29] initially found mostly positive impacts for Indiana EZs. Indiana EZs permanently increased inventory values to 8%, or $3.2 million, more than would have been the case without the zone. Papke[29] also found that unemployment claims declined by 19%, or 1,500 people, for the local labor market following zone designation. However, value of machinery and equipment declined by 13%, or $5 million.

Papke[30] subsequently reversed her positive conclusions, saying that EZs lost an average of about 2,300 people, or 674 households. Per capita income fell 2%. Zone unemployment only dropped from 9.3% to 8%. The percentage of people working in the zone as a place of residence rose only 4%. Firms created 2,897 new jobs in Indiana zones in 1988, with 15% going to EZ residents. Zone residents earned about half as much as non-resident EZ employees. Annual cost of an Indiana EZ job was $4,564, or $31,113 per zone resident. Zones lost more population and experienced a decline in per capita income compared to income growth in non-zones, while unemployment only fell slightly in zones, and fewer zone residents actually worked in zones.

New Jersey Zones

Urbanomics conducted a cost-benefit study of businesses in 11 New Jersey EZs (see also Ref. [31]). Analysts defined benefits as jobs, payroll and production, both directly and through multipliers. The EZ program cost taxpayers $51.6 million, but induced $106.5 million in subsequent tax revenues, totaling $267.4 million with multipliers. The direct tax benefit-to-cost ratio was 2.2:1, and the total tax benefit-to-cost ratio was 5.2:1. Cities that had grown slowly before designation grew faster than comparison cities once the zone was in place.

Boarnet and Bogart,[32] using an econometric model with a panel study design, tested Rubin and Trawinski's conclusions[31] by studying 28 municipalities eligible for zone designation and 7 municipalities that actually became EZs in 1984. Boarnet and Bogart "found no evidence that the urban enterprise zone program in New Jersey had a positive effect on total municipal employment, on sectoral employment or on municipal property values."[32]

Illinois Zones

Sridhar[33] studied 49 Illinois zones. Sridhar found that economic development incentives, on average, yielded net benefits 10 times higher than tax abatement costs. For new jobs created, earnings were highest in low-unemployment zones and lowest in high-unemployment zones. But when earnings were made net of reservation wages, which are the wages necessary to induce people into the labor force, net benefits and benefits per job were greatest in high-unemployment zones. While net benefits and benefits for each job relocated were highest in high-unemployment areas, they were negative in low-unemployment areas. Therefore, positive net social benefits would exist if all jobs were redistributed from average-unemployment areas to EZs.

McDonald[34] argued that Sridhar's work was invalid because it assumed that EZ programs were responsible for all jobs created in a zone. Lambert and Coomes[35] studied one Louisville EZ where more than $560 million in federal and state funding went towards the expansion of Louisville's airport, causing United Parcel Service (UPS) to increase its operations within the EZ. When evaluating Louisville's EZ, Lambert and Coomes write, "Most of the EZ benefits claimed by the proponents are linked to the airport expansion. UPS and other airport-related firms did take advantage of EZ tax advantages; however, it would be far-fetched to claim that the EZ program caused the local economic benefits."[35]

California Zones

Dowall[36] analyzed 13 California zones. Shift-share analysis attributed virtually all employment growth from 1986 to 1990 in zones to countywide growth and industrial mix. Zones actually retarded employment by 5,578 jobs.

Maryland Zones

The General Accounting Office (GAO)[37] studied three Maryland EZs from 1980 to 1987, finding no effect on employment or welfare dependence of workers. Job creation in the zones did not affect costs incurred in subsidizing firms. GAO reviewed comparative case studies, state program evaluations, and broad reviews of program results, concluding that studies either had flaws or failed to focus on program-related changes in employment. Flaws included: 1) reliance on data of unknown or dubious quality such as surveys of zone administrators, 2) measurement of program effects too soon after zone designation, and 3) failure to use an adequate baseline for attributing observed effects to possible influences.

Ohio Zones

Hill[38] studied Ohio's Amended Substitute Senate Bill 19, which reformed the state's EZ program. Hill examined numerous publications and key informant interviews to assess Ohio's EZ program. He concluded that the program is an ad hoc business tax reduction, not true tax reform. The program puts most distressed areas of the state at a competitive disadvantage. Even though the program intends to respond to interstate competition, its major impact was to stimulate intrastate tax competition. The program's exaggerated benefits did not result in net new job formation.

Rural Zones

Few studies examine rural EZ effectiveness, and findings conflict (see Refs. [39–41]). Louisiana zones were declared ineffective.[42] Robinson and Reeder[40] conducted the best research on rural EZs. They reanalyzed the rural zone data in the 1996 HUD survey of zone administrators. Rural zones created or saved 2 jobs per 100-zone residents as compared with 3 jobs per 100 residents in metro zones. Only one of seven zones reported saving any jobs. Rural zone development came almost entirely from expansions within the zone. Most were manufacturing companies. Three-fifths of jobs created went to zone residents and one-half went to unemployed people. Weaknesses in the Robinson and Reeder[40] study include reliance on zone administrator surveys and an inability to determine whether jobs would have been created in the absence of zone incentives. Using the number of jobs saved to measure success is also problematic.

Urban areas often dominate funding for EZ programs. In Florida, 83% of EZ tax incentives went to just three urban zones, while less than one percent of the EZ funding went to the state's twenty rural EZs.[43] Rural and small-town EZs also experience difficulty in the implementation and administration of EZ incentives. While Florida's Miami-Dade County spent approximately $325,000 for

the administration of its EZ program in the 1998-1999 fiscal year, many coastal communities within the state put less than $1,500 each towards EZ management in the same year.[43]

Federal Studies

In the 101st Congress, legislators proposed six EZ bills. Bills provided labor subsidies to reduce wage costs by almost 14% if half of total wages were devoted to economically disadvantaged workers. Some firms might increase EZ investment between 8.5% and 20%, employment between 6.5% to 14%, and output between 7.5% and 15%. But tax-induced increases in investment, employment, and output in EZs would largely be offset by declines elsewhere.[44] EZ investments could earn up to 39% lower pre-tax rates of return than are available from alternative investments, representing a reduction in national income. HUD researchers concluded that job creation could not be attributed to EZs; other factors were responsible.[1]

ARE EZ TAX INCENTIVES WASTED?

Literature is divided on whether investment would have occurred in the absence of an EZ, although the best research suggests that it would have. This literature relies heavily on surveys of firms and administrators, as well as administrative data.

Surveys of Firms and Zone Administrators

Dowall's[36] study of California EZs showed one-half of eligible zone firms did not use incentives. Another fourth tried to access incentives but were unable to do so. 67% of businesses using zone programs stated that traditional factors such as markets, transportation, and worker availability influenced their location or expansion decisions, not EZ incentives. Importantly, many businesses did not discover tax incentives until after making their decisions. Elder and Cohen[45] had identical results in their Illinois zone study. 77% of Louisville's EZ firms that used the most expensive and common EZ benefits made their decisions based on factors other than EZ incentives.[35]

GAO's Maryland study[37] used interviews with several hundred employers to explore the importance of locational factors. GAO presaged Dowall's[37] findings above. At least 60% rated market access, community characteristics, site characteristics and government cooperation as important in their location decision. Transportation, real estate, financial health of region and quality of life were rated as important by at least 50% of employers. Financial incentives were important to only 14%.

Rubin and Trawinski's[31] study of New Jersey zones, by contrast, revealed greater impact. When companies were asked about location decisions, 32% reported that EZ benefits were the only or primary reason for their decision to expand or locate within zones, 38% suggested that EZ benefits provided a secondary reason to consider the zones, and 30% felt that EZ benefits had no impact.

HUD's interviews with zone administrators found that property and corporate income taxes were ranked first in importance by two-fifths of respondents. This contrasts with GAO's conclusions (as reported in Ref. [1]).

Firms differ in their consideration of EZ incentives when making decisions. Firms may misrepresent their motivations for using incentives: some may not need them, but still justify why they used them; some may not need them, but want to show support for zone administrators or the economic development department; and some may truly need them. Skeptics are not convinced that researchers have sorted out these motivations.[46]

Administrative Record Studies

Dowall's[36] report on the results of the California State Franchise Tax Board tax credit study concluded that incentives are not important. Board records showed that 1,719 jobs were created by granting tax credits to zone businesses, a figure representing only 5% of the jobs reportedly created in zones by zone administrators. EZ employment from tax credits contributed only 6% of total net increase in zone employment between 1986 and 1990. Therefore, EZ administrators may exaggerate job creation and retention in order to bolster program support. California EZ businesses claimed $10.6 million in tax credits between 1986 and 1990, while the total net taxable income of zone firms was $2.7 billion: tax credits address a small part of business costs.

DO EZS EXACERBATE TAX WARS AMONG STATES?

Disadvantaged communities offer incentives to attract firms to EZs, but these have a limited effect on interstate competition. Few firms relocate. Effective tax rates overall created competition mostly within rather than across states.[47] The average effective tax rate in cities outside zones was 9.1% as compared to 7.3% inside zones. Average state and local tax burden on new investment, then, was only 19% lower. Considerable variation occurred across cities. Outside zones in low-tax cities, the effective tax rate was 5.6% and 14.7% in high-tax cities. Inside zones, rates dropped to 3.7% to 13.2%, respectively.

Fisher and Peters,[47] using their hypothetical firm approach, offer the best evidence about EZs. Cities with EZs usually offered more generous incentives than cities without zones, but "enterprise zones are little more than geographically targeted versions of standard state and local economic development programs."[47] However, state corporate income tax credits were more prevalent and more generous in EZs than statewide, and policymakers employed jobs credits twice as often as investment credits within EZs (see also, Ref. [48]). Zones tended to offer incentives worth two to three times those available statewide.[47] Within EZs, zone incentives accounted for one-third of the incentives offered.

Most jobs in EZs come from expansions of existing zone businesses and from new businesses, rather than relocations.[21,49] In a study of 357 zones in 17 states, 26% of 1,623 zone firms making new investments were new firms. 8% were new branch plants of non-zone firms and 9% were relocations from outside the zone. "If EZs had been established to nurture new business development, the incentive programs would have been structured quite differently and an emphasis would have been placed on small business incubators, technology transfer programs, management assistance and venture capital provision."[47]

HOW WELL DO EZ INCENTIVES WORK?

Literature suggests that targeted populations and businesses do not necessarily benefit from EZs. Frequently, incentives negatively impact zones.

Incentive Beneficiaries

Job tax credit programs may not induce jobs, because many firms cannot fully use them. Most job tax credits have a statutory ceiling and are one-time credits.[47] For 13 states with job tax credits in Fisher and Peters' study, firms in 6 states used 100% of credits available. But in the other states, firms used only 67% of the credit on average. Job tax credits did not induce employment as expected. Job tax credits may have no price effect at the margin, meaning that all other costs being equal in other locations, these taxes may have little impact on firm costs of business.

People who ought to benefit from EZs may not. Shocks or subsidies in labor markets only temporarily reduced unemployment in targeted areas. In-migration of workers to a targeted area quickly eliminated benefits to original residents. In the long run, new in-migrants to a targeted area took many newly created jobs.[50] Bartik,[51] in reviewing 18 studies, calculated that 60% to 90% of jobs created by employment programs go, in the long-run, to in-migrants rather than the targeted beneficiaries. Ladd (Ref. [52] see also Ref. [53]), in her literature review of EZs, surmised that place-based subsidies and even people-based, place-based subsidies failed to raise employment levels and well being of targeted residents.

Minority businesses were not attracted to EZs. Glover[54] surveyed zone firms and administrators, finding that only 5% of firms were minority-owned.

Capital Investment Incentives

Not all incentives increase employment; some actually decrease it.[22,30,48] Nationally, wide variation exists in the mix of labor and capital incentives inside and outside zones, ranging from 0% to 100% focus on labor.[47] Typical capital incentives clearly have much larger effects on the price of capital goods than average labor incentives have on wages. The exemption of capital equipment from a 6% sales tax reduces its acquisition cost by 4% to 4.5%. A 1% state investment tax credit reduces the price about 0.65%. Average jobs credit per job, represents only 0.2% to 0.5% of present value of wages over 10 years. Maximum jobs credit represents from 1% to 1.6% of present value of wages over this period. Incentives that lower the price of capital goods have both an output effect (production and employment increase because costs are lowered) and a substitution effect (capital is substituted for labor). If the substitution effect is stronger, a capital incentive could reduce employment. Loh[55] looked at county-level growth in Ohio in the 1980s as a function of economic incentives, concluding that capital subsidies to private businesses were more effective than either labor subsidies to private businesses or capital subsidies to communities. However, Loh's work has been roundly criticized.[47]

EZ Size

If every community is an EZ, the program breaks down. For example, an existing EZ in Jefferson County, Kentucky was expanded due to political pressures. The expanded EZ included new zone areas that did not fulfill the minimum socioeconomic requirements put forth in Kentucky's EZ legislation, but the overall zone's economic vital signs were still low enough to qualify.[35] Arkansas and Kansas have EZs that cover the whole state.[2] In 1995, South Carolina designated 90% of the state an EZ. Some states designated entire counties. Critics suggest that this misconstrues the intent of geographically small area targeting. Small area targets do not significantly affect economies, either positively or negatively, so partial equilibrium models apply. When zones get too large, full equilibrium models apply. Full equilibrium suggests that transfers of wealth from one area to another reduces wealth in the entire economy (see Ref. [48]).

REFERENCES

1. Birdsong, B. *Federal Zones*; Urban Institute: Washington, DC, 1989.
2. Lohman, R.; et al. State enterprise zone programs: A survey of the benefits (part I). J. Multistate Tax. Incent. **June 2002**, *12* (3).
3. Key, K.; Smith, J. Trends in state and local economic development incentives. J. State Tax. **1996**, *15*, 1–13.
4. Burnier, D. Becoming competitive: How policy makers view incentive-based development policy. Econ. Dev. Q. **February 1992**, *6*, 1.
5. Noto, N. Trying to Understand the Economic Development Official's Dilemma. In *Competition Among States and Local Government*; Urban Institute: Washington, DC, 1991.
6. Wolman, H. Local economic development policy. J. Urban Aff. **1988**, *10*, 19–28.
7. Ledebur, L.C.; Woodward, D. Adding a stick to the carrot. Econ. Dev. Q. **1990**, *4*, 15–25.
8. Spindler, C.J.; Forrester, J.P. Economic development policy. Urban Aff. Q. **1993**, *29*, 28–53.
9. Clingmayer, J.; Feiock, R. Distribution and redistribution in economic development. J. Polit. **1995**, *57*, 508–520.
10. Gilbert, J. Selling the city without selling out. Urban Lawyer **1995**, *27*, 1–13.
11. Watson, D.J. *The New Civil War*; Praeger: Westport, CT, 1995.
12. Wiewel, W. Response. Econ. Dev. Q. **1999**, *13*, 357–364.
13. Baum, D.N. The economic effects of state and local business incentives. Land Econ. **1987**, *63*, 348–360.
14. Bartik, T.J. *Who Benefits*; Upjohn Institute: Kalamazoo, MI, 1991.
15. Buss, T.F.; Yancer, L.C. Cost-benefit analysis: A normative perspective. Econ. Dev. Q. **1999**, *13*, 29–37.
16. Hartzheim, L.A. State tax incentives. J. State Tax. **1997**, *15*, 51–64.
17. Bartik, T.J. Better evaluation is needed. Econ. Dev. Q. **1994**, *8*, 99–106.
18. Chi, K.S.; Leatherby, D. *State Business Incentives*; Council of State Governments: Lexington, KY, 1997; 8.
19. National Conference of State Legislatures. *A Review of State Economic Policy*; NCSL: Washington, DC, 1997; 1.
20. James, F.J. The Evaluation of Enterprise Zone Programs. In *Enterprise Zones*; Green, R., Ed.; Sage: Newbury Park, CA, 1991; 225–257.
21. Wilder, M.; Rubin, B. Rhetoric versus reality. J. Am. Plan. Assoc. **1996**, *62*. pp. 4, 473–91.
22. Courant, P. How would you know a good economic development program if you tripped over one? Nat. Tax J. **1994**, *47* (4), 863–891.

23. Peters, A.H.; Fisher, P.S. *The Effectiveness of State Enterprise Zones*; W.E. Upjohn Institute for Employment Research: Kalamazoo, MI, 2002a.

24. Engberg, J.; Greenbaum, R. State enterprise zones and local housing markets. J. Housing Res. **1999**, *10* (2), 163–187.

25. Netzer, D. An Evaluation of Inter-Jurisdictional Competition. In *Competition Among States and Local Governments*; Kenyon, D., Kincaid, J., Eds.; Urban Institute: Washington, DC, 1991; 110–132.

26. Buss, T.F. The effect of state tax incentives on economic growth and firm location decisions: An overview of the literature. Econ. Dev. Q. **2001**, *15*, 90–105.

27. Peters, A.H.; Fisher, P.S. *State Enterprise Zone Programs: Have They Worked?*; W.E. Upjohn Institute for Employment Research: Kalamazoo, MI, 2002.

28. Greenbaum, R.; Engberg, J. An Evaluation of State EZ Policies. In *Public Policies for Distressed Communities Revisited*; Redburn, F.S., Buss, T.F., Eds.; Lexington Books: Lanham, MD, 2002; 33–64.

29. Papke, L.E. *Tax Policy and Economic Development*; Working Paper, Boston University, 1991.

30. Papke, L.E. *What Do We Know About Enterprise Zones?*; National Bureau of Economic Research: Cambridge, MA, 1993. Working Paper #4251.

31. Rubin, M.; Trawinski, E. New Jersey's urban enterprise zones. Urban Lawyer **1991**, *23*, 461–471.

32. Boarnet, M.G.; Bogart, W.T. Enterprise zones and employment. J. Urban Econ. **1996**, *40*, 198–215.

33. Sridhar, K.S. Tax costs and employment benefits of enterprise zones. Econ. Dev. Q. **1996**, *10*, 69–90.

34. McDonald, J.F. Comment. Econ. Dev. Q. **1997**, *11*, 222–224.

35. Lambert, T.E.; Coomes, P.A. An evaluation of the effectiveness of Louisville's enterprise zone. Econ. Dev. Q. **2001**, *15*, 168–180.

36. Dowall, D.E. An evaluation of California's enterprise zone programs. Econ. Dev. Q. **1996**, *10*, 352–368.

37. General Accounting Office. *Enterprise Zones: Lessons From the Maryland Experience*; GAO: Washington, DC, 1988.

38. Hill, E.W. *Tax Abatement: War Within a State*; 1994. Unpublished manuscript.

39. U.S. Department of Housing and Urban Development. *State-Designated Enterprise Zones*; HUD: Washington, DC, 1986.

40. Robinson, K.L.; Reeder, R.J. State enterprise zones. Rural Dev. Perspect. **1991**, *7*, 30–35.

41. Wortman, M.S. Impact of Entrepreneurship Upon Rural Development. In *Rural Development Research*; Rowley, T.D., et al., Eds.; Greenwood Press: Westport, CT, 1996.

42. Nelson, A.C.; Whelen, R.W. Do Enterprise Zones Make a Difference? In *A Paper Presented to the Urban Affairs Association*; March 9–12, 1989.

43. Perez, E. Flaws seen in enterprise zones' focus. Wall Street J. **April 19, 2000**.

44. Zimmerman, D. *Federal Tax Incentives for Enterprise Zones*; Congressional Research Service, U.S. Library of Congress, June 15 1989; 89–371E.

45. Elder, A.; Cohen, I. *Evaluation of Effectiveness and Efficiency of Enterprise Zones in Illionois*; Illinois State University, 1988.

46. Netzer, R. Comment. In *New England Economic Review*; Federal Reserve Bank of Boston: New England, Mar/Apr 1997; 131–137.

47. Fisher, P.S.; Peters, A.H. *Tax and Spending Incentives and Enterprise Zones*; Federal Reserve Bank of Boston: New England, Mar/Apr 1997; 131–137.

48. Gravelle, J.G. *Enterprise Zones*; Congressional Research Service, Library of Congress, June 3 1992. CRS Report 92–476S.

49. Erickson, R.A.; Freidman, S.W. *Enterprise Zones*; Center for Regional Business Analysis, Penn State University, 1990.

50. Blanchard, O.; Katz, L. Regional evolutions. Brookings Pap. Econ. Act. **1992**, *1*, 1–75.

51. Bartik, T.J. Who benefits from local job growth. Reg. Stud. **1993**, *27*, 293–311.

52. Ladd, H.F. Spatially targeted economic development strategies. Cityscape **1994**, *1*, 193–218.

53. Erickson, R.A.; Syms, P.M. The effects of enterprise zones on local property values. Reg. Stud. **1986**, *20*, 1–14.

54. Glover, G. Enterprise zones: Incentives are not attracting to spur urban economic development. Rev. Black Polit. Econ. **1993**, *22*, 73–79.

State and Local Public Pension Fund Management

Jun Peng
University of Arizona, Tucson, Arizona, U.S.A.

INTRODUCTION

Public pension funds constitute a very important part of state and local government finance. They are important for at least two reasons. First, they hold an enormous amount of assets. According to the Census Bureau's annual survey of state and local finance, the total value of assets in public pension funds amounted to $2.2 trillion in fiscal year 2002, covering 17 million members in the public sector.[a] Thus the mismanagement of pension assets will affect the well-being of 17 million current and retired public sector employees. Second, pension funds are closely linked with the government operating budgets from which the pension contributions come. Through this connection, mismanagement of pension funds will therefore also affect other aspects of government finance such as the provision of public service. It is therefore critical to have a good understanding of pension management. This article serves to explain the most fundamental aspects of pension management, especially with regard to the measurement of pension fund liability and the main elements of prudent pension management in the public sector.

DEFINED BENEFIT AND DEFINED CONTRIBUTION

The first important thing to understand is the two very different types of retirement programs provided by the government: defined benefit (DB) and defined contribution (DC). In DB plans, government employers guarantee a certain level of retirement benefits to employees when they retire. In DC plans, employers guarantee a certain level of contribution, usually as a percentage of salary, to employees' individual retirement funds while they are working, but are not responsible for their retirement benefits when they retire. Instead, the employees have to be responsible for own future retirement benefits. Although DC has attracted more attention in recent years as many states set up new DC plans and employees can switch to

DC plans from DB plans,[1] DB remains the predominant plan type among state and local government workers. In 1998, there were 12.98 million members in state and local public DB plans,[2] accounting for 80% of the 16.15 million members in all state and local public pension plans in that year.[3] Therefore the remaining of this article is only concerned with management issues related to DB plans.

The next important thing to understand is the funding methods for DB programs. There are two basic ways of funding DB programs: pay-as-you-go (PAYGO) and advance funding. PAYGO means that the current year's benefits to retirees are paid out of current year's contribution from employers and employees. Advance funding means that while an employee is still working, the employer and/or the employee will set aside a certain amount of money every year so that by the time the employee retires, a sufficient amount of funds has been accumulated to pay for all his future benefits. It is quite obvious that at the federal level, social security, although not entirely a retirement program, is funded on a PAYGO basis, as current workers' social security taxes are used to pay for current retirees' social security benefits. The looming social security crisis comes largely as a result of not having enough taxes coming in to pay the retirement benefits in the future. Unlike the federal social security program, state and local pension programs are funded using the advance funding method. With advance funding, the key issue is knowing the amount of funds that needs to be accumulated by the time the employee retires and the amount of funds that needs to be set aside every year so that the required amount will be accumulated by the time he retires. Understanding this issue is the key to understanding almost all other important aspects of public pension management.

ACTUARIAL EVALUATION METHOD

First, how do we know how much to set aside by the time the employee retires? To understand this, we first need to know how the future retirement benefits are calculated. An employee's future benefit is based on a formula like this: final salary × years of service × multiplying factor. An example is if an employee's final salary is $50,000

---

[a]The data can be found at the Census Bureau's website http://www.census.gov/govs/www/retire02.html.

Encyclopedia of Public Administration and Public Policy
DOI: 10.1081/E-EPAP-120010750

Table 1   Iowa public employees' retirement system funding status

Fiscal year	Actuarial value of assets (AVA)	Actuarial accrued liability (AAL)	Percentage funded	Unfunded actuarial accrued liability (UAAL)
2003	16,120,476,011	17,987,374,960	89.62%	($1,866,898,949)

and has worked for the government for 30 years. Suppose the multiplying factor is 2% of an employee's final salary for each year of service, then his annual pension will be $30,000. Second, pension sponsor needs to make an assumption about how long he will receive the pension after he retires. Last, because of the time value of money, a pension paid 30 years after he retires is worth a lot less than a pension of the same amount paid the year he retires. The pension sponsor needs to discount and find the present value of all future pension benefits by the time he retires.[b] It is this present value of all future pension benefits that becomes the amount to be accumulated.

Second, how should this present value of all future benefits be funded over the working life of the employee? The key principle here is that the funding of benefits should be related to the period in which benefits are earned. There are several actuarial cost methods to distribute the cost over time, such as entry age normal, projected unit credit, and aggregate cost. Of these, the most commonly used is the entry age normal method. Under this method, the present value of future benefits is allocated as a level percentage of the individual's projected compensation between the time he starts working and the time he retires. The purpose of such a method is to spread evenly over time the cost of funding. The part of this total cost allocated to the year in which the service is provided is considered that year's normal cost, and the part allocated to future years is considered future normal cost. Once a person has already worked for sometime, then he has earned (or accrued) some benefits which the pension plan has to pay. To evaluate whether the pension for an employee has been funded sufficiently at any time before he retires, the present value of all his future benefits at the time of evaluation is divided into two parts: the present value of benefits already earned (or accrued) as a result of the service provided prior to the date of evaluation, which is now the pension plan's liability, and the present value of benefits yet to be earned. The first part should be covered by the assets already held in the pension plan and the second part should be covered by the present value of all future normal cost.

Now we can use these basic concepts to understand the funding status of a pension plan at any particular time.

Data in Table 1 were taken from Iowa's Comprehensive Annual Financial Report for FY2003. Such format is a standard way of reporting funding status of a pension plan.

In this table, actuarial accrued liability (AAL) is the difference, as of the actuarial evaluation date, between the present value of all future pension benefits and the present value of all future normal costs. AAL can roughly be interpreted as the present value of future benefits already accrued and thus is the liability of the plan. Then AAL is compared to the actuarial value of asset (AVA) on hand. The difference between the two is called unfounded actuarial accrued liability (UAAL). Dividing AVA by AAL, we also get a funding ratio of the plan. If AVA is greater than AAL, then the plan is overfunded. UAAL will be negative and the funding ratio will be greater than 100%. If AVA is less than AAL, then the plan is underfunded. UAAL will be positive, and the funding ratio will be less than 100%. In Iowa's case, because AVA is less than AAL, the plan is underfunded. It has a UAAL of US$1.87 billion and a funding ratio of 90%.

To fully understand the actuarial evaluation method, two more elements need to be discussed: actuarial valuation of asset and assumptions underlying the valuation of liabilities.

The actuarial value of asset is different from the actual value of the asset in a pension fund. Inasmuch as most of the assets in a pension funded are invested in the stocks and fixed-income securities, the value of the assets can fluctuate tremendously from year to year because of the fluctuation in the financial market. Simply comparing AAL to the actual value of the asset will result in big swing in the funding status. To reduce such volatility, a smoothing technique is adopted in valuing the asset. Such technique involves calculating a 4- to 5-year moving average of investment return when valuing the asset. For example, if using a 4-year moving average, then only 25% of the investment gains or losses each year over the past 4 years will be recognized in valuing the assets for the current evaluation year. The rationale is to smooth out the ups and downs in the financial market, leading to a more stable investment return over a 4- to 5-year period. Therefore in some years, the actuarial value can be higher than the actual value of asset, whereas in other years, it can be lower than the actual value of the asset.

It can already be inferred to some extent from the previous discussion that the calculation of future benefits involves a lot of assumptions. These assumptions fall into

---

[b]The discount rate used for such discounting will be discussed later in this section.

two categories, economic and demographic. Economic assumptions include rate of investment return, inflation rate, and salary growth. Demographic assumptions include mortality rate and disability rate, among others.[c] Of all these assumptions, the assumption on the rate of investment return is the most important one by far. The rate of return determines how fast the asset is projected to grow in the future. It is also the rate used to discount the future benefits and future normal costs to the present value. Why should the rate of return be used as a discount rate for calculating the present value of future benefits? That is because allowing the present asset to grow at a certain rate to reach an amount in the future to pay the pension benefits is the same as discounting that future pension payment to the present value using the same rate in order to compare with the value of the asset in the pension today. This assumption is important because different rates can lead to very different present value of future pension liabilities. For the same amount of future pension liabilities, an assumption of a higher rate of return (or discount rate in this case) will lead to a smaller present value of pension liabilities. Because it is the present value, rather than the future value, of pension liabilities that matters in evaluating the funding status of a pension plan, a smaller present value of pension liabilities would leave the plan in a better funding status than otherwise. When evaluating the soundness of a pension plan, one of the key factors a rating agency will look at is the assumed rate of investment return.

Other assumptions are also important in determining the value of future benefits. For example, salary growth projection will determine what a person's final salary will be. Inflation projection will determine what cost of living adjustment for current retirees will be. Mortality rate will determine how long a retiree will receive pension benefits.

PENSION FUND MANAGEMENT

With the basic understanding of the actuarial valuation of pension fund, we can proceed to look at some broader issues concerning pension fund management. The central theme in pension fund management is to make sure that it is sufficiently funded at any time and if UAAL emerges, a plan should be in place to shrink it and eventually eliminate it. There are two basic ways of paying off UAAL: amortization and pension obligation bonds (POBs).

The first and also the most commonly used method, amortization, is the same as paying off a mortgage or car loan. Inasmuch as UAAL is a financial liability of the government, it is no different from other types of debt or loans. To spread out the burden of paying off UAAL,

actuarial requirement typically demands that UAAL be amortized over a 20- to 30-year period. Just like an individual who has to pay interest on the mortgage loan he takes out, the government also has to pay interest on UAAL when paying it off, with the interest rate being the assumed rate of return. The reason a government has to pay interest to the pension plan on its UAAL is because UAAL is the present value of future benefits not covered by current assets. Any portion of UAAL that is not paid off will therefore grow at its discount rate, which is the rate of return. Therefore the UAAL next year will be equal to the unpaid portion of UAAL this year plus the growth on the unpaid portion. This growth is the interest on UAAL. UAAL can also be thought of as the amount of asset that should have been in the pension plan at present. Had this amount been in the plan and invested, it would have grown at the assumed rate of return and earned investment income. Therefore the government has to return not only the asset (the amount equal to UAAL) to the pension plan but also the lost investment income (the amount equal to the interest on UAAL).

The second and less common way is to issue POBs to pay off the UAAL at once and then the government will pay debt service on POBs. POBs does not impose a new debt burden on the government, because it essentially turns a debt owed to the pension plan into a debt owed to the investors in POBs. There is only one factor that should determine whether amortization or POBs should be used: interest rate. With amortization, the government has to pay interest at the rate of return to the pension plans. If the government can issue POBs at a rate below the assumed rate of return, then the issuance of POBs results in interest cost savings to the government. While the assumed rate of return is usually based on historical return and does not change frequently, the interest rate on POBs is determined by the prevailing market interest rate and the issuer's credit rating. With the very low interest rate environment in recent years, the rate on POBs has also fallen considerably, resulting in opportunities for issuing POBs. While POBs can lead to interest cost savings, it is not without any risk. For example, if the proceeds of the POBs are invested and do not earn the assumed rate of return, then a new pension liability is created.[d]

While understanding how to pay off UAAL is important, it is more important to understand why it occurs in the first place. Understanding the various factors for causing UAAL will shed light on how to prudently manage public pension fund. As discussed in the "Actuarial Evaluation Method," the calculation of UAAL consists of three factors: government contribution, asset in the pension plan, and the calculation of future

---

[c]For a more detailed discussion of assumptions, please see Ref. [4].

[d]For a more detailed discussion of the pros and cons of POBs, please see Ref. [5].

Table 2 Public pension funding ratio and asset allocation

	1990	1992	1994	1996	1998	2000	2002
Funding ratio	80.2	82	84.9	88.7	95.2	103.8	96.1
Asset allocation							
Domestic equity	37.8	39.3	40.2	42.0	47.9	45.0	41.1
International equity	2.0	3.7	6.5	10.5	12.0	15.3	13.9
Domestic bonds	44.4	41.4	35.0	34.3	28.6	26.1	33.2
International bonds	0.8	1.8	2.4	2.5	2.0	1.8	1.5
Mortgages and real estate	5.6	6.3	5.4	4.6	4.1	4.8	4.0
Short term	5.8	4.6	4.2	2.9	2.2	2.2	2.2
Other	3.6	2.9	6.3	3.2	3.2	4.8	4.1

pension benefits. The reason for underfunding then has to be found among these three factors.

Annual pension contribution consists of one or two parts. The first part is the normal cost, which is the portion of the future benefits assigned to the year in which it is earned. This should apply to every government with a pension plan. The second part consists of amortization of UAA if a government has one. If normal cost is not fully contributed every year, then it will result in underfunding. If the amortization portion of the contribution is not fully met, then underfunding will worsen rather than improve. Therefore making the required contribution is one key element in making sure the pension fund is properly funded; if it is already underfunded, then such underfunding shrinks over time.

Once the contribution is made, it becomes the asset of the pension plan and will be invested. Investment management thus becomes the second element in ensuring a pension is properly funded. In their book on investment management process, Trone et al.[6] list five key steps in a prudently managed investment process. These five steps are analyzing the current position, designing the optimal portfolio, developing an investment policy statement, implementing the investment strategy, and monitoring the performance of your investment portfolio. While all of these are important steps in making sure the investment is properly manage, what is of particular relevance to this article is designing an optimal portfolio. As pension fund investment has to meet the required rate of return, an optimal portfolio means designing an asset allocation strategy that will allow the pension plans to achieve this rate of return with minimum risk (or least variation from this expected return). Asset allocation refers to dividing pension assets among a variety of investment categories such as equity, bonds, and real estate. For prudent pension management, such asset allocation strategy should be neither very conservative nor very aggressive. A very conservative strategy, such as not allocating a sufficient amount for equity, will make it very difficult for the pension plans to achieve the required rate of return, resulting in funding shortage. A more aggressive strategy,

which tends to invest a very large portion in the stock market, may also lead to substantial decrease in pension funding level during a financial market slump.

On the liability side of the equation, the calculation of future pension benefits can change. Such change comes when government officials increase the level of pension benefits, possibly as a result of negotiations with public sector unions. Because pension benefits are not paid right away, it is potentially easier for politicians to promise an increase in pension benefits than an increase in wages, especially when the pension fund is very well funded. Therefore when government officials increase pension benefits, they need to be mindful how that will affect the pension funding status. If an increase in benefits is not matched by an increase in contribution or an increase in investment return, then a funding shortage can occur.

Because of these three factors, a pension plan that is fully funded today does not necessarily mean it will be fully funded tomorrow. Because of the method UAAL is calculated, to maintain its full funding status, the government still needs to contribute the required amount, earns the required rate of return on investment, and should not make changes in benefits without careful analysis of the impact on the pension funding status.

To complete the discussion of public pension funding status, it is useful to see how public pension funding level has progressed over the years. Every other year since 1990, the Public Pension Coordinating Council (PPCC) has been conducting survey of public pensions. The data on funding level and asset allocation are presented in Table 2.[e]

It is obvious from this table that public pension funding has improved substantially since the early 1990s. The

---

[e]The data in 1990 through 1998 were collected from PPCC pension survey reports published in *Government Finance Review*. Data in 2000 were available at PPCC's website http://ppcc.grsnet.com. Data in 2002 were actually collected by the National Association of State Retirement Administrators and the National Council on Teacher Retirement. The summary of the survey can be found at http://www.nasra.org/presentations/brainardplenary.pdf.

funding ratio increased from 80% in 1990 to 104% in 2000, meaning the pension funds overall were overfunded in that year. It is not a mere coincidence that this improvement happened to go hand in hand with an increase in asset allocation for equity, both domestic and international. That allocation increased from under 40% in 1990 to about 60% in the late 1990s. This increase in allocation for equity happened amid one of the greatest stock market booms in history, thus substantially increasing the value of assets in pension funds. It is no wonder that the 6-year stock market slump starting in 2000 also substantially decreased the value of these assets and lead to deterioration in pension funding level in 2002.

LOOKING FORWARD

Looking into the future, public pension funds will assume more prominence in government finance than in the past. As mentioned in the "Introduction," the annual pension contribution has to come out of the government operating budget. It is therefore in direct competition with other vital public services for the scarce financial resources. Because of the phenomenal investment return in mid to late 1990s, the government could afford to both reduce pension contribution and still maintain a full funding status. The subsequent stock market crash, however, ended such a "holiday" for pension contribution. As can be seen from Table 2, the average pension fund is now underfunded. After years of decreasing pension contributions, many states now are seeing substantial increase in pension contributions, at a time when many states can least afford to do so because of the fiscal difficulty. Because of the underfunding, the government has to pay not only its normal cost but also the amortization of UAAL. The worst has yet to come. Because of the smoothing technique used in valuing the assets in the pension funds, much of the stock market loss between 2000 and 2002 has yet to be filtered into the valuation of the assets. For example, if using a 4-year smoothing technique, a portion of the loss of 2002 will remain in the valuation until 2005. That means the underfunding situation will continue to deteriorate for several more years before it gets better, and the government pension contribution will continue to increase. To make matters worse, the sustained over 20% investment return in mid to late 1990s in the stock market probably will not come back any time soon and the investment return in the future more likely will only match the historical average return. Therefore, on the one hand, the government tries to make up for the investment loss; on the other hand, it also has to make sure that its future investment will meet the required rate of return. Otherwise, even greater funding gap will occur. With the future investment environment not as favorable as the one in the 1990s, it is all the more important for government to stick to the basic prudent pension management practices as laid out in this article.

REFERENCES

1. Fore, D. Going Private in the Public Sector: The Transition from Defined Benefit to Defined Contribution Pension Plans. In *Pensions in the Public Sector*; Olivia, M., Hustead, E.C., Eds.; University of Pennsylvania Press, 2001.
2. U.S. Department of Labor, Bureau of Labor Statistics. *Employee Benefits in State and Local Governments*; 1998. Available at http://www.bls.gov/ncs/ebs/sp/ebbl0018.pdf.
3. U.S. Census Bureau. available at http://www.census.gov/govs/retire/ret98t5.xls.
4. Husteadd, E.C. Determining the Cost of Public Pension Plans. In *Pensions in the Public Sector*; Olivia, M., Hustead, E.C., Eds.; University of Pennsylvania Press, 2001.
5. Burnham, J.B. Risky business? Evaluating the use of pension obligation bonds. Gov. Finance Rev. **June 2003**, *19* (3), 12–17.
6. Trone, D.B.; Allbright, W.R.; Taylor, P.R. *The Management of Investment Decisions*; McGraw-Hill: New York, 1996.

Subnational Counter-Cyclical Fiscal Policy in the United States

Yilin Hou
The University of Georgia, Athens, Georgia, U.S.A.

INTRODUCTION

This article is a review of the counter-cyclical fiscal policy (CCFP) at the subnational level in the United States. The term "subnational" is used in contrast to "national," referring exclusively to the 50 states. Although the literature and data used are restricted to the United States, the academic and practical implications go beyond this country because budgetary stabilization at the subnational level has been a universal topic, bearing significance in many other countries as well.

This article is organized as follows: "Evolution of Theory" examines the origin and development of CCFP in the United States, which, in a period of about 70 years, presents many lessons. "The Practice of CCFP by State Governments" looks into the practice of CCFP by state governments, covering the choice and shift of policy instruments and responses to states' use of CCFP from the capital market, professional organizations, and the United States Congress. "The Future of CCFP" shifts focus onto the future of CCFP. It will consider the ongoing argument about the economic stabilization function of CCFP as well as the fundamental public good of reducing revenue shocks from economic fluctuations. It ends with the proposition that CCFP is not a panacea; politics and basic budgetary discipline are the ultimate baseline.

EVOLUTION OF THEORY

The study of business cycles has a history almost as long as the market economy in the western world. Prior to the 1930s, the dominant economic philosophy was the classical economic theory. In the 1930s, with the work of John Maynard Keynes emerged the theory and practice of CCFP. The Great Depression led to a thorough examination of the monetary policy as well as fiscal policy at the federal and subnational levels. Scholars found that the federal, state, and local sectors behaved perversely during the Depression because both levels were bound by the requirement to balance the annual budget.[1]

In 1932, Leland[2] studied how governments could best meet financial crisis and proposed that "a wise fiscal policy requires... a longer term financial program [than the fiscal year] that should take account of the fluctuations of the business cycle and should control the policy of the annual budget." Leland's proposal was discussed in 1933 by a University of Chicago roundtable as a method that the federal government could use to balance the budget over economic cycles.[3]

In 1941, Hansen further expanded this idea. Hansen observed that to promote security for unemployed workers and economic stability during the Great Depression, the federal government at first relied primarily on monetary policy, but the huge number of the unemployed compelled enormous expenditures. Fiscal policy, more by accident than by design, came onto the front stage.[4] Although an important weapon, monetary policy "has severe limitations and must be supplemented with [fiscal policy, which] includes first a [counter-] cyclically adjusted public spending program and second a [counter-] cyclically administered tax policy."[4]

In 1944, Hansen and Perloff extended the argument for CCFP to the state and local sectors: In periods of depression, tax rates should be reduced, and public expenditure should be high by drawing on accumulated reserves and incurring public debt. The policy, in general, shall be directed toward increasing consumer purchasing power and stimulating investment and business activity. For this purpose, tax rates during economic booms should be high to drain off excess consumer purchasing power and to accumulate reserves for revenue shortfalls in the future; public expenditure, in contrast, should be kept low—at a level just adequate to maintain essential social services. Borrowing for further expansion in such periods should be eliminated, and accelerated repayment of public debt should be pursued if the boom is strong.[1]

Intuitively, the counter-cyclical features of such a fiscal policy make sense, but they are difficult to implement, especially during economic prosperity. Major obstacles may come from three sides. First, states are limited by their constitutions or statutes from accumulating high levels of surpluses. Even in the absence of legal restraints, individual and corporate taxpayers tend to exert spending pressure on elected officials during booms to expand public expenditures and/or reduce tax rates; and elected

Encyclopedia of Public Administration and Public Policy
DOI: 10.1081/E-EPAP 120024102

officials either share the general optimism or simply follow the voters' will to facilitate their own reelections. Finally, the goals of economic development lead to interstate competition for businesses, which induces, or even dictates, reduction of tax rates.

A subnational government can resort to one or more of the following three means in a recession to implement a CCFP, each with its pros and cons. First, because the federal government has monetary policy and controls more and wider taxing power, federal grants are a valuable financial source. However, obtaining such grants is often unreliable. As experience goes, federal grants may not come as early or at the amount states may need and expect. This lesson was confirmed in the 2001 recession: When the national recession coincided with a catastrophic disaster, federal aid dwindled, and the federal government mandated expenditures that added to states' financial burdens. Besides, where a grant is based on a matching ratio, poor states are hit hard. When a state is in fiscal distress, it often has to cut its assistance to local governments.

The capital market is another means of addressing recession pressures because incurring/increasing public debt in downturns is technically sound. However, recession years are the time when states adopt drastic fiscal measures that adversely affect their credit rating, thus eroding their borrowing capacity on the market. Besides, strict debt limitations as prescribed in state constitutions or statutes do not allow state governments indefinite room for incurring debts.

Then, the only means that is consistently reliable, independent of outside control, is own-source reserves. The availability of reserves depends on two internal factors: first, the legal framework-statutory balanced budget requirements on a (bi)annual basis, which offer little room for flexibility in this context; and, second, the human factor; chief elected officials must possess not only the managerial foresight for the necessity of reserves but also the political courage and skill to resist and manipulate spending pressures during prosperity. Once accumulated, reserves must be guarded against any possible raids in boom years. The best means for counteracting these two internal factors is an institutionalized device that provides statutory protection of the reserves.

The July 1949 "Budget Theory Symposium" dealt with legal framework. Conferees succinctly pointed out that "there is no magic" about the 1-year period of the annual budget; that the most important issue is "stabilization of tax expectance [for businesses];" and that "longer projections and more frequent reviews by the legislative body are both desirable...."[5] This statement partially softens the theoretical foundation of the annual budget.

Another round of theoretical exploration came in 1987 when Gramlich reexamined macroeconomic evidence and concluded that conventional wisdom may have been inaccurate (states should not only pursue CCFP but, in fact, adopt such practices to stabilize their budgets) and that we can reasonably assume that subnational fiscal policy can exert at least short-term influence.[6] Gramlich, in 1991, further distinguishes three types of state fiscal policies: neutral, perverse, and stable. The neutral type discourages counter-cyclical policy and advocates automatic fluctuation of taxes and budget surpluses with changes in income. With no counter-cyclical action and no changes to the tax structures over the business cycle, revenues move procyclically. If following a perverse policy, governments would initiate discretionary tax increases and/or expenditure reductions during recessions, cut taxes, and increase spending in boom years. This policy amplifies business cycle fluctuations.[7]

Gramlich advocates a fiscal policy for stability: Governments smoothen the cycle by raising taxes and/or cutting spending during expansion to accumulate reserves, then by lowering taxes and/or increasing spending during recession by decumulating reserves. The budget would then be balanced over the cycle. This is a stronger version of CCFP, involving accumulating reserves and tax rate changes. No states have adopted this version—although saving reserves are common, tax rate changes, especially permanent ones, are much more difficult and thereby less common because tax increases are politically unpopular. A weaker version without tax changes is what many states have practiced.

THE PRACTICE OF CCFP BY STATE GOVERNMENTS

In the world of administration, New York was the first state to respond to the 1944 Hansen and Perloff proposal by establishing a budget stabilization fund (BSF) to stabilize own-source revenues, with funding from annual surpluses;[8] but the concept and adoption of BSF spread very slowly among the states until the 1970s. The earliest state BSFs were designed following the weaker version of CCFP—to save annual surpluses in prosperity but not to raise tax rates in boom and then lower the rates in a recession.

Nevertheless, the practice of CCFP had spread out through a wise use of general fund surplus (GFS) accumulated from boom years, evolving the perverse policies of the 1930s into the rational fiscal policies since World War II. Independent academic research identified this orientation shift in the mid-1960s: "...[T]he patterns of deviations from the trend for state and local receipts were found to have been more and more stabilizing with each succeeding [business] cycle."[9] A report by the United States Advisory Commission on Intergovernmental Relations (ACIR) in the late 1970s confirms this policy change: "...[D]uring each economic downswing since World War II, state and local fiscal behavior was 'correct' [meaning 'counter-cyclical'] because [spending more from reserves] added to aggregate demand [during downturns]."[10]

The severe economic and budgetary difficulties of Michigan from 1974 to 1975 and earlier recessions forced the state to seek a permanent solution. Such efforts led to the creation, in 1977, of the Michigan "counter-cyclical budget and economic stabilization fund," which, in comparison with its earlier counterparts in other states, has two new features. First, it places an economic element in the purpose of the fund—to assist in stabilizing not only governmental revenue during periods of recession but also employment when the rate of unemployment is high. Second, the source and use approval of the fund are by a preset formula—the percentage above the 2% annual growth rate benchmark determines the amount to be transferred into the fund in the next fiscal year, and the percentage of negative annual growth rate determines the amount to be used from the fund in the current fiscal year.[11] The Michigan legislation became a model for many other states. It was "copied" in Ohio, Indiana, and Washington, and it influenced the BSF legislation in many more states. It is not an exaggeration to say that widespread adoption of BSFs among the states started with the 1977 Michigan model legislation accompanied by other social economic factors.

Policy Instruments

Once a CCFP is shown to be rational, state governments face the task of choosing policy instruments that are technically convenient and politically operable while guaranteeing the reserves necessary to handle revenue shocks. The two major ones are the BSF and GFS, although, conceptually, there can be many more possible instruments (some are variations of BSF and GFS in different forms). To practitioners, all forms of reserves, including various contingency funds, can be counted in the BSF category—those that are fine are for one time use and will be returned as soon as the economy recovers. (In fact, the Government Finance Officers' Association (GFOA) lists contingency funds as the same as BSF; see *Recommended Budget Practices—A Framework for Improved State and Local Government Budgeting*, Section 4.1, Ref. [12]).

Although we can assume that, in general, economic differences between BSF, GFS, and other forms of reserves do not exist—because total cash position at times of a budget shortfall is the issue[13,14]—it is important to remember that because budgeting is always closely related to politics, the real test for the above assumption is whether elected officials, and taxpayers collectively, can "administratively and politically" exercise adequate

fiscal self-restraint on a routine basis in times of expansion[15] (i.e., to protect fiscal reserves against current spending pressure for use in a subsequent downturn).

From 1946 to the mid-1980s, the adoption of BSFs among the states was very slow; most states relied on GFS as the policy tool, and even with those states with a BSF, GFS was an indispensable supplement. In the late 1970s, the "tax and expenditure limitation movements," starting with Proposition 13 in California, rapidly spread to other states. A direct consequence of these movements was a strict limit on general fund balance levels. GFS levels plummeted in states with such a limit. In the course of these movements came the severe national recessions of 1980 and 1982, which repeated in state legislatures and state governments, in general, the historical lesson of the chaos that may ensue when inadequate reserves are on hand to ameliorate sudden revenue shocks. Thus the tax and expenditure limitation movements and the recent recessions became the driving force and catalyst in the wider adoption of BSF, triggering a chain reaction among the states. Soon, over a dozen states passed BSF legislation.

The lesson can be best summarized with a quote from the 1981 State of Washington legislation for their "emergency reserve fund": "The current budgetary system of Washington lacks stability. It encourages crisis budgeting and results in cutbacks during lean years and overspending during surplus years." To safeguard the fund against raids, a very strict procedure was put into place: Appropriations from the fund can be made "only if approved by two-thirds of each house and by a vote of the people at [the] next general election." (Revised Code of Washington 43.135.045)[a] Historical data show the shift of state fiscal reserves from GFS to BSF—although the historical average balance of BSFs has increased from the early to the more recent ones, the historical average level of GFS has tended to decrease.

Response from the Congress, Market, and Professional Organizations

Adoption and implementation of CCFP by the states have been welcomed and encouraged by legislators, the debt market, and professional organizations. In 1985, the United States Congress concluded that "the states believe there is a role for [state] government in countering recession, irrespective of Federal action." Three design

---

[a]Revised Code of Washington, Title 43: State Government—Executive, Chapter 43.135: State Expenditures Limitations (formerly Tax Revenue Limitations), Section 045: Emergency Reserve Fund.

issues are prominent: first, state reserve funds have to be large enough to buffer revenue shocks in a recession. There is no uniform level of the reserve proper to all states. The level varies by each state's cyclical economic fluctuation; second, states need a policy of maintaining reserves of a given size to avoid year-to-year debates about the proper size; and, third, the accumulation and release of reserves should be gradual.[16]

In 1990, research by the GFOA argues that establishing a fund balance policy and the BSF can alleviate sudden short revenue shocks or deficits.[13] GFOA advocates CCFP and lists it as a best practice.[12] Credit rating agencies claim that "maintaining an operating reserve is the most effective practice that can enhance an issuer's credit rating" and lists it as the first of 12 best practices that have "significant rating value."[17] Thus CCFP at the subnational level in the United States has been widely accepted and adopted.

THE FUTURE OF CCFP

In the field of macroeconomic theory, the debate about the stabilization policy is yet to conclude. Some economists hold that variations in governmental revenue flows are caused by a combination of multifactors. Fluctuations in the economy (recession and expansion) are but one of them. Others are changes in the tax structure, additions or discontinuations of taxes, and raising or reducing of tax rates, which are results of not only the economy but also, and more often, election politics.[18] Because monetary and fiscal policies can influence these fluctuations and offset shocks, policy makers should act to stabilize the economy to keep output and employment close to their natural rates.

However, some other economists doubt whether the government is able to stabilize the economy. On one hand, between the recognition of a recession for state governments and the start of counter-cyclical fiscal programs, there are long and variable lags that are inherent in economic policy making. On the other hand, our understanding of the economy is still very limited and economic forecasting has repeatedly failed our expectations. Therefore it may not be a bad idea for policy makers simply to passively follow a fixed policy rule.

A more seemingly convincing argument about CCFP goes that: assuming stabilization could be successfully achieved, by the natural rate hypothesis, such a policy can only reduce the magnitude of fluctuations around the natural rate by eliminating the peaks of booms as well as the troughs of recessions so that the average benefit would be small.[19] Finally, the real-business-cycle theory takes fluctuations as the optimal response of the economy to changing technology, and believes that even if

stabilization were possible, policy makers should not pursue this goal.

A direct answer to such doubts is straightforward: Drastic fluctuations of state budgets in history have caused, and will again cause, huge damage and interruption to public life. Revenue shocks from business cycles have repeatedly shown that the subnational sector is prey to economic fluctuations. Public expenditures should not be as subject to cyclical fluctuations as private investments.[20] Therefore, stabilization of state budgets is a big public good, which is worth every effort to achieve. Scholars and practitioners have also been calling for CCFP for decades. The tide has been rising with recessions and ebbing with expansions—the lesson is still not thoroughly learned.

CONCLUSION

However, a rational fiscal policy and proper policy tools are not a panacea to governmental revenue shocks. The policy and policy tools are but the means that must go through the human hands of implementation to be effective, which in turn lies ultimately in the domain of politics. Specifically, a wise fiscal policy may be brushed aside; appropriate policy instruments can run distorted; and fiscal reserves that are adequate by the most sophisticated formula might as well be used off the right target. Therefore, the solution returns to the very basics of fiscal restraint and budgetary discipline. It would be a misconception that a rational policy can solve the problem once and for all.

REFERENCES

1. Hansen, A.H.; Perloff, H.S. *State and Local Finance in the National Economy*; W. W. Norton & Company, Inc.: New York, 1944; 40–55.
2. Leland, S.E. How Governments Can Best Meet the Financial Crisis. In *Conference Paper: Convention of the International City Managers' Association*, Cincinnati, OH, October 24, 1932.
3. *Balancing the Budget—Federal Fiscal Policy During Depression*; Gideonse, H.D., Ed.; The University of Chicago Press: Chicago, 1933.
4. Hansen, A.H. *Fiscal Policy and Business Cycles*; W. W. Norton & Company, Inc.: New York, 1941; pp. 116, 261.
5. Symposium on budget theory. Public Adm. Rev. **1950**, *1* (10), 20–31.
6. Gramlich, E.M. Subnational Fiscal Policy. In *Perspectives on Local Public Finance and Public Policy*; Quigley, J.M., Ed.; JAI Press Inc.: Greenwich, CT, 1987; Vol. 3, 3–27.
7. Gramlich, E.M. The 1991 state and local fiscal crises. Brookings Pap. Econ. Act. **1991**, (2), 249–287. This

tripartite theory traces back to A.H. Hansen and H.S. Perloff, 1944.

8. New York State Consolidated Laws: Chapter 56. State Finance Law: Article VI. Funds of the State. Section 92.

9. Rafuse, R.W. Cyclical Behavior of State-Local Finances. In *Essays in Fiscal Federalism*; Musgrave, R.A., Ed.; The Brookings Institution: Washington, DC, 1965; 118.

10. *Counter-Cyclical Aid and Economic Stabilization*; The United States Advisory Commission on Intergovernmental Relations (ACIR): GPO: Washington, DC, 1978; 6.

11. *Act 76 of 1977 (Repealed), and Act 431 of 1984; also Michigan Compiled Laws: Chapter 18. Department of Management and Budget*. Sections 351–359.

12. *Develop Policy on Stabilization Funds*; GFOA: Chicago, IL, 1999.

13. Allan, I.J. Unreserved Fund Balance and Local Government Finance. In *Research Bulletin—Research and Analysis on Current Issues*; Government Finance Officers' Association: 1990; 4.

14. Sobel, R.S.; Holcombe, R.G. The impact of state rainy day funds in easing state fiscal crises during the 1990–1991 recession. Public Budg. Finance Fall. **1996**, *16*, 30.

15. *States' Use of Surplus Funds*; Congressional Budget Office: Washington, DC, November 1998; 15–16.

16. *Federal and State Roles in Economic Stabilization*, United States House of Representatives. December 31, 1985; 3–14. 99th Congress, 1st Session, Report 99-460.

17. Impact of Management Practices on Municipal Credit. In *Fitch IBCA Special Report in Its Public Finance Newsletter*, May 4, 2000. http://www.fitchibca.com (accessed June 2000).

18. Stonecash, J.M. The Revenue Problem: Revenue Fluctuations and Forecasting, New York State, 1950–1990. In *Case Studies in Public Budgeting and Financial Management*; Khan, A., Hildreth, W.B., Eds.; Kendall/Hunt Publishing Company: Dubuque, IA, 1994; 153–163.

19. Mankiw, N.G. *Macroeconomics*; Worth Publishers: New York, 1992; 486.

20. Musgrave, R. *The Future of Fiscal Policy—A Reassessment*; Leuven University Press: 1978; 31.

Telehealth and State Government Policy

Mary Schmeida
Kent State University, Kent, Ohio, U.S.A.

INTRODUCTION

Telehealth represents a new paradigm in health care. Considered both an administrative reform and regulatory policy, it draws on electronic government and electronic commerce. Although no authoritative consensus on the definition of telehealth has been reached, Congress defines it as the use of electronic information and telecommunications technologies to support long-distance clinical health care, patient and professional health-related education, and public health care and administration.

In the era of technology, state policy makers find telehealth important. Advanced communication technology can provide health care services to state residents. To governments, Internet technology can make product and service delivery both cost-efficient and convenient. As a powerful tool for reshaping government, it is expected to help build economic strength, allowing government to be catalytic and enterprising. State policy makers are incrementally passing telehealth-enabling legislation, and a patchwork of laws exists today.

TELEHEALTH EVOLUTION

History documents the beginnings of telehealth throughout the twentieth century. The Nebraska Project of the 1950s, using closed-circuit television, is generally considered the first comprehensive attempt at telehealth, advancing clinical psychiatry and medical instruction[1] and promoting remote consultation to prisons, courts, and schools. Projects of the 1960s and 1970s involved the U.S. military and the National Space and Aeronautical Administration,[2] with innovations advancing emergency and cardiology care. Recent evolution is dramatic, combining audiovisual components of traditional forms of media with the interactivity and speed of telephone and e-mail, permitting the exchange of patient information regardless of geographic distance; facilitating interaction between practitioners and consumers; transmitting images via satellite to experts for interpretation; and entering surgery, as seen in experimental robotic coronary artery bypass surgery.

CONDITIONS DRIVING TELEHEALTH POLICY

Several conditions are driving telehealth policy across the states. External conditions driving state telehealth-enabling laws include the lack of access to medical specialists, spiraling costs of health care, and growing consumer sophistication and demand for quality health care. Political conditions driving policy are the bureaucratic issues of a top–down government that no longer works to satisfy citizen demands for quality goods and services. A flexible and agile government can respond to the changing external environment, with quick information technologies to meet citizen demands, breaking down bureaus and reshaping government.

Lack of Access to Medical Specialists

Rural states have a great lack of access to specialists. Across the states, rural regions are facing a growing maldistribution of medical specialists, hospitals, and health care resources. Specialists and advanced diagnostics have been more readily accessible in urbanized areas versus remote rural settings. For example, West Virginia is among the most rural, poorest, and most elderly of the states, and has a lower-than-national-average supply of physicians.[3]

The original goal was to improve consumer access to health care. Inequitable distribution of medical resources, in relation to the distribution of need in inaccessible state populations, has led to the expansion of the national information infrastructure, making telehealth a feasible solution to minimize disparities. Rural consumers can now seek video teleconsultation at access points or facilities equipped for telecommunications in remote areas. For example, pediatric populations in rural regions can receive early disease intervention that has been previously delayed due to distance and cost. Although the lack of specialty services in rural regions has driven the telehealth idea in the past, professional shortage areas can also include urban regions of a state because metropolitan isolates can also have difficulty accessing services.

Encyclopedia of Public Administration and Public Policy
DOI: 10.1081/E-EPAP 120027078

Spiraling Costs of Health Care

Spiraling health care costs is a condition underlying telehealth activity. The urban consumer price index shows a rising yearly trend for the cost of health care from 74.9% for 1980, to 162.8% for 1990, to 272.8% for 2001.[4] The growing elderly population demanding costly services is also driving policy. The projected rise in Medicare spending is a function of the aging population's longevity requiring expensive specialized services, the retirement of baby boomers along with the declining ratios of workers to Medicare beneficiaries, and the overall increased costs of health care such as the increased cost of diagnostic equipment.[5] Telehealth as a cost containment strategy for entitlement programs can reduce: opportunity costs, costs associated with overtreatment and medical error, out-of-pocket expenses, and costs for insurance companies. State prison systems using telehealth are not only avoiding costs of security guards and transportation, but increasing public safety.

States are seeking creative financial arrangements. Because initial capital costs can be substantial and there are incremental costs with each use, cooperative initiatives between public, private, and nonprofit sectors can limit start-up and program sustainment costs. For example, Nebraska created a health care trust fund awarding grants for infrastructure development. Creative arrangements have led to consortiums of neighboring states implementing projects. Regional networking can minimize program costs while sustaining projects, inviting interstate commerce, and bringing new telehealth policy ideas to the table.

Growing Demand for Quality Health Care

Telehealth is expected to improve the quality of U.S. health care. Research links poor U.S. health care to underuse, overuse, and misuse of services. With choice as a proxy for quality, government telehealth websites inform residents on options in choosing a health plan and premium, practitioner(s), and hospital setting for services.[6]

Many states are improving the quality of care their residents receive by implementing innovative telehealth ideas, with Texas, Hawaii, North Carolina, California, Virginia, and Michigan as leaders in scope of implementation.[7] For example, telehealth home care can improve quality by: preventing hospital readmissions; predicting and avoiding chronic illness setbacks; and bringing early medical intervention to remote populations, thus improving clinical outcomes.

STATE TELEHEALTH-ENABLING LAWS

There are barriers to expanding the use of telehealth. These include a lack of: uniform statewide physician licensure statutes; laws regarding disclosure of restricted patient information to unauthorized individuals; interstate reimbursement to practitioners; and strict Internet regulation for the dispensing of pharmaceuticals on-line. Enabling laws create the legal environment that makes telehealth feasible. Although federal legislation has tried to create this environment, the states are taking the lead and leaving a patchwork of enabling laws. However, both state and federal telehealth legislations still lag behind the rapid and dramatic change in technology.

Several states are leaders in passing telehealth-enabling laws. Georgia, Kansas, Louisiana, South Dakota, and Texas are leaders, whereas West Virginia has been relatively inactive in initiatives to overall state telehealth policy. Texas has been revolutionary—assuming a formal position among the states in coordinating overall planning for telehealth development, promoting the idea with public utilities, and setting reasonable telecommunication costs and prison telehealth.[8]

Telehealth Medicaid Practitioner Reimbursement Laws

States are enacting Medicaid telehealth practitioner reimbursement laws. This administrative reform policy changes previous policy on unfair fee-splitting arrangements for practitioners and the lack of reimbursement for provision of services to Medicaid recipients. Medicare has been on the forefront on this topic, expanding its reimbursement policy to include a variety of originating telehealth sites, shaping policy for state programs, and as a policy example for the private insurance industry. Some state Blue Cross/Blue Shield plans, among other private insurers, are electing to pay for select telehealth services.

Nineteen states have adopted Medicaid telehealth reimbursement laws. As an innovator, Texas requires that reimbursement not be denied due to lack of in-person consultation and also provides parity between telehealth and in-person health care on deductibles and copayments. All states enacting this law reimburse for medical health needs, whereas California, Kansas, Minnesota, Montana, Texas, and Virginia also reimburse for mental health.[9]

State Health Care Information Privacy Laws

The use of the Internet for patient care is a growing concern. Over the past decade, consumer privacy attitudes have changed, with 60% of Internet users expressing concern that placing medical records on-line can be violated even if password-protected, and 89% of those seeking on-line health information expressing concern that the website may sell or give other institutions information about their activities.[10] Although technology can benefit practitioners, the tradeoffs can jeopardize the integrity of sensitive health information.

States are responding to consumer privacy demands with legislation. Although the Health Insurance Portability and Accountability Act of 1996[11] provides new safeguards in this area, states must also respond. To date, health privacy statutes vary significantly across the states regarding electronic means for disclosing private health information and storing the information. Twenty states have restrictions on disclosure of patient health information by hospitals and health care entities. For example, Rhode Island prohibits medical information from being disclosed regardless of the institution holding the medical record. Most states have not intended statutes to be comprehensive, thus lagging behind the needs of innovative health care.[12]

Interstate Physician Licensure Laws

No uniform state licensure laws exist for governing telehealth practitioners. Updated laws would protect consumers and monitor the telehealth activities of providers regulating the practice of physicians across the states. Recognizing the significance of this issue, 17 states have adopted full telemedicine licensure status for physicians. This allows physicians physically located in their home state or foreign country to perform certain patient care services in another state through the use of telecommunications, or to practice medicine in another state. Colorado allows nothing to prohibit consultation between a Colorado physician and a practicing physician in another state. Nine states allow interstate telehealth by certificate, registration, or special licensure, whereas 24 states have no interstate licensure laws for physicians.[13] Interstate licensure is important to telehealth diffusion because any uncertainty among practitioners about licensure status and associated liability risks will restrict activity.

Internet Pharmacy Regulations

State Internet pharmacy regulations are critical to ensuring quality health care. Internet pharmacy consumers can face injury if prescriptions are electronically issued by pharmacies without knowledge of the consumer's medical history. As an initiative to regulate Internet pharmaceutical activity, President Clinton, in 1999, expanded Food and Drug Administration (FDA) enforcement powers to eliminate unsafe dispensing of drugs on-line. However, the states have traditionally regulated pharmacists and physicians, and are increasingly stepping up to enforce unsafe pharmaceutical electronic commerce activity. Thirteen states are policy innovators, enacting legislation requiring physician initial examinations before prescribing medication on the Internet—Alabama, Arizona, California, Florida, Iowa, Idaho, Kansas, Maine, Mis-

sissippi, Nebraska, New York, Ohio, and Virginia. Although regulations would restrict the pharmaceutical electronic business growth, restrictions would protect consumers and improve the quality of electronic prescription services.[14]

ECOLOGICAL FACTORS EXPLAINING ADOPTION OF LAWS

Several ecological factors are influencing the adoption of telehealth-enabling laws. Policy diffusion literature shows political, economic, intrastate, and interstate policy networks, and demand factors can affect whether states adopt legislation across issue areas. Using 50 state data with statistical controls, Schmeida[15] found that ecological determinants matter in explaining the adoption of the four telehealth-enabling laws discussed above. The presence of designated mental health professional shortage areas is found to influence the adoption of all four laws. State legislative professionalism explains the adoption of all enabling laws, except Internet pharmacy regulations. Greater legislative professionalism increases the likelihood that states will adopt privacy laws, but not necessarily telehealth reimbursement and physician licensure laws.

Particular state ecological factors also explain the adoption of specific telehealth laws. Illustrative of these are the following:

- States with higher information technology administration and management capacity, and populations over the age of 64 years are more likely to adopt Internet pharmacy laws.
- States with greater electronic commerce and business regulations are less likely to adopt physician telehealth licensure laws, but are more likely to adopt full licensure status.
- States with a greater percentage of women in the legislature are more likely to pass privacy laws; this is important because women in politics have historically been instrumental in driving health policy.

Such findings provide policy makers with a foundation for understanding this evolving policy area.

CONCLUSION

As an innovative policy, telehealth is important to the state government. Drawing on electronic government and electronic commerce, it has the potential to improve access to health care services, to contain costs while improving service quality, and to reshape the government. State policy makers are passing enabling legislation, although legislative details vary from state to state. Likely benefits of telehealth policy are cost containment, improved access for underserved populations, and enhanced quality of care.

REFERENCES

1. Smith, H.; Allison, R. *Telemental Health: Delivering Mental Health Care at a Distance*; U.S. Department of Health and Human Services, 1998; 3. http://www.usdhhs.gov (accessed November 2003).

2. Office of Health Affairs, U.S. Department of Defense. *Military Health Services System Information Management/Information Technology Strategic Plan*; Defense Technical Information Center, 1996; 1–5. http://usdod.gov (accessed November 2003).

3. National Conference of State Legislatures. In *Summary and Analysis of State Initiatives to Promote Telemedicine, Volumes 1 and II*; 2003; 1–91. http://www.ncsl.org (accessed September 2003).

4. U.S. Census Bureau Statistical Abstract of the United States: 2002. In *Table No. 483*; U.S. Government Printing Office: Washington, DC, 2003; 453.

5. *Centers for Medicare and Medicaid Services*; 1999; 1–9. http://www.cms.hhs.gov (accessed November 1999).

6. AARP. *Beyond 50.02: A Report to the Nation on Trends in Health Security*; 2001; 91–117. http://www.aarp.org/beyond50/ (accessed January 2003).

7. Schmeida, M.; McNeal, R.; Mossberger, K. *Implementing Telehealth in the American States*; Paper to be presented at the 2004 Midwest Political Science Association Conference, 1–30.

8. National Conference of State Legislatures. In *Summary and Analysis of State Initiatives to Promote Telemedicine, Volumes 1 and II*; 2003; 1–91. http://www.ncsl.org (accessed September 2003).

9. *Centers for Medicare and Medicaid Services*; 2003; 1–7. http://www.cms.hhs.gov (accessed December 2003).

10. House of Representatives Hearing 107-35. *Opinion Surveys: What Consumers Have to Say About Information Privacy*; U.S. Government Printing Office: Washington, DC, 2001; 1–38. 107th Congress, 1st Session.

11. Public Law 104-191. *Health Insurance Portability and Accountability Act of 1996*; US Government Printing Office: Washington, DC, 1996; 1–21. 104th Congress, 2nd Session.

12. National Conference of State Legislatures. In *Summary and Analysis of State Initiatives to Promote Telemedicine, Volumes 1 and II*; 2003; 1–91. http://www.ncsl.org (accessed September 2003).

13. Office for the Advancement of Telehealth. *2001 Telemedicine Report to Congress*; 2001; 1–26. http://telehealth.hrsa.gov/ (accessed June 2003).

14. Office for the Advancement of Telehealth. *2001 Telemedicine Report to Congress*; 2001; 1–26. http://telehealth.hrsa.gov/ (accessed June 2003).

15. Schmeida, M. *Telehealth Enabling Laws: Explaining Adoption and Diffusion Across the American States*; Paper to be presented at the 2004 Midwest Political Science Association Conference, 1–35.

Thailand

Brian Brewer
City University of Hong Kong, Kowloon, Hong Kong

INTRODUCTION

Thailand has experienced frequent changes in its national government over the past 70 years, while the rapid economic growth of the 1970s and 1980s that was halted so dramatically by the 1997 Asian financial crisis has resumed once again. The 1997 constitution, through its reform of the electoral system and the establishment of a range of institutions such as the National Counter Corruption Commission (NCCC), the Constitutional Court, and the Office of the Ombudsman, provides an institutional framework to support principles of good governance. Major public administration challenges include the implementation of public service reforms such as decentralization, a continuous battle against corruption at all levels, ensuring a free media, and facilitating the further development of Thailand's civil society.

GOVERNMENT IN THAILAND

Thailand, with a population of 63.3 million, is generally regarded as a ''middle income'' country and, though less prosperous than its more industrialized neighbor Malaysia or the city-state of Singapore, its 2002 per capita GDP of US$6,900 is higher than other countries in Southeast Asia (http://unstats.un.org/unsd/demographic/social/inc-eco.htm) (Table 1). Poverty tends be more widespread in the countryside as industrial development has concentrated mostly in the Bangkok Metropolitan Region.

The only Southeast Asian country never colonized by a European power, Thailand is a constitutional monarchy with executive power vested in a prime minister and cabinet. Under the terms of the 1997 constitution, the bicameral National Assembly consists of a House of Representatives composed of 400 single-member districts and 100 party-list seats, all directly elected for 4-year terms, and a Senate that has 200 members directly elected for 6-year terms.

The current prime minister, Thaksin Shinawatra, is a telecommunications billionaire who has formed a coalition government from the 248 seats won by his Thai Rak Thai (Thais Love Thais, or TRT) in the 2001 general election together with three smaller parties: two conservative and one centrist. With this comfortable parliamentary majority, Thaksin's government has greater stability than any government in modern Thai history, which between 1932 and 1992 gave rise to 50 different, and often unstable, military and civilian administrations.

There are 76 provinces in Thailand, including metropolitan Bangkok. The governor of Bangkok has been directly elected, whereas all other provincial governors have been career civil servants appointed by the Ministry of the Interior. Under this highly centralized system of public administration, most officials at provincial, district, and subdistrict level have been affiliated with central agencies. Consequently, public policy has traditionally been paternalistically developed within the centrally oriented bureaucracy, while political power has revolved around a narrow set of competing elites in the capital.

1997 CONSTITUTION

Thailand's 1997 constitution is the basis for major structural changes in the Thai political, legal, and administrative systems, although when it was approved overwhelmingly by the National Assembly the vote belied deep divisions between reformers and conservatives. It does, nevertheless, enshrine the principle of constitutional supremacy. Any law, act, or decree contrary to or inconsistent with the constitution is unenforceable, while all branches of the government are bound to ensure that the constitution's integrity is upheld.

A number of constitutional features are designed to undermine corrupt electoral practices and to reduce the fragmentation of political power among too many political parties. All candidates for election either as members of the House of Representatives or the Senate must have at least a Bachelor's degree. This measure is designed to reduce vote buying in rural areas, based on the assumption that many traditional ''godfathers'' (i.e., wealthy local businessmen who dominate political/economic life within a rural district) would be disqualified. All parties contesting a general election must endorse a ''slate'' of 100 candidates so as to help eliminate small splinter factions and, by consolidating power in the hands of a few dominant parties, help ensure governments with a degree of long-term stability.

Encyclopedia of Public Administration and Public Policy
DOI: 10.1081/E-EPAP 120024434

Table 1 Per capita GDP (US$) 2002 (estimated), selected countries in Southeast Asia

Country	Per capita GDP (US$)
Singapore	24,000
Malaysia	9,300
Thailand	**6,900**
Philippines	4,200
Indonesia	3,100
Vietnam	2,250
Myanmar (Burma)	1,660

http://www.worldfactsandfigures.com/gdp_country_desc.php.

ASIAN FINANCIAL CRISIS

The spark igniting the Asian financial crisis in July 1997 was the Thai government's failed attempt to defend the Thai baht, which was linked to the U.S. dollar, against speculators. Thailand's booming economy ground to a halt amid massive layoffs in finance, real estate, and construction that resulted in huge numbers of workers returning to their villages in the countryside and 600,000 foreign workers being sent back to their home countries. The currency was floated and the government agreed to a US$17.2 billion bailout by the International Monetary Fund (IMF)/World Bank subject to conditionalities such as passing laws relating to bankruptcy (reorganizing and restructuring) procedures and establishing strong regulatory frameworks for banks and other financial institutions.

Thailand's economy is once again doing well and the extra tax revenue being generated should allow Thailand to balance its budget in 2004, four years ahead of schedule. Real GDP growth is expected to average 5.9% in 2003–2004, while inflationary pressures are expected to remain low and the baht to continue to be stable (http://www.economist.com/countries/Thailand/profile.cfm?folder=Profile-Forecast).

PUBLIC SECTOR

The Thai public sector is not particularly large. Except for Myanmar, Thailand spends a smaller portion of its GNP on the public sector than its Asian neighbors (Table 2).

Over the years, legislation has been enacted to facilitate the development of a modern civil service. The 1975 Civil Service Act introduced a position classification system and required new recruits to take an entry examination, and the 1992 Civil Service Act outlined the role of the Civil Service Commission as the central human resources agency for the public service. However, the bureaucracy is a traditional pillar of Thai society that has exercised

considerable power and enjoyed high status under both military and civilian regimes. Therefore, reform initiatives have had a limited impact on rectifying a host of shortcomings such as overcentralization, poor coordination, functional overlap (particularly at the subnational level), antiquated work processes, too much delay and discretion in implementing decisions, and lack of responsiveness and accountability to the citizenry. During the 1990s, the public sector's attempt to recruit and retain professionals was undermined by more attractive private sector salaries, particularly in key areas such as law, accounting, and computer science.

The military is also a traditional pillar of Thai society, although its role since 1992 has changed from one of exercising absolute power to that of "system stabilizer." As a more professional military has emerged, it has been less inclined to become involved directly in political affairs. Even the severe economic meltdown of the Asian financial crisis and the strong opposition within the traditional bureaucratic/military establishment to the new constitution did not provoke military intervention.

Public sector reforms designed to reduce the role of the state predate the initiatives flowing from the new constitution, although privatization of state assets was part of a package of reform measure announced when Thailand accepted its financial bailout in 1997. The long-term trend of selling off state-owned enterprises (SOEs), developing joint public/private ventures, and deregulation to encourage market competition has been boosted by the Thaksin administration's determination to move ahead with state enterprise privatization, with the caveat that enterprises responsible for key public services are to remain at least 50% owned by the government. Public utilities, such as electricity and water, are to be under government control even after corporatization.

The 1997 constitution is designed to reduce the control of the central bureaucracy through initiatives such as decentralization and to strengthen good governance principles. The Official Information Act (1997) provides

Table 2 Total expenditure on the public sector, selected countries in Southeast Asia (2000)

Rank order	Country	Expenditure (% of GDP)
1	Vietnam	23.4
2	Indonesia	20.5
3	Malaysia	19.7
4	Philippines	19.5
5	Singapore	19.1
6	**Thailand**	**18.0**
7	Myanmar	8.7

http://www.worldbank.org/data/databytopic/publicsector.html.

greater access to official information. One of the most visible changes in transparency is the policy on asset declaration by government officials—an issue highlighted frequently by the print media. In May 1999, the Cabinet issued its Public Sector Management Reform Plan, outlining the government's vision for institutional change under the supervision of a high-level Public Sector Reform Committee. Greater decentralization of the public sector has been a controversial issue of long-standing between politicians and bureaucrats, and it is now a key component of the democratic reform vision. A Decentralization Committee has been established, and responsibilities and funding are beginning to move away from the center of government toward special or general organizations at the local level. This is particularly the case with health, education, and local government financing.

A new bureaucratic system was launched in October 2002, consisting of 20 ministries, 61 bureaus, and 60 departments. This reform was designed to enhance government efficiency and flexibility, and reduce the chain of command. Primary objectives are to improve interdepartmental coordination and to bring together similar functions from multiple ministries.

Because of his deep distrust of, and increasing impatience with, the Thai bureaucracy's measured procedures, the Prime Minister, Thaksin Shinawatra, has now thrown his support behind the development of a chief executive officer (CEO) system, which would require senior government officials to manage their areas of responsibility like corporate CEOs. Among the first group targeted for training in this approach have been ministry permanent secretaries, department heads, chiefs of state enterprises, and some provincial governors (http://www.kellogg.northwestern.edu/news/hits/030702tnt.htm).

Corruption is a long-standing governance issue in Thailand, where traditional patron–client relationships and gift-giving have been widely accepted in public appointments, dealing with public officials and political campaigning. It has been the norm for government ministers to exercise patronage in relation to promotions and appointments, in particular to semigovernment Boards and authorities. Transparency International's Corruption Perceptions Index 2003 ranks Thailand 75th out of the 133 countries whose levels of corruption were charted (http://www.transparency.org/cpi/2003/cpi2003.en.html) (Table 3).

A major concern about the public reform decentralization initiatives concerns the capacity of the watchdog National Counter Corruption Commission (NCCC) to operate effectively against widespread corruption at the subnational level. However, unlike the corruption agency it replaces, the NCCC is an autonomous agency established apart from the Office of the Prime Minister with its own secretariat, budget, and personnel administration. Its main responsibilities are to ensure the declaration and inspection of assets and liabilities for officials holding political positions and state officials, to undertake corruption prevention and suppression activities (http://www.nccc.thaigov.net/nccc/eng.php). It has the power to overrule the Attorney General and initiate prosecution.

CONSTITUTIONAL COURT

The Constitutional Court is an independent body consisting of 15 full-time judges selected by a complicated process that seeks to ensure they are above political and business interests. It renders judgments on the constitutionality of the provisions of law and other powers as provided for in the Constitution and other laws.

In 2000 the NCCC found Thaksin Shinawatra, Thailand's prime minister, guilty of filing false asset statements when he was deputy prime minister in 1997 and the case was referred to the Constitutional Court for further action. A controversial eight-to-seven split in Thaksin's favor, in August 2001, averted a political crisis by allowing the prime minister to remain in office. It did, however, raise serious questions about whether the rule of law was being undermined by political expediency.

Table 3 Transparency international corruption perceptions index 2003, selected countries in Southeast Asia

Country rank	Country	CPI 2003 score	Surveys used	Standard deviation	High–low range
5	Singapore	9.4	12	0.1	9.2–9.5
37	Malaysia	5.2	13	1.1	3.6–8.0
70	**Thailand**	**3.3**	**13**	**0.9**	**1.4–4.4**
92	Philippines	2.5	12	0.5	1.6–3.6
100	Vietnam	2.4	8	0.8	1.4–3.6
122	Indonesia	1.9	13	0.5	0.7–2.9
129	Myanmar	1.6	3	0.3	1.4–2.0

http://www.transparency.org/cpi/2003/cpi2003.en.html.

OMBUDSMAN

The Ombudsman of Thailand (http://www.ombudsman. go.th) established in April 2000, under the provisions of the 1997 constitution, is empowered to refer any case in violation of the constitution to either the Administrative Court or the Constitutional Court. It also has the authority to inquire into complaints about maladministration by civil servants, members or employees of government bodies, state agencies, state enterprises, or local governments.

CIVIL SOCIETY

Civil society has, during the past 20 years, expanded substantially. Participation in Thai civil society appears to be strongest among rural, older citizens with more traditional attitudes although there is a continuing growth in the numbers of nongovernmental organizations (NGOs), with and without legal status, supporting issues such as environmental and wildlife protection, women's/ children's rights, and student's concerns. Private foundations, business groups, and professional organizations have also developed as vehicles of expression for the concerns of the middle class.

Many civil society groups and organizations participated in the consultation exercises that led to the drafting of Thailand's 1997 Constitution, which recognizes public participation as having a legitimate role to play in shaping national policies (Chapter V, Section 76—http:// www.kpi.ac.th/en/con_th5.asp). Under the new constitution, the Senate, composed of 200 members elected from geographic constituencies, is designed to reduce the influence of the bureaucracy, military, and business groups in favor of individuals more closely aligned with the community.

Thai civil society appears to be increasingly integrated into the participatory processes developed and controlled by the state in line with its ''good governance'' agenda rather than operating as a wholly independent critical force. For example, the government recently established the Community Organizations Development Institute (CODI) as a new type of public organization under the supervision of the Ministry of Finance (http://www.codi. or.th) to promote the development of community organizations and civil society by coordinating the efforts of stakeholders involved in community development.

NATIONAL ECONOMIC AND SOCIAL DEVELOPMENT BOARD

The National Economic and Social Development Board (NESDB) (http://www.nesdb.go.th) is Thailand's economic development agency and ''think tank.'' It is responsible for developing the 5-year National Plans that provide a guideline for the country's medium-term economic development. A series of participatory planning exercises with the private sector, NGOs, and civil society at the regional and local levels was undertaken to develop the 9th National Plan (2002–2006) (http://www. un.or.th/Thailand_Info/Development/plan/plan.html). Its main goals of poverty alleviation, recovery with sustainability and stability, good governance, and strengthening development foundations are essentially Thailand's national priorities. In the latest plan the growing significance of civil society in the decision-making process is emphasized.

MEDIA

The print and nonprint media have been credited with the role of assisting to heighten political consciousness as for example, during the televising of the constitutional debates prior to the approval of the 1997 constitution. However, Freedom House's Global Survey of Media Independence reduced Thailand's 2002 rating from Free to Partly Free because of increased pressure on media outlets by Prime Minister Thaksin Shinawatra's administration (http://www.freedomhouse.org/research/ pressurvey.htm) (Table 4).

Most radio and broadcast television stations are directly or indirectly owned or overseen by either the government or the armed forces, and, by law, radio stations must renew

Table 4 Freedom house freedom of the press survey 2003,[a] selected countries in Southeast Asia

Country	Status
	Free (0–30)
	Partly free (31–60)
	Not free (61–100)
Philippines	Free/21 to 30
Thailand	**Partly free/31 to 40**
Indonesia	Partly free/51 to 60
Singapore	Not free/61 to 70
Malaysia	Not free/71 to 80
Vietnam	Not free/81 to 90
Myanmar	No data

[a]Legal environment: 0–30 points
Political influences : 0–40 points
Economic pressures: 0–30 points
Total score: 0–100 points
http://www.freedomhouse.org/research/ pressurvey.htm.

their licenses annually. As for newspapers, which do scrutinize official policies and report allegations of corruption and human rights abuses, they appear to be exercising a higher level of self-censorship.

CONCLUSION

The electoral system and framework of agencies established by Thailand's enlightened 1997 constitution provide a sound basis for the continuing development of good governance principles in the country. However, critical issues surround how to ensure that either the majority government or the many different ''vested interests'' in the public administration system do not compromise, either overtly or covertly, the potential effectiveness of the new watchdog agencies, progress toward public services reform, freedom of the media, or the active engagement of civil society in policy making processes.

FURTHER READING

Asian Development Bank. 2003. http://www.adb.org/thailand.

Asia Foundation. 2003. http://www.asiafoundation.org/Locations/thailand.html.

Bello, W.; Cunningham, S.; Li, K.P. *A Siamese Tragedy: Development and Disintegration in Modern Thailand*; Zed Books Ltd.: London, 1998.

Bunbongkarn, S. Thailand: Democracy Under Siege. In *Driven By Growth: Political Change in the Asia-Pacific Region (Revised Edition)*; Morley, J.W., Ed.; M. E. Sharpe: Armonk, NY, 1999; 161–175.

CountryWatch. *Thailand: 2003 Country Review. Country Watch: Houston*; 2002. http://www.countrywatch.com.

Uneven Development in South East Asia; Dixon, C., Drakakis-Smith, D., Eds.; Ashgate: Aldershot, 1997.

Klein, J.R. *The Constitution of the Kingdom of Thailand, 1997: A Blueprint for Participatory Democracy*; The Asia Foundation: San Francisco, CA, 1998. (Working Paper #8).

Office of the Council of State, Royal Thai Government. *Constitution of the Kingdom of Thailand*; 1997.

Transparency and Corruption in Southeast Asia

Habib Zafarullah
University of New England, Armidale, New South Wales, Australia

Noore Alam Siddiquee
International Islamic University Malaysia, Kuala Lumpur, Malaysia

INTRODUCTION

In the contemporary world, effective democratic governance is anchored, among other key factors, on the degree of openness that governments exhibit in political and administrative affairs and the amplitude of integrity public administrators demonstrate in performing their official routine. Democracy cannot thrive in an environment of secrecy, as the free flow of information is imperative for people to follow and scrutinize the operations of a representative government, assess the policies and decisions it makes, and appraise the conduct of its personnel. Open government, which can promote a culture of probity within the public service, facilitates the consolidation and gradual deepening of democracy.[1] It strengthens the structures of accountability by applying the wherewithal to reduce malfeasance and corruption in public organizations. The more transparent a government is, the fewer will be the opportunities for public administrators and managers to resort to corrupt practices in the tasks they perform and deeper will be people's capacity to exercise control over arbitrary state power. Framing public policies behind closed doors or adhering to obscure procurement and financial practices can lead to making erroneous choices that may have adverse implications for the community and beyond. The immoderate exercise of bureaucratic discretion in a closed secretive environment or the influence of nontransparent corporate culture and the almost unbound volition of oligopolists to control competition in the market place result in corruption. Thus in the symbiotic relationship between corruption and opacity, discretion and monopoly are critical factors,[2] and the social and economic fallout of inordinate opacity and pervasive corruption can be a bane for democracy and development.[3]

THE SOUTHEAST ASIAN SCENE

The financial crisis of the late 1990s was a watershed in political governance in Southeast Asia. It exposed the imperfections of nondemocratic political structures and illiberal regimes and the failure of governments to either protect their economies from internal uncertainties and external threats or expose them to economic instability.[4] In several countries, it brought to the forefront the inadequacies of the state apparatus in fostering a culture of integrity in both government and the economic market for safeguarding the welfare of the people and in sustaining social and economic development.[5] The crisis, apart from external factors, also stemmed from the recondite operations of governments and markets and their indisposition to share or disseminate information with/to other stakeholders for the effective transaction of governmental or economic business. It also underscored the relevance of openness to accountability for lessening the opportunities for rent seeking, underhand dealings, and other forms of corruption. It highlighted the need for modernizing government by institutional reforms—making the operations of public institutions more transparent and upgrading the mechanisms for enforcing accountability in governments and financial markets.

Among the Southeast Asian nations, Singapore is perceived to be the least corrupt whereas Malaysia, Thailand, the Philippines, Vietnam, Indonesia and Myanmar are alleged to exhibit levels of corruption ranging from high to very high caused by systemic failures and individual dishonesty.[6,7] The level of governmental transparency is fairly low as citizen access to information is restricted because of overbearing legal and extralegal impediments.[8,9] Such low levels of transparency have significantly contributed to high levels of corruption in Southeast Asia.

A variety of social, political, and economic factors have contributed to making corruption pervasive, resulting in the effusion of resources and enervating both development activities and the effective delivery of public service.[10] Most countries in the region have been under authoritarian or pseudo-democratic rule for prolonged periods, and where democratization has been ushered, the consolidation process has been tardy. In government, accountability structures are imperfect or weak in ensuring vertical and horizontal systems of checks and balances.[11] Entrenched elites hardly face

Encyclopedia of Public Administration and Public Policy
DOI: 10.1081/E-EPAP-120024435

any competition, giving them a free will to influence officials to obtain undue advantage to serve their parochial interests. These happen out of the public gaze and often escape social and political oversight.

The economic liberalization programs initiated in the last two decades opened the Asian economies to globalization, spurred corporatization within the public sector, and the privatization of public assets and services. Globalization internationalized corruption as corporate power continues to be raised to high levels in the absence or weakness of civil society, particularly in Indonesia and to a lesser extent in Singapore and Malaysia. Transnational corporations have typically corrupted political and bureaucratic structures for ''exploiting market opportunities.''[12] Asian countries are at risk from such international rackets as money laundering, illegal flight capital, financial crime, and people smuggling.[13]

The media, which can be a powerful influence in creating a sound public integrity system, has not always been free; rather, authoritarian regimes in most of Southeast Asia placed unjustified restrictions on the press in the past and capriciously regulated the electronic media to serve their parochial political interests. Independent information sources have been few and far between, and only recently have they begun to permeate into society and support openness in governance. In countries such as Myanmar, Cambodia, Malaysia, and even Singapore, excessive press censorships are seen as rebuffs on media freedom.[14]

Thus from a democratic governance perspective, it became essential to put in place structures and mechanisms that would decelerate rent seeking and both systemic and individual corruption in government and the marketplace, facilitate public access to information to comprehend the rationale for and the impact of government decisions, enforce rules to activate disclosure practices in the corporate sector, moderate mismanagement in public organizations, narrow the hiatus between citizens and public agencies, and improve both horizontal and vertical accountability in government. All these are imperative to boost public confidence and trust in government.

MEASURES TO IMPROVE TRANSPARENCY AND COMBAT CORRUPTION

Under both domestic pressure and external intervention to improve governance, the Southeast Asian governments have embarked on wide-ranging programs to enhance transparency and curb corruption within their fold as well as in commerce and industry. Some of these initiatives were undertaken even before the financial crises laid bare the structural and procedural deficiencies of

governance on both the state and corporate planes, mainly as responses to the demands of international financial institutions. Nongovernmental efforts, principally by business and industry groups, were heightened postcrisis to institute high levels of corporate ethics, responsibility, and transparency to raise stakeholder confidence in both national and transnational firms' ability to deliver goods and services.

Government, international, regional, and national organizations have initiated open dialogues and comprehensive analyses to locate black spots in governmental structures that incur diminished transparency and weak accountability and to discern the causes of corruption and other forms of political and administrative malfeasance. The international lending institutions are now adopting a hands-on approach to repair institutional weaknesses and freely collaborating with governments in their quest for sound governance. The World Bank, for instance, has been supporting measures that incorporate ''deregulation to reduce opportunities for corruption, enforcement of sanctions through development of special watchdog agencies and robust judicial systems, and through strengthened civil society institutions, such as an independent press to raise public awareness of the corruption problem.''[11] Surveys and analytic reports on corruption in Thailand, Cambodia, Indonesia, and the Philippines have provided directions to combat the malaise as well as enhance transparency.[9]

Anticorruption Strategies

Several Southeast Asian countries have endorsed the Asian Development Bank/Organization for Economic Cooperation and Development (ADB/OECD) sponsored Anti-Corruption Initiative for Asia-Pacific. This action plan incorporates ''a systematic and readily enforceable approach to fight corruption'' to promote ''economic and social stability'' in the region. Basically, this initiative was to underscore the critical significance of developing accountable and transparent systems in public management, designing effective measures to prevent and investigate all forms of corrupt practices, developing an ethical and trustworthy corporate culture, and promoting active citizen participation in anticorruption exercises by stimulating public discussion of the issue and creating mechanisms for easy access to information. Specific country plans are expected to adopt international instruments and standards to design effective public integrity management systems complemented by legal, structural, and administrative reforms.[15]

Institutions of horizontal accountability such as constitutionally mandated ''oversight'' bodies, with varying degrees of operational and fiscal autonomy and, in some instances, with quasi-judicial powers, have been created in several Southeast Asian countries to scrutinize government organizations and investigate corruption and malpractices. For example, the Philippines has a Civil Service Commission to enforce "ethics and accountability" among public servants. The Ombudsman "is mandated to investigate and prosecute the criminal liability of public officials and employees involved in graft and corruption," whereas the Commission on Audit serves as a fiscal vigilante.[16] The Presidential Commission for Good Government was entrusted with the objective of recovering ill-gotten wealth from individuals, whereas other measures were put in place to ensure public disclosure of assets held by public officials.[17] In Thailand, the National Counter-Corruption Commission was granted prosecutorial authority to offset unjust governmental edicts, whereas other similar institutions such as the Constitutional Court, the Ombudsmen, the Election Commission, and the State Audit Commission are responsible to promote transparency and accountability and control corruption in the public sector.[18] Singapore's strong state capacity and committed political leadership have been instrumental in building and enforcing the mechanisms necessary to keep corruption at a low level. The government has established several instruments and has been strict in enforcing laws through an independent Corrupt Practices Investigation Bureau. Periodic review of government procedures also has the effect of obviating opportunities for corruption in public organizations.[19]

Like Singapore, Malaysia has had an anticorruption strategy since the 1960s. However, the Anti-Corruption Agency (ACA), the Public Complaints Bureau, and several departmental committees on integrity, quality, and productivity have struggled in keeping the level of corruption low in the public sector. One limitation of the ACA that catechizes its impartiality and objectivity is its lack of independence from political control.[20] The effectiveness of this strategy is therefore suspect.

Access to Information

Southeast Asian nations have made slow but steady progress in establishing the structures for the free flow of information between government and society. In several cases, the obstacles in information sharing and dissemination have been gradually removed. Thailand and the Philippines have relatively liberal information regimes, and their constitutions are explicit about people's right to obtain information for a variety of purpose—either to check the performance of state officials or to comprehend the basis of policy development. These constitutional provisions have been supplemented by laws and regulations such as the Thai Official Information Act and the Philippine Code of Conduct and Ethical Standards for

Public Officials and Employees. This is similar to the East Asian (e.g., South Korea, Hong Kong) experience of information disclosure by public agencies and citizens' access to governmental information for a variety of purpose and especially to ascertain the outcome of decisions bearing on their lives. While some of these measures appear good on paper, they have not always provided the desired level of access to information nor have they always contributed to enhancing transparency or in curbing malfeasance in government. Both Singapore and Malaysia also fare poorly in disclosing governmental information to the public. Official secret acts and tough regulations on Internet access have restricted information access and disclosure.[10] Other countries in the region are remiss in creating the appropriate structures for freedom of information and in enhancing transparency in government.

ROLE OF CIVIL SOCIETY AND E-GOVERNANCE

In the fight against corruption or in advocating for greater transparency in government and improving public access to information, civil society institutions have been playing a significant role especially in countries where state initiatives have been ineffective in producing results. Similarly, e-governance initiatives have helped improve transparency and information access. Civil society can partner with nongovernmental organizations (NGO) and the business sector in creating a culture of integrity and anticorruption in society by persuading and even compelling governments to institute reforms and creating public awareness of the evil and tackling adverse consequences of corruption. In Thailand, civil society groups and organizations have been active in placing pressure on the government to modify constitutional arrangements and create or strengthen public bodies to combat corruption.[21] Chapters of Transparency International in some Asian countries have initiated purposive moves against corruption through research and surveys, conferences and seminars, publications, and lobbying. Its annual Corruption Perception Index highlights the extent of corruption prevalent in a country and helps mobilize public opinion and stimulate action for strengthening governmental initiatives. As in Korea, where a bold step was taken by the People's Solidarity for Participatory Democracy to frame on its own initiative an anticorruption bill and lobby for its enactment by the national legislature,[22] the Indonesian Coalition for Information Freedom (a coalition of NGOs) drafted a freedom of information act for enabling greater transparency of government business and parastatal and nongovernmental organizations. This was in response to the government's failure to initiate legislation on information access.

The information gap that contributes to the lack of transparency can be substantially reduced by employing information communication technology (ICT) in linking organizational units, the government, the private sector, and the state with the people. Information communication technology can empower the poor and the marginalized in societies by affording relevant information to them and enabling their participation in public affairs through their feedback on public services and the exercise of their ''voice.'' The Internet is being widely used not only to disengage citizens from long queues at service counters and simplify procedures, but also to make administrative practices more transparent and comprehensible. Indeed, e-government links citizens to the state by facilitating communication and enabling a positive relationship between them.

Many Asian governments have afforded ICT high priority and have adopted comprehensive policies to overcome the information divide between the state and citizens. Several governments have gone on-line providing not only a wide array of information on policies and procedure, but also a variety of e-services including easy lodgment of complaints via the Internet and quick retrieval of information.[23] Dedicated Web portals link citizens to ministries and public agencies and the services they provide. The creation of a ''cashless'' payment system and processing of clearance documents by using ICT has vastly reduced corruption in the Philippine Customs Bureau and advantaged customers from its services.[24] Similarly, initiatives in other countries have also yielded useful results.

CONCLUSION

The Asian financial crisis has left its impact on the society and public administration in the region. Apart from causing considerable economic hardship, it also exposed the weaknesses and shortcomings of the existing governmental systems and processes and signified the need for reform to improve governance and public integrity. However, reforms are mainly focused on revamping the institutional mechanisms and strengthening anticorruption legislations without seeking to effect corresponding changes in other areas. In essence, the political systems continue to be largely authoritarian and decision-making processes closed and/or centralized with limited scope for public participation. In some cases, freedom of expression and information is extremely limited, the media continues to be the captive of the government, independent oversight bodies are absent, civil society groups face formidable constraints, and draconian legislations remain firmly in place. With restricted public scrutiny, public officials discreetly cover up mistakes, are arbitrary in

making policy decisions, and indulge in corrupt practices. Because exposure is a powerful deterrent to corrupt practices, Southeast Asian nations need to introduce greater transparency and openness in public management, create independent judiciary and anticorruption bodies with wide power, spare the media from undue restraints, and widen the space for civil society groups to play an effective role. These will benefit society, improve social trust, build public confidence in governments, and contribute to political and economic stability.

REFERENCES

1. UNDP. *Human Development Report 2002*; UNDP: New York, 2002.
2. Klitgaard, R. *Controlling Corruption*; University of California Press: Berkeley, 1988.
3. Kaufmann, D.; Kraay, A.; Zoido-Lobaton, P. Governance Matters. In *Policy Research Working Paper*; World Bank: Washington, DC, 1999; Vol. 2196.
4. Backman, M. *Asian Eclipse: Exposing the Dark Side of Business in Asia*; John Wiley: Singapore, 1999; 23–41.
5. Vishwanath, T.; Kaufmann, D. Toward transparency: New approaches and their application to financial markets. World Bank Econ. Obs. **2001**, *16* (1), 41.
6. Transparency International. *Corruption Perceptions Index 2003*. http://www.transparency.org.
7. OECD. *Public Sector Corruption: an International Survey of Prevention Measures*; OECD: Paris, 1999.
8. PCIJ. *The Right to Know: Access to Information in South East Asia*; The Philippine Center for Investigative Journalism: Manila, 2001.
9. World Bank. *Reforming Public Institutions and Strengthening Governance: Implementation Update. Part 2*; World Bank: Washington, DC, 2002; pp. 16, 21.
10. Transparency International. *Global Corruption Report 2003*; 149. http://www.transparency.org.
11. World Bank. *Reforming Public Institutions and Strengthening Governance: A World Bank Strategy*; World Bank: Washington, DC, 2000; pp. 86, 88.
12. Goudie, A.W.; Stasavage, D. Corruption: The Issues. In *Technical Paper*; OECD Development Center, 1997; Vol. 122, 12.
13. Collins, P. Governance and Development: New Frontiers. In *Applying Public Administration in Development: Guideposts to the Future*; Collins, P., Ed.; John Wiley: London, 2000; 271.
14. RWB. Introduction: Asia and Pacific. In *Annual Report 2003*; Reporters Without Borders, 2003. http://www.rsf.org/article.php3?id_article=6656.
15. ADB/OECD. *Anti-corruption Initiative for Asia-Pacific: Combatting Corruption in the New Millennium*; Asian Development Bank: Manila, 2001.
16. CSCP. *Ethics and Accountability: the Philippine Experience*; Civil Service Commission of Philippines: Manila,

2000. http://unpan1.un.org/intradoc/groups/public/documents/apcity/unpan003218.pdf.

17. Moran, J. Patterns of corruption and development in East Asia. Third World Q. **1999**, *20* (3), 569–587.

18. World Bank. Fostering institutions to contain corruption. PREM Notes **1999**, *24*.

19. Yak, C.C. Good People, Good Laws. In *Progress in the Fight Against Corruption in Asia and the Pacific: Conference Proceedings*; Asian Development Bank: Manila, 2000; 65.

20. Aziz, T.A. International Case Study; Stamping Out Corruption in Malaysia. In *Paper Presented at the 113th International Training Course*; United Nations Asia and Far East Institute: Tokyo, 2002; 399.

21. ADB/OECD. *Progress in the Fight Against Corruption in Asia and the Pacific: Conference Proceedings*; Asian Development Bank: Manila, 2000; 5.

22. Lee, H.-B. Government–nongovernment Organization Interaction in Drafting the Republic of Korea's Anti-corruption Law. In *Anti-corruption Initiative for Asia-Pacific: Combatting Corruption in the New Millennium*; Asian Development Bank: Manila, 2001; 153.

23. Yong, J. *E-Government in Asia—Enabling Public Service Innovation in the 21st Century*; Times Press: Singapore, 2003.

24. Parayno, G.I., Jr. *Reforming the Philippine Customs Services Through Electronic Governance*; Asian Development Bank: Manila, 1999; 61–69.

Truth and Reconciliation Commission

Daryl Balia
Public Service Commission, Pretoria, South Africa

INTRODUCTION

To unearth one's bloody and repressive past is highly risky for a country traveling the road of reconciliation and healing. Not only is the prospect of renewed violence kindled, but also the trauma of painful remembrance, which could so easily infect succeeding generations. South Africa as a sovereign nation decided, however, that a collective search for truth and justice was necessary for uncovering its apartheid past. Apartheid, which is Afrikaans for apartness, was institutionalized racial discrimination and segregation, formally enacted into law in South Africa in 1948 and often repressively enforced. The medium chosen was a Truth and Reconciliation Commission (TRC) which was given legal status through an Act of Parliament in 1995. Such a course was not unique, as the examples of postwar Germany, Chile, Argentina, Haiti, and a handful of other countries illustrate. The emphasis in South Africa's case was to legitimize the moral repugnance of all the traces of apartheid, allow for a degree of justice for victims of human rights abuses, offer qualified amnesty to perpetrators upon individual request, and contribute to building national unity and reconciliation. The truncated past was defined from March 1960 to 10 May 1994, despite the fact that the practice and origins of the apartheid ideology go back centuries earlier.

The TRC itself conducted its work from April 1996 to July 1998 through three committees for human rights violations, amnesty, and rehabilitation and reparation, respectively. It was led by former head of the Anglican Church in South Africa and Noble Peace Prize laureate, Archbishop Desmond Tutu, and signed into law by former President Nelson Mandela.

Tutu was of course assisted by 16 other commissioners, regional officers, a research unit, an investigative unit, a legal department, and a media department. As it was given a two-year time frame to complete its operation, the TRC proceeded with haste in conducting mostly investigations and public hearings. It is noteworthy that only about 10% of the 21,000 statements submitted by victims were used for public hearings. Many victims felt cheated as they would come to a hearing only to learn that their story would not be heard. While for some the Truth Commission seemed to offer hope to form a new collective with those previously disenfranchised (black), for others, it rendered the poor victims voiceless through a process of translation and contextualization. Mostly privileged black males were given time and space to tell their stories at the expense of women who, when given the opportunity, would speak of the sufferings of the voiceless generally. Ultimately, it seems that no redemptive balance was struck about which stories of survival, healing, defiance, torture, killing, or fighting would prevail in defining the TRC outcome.

MODE OF OPERATION

The founding legislation, which was signed by President Mandela on 19 July 1995 and which made the operation of the TRC possible, was the Promotion of National Unity and Reconciliation Act. The broad mandate defined in the act was as follows:

- To establish as complete a picture as possible of the causes, nature, and extent of the gross violations of human rights during the period from 1 March 1960 to the cutoff date.
- To facilitate the granting of amnesty to persons who make full disclosure of all the relevant facts relating to acts associated with a political objective and who comply with the requirements of this act.
- To establish and make known the fate or whereabouts of victims and to restore the human and civil dignity of such victims by granting them an opportunity to relate their own accounts of the violations of which they are the victims and by recommending reparation measures in respect of them.
- To compile a report providing as comprehensive an account as possible of the activities and findings of the commission, which contains recommendations of measures to prevent the future violations of human rights.[1]

The three TRC committees were specifically tasked with functions that would enable the TRC to fulfill its mandate. The Human Rights Violations Committee conducted hearings throughout the country to give apartheid's victims a platform to tell their stories of oppression. On the

Encyclopedia of Public Administration and Public Policy
DOI: 10.1081/E-EPAP 120023430

other hand, the focus of the Amnesty Committee was on the perpetrators, allowing them the possibility of seeking pardon for their individual misdemeanors. The Committee on Reparation and Rehabilitation, apart from making recommendations on such matters, also inquired into measures necessary for the prevention of human rights abuses and the creation of a new society free from racial segregation. Some of the work of the Amnesty Committee would later include outstanding matters of the other two committees when the TRC suspended operations.

MODEL OF MANAGEMENT

A country transitioning from authoritarian rule to democracy faces multiple challenges, one of which is how to deal with a repressive past that could potentially destroy its future. Hayner,[2] an expert on truth commissions, believes that such commissions do have the capacity to give victims space to voice their suffering, promote reconciliation, prevent a repetition of past horrors, and allow for an acknowledgment of transgressions committed. The potential therefore of the TRC process in South Africa, which lasted more than 2 years, as a strategic link in the national management of conflicts needs to be stressed. This is especially in view of the fact that conventional institutions such as the courts, police, political bodies, or defense establishments are not viewed as being neutral enough in a climate of transition. Truth commissions, on the other hand, if they are generally constituted by men and women of honor, are more objectively able to be scribes of history, pursue claims of justice and truth, contribute to personal healing and reconciliation, and institutionalize the emerging culture of human rights than politicians or state bureaucrats. In hindsight, Tutu was convinced that South Africa would serve as an example to the world in matters of conflict management as the verities of hope, peace, and reconciliation had triumphed through the TRC process, despite the evil nature of human beings.[3]

Less sanguine were some of his fellow commissioners who judged that the quota of truth to emerge from the TRC hearings to have been rather too small. Within the TRC, internal bickering often buttressed by issues of race proved an albatross as a few commissioners failed to complete their terms. Under tight financial constraints, and within a limited time frame, the TRC clearly succeeded in producing a five-volume report of its work that has laid the foundation for the new society to be built as a reconciled community. The role of the TRC leader was pivotal to the entire process, despite a strongly held view by some whites that the TRC would not be impartial and operate with an ideological bent. Members of the (black) ruling elite were equally grieved that the TRC

"erroneously" determined that various acts of the liberation struggle constituted human rights violations. Tutu lamented the absence of a white leader who would come forward and say, "We had an evil system...please forgive us."[a] He celebrated the fact that at last, after years of personal struggle, apartheid was unequivocally relegated in history as a crime against humanity. Little wonder then that Nelson Mandela, in his last opening address to parliament, announced that the "doors of the world have opened to South Africa, precisely because of our success in achieving things that humanity as a whole holds dear" (5 February 1999).

IMAGE AND PERFORMANCE

In reliving the memory of the past, the TRC was able at times to offer a theatrical reenactment of pain, as the case of Jeffrey Benzien illustrates. He used to be an investigator in the security branch of the South African police department and was requested by one of his victims to demonstrate the use of the wet blanket method of torture. For many, this was an "archival moment" that would become iconic of the whole TRC process itself. Another involved Desmond Tutu, leader of the TRC, when he broke down in tears after hearing the public testimonies of pain and anguish. Winnie Mandela, former wife of Nelson Mandela, captured the media spotlight by her appearance and confession, under coercion, that "things went horribly wrong" with her Mandela United Football Club that operated more as a vigilante outfit. Thus apart from documents collected, referenced, and preserved by the TRC, there exists the "unofficial" archive of the media images that remain extremely powerful in causing the memory of the past to be made real in the present.

Beyond the image of a legally constituted hearing, which would often lead to a judgment about amnesty, stood the sacred canopy invoking the sounds of solemn assemblies, where confession was elicited, hymns were sung, and prayers were offered often in the presence of Desmond Tutu who dressed in clerical garb as a rule. Performance at these hearings was therefore designed to achieve a cathartic effect, if not to facilitate the public expression of an individual or collective act of forgiveness. The TRC therefore as public performance sought to recreate the past by facilitating testimony that carried the intention of revealing truth and was thus seen as "a theatrical re-presentation of pain suffered and inflicted by victims and perpetrators of apartheid-era violence."[5] Not surprisingly, the work of the TRC became the subject of numerous artistic creations, perhaps provoking individuals

---

[a]See foreword by Ref. [4].

to explore deep-seated memories in less traumatic ways. Most noteworthy was a literary classic by white poet Krog[6] whose ''Country of my Skull'' won international acclaim. Her ''fragmentary'' style of writing seems to have been necessitated by the fact that here was a white Afrikaner writing with empathy about suffering and pain endured by blacks. Krog dreaded closure in the labyrinth of memory evocations, as the road ahead required the restoration of such memory of humanity itself.

AMNESTY AND RECONCILIATION

One of the foundational principles of the TRC process was that truth telling by perpetrators could be exchanged for amnesty, something at odds with international conventions. Apart from seeing this as ''unconstitutional,'' many believed that victims were being denied justice, as perpetrators would go free while the material welfare of victims was slowly being addressed. Because the process was slanted toward individual amnesty, there was little hope of the structural evils of apartheid being held accountable. Apartheid, being a crime against humanity, was to go largely unpunished as the TRC had chosen rather to forgive and forget those making contrite confessions. Many commentators would, as a result, accuse the TRC of sacrificing justice at the altar of truth to the detriment of apartheid's victims. Furthermore, the TRC's doctrine of reconciliation, while deeply Christian, was controversial. The three prerequisites for reconciliation are truth, justice, and reparation, but these were highly contested notions even among TRC commissioners themselves.

When it was achieved, reconciliation usually proved to be an individual experience during the public hearings rather than an overnight national achievement. The TRC had set in motion, through concrete example, a pattern of life for erstwhile enemies in a rejuvenated moral landscape. Frustration and bitterness might have been the lot for many, but the TRC, despite its ''Christian baggage,'' provided an important catalyst for the evolution of the new human rights culture. Hence for Tutu, the TRC is ''at its heart a deeply theological and ethical initiative. For people of faith, the experience of honesty and mercy, confession and forgiveness, justice and peace, repentance and reconciliation is what truth and reconciliation are all about.''[7] Prominent Christian leaders, as a result, saw themselves as being lead agents in a renewed ministry of reconciliation, one where the business of forgiveness was to prevail over the cry for vengeance. Of course, the agreements on amnesty and reconciliation were based on political and moral compromise between leading protagonists of the racial divide who both largely shared the same religious faith. The concept of ''truth'' that was to emerge from the TRC process was thus qualified and vitiated by an impinging political and, perhaps, an historical thirst for the better future of South Africa.

CONCLUSION

The publication of the TRC final report did not signal the end of the historical transition as some had hoped. Political parties, including the ruling African National Congress (ANC), remain unconvinced about its pronouncements, especially its reluctance to cast moral judgments about their struggles. To have the TRC paint both victim and oppressor with the same brush of justice was an anathema. Considered in the modern paradigm of restorative justice in a transitional democracy, the TRC ranks very high as having set an international standard. In a situation where punishing perpetrators through criminal trials was not desirable, but rather national healing and reconciliation together with building a human rights culture, the TRC stepped forward with limited resources in a very restricted time and answered the call of leading a nation on the ''freedom road.''[8] That its work remains unfinished is also true. The TRC had instructed that all information collected should be held by the National Archives, but by September 2003, this was still undone. Numerous applications for reparations and amnesty are still being processed while the TRC remains officially in ''suspension.'' As and when these matters reach finality, it may be possible to begin delving deeper into the lasting significance of the TRC for South Africa and the world.

REFERENCES

1. *Truth and Reconciliation Commission of South Africa Report*; Juta and Co.: Cape Town, South Africa, 2003; Vol. I.
2. Hayner, P.B. *Unspeakable Truths, Confronting State Terror and Atrocity*; Routledge: London, 2000.
3. Tutu, D.M. *No Future Without Forgiveness: A Personal Overview of South Africa's Truth and Reconciliation Commission*; Rider Books: London, 1999.
4. Tutu, D. *TRC Report*; Vol. I–V.
5. Bester, R. *At the Edges of Apartheid Memory; Unpublished Paper*; 6.
6. Krog, A. *Country of My Skull: Guilt, Sorrow, and the Limits of Forgiveness in the New South Africa*; Random House: Parklands, South Africa, 1998.
7. *To Remember and to Heal: Theological and Psychological Reflections on Truth and Reconciliation*; Botman, R.H., Petersen, R., Eds.; Human and Rousseau: Cape Town, South Africa, 1996.
8. Asmal, K.; Asmal, L.; Roberts, R.S. *Reconciliation Through Truth, a Reckoning of Apartheid's Criminal Governance*; David Philip Publishers: Cape Town, South Africa, 1997.

Tuskegee Study

Holona L. Ochs
Andrew B. Whitford
University of Kansas, Lawrence, Kansas, U.S.A.

INTRODUCTION

The Tuskegee Syphilis Study, which was conducted by the U.S. Public Health Service (PHS) through the Tuskegee Institute between 1932 and 1972, sought to examine the "effects of untreated syphilis on the [N]egro male."[1] The study began with at least one good purpose: to consider ways to improve the health of African–American males in the south. It ended with the broad recognition that its means violated the individual rights of study participants, that researchers in the study had been failed by their individual integrity, and that the organization conducting the study did not contain sufficient checks on professional practice to restrict unethical action (described below). Perhaps more importantly, it ended with the recognition that many professionals and decision makers throughout society who knew of this study did not take appropriate protective action (an official history of this study is located at: http://www.cdc.gov/nchstp/od/tuskegee/). This history, along with changes to federal regulations for research projects involving human subjects, document another lasting effect of the Tuskegee Syphilis Study: it changed federal research establishment, especially organizations such as the PHS and the Centers for Disease Control (CDC).

The Julius Rosenwald Fund, which was established in 1928 to promote the health, education, and welfare of African–Americans, provided many of the initial charitable contributions that funded research and treatment for African–American syphilitic subjects in the south.[2] By 1931, the Depression had nearly depleted the Rosenwald fund, and attempts at actual treatment of patients ended. Following this, the PHS decided to use a group of 600 low-income African–American men in Macon County, AL, 399 of whom had syphilis, to determine if syphilis differently affected African–Americans. This began the longest, continued, nontherapeutic medical experiments on human subjects in history.[3]

The policy significance of the Tuskegee study is the fact that the publicity it generated strongly contributed to the development of systematic standards for evaluating research programs involving human subjects. The administrative significance is that, using government authority, officials undertook unethical behavior and implemented unethical policy. The long-term effect of this experiment has been to undermine trust among American minorities in both government and medicine. Of course, because this study was carried out using African–American doctors, nurses, and institutions, repairing this damage is even more complicated. The Tuskegee study remains a potent symbol of the government's abuse of African–Americans in the United States, racism in science, arrogance of the medical community, and misconduct in research involving human participants.

A BRIEF HISTORY OF HUMAN SUBJECTS RESEARCH

Historically, nonconsensual experiments have been regularly performed on captive populations in an institution, particularly when groups of people are seen as "less than human." Examples of unethical research similar to the Tuskegee study include the following:[4]

- Experiments conducted by Nazi physicians during World War II (WWII)
- Experimentation in 1952 on Harold Blauer at the New York State Psychiatric Institute in conjunction with the U.S. Army Chemical Corps
- An experiment conducted in 1953 on a premature infant at the Brooklyn Doctors Hospital without any attempt to obtain informed consent
- The Jewish Chronic Disease Hospital case of 1963 in which 22 chronically ill noncancer patients were injected with cancer cells
- The injection of hepatitis in severely retarded children at the Willowbrook State Hospital in New York
- The Cincinnati radiation experiments on an entirely nonconsensual group of cancer patients of below-average intelligence who were primarily African–American, resulting in acute radiation sickness, severe burns, and premature death
- The study conducted at the Veteran's Administration West Los Angeles Medical Center, which was shut down in 1999 for experimenting both on subjects who had not consented and those who expressly refused consent.

Encyclopedia of Public Administration and Public Policy
DOI: 10.1081/E-EPAP-120024807

The recurring theme is that latent tendencies toward dehumanization exist when any process becomes routinized.[5] The scientific method is a routine, as is much of policy implementation through the application of standard operating procedures.

It has often been argued in the medical community that professional expertise and "compassion" of physicians for human subjects are a better way to protect the rights of patients than external constraints on their behavior, despite evidence that these individual qualities are often ineffective.[3–6] Even with physicians, the effectiveness of an individual's integrity depends on, and interacts with, professional ethical standards and institutional reward systems, as well as formal and informal positions of power and autonomy; such concern-producing conditions sufficient to protect the subject occur rather infrequently.[7] The "compassion" or desire to make good decisions is often misguided or misplaced, particularly when the subjects are regarded by society as "less than human." Dr. John R. Heller, the Director of Venereal Disease for the PHS from 1943 to 1948, claimed, even after penicillin was being used to treat syphilis in 1943 that, "The men's status did not warrant ethical debate. They were subjects, not patients; clinical material, not sick people."[2]

BACKGROUND AND DEVELOPMENT OF THE TUSKEGEE STUDY

The purpose of the study funded by the Rosenwald Memorial Fund, a Chicago-based philanthropic foundation, was to track the prevalence of syphilis among African–Americans in the 1930s as a way of determining the practicability and potential effectiveness of mass control of syphilis. The project began in 1929 as a syphilis control program using the standard therapy of the time—heavy metals treatment.[3] Conducted in six rural counties with diverse social and economic characteristics, this was the first attempt to systematically control venereal disease in rural areas.[8] The study's findings, which were reported at the 1932 Annual Convention of the National Medical Association at Howard University, were that socioeconomic characteristics had a greater impact on the prevalence of the disease than race, and that syphilis is not a racial disease.

Public health officials were concerned with remaining technical issues, such as the evaluation of blood tests for latent syphilis, which required 10–20 years before resulting in an outcome. The Rosenwald study did not resolve questions about the effectiveness of serological evaluations vs. autopsy examinations, and the general belief that syphilis was a "disease of small consequence to the Negro" persisted.[9]

This is the environment within which the Tuskegee study took place. Officials' low confidence in blood tests

for latent syphilis and the broad acceptance of racial hygiene theories contributed to pressures for a study centering on the observation of untreated syphilis in the latent stage through autopsy as a way of verifying the presence of syphilitic destructive lesions.

For the Tuskegee study, PHS selected Macon County, AL—the poorest of the six counties included in the Rosenwald study and the county with the highest syphilis prevalence rate (approximately 40%).[9] The study involved 399 African–American men diagnosed with syphilis and a control group of 201 African–American men who did not have the disease. The men were told by the researchers that they had "bad blood"—a local term describing various common ailments. Informed neither of their actual diagnosis nor the nature of the illness, they were not provided proper treatment.[3] The Tuskegee study disregarded virtually all of the principles of the Nuremberg Code. A copy of the Nuremberg Code is posted at the U.S. Holocaust Memorial Museum's web site. Of particular importance are the unnecessary physical and mental sufferings and injuries, and the continuation of the experiments despite reason to believe that death or disabling injury will occur. The problem of syphilis was already solved, and the risk of death in the study was 100%. Participants were subjected to a painful spinal tap in the initial phase of the study, and researchers documented the untreated pain resulting from a curable disease in 399 men for 40 years.

Dr. Vonderlehr of the PHS began the experiment in 1932 by offering a painful lumbar puncture as a "special free treatment" that was actually a diagnostic procedure performed strictly for the benefit of the researchers.[3] Following this examination, a letter was sent to each of the participants offering special free treatment for "bad blood," and an African–American nurse from the area, Eunice Rivers, was used to convince the men to participate in the study. The participants consisted of rural farmers who owned their homes, renters considered permanent residents, and day laborers. Five hundred twenty of the original 600 men received consistent follow-ups to the point of autopsy.[1] In exchange for participating in the study, the men were offered free medical exams, free meals on the days of the exams, free rides to and from the clinics along with an opportunity to shop or visit friends in town on the return trip, free treatment for minor nonsyphilitic ailments, and burial insurance.[1]

The program involved annual examinations by a "government doctor" in which the men were given a physical examination to document the effects and progression of the disease.[1] They were also assessed for nonsyphilitic conditions and provided with advice and medication (when it was available) for other ailments.[1] The men were given mercurial ointment (which was known to be completely ineffective against syphilis) and dosages of neoarsphenamine or arsenic in amounts short of what would be necessary to stop the infection under the false pretense that the drugs would cure the men of their "bad blood."[3]

The PHS began using penicillin to treat syphilis in 1943, but despite the safe and effective treatment history and general availability by 1953, penicillin was deliberately withheld from the participants.[3] In fact, the PHS went to the extremes to prevent the study participants from receiving any form of treatment for syphilis. PHS distributed lists of names of participants to local physicians instructing them not to provide penicillin to the men involved in the study, and when about 50 of the men were drafted during WWII, PHS requested that the draft board not test or treat the men for syphilis; the board complied.[3] In 1943, when the PHS established "Rapid Treatment Centers" across the country to systematically treat syphilis, no clinic was established in Macon County so as not to disrupt the study.[3]

By not treating the men in the study and by not informing them of the nature of the disease, the PHS contributed to the spread of the disease to many women and infants who acquired congenital syphilis.[3] As such, the PHS, the draft board, the Macon County Medical Society, the Alabama State and Macon County Boards of Health, the Tuskegee Institute, and all of the physicians involved violated Alabama law by failing to treat a communicable disease.[3] As many as 100 of 399 participants are believed to have died from syphilis over the course of the study.[10] In 1950, Dr. Wenger of the PHS noted, "...we have contributed to their ailments and shortened their lives."[3]

In 1968, Peter Bauxum, a PHS venereal disease interviewer and investigator, and others raised concern over the ethics of the Tuskegee study. The CDC responded by reaffirming the need for the study, and gained the official support of the local American Medical Association and the National Medical Association for the study's continuation.[3] The first news articles condemning the study appeared in 1970, and, in 1971, Congress held hearings to investigate the scandal. In 1972, the Assistant Secretary for Health and Scientific Affairs (ASH) appointed an Ad Hoc Advisory Panel to review the study, which concluded that the Tuskegee study was "ethically unjustified." In November 1972, the ASH announced the end of the Tuskegee study.[3]

IMPLICATIONS FOR PUBLIC POLICY AND PUBLIC ADMINISTRATION

The legacy of the study at Tuskegee has reached far and deep in ways that hurt our progress and divide our nation.

We cannot be one America when a whole segment of our nation has no trust in America.[a]

The Tuskegee study remains a primary and widely cited example of research that lacked adequate protection for the participants. The study violated a number of ethical principles that are now regularly applied to human subjects research. The study used disadvantaged, rural black men to study the untreated course of a disease that is not confined to that population, placing an undue burden on that population and placing at risk a broad population. The study not only failed to minimize the risks to the participants, but increased those risks by depriving them of treatment long after it became available. The 600 men involved in the study were not afforded informed consent, even after the Nuremberg Code was written in 1946, codifying the need for voluntary consent. It may be that the lack of education of the participants made informed consent difficult; most were illiterate, many did not even know their last name, and the best educated participants had only completed 8 years of school. However, it is widely accepted that this disadvantaged position only accentuates the need for the protection that administrators have an obligation to serve.

Along with others, this study provided a broad impetus for federal regulations that guide the practice of research. The resulting policy requires research proposals to be reviewed by a human subjects committee; only research meeting the standards for the treatment of human subjects are approved by the committee and capable of being carried out. The Department of Health and Human Services now implements the federal policy for the protection of human subjects, and the policy is integrated into the procedural process of every public and private organization conducting research involving human subjects in the United States. Further, information about the federal human subjects research guidelines can be found at the United States Office for Human Research Protections (http://ohrp.osophs.dhhs.gov/index.htm).

The Tuskegee study also has implications for a lasting difficulty in the evaluation and analysis of medical policy and interventions: the concern among African–Americans that the scientific establishment does not fully address their concerns about the protection federal regulations provide them. "Distrust of the white-dominated medical community, either because of Tuskegee or the long history of subordination of blacks in this country at the hands of whites, obviously plays some role in the reluctance of

---

[a]The formal apology issued by President Clinton on May 16, 1997, taken from Ref. [11].

black people to participate in clinical research... It is critical for black people to become involved in this type of research in order for skilled clinicians to determine if any measures can be taken to reduce the incidence of a number of diseases that befall black people at a far greater rate than whites."[12] The hidden effect of Tuskegee is the inability of evaluators and analysts often to pull together the type of diverse and rich human information about the real effects of health policy across various segments of the population that are necessary to change policy outcomes in the long run.

CONCLUSION

Individual integrity without proper institutional constraints often results in misguided decisions. At least 16 reports on the Tuskegee experiments were published in reputable journals such as *Public Health Reports, Archives of Internal Medicine, Journal of Chronic Diseases, Milbank Fund Memorial Quarterly, American Journal of Public Health, Journal of the American Medical Association,* and *New England Journal of Medicine.*[13] Yet, even though individuals with integrity who read these studies or participated in these experiments may have had compassion and concern for human subjects, that compassion did not result in the ending of the study for 40 years. However, even with external constraints provided by federal regulations for the protection of human subjects, a lack of individual integrity on the part of the researcher can result in unethical practice. Neither compliance nor integrity alone prompts ethical practice, but instead, serving the public interest requires that external institutional accountability and individual integrity reinforce one another.[14]

REFERENCES

1. Rivers, E.; Schuman, S.H.; Simpson, L.; Olansky, S. Twenty years of follow-up experience in a long-range medical study. Public Health Rep. **1953**, *8* (4), 391–395.
2. Thomas, S.B.; Quinn, S.C. The Tuskegee Syphilis Study, 1932 to 1972: Implications for HIV education and AIDS risk education programs in the black community. Am. J. Public Health **1991**, *81*, 1498–1506.
3. Jones, J.H. *Bad Blood: The Tuskegee Syphilis Experiment*; Collier Macmillan 1981; 182.
4. *In the Wake of Terror: Medicine and Morality in a Time of Crisis*; Moreno, J.D., Ed.; MIT Press: Cambridge, 2003.
5. Adams, G.B.; Balfour, D.L. *Unmasking Administrative Evil*; Sage Publications: London, 1998.
6. Barber, B.; Lally, J.J.; Makarushka, J.L.; Sullivan, D. *Research on Human Subjects*; Russell Sage Foundation: New York, 1973.
7. Lally, J.J.; Barber, B. The compassionate physician: Frequency and social determinants of physician–investigator concern for human subjects. Soc. Forces **1974**, *53* (2), 289–296.
8. Public Health Service. *Milestones in Venereal Disease Control: Highlights of Half a Century*, Publication PHS 515; U.S. Department of Health, Education, and Welfare: Washington, DC, 1957.
9. American Medical Association. Unraveling the Tuskegee study of untreated syphilis. Arch. Intern. Med. March **2000**, *160*, 585–598.
10. Jones, **1993**.
11. Gamble, V.N. Under the shadow of Tuskegee: African Americans and health care. Am. J. Public Health **1997**, *87* (11), pp. 1176, 1773.
12. The reluctance of black people to participate in clinical medical research. J. Blacks Higher Educ. **1997**, *17*, 33–34.
13. Yankauer, A. The neglected lesson of the Tuskegee study. Am. J. Public Health **1998**, *89* (9), 1406.
14. Lewis, C.W. *The Ethics Challenge in Public Service: A Problem-Solving Guide*; Jossey-Bass: San Francisco, 1991.

Understanding the Basics of Refunding in the Municipal Bond Market

Jun Peng
University of Arizona, Tucson, Arizona, U.S.A.

INTRODUCTION

Refunding of outstanding debt is probably the most important management activity after the debt has been first issued in the primary municipal bond market, as long as the issuer's debt-paying capacity does not deteriorate. Refunding, in a nutshell, means issuing new debt to retire outstanding debt. The primary purpose of refunding is to lower the borrowing cost.

Although there are key differences, the best analogy of refunding in the municipal bond market is mortgage refinancing in the residential housing market. When mortgage rate goes down, homeowners will take out a new mortgage loan to retire the old mortgage loan, which typically carries a higher mortgage rate, to reduce their monthly mortgage payment. This is, however, where the similarity between municipal bond refunding and mortgage refinancing ends. It is the differences between these two that make municipal bond refunding more complicated. To understand the major differences between the two, it is important to understand the concept of option first.

CALL OPTION AND ITS ROLE IN REFUNDING

In the financial market, option gives the seller of the option the right but not the obligation to engage in certain financial transactions. There are two basic options, call option and put option. Call option gives the issuer the right but not the obligation to purchase some financial products at a certain price and at a certain date, and it will be exercised only when the actual market price of the product is higher than the purchase price agreed upon in the contract. The put option gives the issuer the right but not the obligation to sell some financial products at a certain price and at a certain date, and it will be exercised only when the selling price agreed upon is higher than the actual market price. It goes without saying that such options do not come free of cost. Both issuers of call and put options have to pay a premium to have such kind of right.

It is the call option that is relevant in the case of municipal bond refunding. The vast majority of the municipal bonds are callable bonds. If a bond is callable, it is written in the official statement that the issuer can (although he does not have to) call back (or purchase back or redeem) the bond from the investors at a certain date in the future before the final maturity of the bond. The issuer, of course, has to pay a premium for having such a call option. Such premium is not paid up front when the bond is first sold but rather paid when the bond is purchased back from the investors in the form of call price. The call price is usually expressed as a percentage of the par value of the bond, such as 103% of the par value of the bonds. Therefore an investor with $1000 worth of the bond can obtain $1030 from the issuer when it is called back. The size of this call premium varies positively with the time period between call date and final maturity. The closer the call date gets to the final maturity date, the smaller the call premium will be. As a matter of fact, after some time period, the bond will be called back at par value. For example, if the bond has a final maturity of 30 years, it may be called back at 103% of the par value 10 years after the bond is first sold, whereas it will be called back at par 20 years after the bond is sold.

As mentioned earlier, the primary reason for refunding is interest cost savings. Therefore issuers will buy back old bond with proceeds from the new refunding bond only when the interest rate on the new bond falls below that on the old bond. This is where the call protection period comes in. The call option builds uncertainty into the financial planning of the investors who purchase the bonds. When the bonds are called back, investors are left with proceeds that will be invested at a lower interest rate, thus reducing their future investment income. To reduce that uncertainty, investors need some protection from very early redemption. Call protection stipulates how early the bond can be called (or redeemed). The call protection period usually has a 10-year span, which means that the bond cannot be called within the first 10 years. Call protection has an important impact on how refunding is performed. Whether the refunding bond is sold inside or outside the call protection period determines how the refunding transaction is performed.

Encyclopedia of Public Administration and Public Policy
DOI: 10.1081/E-EPAP-120040642

CURRENT AND ADVANCE REFUNDING

There are two kinds of refunding transactions: current refunding and advance refunding. In a current refunding, the proceeds of the refunding bond need to be used to redeem the old bond within 3 months after the refunding bond is issued. That means that current refunding should happen no later than 3 months before the last day of the call protection. In most cases, current refunding happens when the call protection period is over. When the interest rate drops, the issuer can issue refunding bonds at a lower rate to immediately retire the old bond. Therefore there is no need for investment of the refunding bond proceeds.

What happens when the interest rate drops and there are still several years before the call protection period is over? The issuer cannot do a current refunding because they cannot call back the bond within 3 months. To lock in the low interest rate even when they cannot call back the bond, the issuer needs to do an advance refunding. It is called advance refunding because the refunding bond is issued way in advance of the redemption of the old bond. It is this time lag that makes advance refunding a more complicated transaction because it involves the investment of the advance refunding bond proceeds and the coexistence of two bonds: the new refunding bond and the old bond (now also called refunded bond).

ESCROW ACCOUNT AND FEDERAL REGULATIONS

In an advance refunding transaction, the proceeds of the new bond are invested in an escrow account. The investment income is then used to pay the debt service on the old outstanding bond. At the end of the call protection period, the proceeds in the escrow account will be used to retire the old bond. Because the bond proceeds in the escrow account and the investment income will exactly match the debt service on the old bond till its redemption, the old bond is also considered escrowed to defeasance. Once the old bond is escrowed to defeasance, it is no longer considered a legal obligation of the issuer and will not appear in any financial statement of the issuer. Although there seems to be two bonds, there really is one bond, the new refunding bond, for which the issuer is responsible in terms of debt service payment.

Two aspects of the investment of escrow proceeds make advance refunding unique. One is the risk profile of the securities to be invested in, and the second is the investment yield restriction. In order for the old bond to be fully considered escrowed to defeasance, the proceeds in the escrow account have to be invested in risk-free financial securities so that there is no doubt whatsoever

about its ability to meet the debt service on the old bond. That usually means Treasury securities, which have no risk of default as they are backed by the full faith and credit of the U.S. government or other triple-A-rated fixed-income securities. This is where the yield restriction issue comes in. The yield restriction issue arises because of the tax exemption of municipal bond interest. As the interest on municipal bond is tax exemption, everything else being equal, the yield on municipal bond is lower than those on other financial securities including Treasury securities. Therefore the refunding proceeds in the escrow account will be invested at a yield higher than the yield at which the refunding bond is issued, leading to arbitrage profit for the issuer. Internal Revenue Service thus requires that the yield on the investment should be equal to, or restricted to, the yield on the refunding bond. Such yield restriction makes it very difficult to find the proper investment securities in the open capital market because such securities have to meet a certain profile regarding size, maturity, and yield. To accommodate the specific investment needs of state and local government issuers of advance refunding bonds, the Treasury Department created the State and Local Government Series (SLGS). These are Treasury securities tailored to the specific investment needs of each advance refunding transaction. Both the federal and local governments benefit from the SLGS, as the federal government can issue federal debt at a lower yield, and the local governments can easily meet their investment requirement without worrying about arbitrage.

Such convenience is not without its drawback. The dependence on SLGS for investment purpose renders advance refunding vulnerable to the vicissitudes of the financial market and the financial condition of the federal government. Whereas the yield on Treasury securities is slightly higher than that on the municipal bonds most of the time, it can actually fall below once a while. In 1998, when Russia defaulted on its debt, which led to a world financial crisis, investors sought safety in the Treasury securities. Such "flight-to-quality" substantially increased the demand for the Treasury securities, thus increasing the price and lowering the yield. The yield on Treasury securities fell below that of the municipal bonds, which did not enjoy the benefit of "flight-to-quality." Advance refunding transactions came to a halt because the issuers would be forced to invest the proceeds at a yield lower than that on the refunding bonds. The federal financial condition matters because SLGS is part of the federal government debt and thus counted toward the federal debt limit. When the federal debt limit is reached, which happens when the federal deficit worsens, as it did in fiscal year 2003 and again in 2004, the Treasury Department can no longer issue any debt. The Congress has to pass a bill to increase the debt limit before the

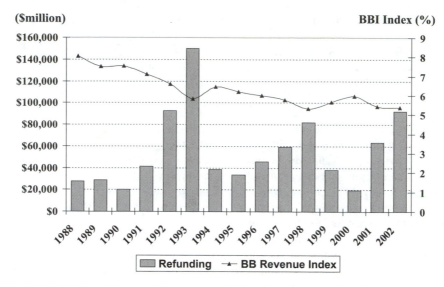

Fig. 1 Refunding volume and interest rate. (*View this art in color at www.dekker.com.*)

Treasury can issue debt (including SLGS) again. Although the Congress never fails to do that, it takes time, and local government advance refunding becomes the victim during the waiting period.

While yield restriction is one federal regulation on refunding, the second federal regulation is that for each municipal bond, the issuer can advance refund only once because of the federal government's fear of overissuance of tax-exempt bonds if state and local governments are allowed unlimited advance refunding opportunities. This is another major difference between municipal bond refunding and mortgage refinancing. A mortgage loan comes with unlimited call options, which means that the homeowner can refinance his mortgage loan as many times as he wants. If the mortgage rate falls after he refinance for the first time, he can refinance again to take advantage of the even lower rate. State and local governments, however, cannot do that. Once they have refunded their bonds, they cannot refund them again even if the interest rate keeps falling. This happens between 2000 and 2003, when the Federal Reserve reduced interest rate many times to a modern-day low. Many issuers refunded their bonds when the interest rate fell early on in this period. When the rates kept falling, they could not do anything to further lowering their borrowing cost. Because of this, U.S. Senators Gordon Smith (Republican, Oregon) and Jon Corzine (Democrat, New Jersey) introduced S.271, the "Municipal Debt Refinancing Act," in January 2003 to permit states and local governments one additional opportunity to advance refund existing tax-exempt bonds within a 2-year window. This bill is still being debated in Congress when this paper is submitted for publication.

OTHER PURPOSES OF REFUNDING

It is mentioned earlier that the primary reason for refunding is to lower the borrowing cost. This purpose can be seen in Fig. 1. The left vertical axis indicates the total national annual refunding volume between 1988 and 2002, whereas the right vertical axis is an annual average municipal bond interest rate index collected by the bond buyer.[a] It is quite obvious that there is a very clear inverse relationship between refunding volume and interest rate.

Whereas lowering borrowing cost is the dominant reason, there are at least two other reasons that can also come into play. One important reason is to relieve pressure on government budget. Although lower borrowing cost is one way for immediate budget savings, restructuring debt service through refunding can also lead to immediate budgetary relief. In this case, the interest rate on the refunding bond may not necessarily be lower than that on the old debt. The primary objective here is to reschedule the debt service by lengthening the final maturity of the bond to lower the debt service payment right away. For example, after 10 years into a 30-year bond, the government decides to refund the old bond that has only 20 years left with a new 30-year bond. As long as the interest rates on the refunding and old bonds are fairly close, such restructuring does not lead to more debt service from a present value point of view, although the nominal amount of debt service will be higher for the

---

[a]Data are collected from the Bond Buyer Yearbook.

refunding bond.[b] The worst-case scenario, however, is that the issuer is so desperate for immediate budget relief from debt service that it refunds the old bond with new bond that carries higher interest rate and longer maturity. Although such a move will lead to smaller debt service payment in the meantime, the issuer will pay substantially more in debt service over the life of the bond.

Another reason for refunding is to remove the restrictive covenants on the old bond. For various reasons, such as low credit quality, when the issuer first issued a bond, it put in place many restrictive covenants, such as requirement for debt reserve fund. Many years later, the issuer might be in a different financial situation and would like to remove these restrictive bond covenants. The only way to remove these restrictive bond covenants, however, is to retire the old bond, along with the restrictive covenants, with a new refunding bond that does not contain any of these restrictive covenants.

AN EXAMPLE

Finally, a basic example is used to illustrate the basic mechanics of an advance refunding transaction. City ABC issued a $1 million 30-year bond at an interest rate of 6%. For reason of simplicity, the debt service is assumed to be level and paid annually. There is a call

---

[b]This is because the present value of future all debt service payments is equal to the face value of the bond, which is the same for the refunded and refunding bonds.

[c]Finding out the annual debt service is a present value of annuity problem, using the formulae

$$PV = A \left[\frac{1 - \frac{1}{(1 + i)^N}}{i} \right]$$

where PV is present value (or the par amount of the bond in this case), A is the annuity (or annual debt service in this case), i is the interest rate, and N is the number of years to maturity. Because we know PV ($1 million), i (6%), and N (30 years), we can solve the problem and find A to be $72,649.

[d]It should be noted that the refunding amount is always greater than the amount to be refunded. This has to be the case because the refunding proceeds in the escrow account are earning at a rate that is lower than that paid on the old bond. To make up for the difference, the principal of the refunding bond has to be greater.

[e]Finding out the present value of total savings is also a present value of annuity problem, as explained in footnote 3. The difference is that now we know A (which is the annual saving of $8105), i (4%), and N (20 years). Solving for PV, we find the present value of total savings to be $126,617.

protection of 10 years. After 5 years, the interest rate dropped to 4%, and the city wanted to refund the bond at 4%. The annual debt service on the old bond was $72,649, and the principal remaining at the end of the 10th year will be $833,277.[c] Therefore the total debt service on the old bond before its redemption will be five annual payments of $72,649 and the final principal payment of $833,277. The present value of this debt service payment stream discounted at 4% will be $1,008,313, which also becomes the par amount of the refunding bonds.[d] This amount will be invested in an escrow account earning 4% to pay the debt service on the old bond before its redemption in another 5 years. The city will then only have to pay debt service on the new refunding bond. When the new bond is amortized over the next 25 years at the rate of 4%, the annual debt service on the new bond comes out to be $64,544, resulting in an annual debt service saving of $8105 for the next 25 years. The present value of total savings discounted at 4% is $126,617.[e]

One factor not considered in this example is issuance cost, which can cost up to 2% of the refunding amount, although it does not change the example in any significant way. Any reduction in interest rate does not immediately translate into an opportunity for refunding. There is cost involved every time when debt is issued, such as underwriting fee, legal fee, and credit rating fee, among others. It is like homeowners incurring closing cost when they refinance their mortgage. The interest rate has to fall to such an extent that at least the present value of future savings should cover all the cost associated with the issuance. Otherwise, it will be financially a net loss. It is probably caused by the concern that refunding should be approached cautiously and not be manipulated for budgetary purposes that some governments require that the refunding transaction can go ahead only if the present value of savings is at least 3% of the refunded bond. In the above example, this 3% rule is easily met even after deducting the issuance cost.

SUGGESTED READINGS

"Refinancing Municipal Debt" at http://www.bergencapital.com/research/files/RefinancingMunicipalDebt.htm.

"Advance Refunding" at http://www.munibondadvisor.com/refunding.htm.

Jordan, L. Understanding current and advance refundings. Gov. Finance Rev. **1992**, *8* (2), 13–15.

Vogt, J. *Capital Budgeting and Finance: A Guide for Local Government*; International City/County Management Association (ICMA), 2004. Chapter 9.

United States Treasury Securities

Theo Edwin Maloy
West Texas A&M University, Canyon, Texas, U.S.A.

INTRODUCTION

Among the many duties of the United States Department of Treasury is managing government accounts and the public debt.[1] The department's Bureau of the Public Debt borrows the money needed to operate the federal government by issuing and servicing marketable, savings, and special securities.

The Bureau of the Public Debt evolved from the Register of the Treasury, becoming the Public Debt Service in 1919. It was designated as a bureau in 1940. With the passage of the Government Securities Act in 1986, the bureau assumed the rulemaking authority for the government securities market. The bureau's functions include the following:

- Borrowing the money necessary to operate the federal government, and accounting for the resulting public debt;
- Receiving, storing, issuing, and redeeming government securities;
- Servicing registered accounts and paying interest when due;
- Maintaining accounting and audit control over public debt transactions and publishing statements;
- Processing claims for securities that are lost, stolen, or destroyed;
- Promoting the sale and retention of United States Savings Bonds.[2]

DEBT INSTRUMENTS

Treasury securities are debt instruments. They are issued to raise the money needed to operate the federal government and to pay off maturing debt obligations. Currently, individuals, corporations, state or local governments, foreign governments, and other entities outside of the United States Government hold just less than US$4 trillion in United States Government debt. Government trust funds, revolving funds, and special funds hold just less than US$3 trillion in United States Government debt, including Federal Financing Bank securities. Treasury securities are a safe and secure investment because the full faith and credit of the United States Government guarantee that interest and principal payments will be paid on time. Interest on Treasury securities is exempt from state and local income taxes.[3–5]

Most Treasury securities are "liquid," which means that they can easily be sold for cash at the prevailing price in a "secondary market"—a public double-auction market where buyers continually offer securities for sale and sellers continually offer to buy those securities. As a group, Treasury securities are often called "marketable Treasury securities," "Treasury securities," or "Treasuries." Individually, they are sometimes called "T-bills," "T-notes," and "T-bonds."[6]

OWNERSHIP OF DEBT INSTRUMENTS

The algebraic sum of all accumulated United States deficits and surpluses is popularly known as the "federal debt." Beginning in 1918, Congress has set a limit on the total dollar amount of debt securities that the Treasury can have outstanding. The current "debt ceiling" is US$7.38 trillion, raised in May 2003 from US$6.4 trillion. Congress may have to increase the debt limit when the federal budget is in surplus on a unified budget accounting basis; the unified budget surplus or deficit only reflects the government's transactions with the public. The debt limit includes Treasury borrowing by government trust funds as well as borrowing by the public.[7]

The current federal debt is approaching US$7 trillion at a rate of increase of approximately US$1.5 billion/day. Foreign and international individuals and institutions hold in excess of US$1.5 trillion of the US$4 trillion in government securities held by entities outside of the United States Government. As the supply of government securities increases, foreign and international holdings of government securities increase at an approximately 22% $year^{-1}$ rate.[8] Asians hold 55% of foreign investments in Treasury securities, and the buying continues. Since the financial crisis of 1997 and 1998, Asian economies have rebounded, in part, by using cheap currencies to boost exports to the United States. In a search for stable investments, the region's central banks have invested trade surpluses in dollar-based securities, primarily United States bonds. In addition, the central banks have sold their currencies for dollars to maintain the weak currency

Encyclopedia of Public Administration and Public Policy
DOI: 10.1081/E-EPAP-120025952

advantage. Many of the dollars, too, are invested in United States securities. Although the buying supports the United States securities markets, international selling—and rumors of selling—has a detrimental effect on American markets. However, the foreign central banks' large holdings of United States Treasury securities are difficult to sell. If large amounts of securities are sold, the value of the banks' remaining securities also declines.[9]

TYPES OF SECURITIES AND THEIR OWNERSHIP

The Bureau of the Public Debt sells Treasury bills, notes, and savings bonds to individual investors. The buyer lends money to the United States Government, and receives the payment of interest in exchange for the loan. Treasury bills and notes are sold in increments of US$1000, with a minimum purchase of US$1000.

All Treasury bills and notes are issued and held by an entry in an electronic ledger, called the "book-entry form." An investor can hold Treasury securities in one of two systems: Treasury Direct or the commercial book-entry system. The security's owner has a direct relationship with the Treasury in the Treasury Direct system. The commercial book-entry system is an indirect holding system where a financial institution, government securities broker, or dealer holds the record of the security for the owner. The commercial book-entry system is a multilevel arrangement that involves the Treasury, the Federal Reserve System (acting as the Treasury's agent), banks, brokers, dealers, and other financial institutions.

Treasury Direct makes principal and interest payments by direct deposit to the security holder's bank account and sends statements to the holder. The Treasury charges no fees for opening an account or buying securities, but it charges a maintenance fee for accounts holding securities with par values in excess of US$100,000. Treasury Direct allows security holders to automatically reinvest the proceeds from most maturing securities.

In the commercial book-entry system, the security investor maintains a relationship with a financial institution, broker, or dealer, and potentially pays fees for its services. The institution will receive the security owner's principal and interest payments from the government. The commercial book-entry system allows an investor to easily buy and sell securities, as well as—unlike Treasury Direct—to use them for collateral. An investor can also hold Treasury securities in stripped form—known as STRIPS or zero-coupon treasuries—in the commercial book-entry system.

STRIPS are Treasury securities that do not make periodic interest payments. Market participants create STRIPS by separating the interest and principal parts of a Treasury note or bond. For example, a 10-year Treasury note consists of 20 interest payments—one every 6 months for 10 years—and a principal payment payable at maturity. When the security is "stripped," each of the 20 interest payments and the principal payment becomes separate securities and can be held and transferred separately. STRIPS can only be bought and sold through a financial institution, broker, or dealer, and held in the commercial book-entry system.

To sell a security held in the commercial book-entry system, the holder arranges a sale through a financial institution, government securities dealer, broker, or investment advisor. Normally, there is a fee for this service. If the investor holds a security in Treasury Direct, it can be transferred to an account in the commercial book-entry system, or it can be sold through the Treasury's Sell Direct program for a fee. Securities can be transferred between Treasury Direct and the commercial book-entry system.[5]

The Treasury Department has not offered a Treasury bond because of the decision in October 2001 to suspend the issuance of 30-year bonds. Bonds issued with coupon rates above current market interest rates are periodically called for early redemption.[10] The Treasury sold noncallable 30-year bonds on February 15 and August 15, and may have subsequently issued an additional amount of a bond at a "reopening." The 30-year bond was the "benchmark" for all debt instruments. Until February 1985, the Treasury issued fixed-principal bonds that are callable 5 years prior to maturity. After providing 4 months' notice, the Treasury can call any callable bond on its first call date, or on any semiannual interest payment date thereafter. The callable bond with the longest remaining period to maturity is the 11.75% bond of November 15, 2009–2014, which was issued in November 1984.[11]

TREASURY BILLS

Treasury bills, or T-bills, are securities that mature in 1 year or less from their issue date. T-bills are bought for a price less than their face value, called the "par value." T-bills can be issued for any period of time less than 1 year, but 28-day, 91-day, and 182-day T-bills are most prevalent. When the T-bill matures, the Treasury pays the purchaser the par value. The interest is the difference between the security's purchase price and what the Treasury pays the owner at maturity. If a T-bill were sold before it matures, a buyer in the open market would pay the seller an amount including the accrued interest. There is an active secondary market for T-bills.

The Treasury usually auctions 13-week and 26-week bills every Monday and a 4-week bill on Tuesdays, for issue on Thursday of that week. It also issues cash management bills from time to time for periods as short as 1 day to maintain the Treasury cash balance, especially immediately before regular tax payment dates.[12]

Although T-bills pay interest, they are sold at a ''discount rate.'' If a 91-day US$1000 Treasury bill were bought at a 0.840% discount, it would be purchased for US$99.788 per US$100 of face value. The discount for a 91-day US$1000 T-bill with a 0.840% discount can be approximated at:

$$2.123 = US\ 1000(\text{discount rate})(\text{days to maturity}/360)$$

The discount rate is not the investment rate, sometimes called the ''bond equivalent yield.'' For a 91-day US$1000 Treasury bill bought at a 0.840% discount, bond equivalent yield can be approximated at:

$$0.008535 = (365 \times \text{discount rate})$$
$$/[360 - (\text{discount rate} \times \text{days to maturity})]$$

The Treasury's Recent Treasury Bill Auction Results lists term, issue date, maturity date, discount rate, investment rate, price per hundred, and the T-bill's Committee on Uniform Securities Identification Procedures (CUSIP) number. A 91-day T-bill with a 0.840 discount would be listed with a 0.854 investment rate and a US$99.788 price per US$100 of face value.[13]

TREASURY NOTES AND BONDS

Treasury notes and bonds are securities that pay a fixed rate of interest every 6 months until the security matures, when the holder receives the par (or face) value. The only difference between a Treasury note and a Treasury bond is their time until maturity. Treasury notes mature in more than a year, but not more than 10 years from their issue date. Bonds, when they are issued, mature in more than 10 years from their issue date. Notes and bonds are usually originally offered at a price close to their par value.

Currently, the Treasury sells fixed-principal and inflation-indexed notes. Both pay interests twice a year, but the principal value of inflation-indexed securities is adjusted to reflect inflation as measured by the Consumer Price Index (the Bureau of Labor Statistics Consumer Price Index for All Urban Consumers). With inflation-indexed notes and bonds, the semiannual interest payments and maturity payment are based on the inflation-adjusted principal value of the security.

The Treasury issues 2-year notes at the end of each month, and 3-year, 5-year, and 10-year notes are issued on February 15, May 15, August 15, and November 15 of each year. The Treasury reopens 5-year notes on the 15th

day of the month after each original issue. An offering is usually announced 1 week before the auction.[14]

BUYING MARKETABLE TREASURY SECURITIES

Treasury bills, notes, and bonds can be purchased in a Treasury auction, or in the securities market. If an investor wants to buy a Treasury security at an auction, the buyer contacts the Treasury, a Federal Reserve Bank, a financial institution, or a government securities broker or dealer. If the buyer wants to buy a Treasury security in the securities market, the investor contacts a financial institution, broker, or dealer.

Each Treasury bill, note, or bond is sold at a public auction. In the Treasury's auctions, all successful bidders are awarded securities at the same price, which is the price equal to the highest rate or yield of the competitive bids that are accepted. A complete explanation of the auction process is published in the Uniform Offering Circular, which is in the Code of Federal Regulations at 31 CFR Part 356. About 1 week before each auction, the Treasury issues a press release announcing the security being sold, the amount being sold, the auction date, and other pertinent information.

For each security that the investor wants to buy, a bid is submitted. The investor can either bid noncompetitively or competitively, but not both in the same auction. A noncompetitive bid receives the bull amount of the security that the buyer wants at the return determined at that auction. An individual cannot bid for more than US$1 million in a bill auction, or US$5 million in a note auction. Most individual investors bid noncompetitively. A competitive bid specifies a ''rate'' for bills, or the ''yield'' for notes. If the return that the bidder specifies is too high, the investor might not receive any securities, or just a portion of what is sought. However, competitive bids can be much larger than noncompetitive bids. Bids can be submitted directly to the Treasury, to a Federal Reserve Bank, or through a financial institution, broker, or dealer. Bids are accepted by mail. Current customers can submit bids via the Internet, or by touch-tone telephone. A financial institution, government securities broker, or dealer can also submit bids on an individual's behalf, probably for a fee.

UNITED STATES SAVINGS BONDS

Savings bonds are Treasury securities that are payable only to the person to whom they are registered. They are not transferable in a secondary market. Savings bonds can earn interest for up to 30 years, but they can be cashed after 6 months if purchased before February 1, 2003; or after 12 months if purchased on or after February 1, 2003.

Series EE and Series E bonds and savings notes are "accrual securities" where the interest is periodically added to the amount the buyer originally paid, to establish their current redemption value. When a buyer cashes a Series EE bond, a Series E bond, or a savings note, the owner receives the redemption value, which is the return of the original investment plus the interest that was earned as the bond was held. The Series EE savings bond increases in value until it is cashed or reaches final maturity in 30 years. The "double E" is the successor to the Series E bond that was issued from May 1941 to June 1980. Investors can purchase up to US$30,000 in Series EE bonds each calendar year.

The amount printed on a Series EE is its denomination, also known as its face amount. Eight denominations are available: US$50, 75, 100, 200, 500, 1000, 5000, and 10,000. The US$50 and 75 denominations are not available through Payroll Savings Plans and other employer thrift plans. Because bonds accrue interest for up to 30 years, the bond's redemption value can exceed its face value. Since December 2001, Series EE bonds have been inscribed as "Patriot Bonds" as part of the county's antiterrorism effort.[15–17]

Series HH and Series H bonds are current-income securities issued with face values of US$500, 1000, 5000, or 10,000. The redemption value of the bonds remains constant at the amount the buyer invested, and the interest is paid to the holder every 6 months. When the owner cashes a Series HH or Series H bond, the original investment is returned. There is no limit on how much a person can invest in Series HH bonds.[17,18]

Series I bonds are a new type of accrual security bond designed for investors seeking to protect the purchasing power of their investment and earn a guaranteed real rate of return. Series I bonds are sold at face values of US$50, 70, 100, 200, 500, 1000, 5000, and 10,000, and they grow in value with inflation-indexed earnings for up to 30 years. An investor can purchase up to US$30,000 in Series I bonds during a calendar year. The bonds offer a fixed rate combined with semiannual inflation adjustments to help protect purchasing power. The fixed rate of return is announced by the Treasury Department each May and November. The fixed rate of return announced in May is the same over the entire life of the Series I bonds purchased between May 1 and October 31 of that year. The fixed rate of return announced in November applies to the entire life of Series I bonds purchased between November 1 and April 30 of the following year. The semiannual inflation rate is also announced each May and November by the Treasury Department. The semiannual inflation rate is based on changes in the Consumer Price Index. The semiannual inflation rate announced in May is

a measure of inflation over the preceding October through March. The inflation rate announced in November is a measure of inflation over the preceding April through September. The semiannual inflation rate is combined with the fixed rate of a Series I bond to determine the Series I bond's earnings rate for the next 6 months. Series I bonds increase in value each month, and interest is compounded semiannually. They earn interest for up to 30 years. In the unlikely event that the Consumer Price Index is negative, the value of Series I bonds would remain the same until the inflation rate becomes greater than zero. In addition to earnings being exempt from state and local income taxes, Series I bonds' federal income taxes can be deferred for up to 30 years, until redemption or other taxable disposition. Taxpayers who qualify can exclude all or part of Series I bonds' interest from income as long as the proceeds are used to pay for tuition and fees at eligible postsecondary educational institutions.

Two types of savings bonds can be bought for cash— the Series EE bonds and the Series I bond. Series HH bonds can only be bought in exchange for Series EE, Series E, and savings notes, or when the owner reinvests the proceeds of matured Series H bonds.[19]

OTHER SECURITIES

Government Account Series securities are issued because various government trust fund statutes provide for interest-earning investments of money that is not needed immediately for the purposes of the fund. Growth in the trust funds is attributable to returns on these investments and current contributions to the funds. Interest rates on par-value Government Account Series securities are prescribed in statutes that provide the investment authority for government trust funds, which include the Social Security trust funds, the Civil Service Retirement and Disability Fund, the Federal Hospital Insurance Trust Fund, and the Federal Retirement Thrift Savings Fund (G Fund). Generally, the Treasury pays interest semiannually on par-value Government Account Series securities. The G Fund invests in overnight par-value securities, and interest is compounded each day. Similar, the Treasury started to issue market-based securities in 1974 to provide an investment mechanism within the government for federal accounts that are authorized to invest in securities that are issued or fully guaranteed as to principal and interest by the United States. These accounts, which number over 200, include retirement fund assets managed by the Pension Benefit Guarantee Corporation, Federal Housing Administration mortgage insurance funds, and the Bank Insurance Fund. The statutes of federal agencies and funds that invest in market-based securities authorize investments but do not authorize investing in par-value Government Account Series securities.[20]

The Treasury sells State and Local Government Series securities to issuers of federally tax-exempt securities as an investment for the gross proceeds of a tax-exempt issue, or any other amount that assists the state or local government to comply with provisions of the Internal Revenue Code related to the tax exemption. The book-entry securities are not transferable. The purchaser can designate the interest rate on a time deposit security, but the rate cannot exceed the maximum interest rate. The maximum rates are "five basis points" (five one-hundredths of 1%, or 0.0005) below the current Treasury borrowing rate for a Treasury security of comparable maturity. The interest rate for a time deposit security that matures in more than 30 years, up to and including 40 years, is the maximum rate on a 30-year State and Local Government Series security. The interest rate for demand deposit securities is a variable rate that the Treasury calculates by using the investment yield on 13-week Treasury bills in the most recent weekly auction, adjusted by the estimated marginal tax rate of investors in tax-exempt securities and adjusted for Treasury administrative costs. Interest is added to the principal and is reinvested daily until redemption.[21]

The Treasury has issued dollar-denominated Foreign Government Series securities directly to foreign governments since 1962. It has also issued foreign currency-denominated foreign series securities on several occasions between 1961 and 1980, but none of them remains outstanding. Special operations, mostly involving United States Government loans to foreign countries for military purchases in the United States, necessitate dollar-denominated securities as temporary investments for the borrowed funds. The Treasury also issued long-term zero-coupon securities to foreign governments on several occasions between 1988 and 1994 to assist them in restructuring their obligations under the Brady Plans. The proceeds of the zero-coupon securities were pledged to pay the principal amount of bonds issued by the foreign governments.[22]

Domestic Series securities were issued in 1989 as an investment for Refcorp under the Federal Home Loan Bank Act. Proceeds of the 30-year and 40-year zero-coupon bonds were pledged to pay the principal amount of marketable Refcorp bonds. The Treasury has not issued Domestic Series securities to another entity.[23]

The Federal Financing Bank is a government corporation, created by Congress in 1973, under the general supervision of the Secretary of the United States Treasury, established to centralize and reduce the cost of federal and federally assisted borrowings from the public. The bank aids federal agencies and other borrowers whose debt is guaranteed by the federal government. The Federal Financ-

ing Bank was also established to deal with federal budget management problems that occurred when offbudget financing flooded the government securities market with offers of a variety of government-backed securities that competed with Treasury securities. The bank has the authority to purchase any obligation issued, sold, or guaranteed by a federal agency to ensure that fully guaranteed obligations are financed most efficiently.[24]

Other miscellaneous federal debts exist, including Adjusted Service Bonds from World War I and Armed Forces Leave Bonds from World War II.[25]

CONCLUSION

Federal government yearly deficits result from expenditures exceeding revenues. The Treasury borrows money to finance the accumulated deficit. In an effort to increase demand for government debt instrument, the Treasury offers a variety of debt types and maturities. As financial markets develop and mature, the Treasury will create new debt instruments to make U.S. government debt more attractive to domestic and foreign investors and governments.

REFERENCES

1. http://www.treas.gov/education/duties/index.html.
2. http://www.treas.gov/education/duties/bureaus/public-debt.html.
3. http://www.publicdebt.treas.gov/opd/opdpdodt.htm.
4. http://www.publicdebt.treas.gov/opd/opdfaq.htm#opdfaq32.
5. http://www.publicdebt.treas.gov/of/ofbasics.htm.
6. http://www.publicdebt.treas.gov/sec/secfaq.htm#secfaq1.
7. http://www.publicdebt.treas.gov/com/comlimit.htm.
8. http://www.fms.treas.gov/bulletin/.
9. http://online.wsj.com/article/0,,SB106000774754160200-email,00.html.
10. http://www.publicdebt.treas.gov/com/combills.htm.
11. http://www.publicdebt.treas.gov/com/combonds.htm.
12. http://www.publicdebt.treas.gov/sec/seccall3.htm.
13. http://www.publicdebt.treas.gov/AI/OFBills.
14. http://www.publicdebt.treas.gov/com/comnotes.htm.
15. http://www.savingsbonds.gov/sav/savseree.htm.
16. http://www.savingsbonds.gov/sav/savpayme.htm.
17. http://www.publicdebt.treas.gov/sav/savpatriotbond.htm.
18. http://www.savingsbonds.gov/sav/sbhglanc.htm.
19. http://www.savingsbonds.gov/sav/sbifaq.htm.
20. http://www.publicdebt.treas.gov/com/comgas.htm.
21. http://www.publicdebt.treas.gov/com/comslg.htm.
22. http://www.publicdebt.treas.gov/com/comfor.htm.
23. http://www.publicdebt.treas.gov/com/comdom.htm.
24. http://www.ustreas.gov/ffb/.
25. http://www.publicdebt.treas.gov/.

Urban Planning and Ethics

Carlos Nunes Silva
University of Lisbon, Lisbon, Portugal

INTRODUCTION

Urban and regional planning faces complex ethical dilemmas related to public interest; professional integrity; obligations toward the community, clients, employers, and colleagues; intellectual property; as well as the environment, other forms of life, and future generations, both in strategic and daily decisions. Therefore, besides the fact that they have to obey and implement the law, the mission of planning professionals includes complex judgements over conflicting land uses, which makes this one of the areas in public administration and public policy where decisions are embedded in highly complex, multilayer, and multiactor decision-making processes. A planner often has to weigh personal values against those established in one's professional organization, or in the society. In spite of this, the discussion of ethical principles in urban and regional planning is a relatively recent fact, even in countries where the planning profession has been organized for a long time.

THE RISE OF ETHICS IN THE PLANNING PROFESSION

The pioneering studies of Howe and Kaufman[1,2] on planners' values and ethics showed that planners acted differently according to their values and ethical principles, but, contrary to what could be expected from these results, the issue was not on top of the agenda in planning theory discussions at that time. Notwithstanding the fact that planners commonly did not acknowledge explicitly that they were considering ethical principles (e.g., when planning new land uses), they were in fact reasoning usually as consequentialists (or utilitarians), weighing the "good" and the "bad" of the outcomes of their decisions through planning techniques such as cost–benefit analysis. That planning has been guided somehow by values seems to be a fact throughout the history of urban planning, at least in its utopian proposals.

But only in the last two decades has a clear interest in the ethical dimension of planning been developed as a result of different factors, as numerous authors such as Kaufman,[3–5] Khakee and Dahlgren,[6] and Hendler[7] show. First, it is a consequence of the conviction that the allocation of different land uses is an ethical problem, in the sense that decisions about land use have economic, social, cultural, and environmental consequences. Second, the emergence of new visions of planning, in reaction to the then-dominant "rational planning model," led to the recognition that decisions about land use are not value-neutral; it is through the political process that some groups or individuals gain and others lose, according to their power resources. This interest in the political dimension of planning was further reinforced by the theory of justice by Rawls[8] and the justification for the minimal state by Nozick,[9] which together helped the development of a strong interest in the ethical dimension of planning in the late 1970s onward. In fact, unlike many other professions, planning involves choices on key social facets of collective life. For example, planners have to decide what are good or bad public spaces, or on housing estate characteristics, or on a transport solution. Thus they need to know how to decide among different claims, taking into consideration multiple and contradictory dimensions. Third, the growing number of professionals in this field increased the social relevance of this activity, further augmented by a more demanding citizenship. Fourth, the social impact of incorrect professional behaviors forced professional organizations to make explicit ethical guidelines in the form of codes of conduct. Finally, the increasing relation between the public sector and the private sector, as a consequence of the liberal economic policies after the 1970s, challenged traditional public administration values and legal control procedures. This and the conviction that different people in the same service can behave differently encouraged governments and international organizations dealing with public policy to adopt ethical standards.[a]

The adoption of codes of ethics in planning, if centered on human rights and on the environment, is commonly seen as having practical relevance. It not only facilitates

---

[a]For example, for a brief review of measures proposed in Organization for Economic Cooperation and Development (OECD) countries, refer to Refs. [10–12]. For the kind of measures proposed by the United Nations for the public sector, in general, refer to Refs. [13] and [14]. For a similar review in the case of local government, refer to Ref. [15]. See also the Organization of American States for its anticorruption measures and the World Bank's "Code of Professional Ethics."

Encyclopedia of Public Administration and Public Policy
DOI: 10.1081/E-EPAP-120023434

the resolution of moral problems which professional planners face, but is seen also as a self-regulation reference for professional conduct; it helps to find an ideal for the profession, states the profession core values, and reinforces the profession's status in society; it informs employers, clients, and the population, in general, about the kind of responsibilities and obligations a planner has toward them; it helps to create an environment of fairness in which ethical conduct will be the norm, as the works of Kaufman,[3–5] Hendler,[16,17] and Lawton[18] suggest. Additionally, it is widely believed that professional behavior is conditioned by the organization's ethical environment and the ethical culture of that specific group. Therefore, to have an ethical code of professional conduct, explicit moral norms is seen as a positive factor for the definition and prevention of unacceptable behavior. Indeed, if a certain professional conduct is seen as unacceptable, then it will be less probable that it will be practiced by many members.

Codes of professional ethics in planning are relatively recent, even in countries where the discussion of ethical principles inside professional organizations has a long-standing tradition, as Kaufman,[3–5] Mahoney,[19] and Fisher[20] point out. Notwithstanding, there are several examples of professional organizations related to planning that adopted codes of conduct long ago, although usually with only very general guidelines. For example, in 1914, the American Society of Civil Engineers (ASCE) adopted a code of ethics (www.asce.org), amended several times afterward. In 1924, the International City–County Management Association (ICMA) adopted a Code of Ethics that was subsequently revised on several occasions. The Town Planning Institute in the United Kingdom (www.rtpi.org.uk) adopted in the 1930s a code of professional conduct. The predecessor of the American Institute of Certified Planners (AICP) (www.planning.org/aicp), the American Institute of Planners (AIP), adopted a code of ethics and professional conduct in 1971, which was revised in 1978 by the new AICP and subsequently revised again in 1981. The American Planning Association (APA) (www.planning.org) adopted a ''Statement of Ethical Principles'' in 1987 as a guide for all its members, replacing the 1962 code of the preceding organization, the American Society of Planning Officials (ASPO). In 1992, the APA adopted a ''Statement of Ethical Principles in Planning'' to serve as a guide of ethical conduct for all those involved in the planning process.[3,21] In Canada, in 1994, the Canadian Institute of Planners adopted also a code of conduct for its members (www.cip-icu.ca).

In Europe, the European Council of Town Planners (ECTP) in 1985 adopted guidelines for professional conduct to be developed by each national association of planners in each member country.[22] In the European Union (EU), there were additional reasons for the har-

monization of professional codes related to the increased labor mobility in the EU market—a situation that affected several professional groups related to urban and regional planning; this led the ECTP to recognize the need for some sort of deontological harmonization within Europe (www.ceu-ectp.org).

A similar process toward the adoption of professional codes of conduct by planners can be found in many other countries around the globe such as, for example, Australia (www.planning.org.au), New Zealand (www.nzplanning.co.nz), India (www.itpindia.org), Brazil (www.arquitetofna.org.br), and South Africa (www.saplanners.org.za).

Other professional groups involved in urban and regional planning also adopted codes of professional conduct in the same period, such as Landscape Architecture (www.asla.org), Architects (www.aia.org/), Civil Engineer (www.asce.org), Geographers (www.aag.org), Sociologists (www.asanet.org), among others. Most of these codes deal with issues of professional conduct but say little about the major aims of planning. A search of North American professional organizations in other fields of activity also shows that the 1990s was a period during which most of them revised their previous code of ethics and professional conduct,[b] which were initially adopted, in most cases, in the 1970s or 1980s. This means that we are talking of a practice that—in most professions related to urban and regional planning—has been in effect for only around three decades.

But probably the situation in all these professional organizations in the early years of professional ethics codification was not much different from the one described by Kaufman[3] and related to the AICP case: ''While some American planners were probably aware that their respective planning organizations adopted ethics codes in the 1980s, few probably knew what was in these codes. This is not meant as a criticism of planners because codes tend to be exceedingly dry and uninspiring documents to read.'' But since then, the situation seems to be changing. Indeed, since the 1980s, the subject of planning ethics has been introduced in several graduate planning programs in the United States, Europe, and other parts of the world, including a discussion on how best to teach planning ethics. At the same time, numerous empirical studies of the ethics of planners were performed and the results were published, as a consequence of the growing

---

[b]For example, that was the case of the American Historical Association, in 1990; American Evaluation Association, in 1994; Archaeological Institute of America, in 1994; American Mathematical Society, in 1995; American Psychological Association, in 1997; American Society of Landscape Architecture, in 1998; and American Statistical Association, in 1999.

concern with the political and ethical dimensions of planning as Kaufman,[4,5] Klosterman,[23] and Hendler[7] point out. It also became common to find seminars dedicated to these topics in programs of professional planning conferences and congresses, as well as special training sessions organized by planners' professional associations.

Despite planning professionals' general acceptance of ethic codes, they often also are seen as an unsatisfactory set of recommendations—vague and paternalistic, and based on a naive view of planning theory and on a simplistic conception of power relations, as Lucy[24] and Fisher[20] argue. As planning is a multidisciplinary field and a multiactor activity, having a code of conduct specific for planners risks ignoring other key stakeholders' concerns and impacts. This view argues for a more comprehensive approach to professional ethics codification. On the other side, the code's effectiveness depends on several conditions not always practiced by all professional organizations. Examples include the implementation of ethics education programs, hotlines for reporting wrongdoings, adoption of a legal framework to support ethical standards, and concomitant appropriate sanctions to deal with misconduct.

ETHICAL PRINCIPLES APPLIED IN PLANNING

There are two main groups of ethical perspectives to be considered in urban planning. The first group includes the consequentialist and deontological perspectives, and the second includes the anthropocentric and nonanthropocentric perspectives.[25,26]c If both dimensions are combined simultaneously, then four major categories of perspectives can be considered.

For the consequentialist perspective, it is the outcome of an action or behavior that determines if it is correct or not, or if it is "good" or "bad." Utilitarianism is an example of the consequentialist perspective. On the contrary, deontological theories see any action or behavior as having a value in itself, independently of its consequences. An ethical urban and regional planning has to consider and contrast ends-oriented ethics (consequentialist ethics) with means-oriented ethical principles (deontological ethics), as both sets of principles are

morally relevant in addressing dilemmas faced by urban and regional planners.

A second dimension is related to the importance given to *Homo sapiens* in the definition of the moral community. For anthropocentric perspectives, only *H. sapiens* matter for that purpose; whereas for nonanthropocentric perspectives, other forms of life and the environment are also valued independently of the importance they have for human beings.

Therefore the professional practices of planners can be rather different from each other depending on the ethical perspective adopted, as research works by Howe and Kaufman,[1,2] Khakee and Dahlgren,[6] and others showed.

From a deontological and nonanthropocentric perspective, for example, ethical urban and regional planning seeks to maximize the public interest, without compromising other moral duties in relation to other forms of life, the environment, and future generations. Therefore it should seek to create a more just society and to improve redistributive justice among individuals, groups, and territories, following the theory of justice and communitarian perspectives by Rawls, but at the same time care about the impact on the environment.[31] This can be performed through the choices made for the provision of housing, education, culture, employment, and health facilities, for example. Thus planning should protect the interests of the disadvantaged (disabled, aged, children, women, and minorities). Planning proposals should respect basic human rights, including the right to a minimum of social benefits available to all, irrespective of economic capacity, and should also prevent harm to people or communities and the environment. Deep Ecology, first proposed by Aarne Naess, is one example of a deontological and nonanthropocentric perspective relevant to the discussion of urban planning ethics.[32]

Whatever the ethical perspective adopted, planners face three main sets of ethical dilemmas. One is related to individual rights, with the tensions between freedom and autonomy on one side, and governmental regulations on the other. The second is related to the overall society, with the tensions, for example, between economic efficiency and social justice. The third relates to the environment and the conflicts between, for instance, environmental protection and development.

The first one (planning and individual rights) has to do, for example, with the preservation of the characteristics of the locality and the choice of lifestyles, with paternalism in planning decisions and the need to prevent or minimize damages, or with limits imposed on private propriety.[26,33] In fact, in urban planning decision-making processes, there are frequently controversies regarding the location of certain activities, or about certain local characteristics (landscape beauty, architectural styles, etc.), or about the limits imposed on owners of private properties.

---

cRefer to Ref. [27] for a review of classical texts (Jeremy Bentham, John Stuart Mill, etc.), as well as contemporary expressions of consequentialism (Richard Brandt and Robert Adams, etc.); for a discussion of utilitarianism, see, among others, Refs. [28] and [29]. Refer to Ref. [30] for a review of classical texts on deontology (Immanuel Kant, W. D. Ross, etc.) and also its contemporary expressions (Robert Nozick, Thomas Nagel, Stephen Darwall, etc.).

Urban growth controls, such as building restrictions that stimulate higher prices, can be seen in some cases as an instrument to protect the character of an area by reducing the ability of low-income families to move in. This and community opposition to the location of poor families, homeless, mentally disabled, or ethnic minorities in the neighborhood are two examples of the social forces that a planner has to face and balance, and which can directly affect individual rights. The balance between national security and individual liberties is also becoming an important ethical issue for planners, in part related to the increasing use of electronic surveillance device in public spaces.

Some planners consider it acceptable and desirable to preserve certain characteristics of the community and to restrict land use, new buildings, or reconstruction of old ones; this requires sensitivity to place identity. Other planners maintain that, if there are no strong arguments such as public health or security reasons, people should be left free to carry out their own choices.[d] However, the argument for the protection of local characteristics should not imply the creation of a monolithic community; therefore urban planning should facilitate the multiple lifestyles that may exist. Moreover, a fair and equitable public participation procedure should always be put in practice to ensure equal opportunities for all interests to be considered. Such procedures may include the use of a local referendum, but this is an uncommon practice.

The possibility of damages on third parties caused by individual decisions, such as those resulting from conflicting land uses, is another type of situation that justifies public intervention and concomitant restrictions on property rights.[e] If some of the negative consequences created by private actions cannot be avoided, it is important, according to this perspective, to seek compensation for such damages from those that caused them.

Restrictions and benefits imposed by a plan zoning on private property need to be balanced fairly. In this case, it is commonly considered correct to apply a system of transfer of development rights from new development areas to compensate owners not being allowed to build, or owners allowed to build less than average, and also to compensate owners of rural land as a form of compensation for the preservation of agricultural and forest lands.

The second group of ethical dilemmas has to do with the social responsibility of planners. In fact, it can be argued from a deontological perspective that planners also have redistributive obligations toward different social groups if we take, for instance, Rawls' contractarian theory of justice. Urban planning should seek to reduce economic and social inequalities through maximization of benefits for the most disadvantaged social groups. From a deontological perspective, ethical urban and regional planning achieves the maximum well being for the majority of citizens, which means that the utilitarian dimension of a plan has to be conditioned by other moral obligations (such as those related with certain human rights) as part of the social contract. Therefore there is a moral obligation for the content of an urban plan to maximize the net benefits for the most discriminated or oppressed in society.[26,35,36] A planner who values children, the aged, the disabled, or women, for instance, will certainly design urban environments that are different from those who do not, or will not endorse or approve developments that do not meet these criteria.

From this point of view, planners also have ethical obligations in relation to future generations,[f] especially due to the fact that few professions have a greater influence on the human habitat and on the quality of people's life. Therefore they should consider the cumulative impact of their decisions and prevent the destruction of built or natural patrimony, and avoid, when possible, all decisions with irreversible consequences. From this perspective, planners have a moral obligation to keep children and young people at the center of planning options, as they will be the generation that will receive the consequences of today's decisions. Nevertheless, there are arguments against the existence of obligations to future generations on the part of planners.

Finally, a third category of ethical dilemmas faced by planners is related to the environment and urban sustainability. In an irreversibly and increasingly urban world, professional planners have a moral obligation to plan for a sustainable city, which cannot be achieved without social equity and social inclusion, and is an additional reason for urban planning to be redistributive.[37] For this, it is necessary to incorporate new values and a different relationship with nature. Such an aim requires a shift in the dominant urban sprawl model of development toward a more compact city—a condition to achieve sustainability.[g] Because part of biodiversity loss is

---

[d]A classical reference for this point of view is Ref. [34].

[e]That is the case of the so-called NIMBY (Not In My Back Yard) or LULU (Local Unwanted Land Uses) type of land use conflicts. A socially responsible planner has a moral obligation to overcome these practices and to promote inclusive communities, reversing the NIMBY to a YIMBY attitude (Yes In My Back Yard).

[f]See Rawl's just saving principle; refer to Ref. [8].

[g]We consider here the following widely used definition of sustainable development: "Development that meets the needs of the present without compromising the ability of future generations to meet their own needs."

due to pollution, destruction of natural habitats, and other man-created conditions, it is necessary to integrate development with conservation. But defining sustainable development in that way seems not enough. Indeed, as Cafaro[38] argues, "massive biodiversity loss is sustainable, provided future generations can meet their self-defined needs." Therefore, from a nonanthropocentric and deontological perspective, planners have a moral obligation to protect and preserve the environment for *H. sapiens* and also for other forms of life in this generation and in future generations.[26,39] These contradictory aims that planners have to address between environmental protection and development are but one more example of the ethical dilemmas that these professionals have to deal with in their daily decisions.

From a deontological perspective, it can be argued that communities have a right to live in a clean environment, which means that there is an ethical duty for planners to minimize the ecological footprint of cities and to promote a model of urban development contrary to urban sprawl. In this model, urban development is more compact, with priority for the redevelopment of brownfield zones instead of occupation of new natural areas, which should only be urbanized when there is no alternative. Therefore it is necessary to develop new ethics for the built environment; reduce urban sprawl associated with the use of individual cars; promote more compact urban patterns, through increase of urban densities and mixing of activities; and create a city that is both safer and easily accessible on foot, as the "New Urbanism" movement claims in its statement of principles.[40] If initially and for most people these ethical obligations for the promotion of an eco-friendly urban and regional development had essentially an anthropocentric justification, they now need to be seen also in relation to other forms of life, thereby enlarging the moral community. Partially related to this is also an ethical duty to coordinate with nearby local or regional authorities and to estimate the impact of local decisions on neighboring administrative areas—a situation that calls for and justifies planning at metropolitan or regional scales.

In planning procedures from a deontological perspective, every citizen has the right to be treated fairly and with equity in the planning process, which means equal treatment by the plan for those in the same condition and the inclusion of those for whom a plan is being prepared. Nonetheless, this sometimes can be an unfair process because of the unequal power relations of those involved in the participation process. In practice, an ethical process of public participation in planning requires that those in a more unfavorable social condition be able to make themselves heard in the decision-making process, as the concept and practice of "advocacy planning," proposed by Paul Davidoff in the 1960s, tried to introduce into mainstream planning. Planners, like other professionals, not only should take into consideration the interests of all stakeholders, but also have an obligation of professional integrity; therefore they should not take personal gains from the decision-making process.

CONCLUSION

Whether dealing with inner-city processes or with natural areas, urban and regional planning inevitably faces conflicting interests and values. The idea of a value-neutral and rationalist planner is no longer a consensual description of mainstream professionals in this field. New ethics concerned with human rights and social justice, and with a deeper green consciousness emerged gradually in the planning profession worldwide in the last two decades. This new ethics replaced the traditional utilitarian and anthropocentric type of criteria in land-use decisions. Like other domains of public policy, urban and regional planning faces a wide range of values, often in conflict with each other. As a result, the task of deciding in practice what is wrong and right is a rather difficult enterprise. In recognition of this complexity and diversity of issues, planners' professional organizations and schools of planning all over the world have been promoting the integration of ethics into their activities and teaching programs since the 1980s. If a driving idea emerges from discussions on these issues, it is certainly that ethics should guide urban and regional planning aimed at restoring the equilibrium of the natural, social, and built environments by reducing the ecological footprints of cities and making them more livable and inclusive places for the present and future generations, with due consideration for human and nonhuman forms of life and ecosystems.

REFERENCES

1. Howe, E.; Kaufman, J. The ethics of contemporary American planners. J. Am. Plan. Assoc. **1979**, *45* (3), 243–255.
2. Howe, E.; Kaufman, J. The values of contemporary American planners. J. Am. Plan. Assoc. **1981**, *47* (3), 266–278.
3. Kaufman, J. American Codes of Planning Ethics. Content, development and after-effects. Plan Can. **1990**, *30* (5), 29–34.
4. Kaufman, J. Reflections on Teaching Three Versions of a Planning Ethics Course. In *Planning Ethics*; Hendler, S., Ed.; Center for Urban Policy Research: New Brunswick, 1999.

5. Kaufman, J. Is the Increased Output of Planning Ethics Knowledge in North America Affecting Those Who Practice Planning? An Exploratory Investigation, Paper Presented at World Planning Schools Congress, Xangai, China, 2001.

6. Khakee, A.; Dahlgren, L. Ethics and values of Swedish Planners: A replication and comparison with an American study. SHPR **1990**, *7*, 65–81.

7. *Planning Ethics*; Hendler, S., Ed.; Center for Urban Policy Research: New Brunswick, 1999.

8. Rawls, J. *Uma Teoria da Justiça*; Editorial Presença: Lisbon, 2001. (''A Theory of Justice,'' Harvard University Press, Cambridge, MA, 1971; first published in 1971, based on the author's papers published in the previous 12 years.)

9. Nozick, R. *Anarquia, Estado e Utopia*; Zahar Editores: Rio de Janeiro, 1991. (''Anarchy, State, and Utopia,'' Basic Books, New York, 1974.)

10. OECD. *Principles for Managing Ethics in the Public Service*; OECD: Paris, 1998.

11. OECD. *Building Public Trust: Ethics Measures in OECD Countries*; OECD: Paris, 2000.

12. Washington, S. L'étique et le service public. Obs.-OCDE **1997**, *204*, 15–17.

13. UN. *Professionalism and Ethics in the Public Service: Issues and Practices in Selected Regions*; United Nations: New York, 2000.

14. UN. *Promoting Ethics in the Public Service*; United Nations: New York, 2000.

15. IULA. *Local Government Associations: Promoting Ethics in Local Government*; International Union of Local Authorities: The Hague, 1999.

16. Hendler, S. Moral theories in professional practice: Do they make a difference? Environments **1990**, *20* (3), 20–30.

17. Hendler, S. Do Professional Codes Legitimate Planners' Values? In *Dilemmas of Planning Practice. Ethics, Legitimacy and the Validation of Knowledge*; Thomas, H., Healey, P., Eds.; Avebury: Aldershot, 1991.

18. Lawton, A. Developing and Implementing Codes of Ethics. Paper Presented at the European Group of Public Administration's Conference, Oeiras, 2003.

19. Mahoney, J. *Teaching Business Ethics in the UK, Europe and the USA. A Comparative Study*; The Athlone Press: London, 1992.

20. Fisher, S. How to Think About the Ethics of Architecture. In *Fox, Warwick, Ethics and the Built Environment*; Routledge: London, 2000; 170–182.

21. Barrett, C. *Everyday Ethics for Practicing Planners*; American Institute of Certified Planners: Washington, 2001.

22. ECTP. *International Agreement and Declaration by the National Institutes and Associations of Professional Town Planners Within the European Economic Commu-*

nity. Appendix C—Professional Conduct Requirements; European Council of Town Planners, 1985.

23. Klosterman, R. Ethical Theory and Planning Education. Introduction. In *Planning Ethics*; Hendler, S., Ed.; Center for Urban Policy Research: New Brunswick, 1999.

24. Lucy, W. APA's Ethical Principles Include Simplistic Planning Theories. In *Readings in Planning Theory*; 1st Ed.; Campbell, S., Fainstein, S., Eds.; Blackwell: Oxford, 1997; Vol. 54 (2). (JAPA, 1988).

25. Howe, E. Normative ethics in planning. J. Plan. Lit. **1990**, *5* (2), 123–150.

26. Beatley, T. *Ethical Land Use. Principles of Policy and Planning*; The John Hopkins University Press: Baltimore, 1994.

27. *Consequentialism*; Darwall, S., Ed.; Blackwell: Oxford, 2003.

28. Sen, A. Utilitarianism and Welfarism. In *Consequentialism*; Darwall, S., Ed.; Blackwell: Oxford, 2003.

29. Rawls, J. 5. Classical Utilitarianism. In *Consequantialism*; Darwall, S. Ed.; Blackwell: Oxford, 2003. Chap. 1.

30. *Deontology*; Darwall, S., Ed.; Blackwell: Oxford, 2003.

31. Blanco, H. Community and the Four Jewels of Planning. In *Planning Ethics*; Hendler, S., Ed.; Center for Urban Policy Research: New Brunswick, 1999; 66–82.

32. Devall, B. The deep, long-range ecology movement: 1960–2000—A review. Ethics Environ. **2001**, *6* (1), 18–41.

33. Brook, I. Can 'Spirit of Place' Be a Guide to Ethical Building? In *Ethics and the Built Environment*; Fox, W., Ed.; Routledge: London, 2000; 139–151.

34. Mill, J.S. *On Liberty and Others Writings*; Collini, S., Ed.; Cambridge University Press: Cambridge, 1993. (''On Liberty,'' first published in 1859.)

35. Hendler, S. Feminist planning ethics. J. Plan. Lit. **1994**, *9* (2), 115–127.

36. Ritzdorf, M. Feminist Contributions to Ethics and Planning Theory. In *Planning Ethics*; Hendler, S., Ed.; Center for Urban Policy Research: New Brunswick, 1999.

37. Talbot, R.; Magnoli, C. Social Inclusion and Sustainable City. In *Fox, Warwick, Ethics and the Built Environment*; Routledge: London, 2000; 91–101.

38. Cafaro, P. For a grounded conception of wilderness and more wilderness on the ground. Ethics Environ. **2001**, *6* (1), 1–17.

39. Girardet, H. Greening Urban Society. In *Ethics and the Built Environment*; Fox, W., Ed.; Routledge: London, 2000; 15–30.

40. Silva, C.N. A Carta do Novo Urbanismo e a Nova Carta de Atenas: A Utopia Urbana do Século XXI? (Chart of New Urbanism and the New Chart of Athens: The Urban Utopia of the XXI Century?) Cad. Munic.-Rev. Acção Reg. Local **2002**, *XVI* (79), 35–47.

Using Model Contracts to Reduce the Risks in Complex Information Technology Procurements

Michael Asner
*Michael Asner Consulting, Surrey,
British Columbia, Canada*

INTRODUCTION

Model contracts are valuable tools. Their use can reduce the risks associated with complex contracts, identify issues for consideration and resolution during the negotiation process, and serve as models for similar procurements in other jurisdictions.

Contract negotiation is an important and critical element in dealing with suppliers. It is part of the procurement process. There is little point in including an incomplete or poorly drafted contract in the request for proposal (RFP) stage, or introducing it into the negotiation process. It is the contract that formalizes the intent and agreement of the parties and must therefore accurately document all the terms and conditions. The contract must be enforceable in court. It must also reflect the understanding and expectations of both parties.

In many RFP processes, it is the procurement professionals who have the responsibility of ensuring that the contract protects the agency, and reflects a shared understanding of the entire business deal. Traditionally, procurement officers have been at a disadvantage when dealing with suppliers. Few procurement officers are lawyers; in contrast, suppliers are very knowledgeable about protecting their rights and the nuances of the law. Often, procurement personnel are dealing with unfamiliar technology, and to make matters worse, many procurement teams have limited access to legal help during the contract development phase of procurement. Simply stated, procurement professionals are at a disadvantage.

OVERVIEW

Model contracts are an attempt by organizations to ensure that their rights are protected, without relying heavily on expert legal help for each new contract. A model contract serves as a template for developing a specific contract.

There is a high initial cost associated with developing a model contract for use throughout an organization. Ideally, the model contract is accompanied by some training, a set of instructions, and possibly a web-based, fill-in template. It is more than simply a list of contract clauses.

Model contracts are only developed for commonly recurring complex purchases, e.g., the acquisition of a new computer system, software, or a systems integrator. Almost all model contracts are for information systems and technology because of the volume and frequency of technology-based RFPs, the high value of the procurement, and the inherent complexity of information technology (IT) acquisitions. They serve as a starting point for development of the specific and complete contract to be included in the RFP.

Most procurement personnel are not lawyers, nor are they subject experts knowledgeable about network protocols, e.g., systems integration or bridge construction. Over the years, many organizations have expended great amounts of time and energy to develop model contracts. The use of these contracts reduces the risks to buyers by identifying issues, risks, and remedies. "Home-grown" contracts are simply too risky, and they prolong negotiations, increase prices, and often abandon remedies which would be available to the agency.

In many jurisdictions, the procurement authority has prepared a set of model contracts designed to meet the majority of the needs of their agencies and departments. These needs are not unique to procurement in the United States; they exist in many other places including Australia, Canada, Hong Kong, and the United Kingdom. In Australia, one of the state governments has developed a set of principles for their model contracts. These principles can be applied in other jurisdictions. They believe that contracts should be based on the following:[1]

- terms and conditions that are fair to all parties—the contract should incorporate a spirit of mutual trust;

Encyclopedia of Public Administration and Public Policy
DOI: 10.1081/E-EPAP 120019219

- schedules and annexes that allow users flexibility in customizing contracts to suit their individual requirements;
- a format that is user-friendly and in "plain English" style;
- a style and language suited to the end users of the products and services;
- consistency in terminology, definitions, and style;
- inclusion of the following elements:

  - a dispute resolution mechanism (e.g., appointment of adjudicator, referee, or expert),
  - performance incentives,
  - allocation of risks.

The last word on this topic goes to the State of Victoria, Australia, where its purchasing board cautions the agency procurement people about using standard or model contracts. They state that the use of the model contracts is not a substitute for:[1]

- people thinking about, then clearly stating what they require;
- negotiation of terms to suit particular circumstances, where necessary;
- proper planning early in the tendering process;
- careful selection of the supplier;
- competent contract management; and
- creating and maintaining a working relationship with a supplier.

A BRIEF SURVEY OF SEVERAL JURISDICTIONS

A model contract is much more than a standardized set of terms and conditions which is the basis for a purchase of goods. It is complete, fully describing specific types of procurements such as computer applications software. Models differ in their level of detail, the amount of instruction and tutorial material provided, and the topics covered.

Many jurisdictions provide good examples of these model contracts and can be major sources of information. For example, the state of Victoria, Australia, has developed model contracts, a checklist of contract clauses, and a 35-page user guide.[1] The state of Washington, U.S.A., has an 8-page guide that includes a checklist of clauses, and four model contracts for information technology.[2] In 1999, California developed new draft model for IT contracts.[3] All of these resources can help public procurement professionals in planning the RFP process and in negotiations.

In the remainder of this section, we will provide a brief survey of how model contracts are dealt with in several representative jurisdictions. All of these contracts deal with different aspects of information technology, reflecting the frequency, volume, and complexity of procurement acquisitions. Each of these examples is web-based, so that the information can be centrally managed and, at the same time, easily accessible by people throughout the organization.

We begin with the **State of Montana**.[4] This is the starting point for the development of a complete, robust, easy-to-use model contract facility. Their web site contains the minimum amount of data, a table of 84 "Standard Contract Language and Forms." There are two types of entries. First, contract elements which should be used by all state agencies "in every bid, proposal, purchase order, or contract." An example is the clause dealing with Access and Retention of Records. The second type of entry is contract elements, which are to be used as required. An example is the clause dealing with "alternate bids," which is only used in certain types of procurements.

The system in the **State of New York** contains much more data than that in Montana.[5] It is further along the road to the ideal model contract facility. The Procurement Services professionals in New York provide their users with a 7-page guideline to promote "a better understanding of the types of contracts available and a "blueprint" for effectively utilizing the many types of technology contracts used." These guidelines deal with the different types of contracts and different procurement strategies. It provides guidance on establishing technology contracts, and on how to process a known requirement. While it does not contain model contracts, it does provide access to all current technology contracts, and their underlying RFPs.

The **State of California** has developed a set of model information technology contracts.[6] To build a draft contract, a purchasing official simply uses an approved "Standard Agreement Form" and attachments. The attachments consist of a Statement of Work for the services required, and terms and conditions selected from five Model IT contracts:

- Information Technology General Terms and Conditions,
- Information Technology Purchase Special Provisions,
- Information Technology Maintenance Special Provisions,
- Information Technology Software License Special Provisions,
- Information Technology Personal Services Special Provisions.

According to the Procurement Division, the benefits of using the new model include the following:

- The use of one model for all IT goods and/or services purchases, whether using a formal bid exceeding $500,000 or informal bids below $500,000.
- Statewide standardization.
- Increased familiarity with the elements and provisions of the model.

Washington State[7] provides another example of a model contracts facility for information technology. It is composed of a set of instructions and model contracts for equipment, software, purchased services, and personal services. Each contract, with its embedded instructions, is between 40 and 60 pages in length. The model contract for software, for example, contains 71 clauses, 3 schedules, and 2 exhibits. Obviously, not every clause will be required in every contract, nor will this contract deal with every issue related to a specific software acquisition. The instructions caution the agency that contracts should be created from the model plus other sources to meet specific needs.

The model contracts and instructions are available from the state's web site. The contracts contain color-coded instructions and fill-in-the-blanks so that agencies can create draft contracts without a separate set of instructions. While specific laws and legal requirements vary from jurisdiction to jurisdiction, these contracts can be used as a starting point—a checklist of issues—by procurement professionals outside the state of Washington.

The **Government of Australia** has set the standard for model contracts.[8] It has developed a Government Information Technology and Communications (GITC) contracting framework. This was performed as a cooperative effort between industry and the Australian federal and state governments. The GITC web site contains extensive information useful in developing contracts, including the model contracts themselves. This version (Version 4) was developed to achieve the following outcome:

- Simplifying the contracting process for the purchase of IT-related products and services.

After developing their model contracts and user documentation, they made all of the information available via the Web. To increase the ease-of-use and access to this information, they implemented two innovations:

1. There is a web-based interactive program which anyone can use to develop a contract. You simply log on to the site and proceed to select contract clauses and input data. At the end, you save your contract. The program provides significant content and functionality:[a]

- Creating a new contract,
- Editing the contract details,
- Saving the contract,
- Printing the contract,
- Adding or removing categories from the contract,
- Opening an existing contract.

2. One can download a file, their "User Guide," which is in fact their entire web-based model contracting system. As soon as this file is downloaded, the user can have access to their model contracting system through the user's own computer without having to access the Internet. Information includes:

User Guide
Frequently Asked Questions
Contacts
About GITC
Head Agreement
Terms and Conditions
Appendices

The amount of information that this site provides is excellent, and the web site design makes it easy to access, locate, and use this information.

CONCLUSION

Model contracts are used increasingly by various parties. They are a good investment in any jurisdiction that purchases lots of information technology goods and services. With increasing public scrutiny, more litigation actions from aggrieved suppliers, fewer procurement staff, and decentralization of contracting, model contracts will become a major tool for imposing standards on the procurement process.

---

[a]The GITC web site provides a mechanism for building contracts. With the introduction of GITC 4, this feature has been extended to provide the following additional functionality:

- Contracts can be saved (as XML) for later on-line editing.
- Contracts can be opened (uploaded) for editing.
- The products and services categories covered by the contract can be changed as soon as the contract has been created.

REFERENCES

1. Government Information Technology Conditions, Terms and Conditions Guidelines, Victoria Government Purchasing Board, www.vgpb.vvic.gov.au/polguid/guid2g.htm.
2. IT Portfolio Management, Policy, Standards and Guidelines, Department of Information Services, State of Washington, www.wa.gov/dis/portfolio.
3. June 1999 New Draft Model I.T. Contracts, California Department of General Services, www.pd.dgs.ca.gov/acqui/itcmnew.asp.
4. State of Montana, Standard Contract Language and Forms, 26 pages, http://www.discoveringMontana.com/doa/ppd/stst.htm.
5. New York State Office of General Services, Procurement Services, Purchasing Memorandum, Sept. 18, 1998, 7 pages, http://www.ogs.state.ny.us/purchase/snt/CL301_0.htm.
6. California Department of General Services, Procurement, June 1999 New Draft Model I.T. Contracts, 4 pages, http://www.pd.dgs.ca.gov/acqui/itcmnew.asp/.
7. Washington State, IT Portfolio Management, Policy, Standards and Guidelines, http://www.wa.gov/dis/portfolio/.
8. GITC 4 is version four of the Government Information Technology and Communications contracting framework. The web site containing this information is called "GITC 4" and can be found at: http://www.gitc.fianance.gov.

Values and Policy Analysis

Steven A. Peterson
The Pennsylvania State University at Harrisburg, Middletown, Pennsylvania, U.S.A.

INTRODUCTION

Policy analysts cannot avoid the importance of values in their work. Policy analysis is grounded in values. This entry focuses on a number of issues: the role of values held by the policy analyst, by policy-makers, and by the larger society. Values at each of these levels affect the nature of policy analysis and the conclusions that emerge from such analysis. Value conflicts can arise from this situation, and the variety of responses available to policy analysts when conflicts occur are described. In a very real sense, there can be no ''value free'' policy analysis.

INTRODUCTORY COMMENTS

Values are an integral part of the process of policy analysis—from selecting questions to be asked or problems to be addressed, to selecting items for the policy agenda, to determining which policy option appears most likely to meet problems identified as worthy of government action.

Indeed, in one of the seminal essays regarding policy analysis, Harold Lasswell was quite explicit regarding the role of values. For instance, he notes that ''The policy-science approach not only puts the emphasis upon basic problems and complex models, but also calls forth a very considerable clarification of the value goals involved in the policy.''[1] In a larger sense, the value of democracy is central for Lasswell's policy orientation. As he says, ''It is probable that the policy-science orientation in the United States will be directed toward providing the knowledge needed to improve the practice of democracy. In a word, the special emphasis is upon the policy sciences of democracy, in which the ultimate goal is the realization of human dignity in theory and fact.''[1]

INDIVIDUAL VALUES AND THE POLICY ANALYST

Paris and Reynolds observe that each person has values that are central to himself or herself. They refer to these as ''Individual Overriding Values'' (or IORVs). These tend to be stable and they rank very highly in a person's hierarchy of values. Paris and Reynolds further note that ''They are called overriding because owing to their features, they can be used to override other lesser values and to resolve conflicts between other values when these occur.''[2] When we examine the world of the policy analyst, IORVs become valuable to understand, as there may be times when the analyst's fundamental values come into conflict with those of policy-makers. At such times, value conflict can prove to be a challenge for the analyst.

What is apt to be the outcome of such conflicts? Weimer and Vining[3] use the work of the economist A.O. Hirschman[4] to outline the options available under such conditions. They assert that the analyst has three choices—exit, voice, and disloyalty. For example, if key political figures demand ''cooked results'' (i.e., that the analyst skew results to fit the politicians' desires) or if political figures misrepresent results of policy analysis in public statements, what is to be done?

Exit would be the situation where the analyst feels that he or she has been so compromised that it is necessary to leave the organization. Voice would represent those circumstances where the analyst would make the effort of working from within an organization to change its way of doing business. Finally, and perhaps most dramatically, disloyalty. For instance, if the agency were trying to suppress a policy analysis that questioned the choice actually made by the organizational leaders, then the individual might leak the original results to the media. Thus if an individual's values were violated by the organization's behavior, he or she could exercise exit, voice, or disloyalty.[3]

VALUES OF POLICY-MAKERS AND POLICIES

Traditionally, a small array of values has been described as most salient for policy-makers' selection of policy choices. Among the most important: equity, efficiency, and effectiveness. Equity is normally defined rather straightforwardly as ''treating likes alike.''[5] Another view is that equity is to be defined in terms of ''fairness.''[3] Or, as Peters puts it, ''...it is argued that government has the legal and economic capacity to

Encyclopedia of Public Administration and Public Policy
DOI: 10.1081/E-EPAP 120010895

redress inequities in the distribution of goods and services that result from the operation of the marketplace."[6] Unfortunately, once one gets past these generic definitions, the actual means by which one applies equity to policy choices is not always clear. Stone has used the example of dividing up a piece of pie "fairly" in her college class. Should everyone get the same sized piece? What about those who do not attend class regularly? If those people get the same sized piece of pie, is that fair to the regular attendees? What if a student is allergic to chocolate? That person is being deprived of a good that others are receiving. Should some compensatory treat be provided to that person?[5]

Efficiency refers to producing the most units of service for the best price, or, as Stone puts it, "getting the most output for a given input."[5] Market-oriented policy choices are often advanced as solutions because they may be more efficient. However, efficiency may not always translate into fairness or effectiveness (i.e., policies that have a desired effect on the original problem). Thus the concept of tradeoff is introduced. Emphasizing one value may lead to a diminution of other values. We may have to trade off some effectiveness or equity in return for enhancing efficiency.

Effectiveness would be defined as the extent to which policy choices meet goals and address problems. Effective programs are those that solve problems. However, as noted before, this may produce tradeoffs. We might be able to assure decent housing for all, by giving everyone who has inadequate housing a voucher for, let us say, $50,000 to purchase adequate housing. This would create a market for housing and, theoretically, address the problem. However, this might be considered to raise issues of equity (What about those who are not so well off who have been able to purchase decent housing while making other sacrifices?) or of efficiency (Is this a cost-effective approach to housing?).

SOCIETAL VALUES

Paris and Reynolds refer to the salience of Societal Overriding Values (SORVs, to use their acronym). These are values held by a large majority of citizens and represent basic societal orientations. As the authors suggest, "For a value to count as an SORV there must be a consensus, or something close to it, on just exactly what counts as satisfying the value."[2]

In political scientist E.E. Schattschneider's view, biases are built into the political system. He has pointed out that "All forms of political organization have a bias in favor of some kinds of conflict and the suppression of others because organization is the mobilization of bias. Some issues are organized into politics, while others are organized out."[7] In a sense, these biases are SORVs, in that they are broadly diffused throughout society and structure discourse (i.e., people use the biases to make decisions without realizing that, in fact, these biases are arbitrary and a construction of the particular society—not based on a priori universal truth).

Any political unit's SORVs will narrow the range of issues considered appropriate for agenda placement. For instance, in the states of the Deep South before the 1960s, white supremacy values would make it literally impossible for the governor of one of those states to suggest placing on the agenda the issue of integration of racially segregated schools. This issue would be "mobilized out" of consideration for agenda placement, as it went against basic values accepted by whites and their elected representatives. Biases, then, can reduce the scope of debate in the political process radically and prevent certain policy alternatives from ever being examined, no matter their objective merits.

CONCLUSION

Thus values have a role to play in the process of policy analysis. Indeed, it would be amazing if this were not so. The world of the policy analyst is one in which values structure the process and shape outcomes.[8]

REFERENCES

1. Lasswell, H.D. The Policy Orientation. In *The Policy Sciences*; Lerner, D., Lasswell, H.D., Eds.; Stanford University Press: Stanford, 1951; pp. 9, 15.
2. Paris, D.C.; Reynolds, J.F. *The Logic of Policy Inquiry*; Longman: New York, 1983; 60.
3. Weimer, D.L.; Vining, A.R. *Policy Analysis*, 3rd Ed.; Prentice-Hall: Upper Saddle River, NJ, 1999; pp. 14, 48–53.
4. Hirschman, A.O. *Exit, Voice, and Loyalty*; Harvard University Press: Cambridge, MA, 1970.
5. Stone, D. *Policy Paradox*; Norton: New York, 2002. Revised edition, pp. 37, 40–41.
6. Peters, B.G. *American Public Policy*, 3rd Ed.; Chatham House: Chatham, NJ, 1993; 373.
7. Schattschneider, E.E. *The Semi-Sovereign People*; Dryden Press: Hinsdale, IL, 1975; 69, reissue edition.
8. Heineman, R.A.; Bluhm, W.T.; Peterson, S.A.; Kearney, E.N. *The World of the Policy Analyst*, 2nd Ed.; Chatham House: Chatham, NJ, 1997.

Whistle-Blowing: Corporate and Public Policy

Michael W. Austin
University of Colorado at Boulder, Boulder, Colorado, U.S.A.

Michael A. Harper
University of Arkansas, Fayetteville, Arkansas, U.S.A.

INTRODUCTION

The phenomenon of whistle-blowing may stir up images of the uncovering of unethical practices in various businesses, but in a loose sense, it has occurred since the mid-1800s within corporate organizational structures. Generally, it is someone telling the truth about wrong actions taken by an entity to some agency, which can bring to bear some type of ramifications on the entity at hand. To better understand what whistle-blowing is, we consider the salient features of a few contemporary definitions, the context in which it occurs, and the ethical tensions involved. We then turn to important public policy questions related to whistle-blowing.

SALIENT DEFINITIONS

Jubb[1] offers an analysis of contemporary definitions and one's definition of whistle-blowing. Jubb's definition is: "Whistle-blowing is a deliberate nonobligatory act of disclosure, which gets onto public record and is made by a person who has or had privileged access to data or information of an organization, about nontrivial illegality or other wrongdoing whether actual, suspected, or anticipated, which implicates and is under the control of that organization, to an external entity having potential to rectify the wrongdoing."

Jubb's definition flows from the understanding that whistle-blowing at the core presents ethical dilemmas for the agent involved in the action. First, a dilemma emerges for the agent with respect to the organization's wrongdoing in light of an organization's established values and/or the agent's personal values. If the organization decides to assent to the wrongdoing over its established values, the dilemma will pit the organization as a whole against the personal values of the agent. This is viewed as an explicit form of dissent within the organizational structure. For Jubb, the central dilemma that an agent faces hinges on one's loyalties to the organization versus loyalties to oneself and/or other entities. This dilemma is set in a context of loyalty that is often implicit within the structure of an organization that hires a person to become an employee with access to the confidentiality surrounding ideas, information, and products. Thus the agent must pit one's loyalties to an organization that has provided employment against loyalties to oneself, colleagues, the profession, family, or the general public.

The last crucial element that must be underscored in Jubb's definition is that the wrongdoing must be disclosed to an external entity; otherwise, no ethical dilemma will arise for the agent. If the agent is not put in a position to choose to override the loyalty created by being able to access confidential materials as an employee, then the dilemma fails to materialize; thus the conditions seen as sufficient for the definition also are lacking. The formulation of a loyalty dilemma is a vital component for Jubb's definition and is the salient feature that requires emphasis.

Our second definition is expressed by Davis[2] and shifts the central feature away from loyalty dilemmas toward understanding an agent's complicity in organizational activities that may involve wrongdoing. Davis' definition, which he calls a theory, is as follows: "You are morally required to reveal what you know to the public (or to a suitable agent or representative of it) when:

(C1) What you will reveal derives from your work for an organization
(C2) You are a voluntary member of that organization
(C3) You believe that the organization, although legitimate, is engaged in a serious moral wrong
(C4) You believe that your work for that organization will contribute (more or less directly) to the wrong if (but not only if) you do not publicly reveal what you know
(C5) You are justified in beliefs (C3) and (C4)
(C6) Beliefs C3 and C4 are true."

Davis sees his definition of whistle-blowing as differing primarily and most importantly in (C4). Here, Davis expresses what he means by complicity. Complicity is important because it is the feature that ties the agent's work with the internal actions of the organization. An agent in an organization will remain an accomplice if

Encyclopedia of Public Administration and Public Policy
DOI: 10.1081/E-EPAP 120025919

he/she overlooks and remains with the organization and even if he/she quits. Whistle-blowing occurs when the agent is put in a position in which taking this revelatory action is the means to break these ties. The action of going public with the wrongdoing prevents complicity on the agent's part. Davis recognizes the issue of loyalty, but he sees complicity as a key feature encountered in many and various whistle-blowing cases, whereas on the other hand, Jubb also recognizes complicity but places emphasis on the need for an ethical dilemma to be formed for whistle-blowing to occur. These are two novel definitions of whistle-blowing that attempt to point out salient features of whistle-blowing. This is not an exhaustive list, but does hone in on important aspects of whistle-blowing that help us understand what it is.

TENSIONS FACING THE WHISTLE-BLOWER

Without reflection, it may seem like the whistle-blower sees the wrongdoings within one's organization and does what is right, but the tensions faced by the whistle-blower are often more substantive than just seeing the wrong and then doing the right thing. Any time issues that involve loyalty and means to a livelihood are at stake, moral and practical tensions will likely follow.

The seemingly most obvious aspects of whistle-blowing involve the moral criteria being brought to bear on the wrongdoing and the practical ramifications that might occur from the "disloyal" action. Nonetheless, Jensen[3] highlights five substantive issues that reveal the deeper moral tensions. Generally, these moral tensions are as follows:

Moral obligations to organization and colleagues
Ethical standards of, and obligations to, a profession
Adverse effects of the action on family or primary groups
Moral obligations toward oneself
Ethical obligations toward the general public
Effects on bedrock values.

When considering moral tensions, it is obvious that some very practical matters seem to fall out, such as the possibility of financial hardships that could occur for the employer and employee. Further thought on these moral tensions can reveal more practical tensions. First, if loyalty is established between the employer and the employee at hiring, then that loyalty is placed under stress when whistle-blowing occurs. This can result in the suspension of the benefits the company provides the employee and vice versa. So not only are the whistle-blower's personal interests affected, but many times the agent also considers the various ramifications that can result for an organization. Those damages can be sig-

nificant—ranging from disruption of normal business functions, to loss of profits, to damaged internal and external credibility, to moral tensions that emerge for the agent's colleagues in that they can be adversely affected by the act. Of course, this may be superceded by the idea that long-term benefits will result, but it is not guaranteed. Second, a tension will exist between the need for an organization to make a profit and the credibility that certain professions may need when looked on by the public, such as medicine or law. Third, there will be potential for tensions from within and without the family of the agent, with the potential for increased publicity, financial hardship, loss of friends, and cruelty toward family members, which need to be weighed. Fourth, the agent should consider the personal risk taken in such actions, which may result in loss of a job, respect, confidence from others, and in oneself, as well as difficulties in future employment. Fifth, public reaction could be mixed regarding the revelation of the wrongdoing. The agent should consider the short-term and long-term ramifications of the act on the public. Lastly, Jensen considers that some deeply held values might encounter friction. For example, the difficult choice and potential consequences of telling the truth in a whistle-blowing scenario may be chosen over the friendship of a peer within the organization. Again, the issue of loyalty is a centerpiece for the culmination of moral tensions, and the practical ramifications of being implicated in wrongdoings within the company drive many of the practical tensions that accompany whistle-blowing.

PUBLIC POLICY AND WHISTLE-BLOWING

The ultimate goal with respect to public policy and whistle-blowing should be to eliminate as much as possible the need for engaging in it, by reducing its legitimate causes.[4,5] Given the moral and legal failures of business scandals (e.g., Enron and MCI Worldcom), we must do all that we can, both institutionally and legally, to encourage the practice when it is justifiable or obligatory. Having good institutional procedures and policies in place, which reduce the need to go public or to the court, is highly desirable. Until then, laws (or regulations) could be formulated so that the potential whistle-blower is required by law (or regulations) to do so, which could remove some of the burden from the individual, as could anonymous hotlines, ombudsmen, and government inspectors general. For example, the Toxic Substances Control Act of 1977 requires companies that produce chemicals to direct their employees to report chemicals that constitute a substantial risk to people's health or to the environment.

When is whistle-blowing morally justifiable and, hence, legitimate? DeGeorge[6] has addressed this issue, and offers three conditions that must be met for whistle-blowing to be morally justifiable. First, the issue must involve a serious harm to the public or to particular segments of the public. For example, if an employee becomes aware of one's company manufacturing and selling unsafe tires as those of high quality, there is an obvious risk to the public. Second, an employee must first report the concern to one's immediate superior. An advantage of this condition is that, if the issue can be handled internally, this preserves loyalty to the company as well as the protection of the public interest. Third, if an employee sees that nothing is done to address the problem, he/she can take her concern up the ladder as far as necessary. If no satisfactory response ensues, then the employee can go public with the concern, whether it be to the media, the government, or some other group that can apply pressure on the company.

Of course, whistle-blowers have been subject to penalties, demotions, isolation in the company, black-balling in the industry, and discharge from their jobs. With this in mind, consider the other points regarding whistle-blowing raised by DeGeorge. It is arguably easier to change laws than it is to change the practices of all corporations, and so issues related to whistle-blowing must be addressed by the law. For example, it should be illegal for a company to fire or take other punitive actions against a whistle-blower, at any time, if the employee has satisfied the set of conditions discussed above. Additionally, the law could include penalties for those individuals within a corporation who are responsible for the defect or harm, instead of just fining the company and leaving the people who are actually morally responsible untouched. Another suggestion is that all companies of a certain size or larger could have (mandated by law) an inspector general whose job is to look for immoral and illegal practices, and be a resource for employees to go to to voice their concerns. Unfortunately, prohibiting the punitive treatment of whistle-blowers by corporations cannot be entirely accomplished by the law, given the subtle ways a company can punish a whistle-blower. However, some of the immoral treatments of whistle-blowers can be stopped by the practices discussed above. Another strategy for encouraging and protecting whistle-blowers is for unions and professional organizations to provide channels for whistle-blowing, as well as protection of those who call attention to an immoral or illegal corporate practice. Generally, professional organizations and societies have failed to protect their members. The problem is that such organizations may not have sufficient resources, or sufficient power, to do anything, which again stresses the need for legal sanctions and motivations for ethical corporate behavior and protection of whistle-blowers.

The need for laws and regulations to promote ethical behavior in business is exacerbated by the complexity and new forms of business conduct.[7] These complexity and newness may make an appeal to traditional ethical precepts less effective than in the past. In 1991, the United States Corporate Sentencing Guidelines went into effect, enjoining both uniform and severe penalties for corporations found guilty of criminal misconduct. In the guidelines, corporations are given incentives for the adoption of ethics programs. If they have such programs, the penalties are significantly reduced if and when a corporation is convicted of an offense but have a program in place prior to that offense. Additionally, it is often the case that both federal and state prosecutors consider refraining from prosecuting a company for misconduct if an ethics program was in place prior to the offense.

The Corporate Sentencing Guidelines offer seven steps to help guide the formation of an ethics program that will both meet government approval and be an effective deterrent of wrongdoing. First, a company's ethics standards and procedures must be specifically constructed so as fit to the company's particular business and needs. Second, particular individuals who are high-ranking officials in the company must be personally involved and responsible for compliance, legitimizing the company's stated ethical goals. Third, companies are to avoid delegating significant discretionary authority to individuals who have shown themselves to be inclined to illegal conduct. Fourth, company leaders should seek to communicate in an effective manner ethics policies and procedures to employees and other agents of the company. Fifth, companies should work for compliance with the standards through monitoring, audits, and a working reporting system. It is important that companies target likely offenses in their monitoring, and they also should have a functioning disciplinary process in place when misconduct is discovered. Establishing a culture of morality and compliance with the law can do much to discourage immoral and illegal behavior. Sixth, companies must have disciplinary procedures in place for enforcing the ethics program. This might include reprimands, fines, suspension, or firing. Lastly, companies must respond to offenses and seek to deter further ones. When misconduct does occur, it should be reported to the government. In addition, companies should modify their ethics programs and other policies, procedures, and structures, as needed, to avoid future problems.

Governmental agencies such as the Environmental Protection Agency, the Nuclear Regulatory Commission (NRC), and the Department of Health and Human Services can be instructive when seeking to develop effective ethics programs. For instance, with respect to whistle-blowing, the NRC gives more specific and detailed guidelines than the Corporate Sentencing Guidelines to the nuclear industry, partly because of the significant harm that could be avoided by whistle-blowers coming forward. NRC policy includes the training of supervisors to understand the value of whistle-blowers to the corporation, and it pushes the importance of having incentive programs in place that will encourage whistle-blowers to report dangerous, immoral, or illegal practices.

How Effective Are Whistle-Blowing Laws?

The level of corporate change regarding whistle-blowing policies in response to legal changes has been analyzed.[8] According to the research of Near and Dworkin, protective legislation at the state level has not been effective. When whistle-blowers suffer retaliation, the majority continues to employ wrongful firing tort suits instead of seeking legislative protection via state statutes. Near and Dworkin explore whether the whistle-blowing statutes enacted by many states caused firms within those states to establish internal mechanisms for reporting wrongdoing as a possible explanation of the fact that no increase in the number of whistle-blowers seeking legislative protection has occurred.

Near and Dworkin surveyed a representative sample of *Fortune 1000* firms with headquarters in states where legislative protection of whistle-blowers exists. From the data they compiled, they conclude that the majority of firms continued to do business as usual, such that the passage of the whistle-blower statutes had little effect on corporate whistle-blowing policies and mechanisms. Most companies that responded heavily relied on an open-door policy, which Near and Dworkin argue is equivalent to no policy at all because employees feel that such policies are neither effective nor protective. Moreover, the policies of the majority of companies responding to the survey do not meet the Corporate Sentencing Guidelines because an open-door policy is not sufficiently specific, lacks the involvement of high-level officials, and does not include protection from retaliation against whistle-blowers. Companies surveyed failed to meet the guidelines with respect to the dissemination of information regarding their ethics statements and open-door policies. Because of this, then, they would be susceptible to harsher sentences and fines, unless they instituted new policies in line with the guidelines. Lastly, the research of Near and Dworkin shows that whistle-blowing statutes enacted by many states did not cause firms within those states to establish internal mechanisms for reporting wrongdoings, given that only a fifth of the firms responding to their survey indicated that they had established such mechanisms in response to the changes in state statutes. To remedy this situation, Near and Dworkin suggest that: 1) legislation, which effectively encourages employees who become aware of wrongdoing to blow the whistle, must be enacted; and 2) governmental incentives, which encourage firms to construct internal channels for whistle-blowers to employ, must be put into place.

CONCLUSION

Whistle-blowers who are justified in bringing wrongdoings to light arguably deserve protection from the backlash that often occurs. Although legislative changes are important, it appears that more must be done to encourage change within corporate structures such that whistle-blowing, when justified, is not only allowed but encouraged. Public confidence in corporations as well as the public interest require nothing less.

REFERENCES

1. Jubb, P.B. Whistleblowing: A restrictive definition and interpretation. J. Bus. Ethics **1999**, *21*, 78.
2. Davis, M. Whistleblowing. In *The Oxford Handbook of Practical Ethics*; LaFollette, H., Ed.; Oxford University Press: Oxford, 2003; 549.
3. Jensen, J. Vernon ethical tension points in whistleblowing. J. Bus. Ethics **1987**, *6*, 324–326.
4. Bok, S. Whistleblowing and professional responsibility. N. Y. Educ. Q. **1980**, *11*, 2–10.
5. *Beyond Integrity*; Rae, S., Wong, K., Eds.; Zondervan Publishing House: Grand Rapids, MI, 1996; 295–304.
6. DeGeorge, R.T. *Business Ethics*; Macmillan Publishing: New York, 1982.
7. Kaplan, J.M.; Rebecca, S. Walker Ethics and the Regulatory Environment. In *A Companion to Business Ethics. Blackwell Companions to Philosophy*; Frederick, R., Ed.; Blackwell Publishers: Malden, MA, 1999; 366–373.
8. Near, J.P.; Dworkin, T.M. Responses to legislative changes: Corporate whistleblowing policies. J. Bus. Ethics **1998**, *17*, 1551–1661.

Index

Accounting and reporting for private nonprofit
    organizations, 1–7
  costs of activities, 6
  definition, 1
  financial statements, 3–5
    activities, 5
    cash flow, 5
    position, 4–5
  investments, 6
  transfer of assets, 6
Acquiring resources: a public sector approach, 8–11
  procurement and market conditions, 10–11
    pricing of goods, 10–11
    services, 11
  vertical integration vs. outsourcing, 9–10
Administrative law judges and agency adjudication, 12–15
  procedures, 12–13
  state, 13–14
Alternative dispute resolution process, 21–25
  consensual, 22–24
    conciliation, 23
    conflict assessment, 23
    early neutral evaluation, 24
    facilitation, 23
    mediation, 23
    minitrials and summary jury trials, 24
    negotiated rulemaking, 23
    policy dialog, 23
  quasi-adjudicatory, 24–25
    arbitration, 24
    settlement judges, 24
  unassisted negotiation, 22
    partnering, 22

Budget stabilization fund, 34–38
  adoption, 38
  defining, 35
    countercyclical reserves fund, 36
    enabling legislation, 35
  evolution, 34
    contingency funds to general fund balances, 34
  fund data, 38
  origin, 34
Bureaucratic reform on state government administration,
    impact of, 148–152
  accessibility via E-government, 150–151
  internal management subsystems, 148–149
  results orientation, 149–150

Capital purchases, 48–51
  cycle, 48
    contract administration, 50

    disposal, 50
    maintenance and service, 50
    planning and budgeting, 48–49
    source selection, 49–50
Community-based planning for
    HIV/AIDS, 52–60
  background, 52–53
  coordination of services, 56–57
  implications of the Oakland study, 57–58
  integrated theoretical model, 53–54
  organizational environment and form,
    54–56
Constructive change proposals, assessing the
    validity of, 26–29
  contents of, 27–28
  recoverable costs, 29
Cooperative purchasing, 61–62
  benefits, 62
  drawbacks, 62
  historical background, 61–62
Court system strategic planning, 63–68
  federal courts, 64
  models, 64–67
    issues and future directions, 67
    other tools, 66–67
  public sector, 63
  state and local court systems, 64

Democracy and public policy, 78–84
  attributes, 79–81
  definitions, 78–79
  purposes, 81–83

Environmental policy, 90–93
  National Environmental Policy Act, 91–92
Ethics and administrative reform, 94–98
  concerns, 94
  four points of view, 94–97
    ethics management, 96–97
    new public management, 95
    new public service, 95–96
    traditional public administration, 95
Ethics and information and communication
    technology, 99–103
  importance in society, 99
  limitations on freedom, 99
  online defamation, 100
  privacy and confidentiality, 101–102
  promise and the challenge of the
    Internet, 99–100
  protecting minors from sexually explicit content,
    100–101

Financial condition, 104–109
   difference between financial condition and position
      analysis, 106
   factors and indicators used, 105–106
   ten-point test, 106
FOIA. *See* Freedom of Information Act—Federal.
Foreign policy analysis, 110–113
   emergence, 110–111
   social constructivism, 112–113
   traditional models, 111–112
Freedom of Information Act—Federal, 114–117
   legislative history, 114–115

Government-sponsored enterprises, 118–121
   beginning, 118–119
   current issues, 121
   function, 119–120
GSEs. *See* Government-sponsored enterprises.

Health care, 123–128, 129–132, 133–137, 138–141
   assessment and evaluation of, 123–128
      background, 123
      examples, 124–126
      process, 126–128
      methodology, 127
   decision analysis, alternatives in, 129–132
      alternative approaches, 130–131
      choosing framework, 131
      clinical decision making, 129–130
   decision making behavior, 133–137
   policy, 138–141
Humanitarian intervention, 142–147
   criteria, 144–145
   objectives, 142–143
   overview, 142
   state sovereignty and human rights, 143–144

Information sources and state policy making, 157–161
   interstate policy diffusion, 158–159
   legislative leaders, 159
   legislative reforms, 157
Integrated health care systems, 162–165
   background, 162–163
   emerging trends and models, 163–164
      legal structure, 163–164
      organizational evolution, 164

Logistics and transportation, 174–178
   carrier selection, 175–176
   definitions, 174
   evolution, 174–175
   modes, 176–177
   statistics, 175

Milgram experiments, 184–187
   historical contexts, 184–185
   methodology, 185–186
Model contracts in information technology, 317–320
   overview, 317–318
   survey of several jurisdictions, 318–319

National security policy, 192–196
   Clinton's post-Cold War, and, 193–194
   George W. Bush and September 11th, and, 194–195
   and options, 192

Ombuds and ombuds programs, 197–199
   benefits and risks, 198–199

Pay-as-you-go financing, 200–203
   capital outlay budgets, 201
   capital outlay examples, 202
   comparison with debt financing, 201–202
   potential sources, 203
Policy design, 204–208
   approaches, 204–205
   target populations, social constructions, and
      elements, 205–207
Policy implementation, 209–212
   first-generation studies, 209–210
   second-generation research, 210–211
Policy networks, 213–216
   administration, 213–214
   governance, 215
   performance, 214–215
Policy process, models of, 188–191
   early theories, 188
   modern theories, 188–189
Postpositivist perspectives, 217–220
   applications of, 218
   assumptions of, 217
   and critique in philosophy, 218
   in policy analysis, 218–219
Privatization, 221–223
   criteria, 223
   definition of, 221
   forms of, 221–223
      contracting out, 221–222
      franchising, 222
   weakness of, 222–223
Public–private partnerships
   in developing countries, 224–228
      constraints to, 226–227
      decline of statist thinking, 224–225
   models for service delivery, 231–232
   strategies to achieve growth, 229–231
      financial incentives, 229–230
      nonfinancial incentives, 230–231
      tax environment, 230
   trends and directions of, 232
Public procurement ethics, 234–238
   fairness, 234–235
   probity, 236–237
   transparency, 237
Public reporting, 239–243
   definition, 240
   direct, 241
   indirect, 240
   origins of, 239–240

Rawls, John, 166–169
   criticism of, 168
   public administration, and, 168

Reciprocal relations, 244–247
  historical development, 245–246
  nuclear arms, 247
  seceding, 246
  ten causal relations, 244
Refunding in municipal bond market, basics of, 302–305
  call options and its role in, 302–303
  escrow account and federal regulations, 303–304
Restorative justice, 248–254
  initiatives, 249
    circle sentencing, 252–253
    community reparative boards, 252
    victim–offender mediation, 249–251
Risk management, 255–258
  administration, 257
  benefits, 257
  concepts, 255–256

South East Asia
  administrative reform, 16–20
    causes and implications of, 18–19
    features and trends, 16–18
  Association of Southeast Asian Nations, 30–33
    key components of ACCSM, 31
    obstacles to cooperation, 31–32
  bureaucrats and politicians, 39–43
    colonial legacy, 39–40
    newly industrializing contexts, 40–41
    pressures for reform, 41–42
  Cambodia, 44–47
    civil society and private sector, 46
    public sector, 44–46
  crisis policy making and management, 69–73
    comparing characteristics, 70–71
    decision and governance characteristics, 69–70
    implications, 72
    responding to unknown proportions, 71–72
  decentralization, 74–77
    growth of democracy and devolution, 75–76
    impact of colonialism, 75
    principal concepts, 74–75
  development administration, 85–89
    administration to management, 85
    decentralization, 88–89
    public administration and reform, 87–88
  Indonesia, 153–156
    background and tradition, 153
    civil service, 153–154
    public administration reform, 155–156
  Lao People's Democratic Republic, 170–173
    background, 170
    public sector, 170–173
    private sector, civil society, and the media, 173
  Malaysia, 179–183
    governmental system, 179
    public administration, 181
    reform and modernization efforts, 180–181
  Singapore, 259–263
    public administration, 259
  Thailand, 285–289
    1997 constitution, 285–286

    Asian financial crisis, 286
    transparency and corruption, 290–294
      measures to improve, 291–292
      role of civil society and e-governance 292–293
State and local public pension fund management, 271–275
  actuarial evaluation method, 271–273
  benefit and contribution, 271
State enterprise zones, 264–270
  growth of, 265
    multi-state studies, 265–267
    status of program evaluation, 264
    tax wars, 268
Subnational counter-cyclical fiscal policy in the United States, 276–280
  evolution, 276–277
  practice, 277–278
    future, 279
    policy instruments, 278
    response, 278

Telehealth and state government policy, 281–284
  conditions, 281–282
  ecological factors, 283
  evolution, 281
  state enabling laws, 282–283
Theory of Justice. See Rawls, John.
Truth and Reconciliation Commission, 295–297
  amnesty and reconciliation, 297
  image and performance, 296–297
  mode of operation, 295–296
  model of management, 296
Tuskegee Study, 298–300
  background and development of, 299
  history of human subjects research, 298–299
  implications for public policy and public administration, 300

United States treasury securities, 306–310
  bills, 307–308
  buying marketable treasury securities, 308
  debt instruments, 306
  notes and bonds, 308
  ownership of, 306–307
  savings bonds, 308–309
Urban planning and ethics, 311–316
  ethical principles, 313–315
  rise of ethics, 311–313

Values and policy analysis, 321–322
  individual values, 321
  societal values, 322

Whistle-blowing, 323–326
  definitions of, 323
  public policy and, 324–326
  tensions of whistle-blower, 324